Elements of Language

Second Course

Lee Odell

Richard Vacca

Renée Hobbs

Judith L. Irvin

Grammar, Usage, and Mechanics Instructional Framework by

John E. Warriner

HOLT, RINEHART AND WINSTON

A Harcourt Education Company

Orlando • **Austin** • New York • San Diego • London

Acknowledgments and other credits, which are extensions of the copyright page, appear at the end of the book.

Printed in the United States of America

ISBN 0-03-079679-2

6 048 08 07

A STUDENT'S GUIDE FOR LANGUAGE ARTS SKILLS AND STRATEGIES AND COUNTDOWN TO TESTING

Language Arts Skills and Strategies

Throughout your school career, you've become familiar with the language arts skills and strategies that help you read, write, and create and analyze presentations or media messages. These skills not only help you do well in your classes and on state tests, but also help you communicate effectively with others.

For a list of the most common language arts skills and strategies, take a look at the chart on the next seven pages. This chart provides definitions with specific examples from *Elements of Language* for each skill and strategy. Use this list as a quick reference to the skills and strategies you will practice this year.

Countdown to Testing

One way to show that you know language arts skills and strategies is to take a test. In fact, many states require that students take standardized tests to show mastery of these language arts skills. To help you prepare for such a test, use the weekly Countdown to Testing activities that appear on pages S9–S32.

The Countdown to Testing section consists of 20 weeks of questions. During each week, you will answer one multiple-choice question each day. Here are a few important points to remember about the questions.

- Some of the questions refer to a passage, and if they do, the directions at the top of each page will direct you to the passage.
- Some of the questions include sentences or graphics you must analyze in order to answer the question.
- All of the questions have a page reference showing you where to go in your textbook to find more information about the skill or strategy the question covers.

By answering these questions in Countdown to Testing, you'll have more practice using language arts skills and strategies, and you'll be better prepared for standardized tests.

LANGUAGE ARTS SKILLS AND STRATEGIES

The following chart lists the four strands of language arts, plus the skills and strategies within these strands that are commonly addressed in language arts classrooms. Each skill or strategy appears in a yellow-tint box. To the right of each skill or strategy you'll find a specific example from your textbook.

READING

Comprehension

Skill or Strategy	Example
Identifying Main Idea and Details: identifying the most important point or focus of a passage and the details that support or explain that focus	The **Reading Skill** on pages 21–22 gives instructions, examples, and practice on identifying an implied main idea. The **Test-Taking Mini-Lesson** on page 26 gives instruction on and examples of identifying main ideas on reading tests. For instruction on identifying details, see pages 782–783.
Forming Generalizations: creating a statement based on specific situations or people that applies to many individuals or situations	The **Reading Focus** on pages 122–123 gives instructions, examples, and practice on forming generalizations.
Summarizing: noting the most important ideas of a text using only as few words as possible	The **Writing Mini-Lesson** on page 129 gives step-by-step instruction, examples, and practice on summarizing. For additional instructions and examples, see page 783.
Drawing Conclusions: adding information you already know to information in a text in order to make a judgment	The **Test-Taking Mini-Lesson** on page 57 gives instruction on and examples of drawing conclusions on reading tests. For additional instruction and examples, see page 779.
Determining Author's Purpose: noting the author's reason for writing about a subject—to inform, persuade, entertain, or express oneself	The **Reading Focus** on pages 22–24 gives instruction, examples, and practice on determining an author's purpose.
Distinguishing Fact and Opinion: being able to tell the difference between information that can be proved and personal beliefs	The **Reading Skill** on pages 162–164 gives instruction, examples, and practice on telling the difference between facts and opinions. The **Test-Taking Mini-Lesson** on page 168 gives instruction on and examples of identifying facts and opinions on reading tests.
Making Predictions: the act of deciding what you think will happen next in a text	The **Reading Skill** on pages 85–86 gives instruction, examples, and practice on using text features for predicting.

Identifying Causes and Effect: noting the difference between causes (what make something happen) and effects (what happens as a result of a causes)	The **Reading Focus** on pages 90–93 gives instruction, examples, and practice on identifying cause and effects. The **Critical-Thinking Mini-Lesson** on page 103 gives instruction, examples, and practice on identifying false cause-and-effect statements.
Identifying Point of View: determining an author's attitude about a subject	The **Reading Skill** on pages 246–247 gives instructions, examples, and practice on identifying point of view. The **Test-Taking Mini-Lesson** on page 249 gives instruction on and examples of identifying point of view on reading tests.
Analyzing Text Structures: recognizing the organizational patterns authors use to present their ideas	The **Test-Taking Mini-Lesson** on pages 95–96 gives instruction on and examples of answering comparison-contrast questions on reading tests. The **Reading Skill** on pages 85–86 gives instruction and practice on analyzing text structures. See pages 783–784 for additional instruction and examples.
Making Inferences: making educated guesses about ideas and details not directly stated in a text	The **Reading Skill** on pages 54–55 gives instructions, examples, and practice for inferring. The **Test-Taking Mini-Lesson** on page 125 gives instruction on and examples of inferring on reading tests.
Paraphrasing: restating in your own words ideas you have read	The **Critical-Thinking Mini-Lesson** on page 179 gives step-by-step instruction, examples, and practice on paraphrasing. See pages 780–781 for additional instruction and examples.
Analyzing Persuasive Techniques: identifying methods authors use to persuade their readers	The **Critical-Thinking Mini-Lesson** on page 254 gives instruction, examples, and practice on analyzing persuasive techniques. The **Test-Taking Mini-Lesson** on page 249 gives instruction on and examples of analyzing persuasive devices on reading tests.
Taking Reading Tests: answering reading questions on standardized tests	For strategies and practice on answering multiple-choice questions and extended response questions, see pages 3–10 and 814–820. The **Test-Taking Mini-Lessons** on pages 26, 57, 95, 125, 168, 211, and 249 give examples and instruction on how to answer reading test questions.

Vocabulary

Using Context Clues: determining the meaning of words through the surrounding text	The **Vocabulary Mini-Lessons** on pages 25 and 94 give instruction, examples, and practice on using context clues. See page 787 for additional instruction and examples.
Analyzing Word Structure: looking at a word's root, prefix, or suffix to help figure out its meaning	The **Vocabulary Mini-Lessons** on pages 56 and 124 give instruction, examples, and practice on analyzing word structure. See pages 789–791 for additional instruction and examples.
Using Multiple-Meaning Words: looking at the context of words with multiple meaning in order to define them	The **Vocabulary Mini-Lesson** on page 167 gives instruction, examples, and practice on multiple-meaning words. See page 789 for additional instruction and examples.

Understanding the Origins of English Words: studying the history of the English language	To learn about the history of English, see pages 766–768.
Understanding Connotation and Denotation: understanding the difference between word associations and word definitions	The **Vocabulary Mini-Lesson** on page 248 gives instruction, examples, and practice on connotation and denotation.

WRITING

Writing Strategies

Progressing through the Writing Process: using the four stages of writing to create texts	See pages xxxii–xxxiii for instruction on the writing process.
Considering Audience and Purpose: choosing words and sentences to address the reason for writing a text and the people you are writing for	See pages 844–845 for instruction on and examples of analyzing audience and purpose.
Evaluating and Revising for Coherence and Unity: assessing writing to improve the way details are connected in a text	See pages 301–311 for instruction, examples, and practice on improving unity and coherence.
Evaluating and Revising for Content and Organization: assessing writing to improve the development and order of the ideas in a text	Each of the **Writing Workshops** on pages 36, 68, 107, 138,187, 225, and 263 gives instruction, examples, and practice on revising content and organization.
Evaluating and Revising for Conciseness and Clarity: assessing writing to improve the precision of word choice and sentences in a text	The **Focus On** features on pages 38, 70, and 189 give instruction, examples, and practice on revising to improve word choice and sentence structure. **Chapter 8,** pages 279–293, gives instruction, examples, and practice on improving sentence style.

Writing Applications

Writing Narrative Texts: producing texts that tell a story	The **Connections to Literature** on pages 231–232 gives instruction, examples, and practice on the process of writing a short story.
Writing Expository Texts: producing texts that explore or explain	The **Writing Workshops** on pages 58, 97, and 269 give instruction, examples, and practice on the process of writing a process essay, a cause-and-effect essay, and a research report, respectively.

Writing Persuasive Texts: producing texts to convince readers to think or act in a particular way	The **Writing Workshops** on pages 212–229 and 250–267 give instruction, examples, and practice on the process of writing a persuasive essay and a brochure, respectively.
Writing Expressive Texts: producing texts to share feelings and thoughts	The **Writing Workshop** on pages 27–40 gives instruction, examples, and practice on the process of writing a personal narrative.
Writing Responses to Literature: producing texts that respond to a piece of literature	The **Writing Workshop** on pages 125–144 gives instruction, examples, and practice on the process of writing a book review. The **Connections to Literature** on pages 147–149 gives instruction, examples, and practice on the process of writing an analysis of a poem.
Writing Creative Texts: producing texts that use language in an original and imaginative way	The **Connections to Literature** on pages 188–189 and 231–232 give instruction, examples, and practice on the process of writing a poem and a short story.
Writing Descriptive Texts: using sensory details to support a dominant impression of a subject	The **Connections to Literature** on pages 41–42 gives instruction, examples, and practice on the process of writing a descriptive essay about a place.
Writing Correspondence: using the correct format to write business and personal communications	For instruction and examples on writing e-mails and letters, see pages 834–839.
Taking Writing Tests: answering multiple-choice writing questions and responding to on-demand writing prompts	For strategies and practice on responding to writing tests, see pages 11–15, 736–739, and 748–751. The **Test-Taking Mini-Lessons** on pages 43, 76, 143, 192, and 230 give instruction on and examples of responses to various types of writing prompts.

Writing Language Conventions

Proofreading for Correct Modifier Usage: reading a final text to identify and correct errors in comparison and placement	**Chapter 20,** pages 554–579, gives instruction, examples, and practice on using modifiers correctly.
Proofreading for Correct Verb Usage: reading a final text to identify and correct errors in tense shift, subject-verb agreement, and irregular verbs	**Chapter 17,** pages 474–503, and **Chapter 18,** pages 504–533, give instruction, examples and practice on using verbs correctly.
Proofreading for Correct Pronoun Usage: reading a final text to identify and correct errors in case and pronoun-antecedent agreement	**Chapter 17,** pages 474–503, and **Chapter 19,** pages 534–553, give instruction, examples, and practice on using pronouns correctly.

Proofreading for Fragments and Run-On Sentences: reading a final text to identify and correct errors in sentence structure	**Chapter 8,** pages 274–279, gives instruction, examples, and practice on correcting fragments and run-on sentences.
Proofreading for Correct Spelling: reading a final text to identify and correct errors in spelling	**Chapter 25,** pages 686–714, gives instruction, examples, and practice for spelling correctly.
Proofreading for Correct Punctuation: reading a final text to identify and correct errors in punctuation	**Chapters 23** and **24,** pages 628–685, give instruction, examples, and practice on correct punctuation. Each of the **Grammar Links** on pages 39, 71, 110, 141, and 266 gives instruction, examples, and practice on correct punctuation.
Proofreading for Correct Capitalization: reading a final text to identify and correct errors in capitalization	**Chapter 22,** pages 602–627, gives instruction, examples, and practice on using capital letters correctly.
Proofreading for Correct Manuscript Style: reading a final text to correct errors in indentation and spacing	For guidelines on manuscript style, see page 756.

Grammar

Understanding and Identifying the Parts of Speech: recognizing the eight parts of speech	**Chapter 11,** pages 344–369, and **Chapter 12,** pages 370–397, give instruction, examples, and practice for identifying and using the eight parts of speech.
Understanding and Identifying the Parts of a Sentence: recognizing subject, predicate, and complements of a sentence	**Chapter 10,** pages 322–343, and **Chapter 13,** pages 398–413, give instruction, examples, and practice for identifying and using the subject, predicates, and complements of a sentence.
Understanding and Identifying Phrases and Clauses: recognizing phrases and clauses	**Chapter 14,** pages 414–437, and **Chapter 15,** pages 438–457, give instruction, examples, and practice for identifying and using phrases and clauses.
Understanding and Identifying Sentence Structure: recognizing kinds of sentences and the four basic sentence structures	**Chapter 10,** pages 339–339, and **Chapter 16,** pages 458–473, give instruction, examples, and practice on classifying sentences and the four basic sentence structures respectively.

SPEAKING AND LISTENING

Speaking and Listening Strategies

Understanding the Techniques of Clear and Distinct Speech: studying the strategies of an effective speaker	For instruction and strategies for effective speaking, see pages 794–799.
Analyzing Oral Texts: listening to an oral presentation in order to understand its message and purpose	For instruction and strategies for analyzing oral texts, see pages 804–807.
Understanding the Listening Process: studying the skills involved in an effective listening process	For instruction and strategies for the listening process, see pages 803–804.

Speaking and Listening Applications

Giving and Listening to an Informative Speech: presenting and listening to a speech that explains	The **Connections to Life** on pages 195–196 gives instruction, examples and practice on giving an informative speech. For additional instruction and strategies on speaking and listening, see pages 794–804 and 807.
Giving and Listening to a Persuasive Speech: presenting and listening to a speech that presents a position	The **Focus on Speaking and Listening** on pages 233–236 gives instruction, examples and practice on presenting and listening to a persuasive speech. For additional instruction and strategies for a formal speech, see pages 794–799.
Giving and Listening to a Narrative Speech or an Oral Interpretation: presenting and listening to a story or a reading of a literary selection	The **Focus on Speaking and Listening** on pages 44–46 gives instruction, examples, and practice for telling and listening to a story. Pages 801–802 give instruction and strategies for presenting an oral interpretation of a literary selection. Pages 804–805 give instruction and strategies for listening to literature.
Participating in an Oral Discussion: presenting and listening to discussions	For instruction and strategies for a group discussion, see pages 799–800.
Holding a Panel Discussion: presenting and listening to a panel to present information or give a forum	For instruction, examples, and practice on how to hold a panel discussion, see the **Focus on Speaking and Listening** on pages 150–151.
Presenting and Listening to an Adaptation of a Scene: presenting and listening to a presentation of a scene	For instruction, examples, and practice on how to produce and present a scene, see the **Focus on Speaking and Listening** on pages 152–154. For instruction on listening to appreciate, see pages 804–805.
Giving and Listening to an Impromptu Speech: presenting and listening to an impromptu speech	For instruction and strategies for an impromptu speech, see page 800. For instruction and strategies for listening to a speech, see pages 802–804 and 807.

VIEWING AND REPRESENTING

Viewing and Representing Strategies

Understanding Electronic Media Terms: studying terms used by the electronic media	To help you understand electronic media terms, see pages 821–828 for instruction and examples.
Understanding Print Media Terms: studying terms used by the print media	To help you understand print media terms, see pages 824–831 for instruction and examples.
Understanding Type Styles, Visuals and Graphics, and Page Layout: studying how writers use nonverbal elements such as font, graphics, and columns	The **Designing Your Writing** features on pages 66, 111, 142, 181, 219, and 259 give instruction on and examples of the effective use of type styles, graphic elements, and layout. Pages 757–765 give instruction on and examples of key concepts in document design.
Analyzing Print Media: looking at print media in order to figure out the message and purpose	The **Connections to Life** on pages 268, 113–114, and 269 give instruction, examples, and practice on comparing ads, analyzing graphics and analyzing a caricature, respectively. For instruction and strategies for analyzing media messages, see pages 808–809. The **Reading Focus** on pages 245–246 explains and gives instructions for using analyzing illustrations.
Analyzing Electronic Media: looking at electronic media in order to figure out the message and purpose	For instruction, examples, and practice on analyzing electronic media, see **Connections to Life** on page 112. For instruction and strategies for analyzing media messages, see pages 808–809.

Viewing and Representing Applications

Creating Print Media: producing print media texts	The **Focus on Viewing and Representing** on pages 77–80 gives instruction, examples, and practice on creating graphics for a print text. The **Writing Workshop** on pages 250–267 gives instruction, examples, and practice on using the writing process to produce a brochure.
Creating Electronic Media: producing electronic media texts	The **Focus on Viewing and Representing** on pages 197–200 gives instruction, examples, and practice for designing a web site. The **Connections to Literature** on pages 145–146 and 195–196 give instruction, examples, and practice for creating a slide show and giving a multimedia presentation, respectively.

DIRECTIONS **Answer each question below on the day of the week assigned to it.**

MONDAY

Choose the word that means the same, or about the same, as the underlined word in the sentence below.

Something that is <u>routine</u> is

A difficult.
B natural.
C boring.
D ordinary.

Vocabulary Mini-Lesson, page 94

TUESDAY

Read the following sentence. Choose the response that fixes the underlined error. If there is no error, choose *D*.

Diane accepted the award and <u>said, I am deeply honored.</u>

A says, "I am deeply honored."
B said I am deeply honored.
C said, "I am deeply honored."
D correct as is

Chapter 24, page 662

WEDNESDAY

There may be a style problem in the sentence below. Select the <u>best</u> revision, or choose *D*.

Before coming to class, school supplied must be bought.

A You must buy school supplies before coming to class.
B School supplies before coming to class must be bought.
C Coming to class before school supplies must be bought.
D correct as is

Writing Workshop, page 109

THURSDAY

Which of the following is an opinion?

A Lewis Carroll is the pen name of C. L. Dodgson.
B C. L. Dodgson wrote *Alice's Adventures in Wonderland.*
C The book has been made into an animated film
D Children enjoy the book because it has no moral.

Test-Taking Mini-Lesson, page 168

FRIDAY

Ramon is writing a research report about Yosemite National Park for a class publication. Which of these is <u>least</u> likely to be a helpful source of information about the park?

A an encyclopedia
B an authoritative Internet source
C a fictional book about the park
D a magazine article about the park

Quick Reference Handbook, page 773

DIRECTIONS **Read the following article.**

La Salle's Expedition

In the summer of 1995, explorers discovered the wreck of a ship more than three hundred years old. It was found under twelve feet of muddy water in Matagorda Bay off the coast of Texas. The *Belle* was one of René-Robert Cavalier, Sauer de La Salle's ships. Who was this man La Salle, what was he doing so far from his native France, and how did his expedition affect Texas history?

Between 1669 and 1684, as a young French adventurer, La Salle explored the length of one of the largest rivers in the New World, the Mississippi. The group of men that accompanied La Salle was small but brave. La Salle survived diseases, battles with powerful Indian tribes, and the jealousy of many who had once been his friends. He seemed so <u>invincible</u> that the king of France, Louis XIV, gave him four new ships.

In 1684, La Salle sailed from France to the Gulf of Mexico. His plan was to build a colony with a fort to establish and protect French trade in that part of the New World. He also wanted to explore parts of Mexico, which was dominated by Spain. La Salle thought that the mouth of the great Mississippi was closer to Mexico than it actually was. He directed his ships more than four hundred miles west of the river and finally went ashore in what is now the state of Texas.

In another part of the Texas territory, Spanish explorers had built one settlement, near El Paso. When they learned of La Salle's plans, they quickly sent out several expeditions to find and destroy La Salle's French colony. Between 1686 and 1689, six expeditions went by land, and five went by sea.

In the meantime, La Salle's little settlement met with one disaster after another. Two of the ships, loaded with supplies, were lost in Matagorda Bay. Many of the settlers were killed by Indians. Others died from disease and starvation. A few simply abandoned La Salle and disappeared into the marshy coastland. Finally, on March 19, 1687, La Salle was murdered by two men from his own colony.

One of the Spanish land expeditions that sought to destroy La Salle's colony was led by a commander named Alonzo de Leon. He and his men marched from Coagula, Mexico, to Matagorda Bay. De Leon eventually found what was left of La Salle's colony. There were only a few houses, the remains of a fort, a wrecked ship out in the bay, and a handful of survivors.

The doomed French colony however, did impact the early history of Texas in significant ways. Historians agree that its brief existence caused the Spanish to establish many beautiful <u>missions</u> and to spread the Spanish culture we know today. If La Salle had succeeded in establishing his colony, French might be the second language in Texas today instead of Spanish, and there might never have been an Alamo for Texans to remember.

WEEK 2

DIRECTIONS **The questions below refer to the article "La Salle's Expedition" on page S10. Answer each question below on the day of the week assigned to it.**

MONDAY

What does the word <u>invincible</u> in line 18 mean?

A undefeatable
B gullible
C invisible
D conquerable

Vocabulary Mini-Lesson, page 94

TUESDAY

In which year did La Salle set out to establish a colony?

A 1669
B 1684
C 1687
D 1689

Quick Reference Handbook, page 782

WEDNESDAY

Which is an opinion expressed in the passage?

A In the summer of 1995, explorers discovered a wrecked ship.
B The group of men that accompanied La Salle was small but brave.
C The king of France, Louis XIV, gave La Salle four new ships.
D Two of the ships, loaded with supplies, were lost in Matagorda Bay.

Test-Taking Mini-Lesson, page 168

THURSDAY

What is the fourth paragraph <u>mostly</u> about?

A the Spanish reaction to La Salle's expedition
B La Salle's earliest expeditions
C problems the colonists had
D the discovery of the wrecked ship

Test-Taking Mini-Lesson, page 26

FRIDAY

According to the passage, what was the most significant result of De Leon's expedition?

A the mapping of the area
B the discovery of gold and silver
C the destruction of La Salle's colony
D the spread of Spanish influence and culture

Reading Workshop, page 90

WEEK 3

DIRECTIONS **The questions below refer to the article "La Salle's Expedition" on page S10. Answer each question below on the day of the week assigned to it.**

MONDAY

Why does the writer ask a question in lines 7–9?

A to guide his or her research
B to convince the reader to write back
C to grab the reader's attention
D to point to future research topics

Quick Reference Handbook, page 832

TUESDAY

What was La Salle's main purpose for establishing a colony?

A to steal Spanish gold and silver
B to settle the Mississippi River basin
C to establish French trade in the area
D to become famous

Reading Workshop, page 90

WEDNESDAY

Which of the following is the most likely reason that Spanish set out to destroy La Salle's colony?

A They did not want competition in the area.
B They knew La Salle to be a hostile aggressor.
C They wanted to protect the traditions and customs of the area's native people.
D They were tricked into doing it by the area's native people.

Reading Workshop, page 54

THURSDAY

In line 62, mission means

A relating to a style of plain, heavy oak furniture.
B groups of people sent to carry out an activity.
C specific tasks for which a person or group is responsible.
D buildings where ministers work to spread a religion or do good work.

Vocabulary Mini-Lesson, page 167

FRIDAY

What was the author's main purpose for writing this passage?

A to explain why La Salle was killed
B to describe what life was like in the 1600s
C to tell the history behind a modern discovery
D to convince students to become archaeologists

Reading Workshop, page 22

DIRECTIONS **Answer each question below on the day of the week assigned to it.**

MONDAY

Read the following sentence. Choose the response that fixes the underlined error. If there is no error, choose *D*.

Ling led us in <u>singing The Star-Spangled Banner.</u>

A singing, "The Star-Spangled Banner."
B singing 'The Star-Spangled Banner.'
C singing "The Star-Spangled Banner."
D correct as is

Chapter 24, page 666

TUESDAY

Choose the response that correctly combines the two word groups below.

This is the pond designed by Taniguchi.
It contains the colorful fish.

A This pond, it contains the colorful fish designed by Taniguchi.
B This pond designed by Taniguchi contains the colorful fish.
C This pond that Taniguchi designed it contains the colorful fish.
D By Taniguchi designed containing colorful fish.

Chapter 8, page 281

WEDNESDAY

Look at the underlined word in the sentence below. Choose the response that identifies the word correctly.

The two women <u>lowered</u> themselves by rope into the spectacular ice cave.

A pronoun
B adjective
C verb
D adverb

Chapter 12, page 371

THURSDAY

Juni's teacher has asked the class to write a personal narrative about a family activity that was important to them. The purpose of this personal narrative would <u>most</u> likely be to

A persuade the reader.
B describe a cause and effect.
C solve a problem.
D tell about an experience.

Writing Workshop, page 29

FRIDAY

Read the following sentence. Then choose the answer in which the underlined word is used in the same way.

The passengers waited to <u>board</u> the planes.

A We will <u>board</u> the windows before the storm.
B Frank used a <u>board</u> to make a shelf.
C The school <u>board</u> will decide the issue next week.
D You must have a ticket to <u>board</u> the ship.

Vocabulary Mini-Lesson, page 167

WEEK 5

DIRECTIONS **Answer each question below on the day of the week assigned to it.**

MONDAY

Look at the underlined word in the sentence below. Choose the response that identifies the word correctly.

Where did you find those <u>colorful</u> polished rocks?

A adjective
B adverb
C preposition
D verb

Chapter 11, page 358

TUESDAY

Choose the word that means the same, or about the same, as the underlined word in the sentence below.

To <u>compel</u> is to

A join.
B force.
C attract.
D hold.

Vocabulary Mini-Lesson, page 94

WEDNESDAY

Look at the series of pictures below. Why does the runner look tired in the middle frame?

A He can't believe how much farther he has to go.
B He can't believe how far he has gone—until he sees that the sign is broken.
C He isn't wearing the right kind of shoes.
D He had planned to drink the lake water.

Focus on Viewing and Representing, page 244

THURSDAY

Read the following sentence. Choose the response that fixes the underlined error. If there is no error, choose *D*.

Although the <u>day was rainy we</u> held the carnival.

A day, was rainy we
B day was rainy, we
C day was rainy; we
D correct as is

Chapter 23, page 654

FRIDAY

Choose the response that correctly combines the two sentences below.

Raul held the flashlight. Sonia searched for her keys.

A Raul held the flashlight Sonia searched for her keys.
B Raul held the flashlight, Sonia searched for her keys.
C While Raul held the flashlight, Sonia searched for her keys.
D While Raul held the flashlight Sonia searched for her keys.

Chapter 8, page 285

WEEK 6

DIRECTIONS **Answer each question below on the day of the week assigned to it.**

MONDAY

Read the following sentence. Choose the response that fixes the underlined error. If there is no error, choose *D*.

Jalal and Ben gave <u>his</u> movie tickets to the volunteers.

A its
B them
C their
D correct as is

Chapter 17, page 493

TUESDAY

Read the following sentence. Choose the response that fixes the underlined error. If there is no error, choose *D*.

<u>Forty-seven students</u> tried out for the part of Hamlet in the school play.

A Forty-seven-students
B Forty seven-students
C Forty seven students
D correct as is

Chapter 24, page 676

WEDNESDAY

There may be a problem in the structure of the word group below. Select the <u>best</u> revision, or choose *D*.

The heavy rains and resulting mudslides in California.

A In California, the heavy rains and resulting mudslides several homes.
B The heavy rains and resulting mudslides in California during March.
C The heavy rains in California and the resulting mudslides destroyed several homes.
D correct as is

Chapter 8, page 275

THURSDAY

There may be a problem in the style of the word group below. Select the <u>best</u> revision, or choose *D*.

The movie that we saw was about wild horses that were tamed for use on ranches.

A The movie was about wild horses tamed for use on ranches that we saw.
B We saw a movie about wild horses tamed for use on ranches.
C Seeing the movie, it was about wild horses that were tamed for use on ranches.
D correct as is

Writing Workshop, page 189

FRIDAY

Choose the response that correctly combines the two sentences below.

E. B.White wrote *Charlotte's Web.* He was a skilled essayist.

A E. B. White, who wrote *Charlotte's Web,* was a skilled essayist.
B E. B. White wrote *Charlotte's Web*, he was a skilled essayist.
C E. B. White wrote *Charlotte's Web* and he was a skilled essayist.
D Being a skilled essayist E. B. White wrote *Charlotte's Web.*

Chapter 8, page 286

WEEK 7

DIRECTIONS **Answer each question below on the day of the week assigned to it.**

MONDAY

Read the following sentence. Then choose the answer in which the underlined word is used in the same way.

At noon, the president will pose for photographs.

A Tran saw through Bill's confident pose.
B Will you pose for a watercolor portrait?
C Higher gas prices pose a problem for drivers.
D She listened with a thoughtful pose.

Vocabulary Mini-Lesson, page 167

TUESDAY

Read the following sentence. Choose the response that fixes the underlined error. If there is no error, choose *D*.

Marlo has practicing every day this week.

A has practiced
B have practice
C have practiced
D correct as is

Chapter 17, page 372

WEDNESDAY

Look at the underlined word in the sentence below. Choose the response that identifies the word correctly.

The mayor seemed to take Cory's suggestions seriously.

A preposition
B verb
C adjective
D adverb

Chapter 12, page 381

THURSDAY

Choose the word that means the same, or about the same, as the underlined word in the sentence below.

Something that is authentic is

A valuable.
B unusual.
C pleasing.
D genuine.

Vocabulary Mini-Lesson, page 94

FRIDAY

Read the following sentence. Choose the response that fixes the underlined error. If there is no error, choose *D*.

Emilio he taught himself to play the guitar—has been accepted to a famous music school.

A Emilio—he taught himself to play the guitar—has
B Emilio, he taught himself to play the guitar—has
C Emilio—he taught himself to play the guitar, has
D correct as is

Chapter 24, page 680

DIRECTIONS **Answer each question below on the day of the week assigned to it.**

MONDAY

Read the following sentence. Choose the response that fixes the underlined error. If there is no error, choose *D.*

Gil thought that the movie remained true to the book; Lyle strongly disagreed.

A book, Lyle
B book—Lyle
C book Lyle
D correct as is

Chapter 23, page 649

TUESDAY

Decide if one of the underlined words below is misspelled. If there is no mistake, select *D.*

A The movie was filmed in the desert.
B She regretted the choice immediately.
C That is a lovly vase.
D no mistake

Chapter 25, page 691

WEDNESDAY

Choose the response that best combines the two sentences below.

Angel helps third-grade students. Angel is a tutor at Zavala Elementary School.

A Angel helps third-grade students and he is a tutor at Zavala Elementary School.
B Angel helps third-grade students, and Angel is a tutor at Zavala Elementary School.
C Angel, a tutor at Zavala Elementary, helps third-grade students.
D Angel helps third-grade students, is a tutor at Zavala Elementary School.

Chapter 8, page 281

THURSDAY

The sentence below may contain an error. Select the best revision, or pick *D.*

Freshly mowed and watered, Kai admired the lawn of his new house.

A The lawn of his new house was freshly mowed and watered, Kai admired it.
B Kai admired the freshly mowed and watered lawn of his new house.
C The lawn was admired by Kai, freshly mowed and watered of his new house.
D correct as is

Chapter 20, page 572

FRIDAY

The sentence below may contain an error. Select the best revision, or pick *D.*

Glenn feels miserably about leaving his friend's CD player on the park bench.

A Glenn feels miserable about leaving his friend's CD player on the park bench.
B Leaving his friend's CD player on the park bench, Glenn feels miserably.
C Miserably, Glenn feels about leaving his friend's CD player on the park bench.
D correct as is

Chapter 12, page 374

DIRECTIONS **Read the following fable.**

The Eagle, the Cat, and the Wild Sow

An Eagle made her nest at the top of a lofty oak; a Cat, having found a convenient hole, moved into the middle of the trunk; and a Wild Sow, with her young, took shelter in a hollow at its foot. The Cat cunningly resolved to destroy this chance-made colony. To carry out her design, she climbed to the nest of the Eagle and said, "Destruction is preparing for you, and for me too, unfortunately. The Wild Sow, whom you see daily digging up the earth, wishes to uproot the oak, so she may on its fall seize our families as food for her young." Having thus frightened the Eagle out of her senses, she crept down to the cave of the Sow and said, "Your children are in great danger. As soon as you go out with your litter to find food, the Eagle is prepared to pounce upon one of your little pigs." Having instilled these fears into the Sow, she went and pretended to hide herself in the hole in the middle of the tree. When night came she went forth with silent foot and obtained food for herself and her kittens, but feigning to be afraid, she kept a lookout all through the day. Meanwhile, the Eagle, full of fear of the Sow, sat still on the branches, and the Sow, terrified by the Eagle, did not dare to go out from her cave. And thus they both, along with their families, perished from hunger, and afforded ample provision for the Cat and her kittens.

WEEK 9

DIRECTIONS **The questions below refer to the fable "The Eagle, the Cat, and the Wild Sow" on page S18. Answer each question below on the day of the week assigned to it.**

MONDAY

Apparently, the Cat's goal in the fable is to

A have the tree for herself and her kittens.
B be friends with the Eagle and the Sow.
C move into a hole in the tree.
D find home for her family.

Reading Workshop, page 54

TUESDAY

In this fable, the Cat is <u>most</u> likely motivated by

A pride.
B loneliness.
C anger.
D greed.

Reading Workshop, page 54

WEDNESDAY

In line 7 of this fable, <u>design</u> means

A pattern.
B to create.
C plan.
D fashion.

Vocabulary Mini-Lesson, page 167

THURSDAY

This fable is about

A trying to get along with others.
B learning to live in a community.
C deceiving others to get what you want.
D how mothers protect their babies.

Reading Workshop, page 21

FRIDAY

If you were to present an oral interpretation of this fable, which of the following tones would <u>best</u> match the feeling of the fable?

A sarcastic
B matter-of-fact
C outraged
D cheerful

Quick Reference Handbook, page 798

DIRECTIONS **The questions below refer to the fable "The Eagle, the Cat, and the Wild Sow" on page S18. Answer each question below on the day of the week assigned to it.**

MONDAY

The moral of this fable is that

A some people are too quick to believe the worst about others.
B most people are good judges of others' character.
C stories about others are never true.
D sows are smarter than people.

Connections to Literature, page 231

TUESDAY

In this fable, <u>feigning</u> is closest in meaning to

A watching.
B pretending.
C fearing.
D deceiving.

Reading Workshop, page 122

WEDNESDAY

In this fable, the writer seems to convey the point of view that

A too many trees are being destroyed by humans.
B humans are a greater threat to animals than are other animals.
C physical strength is more important than intelligence.
D some people can be easily frightened.

Test-Taking Mini-Lesson, page 249

THURSDAY

The tree is an important detail of a setting because it

A is very tall.
B can house several different animals.
C is about to be uprooted by the Sow.
D is a source of food for animals.

Critical-Thinking Mini-Lesson, page 31

FRIDAY

The purpose of the fable is <u>mainly</u> to

A entertain and instruct.
B reveal a process.
C spur readers to action.
D express an emotion.

Connection to Literature, page 231

DIRECTIONS **Read the following passage from a student draft.**

(1) Although more American students are getting high school diplomas than at any other time in the past, the high school dropout rate is still too high. (2) Various estimates place it between 12 and 25 percent. (3) The unemployment rate for high school dropouts is greater than that for graduates. (4) Dropping out of high school reduces one's employment opportunities. (5) Since many jobs today require specialized skills, dropouts may be forced into a labor market that is unstable.

(6) To help "at risk" students stay in school, we need to consider a range of proposals and leave no stone unturned. (7) First, we need to offer career counseling to students, beginning in the ninth grade. (8) Second, we should provide stimulating, quality education that will give students incentives to complete their schooling. (9) And third, we must get parents more involved in school programs and policies.

WEEK 11

DIRECTIONS **The questions below refer to the student draft on page S21. Answer each question below on the day of the week assigned to it.**

MONDAY

According to the author of this essay, why is the current drop-out rate a problem?

A Dropouts have trouble finding stable employment.
B Dropouts earn less money than college graduates.
C Dropouts often get involved in crime.
D Dropouts are leaving school at higher rates than ever before.

Quick Reference Handbook, page 781

TUESDAY

What sources might this writer consult to get statistics to support the statements in the first paragraph?

A Census Bureau
B Educational Resources Information Center
C National Center for Education Statistics
D all of the above

Writing Workshop, page 216

WEDNESDAY

Which of the following statements might the writer use to elaborate on Sentence 5?

A "A technical education can increase one's chances of qualifying for a well-paying job."
B "Many dropouts become discouraged about work."
C "Dropouts should consider getting their general equivalency diplomas."
D "For example, one area of employment for dropouts has been the construction industry, which is strongly affected by changes in the economy."

Writing Workshop, page 219

THURSDAY

Which sentence is repetitive and can be dropped?

A Sentence 2
B Sentence 4
C Sentence 8
D Sentence 9

Chapter 8, page 290

FRIDAY

The audience for the essay probably includes all of the following groups <u>except</u>

A parent-teacher associations.
B local community boards.
C conservation groups.
D guidance counselors.

Writing Workshop, page 214

WEEK 12

DIRECTIONS **The questions below refer to the student draft on page S21. Answer each question below on the day of the week assigned to it.**

MONDAY

Based in this passage, which of the following is the best title for the essay?

A Myths about Dropouts
B The Increasing Dropout Rate
C Dealing with the Dropout Rate
D Dropping Out: One Teen's Story

Test-Taking Mini-Lesson, page 26

TUESDAY

Which of the following points, if added to the paper, would help persuade the audience of the advantages of staying in school?

A High school graduates earn $200,000 more over their lifetimes than drop-outs.
B Dropouts head about half the families on welfare.
C Half of the prison population consists of dropouts.
D all of the above

Writing Workshop, page 216

WEDNESDAY

Suppose the writer's audience consists mainly of parents. Which sentence describes a solution that would be most relevant to that audience?

A Sentence 6
B Sentence 7
C Sentence 8
D Sentence 9

Writing Workshop, page 214

THURSDAY

How should the writer revise Sentence 6 to eliminate wordiness?

A Delete the term "'at risk.'"
B Cut "and leave no stone unturned."
C Delete "stay in school."
D Cut "we need to consider a range of proposals."

Chapter 8, page 290

FRIDAY

If this passage were to become part of a persuasive speech, which of the following visuals would best support the speaker's purpose?

A a graph comparing the employment rates of graduates and dropouts in various fields
B a line graph showing the decline in dropout rates over the years
C a caricature of a group of dropouts
D a word-for-word copy of the speech on an overhead transparency

Focus on Speaking and Listening, page 234

WEEK 13

DIRECTIONS **Answer each question below on the day of the week assigned to it.**

MONDAY

There may be a problem in the structure of the word group below. Select the best revision, or choose *D*.

After Catherine painted the portrait and presented it to Joseph.

A After Catherine painted the portrait and presenting it to Joseph.
B After Catherine painted the portrait, she presented it to Joseph.
C Presenting to Joseph the portrait Catherine had painted.
D correct as is

Chapter 8, page 275

TUESDAY

Read the following sentence. Choose the response that fixes the underlined error. If there is no error, choose *D*.

Kevin and Lisa has noticed the advertisement in the paper.

A has notice
B have noticed
C have noticing
D correct as is

Chapter 17, page 483

WEDNESDAY

Look at the underlined words in the sentence below. Choose the response that identifies the words correctly.

Margaret Ann Farrell has been nominated for the annual literary prize.

A transitive verbs
B action verbs
C helping verbs
D linking verbs

Chapter 12, page 372

THURSDAY

Decide if one of the underlined words below is misspelled. If there is no mistake, select *D*.

A Val swam slowly across the pool.
B My errors were caused by lazyness.
C The statement cause quite a commotion.
D no mistake

Chapter 25, page 692

FRIDAY

Read the following sentence. Choose the response that fixes the underlined error. If there is no error, choose *D*.

Her report was about the World Trade center.

A The World Trade Center
B the world trade center
C the World Trade Center
D correct as is

Chapter 22, page 611

WEEK 14

DIRECTIONS Answer each question below on the day of the week assigned to it.

MONDAY

Choose the response that fixes the error in the closing below. If there is no error, choose *D.*

sincerely yours,

A Sincerely Yours,
B Sincerely yours,
C sincerely Yours,
D correct as is

Chapter 22, page 605

TUESDAY

Choose the word that means the same, or about the same, as the underlined word in the sentence below.

To <u>capsize</u> is to

A change.
B steady.
C cover.
D overturn.

Vocabulary Mini-Lesson, page 94

WEDNESDAY

Read the following sentence. Choose the response that fixes the underlined error. If there is no error, choose *D.*

Ella <u>lays</u> the stack of books on Jim's desk.

A has lain
B is lying
C lies
D correct as is

Chapter 18, page 523

THURSDAY

Read the following sentence. Choose the response that fixes the underlined error. If there is no error, choose *D.*

A flock of <u>birds are</u> on the pond.

A birds is
B birds to be
C bird are
D correct as is

Chapter 17, page 489

FRIDAY

Read the following sentence. Then choose the answer in which the underlined word is used in the same way.

I will <u>mold</u> the clay into round forms.

A The dessert was formed into a <u>mold</u>.
B Some ads try to <u>mold</u> public opinion.
C <u>Mold</u> the loaves of bread before baking them.
D A type of <u>mold</u> grew from the damp ground.

Vocabulary Mini-Lesson, page 167

DIRECTIONS **Answer each question below on the day of the week assigned to it.**

MONDAY

There may be a problem in the structure of the word group below. Select the best revision, or choose *D.*

Under the table in the dining room.

A James lying under the table in the dining room.
B His book under the table in the dining room.
C James found his book under the table in the dining room.
D correct as is

Chapter 8, page 275

TUESDAY

Read the following sentence. Choose the response that fixes the underlined error. If there is no error, choose *D.*

My mother is taking my brothers and I to Redwood National Park this summer.

A I and my brothers
B my brothers and me
C my brothers and myself
D correct as is

Chapter 19, page 541

WEDNESDAY

Shanta's science homework is to write instructions for operating a tool. Which of these actions would best help her organize her ideas before writing?

A numbering the steps in the instructions
B calculating how long the procedure takes
C comparing the tool with another tool
D defining each unfamiliar word

Writing Workshop, page 61

THURSDAY

Read the following sentence. Choose the response that fixes the underlined error. If there is no error, choose *D.*

Drawing on her recent experiences in a mining town, aunt Lilly wrote a novel.

A Mining Town, aunt Lilly
B mining town, Aunt Lilly
C mining town, aunt lilly
D correct as is

Chapter 22, page 619

FRIDAY

Look at the underlined words in the sentence below. Choose the response that identifies the words correctly.

Both Mimi and Chu will attend the awards ceremony.

A relative pronouns
B correlative conjunctions
C coordinating conjunctions
D linking verbs

Chapter 12, page 390

WEEK 16

DIRECTIONS Answer each question below on the day of the week assigned to it.

MONDAY

Decide if one of the underlined words below is misspelled. If there is no mistake, select *D*.

A The water was bubbling over the edge.
B Do you beleive this story?
C The problem occurred after our discussion.
D no mistake

Chapter 25, page 688

TUESDAY

Read the following sentence. Choose the response that fixes the underlined error. If there is no error, choose *D*.

This is the driest summer I can remember.

A most driest summer
B more drier summer
C most dry summer
D correct as is

Chapter 20, page 560

WEDNESDAY

There may be a problem in the structure of the sentence below. Select the best revision, or choose *D*.

After graduation he moved to Colorado then he started a software business.

A After graduation he moved to Colorado, and then he started a software business.
B After graduation, he moved to Colorado then he started a software business.
C After graduation he moved to Colorado, then he started a software business.
D correct as is

Chapter 8, page 277

THURSDAY

Read the following sentence. Choose the response that fixes the underlined error. If there is no error, choose *D*.

What did you think of the movie *The Bridge On the River Kwai?*

A *The Bridge On The River Kwai?*
B *The Bridge on the River Kwai?*
C *The Bridge on the river Kwai?*
D correct as is

Chapter 22, page 620

FRIDAY

Look at the graphic at right. What type of cause-and-effect relationship does it most likely describe?

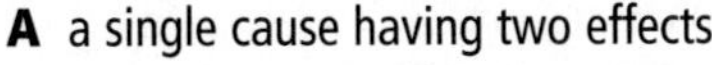

A a single cause having two effects
B a lengthy cause-and-effect chain
C two causes leading to a single effect
D the three causes of the Civil War

Reading Workshop, page 90

DIRECTIONS **Answer each question below on the day of the week assigned to it.**

MONDAY

Ana's English teacher has asked students to write a descriptive essay about a special place. Which of these would best help Ana prepare to write about her special place?

A reading stories about places she wants to visit
B closing her eyes and picturing her place
C listing places that her friends have seen
D watching a video about top vacation sites

Connections to Life, page 42

TUESDAY

Read the following sentence. Choose the response that fixes the underlined error. If there is no error, choose *D*.

The audience could see that colonel Edmund Hallman had no intention of delivering a brief speech.

A Colonel Edmund Hallman
B colonel Edmund hallman
C colonel edmund hallman
D correct as is

Chapter 22, page 619

WEDNESDAY

Read the following sentence. Then choose the answer in which the underlined word is used in the same way.

The core of the pineapple is too tough to eat.

A No one questioned his core beliefs.
B The core of his argument has flaws.
C Use this knife to core the apple.
D A golf ball can have a liquid core.

Vocabulary Mini-Lesson, page 167

THURSDAY

Read the following sentence. Choose the response that fixes the underlined error. If there is no error, choose *D*.

Jason's feet were starting to sink into the thick mud.

A feet was starting
B feet were start
C feet were started
D correct as is

Chapter 17, page 476

FRIDAY

There may be a problem in the structure of the word group below. Select the best revision, or choose *D*.

Designed by a team of architects who trained under Philip Johnson.

A The building was designed by a team of architects who trained under Philip Johnson.
B Conceived and designed by a team of architects who trained under Philip Johnson.
C Designed by a team of architects and builders who trained under Philip Johnson.
D correct as is

Chapter 8, page 275

DIRECTIONS **Read the following article, "Many Ways to Be Smart."**

Many Ways to Be Smart

How many ways can people be smart? Many educators once thought the most important way to be smart was through different school subjects, like math, science, and language arts. Now many experts are refuting the ideas that people can be smart in only one or two ways. Among these experts is Howard Gardner, a professor of education at Harvard University.

Gardner says that most people are smart in several different ways, and he describes eight different kinds of intelligence. Instead of asking *How smart am I?* Gardner's theory asks, *How am I smart?* In Gardner's theory, the human mind can be thought of as a pie cut into eight slices. Each slice has its own unique flavor, and each slice allows people to do very different activities. Look at this list and ask yourself, *How am I smart?*

- **Logical-Mathematical Intelligence** You work easily with numbers. You use reasoning to solve problems and easily figure out patterns between concepts and things. This intelligence occurs in scientists, mathematicians, accountants, computer programmers, lawyers, and bankers.
- **Linguistic Intelligence** You easily read or use words to express yourself or to communicate with others. You entertain yourself and others telling jokes or stories. This intelligence is found in poets and rappers, playwrights, novelists, journalists, public speakers, and comedians.
- **Bodily-Kinesthetic Intelligence** It is normal for you to express ideas and feelings with your body, as an actor or a dancer does. You are a "natural athlete" and can use your body to play sports or communicate. Perhaps you create or transform things with your hands, as inventors, mechanics, surgeons, chefs, and craftspeople do.
- **Visual-Spatial Intelligence** You easily form pictures in your mind and can mentally see objects from many different angles. Architects, graphic designers, map-makers, navigators, interior decorators, painters, photographers, and sculptors fit into this category.
- **Musical-Rhythmic Intelligence** You sing, play a musical instrument, or write music. Musicians, singers, DJs, and music teachers fall into this group.
- **Interpersonal Intelligence** You are a "people person," acutely aware of others' feelings. You work well with people because you understand them and their special traits. Counselors, teachers, politicians, religious leaders, and successful sales people often have highly developed interpersonal intelligence.
- **Intrapersonal Intelligence** You have a strong sense of yourself. You dream, and you act to make your dreams come true. Strong intrapersonal intelligence occurs in philosophers, entrepreneurs, psychiatrists, therapists, and spiritual teachers.
- **Naturalistic Intelligence** You notice patterns in nature and have a strong interest in plants, animals, and the earth. Geologists, animal researchers, and gardeners use naturalistic intelligence.

WEEK 18

DIRECTIONS **The questions below refer to the article "Many Ways to Be Smart" on page S29. Answer each question below on the day of the week assigned to it.**

MONDAY

What is the meaning of <u>refuting</u> in line 5?

A embracing
B struggling with
C disproving
D obscuring

Vocabulary Workshop, page 94

TUESDAY

Which of the following <u>best</u> describes the traditional way of thinking about intelligence?

A Intelligent people do well in school.
B People are smart in multiple ways.
C No one is smart in more than one way.
D Being a good dancer is a sign of intelligence.

Reading Workshop, page 54

WEDNESDAY

If the writer of this article were to present it as a speech, which type of graphic would be <u>best</u> suited to illustrating the eight types of intelligence?

A bar graph
B pie chart
C line graph
D flow chart

Focus on Viewing and Representing, page 114

THURSDAY

The main idea of the second paragraph is that, in Gardner's theory,

A it is impossible to measure intelligence.
B intelligence is like an apple pie.
C most people are smart in several different ways.
D Gardner's theory is radical and controversial.

Quick Reference Handbook, page 782

FRIDAY

According to Gardner's theory, which type of person would most likely possess great bodily-kinesthetic intelligence?

A a teacher
B a singer
C a poet
D a tailor

Reading Workshop, page 122

WEEK 19

DIRECTIONS **The questions below refer to the article "Many Ways to Be Smart" on page S29. Answer each question below on the day of the week assigned to it.**

MONDAY

The purpose of "Many Ways to Be Smart" is to

A instruct readers on how to increase their I.Q.'s.
B entertain readers with a fanciful hypothesis.
C persuade readers that there are multiple ways to be smart.
D inform readers about Dr. Gardner's theory.

Reading Workshop, page 22

TUESDAY

In line 52, acutely means

A keenly.
B hardly.
C gradually.
D smoothly.

Vocabulary Mini-Lesson, page 25

WEDNESDAY

The pie chart at right show important ideas from the article. Which ideas are missing?

A interpersonal, naturalistic
B logical-mathematical, interpersonal
C naturalistic, visual-spatial
D musical-rhythmic, linguistic

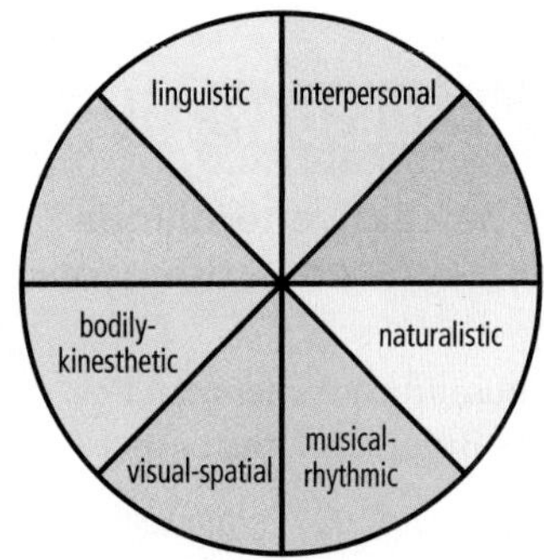

Focus on Viewing and Representing, page 114

THURSDAY

According to Gardner, someone like the late oceanographer Jacques Cousteau would most likely be diagnosed with a high level of

A linguistic intelligence.
B musical-rhythmic intelligence.
C interpersonal intelligence.
D naturalistic intelligence.

Reading Workshop, page 122

FRIDAY

Someone who has struggled in school will most likely find Gardner's theory

A confidence-boosting.
B counter-intuitive.
C depressing.
D awe-inspiring.

Reading Workshop, page 122

DIRECTIONS **Answer each question below on the day of the week assigned to it.**

MONDAY

Choose the response that correctly combines the two sentences below.

Ramon worked at the San Diego Zoo.
He studied elephants.

A Ramon worked at the San Diego Zoo where he studied elephants.
B Ramon worked at the San Diego Zoo, he studied elephants.
C Working at the San Diego Zoo, studying elephants.
D Ramon worked at the San Diego Zoo, studied elephants.

Chapter 8, page 285

TUESDAY

Decide if one of the underlined words below is misspelled. If there is no mistake, select *D*.

A I might be persuaded to change my vote.
B We stared in dissbelief.
C The occasion was grand!
D no mistake

Chapter 25, page 690

WEDNESDAY

Which type of persuasive technique has the creator of the advertisement below used?

Five hundred thousand customers can't be wrong—Barbara's Burgers are the best!

A testimonial
B logical appeal
C "plain folks" appeal
D bandwagon

Critical-Thinking Mini-Lesson, page 254

THURSDAY

Read the following sentence. Choose the response that fixes the underlined error. If there is no error, choose *D*.

Natalie and Chase was racing to the train.

A was raced
B were race
C were racing
D correct as is

Chapter 17, page 483

FRIDAY

There may be a problem in the structure of the word group below. Select the best revision, or choose *D*.

As Alonzo watched the tractor approach the gate to the ranch.

A As Alonzo watched the tractor approach the gate to the ranch, he called to his father.
B As Alonzo watched the tractor approach the gate to the ranch in Wyoming.
C As Alonzo and his father watched the tractor approach the gate to the ranch.
D correct as is

Chapter 8, page 275

PROGRAM AUTHORS

LEE ODELL helped establish the pedagogical framework for the composition strand of *Elements of Language.* In addition, he guided the development of the scope and sequence and pedagogical design of the Writing Workshops. Dr. Odell is Professor of Composition Theory and Research and, since 1996, Director of the Writing Program at Rensselaer Polytechnic Institute. He began his career teaching English in middle and high schools. More recently he has worked with teachers in grades K–12 to establish a program that involves students from all disciplines in writing across the curriculum and for communities outside their classrooms. Dr. Odell's most recent book (with Charles R. Cooper) is *Evaluating Writing: The Role of Teachers' Knowledge about Text, Learning, and Culture* (1999). He is Past Chair of the Conference on College Composition and Communication and of NCTE's Assembly for Research.

RICHARD VACCA helped establish the conceptual basis for the reading strand of *Elements of Language.* In addition, he guided the development of the pedagogical design and the scope and sequence of skills in the Reading Workshops. Dr. Vacca is Professor of Education at Kent State University. He recently completed a term as the forty-second President of the International Reading Association. Originally a middle school and high school teacher, Dr. Vacca served as the project director of the Cleveland Writing Demonstration Project for several years. He is the co-author of *Content Area Reading; Reading and Learning to Read;* and articles and chapters related to adolescents' literacy development. In 1989, Dr. Vacca received the College Reading Association's A. B. Herr Award for Outstanding Contributions to Reading Education. Currently, he is co-chair of the IRA's Commission on Adolescent Literacy.

RENÉE HOBBS helped develop the theoretical framework for the viewing and representing strand of *Elements of Language.* She guided the development of the scope and sequence; served as the authority on terminology, definitions, and pedagogy; and directed the planning for the video series. Dr. Hobbs is Associate Professor of Communication at Babson College in Wellesley, Massachusetts, and Director of the Media Literacy Project. Active in the field of media education, Dr. Hobbs has served as Director of the Institute on Media Education, Harvard Graduate School of Education; Director of the "Know TV" Project, Discovery Networks and Time Warner Cable; and Board Member, The New York Times Newspaper in Education Program. She works actively in staff development in school districts nationwide. Dr. Hobbs has contributed articles and chapters on media, technology, and education to many publications.

JUDITH L. IRVIN also helped establish the conceptual basis for the reading strand of *Elements of Language.* Dr. Irvin taught middle school for several years before pursuing graduate studies in Reading-Language Arts. She now teaches courses in curriculum, middle school education, and educational leadership at Florida State University. She chaired the Research Committee of the National Middle School Association and was the editor of *Research in Middle Level Education Quarterly* for six years. Dr. Irvin writes a column, "What Research Says to the Middle Level Practitioner," for the *Middle School Journal.* Her many publications include *What Research Says to the Middle Level Practitioner* and *Reading and the Middle School Student: Strategies to Enhance Literacy.*

JOHN E. WARRINER was a high school English teacher when he developed the original organizational structure for his classic *English Grammar and Composition* series. The approach pioneered by Mr. Warriner was distinctive, and the editorial staff of Holt, Rinehart and Winston have worked diligently to retain the unique qualities of his pedagogy. For the same reason, HRW continues to credit Mr. Warriner as an author of *Elements of Language* in recognition of his groundbreaking work. John Warriner also co-authored the *English Workshop* series and was editor of *Short Stories: Characters in Conflict.* Throughout his career, however, teaching remained Mr. Warriner's major interest, and he taught for thirty-two years in junior and senior high schools and in college.

PROGRAM CONSULTANTS

The program consultants reviewed instructional materials to ensure consistency with current research, classroom appropriateness, and alignment with curriculum guidelines.

Ann Bagley
Senior Administrator for Secondary English
Wake County Public Schools
Raleigh, North Carolina

Vicki R. Brown
Professor of Education
Grambling State University
Principal, Grambling Middle School
Grambling, Louisiana

Max Hutto
Supervisor of Middle School Language Arts
Hillsborough County Schools
Tampa, Florida

Beth Johnson
Supervisor of Language Arts
Polk District Schools
Bartow, Florida

Kathleen Jongsma
Associate Professor, Department of Education Chair
Texas Lutheran University
Seguin, Texas

Kaye Price-Hawkins
Language Arts Consultant
Abilene, Texas

Lanny van Allen
Consultant, Texas Center for Reading and Language Arts
The University of Texas at Austin
Austin, Texas

CRITICAL REVIEWERS

The critical reviewers read and evaluated pre-publication materials for this book.

Ann B. Adams
Alameda Junior High School
Pocatello, Idaho

Liza G. Bryant
Deerlake Middle School
Tallahassee, Florida

Karen Chaffin
Morningside Middle School
Ft. Worth, Texas

Judy Champney
Science Hill High School
Johnson City, Tennessee

Karen L. Gamble
Labay Middle School
Houston, Texas

Raffy Garza-Vizcaino
Brooke Elementary School
Austin, Texas

Gail Hayes
South Florence High School
Florence, South Carolina

Heidi Huckabee
Mesa Middle School
Roswell, New Mexico

Martha Dixon Kearse
Providence High School
Charlotte, North Carolina

Thomas F. Lathinghouse
Bruner Middle School
Fort Walton Beach, Florida

Nancy Levi
Oakland High School
Murfreesboro, Tennessee

Gary McCloskey
Walter Stiern Middle School
Bakersfield, California

Mary Mikel
Okaloosa County School District
Crestview, Florida

Elizabeth G. Pope
Memorial Middle School
Sioux Falls, South Dakota

Beverly E. Sparks
Chemawa Middle School
Riverside, California

Lynn Fry Striepe
Indian Trails Middle School
Winter Springs, Florida

Betty Templeton
Riverside High School
Greer, South Carolina

Michael J. Wallpe
Metropolitan School District
Indianapolis, Indiana

Julie Wright
Carr Intermediate School
Santa Ana, California

TEACHER/STUDENT CONTRIBUTORS

The following teachers and students worked with HRW's editorial staff to provide models of student writing for the book.

Teachers

Marjorie A. Bloom
DeLaura Middle School
Satellite Beach, Florida

Karen Chaffin
Morningside Middle School
Ft. Worth, Texas

Karyn Gloden
Wake County Public School System
Raleigh, North Carolina

Shannon Niemeyer
Edward E. Drew, Jr. Middle School
Falmouth, Virginia

Karyn Pappert
Linton Middle School
Penn Hills, Pennsylvania

Judi Thorn
Jenks East Middle School
Tulsa, Oklahoma

Julie Wright
Carr Intermediate School
Santa Ana, California

Students

Julie Clift
DeLaura Junior High School
Satellite Beach, Florida

Anthony J. Falso
Linton Middle School
Penn Hills, Pennsylvania

Armando Hernandez
Morningside Middle School
Ft. Worth, Texas

Chris Janney
Edward E. Drew, Jr. Middle School
Falmouth, Virginia

Lindi Martin
Jenks East Middle School
Tulsa, Oklahoma

Carolyn Paisie
Davis Drive Middle School
Apex, North Carolina

Arlyne Torres
Carr Intermediate School,
Santa Ana, California

FIELD TEST PARTICIPANTS

The following teachers participated in the pre-publication field test or review of prototype materials for the *Elements of Language* series.

Nadene Adams
Robert Gray Middle School
Portland, Oregon

Carol Alves
Apopka High School
Apopka, Florida

Susan Atkinson
O. P. Norman Junior High School
Kaufman, Texas

Sheryl L. Babione
Fremont Ross High School
Fremont, Ohio

Jane Baker
Elkins High School
Missouri City, Texas

Martha Barnard
Scarborough High School
Houston, Texas

Jennifer S. Barr
James Bowie High School
Austin, Texas

Leslie Benefield
Reed Middle School
Duncanville, Texas

Gina Birdsall
Irving High School
Irving, Texas

Sara J. Brennan
Murchison Middle School
Austin, Texas

Janelle Brinck
Leander Middle School
Leander, Texas

Geraldine K. Brooks
William B. Travis High School
Austin, Texas

Peter J. Caron
Cumberland Middle School
Cumberland, Rhode Island

Patty Cave
O. P. Norman Junior High School
Kaufman, Texas

Mary Cathyrne Coe
Pocatello High School
Pocatello, Idaho

Continued

Geri-Lee DeGennaro
Tarpon Springs High School
Tarpon Springs, Florida

Karen Dendy
Stephen F. Austin Middle School
Irving, Texas

Dianne Franz
Tarpon Springs Middle School
Tarpon Springs, Florida

Doris F. Frazier
East Millbrook Magnet Middle School
Raleigh, North Carolina

Shayne G. Goodrum
C. E. Jordan High School
Durham, North Carolina

Bonnie L. Hall
St. Ann School
Lansing, Illinois

Doris Ann Hall
Forest Meadow Junior High School
Dallas, Texas

James M. Harris
Mayfield High School
Mayfield Village, Ohio

Lynne Hoover
Fremont Ross High School
Fremont, Ohio

Patricia A. Humphreys
James Bowie High School
Austin, Texas

Jennifer L. Jones
Oliver Wendell Holmes Middle School
Dallas, Texas

Kathryn R. Jones
Murchison Middle School
Austin, Texas

Bonnie Just
Narbonne High School
Harbor City, California

Vincent Kimball
Patterson High School #405
Baltimore, Maryland

Nancy C. Long
MacArthur High School
Houston, Texas

Carol M. Mackey
Ft. Lauderdale Christian School
Ft. Lauderdale, Florida

Jan Jennings McCown
Johnston High School
Austin, Texas

Alice Kelly McCurdy
Rusk Middle School
Dallas, Texas

Elizabeth Morris
Northshore High School
Slidell, Louisiana

Victoria Reis
Western High School
Ft. Lauderdale, Florida

Dean Richardson
Scarborough High School
Houston, Texas

Susan M. Rogers
Freedom High School
Morganton, North Carolina

Sammy Rusk
North Mesquite High School
Mesquite, Texas

Carole B. San Miguel
James Bowie High School
Austin, Texas

Jane Saunders
William B. Travis High School
Austin, Texas

Gina Sawyer
Reed Middle School
Duncanville, Texas

Laura R. Schauermann
MacArthur High School
Houston, Texas

Stephen Shearer
MacArthur High School
Houston, Texas

Elizabeth Curry Smith
Tarpon Springs High School
Tarpon Springs, Florida

Jeannette M. Spain
Stephen F. Austin High School
Sugar Land, Texas

Carrie Speer
Northshore High School
Slidell, Louisiana

Trina Steffes
MacArthur High School
Houston, Texas

Andrea G. Freirich Stewart
Freedom High School
Morganton, North Carolina

Diana O. Torres
Johnston High School
Austin, Texas

Jan Voorhees
Whitesboro High School
Marcy, New York

Ann E. Walsh
Bedichek Middle School
Austin, Texas

Mary Jane Warden
Onahan School
Chicago, Illinois

Beth Westbrook
Covington Middle School
Austin, Texas

Char-Lene Wilkins
Morenci Area High School
Morenci, Michigan

CONTENTS IN BRIEF

CONTENTS

CHAPTER 2

Explaining a Complex Process

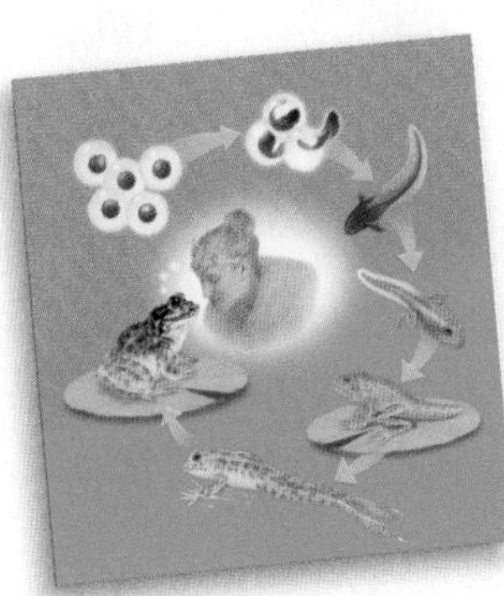

CHAPTER

Explaining Cause and Effect

Informational Text

Exposition

CHAPTER 4

Analyzing a Book

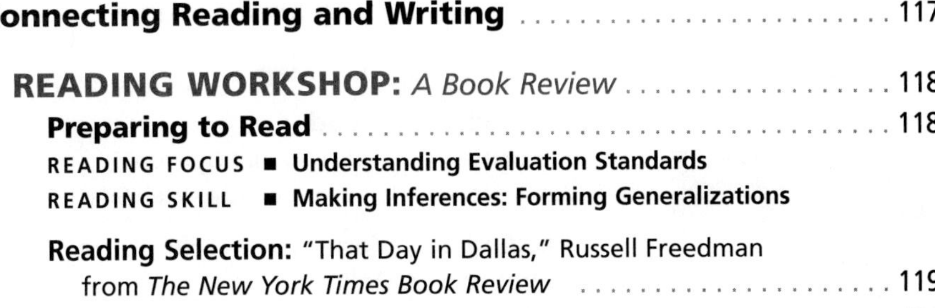

Informational Text

Exposition

CHAPTER

Reporting Your Research 156

Informational Text

Exposition

CHAPTER

Sharing an Opinion 202

Informational Text

Persuasion

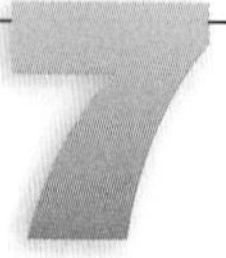

CHAPTER 7

Using Brochures 238

Informational Text

Persuasion

PART 2 Sentences and Paragraphs 272

PART 3 Grammar, Usage, and Mechanics

CHAPTER 10

The Sentence

CHAPTER 11

Parts of Speech Overview

CHAPTER 13

Complements

Direct and Indirect Objects, Subject Complements 398

CHAPTER 14

The Phrase

Prepositional, Verbal, and Appositive Phrases 414

CHAPTER 15

The Clause

Independent and Subordinate Clauses 438

CHAPTER 16

Sentence Structure

CHAPTER 17

Agreement

CHAPTER 18

Using Verbs Correctly

Principal Parts, Regular and Irregular Verbs, Tense, Voice 504

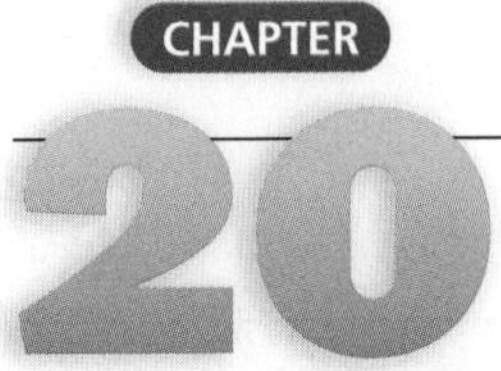

Jump Start reprinted by permission of United Feature Syndicate, Inc.

CHAPTER 21

A Glossary of Usage

Common Usage Problems 580

CHAPTER 22

Capital Letters

Rules for Capitalization 602

Punctuation

End Marks, Commas, Semicolons, and Colons 628

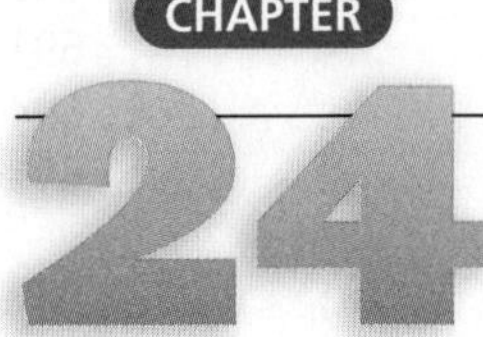

Punctuation

Underlining (Italics), Quotation Marks, Apostrophes, Hyphens, Parentheses, Brackets, Dashes 658

CHAPTER 25

Spelling

CHAPTER 26

Correcting Common Errors

PART 4 Quick Reference Handbook 752

MODELS

READING SELECTION

- The Conservancy of Southwest Florida, ***The Wildest Places in Southwest Florida***
- Mark Derr, **"If You're a Bear, These Dogs Will Give You Paws,"** from *Smithsonian*
- **"Egyptian Mummies,"** Smithsonian Institution Web site
- Russell Freedman, **"That Day in Dallas,"** from *The New York Times Book Review*
- Bob Hugel, **"I Can't Hear You! Listen Up: Save Your Hearing by Acting Now,"** from *Scholastic Choices*
- Ben Mikaelsen, **"Bear in the Family,"** from *Voices from the Middle*
- Charol Shakeshaft, **"Should Public School Students Wear Uniforms?"** from *Newsday*
- **"Special Effects: Titanic and Beyond,"** NOVA *Online*

WRITING MODELS

- Aesop, **"The Dog and His Shadow"**
- Maya Angelou, ***I Know Why the Caged Bird Sings***
- Harry Behn, **"Growing Up"**
- Myrna Daly, **"Pocahontas: A Bridge Toward Peace,"** *Boys' Life*
- Gerald Durrell with Lee Durrell, ***The Amateur Naturalist***
- Leonard Engel, ***The Sea***
- Colin Fletcher, ***The Secret Worlds of Colin Fletcher***
- Esther Forbes, ***Johnny Tremain***
- John Langone, ***In the Shogun's Shadow***
- Michael D. Lemonick, **"Under Attack,"** *Time*
- David Louis, ***2201 Fascinating Facts***
- Nancy Mohr, **"A Long Shot Pays Off,"** *Smithsonian*
- Ken Nesbitt, **"Don't Bring Camels in the Classroom"**
- Marian T. Place, ***Mount St. Helens: A Sleeping Volcano Awakes***
- Jack Prelutsky, **"An Elephant Is Hard to Hide"**
- Esmeralda Santiago, ***When I Was Puerto Rican***
- Marilyn Singer, ***It's Hard to Read a Map with a Beagle on Your Lap***
- Monica Sone, ***Nisei Daughter***
- William Wise, **"Strange and Terrible Monsters of the Deep,"** *Boys' Life*
- **"Word Stories: Brazil,"** *Calliope*
- Jean Wyrick, ***Steps to Writing Well***

STUDENT MODELS

- Julie Clift, **"Team Sports"**
- Anthony Falso, **"The Yard Doctors"**
- Armando Hernandez, **"How Do CDs Work?"**
- Chris Janney, **"Tracking Hurricanes"**
- Lindi Martin, **"Conquering Your Fears"**
- Carolyn Paisie, **"Remembering Childhood"**
- Arlyne Torres, **"Viewing Violence"**

STUDENT'S OVERVIEW

***Elements of Language* is divided into four major parts.**

PART 1 Communications

This section ties together the essential skills and strategies you use in all types of communication—reading, writing, listening, speaking, viewing, and representing.

Reading Workshops In these workshops, you read an article, a story, an editorial—a real-life example of a type of writing you will later compose on your own. In addition, these workshops help you practice the reading process through

- a Reading Skill and Reading Focus specific to each type of writing
- Vocabulary Mini-Lessons to help you understand unfamiliar words
- Test-Taking Mini-Lessons targeting common reading objectives

Writing Workshops In these workshops, you brainstorm ideas and use the writing process to produce your own article, story, editorial—and more. These workshops also include

- Writing and Critical-Thinking Mini-Lessons to help you master important aspects of each type of writing
- an organizational framework and models to guide your writing
- evaluation charts with concrete steps for revising
- Connections to Literature and Connections to Life, activities that extend writing workshop skills and concepts to other areas of your life
- Test-Taking Mini-Lessons to help you respond to writing prompts for tests

Focus on Speaking and Listening
Focus on Viewing and Representing

This is your chance to sharpen your skills in presenting your ideas visually and orally and to learn how to take a more critical view of what you hear and see.

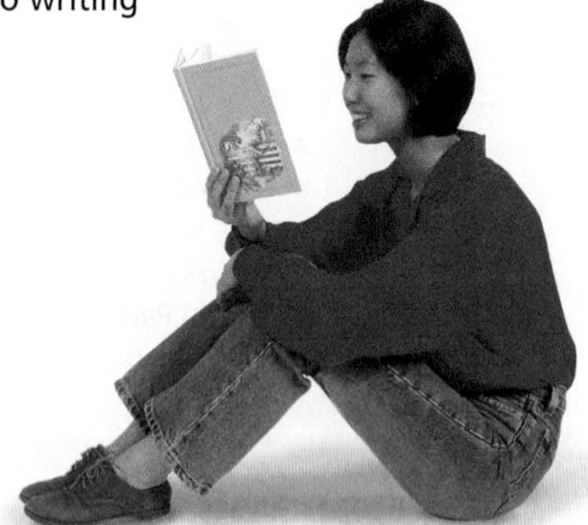

PART 2 Sentences and Paragraphs

Learn to construct clear and effective sentences and paragraphs—what parts to include, how to organize ideas, and how to write these essential parts of compositions with style.

PART 3 Grammar, Usage, and Mechanics

These are the basics that will help you make your writing correct and polished.

Grammar Discover the structure of language—the words, phrases, and clauses that are the building blocks of sentences.

Usage Learn the rules that govern how language is used in various social situations, including standard versus nonstandard and formal versus informal English.

Mechanics Master the nuts and bolts of correct written English, including capitalization, punctuation, and spelling.

PART 4 Quick Reference Handbook

Use this handy guide in and outside school anytime you need concise tips to help you communicate more effectively—whether you need to find information in a variety of media, make sense of what you read, prepare for tests, or present your ideas in a published document, speech, or visual.

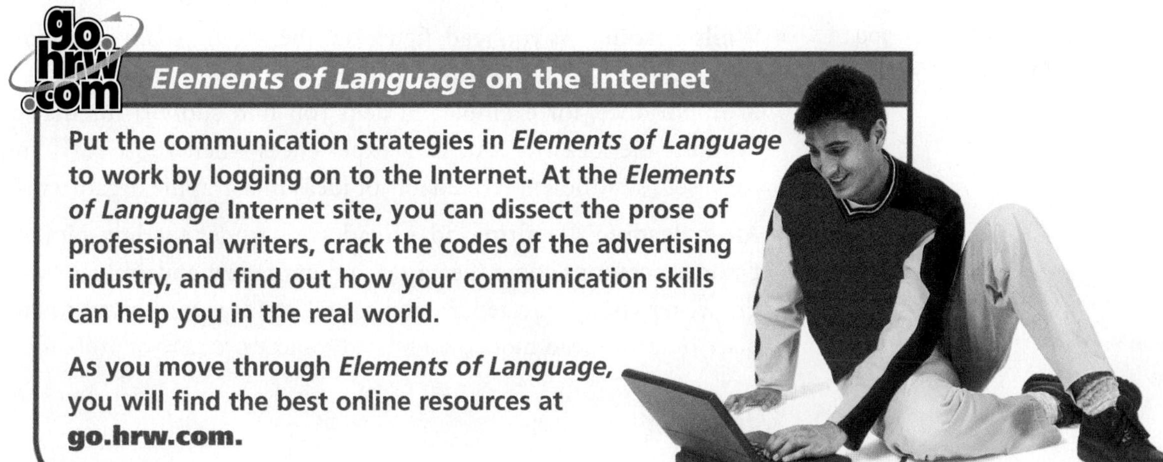

Elements of Language on the Internet

Put the communication strategies in *Elements of Language* to work by logging on to the Internet. At the *Elements of Language* Internet site, you can dissect the prose of professional writers, crack the codes of the advertising industry, and find out how your communication skills can help you in the real world.

As you move through *Elements of Language*, you will find the best online resources at go.hrw.com.

The Reading and Writing Processes

Do these situations sound familiar? While reading, you suddenly realize you have read the same sentences several times without gaining any meaning from them. While writing, you stare at the single sentence you have written, unable to think of anything else to write. When you find yourself stuck, step back and look at the processes of reading and writing.

Reading

The reading you do in school requires you to think critically about information and ideas. In order to get the most from a text, prepare your mind for the task before you read, use effective strategies while you read, and take time to process the information after you read.

TIP Reading and writing are both recursive processes—that is, you can return to earlier steps when needed. For example, you might make new predictions while you are reading a text or you might develop additional support for ideas when you are revising a piece of writing.

- **Before Reading** Get your mind in gear by considering your purpose for reading a particular piece of writing and by thinking about what you already know about the topic. Preview the text by skimming a bit and considering headings, graphics, and other features. Use this information to predict what the text will discuss and how challenging it will be to read.
- **While Reading** As you read, figure out the writer's main idea about the topic. Notice how the text is organized (by cause and effect or in order of importance, for example) to help you find support for that point. Connect the ideas to your own experiences when you can. If you get confused, slow down, re-read, or jot ideas in a graphic organizer.
- **After Reading** Confirm and extend your understanding of the text. Draw conclusions about the writer's point of view, and evaluate how well the writer communicated the message. Use ideas in the text to create a piece of art, to read more on a related topic, or to solve a problem.

Writing

A perfect text seldom springs fully formed from your mind; instead, you must plan your text before you write and work to improve it after drafting.

- **Before Writing** First, choose a topic and a form of writing, such as a poem or an editorial. Decide who your readers will be and what you want the text to accomplish. Develop ideas based on your knowledge and on research. Organize the ideas, and jot down your main point.
- **While Writing** Grab attention and provide background information in an introduction. Elaborate your ideas to support your point, and organize them clearly. Then, wrap things up with a conclusion.
- **After Writing** To improve a draft, evaluate how clearly you expressed your ideas. Ask a peer to suggest areas that need work. Then, revise. Proofread to correct mistakes. Share your finished work with others, and reflect on what you learned.

You may have noticed that the reading and writing processes involve similar strategies. The chart below summarizes these similarities.

The Reading and Writing Processes

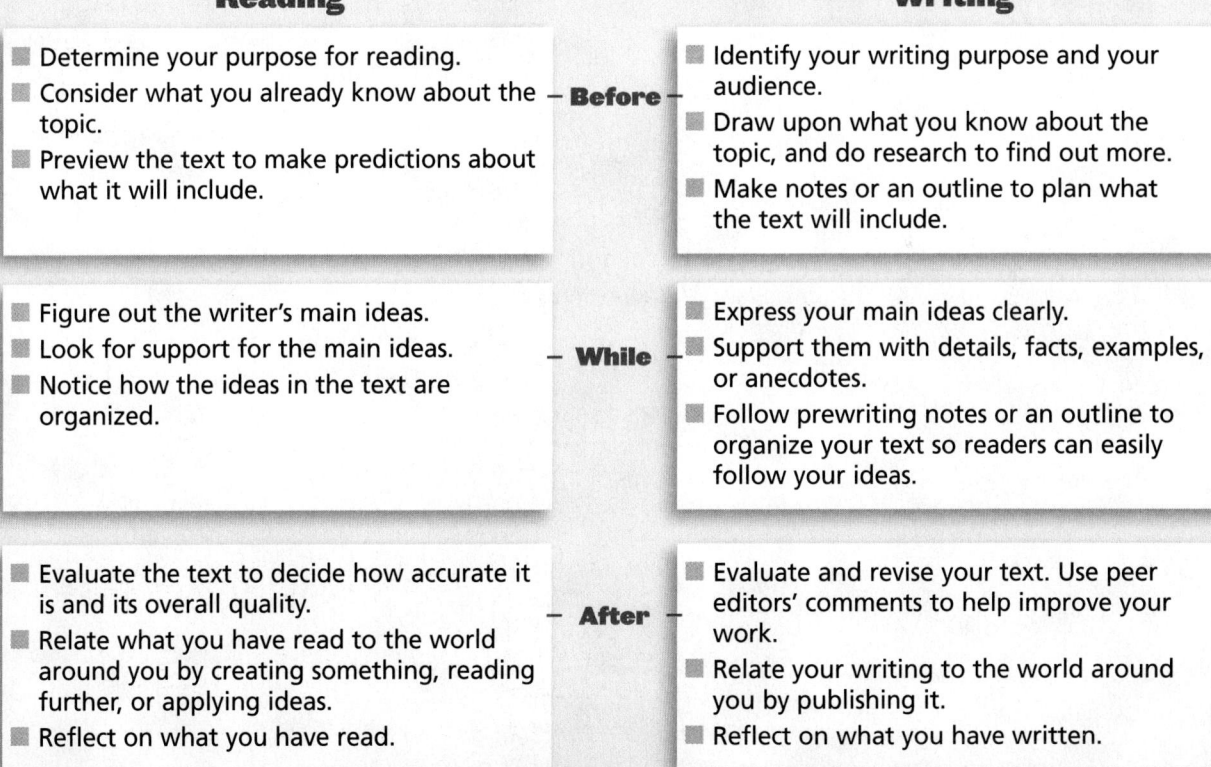

Reading		Writing
■ Determine your purpose for reading. ■ Consider what you already know about the topic. ■ Preview the text to make predictions about what it will include.	**Before**	■ Identify your writing purpose and your audience. ■ Draw upon what you know about the topic, and do research to find out more. ■ Make notes or an outline to plan what the text will include.
■ Figure out the writer's main ideas. ■ Look for support for the main ideas. ■ Notice how the ideas in the text are organized.	**While**	■ Express your main ideas clearly. ■ Support them with details, facts, examples, or anecdotes. ■ Follow prewriting notes or an outline to organize your text so readers can easily follow your ideas.
■ Evaluate the text to decide how accurate it is and its overall quality. ■ Relate what you have read to the world around you by creating something, reading further, or applying ideas. ■ Reflect on what you have read.	**After**	■ Evaluate and revise your text. Use peer editors' comments to help improve your work. ■ Relate your writing to the world around you by publishing it. ■ Reflect on what you have written.

The Reading and Writing Workshops in this book provide valuable practice for strategies that will help you effectively use these related processes.

PART 1

Communications

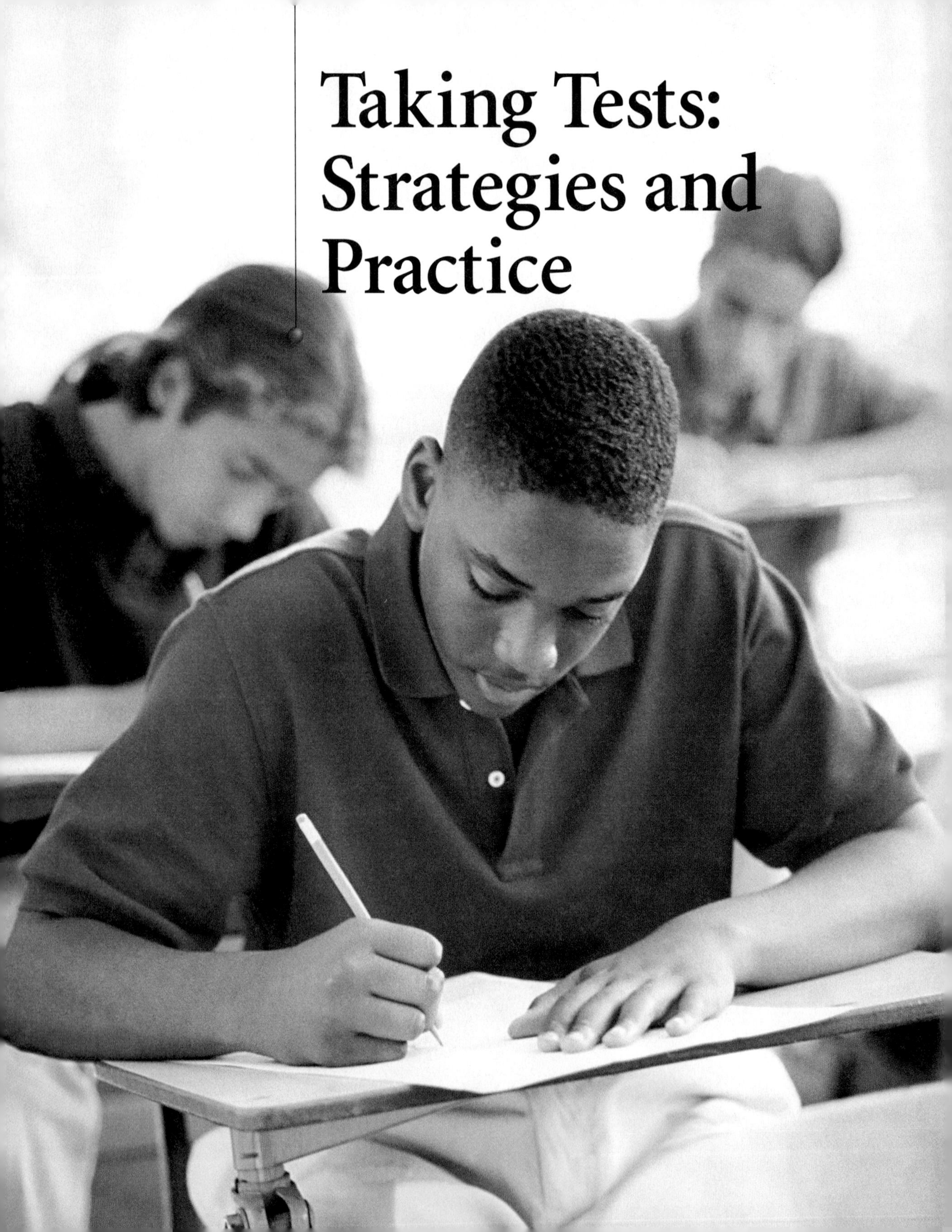

Taking Tests: Strategies and Practice

Taking Reading Tests

Every so often, you get the chance to show what you know about reading and writing by taking a **standardized test.** A standardized reading test contains **reading passages** followed by **multiple-choice questions** and sometimes an open-ended **essay question.** In this section, you'll find strategies and practice to help you boost your scores on the reading sections of standardized tests.

THINKING IT THROUGH

Reading Test Strategies

STEP 1 **Watch your time.** Divide the total test time by the number of questions to estimate how much time you can spend on each question. Check every five or ten minutes to see if you need to speed up.

STEP 2 **Concentrate.** Carefully read the directions and any introduction to the reading passage. Don't let your attention wander as you read the passage. If you're allowed to mark the test booklet, underline or circle key words and phrases.

STEP 3 **Understand the question.** Look for tricky words like *not* and *except;* they require you to choose an answer that is false or opposite in some way. Don't fall for answers that make true statements but don't answer the question that's being asked. Most important, never choose an answer until you've read *all* of the answer choices.

STEP 4 **Make educated guesses.** You may recognize the correct answer easily. If not, first get rid of the one or two answers you know are wrong. Then, from the remaining answers, choose the one you think is most likely to be right. Learn to trust your educated guesses.

STEP 5 **Keep going.** Don't get stuck. Skip difficult questions you can't answer. You can go back to them later if you have time at the end.

STEP 6 **Don't lose your place.** Before you bubble in an answer, match each question to the number on the answer sheet. If you skip a question, be sure to skip that number on the answer sheet.

STEP 7 **Take another look.** Before time runs out, try answering questions you skipped, and check your answers. Erase any stray marks.

TIP Before the test, ask about how the test is scored. If no points are taken off for wrong answers, plan to answer every question. If wrong answers count against you, answer questions you know and those you can answer with an educated guess.

Read the following passages carefully. Then, choose the best answer to each question.

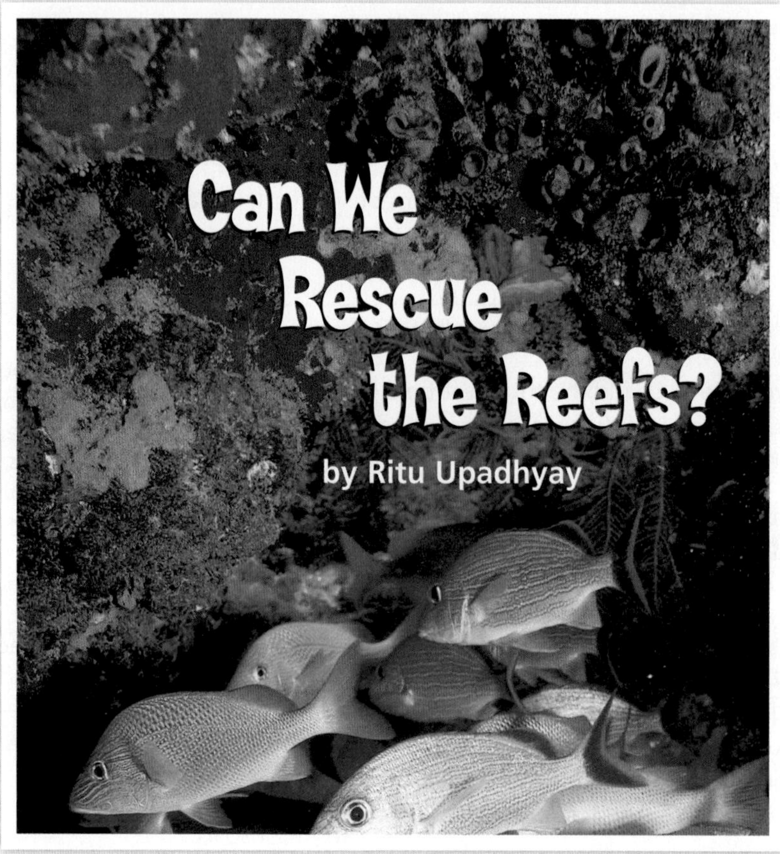

Can We Rescue the Reefs?

by Ritu Upadhyay

Under the clear blue sea, bustling communities of ocean creatures live together in brightly colored, wildly stacked structures called coral reefs. These silent, majestic underwater cities are home to 4,000 different species of fish and thousands of plants and animals. For millions of years, marine creatures have lived together in reefs, going about their business in their own little water worlds.

But danger looms. At an international meeting on coral reefs, scientists issued a harsh warning. More than a quarter of the world's reefs have been destroyed by pollution and careless human behavior. Unless drastic measures are taken, the remaining reefs may be dead in 20 years. "We are about to lose them," says Clive Wilkinson of the Coral Reef Monitoring Network.

Precious Underwater Habitats

The destruction of coral reefs, some of which are 2 1/2 million years old, would have a very serious impact on our oceans. Though coral reefs take up less than one percent of the ocean floor, they are home to 25% of all underwater species. Wiping them out would put thousands of creatures at risk of extinction. It would also destroy one of our planet's most beautiful living treasures.

Though it's often mistaken for rock because of its stony texture, coral is actually made up of tiny clear animals called coral polyps. Millions stick together in colonies and form a hard outer shell. The colonies eventually grow together, creating large reefs. When coral die, their skeletons are left behind, and new coral build on top. Reefs grow into complex, mazelike structures with different rooms, hallways, holes, and crevices for their inhabitants to live in. Over the years, the ancient Great Barrier Reef off Australia's coast has grown to 1,240 miles long!

Sucking the Life out of the Reefs

Coral may look and feel tough, but it is extremely sensitive to environmental changes. A major cause of recent reef destruction is the gradual warming of the oceans. The El Niño climate shift in 1998, in particular, heated seas and did terrible damage to coral reefs.

Warm water causes a deadly situation called coral bleaching. Coral contains tiny algae, or water plants, that give coral its vibrant color. Coral also uses the algae to create its food. This mutually helpful relationship between two beings is called symbiosis (sim-by-oh-sis). At high temperatures, though, coral releases the algae. Without it, not only does coral lose its beautiful color—it dies.

Global warming is believed to be caused by certain polluting gases that trap heat close to the earth's surface. Unless something is done, warns scientist Ove Hoegh-Guldberg, the oceans will grow so warm over the next 20 years that the reefs will be cooking in a "hot soup."

Not Such a Dynamite Idea

While warming may be the biggest threat to coral reefs, it is not the only one. Fishermen do enormous damage. The fish that live in reefs are very valuable as pets and food. To trap these fish, some fishermen enjoy "blast fishing"—shattering reefs with dynamite. Others drop cyanide poison into the water to stun fish so they are easier to catch. Most of the reefs in the Philippines have been destroyed by such fishing techniques. Pollution from oil slicks, garbage, and pesticides has also taken a toll. It messes up the delicate balance among algae, coral, and other reef species.

The outlook for reefs is not hopeless, however. Scientists believe reefs can be rescued if governments control pollution and ban practices like blast fishing. Says Wilkinson: "The world's attitude must change."

1. Which sentence **best** states the main idea of the passage?

A. Swift action is needed to save coral reefs, which are dying.

B. Coral reefs are home to more than 4,000 species.

C. Coral reefs are made up of colonies of tiny animals called coral polyps.

D. Global warming has been raising the ocean's temperature.

2. The writer's main purpose is to

F. describe

G. entertain

H. tell a story

J. give information

continued

3. How does the author support the point that reefs are being destroyed?

A. by explaining how reefs form

B. by describing reef fish

C. by noting reef locations

D. by quoting experts

4. What does *crevices* mean in this sentence from the article?

> "Reefs grow into complex, mazelike structures with different rooms, hallways, holes, and crevices for their inhabitants to live in."

F. homes

G. buildings

H. cracks

J. nests

5. The three paragraphs under the subhead "Sucking the Life out of the Reefs" have the organizational pattern of

A. chronological order

B. order of importance

C. cause and effect

D. comparison and contrast

6. Which is an example of *symbiosis?*

F. Coral build on top of skeletons of other coral.

G. Fishers use poison to stun the fish living in reefs.

H. Coral and algae live together and help each other.

J. Warm water kills the algae that live on coral reefs.

7. We can infer that any disease that kills the algae that live in coral will also

A. kill the coral animals

B. kill fish and other plants

C. make the reefs more beautiful

D. keep divers away from the reefs

8. *Coral bleaching* is a term used to describe what happens when

F. fish and other species begin to inhabit the reefs

G. the coral release the algae that live in the reef

H. common fishing techniques kill the coral

J. the coral animals turn bright, beautiful colors

Write several paragraphs in response to *one* of the following questions:

9. Identify the causes of reef damage that can be controlled by people. Then, tell what you personally can do to help rescue coral reefs. What other steps do you think can or should be taken? Support your statements with reasons and evidence.

10. You have just won a trip to scuba dive in a coral reef. Describe everything you see on your dive—sea life, reef formations, damaged areas, and human activities. Be sure to include sensory details.

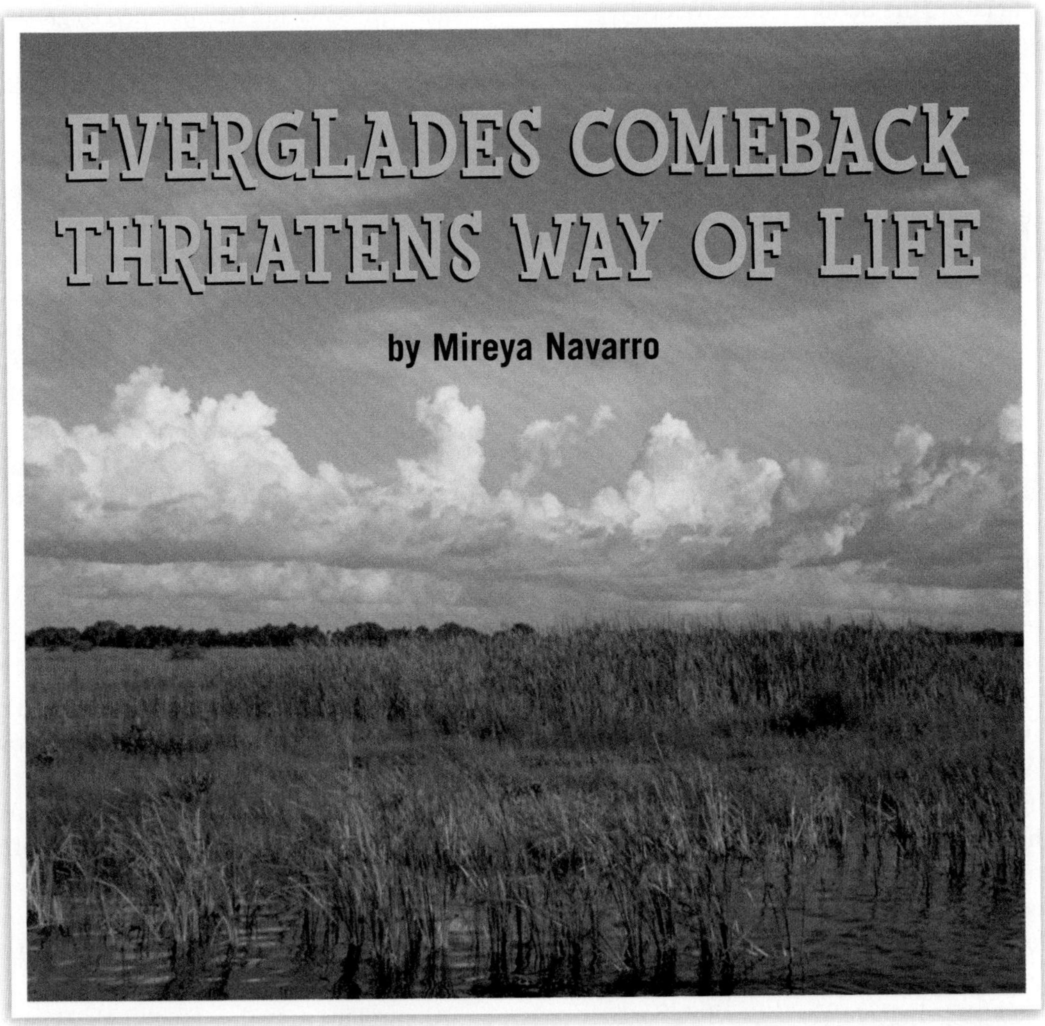

EVERGLADES COMEBACK THREATENS WAY OF LIFE
by Mireya Navarro

The way some residents tell it, the area on the edge of the Everglades National Park known as East Everglades can have all the charm of a swamp: flooding, mosquitoes, remoteness. But the same residents describe the bright side of the neighborhood as "magical" and "breathtaking."

"The privacy, the quality of the air, the low noise, the safety, the spiritual contact with nature," said Jose Exposito, 38, an East Everglades resident and the owner of an orchid business, "it's just a way of life you don't find anywhere."

That way of life is about to end for the area, about 25 miles west of Miami. Mr. Exposito's rural neighborhood, government officials say, stands as one of the obstacles to a comprehensive[1] effort to repair the vast expanse of wetlands that is the Everglades.

Officials of the South Florida Water Management District, the agency that oversees flood protection and water supply for 16 counties, voted last month to spend about $120 million to buy out the 1,400 landowners in the East Everglades area by the year 2002. Those who refuse to sell will have their properties condemned,[2] officials said.

Officials of the water management agency say plans are for most of the area of 6,000 acres to have continuous standing water once the residents are gone, as efforts are begun to restore the flow of water to the Everglades National Park.

"This is one of these crucial components"[3] for restoration, said Mark Kraus, conservation director for the Everglades office of the National Audubon Society, "and the people living in the area are victims of circumstance."

"We support the plan for buyout," Mr. Kraus said, "but we know there's a human factor here, and there ought to be fair treatment, including relocation costs."

East Everglades neighbors say money does not begin to compensate[4] them for wiping out their homes and businesses, which started developing in the 1950's. The area, an eclectic[5] collection of small farms, ranches, and concrete-block homes on plots of several acres, oozes self-sufficiency. . . .

Businesses include Mr. Exposito's Soroa Orchids, whose motto, "an exquisite encounter with nature," is a promise he said he might not be able to keep somewhere else. And neighbors include Berta and Humberto Valdes, who built their 2,800-square-foot home in 1979 as a haven[6] to raise five sons and had planned to grow mamey[7] trees to support their retirement.

"You can't compensate 20 years of a lifetime," said Mrs. Valdes, 48, a teacher. "We did everything right to build our family house, our retirement house. Our future retirement income is gone."

The community has become a casualty of an effort to correct what Everglades preservationists call a monumental environmental mistake: ditching and draining that started in 1947 as a flood-control project mandated by Congress. . . .

Many East Everglades residents and their supporters said that as nature lovers they would understand the need to give the land back to the Everglades to insure its health. But many refuse to believe that their displacement[8] is necessary to restore water flow to the Everglades National Park.

Some note that the Army Corps of Engineers had proposed at one time a less costly alternative: building a levee[9] around the area to allow it to survive as more water was released into the park.

Richard Bonner, a deputy district engineer for the Army Corps in Florida, said state officials had decided against that option for fear that such protection would induce more population growth and ultimately become more of a barrier to getting water to the park.

"Controlling growth is tough," Mr. Bonner said. "It's hard to keep people out." . . .

---

1. **comprehensive:** complete.
2. **condemned:** taken by the government for public use.
3. **crucial components:** extremely important parts or elements.
4. **compensate:** pay for.
5. **eclectic:** varied.
6. **haven:** safe place.
7. **mamey:** a tropical fruit tree.
8. **displacement:** removal.
9. **levee:** a wall of earth to stop high water from flooding land.

Hector and Georgina Beceiro, who moved into the area in 1975, spending five years building their house on two and a half acres, where they grow plantains and tangerines, say it will take a court order to get them out. The ashes of her father, who once lived with them, are scattered around the property according to his wishes, the family said.

"I'm 67," Mr. Beceiro, a retired salesman, said. "Do you know what it's like to have to start over at 67? Can the government pay me for all the hours of work over 23 years?" . . .

11. Which sentence **best** states the main idea of the passage?

- **A.** East Everglades is a magical place to live, unlike anywhere else in Miami.
- **B.** Soon the East Everglades will be flooded with standing water.
- **C.** The Everglades was damaged when the Army Corps of Engineers built ditches and drained the water.
- **D.** Residents will be forced to leave businesses and homes because of conservation efforts.

12. Who has control over what will happen to the East Everglades?

- **F.** the residents of the East Everglades
- **G.** the Army Corps of Engineers
- **H.** the South Florida Water Management District
- **J.** the Everglades office of the National Audubon Society

13. Mrs. Valdes and Mr. Beceiro both believe that

- **A.** the government can't compensate them for their time
- **B.** restoring the Everglades is not important
- **C.** the Army Corps of Engineers is to blame for the water problem
- **D.** flooding could destroy their homes and businesses

14. Why did state officials decide **not** to build a levee?

- **F.** It would be too expensive and take too much time to build.
- **G.** It couldn't hold back the amount of water released into the park.
- **H.** It might encourage more people to move into the area.
- **J.** It would cause further damage to the Everglades.

15. Why does the author quote East Everglades residents as well as officials?

- **A.** to make clear the article's structure
- **B.** to present both sides of a controversial issue
- **C.** to support the author's personal opinion
- **D.** to persuade the government to change its policy

16. *Restoration* (in paragraph 6) means

- **F.** returning someone to health and strength
- **G.** putting something back the way it was
- **H.** imitating an old object, such as an antique piece of furniture
- **J.** putting a person back in a place or rank

continued

17. From this passage, we can infer that people from the East Everglades will probably

A. move out quickly with few objections

B. object to having to move

C. refuse to move

D. move to another swamp area

Comparing the Passages

18. The main thing that both passages have in common is that they

F. discuss an environmental problem and possible solutions

G. oppose a plan to solve an environmental problem

H. try to persuade the reader to take a specific action

J. express the writer's personal opinion on a controversial issue

Write several paragraphs in response to *one* of the following questions:

19. At the end of the first passage, Clive Wilkinson says, "The world's attitude must change." Explain what you think he means by that statement and what actions the passage suggests must be taken. Do you think Mark Kraus feels the same way or differently about the attitudes expressed by East Everglades residents in the second passage? Explain, and give details from the passages to support your statements.

20. Do you think the authors of these two passages have different purposes for writing, or is their purpose the same? Explain what you think each author's purpose is. Use details and information from the passages to support your view.

Taking Writing Tests

Standardized tests measure your writing skills in two ways:

- An **on-demand writing prompt** gives you a situation and asks you to write a coherent, well-developed **essay** in a limited time, usually less than an hour. The prompt may ask you to write a narrative, expository, or persuasive essay.
- **Multiple-choice questions** test your knowledge of sentence construction and revision and paragraph content and organization.

Use the following strategies to write any type of essay. You'll recognize these steps as the familiar steps of the writing process.

THINKING IT THROUGH: Writing Test Strategies

STEP 1 **Read the writing prompt carefully.** Underline key verbs (such as *analyze, argue, explain*) that tell you what to do. (Before the test, review the chart of **key verbs that appear in essay questions,** page 816.) Cover all parts of the prompt—including identifying your audience—or you'll lose points.

STEP 2 **Think before you write.** If you have forty-five minutes to write, take ten minutes or so for prewriting. Use scratch paper to brainstorm ideas, make a cluster diagram or a rough outline, or gather details. Plan how you'll organize your essay.

STEP 3 **Draft your essay.** Spend about two thirds of your time drafting your essay. Express your ideas as clearly as you can. Write a strong opening paragraph and a definite closing, and use specific details to support and elaborate your main points.

STEP 4 **Edit and revise as you write.** Re-read your draft. Try to use transitions or combine sentences to make the ideas flow together more smoothly. To add a word or a sentence, use a caret (^) and insert it clearly and neatly.

STEP 5 **Proofread your essay.** Correct all errors in grammar, usage, mechanics, and spelling. Your score partly depends on how well you follow these conventions of standard English.

TIP Don't skip this prewriting step. Using prewriting strategies will result in a stronger, more interesting essay.

Narrative Writing

Sample Writing Prompt *Tell a brief story (a true story or a fictional one) about an incident involving a contest, a race, or another kind of competition. Introduce main characters, and tell what happened. Add dialogue and details about the setting to your story.*

Reference Note

For more on writing a **personal narrative,** see pages 27–38.

A story map like the one below can help you plan a short story or an autobiographical incident. Be sure to do what the prompt asks you to do—add dialogue and details about the setting and characters. (See **using and punctuating dialogue** on page 39.)

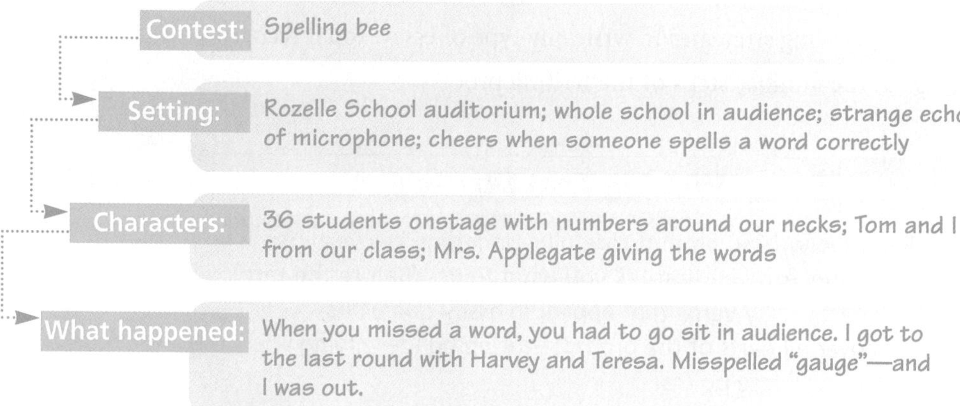

Contest: Spelling bee
Setting: Rozelle School auditorium; whole school in audience; strange echo of microphone; cheers when someone spells a word correctly
Characters: 36 students onstage with numbers around our necks; Tom and I from our class; Mrs. Applegate giving the words
What happened: When you missed a word, you had to go sit in audience. I got to the last round with Harvey and Teresa. Misspelled "gauge"—and I was out.

Expository Writing

Sample Writing Prompt *Your classmates are preparing a pamphlet for sixth-graders entering middle school. Write a brief article for that pamphlet, explaining how to do something that will help them succeed in school. Identify the skill, and explain each of the steps in the process. Provide details that elaborate on each step.*

Reference Note

For more on **explaining a complex process,** see pages 58–71.

This prompt asks you to write a "how-to" essay (sometimes called a process essay). In your opening paragraph, you'll identify the process or skill and then discuss each step in the order it is performed. Don't forget to give details about each step.

How to Evaluate an Internet Web Site

1. Check for reliability and bias. Who is posting the information? Is it someone's personal Web site (address ends in .net or .com), a government agency (.gov), a for-profit (.com) or not-for-profit organization (.org), or an educational institution (.edu)?
2. Check for how recent the information is. Look for the date it was posted and/or updated.
3. Check for accuracy. Don't believe everything you read. Double-check facts by finding the same information in another source.

Persuasive Writing

Sample Writing Prompt *The city council is considering a law banning bicycling on all sidewalks. Consider the effects such a law will have, and decide whether you support or oppose the proposed law. Then, write an essay in which you clearly express and support your opinion.*

You can use the T.H.E.M.E.S. strategy to brainstorm ideas for your persuasive essay: T = time; H = health; E = education; M = money; E = environment; and S = safety. Here's a cluster diagram by a student who opposes the law.

Reference Note

For more on writing a **persuasive essay,** see pages 212–229.

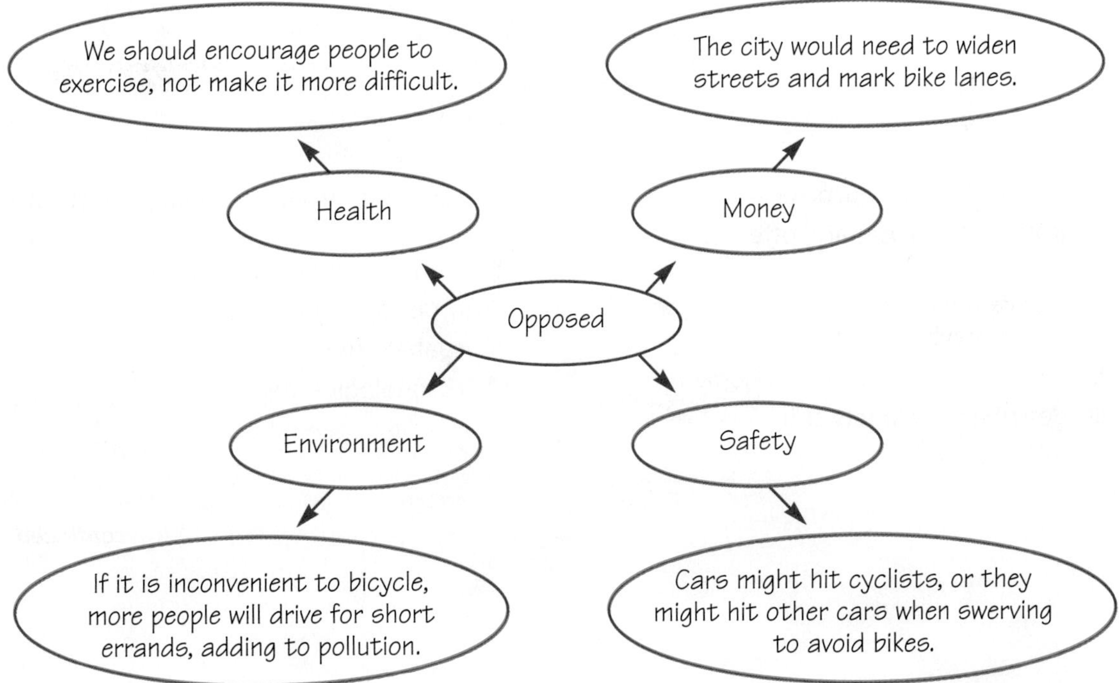
We should encourage people to exercise, not make it more difficult.
The city would need to widen streets and mark bike lanes.
Health
Money
Opposed
Environment
Safety
If it is inconvenient to bicycle, more people will drive for short errands, adding to pollution.
Cars might hit cyclists, or they might hit other cars when swerving to avoid bikes.

TIP Review the strategies on page 3, which also apply to multiple-choice writing questions.

Multiple-Choice Writing Questions

In some standardized tests, multiple-choice writing questions test your understanding of sentence and paragraph structure, and the conventions of standard English (grammar, usage, punctuation, capitalization, and spelling). You may find questions like the ones below.

Read the following paragraph. Then, choose the best answer for each question.

(1) The force that makes objects fall to the ground is also the force that keeps the planets in their orbits around the sun. **(2)** Isaac Newton was the first person to realize this. **(3)** The ancient Greeks thought that objects fell because they were seeking their natural places, and that the planets were moved by invisible crystal spheres. **(4)** Even Johannes Kepler, who showed in 1609 that the planets moved in elliptical, or slightly oval-shaped, orbits, thought that they were being supported by an invisible framework. **(5)** In 1687 Newton proved in his book *Principia* that the planets orbit around the sun because there is a long-range force—gravity—attracting them toward the sun. **(6)** He was also able to show that the force of gravity between the sun and a planet depends on the distance between the two. **(7)** A planet twice as far from the sun as another will experience only one-quarter of the force; if it is three times as far away, the force will be one-ninth, and so on. **(8)** Newton also showed that the force of gravitational attraction between two objects depends on their masses. **(9)** The greater the mass of the objects, the greater the force pulling them together.

1. The writer's main purpose is to
- **A.** explain the causes and effects of gravity
- **B.** discuss the history of our understanding of gravity
- **C.** discuss the history of astronomy
- **D.** describe the planets and workings of our solar system

2. What is the organizational pattern of sentences 3–5?
- **F.** comparison-and-contrast order
- **G.** order of importance
- **H.** spatial order
- **J.** chronological order

continued

3. Sentence 6 makes a statement that sentence 7 supports with two
   A. examples
   B. reasons
   C. causes
   D. opinions

4. A *framework* (sentence 4) is a
   F. long-range plan
   G. structure that holds something up
   H. decorative border around a picture
   J. protective wall

5. We can understand what *elliptical* (sentence 4) means because the writer
   A. gives examples of elliptical objects
   B. contrasts elliptical and round shapes
   C. gives the word's origin
   D. provides a definition after the word

6. In sentence 1, the word *orbits* is
   F. a verb
   G. an adverb
   H. a noun
   J. an adjective

7. In sentence 1, the word *force* appears twice. The first time, it functions as
   A. the subject of the sentence
   B. a direct object
   C. an indirect object
   D. a predicate adjective

8. Which word is misspelled?
   Newton supposedly (**F**) thought of his theory (**G**) of universal (**H**) gravity when he saw an apple fall from a tree. NO ERROR (**J**)

9. How should this sentence be corrected?
   Using Newton's ideas about the orbits of comets Edmond Halley accurately predicted the return of a comet in 1758.
   A. Change *Newton's* to *Newtons.*
   B. Add a comma after *comets.*
   C. Change *accurately* to *acurately.*
   D. Make no change; correct as is

10. Which source would provide the **best** information about recent experiments concerning gravity?
    F. Sir Isaac Newton's book *Principia*
    G. an article on space station research about the effects of weightlessness
    H. a research report about gravity published online by a college student
    J. an encyclopedia article about gravity

Reference Note

For more on preparing for reading and writing tests, see the **Test-Taking Mini-Lessons** in each Part 1 chapter and **Studying and Test Taking** on pages 810–820.

CHAPTER

1 Sharing Your Life

Reading Workshop

Reading a Personal Narrative

Writing Workshop

Writing a Personal Narrative

Speaking and Listening

Telling a True Story

Narration/ Description

"You had better have a good story," your friends say when you show up late. You do. You explain the whole series of events that delayed you. You tell all the details about the lost dog you found, the struggle to catch it, and the thrill of finding its owner and collecting a reward. Your friends are impressed not only by your good deed but also by the way you told them about it.

A **personal narrative** is a story of an experience in someone's life. It focuses on the details—the smells, sights, and sounds associated with the experience. A personal narrative is an example of **expressive writing** because through the telling of the story, the author expresses his or her thoughts and feelings about the experience.

YOUR TURN 1 Discovering Personal Narrative

Get together with other students to share memorable experiences. Try to focus on a single experience, such as playing in an important game or auditioning for a school play or talent show. Include the following as you retell your experience.

- details about your experience (smells, sounds, colors, tastes)
- your feelings during the experience (Were you nervous? happy? excited? scared?)
- how you felt after the experience (Were you relieved? exhausted? proud? embarrassed?)

Reading a Personal Narrative

WHAT'S AHEAD?

In this section you will read a personal narrative. You will also learn how to

- **identify an implied main idea**
- **discover a writer's purpose for writing**

Most pet owners you know probably have a dog, a cat, or maybe some fish. Ben Mikaelsen, the author of the personal narrative on the next page, prefers a different kind of pet. His pet, Buffy, is a lot bigger than your average dog. However, Buffy's size is not the only thing that makes him interesting. As you read about Mikaelsen's life with Buffy, consider these questions: What did the author learn about himself from his experience with his pet? Why do you think the author wants to share his experience with others?

Preparing to Read

READING SKILL

Implied Main Idea A **main idea** is the most important point in a piece of writing, but it is not always stated directly by the author. To identify an **implied main idea,** you have to use the clues that the author provides. These clues include details about the subject. The clues add up to an overall impression in the reader's mind about the main point the author wants to make. Ben Mikaelsen, the author of the following personal narrative, makes several points about his pet. As you read, decide for yourself what the most important point is.

READING FOCUS

Author's Purpose An **author's purpose** is the reason he or she writes a particular article or essay. An author might want to share information, express his or her feelings, influence you, or entertain you. As you read "Bear in the Family," think about what the author wants you to know about himself or his experience. Then, consider why he might want to share his experience with you.

Reading Selection

Read the following personal narrative. In a notebook, jot down answers to the numbered active-reading questions in the shaded boxes. Underlined words will be discussed in the Vocabulary Mini-Lesson on page 25.

from Voices from the Middle

Bear in the Family

by Ben Mikaelsen

1 A knock on the front door brings Nicky, our dog, to her feet. Behind her, rising more slowly, is Buffy, our ten-year-old, six-hundred-pound black bear. Visitors seldom venture this far up the mountain. Our rustic log cabin, nestled up a winding canyon, is miles from the nearest paved road.

2 Nicky growls softly, and I praise her for alerting me. Buffy, however, lumbers over to the big arched door and stands up. He wraps a large paw around the elk-antler door handle and swings the thick panel open with an easy tug.

3 Today the visitor is a neighbor wanting to borrow eggs. Towering seven feet tall, Buffy blocks her entrance. As usual, the elderly lady comes armed with a marshmallow. Buffy lips it gently from her hand and moves aside. She tosses another treat to our dog.

4 It's humorous when Buffy opens the door to a stranger. The occasional proselytizer[1] or salesperson can barely remember his or her name with a mountainous unchained bruin[2] looming over them. They do not see Buffy as I do—as a young, innocent child.

5 This child came to us ten years ago. Harboring an insatiable fascination for bears, I jumped at the chance to care for a young cub returned from a research facility. My wife Melanie agreed to help adopt this creature we had never met.

6 Before picking up our baby, we read dozens of books on bears and secured necessary licenses. I built a sturdy chain-link facility around two sides of the house. Our Buffy would have a spring-fed pond, a playground, a den, and plenty of running room. Finally, we were ready—we thought.

7 The twenty-pound, sixteen-week-old rascal who joined our family caught us unprepared. The first night, I lay in bed listening to his haunting cry, a

1. How is Buffy like a child? Watch for more details.

1. **proselytizer:** a person seeking to convert others to his or her religion.

2. **bruin:** a bear.

lost, mournful little sound. I crept out and sat near him in his den. After a few minutes he crawled on my lap and sucked the pads on his front feet, voicing his fear with a high-pitched clucking sound. I began to hum and rock him. When he finally fell asleep, I tucked him into the straw.

8 The first six months that Buffy lived with us, I rocked him to sleep every night. I spent hours feeding him, playing with him, observing him. At first, every utterance[3] and gesture puzzled me. Because Buffy's muscle structure and coordination resembled that of a human, his play was very humanlike. Emotionally the puzzle was much more complex. One moment he would stand and shake his head playfully at a neighbor's Angus bull. The next moment he cowered behind me at the sight of a small bum[4] lamb.

9 Originally Buffy nursed from a bottle. When I tried to wean him, he refused to switch over to solid foods. Melanie solved the problem by substituting water. Buffy took one suck and angrily threw the bottle across the pen. Then he ran to retrieve it and sucked hopefully. A second time he flung it. By that night he had abandoned his beloved bottle. . . .

2. What do you think is the point of this story about Buffy?

10 Our friendship with Buffy grew painfully slowly. His distrust made him reclusive. I realized that friendship depended on us somehow joining him in his world. That opportunity came all too soon.

3. What feelings do the details in the paragraph below describe?

11 On a midsummer's evening, I discovered a wild male black bear tearing at Buffy's pen. He had nearly broken down the gate. I shouted and threw rocks until the bear lumbered off; then I crawled in with little Buffy. The cub's tiny front feet pumped out from under his fuzzy rump as he ran frantically in circles. Fear quivered in every bawl. Finally he slowed and stared at me. Shaking, he clambered onto my lap and hugged me. I found myself crying. What instincts had caused a bruin to almost kill my Buffy?

4. Do you think that this event was important to the author? Why?

12 We cuddled for a long while, Buffy nuzzling and hugging me. When he finally slept, I moved to set him down. He awakened and clung to me. I slept with him that night, cementing our friendship. Overnight we bonded and became family. Overnight I became his guardian, not only his provider.

---

3. **utterance:** a sound made by someone; speech.

4. **bum:** sickly, lame.

First Thoughts on Your Reading

1. What is your overall impression of Buffy? of the author? What gives you this impression?
2. How do you think the author's experiences with the bear changed the author?

Implied Main Idea

READING SKIL L

What's the Big Idea? When you look for the main idea of a piece of writing, you are trying to identify the author's most important point. The main idea is usually only suggested, or **implied,** in personal narratives. In other words, the author does not want to tell you the main idea outright. Instead, the author wants you to discover the main idea by experiencing the events just as he or she did. It is up to you to look at the details and decide what one idea they all seem to support. Use the Thinking It Through steps below to find the implied main idea of paragraph 8 in "Bear in the Family." (It begins, "The first six months that Buffy lived with us . . .")

Identifying the Implied Main Idea

STEP 1 Read the paragraph and decide what important point the author seems to be making about the subject. This might be the main idea.

As a young bear, Buffy seems to act a lot like a human baby.

STEP 2 Identify details that support your guess about the paragraph's main idea.

Buffy has to be rocked to sleep. He plays like a human, and he gets scared easily.

STEP 3 Return to Step 1 and revise your guess if

- few details support your guess, or
- many details seem to support some other point

The part about shaking his head at the neighbor's bull doesn't seem like something a baby would do, but a bear might. My revised main idea is that in some ways, Buffy acts like a human baby, and in others he acts like a little bear.

The Big Picture Eventually, you will need to identify the implied main idea of the entire personal narrative. You can use the same process that helps you find the implied main idea of a paragraph (or section). Determine what point the author seems to be making in the narrative. Then, look for details throughout the narrative that support that point. If you find little support for the main idea you have chosen, revise your main idea. Look for the point that most of the details seem to support. A graphic organizer like this one can help you see how supporting details point to a narrative's implied main idea.

TIP Since not every paragraph has a main idea, you might want to examine a few paragraphs at a time and determine the main idea of each section.

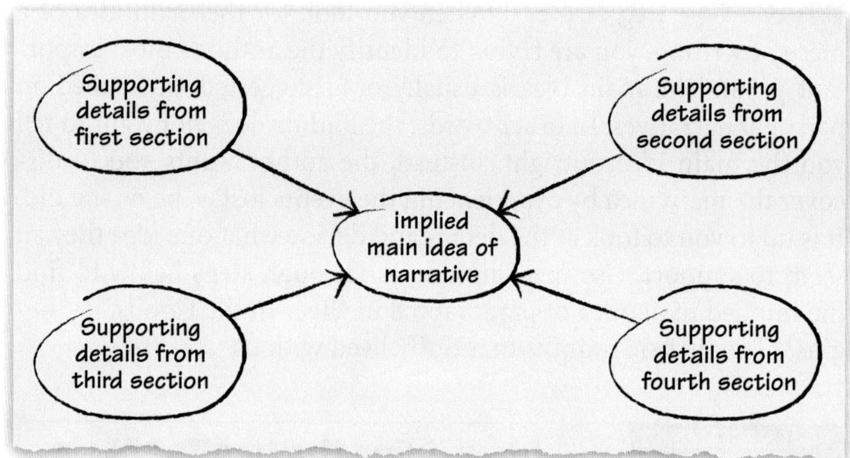

YOUR TURN 2 Identifying the Implied Main Idea

- With a partner, identify the implied main idea in "Bear in the Family," which begins on page 19.
- Divide the selection into four sections of equal length. With your partner, find details that support the main idea you identified. You may need to revise your main idea statement until you find support for it from each section.
- Finally, make a graphic organizer like the one above to record the implied main idea and the details that support it.

READING FOCUS

Author's Purpose

Be Reasonable All writers have at least one reason, or **purpose,** for writing. You may find that many items you read are written for more than one purpose. When this happens, one purpose is the main purpose and the others are secondary, or less important, purposes. Understanding why a piece was written helps you be a more aware reader. For example, an advertisement might make you laugh, but if you are aware that it is mainly trying to sell you something, you will understand the message better and be a better judge of the product. Here are the purposes writers use.

	Purposes for Writing
to inform	to give other people information that they want or need; to share a special knowledge
to influence	to convince other people to do something or to believe something
to express	to get to know oneself and to find meaning in one's own experiences
to entertain	to create a literary work or to say something in a unique way

As a reader, you can watch for clues about the purpose or purposes a writer is using in a piece. These clues can include

- illustrations, diagrams, maps, charts, headings, and bulleted or numbered items (**to inform**)
- words like *should* and *must,* and words that assign value such as *worst* and *best* (**to influence**)
- frequent use of the word *I* and emotional words (**to express**)
- use of vivid descriptions, dialogue, rhymes, drama, or humor (**to entertain**)

The type of writing can also help you determine a writer's main and secondary purposes. For example, a comic-book writer's main purpose is to entertain, but the writer may also want to inform. An author of a magazine article usually wants to influence. Sometimes, though, he or she will also want to entertain readers.

Read the paragraph on the next page from Esmeralda Santiago's autobiography, *When I Was Puerto Rican,* and see if you can figure out her purpose(s) for writing. If you have trouble, use the Thinking It Through steps that follow the paragraph.

TIP A writer may have only one purpose for writing, one main purpose and one secondary purpose, or even one main purpose and two or three secondary purposes.

It was raining in Brooklyn. Mist hung over the airport so that all I saw as we landed were fuzzy white and blue lights on the runway and at the terminal. We thudded to earth as if the pilot had miscalculated just how close we were to the ground. A startled silence was followed by frightened cries and *aleluyas* and the rustle of everyone rushing to get up from their seats and out of the plane as soon as possible.

Esmeralda Santiago, *When I Was Puerto Rican*

THINKING IT THROUGH

Identifying the Author's Purpose

STEP 1 Look for clues such as those listed on page 23 to help determine whether the author is

■ providing information	She provides some information about why the flight was scary.
■ trying to influence you	No, she doesn't say not to fly, just that this flight was bad.
■ expressing personal feelings	No, she describes the situation and the reactions of the other passengers, not her own.
■ trying to entertain you	Yes, she tells what happened in a dramatic way, using vivid descriptions and details.

STEP 2 Based on your answers, decide which purpose or purposes the author may have had for writing this piece.

Because she describes the scene vividly, I think the main purpose is to entertain. A secondary purpose may be to inform.

YOUR TURN 3

Identifying the Author's Purpose

Use the Thinking It Through steps above to help you determine the author's purpose(s) for writing "Bear in the Family," on pages 19–20.

MINI-LESSON VOCABULARY

Context Clues

Writers of personal narratives use precise words to communicate their experiences vividly. Some of these words may be unfamiliar to you, though. You can figure out an unfamiliar word by looking at **context clues**—clues from the words and sentences that surround the unfamiliar word. Try using context clues to understand the underlined word in this sentence beginning at the bottom of page 19.

> The first night, I lay in bed listening to his haunting cry, a lost, mournful little sound.

If you need help, the Thinking It Through steps below can show you what to do.

THINKING IT THROUGH Using Context Clues

STEP 1 Skim the word's context to see how many times the word appears. Look at all of the clues to its meaning.

The word appears only once, so there is only one group of clues to help me figure out its meaning.

STEP 2 Look carefully at all of the details that might provide a clue about the meaning of the word. Decide how the clues might be related to the unfamiliar word, and make a guess about its meaning.

The words cry, haunting, and lost appear near the word. Haunting sounds scary, and cry and lost sound sad. Maybe Buffy is scared or sad. The sentence describes the sounds Buffy is making. He is lonely and afraid. I guess mournful means "sad."

STEP 3 Use your definition in place of the word in the passage. Check to see that it makes sense.

". . . his haunting cry, a lost, sad little sound." Sad seems to fit in the sentence, and it makes sense with the rest of the paragraph.

PRACTICE

Using the steps listed above, figure out the meanings of the words below. The words are underlined in "Bear in the Family" to help you see the context.

1. lumbers (page 19)
2. insatiable (page 19)
3. cowered (page 20)
4. reclusive (page 20)
5. clambered (page 20)

MINI-LESSON **TEST TAKING**

Identifying Implied Main Ideas

When you take a reading test, you may be asked to identify the implied main idea of a reading passage. The passage will usually be two or more paragraphs long. If the following passage and question were on a reading test, how would you approach them?

Bats have many helpful features. Since bats have a good sense of smell, they can easily find food and their roosts. While some bats can see to move about and find food, other bats that cannot see well depend on echoes. As they fly, the bats that use echoes make high-frequency sounds that bounce back to them, telling them the locations of objects around them. Five hook-like claws on each foot allow bats to hang safely from rocks and trees.

Although bats have a reputation for being dangerous, they tend to be shy. They come out only at night, and they live in dark places. Bats use their special features to avoid contact with predators. Bats stay away from predators such as cats, snakes, and owls by hanging from their claws in high places.

Which of the following is the implied main idea of the passage?

A. Bats are dangerous to humans.

B. Bats are well equipped to survive in the wild.

C. Bats are vulnerable because they cannot see or smell.

D. Bats are afraid of most other living things.

THINKING IT THROUGH — Identifying Implied Main Ideas

STEP 1 Figure out the main point the passage seems to be making. This might be the passage's main idea.

Bats have features that help them survive in the wild.

STEP 2 Look for details in the passage that support this main idea, and reconsider your answer if necessary.

Bats have a good sense of smell; some bats see well, and others use echoes to move and get food; claws help them hang in high places where predators cannot reach them.

STEP 3 Eliminate answer choices that do not fit your answer. Then, select the choice that the passage supports best.

Choice A is wrong because bats are shy and avoid humans. Choice B sounds like my answer and has a lot of support. Choice C is wrong because bats have a good sense of smell and some can see. Choice D may be true, but there is no information here about that. I'll choose B.

Writing a Personal Narrative

WHAT'S AHEAD?

In this workshop you will write a personal narrative. You will also learn how to

- **organize ideas in chronological order**
- **choose relevant details**
- **eliminate stringy sentences**
- **punctuate dialogue**

"I remember that!" Have you ever said that while looking at old photographs of yourself and your friends or family? Looking back at yourself reminds you of what you were once like, what interested you, and what your dreams were. It also makes you think about important experiences that have made you unique.

A **personal narrative** is a story of a life experience that taught you something about yourself. In this workshop you will share a meaningful experience from your life by writing a personal narrative.

Prewriting

Choose and Evaluate an Experience

Memory Lane A personal narrative is your memory of an important experience. Tap into your personal store of memories by

- looking through old photographs, journals, diaries, or letters
- asking family members or friends for stories about you
- looking at mementos, such as souvenir buttons or play programs

As you review your experiences, be aware of your thoughts and feelings. A strong reaction means that the experience was important to you. One student listed his important memories below.

my first crush	catching a four-pound bass
working at a snack bar	winning a pepper-eating contest

TIP Be careful not to choose memories that might be too personal to share with your classmates or teacher. If you think you might be uncomfortable sharing an experience, you might want to choose something else.

Put It to the Test Now that you have listed some experiences, choose one you might want to explore in writing. Then, use the Thinking It Through steps below to decide whether your favorite choice will work for this assignment.

THINKING IT THROUGH Evaluating an Experience

STEP 1 Summarize what happened. If you have a hard time restating the experience in a sentence or two, then it is probably too complicated for this paper.

The first time I worked at the snack bar at the citywide garage sale, I thought I would mess everything up, but I did fine and I learned a lot.

STEP 2 Map out what happened. Make sure you can recall the events clearly and in order. If there are big gaps in your narrative, your readers will have trouble following you.

1. I found out I had to work at the snack bar.
2. I had no experience, so I knew I would make a mess of it.
3. My math teacher helped, and I did a good job.

STEP 3 Tell what you learned from your experience. If you have no clear answer, the experience may not be important enough to choose as a topic.

I learned how important practical math is, and I learned to believe in myself more.

STEP 4 Quiz yourself. Will you be comfortable sharing your experience with others? What might they learn from you?

I can share this. Reading about my experience might inspire someone else to take on a challenge that looks too difficult.

YOUR TURN 4 Choosing and Evaluating an Experience

Brainstorm a few experiences you might write about and evaluate your favorite experience, using the Thinking It Through steps above. If the experience does not work with all four steps, try another one that matters to you.

Think About Purpose and Audience

What's It All About? In a personal narrative, your main purpose is to express yourself. Keep these *characteristics of expressive writing* in mind as you plan your narrative.

- is written in the first person ("I")
- includes vivid details of people, places, events, and things
- tells the events of an experience in the order in which they happened (first, second, third, and so on)
- includes the writer's thoughts and feelings during the experience

You may discover a secondary purpose as you write your paper. In addition to expressing yourself, you may find yourself also trying to entertain, to inform, or even to influence your readers.

Reference Note

For more on **author's purpose,** see page 23.

Who Wants to Know? Now that you have identified an experience to share, consider with whom you are comfortable sharing it. If you write about your first crush, will you share that experience in the school newspaper, or would you rather share it with only a close friend? Choose the most appropriate **audience** for your narrative. Keep in mind your audience could be someone close to you, or it could be readers you have never met. (Remember that your teacher is automatically part of your audience, so be sure you are comfortable sharing this experience with him or her.)

TIP Much of the writing you do for school is informative. Informative writing is usually in the third person, so you seldom use "I" or "me." When you write with an expressive purpose, however, you can use your natural voice. Your writing **voice** reveals your feelings about your topic and your general attitude.

YOUR TURN 5 Thinking About Purpose and Audience

Your purpose for writing a personal narrative is to express yourself to others. Use the following steps to identify an appropriate audience.

- First, list several different audiences.
- Then, choose one audience with whom you are comfortable sharing this experience.

Recall and Arrange Details

Make It Real To get your readers involved in your narrative, you need to show them events as you experienced them. **Details are the heart of an interesting story.** Details can include the kinds of information listed on the next page.

KEY CONCEPT

TIP Adding details can make an ordinary event a memorable one.

Ordinary: It began to rain.

Memorable: The clouds suddenly turned thick and gray, and huge silver droplets began to fall.

- smaller events that were part of the experience you are retelling
- what you observed by using your senses (hearing, touch, smell, taste, and sight)—in other words, **sensory details**
- specific information about other people involved in the experience, including **dialogue,** or what people said
- the time and place the experience happened
- your thoughts and feelings during the experience

Walk This Way Consider how you will arrange your details. KEY CONCEPT **Most narratives are written in chronological order. That is, events are told in the order in which they happened.** To make sure you retell your experience in chronological order, you can number the events and details in a chart, or you can make a **time line** like the one below.

Time	Event	Details
8:00	went to set up garage sale	cold, rainy Saturday morning in April, inside a big and empty firehouse, sounds echoed
8:30	was told I had to work the snack bar	Mom told me to fill in. I argued because I'm bad with money. Mom said, "Nonsense. You can do it."
9:00–12:00	sale started; the snack bar got really busy	Everyone wanted hot food and drinks. I was slow; they were impatient. I was so nervous I spilled a drink. My math teacher showed me how to make change.
12:00–4:00	I got better at working the snack bar	felt more comfortable; made change quickly; I wished it would stay busy. Mom said she was proud of me.

TIP Use the *5W-How?* questions (*Who? What? When? Where? Why?* and *How?*) to recall details about an event. Answer questions such as *"Who was involved?"*

YOUR TURN 6 Recalling and Arranging Details

In chronological order, list as many details as you can recall about your experience. You can make a time line or create a chart. Include smaller events, your thoughts and feelings, and sensory details.

MINI-LESSON **CRITICAL THINKING**

Choosing Relevant Details

On my first day at my new school, I was nervous. The school was at the end of a narrow, winding street. I went to the main office to sign up. It was crazy, with kids running everywhere holding pink permission slips. In comparison, I felt like I was moving in slow motion.

Are all the details in this passage *relevant*? In other words, do they make the experience clear, or do they just clutter up the narrative?

Relevant details help readers focus on the main idea: the writer is nervous. The details about the main office show how busy and confusing the school is.

Irrelevant details take readers away from the main idea. The narrow, winding street may add to the picture in your mind, but it does not relate to the writer's main idea.

THINKING IT THROUGH

Testing Details for Relevance

Here is how a writer determined that the details about the school office were relevant to his story.

STEP 1 Identify the main idea of the narrative.

The main idea is how awkward and nerve-racking the first day of school was.

STEP 2 Make sure the details relate to the main idea.

The scene in the office was the first sign that I would be out of step with everybody the whole day.

STEP 3 Make sure that the details will help the reader create a mental picture.

The kids running around made me feel like I was in a circus. I want readers to see that.

PRACTICE

Identify at least five details in the following paragraph. Using the steps above, classify each detail as relevant or irrelevant.

Last Tuesday, my friend Marika's birthday, we went on a field trip to the aquarium. Inside the aquarium it was gloomy. The only light came from the fish tanks, which were like giant, silent TV screens. My grandmother eats fish on Friday. Hammerhead sharks soared across the tank in front of us. Our class quietly watched the eerily gliding twenty-foot fish.

Writing

Personal Narrative

Framework	Directions and Explanations
Introduction ■ Attention-grabbing opening ■ Details that set the scene	Grab your reader's attention right away with an interesting beginning. Look at professional authors' opening lines for ideas. Also, include enough **details to set the scene** for your readers by noting where and when the experience happened.
Body ■ Event 1 (details) ■ Event 2 (details) ■ Event 3 (details) and so on	■ Arrange the events of your narrative and their details **in the order in which they occurred.** Start at the beginning and work your way to the end. Connect the events using transitional words such as *first*, *next*, *then*, and *finally*. ■ Use **details** to **elaborate** on each event in the narrative. Include sensory details, details about people who were involved, and **dialogue.** Most important, include just enough details about your feelings at the time to keep your audience in **suspense.** Save your explanation of the meaning of the experience until the very end.
Conclusion ■ Meaning of the experience for the narrator	Let your readers know the **meaning of the experience** for you—how it changed you or what it taught you.

YOUR TURN 7 Drafting Your Personal Narrative

Now it is your turn to draft a personal narrative. As you write, refer to the framework above and the Writer's Model on the next page.

A Writer's Model

The final draft below closely follows the framework for a personal narrative on the previous page.

A Valuable Lesson

"Two cups of coffee, a bagel with cream cheese, and a hot pretzel." It was a typical order at the snack bar at the citywide garage sale my parents helped run every April. The event was supposed to raise money for the local playground. Every year we made enough money to make some improvement. This was my first year at the snack bar, though, and I was worried that instead of raising money, I would end up owing it.

Attention-grabbing opening

Details that set the scene

We got to the firehouse early to set up everything. Usually, people set up tables and sold their "treasures" outside. Because the weather that day was rainy and cold, we moved inside. We set up in the garage where the fire-trucks were usually parked. Without them, the room seemed huge, with a sky-high ceiling and a smooth, gray cement floor. Our voices and footsteps echoed off the bare walls and floor and sounded unfamiliar and loud.

Event 1

Details (sensory details)

I was carrying boxes when my mother told me to fill in at the snack bar because one of the workers had the flu. I protested. I said, "No way. I'll mess it up. You know I'm no good with money, and I'll never remember the orders. Please, Mom, don't make me."

Event 2

Details (thoughts and feelings)

"Nonsense. You can do it. Besides, you won't get much business until lunch," said my mother, "and then I'll help you." I shrugged my shoulders and scraped the sole of my wet sneaker against the cement floor, making a loud squeak. I thought the idea was a bad one, but I went.

Details (what others said)

My mother was completely wrong. Because the weather was bad, people wanted hot snacks and drinks. I was swamped with orders. At first, I was really slow at taking the orders and making change. The line of people grew, and everybody seemed impatient. I was so nervous

Event 3

Details (smaller events)

(continued)

(continued)

that my hands shook, and I spilled orange juice on the floor. What a sticky mess! Then Ms. Muñoz, my math teacher, showed me how to make change by counting up to the total amount I was given. If someone gave me five dollars for something that cost $3.25, I handed over three quarters and a dollar and said, "Seventy-five cents makes four dollars, plus one dollar makes five." Things went more smoothly after that.

Meaning of experience

By the end of the day, I could pour hot coffee, slice a bagel, add up the bill, and make change quickly with a smile. I was even a little disappointed when the sun came out and dried up business. My mom said that she was proud of me, and when she suggested that I work the snack bar again next year, I did not even shrug. I was too busy imagining the restaurant I would open one day.

TIP If you use dialogue in your narrative, it should reflect the way people really talk. In other words, even though you might normally avoid using contractions (*isn't, it's, we'll*) in your writing, it will sound more natural to use them when you are quoting someone's exact words.

A Student's Model

A tough experience can teach us something important. Lindi Martin, a student at Jenks East Middle School in Tulsa, Oklahoma, describes such an experience in the following passages from her personal narrative.

Conquering Your Fears

by Lindi Martin

I was only eight, but I remember it like yesterday. I was sitting in the doctor's office when they gave my parents and me the shocking news. "I am sorry to tell you this, but your daughter's condition is getting worse. The only way to fix it is by surgery."

Attention-grabbing opening

. . . It was now time for surgery. They sent a surgical nurse down to my room with a gurney. Being the scared little girl that I was, I thought the moment I got up on it, they would hurt me. So I decided that my teddy bear, Rainbow, and I would follow along behind it, very defiantly, with my parents. When the doctors saw me walk in, they started to laugh, and I realized that everyone else who had seen me probably had laughed, too. What was comic relief to them was no comedy at all to me. So I simply put my nose into the air and kept walking.

Event 1

Details (thoughts and feelings)

The nurse prepped me and had me lie down on the operating table. The doctor asked me what "flavor" of anesthesia I wanted; I thought for a while and answered, "Strawberry." He then asked me to count backward from one hundred as he lifted the mask over my face. I woke up a few hours later, feeling woozy and very sore. I saw my parents and drifted back to sleep. . . .

Event 2

Details (smaller events)

My experience has taught me a lot. I discovered that in order to conquer your fears, you must face them first. In a way I am thankful for my surgery, because I conquered a lot of my fears.

Meaning of experience

Revising

Evaluate and Revise Content, Organization, and Style

COMPUTER TIP

If you are using a computer, format a draft with wide margins and double-spaced lines to allow space for revisions.

Checking It Twice To evaluate a peer's writing (if you collaborate or have a writing conference) or to evaluate and revise your own work, you will need to do at least two readings. The first reading will examine content and organization, using the guidelines below. In the second reading you will improve style, using Focus on Sentences on page 38.

First Reading: Content and Organization Use this chart to evaluate and revise your narrative so that it is easy to understand.

Guidelines for Self-Evaluation and Peer Evaluation

Evaluation Questions	Tips	Revision Techniques
1 Does the beginning of the narrative grab the audience's attention?	**Put stars** next to quotations, surprising details, or statements that would interest the audience.	If needed, **add** a quotation, a surprising detail, or a statement to the introduction.
2 Does the introduction set the scene for the reader with details?	**Circle** details that show when and where the experience happened.	**Add** details about where and when the event happened to help readers picture the scene.
3 Are the events in chronological order?	**Number** the events as they appear in the paper. Compare the numbered events to the actual order of events.	**Rearrange** the events to put them in the order in which they actually happened, if necessary.
4 Does the narrative include details that make the people, places, and events seem real?	**Highlight** sensory details and dialogue in the paper. In the margin, note to which senses the sensory details appeal.	If necessary, **elaborate** with dialogue or sensory details: sights, sounds, smells, textures, and tastes.
5 Does the writer include thoughts and feelings in the narrative?	**Put a check mark** next to any statement of the writer's feelings or thoughts.	If necessary, **add** specific details about thoughts and feelings.
6 In the conclusion, does the writer state why the experience is meaningful?	**Underline** the writer's statement of why the experience is meaningful.	**Add** a statement that explains why the experience is important, if needed.

ONE WRITER'S REVISIONS This revision is an early draft of the narrative on pages 33–34.

> Usually, people set up tables and sold their "treasures" outside. Because the weather that day was rainy and cold, we moved inside. We got to the firehouse early to set up everything. We set up in the garage where the firetrucks were usually parked. Without them, the room seemed huge, with a sky-high ceiling and a smooth, gray cement floor. Our voices and footsteps echoed off the bare walls and floor and sounded unfamiliar and loud.

rearrange

elaborate

elaborate

Responding to the Revision Process

1. Why did the writer move a sentence in the paragraph?
2. Why did the writer add phrases to the last two sentences?

PEER REVIEW

As you read a peer's paper, ask yourself:

- What event or detail of this narrative is most vivid?
- What events do I have trouble picturing?

Second Reading: Style In your first reading, you looked at *what* you said and *where* you said it in your narrative. Now you will look at *how* you expressed your thoughts in each sentence. For instance, did you include *stringy sentences* in your personal narrative? A **stringy sentence** contains many thoughts connected by *and, but,* or *so.* However, not all sentences that contain more than one *and, but,* or *so* are stringy. Look at the last sentence in the example above. Then, find and eliminate stringy sentences in your personal narrative, using the following technique.

When you evaluate your narrative for style, ask yourself whether your writing contains any stringy sentences. As you re-read your essay, draw a wavy line around the words *and, but,* and *so.* Sentences that use *and, but,* or *so* more than once may be stringy. If necessary, break one or more stringy sentences into separate sentences, or turn some complete ideas into subordinate clauses. The Focus on Sentences on the next page can help you learn to revise stringy sentences.

Sentences

Stringy Sentences

When people retell events, they sometimes cram sentences with too many details. A narrative can develop a breathless pattern of "and this happened, so then I did this, but then this happened." A sentence with too many ideas strung together by the words *and*, *but*, or *so* is called a **stringy sentence.**

Stringy The phone rang, and I got up to answer it, but my brother picked it up first.

You can fix a stringy sentence by breaking the sentence into at least two sentences, or you can turn an independent clause into a phrase or a subordinate clause.

Revised The phone rang. I got up to answer it, but my brother picked it up first. [two sentences]

Revised I got up to answer the phone **when it rang,** but my brother picked it up first. [subordinate clause]

TIP Subordinate clauses often begin with words such as *when, after, because, that,* and *if*.

Reference Note

For more information and practice on **independent clauses,** see page 440. For more information and practice on **subordinate clauses,** see page 441.

ONE WRITER'S REVISIONS

Because The weather was bad, ~~and~~ people wanted hot snacks and drinks, ~~and~~ I was swamped with orders.

Responding to the Revision Process

How did the writer improve the sentence above?

YOUR TURN 8 Evaluating and Revising Your Personal Narrative

- Evaluate and revise the content and organization of your narrative using the guidelines on page 36.
- Use the Focus on Sentences above to improve any stringy sentences.
- If peers evaluated your paper, consider their comments as you revise your narrative.

Publishing

Proofread Your Personal Narrative

Two Heads Are Better Than One If you have another person proofread your narrative, you will be more likely to catch mistakes that can distract readers. Have this second reader look for common mistakes, such as spelling, capitalization, and punctuation errors. One common error you might find in personal narratives involves punctuating dialogue.

TIP Another **resource** you can use to catch mistakes is a dictionary. Keep one handy to check your spelling.

Grammar Link

Using and Punctuating Dialogue

Punctuating dialogue can be tricky. Here are some rules to help you handle some typical problems with dialogue.

A person's exact words go inside quotation marks, and so do commas and periods. Question marks and exclamation points go inside quotation marks only when what the person said is a question or an exclamation.

"Nonsense**!"** said my mother.

"What**?"** I cried.

Can you believe she said **"**Do it now**"?**

A sentence in quotation marks is often interrupted to identify who is speaking. The second part of the quotation begins with a lowercase letter.

"You won't get much business until lunch," said my mother, "**a**nd then I'll help you."

When the second part of an interrupted quotation is a complete sentence, it begins with a capital letter.

"Nonsense," said my mother. "**Y**ou can do it."

PRACTICE

On your own paper, revise the following sentences by adding quotation marks and correcting capitalization where necessary.

Example:

1. Let me help you, Ms. Muñoz said. I can teach you an easy way to make change.

1. "Let me help you," Ms. Muñoz said. "I can teach you an easy way to make change."

1. I can do this, I thought.

2. Would you like cream, I asked, or sugar in your coffee?

3. He said, I need a napkin to wipe up this spill.

4. Here is your change, I said. Thank you for coming and enjoy your day.

5. What will I call my future restaurant? I wondered aloud.

For more information and practice on **punctuating dialogue**, see page 666.

Publish Your Personal Narrative

Reference Note

For more on **oral interpretation,** see page 801 in the Quick Reference Handbook.

Sharing Your Experience Now is the time to share your personal narrative with the audience you identified in prewriting. Depending on who is in your audience and how comfortable you are with sharing this experience, you may try one of these ways to publish your personal narrative.

- Give a copy to a friend or a trusted adult.
- Share your personal narrative in an oral presentation to your class.
- Turn your personal narrative into a book. Give each event its own page, and add photographs or illustrations.

Reflect on Your Personal Narrative

Building Your Portfolio Taking time to reflect on your personal narrative will help you improve as a writer. Consider how well you achieved your purpose and reached your audience. Then, answer the following questions about what you wrote and how you wrote it.

- What was the clearest or most exciting detail in your narrative? What makes you think so?
- Which techniques did you use to spur your memory of specific details? (See Recall and Arrange Details, page 29.) How helpful were the techniques? Which would you use again?

TIP Writing a response to the Reflect on Your Personal Narrative questions above is an example of **expressive writing,** just as your personal narrative itself is. You write expressively when you **write to discover** or **to reflect on ideas.** You also write expressively when you **write to solve problems.** If you have ever written a letter to a friend just to "talk out" a problem, you have used expressive writing.

YOUR TURN 9 Proofreading, Publishing, and Reflecting on Your Personal Narrative

- Correct grammar, usage, and mechanics errors.
- Publish your personal narrative for your target audience.
- Answer the questions from Reflect on Your Personal Narrative above. Record your responses in a learning log, or include them in your portfolio.

A Descriptive Essay About an Important Place

You have written about an important event in your life. Now, think about a *place* in your life that matters to you. Maybe that place is your own room with the stereo blasting, a quiet corner of the public library, or the kitchen at your grandmother's house. Wherever your important place is, you will have a chance to describe it in detail by writing a *descriptive essay*. A **descriptive essay** magnifies a single subject, revealing many sensory details and describing the writer's feelings about the subject.

Details, Details The key to a good descriptive essay is the details. The chart below explains a few details that help make a description vivid.

Type of Detail	Definitions and Examples
Figure of Speech	makes vivid comparisons
Simile	compares two things using *like* or *as* *The terrible news hit us like a tidal wave.*
Metaphor	compares two things by saying that something is something else *The dog's wagging tail was a welcoming smile.*
Personification	gives human characteristics to nonhuman things *The sun smiled down on our soccer game.*
Sensory Description	describes with words that appeals to the five senses ▪ sights — *the blinding lightning* ▪ sounds — *the crack of the baseball bat* ▪ smells — *the sweet perfume of roses* ▪ tastes — *fiery jalapeños* ▪ sensations — *gritty sandpaper*
Measurement	estimates size to give the reader some perspective *The grass snake was no bigger than a pencil.*

On the next page is part of a description by Monica Sone. She and her family were sent to an internment camp for Japanese Americans during World War II. Sone uses measurements, figures of speech, and sensory details to describe her family's home there.

We were assigned to apartment 2-I-A, right across from the bachelor quarters. The apartment resembled elongated, low stables about two blocks long. Our home was one room, about eighteen by twenty feet, the size of a living room. There was one small window in the wall opposite the one door. It was bare except for a small, tinny wood-burning stove crouching in the center. The flooring consisted of two-by-fours laid directly on the earth, and dandelions were already pushing their way up through the cracks. Mother was delighted when she saw their shaggy yellow heads. "Don't any-one pick them. I'm going to cultivate them."

Monica Sone, *Nisei Daughter*

Show Me How do you **develop** and **record details** about a place *you* would like to describe? If possible, go to the place. If you are unable to go there, close your eyes and picture the place. Then, answer the following questions.

- Look around. What do you see?
- Listen to the sounds. What do you hear?
- Take a deep breath. What do you smell? Can you taste anything?
- Move around. What can you touch? Do things feel smooth or rough or sharp?
- What are your feelings about this place?

Order in the Court Once you have all the details, you will need to arrange them. You can organize details in these ways.

- **Spatial order** Details appear in the order that you see them. Often, the author describes the relationship of one detail to another using prepositions, such as *near, below,* and *behind.* Monica Sone used spatial order in her description.
- **Order of importance** When writers organize details in this way, the most important detail usually appears last. If the place you will describe has a surprising feature, you may want to organize your ideas so that they lead up to this detail.

Pen to Paper In your first draft you will use your notes about details and organize them in a way that makes sense. Then, you should have a classmate read your essay and answer these questions. The answers will help you revise your essay.

- Does the description create a vivid picture in my mind?
- Is it clear why this place is significant to the writer?

YOUR TURN 10 Writing a Descriptive Essay

Follow the steps above to write and revise a descriptive essay about an important place. Then, make a clean copy of your essay, and share it with your class.

MINI-LESSON TEST TAKING

Answering Prompts That Ask You to Describe

A writing test may ask you to describe something important to you. In a test-taking situation you have a limited amount of time to analyze the prompt, plan your answer, and write a response. You must work quickly and thoughtfully. Suppose the following prompt appeared on a writing test. How would you approach it?

Write a letter to a friend describing a pet in detail. You may describe your own or someone else's pet, or the pet you wish you had.

TIP Whether you **print** or write in **cursive,** make sure you use your most legible handwriting when taking a writing test.

THINKING IT THROUGH Writing a Description

STEP 1 Read the prompt at least twice. Look for key words in the prompt to decide what it is asking you to do.

I should write a letter to my friend describing a pet.

STEP 2 Identify the task. The prompt has given you important clues about the audience, purpose, and format of your answer.

My audience is a friend. My purpose is to describe something. The format for this response is a letter.

STEP 3 Use your own experiences. Test-taking prompts cannot ask you to do research, so you must base your answer on what you already know or can imagine. To develop details—including sensory details—use a list or a **conceptual map** like the one to the right.

Before you begin, make sure you know how much time you have to respond to the prompt. Plan to spend about half of your time prewriting.

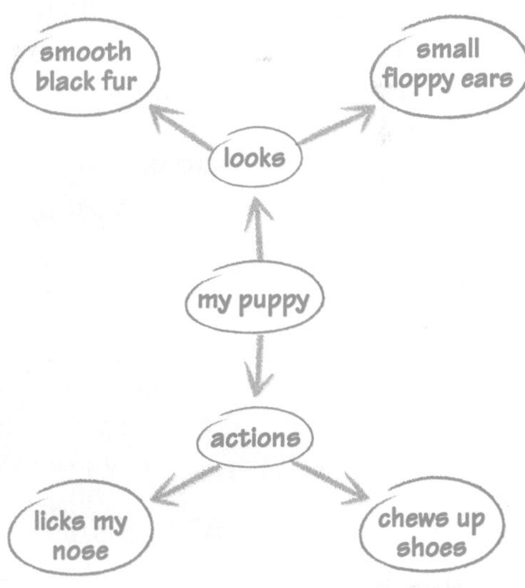

STEP 4 Write your response. Put details in an order that makes sense, such as spatial order or order of importance. Check your response for grammar and spelling errors.

WHAT'S AHEAD?

In this section you will present an oral narrative. You will also learn how to

- **identify differences between oral and written narratives**
- **select an appropriate narrative for oral presentation**
- **create a script with notes for delivering an effective oral presentation**

Telling a True Story

"Once upon a time" is the way many stories you heard as a child began. When you heard those words, you knew a good story would follow, and you settled down to listen. Now that you are older, you know that a good story does not always begin with those words or feature princesses and magical events. Good stories can be true stories about experiences that real people like you have lived through. Personal narratives make interesting storytelling. In this section, you will discover how to turn a personal narrative into an oral presentation.

Written vs. Oral Storytelling

You may not think that there is much difference between a narrative that is written and one that is told orally, but there is. Writers and storytellers have different skills, and readers and listeners have different ways of following a narrative, as you can see below.

Written Narrative	Oral Narrative
Writers may use many words to describe a gesture, a sound, or an idea.	**Storytellers** may use their voices, faces, and gestures to convey ideas.
Readers often enjoy long passages of description because they have time to pause and reflect.	**Listeners** usually cannot go back and listen again. Too much description may distract them from what is going on in the narrative.

Reference Note

For more on **oral interpretation,** see page 801 in the Quick Reference Handbook.

A written personal narrative may sometimes sound flat or wordy when it is read aloud. This is because a writer may need many words to describe something that a storyteller can simply act out. Read the example on the next page.

Written Narrative	Oral Narrative
"He shrugged and turned away as he sadly said goodbye."	"Goodbye."

Do you see the difference? The storyteller only has to say goodbye because he or she can act out the rest—by shrugging, turning away, and using a sad voice. Keep in mind the differences described above as you adapt a written personal narrative into an oral narrative.

From Written to Oral Narrative

Follow these steps to prepare an oral version of a personal narrative, either your own or one written by a professional writer.

Reference Note

For more on adapting language to fit the **audience, purpose,** and **occasion,** see pages 794–95 in the Quick Reference Handbook.

1. **Make sure the narrative you have chosen fits your audience and your purpose.** Ask these questions about your narrative:
   - Is the selection enjoyable and well written?
   - Will the selection appeal to my audience?
   - Are the selection's language and topic appropriate for the occasion? (Avoid topics or words that might offend members of your audience or get you into trouble.)
   - Is the selection a good length? Can the selection be presented within the time limit set by your teacher?
2. **Read and edit the narrative.** Make a copy of the selection and read it aloud. Cross out any words, phrases, or sentences you can leave out of your presentation. Remember, acting out information is an effective way to get an idea across to an audience. For example, instead of telling your audience that a character is angry, you can show them by using **gestures,** such as stomping your foot and putting your hands on your hips. You can also raise the **pitch** of your voice to a shrill level and change the **tone** of your voice to sound irritated. Just jot a note in the margin to remind yourself to act out the missing information.

TIP Be careful not to cut words and phrases that will enliven your presentation. They include **sensory details, precise language, action verbs,** and **colorful modifiers** (adjectives and adverbs).

3. **Write a script and make delivery notes for the selection.** Once you have decided what parts to cut and where to change your pitch or your tone or to make gestures, you are ready to write your script. Leave plenty of space between lines to make notes about how your voice or actions will be used to enhance the narrative. For other delivery notes, you might underline a word you want to

emphasize or put a slash mark (/) where you want to pause. Here is part of one student's script.

{point to self}
This was my first year at the snack bar, though, / and I was worried
{exasperated}
that instead of raising money, / I would end up owing it.

TIP As you write your script, include an introduction to your narrative that gives the reason why you chose the story and that identifies the author (if the author is not you). If you are presenting an excerpt from a longer piece, set the scene by describing some important events that have already taken place.

TIP Telling true stories aloud is an important part of life in many families. Through this **oral tradition,** family history is passed from generation to generation in the form of stories told aloud. Who continues the oral tradition in your family? Find your family's storyteller, and have him or her help you generate criteria, or standards, for what makes a good oral story.

4. **Rehearse your narrative several times.** Time your presentation if you will have a time limit. Practice your presentation in front of a mirror, then try a rehearsal in front of friends. Listen to their feedback. You may not take all of their suggestions, but do consider their ideas as you practice and improve your presentation.

Speaking Effectively

Here are some ways to make your presentation effective.

- Rehearse your script several times so that you know it well. This will give you confidence to perform and will allow you to make eye contact with your audience.
- Speak loudly enough for everyone to hear you. The **volume** of your voice may sound unnaturally loud to you, but the people sitting in the back of the room will be able to hear you.
- Keep an eye on your audience. Notice people's reactions. If they seem bored, it may be because they cannot hear you. If they nod and smile, then you know that you are on the right track.

YOUR TURN 11 Preparing an Oral Personal Narrative

Follow the steps listed on pages 45–46 to turn your own personal narrative or one from a language arts textbook into a script. Then, present it to your class or to another group of interested people.

CHAPTER

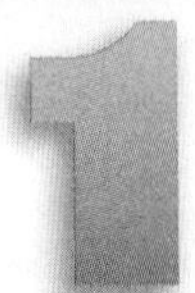

Choices

Choose one of the following activities to complete.

CROSSING THE CURRICULUM: ART

1. Say Cheese! Create a **photo collage** of an important event in your life. Collect images that fit the event from magazines and newspapers, and arrange them in an eye-catching way. Share your experience with other classmates by explaining how the images tell the story.

CAREERS

2. Twenty Questions Interview an adult you know about the events that led to his or her career. Here are some questions you might ask.

- Why did you choose the career you have now?
- What education or training did you receive?

Take notes or tape-record the interview and write a short **narrative** based on your notes.

DRAMA

3. Curtain Call Alone or in a group, act out another person's experience. Do a **dramatic interpretation** of a scene from a play based on a real person, such as *The Diary of Anne Frank.* Choose a scene and select roles within your group. Then, rehearse your lines and present your scene to your class.

WRITING

4. Once Upon a Time, I . . . Create a **children's book** based on an experience that is meaningful to you and suitable for youngsters. Keep your audience in suspense by saving any surprises for the conclusion. Include vivid details, limit the number of words on a page, and add colorful illustrations. If you wish, bind your storybook, and give it to a younger class.

CROSSING THE CURRICULUM: MUSIC

5. Singing the Blues Blues and folk songs let songwriters share their experiences and are often passed from one generation to the next as part of an **oral tradition.** Choose a favorite blues song or folk song, and write a **summary** of the songwriter's experience. Then, form a group with others who chose this activity, compare the different experiences, and summarize your discussion.

CHAPTER

Explaining a Complex Process

Reading Workshop

Reading About a Complex Process

Writing Workshop

Writing About a Complex Process

Viewing and Representing

Creating Graphics

Informational Text

Exposition

Have you ever wondered how a refrigerator keeps food cold or how tornadoes form? Maybe a young child has asked you how plants make food or how a CD makes music. These are all basic questions, but none of them has a simple answer. To find answers, you would turn to **expository,** or informative, writing.

The answers to the questions above involve *complex processes.* A **complex process** has several steps that usually must occur in a certain order for the process to work. You might one day need to examine complex processes because understanding a process is crucial to your job: to help you save a life, for example, or repair a machine or grow a crop. You might also read and write about complex processes—like those explained in science magazines, for instance—simply to satisfy your curiosity.

YOUR TURN 1 Discovering Complex Processes

With a group of other students, discuss the following questions to consider how people learn about complex processes.

- What are some processes you have learned about?
- Were these processes easy to understand? Explain.
- Based on your group's discussion so far, what makes an explanation of a process easy to understand? What makes it difficult?

GO TO: go.hrw.com
KEYWORD: EOLang 8-2

Reading About a Complex Process

WHAT'S AHEAD?

In this section you will read an article explaining a complex process. You will also learn how to
- **draw conclusions**
- **find chronological order**

In movies, mummies come to life and lurch toward nosy intruders who disturb their tombs. In reality, though, mummies provide us with a glimpse into the lives and beliefs of ancient cultures. One of the most interesting things scientists have learned from unearthing tombs of the ancient Egyptians is how the mummies themselves were made. The following article explains, step by step, the process the Egyptians used. As you read, consider two questions. What parts of this process does the author expect you to figure out for yourself? How are the ideas in the article organized?

Preparing to Read

READING SKILL

Making Inferences: Drawing Conclusions Sometimes when writers provide information, they trust that their readers can figure out certain things. Rather than explaining every idea in detail, they will provide readers with enough clues to see the connections between ideas and fill in the gaps for themselves. As you read the article that begins on the following page, consider how you **draw conclusions,** or make judgments, about the gaps the writer has left between some ideas.

READING FOCUS

Chronological Order To help readers follow the steps of a process, writers of process articles will often use **chronological (time) order.** Words such as *first, then,* and *next* show chronological order. Watch for clues in the following article that tell in what order the steps of the mummification process took place.

Reading Selection

Read the following process article, an excerpt from the Frequently Asked Questions (FAQs) section of the Smithsonian Institution's Web site. In a notebook, jot down answers to the numbered active-reading questions in the shaded boxes. The highlighted words will appear in the Vocabulary Mini-Lesson on page 56.

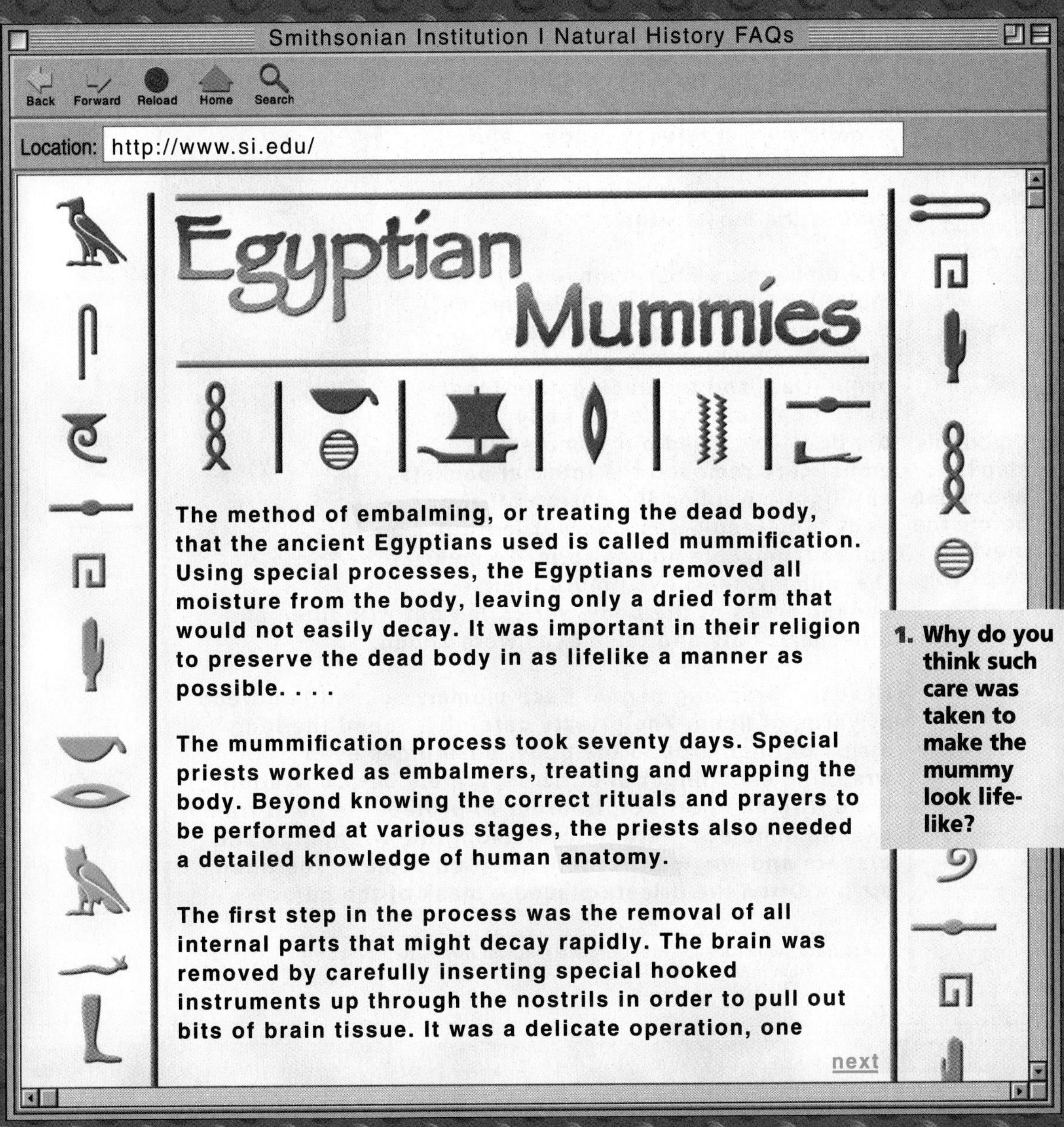

Egyptian Mummies

The method of embalming, or treating the dead body, that the ancient Egyptians used is called mummification. Using special processes, the Egyptians removed all moisture from the body, leaving only a dried form that would not easily decay. It was important in their religion to preserve the dead body in as lifelike a manner as possible. . . .

1. Why do you think such care was taken to make the mummy look life-like?

The mummification process took seventy days. Special priests worked as embalmers, treating and wrapping the body. Beyond knowing the correct rituals and prayers to be performed at various stages, the priests also needed a detailed knowledge of human anatomy.

The first step in the process was the removal of all internal parts that might decay rapidly. The brain was removed by carefully inserting special hooked instruments up through the nostrils in order to pull out bits of brain tissue. It was a delicate operation, one

next

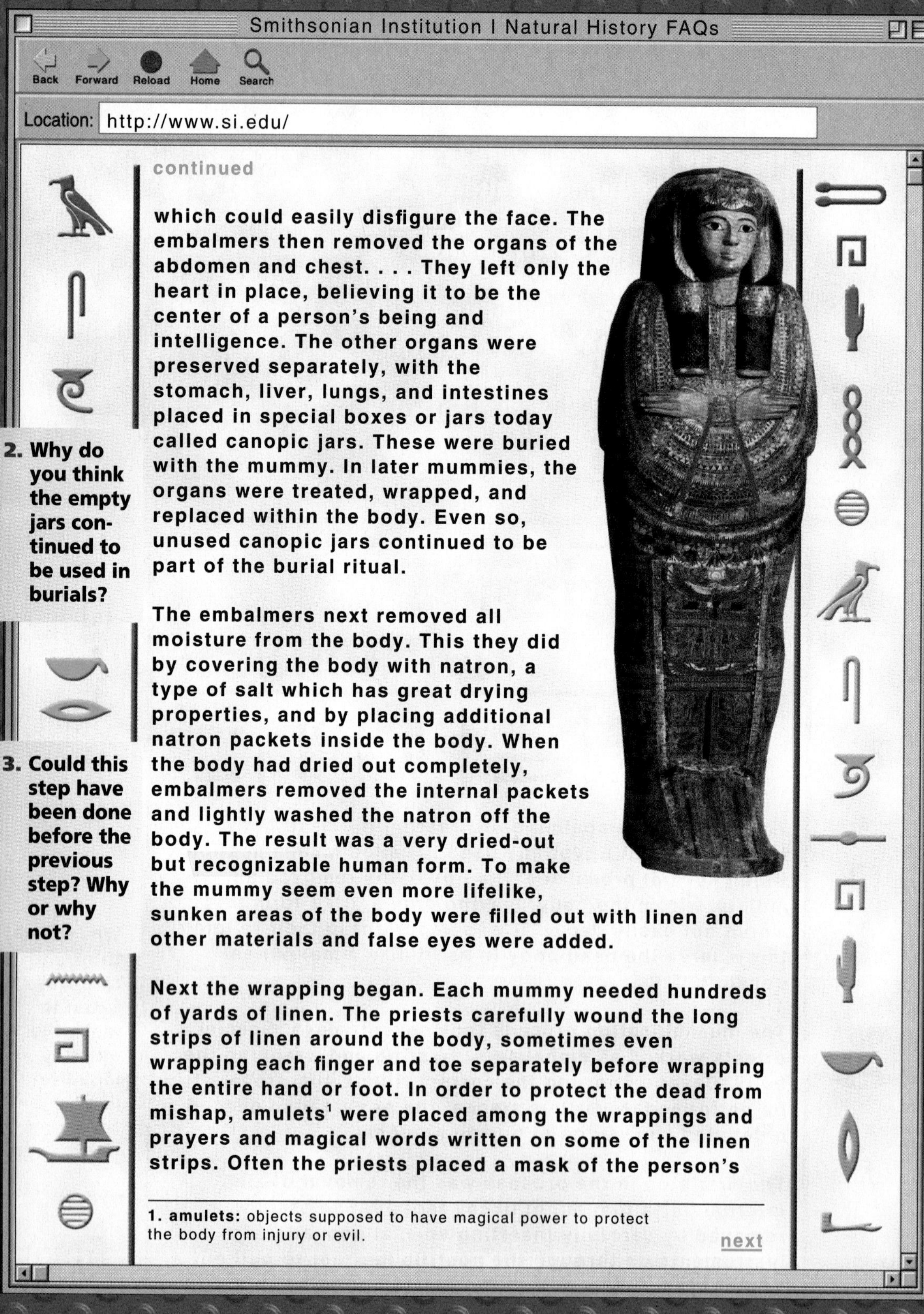

continued

which could easily disfigure the face. The embalmers then removed the organs of the abdomen and chest. . . . They left only the heart in place, believing it to be the center of a person's being and intelligence. The other organs were preserved separately, with the stomach, liver, lungs, and intestines placed in special boxes or jars today called canopic jars. These were buried with the mummy. In later mummies, the organs were treated, wrapped, and replaced within the body. Even so, unused canopic jars continued to be part of the burial ritual.

2. Why do you think the empty jars continued to be used in burials?

The embalmers next removed all moisture from the body. This they did by covering the body with natron, a type of salt which has great drying properties, and by placing additional natron packets inside the body. When the body had dried out completely, embalmers removed the internal packets and lightly washed the natron off the body. The result was a very dried-out but recognizable human form. To make the mummy seem even more lifelike, sunken areas of the body were filled out with linen and other materials and false eyes were added.

3. Could this step have been done before the previous step? Why or why not?

Next the wrapping began. Each mummy needed hundreds of yards of linen. The priests carefully wound the long strips of linen around the body, sometimes even wrapping each finger and toe separately before wrapping the entire hand or foot. In order to protect the dead from mishap, amulets[1] were placed among the wrappings and prayers and magical words written on some of the linen strips. Often the priests placed a mask of the person's

1. **amulets:** objects supposed to have magical power to protect the body from injury or evil.

next

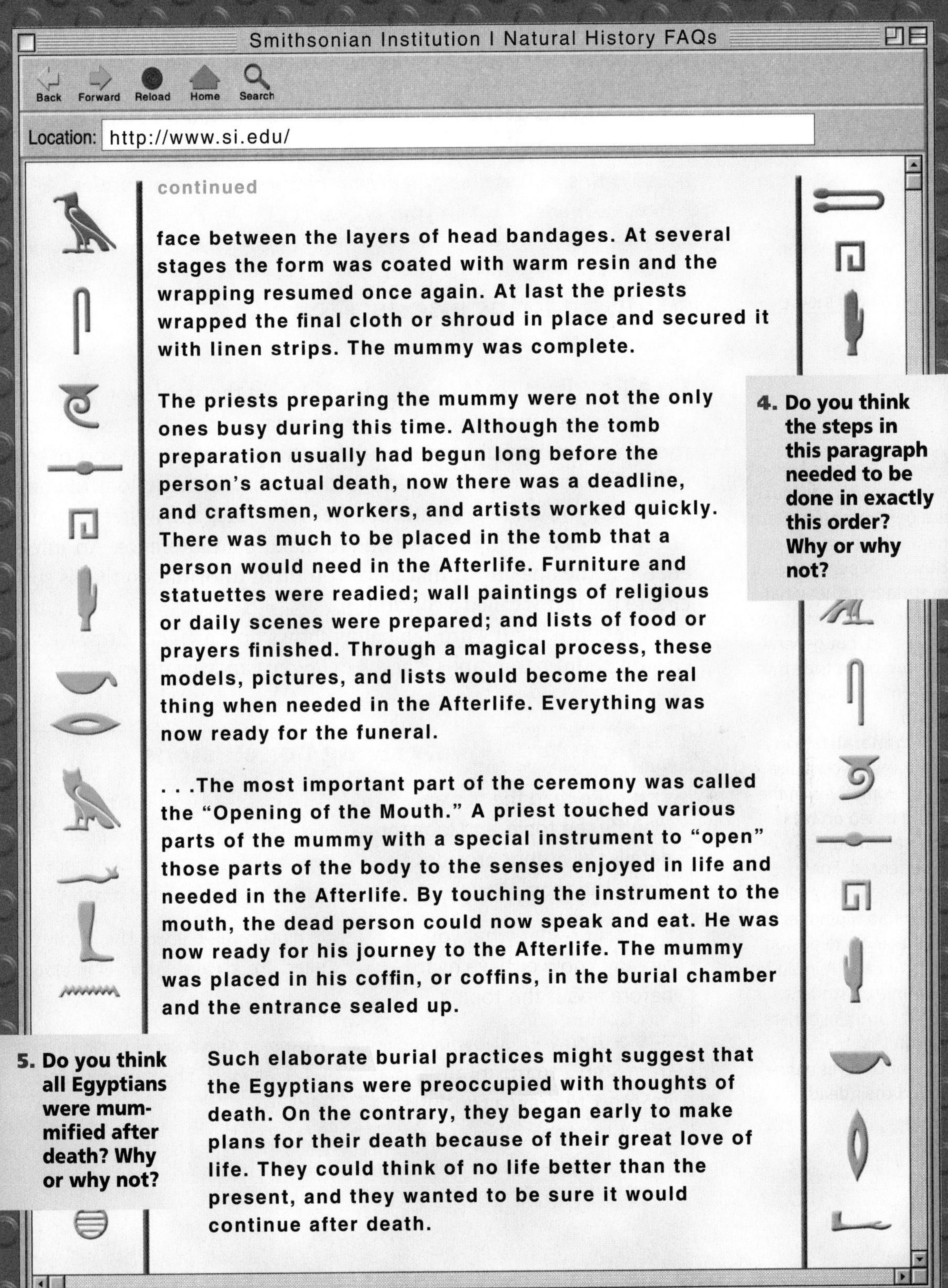

continued

face between the layers of head bandages. At several stages the form was coated with warm resin and the wrapping resumed once again. At last the priests wrapped the final cloth or shroud in place and secured it with linen strips. The mummy was complete.

The priests preparing the mummy were not the only ones busy during this time. Although the tomb preparation usually had begun long before the person's actual death, now there was a deadline, and craftsmen, workers, and artists worked quickly. There was much to be placed in the tomb that a person would need in the Afterlife. Furniture and statuettes were readied; wall paintings of religious or daily scenes were prepared; and lists of food or prayers finished. Through a magical process, these models, pictures, and lists would become the real thing when needed in the Afterlife. Everything was now ready for the funeral.

4. Do you think the steps in this paragraph needed to be done in exactly this order? Why or why not?

. . .The most important part of the ceremony was called the "Opening of the Mouth." A priest touched various parts of the mummy with a special instrument to "open" those parts of the body to the senses enjoyed in life and needed in the Afterlife. By touching the instrument to the mouth, the dead person could now speak and eat. He was now ready for his journey to the Afterlife. The mummy was placed in his coffin, or coffins, in the burial chamber and the entrance sealed up.

5. Do you think all Egyptians were mummified after death? Why or why not?

Such elaborate burial practices might suggest that the Egyptians were preoccupied with thoughts of death. On the contrary, they began early to make plans for their death because of their great love of life. They could think of no life better than the present, and they wanted to be sure it would continue after death.

First Thoughts on Your Reading

1. What parts of the mummification process would you like to know more about?
2. Did this article give you a clear picture of how mummies were made? Explain your answer.

READING SKILL

Making Inferences: Drawing Conclusions

Be a Reading Detective Imagine that the article you are reading mentions a person who wears a white lab coat and works with test tubes. You can probably figure out that this person is some sort of scientist. The writer expects readers to know what scientists look like and do. When you make a connection between clues the writer provides and what you already know, you are making an **inference.** An inference, like the one above, that helps you fill in information that is specific to the text is called a **conclusion.**

The Thinking It Through below shows how a reader drew a conclusion about paragraphs 2 and 3 of "Egyptian Mummies."

TIP Another type of inference you can make is a *generalization.* Both generalizations and conclusions depend on your putting together what you know and what you have read, but generalizations go outside the text, into the larger world.

A **generalization** is a judgment you make about something in the world based on what you have read, seen, or experienced. For example, after reading "Egyptian Mummies" and seeing a television program about Incan ice mummies, a student might form the generalization that many ancient cultures mummified their dead.

THINKING IT THROUGH — Drawing Conclusions

STEP 1 Re-read the passage, identify the topic, and look for details the author provides about the topic.

This passage is about the priests who mummified people and the first step in the process, removing the internal organs.

STEP 2 Consider what you already know or have heard before about this topic.

In pictures I've seen, the mummies are always wrapped in cloth.

STEP 3 Add your knowledge from Step 2 to the information in Step 1 to draw a conclusion about the topic.

Wrapping the body in cloth is a later stage in the mummification process.

YOUR TURN 2 Drawing Conclusions

- Draw a conclusion about the fifth paragraph of "Egyptian Mummies" by using the Thinking It Through steps on the previous page and answering this question: Why do you think amulets and careful wrapping were important?
- Then, draw another conclusion about the sixth paragraph of the text. Be sure to tell what evidence in the text led you to draw this conclusion.

READING FOCUS

Chronological Order

It's about Time Most process pieces are written in **chronological order** to explain the steps of a process in the order in which they take place. To tell whether an article is written in chronological order, look for *signal words* or *transitions* such as these:

after	before	first	once	until
as	during	next	second	when
at last	finally	now	then	while

These **signal words** or **transitions** can help you put together the small parts of the big picture. You can map out the big picture by using a time line. For example, the time line below shows, in chronological order, the steps British archaeologist Howard Carter and his team took in 1922 to discover the tomb and mummy of the Egyptian pharaoh Tutankhamun.

November 1:	Nov. 4:	Nov. 5:	Nov. 25:	Nov. 26:
began search in desert	found tomb entrance	uncovered steps to door	opened door; cleared passage	opened next door; found tomb

YOUR TURN 3 Finding Chronological Order

Look for words that signal chronological order in "Egyptian Mummies" on pages 51–53. Then, make a time line showing the steps in the process of mummification, in chronological order. Unlike the time line above, your time line will not include dates.

MINI-LESSON **VOCABULARY**

Greek and Latin Roots

Complex process papers often contain unfamiliar words. A **word root,** which is the main part of a word, carries the core meaning of a word. Knowing common Latin and Greek word roots, such as the ones in the chart to the right, can help you figure out the meanings of these unfamiliar words.

Here is how to figure out the meaning of the word *elaborate* from the selection "Egyptian Mummies."

Root	Meaning	Example
–balm– *L.*	soothing oil	lip balm
–cogn– *L.*	to know	incognito
–figur– *L.*	form	configure
–occup– *L.*	to possess	occupation
–tom– *G.*	to cut	appendectomy

THINKING IT THROUGH

Using Greek and Latin Roots

Sentence: Such *elaborate* burial practices might suggest that the Egyptians were preoccupied with thoughts of death.

STEP 1 Identify and define the word root.

The Latin root -labor- means "to work."

STEP 2 Use the word's context and the meaning of the root to define the word.

The writer talks about how much work the Egyptians put into burying people. I think elaborate means "to put a lot of work into something."

STEP 3 Substitute your definition for the word. You may have to adjust the wording of your definition to make it fit.

"Such to put a lot of work into something burial practices . . ." sounds funny. "Such thoroughly worked out burial practices . . ." sounds right.

PRACTICE

Define these words by using the steps above. The words are highlighted in "Egyptian Mummies." Meanings of prefixes are noted where needed.

1. embalming (*em*–: into), page 51
2. anatomy (*ana*–: up), page 51
3. disfigure (*dis*–: cause to be the opposite of), page 52
4. recognizable, page 52
5. preoccupied, page 53

MINI-LESSON **TEST TAKING**

Answering Questions About Drawing Conclusions

On a reading test, you may be asked to draw a conclusion about a passage. Consider the passage below and the question that follows it.

> In 1999, archaeologists discovered three perfectly preserved Incan mummies high atop a volcano in the Andes mountains of Argentina. Unlike many other mummies, these mummies were preserved by nature, not by the efforts of humans. The extreme cold of the mountains "freeze-dried" the boy and two girls 500 years ago. Buried with the mummies were valuable artifacts, including gold and silver statues, beautiful fabrics, and pots of food. Ancient cultures as far away as Siberia and Egypt surrounded their mummies with similar treasures.

Based on the passage, what do the frozen Incan mummies have in common with mummies preserved by humans?

A. Five hundred years ago, people were creating both kinds of mummies.

B. Both methods of mummification were used by most ancient cultures.

C. Both were considered important enough to be buried with valuable objects.

D. Children, as well as adults, were made into both kinds of mummies.

THINKING IT THROUGH

Drawing a Conclusion

STEP 1 Read the question or stem to identify the topic of the question.

The topic of the question is what the two kinds of mummies have in common.

STEP 2 Study the answer choices, ruling out those choices that are clearly wrong.

I think choice A is wrong because the passage doesn't mention when the Egyptian mummies were made. Choice D is wrong because the passage doesn't mention adults at all.

STEP 3 Re-read the passage and look for evidence that supports the remaining answer choices.

The writer does not say that other cultures used both methods, so choice B is wrong. There is evidence for choice C because in the last sentence the writer says that other cultures also surrounded their mummies with treasures. Both kinds of mummies must have been important, or they wouldn't have been buried with so many valuables. Choice C is correct.

Writing About a Complex Process

WHAT'S AHEAD?

In this workshop you will write an essay about a complex process. You will also learn how to

- **organize details in chronological order**
- **eliminate jargon from your writing**
- **choose precise words**
- **punctuate introductory words and phrases**

You may have once wondered in amazement how the caterpillar that went into a chrysalis came out as a butterfly a few weeks later. You might also have once taken apart a radio or watch to figure out how it worked. Finding out what goes on behind the scenes usually starts with a simple question such as "How did *that* happen?" or "What makes *this* work?" The answers to these questions, though, are often complex.

An essay about a complex process is a type of **expository writing** because it explores and explains the answers to these questions. In this workshop you will share your own behind-the-scenes knowledge about a process. That process might be one you already understand well, or it might be one you will learn about as you plan your essay.

Prewriting

Find a Topic

How Does It Work? Use the following ideas to brainstorm a list of topics for your essay.

- how things work, from household appliances to the space shuttle
- why things happen, especially in nature, or
- where ordinary objects such as erasers or toothpicks come from

You should consider topics in the form of *how* or *why* questions such as those on the next page.

- How does an airplane get off the ground?
- Why does the outside of a glass of cold water get wet?
- How is vinegar made?
- How does e-mail get from one computer to another?

Do not worry about whether you know the answers to the questions you brainstorm. Just jot down any ideas that interest you.

Evaluate Your Topic

Judge for Yourself Once you have considered a few processes, take time to evaluate your choices. A good topic for your essay will meet all of these requirements:

- **It concerns a process, not a single event.** For example, the reason the sky is blue has to do with a single event—air molecules scattering sunlight—rather than a series of events.
- **It is not a "how-to" topic;** you will explain how or why something happens, not teach readers how to do something.
- **It concerns the larger world,** rather than focusing on yourself.
- **It should be a process familiar to you,** if possible.

TIP You should plan to explore a process in depth, not state the obvious. For example, rather than simply saying that water boils when it gets hot enough, you would explain what happens to water molecules when they reach 100 degrees Celsius. What appears to be a simple process—for example, why ice melts—may actually be quite complex.

How do you do an ollie on a skateboard?	No—"how-to"
Why is the sky blue?	No—not really a process
How does lake water get clean enough to drink?	Yes—meets all four requirements
How do I clean my room?	No—only concerns me

YOUR TURN 4 Choosing a Process

Brainstorm and write down several topics for complex processes by asking *how* and *why* questions about everyday events. From your list of potential topics, choose the one that best meets the four requirements above. If you have more than one good topic, consider which one is more unusual, or which one most people have probably not considered before.

Identify Your Purpose and Audience

What's My Motivation? You might wonder why people write about complex processes. Whether a doctor writes an explanation of the circulatory system for medical students or an auto expert writes an engine manual for mechanics, the purpose is the same. **People write complex process explanations for the *purpose* of sharing information with an *audience* of curious readers.** To capture audience interest, a writer must give readers a reason to learn about the process being explained. In your essay you will explain a process to readers who do not yet understand how that process works. Answer these questions to identify this audience:

KEY CONCEPT

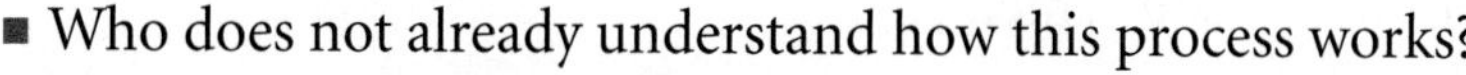

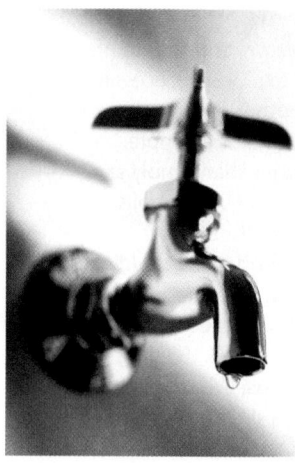

- Who does not already understand how this process works?
- Who is interested in this topic?

Here are notes one student made about her audience.

> Kids my age may not know where we get our drinking water. They'll be interested if I tell them how dirty it is at first. I can keep them interested by not being too technical. If I keep the explanation simple and compare it to things most people understand, they should get it.

TIP Your **voice** is the way your writing sounds. To create an effective voice for a complex process essay, choose your words carefully. If you use words that are too difficult or that do not mean exactly what you want to say, your readers may have a hard time understanding the process. To create an effective voice for this piece, you should also avoid using humor that may not come across in your writing. Humor could distract your readers, which may cause them to miss important information. Humor could also give your audience the impression that you do not take your topic seriously.

YOUR TURN 5 Identifying Audience

Identify your audience by answering the questions above. Then, consider the following questions and jot down any ideas that occur to you.

- What does my audience already know about the process?
- What basic information will they need to understand the process?

Gather Information

May the Source Be with You To explain your topic well, you may need to do some research. You can ask someone who knows more about the process than you do, look in the library or on the Internet, or watch a television program or video on the topic. Wherever you get your information, take careful notes in your own words, and be sure to keep a list of the sources you have used. Here are the types of information you should look for when researching your process.

- detailed explanations of each step of the process, why each step occurs, and how the steps fit together
- definitions of terms your audience might not understand
- background information about the process—what causes it to happen, why it is important, or what might happen if it did not occur

TIP You may find in researching your topic that the process is too complicated to explain thoroughly in a few pages. Consider focusing on just one part of the whole process or changing to a different, less complex topic.

Plan Your Essay

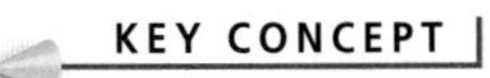

Chart Your Progress The type of process you will explain is called "complex" for a good reason—**it involves many steps and detailed information.** To organize the information you gathered while researching your process, use a **time line, chart,** or some other **graphic organizer.** A helpful graphic organizer, such as the chart on page 62, will show a summary of the steps in chronological order and the details needed to understand the steps. Your graphic organizer will serve as a guide for writing your essay. You will discuss the steps of the process in the body of your essay. You can use the introduction and conclusion of your essay to explain what happens before and after the process.

TIP Have a few classmates read your chart and ask questions when they need more information. Jot down words you need to define and details or background information they need to understand the process. You might include a column for this information in your chart.

Fine Tuning Once you have listed what you know on paper, you can use the following tips to see where you need to add, delete, or change information.

- If a step has little or no elaboration next to it, add some details.
- If there seems to be a large gap between steps, check your notes to see if you should include another step.
- If a step will seem obvious to your audience, cross it out.
- If your steps do not show a logical **progression** from one idea to the next, rearrange the steps so that they are in **chronological order,** or time order.

Reference Note

For more on **chronological order,** see page 55.

Here is one student's revised chart:

Steps of the Process	Details About Steps	
Beginning Water enters the treatment plant.	It comes from lakes, rivers, or ground water. These sources might be contaminated.	
1. Chemicals help large particles fall to the bottom.	Chemicals break down and attract large particles of dirt. Dirt sticks to bits of the chemical, forming clumps heavy enough to fall to the bottom. Water sits still to let particles fall.	*(aluminum sulfate or ferric sulfate)* *for 2–3 hours*
2. Water passes through a series of filters.	Water is forced through filters. Filter layers may include very fine sand, gravel, anthracite coal, or charcoal.	*to eliminate small particles that make water cloudy.*
3. Chlorine is added to kill harmful microorganisms.	Chlorine kills dangerous bacteria and prevents later growth of additional bacteria or algae.	*It takes a fairly small amount of chlorine to do this.*
End Water is clean enough to drink.	Treatment plant adjusts the pH level ~~Water travels through pipes to customers.~~	*by carbonating the water; this improves the taste.*

Reference Note

For more on taking **notes,** see page 811 in the Quick Reference Handbook.

YOUR TURN 6 Planning Your Essay

- Make thorough notes about the process you have chosen to explain.
- Then, create a chart like the one above to list everything you know or have learned through research about your process.
- Finally, check the steps and details in your chart, and add or delete information if necessary. You can use your revised chart as a guide for writing your essay.

MINI-LESSON **WRITING**

Eliminating Jargon

Jargon is specialized vocabulary used in a particular field. You might have trouble understanding jargon if you know little about the field. A reader unfamiliar with the workings of airplanes would not understand the term *aileron*, for example.

Eliminating jargon is important in writing about a complex process. Remember, your audience is reading to learn about the process, so they are unlikely to know the jargon associated with it.

Here is a jargon-filled paragraph. How many of the words do you understand?

> Torpedoed in 1942, the freighter *Manuela* now rests on the floor of the Atlantic Ocean on its starboard side. Pictures show that the freighter is broken into three main sections: the bow, the hull amidships, and the stern. The debris field lies in a circular area in the middle of the three sections.

While this passage would make sense to someone who knows about shipwrecks, you would have trouble navigating it without understanding the terms *starboard*, *bow*, *hull*, *amidships*, *stern*, and *debris field*.

Here are two ways you can help readers understand technical terms.

- **Add a definition, either right before or right after the term.**
- **Eliminate the jargon by stating the idea in words your audience will understand.**

The following example puts jargon into words that make sense to readers who know little about shipwrecks.

> Torpedoed in 1942, the freighter *Manuela* now rests on the floor of the Atlantic Ocean on its starboard, or right, side. Pictures show that the freighter is broken into three main sections: the front, the middle section of the ship's outer shell, and the rear. Smaller pieces of the ship lie in a circular area in the middle of the three sections.

PRACTICE

Clarify the meaning of the italicized word in each sentence by either adding a definition or rephrasing the idea. You may check a dictionary to define unfamiliar terms.

1. Ancient bacteria can be revived because their *spores* have survived in amber.
2. Workers at the motorcycle plant *true* the wheels and then adjust the spokes.
3. A rainbow is formed when light passing through water droplets is *refracted*.
4. The success of the football team will depend on the effectiveness of its *red zone* defense.
5. The bat's *sonar*, which makes it an excellent hunter, is more accurate than the navy's.

Writing

Complex Process Essay

Framework	Directions and Explanations
Introduction ■ Reason why people should understand this process ■ Clear topic statement ■ Background information	Your introduction should clearly tell your audience **what process you will explain** and give a **reason for learning how this process works.** If necessary, provide any **background information** readers might need to understand the importance of the process or events that led up to the process.
Body ■ First step plus elaboration ■ Second step plus elaboration and so on	Use your prewriting chart to help you arrange the steps of your process in **chronological order.** Create **coherence** by connecting steps or ideas with **transitions,** such as those on page 55. Remember to **define any terms** that readers might not already know the first time you use them. **Elaborate on each step.** For example: ■ Explain each step in detail by describing the smaller steps that are part of it or by using sensory description ■ Show how the step relates to the rest of the process
Conclusion Final comment about the process and/or Restatement of its importance	Tell your readers an interesting fact about the process, such as how the product of the process is used or what happens after the process is complete. You might also remind readers **why the process is important.**

YOUR TURN 7 Drafting Your Complex Process Essay

Now it is your turn to draft a complex process essay. As you write, refer to your notes, the framework above, and the Writer's Model on the next page.

A Writer's Model

The final draft below closely follows the framework for a complex process essay.

Polluted to Pristine: The Water Treatment Process

I have never learned as much on a field trip as I did when our class went to the water treatment plant last month. Like most people, I had never thought about where our drinking water comes from. Most drinking water starts out in a river, in a lake, or underground. You would not want to drink directly from those sources, though. The water could be contaminated with bacteria, algae, and even chemicals or sewage that has run into the water source. Your tap water is safe to drink, however, thanks to the water treatment process. Here is how a typical water treatment plant cleans the water you drink.

Background information

Reason for learning

Statement of topic

After the water arrives at the plant, the big pieces of dirt are removed by adding a chemical (aluminum sulfate or ferric sulfate) to the water. This chemical acts as a coagulant, or sticky substance, for the floating dirt and minerals. The pieces of dirt clump together around the chemicals, and these clumps get so heavy that they fall to the bottom of the water tank. After the particles have had time to fall to the bottom, the clear water above the layer of dirt is skimmed from the tank .

Step 1

Elaboration

The much cleaner (but still not clean enough to drink) water then moves on to the next step of the process, filtration. Here, particles too small or stubborn to be caught by the sticky chemicals are removed by several filters. Now, instead of sitting still to get cleaner, the water has to move to get clean. It may pass through layers of very fine sand, gravel, anthracite coal, or charcoal. These layers catch most of the remaining particles, leaving water that looks clear and drinkable.

Step 2

Elaboration

It takes one last step to make the treated water safe for you to gulp down after gym class. Even though the water

Step 3

(continued)

(continued)

looks clean, there may still be microscopic bacteria in it. These bacteria can really ruin your day if you drink them. To kill them, a small amount of chlorine is added—like the chlorine in swimming pools. The amount of chlorine needed to make this filtered water safe for you to drink is not enough to make it taste bad. It *is* enough to prevent the growth of new bacteria and algae after the water leaves the plant.

Elaboration

Now the water is safe to drink. Before it heads to your house, though, water treatment plants eliminate any bitter taste and adjust the pH (acidity) level of the water. They do this by bubbling carbon dioxide, which also makes sodas fizzy, through the water. Finally, safe and good-tasting water is delivered to your house.

Interesting fact

Restatement of reason

Designing Your Writing

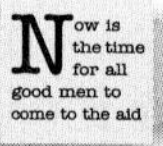

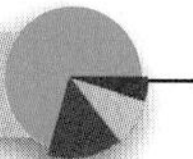

Text Features **Text features** are tools writers use to make their ideas stand out. You can use text features to make your complex process essay even easier for readers to understand. Here are some ideas.

- Separate a group of short steps from the rest of your essay in a **numbered list** or a **bulleted list** like this one. You can use word-processing features or create the numbers or bullets by hand.
- Make any words you define stand out, either by underlining them or by using your word processor to print them in *italics.*

A Student's Model

Notice that in the following excerpt Armando Hernandez, a student at Morningside Middle School in Ft. Worth, Texas, explained two complex processes: how a CD is recorded and how a CD produces sound.

How Do CDs Work?

When explaining how to play a CD, you probably think of two main steps: 1) Insert the CD. 2) Press "play." What you may not know is that a lot goes on before and after you press "play." It is much more complex than it seems.

Statement of topic

First, you must record a CD. During recording, a microphone turns live music into electrical signals. The signals are broken into segments, and each segment becomes a digital code. A laser then uses this code to produce a pattern of microscopic bumps and pits into a CD.

Step 1 in recording

Step 2

Step 3

Playing a CD is almost the opposite of producing one. First, there is a turntable drive motor. A CD sits on the turntable. The motor spins the turntable when you press "play."

Step 1 in playing

Next, a low-powered laser beam focuses on the bottom of the CD where the bumps and pits are. The brightness of the reflected light of the laser beam changes as the beam bounces off the bumps and pits. The light hits a device that translates the differences in brightness into an electrical signal.

Step 2

Step 3

Finally, the CD player decodes the signal and reproduces the original sound that you can hear through loudspeakers or headphones. . . .

Step 4

Works Cited

Feldman, Leonard. "Compact Disc." Academic American Encyclopedia. 1989 ed.

Pohlmann, Ken C. "Compact Disc." The World Book Encyclopedia. 1995 ed.

Revising

Evaluate and Revise Content, Organization, and Style

COMPUTER TIP

To move a step without retyping it, use the cut and paste function on your word processor or use your mouse to highlight the text and drag it to the right place.

Do a Double Take To evaluate your own writing or a peer's, look over the essay at least two times. The first time you will look at the big picture: what you included in the essay and how you organized it. Use the guidelines below to **edit** the content of your essay. In your second reading, you will concentrate on individual sentences. The Focus on Word Choice on page 70 will help you to use more precise wording in your writing.

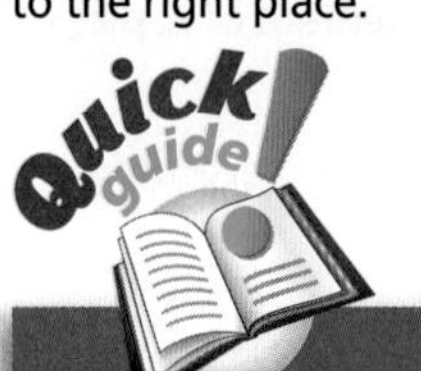

First Reading: Content and Organization Use this chart to evaluate and revise your own complex process essay or a classmate's.

Guidelines for Self-Evaluation and Peer Evaluation

Evaluation Questions	Tips	Revision Techniques
1 Does the introduction clearly state the process that the paper will explain?	**Highlight** the sentence that states the paper's topic.	If needed, **add** a topic sentence, or **replace** it with a clearer statement of the process.
2 Does the introduction give readers a reason to learn about the process?	**Underline** the sentence that tells why readers should know how this process works.	If needed, **add** a reason for reading to the beginning of the essay.
3 Do transitions give the essay coherence and help show a logical progression of ideas?	**Number** the steps of the process as you read them.	**Rearrange** the steps of the process, or **add** transitions to make the connection between steps or ideas clearer.
4 Do details provide enough elaboration to make each step of the process clear?	**Put a check mark** next to each detail that elaborates on a step or idea.	As needed, **elaborate** on any step with fewer than two check marks.
5 Does the conclusion make a final comment about the process or restate why people should understand it?	**Underline** the final comment or restatement of why readers should know about this process.	If necessary, **add** a final comment or a restatement of why the process is worth understanding.

ONE WRITER'S REVISIONS Here is a revision of an early draft of the complex process essay on pages 65–66.

After the water arrives at the plant, ~~T~~the big pieces of dirt are removed by adding a chemical (aluminum sulfate or ferric sulfate) to the water. This chemical acts as a coagulant, or sticky substance, for the floating dirt and minerals. After the particles have had time to fall to the bottom, the clear water above the layer of dirt is skimmed from the tank. The pieces of dirt clump together around the chemicals, and these clumps get so heavy that they fall to the bottom of the water tank.

add

add

rearrange

Responding to the Revision Process

1. Why do you think the writer added to the first and second sentences?
2. How did moving the last sentence make the process clearer?

PEER REVIEW

As you read a peer's essay, ask yourself these questions:

- How clearly can I picture the whole process?
- What parts of the process are confusing or unclear?

Second Reading: Style Now that you have improved the content and organization of your essay, take a look at the style of your essay. The style of your essay involves the way you express your ideas. One way to edit the style of your writing is to replace vague words with precise words. Choosing a precise word with a crystal-clear meaning instead of a vague word with a fuzzy meaning will help you achieve your purpose by making it easy for your audience to understand your ideas.

When you evaluate your essay for style, ask yourself whether the paper uses precise words to express its ideas clearly. As you re-read your essay, circle any words you think readers might picture in many different ways. Can you help readers picture what you picture? If so, replace vague words with more precise, descriptive language. The Focus on Word Choice on the next page can help you choose precise words.

Word Choice

Choosing Precise Words

No two words have exactly the same meaning. Your readers will get a clearer picture of the process you are explaining if you choose your words precisely. Here are two traps to avoid:

- **Trap 1: Choosing vague rather than precise wording.** Readers may picture something very different from what you had in mind if you use vague wording, such as *car,* instead of more precise language, such as *1950s wood-paneled station wagon.*
- **Trap 2: Choosing a precise word that does not fit the situation or feeling of a passage.** For example, *murmur* and *mutter* both refer to a low flow of words or sounds, but *mutter* usually suggests anger. An unhappy customer would probably *mutter* about a bill, but a happy mother would *murmur* (not *mutter*) to her baby.

TIP If you have chosen a word whose meaning does not quite fit the feeling of your passage, try looking this word up in a thesaurus. A thesaurus will probably list several synonyms for your word, and one of these synonyms may be the exact word you need.

ONE WRITER'S REVISIONS

It takes one last step to make the treated water safe for you to ~~sip~~ gulp down after gym class. Even though the water looks clean, there may still be ~~tiny~~ microscopic bacteria in it.

Responding to the Revision Process

How did the changes the writer made improve this passage? Why do you think so?

YOUR TURN 8 Evaluating and Revising Your Complex Process Essay

Evaluate and revise your essay using the guidelines on page 68 and the Focus on Word Choice above. If a peer evaluated your paper, think carefully about each of your peer's comments as you revise.

Publishing

Proofread Your Essay

A Fresh Set of Eyes Errors in your final paper will make it harder for your reader to focus on understanding your process. If you have another person help you proofread your essay, you will be less likely to miss any mistakes.

Grammar Link

Punctuating Introductory Words and Phrases

When you use chronological order, you will often start sentences with introductory words and phrases. To determine if you need to use a comma to separate these words and phrases from the rest of the sentence, follow these rules.

1. **If the meaning of the sentence is clear, the comma is optional.**

Comma Optional	In two weeks, the county will pave the road.

2. **Use a comma after a short phrase if the sentence might be misunderstood without it.**

Comma Needed	In the winter, snow often causes delays in road work.

3. **Use a comma after introductory words such as *yes, no,* and *well.*** A comma lets readers pause where a speaker would.

Incorrect	Yes the road is now ready.
Correct	Yes, the road is now ready.

4. **Use a comma after any long phrase that begins a sentence.** A comma separates a sentence into chunks of meaning.

Incorrect	After the wear and tear of several years of traffic the road will need to be resurfaced.
Correct	After the wear and tear of several years of traffic, the road will need to be resurfaced.

PRACTICE

Correct the following sentences by adding commas where necessary. Write a *C* next to sentences that are already correct. For each sentence, note which rule you are applying.

1. Clearly eating a meal is only the first part of the digestive process.
2. To move food along the esophagus contracts.
3. For several hours food is digested in the stomach.
4. Through tiny openings in the walls of the small intestine nutrients enter the bloodstream.
5. Finally you have the energy you need.

For more information and practice on using **commas after introductory words and phrases,** see page 644.

Reference Note

To add **graphics** to your essay, see page 77.

TIP Give your essay a title that creatively and accurately reflects your topic.

PORTFOLIO

Publish Your Essay

Facing the Audience Now you can share your explanation of a complex process with your audience. Depending on who that audience is, you might try one of these publishing ideas.

- Give a presentation about the process, to your class or to younger students, using illustrations or demonstrating the process if possible.
- With your class, create a "How It Works" manual with explanations of many different processes. This manual can be kept in class or in the library for other students to consult.

Reflect on Your Essay

Building Your Portfolio Finally, think about your essay. Answer the following questions to build on your writing skills.

- How did you fit your explanation to your audience?
- What sources did you consult for information about your process? Which were helpful? Which might you use again?
- How well did you achieve your purpose of sharing information with your audience? Do you think your audience fully understood your essay? Explain.

YOUR TURN 9 Proofreading, Publishing, and Reflecting on Your Essay

- Correct grammar, usage, and mechanics errors.
- Publish your essay for your target audience.
- Answer the questions from Reflect on Your Essay above. Record your responses in a learning log, or include them in your portfolio.

A Humorous "How-to" Poem

Process writing is not all serious business. Here is an opportunity to use your writing skills to explain another type of process in a fun way. "How-to" writing is a kind of process writing you have probably done before—it involves giving readers instructions for making or doing something. In this section, you will write a funny "how-to" poem for younger readers.

The Rhyme and Reason of It The chart below shows three of the many techniques poets use to get their ideas, whether serious or funny, across to readers. Although many poems do not use rhyme or rhythm, younger readers tend to prefer poems that use both. Because you are writing for younger readers, you should try to use rhyme and rhythm in your poem. Effective use of rhyme and rhythm can give a poem a songlike quality that makes the poem easy to read and pleasing to hear. Your teacher can provide more examples of irony or suggest other poetic techniques you might use.

The chart below explains the poetic techniques of rhyme, rhythm, and irony. In the first example, rhyming words are printed in boldface. In the second, the boldface letters show stressed syllables that create rhythm.

Poetic Technique	Definition	Example
Rhyme	the use of syllables that sound alike to form a pattern, usually at the ends of lines of poetry	I wouldn't want to **tackle** An irritated **jackal**
Rhythm	a repeated pattern of stressed and unstressed syllables in poetry	**I** con**fess** I'd **care** to **mess** **With** a **wolf** pack **e**ven **less**
Irony	a difference between what the reader expects to happen and what actually happens, or a difference between what the author says and what the author means	But I'd rather face their wrath Than give my basset hound a bath Marilyn Singer, *It's Hard to Read a Map with a Beagle on Your Lap*

On the following page is an example of a humorous "how-to" poem for younger readers by Jack Prelutsky. As you read, notice the way the author uses rhyme and rhythm. Also, notice the poet's twist: Instead of giving his readers specific instructions for how to do something, the poet explains how *not* to hide an elephant, step by step.

An Elephant Is Hard to Hide

by Jack Prelutsky

An **ele**phant is **hard** to **hide**,
it's **ra**ther **tall**, it's **fair**ly **wide**,
it **occupies** a **lot** of **space**,
you **just** can't **put** it **anyplace**.
It's quite an unrewarding **chore**
to try and cram it in a **drawer**,
a closet's somewhat better, **but**
you're apt to find the door won't **shut**.

Rhythm—stressed syllables are boldfaced

Rhyme

An elephant beneath your bed
will manifest[1] both tail and head,
and in the tub, there's little doubt
that it will soon be singled out.
An elephant won't simply sit,
it tends to move about a bit,
this trait, when coupled with its size
makes it a nightmare to disguise.

Irony—Of course an elephant would be found, and quickly!

An elephant, if kept around
is almost certain to be found,
your parents may suspect one's near
when peanuts start to disappear.
An elephant is hard to hide,
I know it's so, because I've tried,
my family should detect it soon . . .
I brought it home this afternoon.

1. **manifest:** reveal or clearly show.

You can see that Prelutsky used rhyme and rhythm in his poem. He also used irony, making it sound as though an elephant is only a little bit too big to fit in a drawer, for example.

A Poet? You Know It! Now that you have taken a closer look at a humorous "how-to" poem, it is your turn to write one. Remember that your audience for this poem is younger readers, so choose a topic that will appeal to them. You can

- explain a silly process, such as how monsters get under little kids' beds at night, or
- explain in a silly way a real process, such as how to keep your brother or sister out of your belongings

Once you have brainstormed several ideas, choose the one you think is funniest.

Step by Step Before you dive into your poem, list the major steps of the process you have chosen. What steps do you want to include because they are funny? What silly steps can you make up? What steps should be skipped because they are too obvious or dull? List all the steps you want to include, in order.

Rhyme Time In planning your poem, you may want to jot down words that rhyme with words you know you will need to use (for example, "stay out of my *room*, or you will meet your *doom*"). Your teacher or librarian may have a rhyming dictionary to help you find other words that rhyme with words in your poem.

We've Got the Beat Besides rhyme, a poem written for younger readers needs a consistent rhythm to make it sound like poetry. In every word or sentence you say, some syllables are stressed and some are unstressed. Poets usually make sure that the patterns of stressed and unstressed syllables are the same in every line or every other line. Prelutsky matches the pattern in every line of his poem. In the following excerpt from Kenn Nesbitt's poem "Don't Bring Camels in the Classroom," the rhythm alternates. The first and third lines have one pattern of stressed and unstressed syllables, and the second and fourth lines have a slightly different pattern (stressed syllables are printed in boldface).

> **Pull** your **pen**guin **off** the **play**ground.
> **Put** your **py**thon **in** a **tree.**
> **Place** your **platypus** wher**ev**er
> **You** think **platypi** should **be.**

Look Before You Leap The way a poem looks on the page is just as important as how it sounds. Unless it looks like poetry, your readers will read it as an essay and miss out on the work you have put into rhyming words and using a consistent rhythm. As you can see in the Prelutsky poem, poetry is organized in lines and stanzas (chunks of lines about the same part of the subject), not sentences and paragraphs. Rhyming words are placed at the ends of lines to draw readers' attention.

YOUR TURN 10 Writing a Humorous "How-to" Poem

Refer to the examples and follow the instructions on pages 73–75 to find a topic and write a short, funny poem for younger readers that explains how to do something. Then, share your work with your target audience by performing a **dramatic interpretation** of your poem. Have fun with your performance by reading your poem in a funny voice or by wearing an appropriate costume.

MINI-LESSON **TEST TAKING**

Explaining "How-to"

When you take a writing test you may be asked to explain how to do something. Because you cannot do research during a test, you will already know all of the information you need to answer the prompt. How might you handle a prompt such as the one to the right?

You have learned many skills, such as how to study for a test, that help you succeed in school. Write a letter to a younger child explaining how to do something that helps you succeed in school. Explain the steps involved and provide details that elaborate on each step.

THINKING IT THROUGH

Explaining "How-to" for Tests

▶ **STEP 1** **Identify the task.** The prompt gives you important clues about the audience, purpose, and format of your answer.

Audience: a child in elementary school
Purpose: to explain how to do something
Format: a letter

▶ **STEP 2** **Choose a topic.** Many prompts will let you choose a topic within the required format. Brainstorm a few topics that fit the prompt and select your favorite.

Skills that help me succeed in school:
- making friends
- using time between classes efficiently
- ✓ finishing homework on time

▶ **STEP 3** **Organize your ideas.** You will have space to jot down the steps you want to explain. A **time line** can help you put your ideas in chronological order.

Time line for finishing homework on time

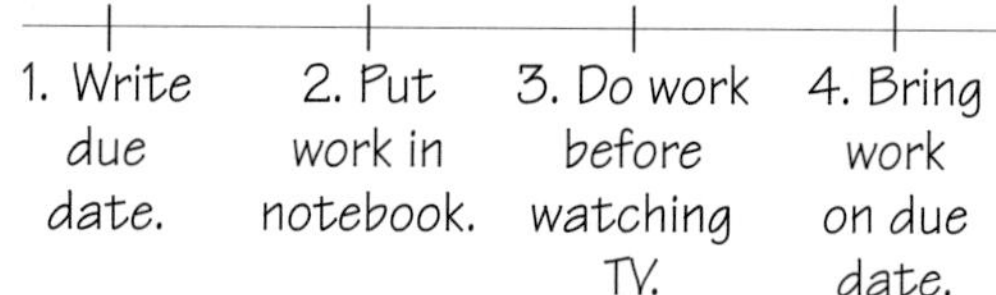

1. Write due date.
2. Put work in notebook.
3. Do work before watching TV.
4. Bring work on due date.

▶ **STEP 4** **Write your response.** Keeping your audience and purpose in mind, list the steps in chronological order, and elaborate on each step.

Possible elaborations:

Step 1: Tell students to do this so they will not forget when assignments are due.

Step 2: Explain that they should do this to keep from losing assignments.

Step 3: Tell them that doing homework right away will be easier than trying to do it late at night when they are sleepy.

Step 4: Explain that this will keep them from losing points for late work.

Creating Graphics

WHAT'S AHEAD?

In this section you will create graphics for your essay. You will also learn how to

- **choose the best form for your graphics**
- **use words to make your graphics clearer**

No matter how clear your explanation, graphics can make a process even clearer to your readers. Providing graphics gives readers a tool for creating their own mental picture of the process you explain, and it also helps your words make more sense.

Looking at Graphics

Some graphics are more helpful than others. Graphics that are cluttered or unclear can confuse readers. Look at the following graphics. Which is helpful? Which is confusing?

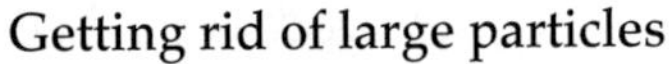
Getting rid of large particles

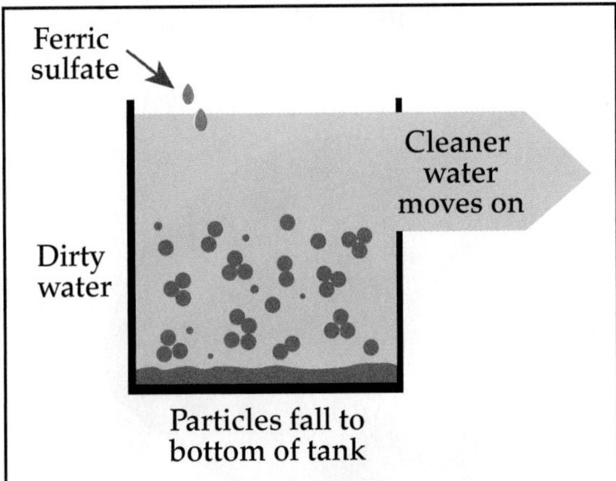

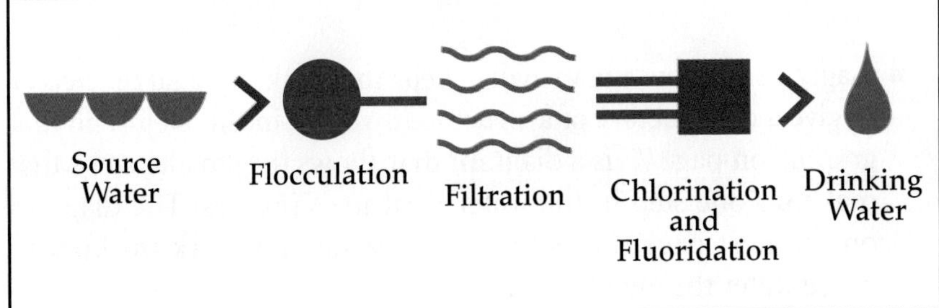

YOUR TURN 11 Looking at Graphics

Identify which graphic on page 77 might help readers understand a process better and which might confuse readers. Then, list the characteristics of the more helpful graphic.

Creating Effective Graphics

You will use the four steps on the following pages to create graphics to make your explanation of a complex process clearer.

1. **Decide what part of your essay should be illustrated.** Think about what parts of the process or which structures involved in the process confused you at first. Your graphics should show an important structure or part of the process that might confuse readers.
2. **Select the best way to illustrate the part you have chosen.** Here are the three most useful options:
   - **illustrations to sketch one item involved in the process.** For example, in an essay on the process of digestion, a writer might use this drawing to illustrate the various types of teeth.

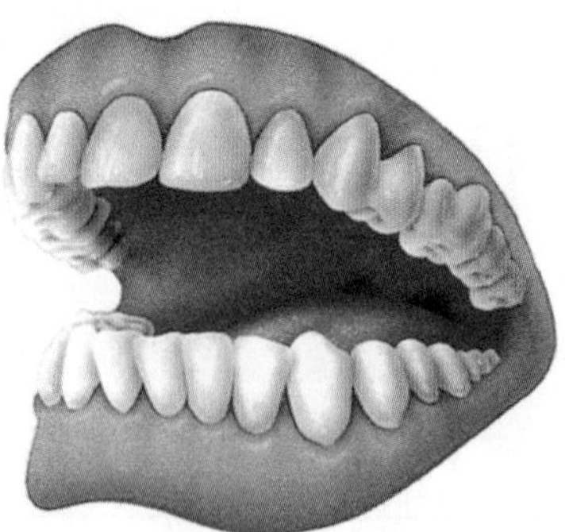

   - **diagrams to show a few smaller steps that make up a larger step or to give a clear picture of a structure involved in this step.** The first graphic on page 77 is a diagram that shows the smaller steps that make up one step in the water treatment process. The diagram on the next page shows how plant structures work together to move water through the plant.

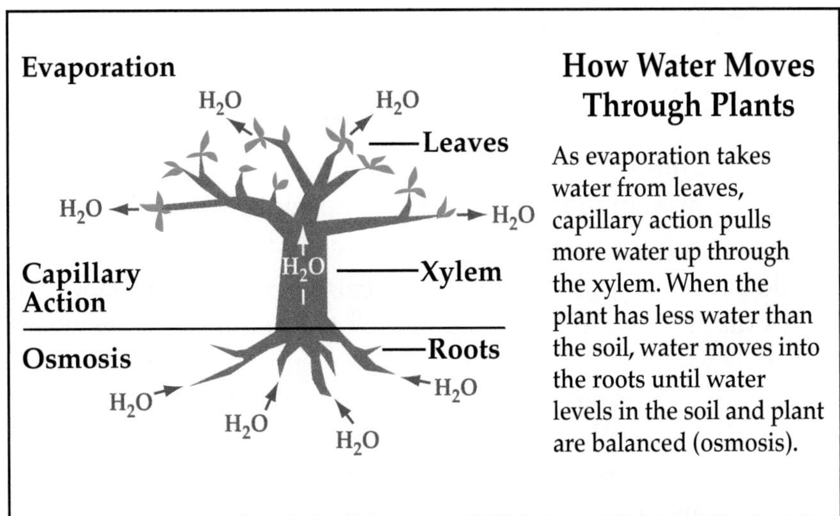

Evaporation
H_2O
H_2O
Leaves
H_2O
H_2O
Capillary Action
H_2O
Xylem
Osmosis
Roots
H_2O
H_2O
H_2O
H_2O
How Water Moves Through Plants
As evaporation takes water from leaves, capillary action pulls more water up through the xylem. When the plant has less water than the soil, water moves into the roots until water levels in the soil and plant are balanced (osmosis).

- **flowcharts with words and symbols to show the major steps in the process.** The second graphic on page 77 shows the major steps in the water treatment process. Here is a flowchart showing the major steps involved in amending the U.S. Constitution.

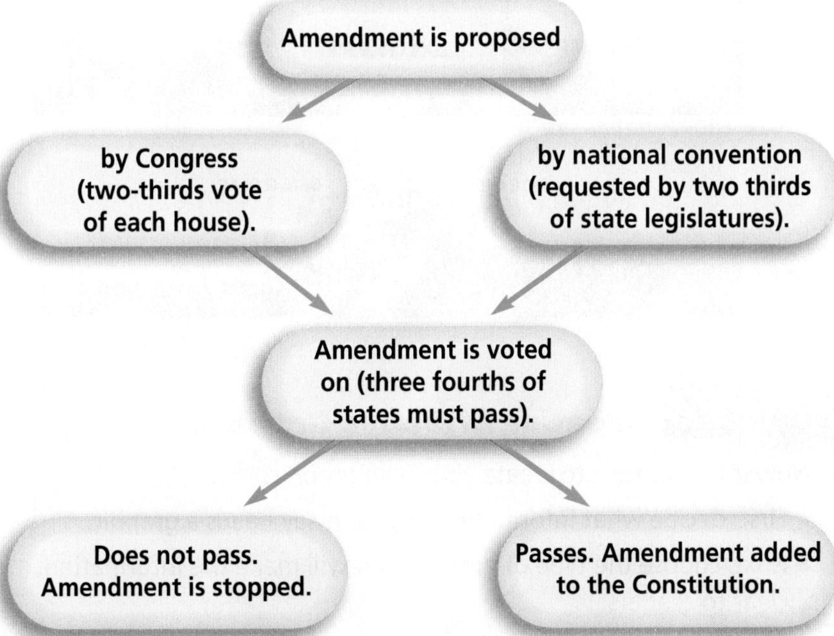

Make a rough sketch of your ideas to make sure the form you have chosen will work. You may have a few false starts before you figure out the sizes and shapes of items that will work best in your graphic.

3. **Create graphics by hand or by using a computer.** Choose the clearest (and easiest) way to communicate your ideas and create your graphics by hand or by using a computer graphics program. Make them bold and clear, not cluttered with unnecessary information or decorations. Use color only if it will make your message clearer. You might want to make the most important part of your graphic a bright color in order to draw attention to it.
4. **Add a title. Also, add captions and labels to explain important parts of your graphic.** Your title should tell readers in just a few words exactly what this graphic shows. Use a one-sentence caption to remind readers about what is happening at a particular point in the graphic or to explain something you cannot show. Identify objects in the graphic using labels. Make your labels no more than a few words long and place them as close as possible to the parts they name without covering any of your graphic. You may also want to draw a line connecting each part to its label.

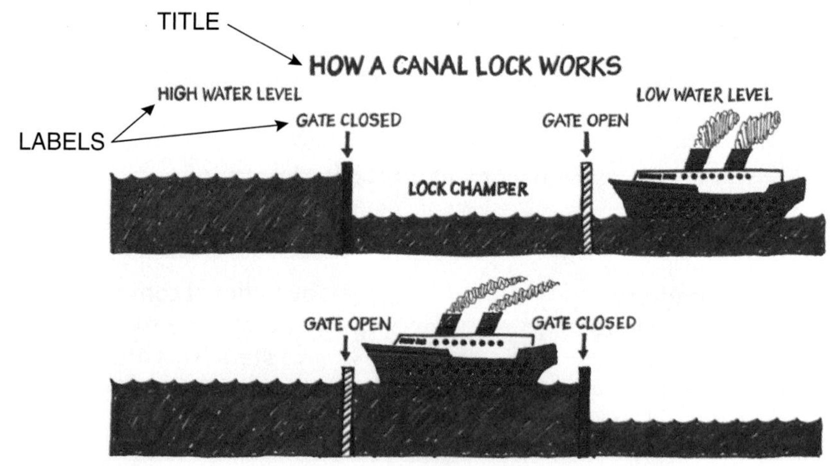

CAPTION

Engineers can raise the water level inside the lock chamber to the higher water level or lower it to the lower water level to allow ships to pass.

YOUR TURN 12 Creating Effective Graphics

Now it is your turn to create your own graphic.

- First, decide what information in your essay needs a graphic.
- Next, choose the type of graphic that will make the information clear to readers.
- Remember that you can create your graphic by hand or by using a computer.
- Finally, add titles, captions, or labels to explain your graphic.

Choices

Choose one of the following activities to complete.

▶ CROSSING THE CURRICULUM: ART

1. Before and After Create a **painting, drawing,** or **sculpture** that shows both the beginning of a process and its end. For example, you might show the formation of a tornado and the destruction it leaves behind. Your depiction might be realistic, or you might use symbols to represent things that are difficult to illustrate. Include a brief explanation of what the symbols in your art represent and why you chose them.

▶ CROSSING THE CURRICULUM: WORLD LANGUAGES

2. Do You Know the Way to San José? Use another language to give simple **directions.** You may explain how to get somewhere or how to do something in any language from Spanish to American Sign Language, as long as it is not your first language. Then, ask your listener to repeat your directions to you in English (or in your first language). Write a **paragraph** evaluating how accurate and clear your directions were.

▶ VIDEO PRODUCTION

3. Show Them How It's Done Create an **instructional video** by taping a demonstration showing how to assemble, use, or fix a mechanical device such as a bicycle pump or a complicated toy. Read a manual or instruction booklet for the device to help you plan your demonstration. Provide narration to explain how to use the device. You might zoom in to give viewers a closer look at part of the device or show a product that can be made with the device.

▶ CAREERS

4. On-the-Job Training Write an **explanation** of a procedure that might be followed in the career of your choice. To get some topic ideas or learn about a particular procedure, you might talk to someone who works in your chosen field. Example topics include procedures for creating a spreadsheet, changing a spark plug, or setting a broken bone. Try to explain the procedure in enough detail that someone else could use your explanation as a guide.

CHAPTER 3 Explaining Cause and Effect

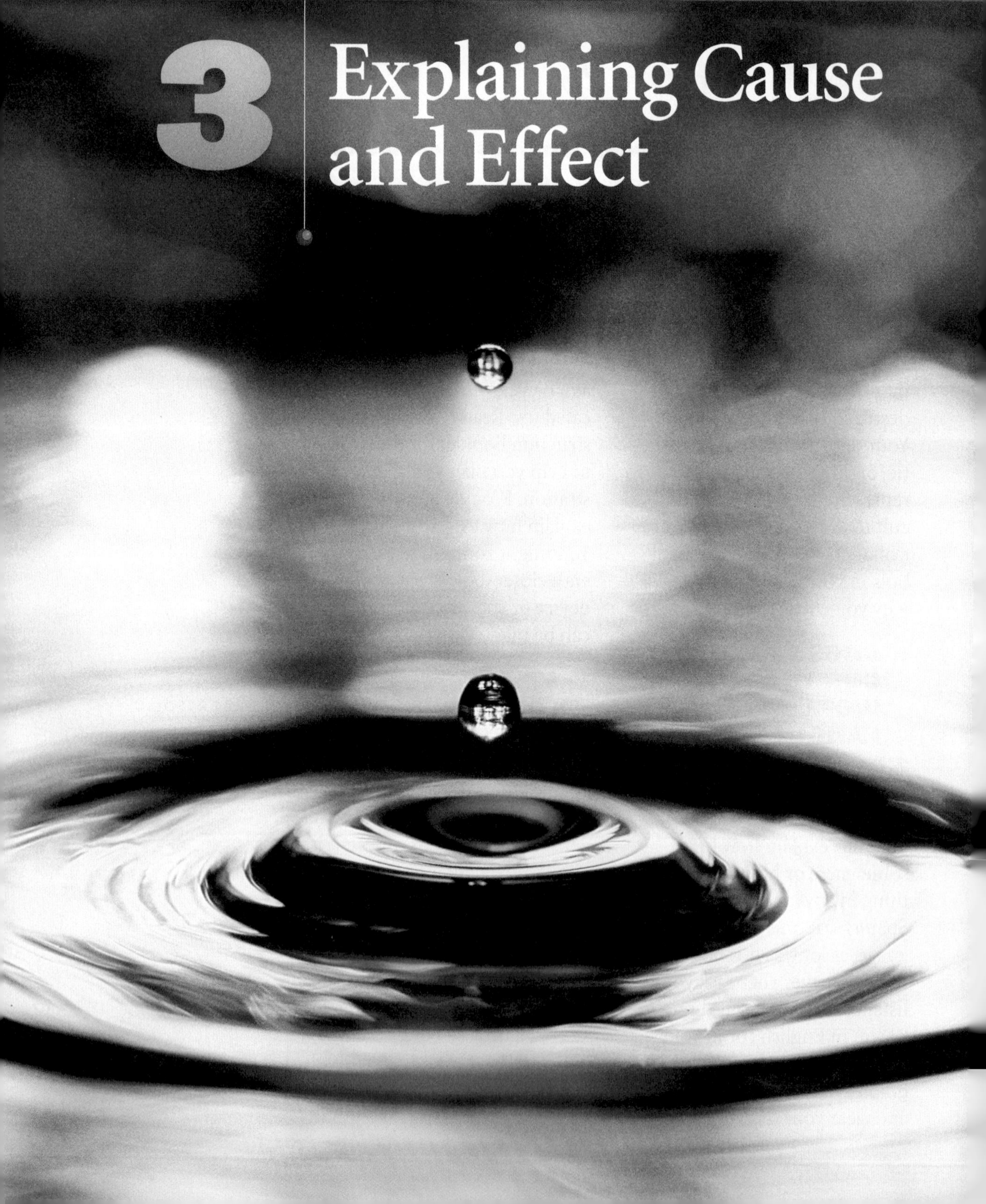

Reading Workshop

Reading a Cause-and-Effect Article

Writing Workshop

Writing a Cause-and-Effect Essay

Viewing and Representing

Analyzing Graphics

Informational Text

Exposition

What will happen if you watch TV instead of studying? Why did your favorite shirt shrink in the wash? As you ponder these questions, you are considering the *causes* and *effects* of events.

Thinking and writing about causes and effects helps you explore the world from two angles. When you wonder about **causes,** you are looking for answers about why something happens. Looking at **effects** helps you understand the results that follow a certain cause. History, science, and the news often focus on causes, effects, or both. You might, for instance, watch a TV documentary about the causes and effects of volcanic eruptions. Learning to identify causes and effects will help you to make sense of the world around you.

YOUR TURN 1 Exploring Cause and Effect

Make a three-column chart like the one below. In the center column, list three events. For each event, write a cause of the event in the first column and one effect in the third column. Here is an example:

Cause	Event	Effect
My alarm clock is broken.	I was late for school.	I missed a quiz in my first class.

GO TO: go.hrw.com
KEYWORD: EOLang 8-3

Reading a Cause-and-Effect Article

WHAT'S AHEAD?

In this section you will read a cause-and-effect article. You will also learn how to

- **make predictions based on text features**
- **identify cause-and-effect relationships**

Do you go to many concerts? When you listen to a personal stereo, do people have to yell to get your attention? If you answered *yes* to these questions, you may be at risk for hearing loss. The article on pages 87–89 is titled "I Can't Hear You!" As you read it, look for information about behaviors that can endanger your hearing.

Preparing to Read

READING FOCUS

Cause-and-Effect Relationships A **cause-and-effect relationship** shows *how* one thing leads to another. Bob Hugel, the author of "I Can't Hear You!" discusses the relationship between the causes and the effects of hearing loss. In other words, he shows how one thing (a cause) leads to hearing loss, which leads to another thing (an effect). As you read, look carefully to see where he shows connections between cause and effect.

READING SKILL

Predictions Based on Text Features Many informative texts include **text features,** such as titles, heads, boldface words, and illustrations. Writers include these features to highlight and clarify important ideas and information. You can use these features to figure out, or **predict,** what kind of information a text will contain. Text features not only help you make predictions, but they also guide you through the text and help you to understand what you are reading. As you read, pay attention to these features and think about the information they give you.

Predictions Based on Text Features

You have just finished reading the introduction to an article on the effects of beginning an exercise plan. What topics do you think you might read about in the rest of the article? Will you read about more energy? better muscle tone? weight loss? Experience tells you that one or more of these topics may appear in an article on the effects of exercise. When you use your experience and information from the text to figure out what will come next, you are making a **prediction.** Look at the example below.

Example: **Information from text:** Exercise has many benefits.

\+ **What you know:** My brother became stronger when he started his exercise program.

Prediction: I think the author will talk about how exercise can make you stronger.

You can also use *text features* to make predictions about what you are reading. **Text features** work as signs to guide a reader through new information by highlighting the most important points and clarifying information. The following chart lists some common text features and explains how you can use them to make predictions.

Text Features	Information They Give	How to Use Them to Make Predictions
Titles	tell (or hint at) the topic of the entire reading	Before you start reading, review what you already know about the topic. Ask questions about the topic and decide how you think the author will answer those questions.
Heads and Subheads	show how a reading breaks up into parts	Use them as stopping points where you can sum up what you have read and predict what is to come. Try turning them into questions that you answer as you read.
Boldface and Italicized Words	tell which words or terms are most important	These words are essential for understanding the ideas in this section. Use these words to predict the important ideas.
Photos and Illustrations with Informative Captions	illustrate important information	Look for hints about information that may be explained more fully in the reading.

When you **scan** a text, you do not read every word. Instead, you read very quickly as you look for specific items. The chart below shows how one student began to make predictions about the reading selection on pages 87–89. First, he scanned the selection to find the text features. Then, he made predictions based on these features.

Feature	What I Can Predict
Title: "I Can't Hear You! Listen Up: Save Your Hearing by Acting Now"	I think this article will be about what you can do to prevent hearing loss.
Heads and Subheads:	
Boldface and Italicized Words:	
Photos and Illustrations:	

TIP Why is it important to make predictions as you read? Making predictions gives you a **purpose** for reading—you read to see whether your predictions are correct. Whenever you read with a purpose, you are much more likely to understand and remember what you read.

Think of yourself as a reading detective. Start by predicting what you will learn when you read an article or chapter in a textbook. If you are reading a short story or a novel, after the first few paragraphs try to predict what big problem the main character will face. As you continue reading, keep adjusting your predictions and continue to make new ones.

YOUR TURN 2 Using Informative Text Features to Make Predictions

Scan the following article, looking for the features listed in the chart on page 85. Use each feature to make a prediction about the information in the article. Make a chart like the one above of the text features you find and the predictions you make.

Reading Selection

Read the following article. In a notebook, jot down answers to the numbered active-reading questions in the shaded boxes. The underlined words will be discussed in the Vocabulary Mini-Lesson on page 94.

from *Scholastic Choices*

I Can't Hear You!

Listen Up: Save Your Hearing by Acting Now

BY BOB HUGEL

Kate LaVail stood in the packed arena, the crowd around her screaming in sync with the pulsating music blasting from giant speakers. Onstage, an alternative rock group jammed in concert. The house was rocking. Kate, a huge music fan and budding guitar player herself, should have been ecstatic. After all, the San Francisco teen loved concerts and went to as many live shows as possible. Here she was, face-to-face with one of the hottest bands in the country.

But as it turned out, Kate would have traded places with anyone in a beat. Less than halfway through the concert, she walked out. "It was too loud," she says. "My ears were killing me."

1. The thesis, or main idea, of this article is not stated directly. Read the first three paragraphs. What is the main idea?

Kate, seventeen, suffers from *tinnitus*, a constant ringing in her ears. She says the disease has built up gradually over years of listening to loud noises, including shrill machinery at a factory where she worked, and blaring music. Audiologists, or hearing specialists, identify both as leading causes of hearing problems.

Americans, they say, play their personal and car stereos too loud, expose themselves to gun blasts too often, and fail to complain about uncomfortably loud work environments.

2. How do Americans cause their own hearing loss?

As a result, twenty-eight million Americans suffer from impaired hearing. . . . Many rock-and-rollers over forty have been diagnosed with hearing loss and have begun wearing hearing aids. . . .

3. What may have caused hearing loss in many people over forty?

A hearing loss in middle age is bad enough. But now even teens are developing hearing problems. Kate first noticed her tinnitus when she was thirteen. Four years later, she says that the ringing is worse and that she often has difficulty hearing what people say. Especially loud noises, like the rock concert, actually cause her pain.

Kate is hardly alone: A study by University of Florida researchers last year showed that 17 percent of middle and high school students nationwide have suffered some degree of hearing loss. In similar studies twenty years ago, only 2.5 percent of kids the same age reported such problems.

Audiologist Alice Holmes, a University of Florida associate professor of health, who worked on the new study, says the results should serve as a warning. "Today's young people, who often have their headphones or car stereos cranked up high, are at great risk for losing some of their hearing in coming years," Holmes says. She warns: Turn down the music while you can still hear it.

4. According to audiologist Alice Holmes, how can people prevent hearing loss?

Hearing Loss: No Cure

How does loud music cause hearing loss? Start with the inner ear, which contains a snail-shaped area filled with fluid, called the *cochlea*. (The outer ear is the part attached to your head; the middle ear includes the eardrum.) The cochlea has thousands of tiny hairlike structures called *cilia*, which pick up vibrations from the fluid and transmit them to the auditory nerve. The auditory nerve carries the sounds to the brain, which interprets them.

The problem is that intense sound waves damage the cilia, which then bend and sometimes break. This damage is permanent. Once it occurs, the cilia can never recover 100 percent and are susceptible to further harm from repeated exposure to strong sound waves.

Eventually, the cells attached to the cilia die, and the process that sends the signals to the brain is permanently damaged. The result is hearing loss, ranging from tinnitus to deafness. And there's no cure.

5. In this section the writer describes how hearing loss is caused by a series of linked events. List the four linked events.

"People think that hearing aids will take care of the problem," says Holmes. "Hearing aids are wonderful, but they don't restore your hearing completely." Hearing-aid wearers also often complain that irksome background noise is amplified to deafening levels, while people's voices, a few feet away, are muffled.

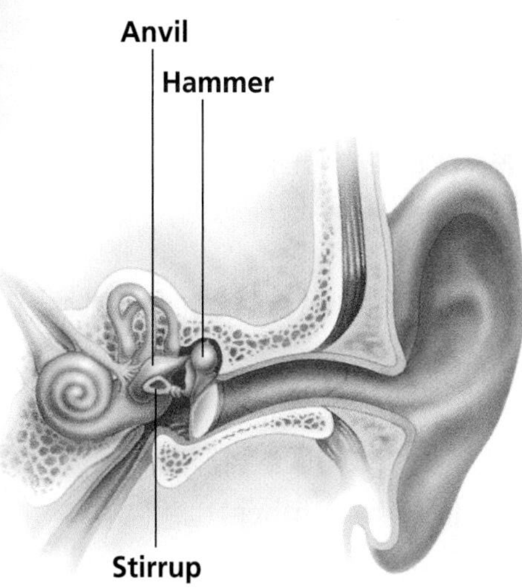

Researching the problem, meanwhile, is tricky, because no one has pinpointed how many incidents it takes to develop a hearing problem. "For some people, one incident of listening to loud music is enough to cause a problem," says audiologist Holly Kaplan, who works with the American Speech-Language Hearing Association. One gunshot or rock concert can partially rob you of your precious ability to hear.

How loud is too loud? When should you turn down the music or wear earplugs? The measurement tool is the *decibel.* Decibels measure the amount of energy produced by sound. Experts say that exposing yourself continuously to sound over 85 decibels is dangerous. The Occupational Safety and Health Administration (a federal agency) recommends no more than eight hours a day of exposure to 90 decibels in the workplace.

Hearing experts acknowledge that determining the noise levels that cause hearing damage is complicated. Holmes, the Florida audiologist, says that two individuals, working side by side in the same factory, could show very different effects from high-decibel noise exposure: one becoming severly hearing impaired while the other is not affected at all.

Still, it's best to opt for safety. Consider, for example, that three-hour rock concerts typically produce sound levels between 110 and 120 decibels, according to the organization Hearing Education and Awareness for Rockers (HEAR). HEAR is dedicated to raising awareness about hearing loss caused by exposure to excessively loud music. . . .

Earplug Power

Kate LaVail, meanwhile, has made it her mission to hand out earplugs to teens heading to concerts. She says she's low-key about her activism but hopeful she can make a difference. "It's a wacky concept to have someone just hand you earplugs for no reason," Kate acknowledges. But, she adds proudly, "If there's a possibility that they'll use the plugs, I've done my part. I've made the effort, and all I can hope is that *they* will."

TIP If the text directly supports your prediction, then your prediction has been confirmed. If you cannot confirm your prediction, you can revise it, using new information from the text.

First Thoughts on Your Reading

1. **What did you predict about "I Can't Hear You!" by examining the article's text features?**
2. **What predictions did you confirm or revise as you read the article?**
3. **What physical effects does Kate link to her hearing loss?**

READING FOCUS

Cause-and-Effect Relationships

What? Why? How? A **cause** is an action or event that makes something else happen. An **effect** is the result of a cause. Cause-and-effect articles explain

- *why* or *how* one thing leads to another
- *what happens* as a result of a certain action or event

Many cause-and-effect articles contain cause-and-effect **clue words.** Causes and effects are often signaled by transitions and other clue words and phrases such as *affect, because, consequently, effect, leads to,* and *results in.*

Example:

cause cause clue word effect
Regular exercise and good eating habits ***result in*** better health.

clue word cause effect
One ***effect*** of going to loud concerts may be a ringing in your ears.

TIP Even if there are no clue words in an article, you can still identify a cause-and-effect relationship. Ask: Is the author explaining *why* or *how?* If so, the author is helping you discover a *cause.* Is the author explaining the *result* of something? If so, the author is helping you see an *effect.* Study this example:

> Last weekend at the beach, I saw people leaving plastic bags full of wrappers, glass bottles, cans, and leftover food on the ground. Trash is not good for people or ocean wildlife. Fish and other creatures can get caught in plastic bags and be killed or badly hurt. Litter is also a hazard for people. Last year while at the beach, I stepped on broken glass and I cut myself badly.

Although there are no clue words, you can see that this passage is about the possible effects of littering a beach.

One Thing Leads to Another You may encounter several cause-and-effect patterns as you read. Writers may explain causes only, effects only, or a cause-and-effect chain. You can see these organizational patterns in the following maps.

Causes Only: This type of explanation focuses on two or more causes of one effect.

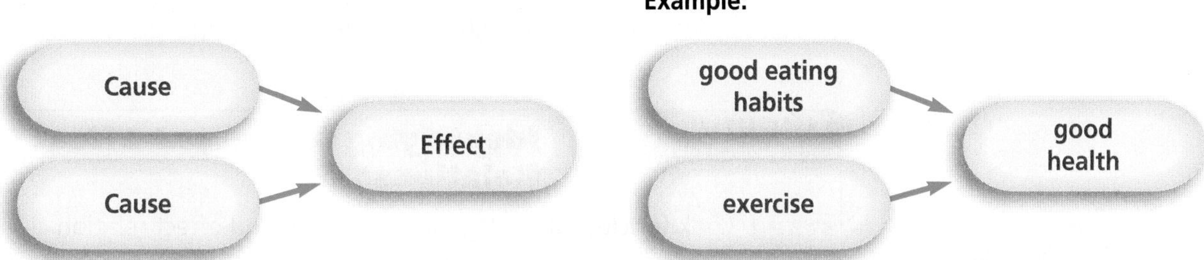

Effects Only: This type of explanation focuses on two or more effects of one cause.

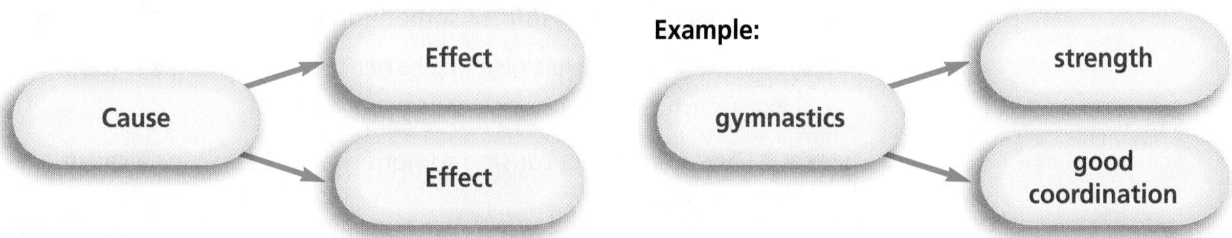

Cause-and-Effect Chain: In this explanation, one cause leads to an effect, which causes another effect, and so on.

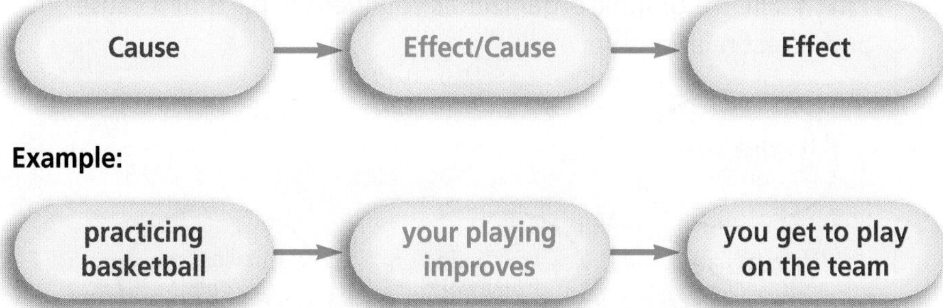

Now that you know the three cause-and-effect patterns, try to identify the cause-and-effect relationships in the paragraph on the following page. If you get stuck and need help, use the Thinking It Through steps that follow the paragraph.

When we get home from school, my brother turns on the TV. Unfortunately for me, he channel-surfs a lot, and I hear snippets from one hundred two different channels. My sister goes into the family room and turns on the stereo full-blast. She listens to the same tape over and over till I want to scream. As a result of all this noise, I can't concentrate on my homework. Now my grades are starting to slip.

THINKING IT THROUGH

Identifying Cause-and-Effect Relationships

Reference Note

For more on **cause-and-effect** clue words, see page 779 in the Quick Reference Handbook.

STEP 1 Look for clue words that signal a cause-and-effect relationship.

"As a result" is a cause-and-effect clue.

STEP 2 Ask: Is the writer explaining *how* or *why* (causes)? Is the writer explaining the *results* of something (effects)?

At first, the writer is explaining why he can't focus on his homework (causes). Then he says he can't concentrate (effect).

STEP 3 Ask: Is an effect *causing* something else? Look for a cause-and-effect chain.

In the last sentence the writer focuses on his slipping grades. There are no clue words, but it's clear that this is the effect of not focusing on homework.

STEP 4 Fill in a graphic organizer as you identify parts of a cause-and-effect relationship.

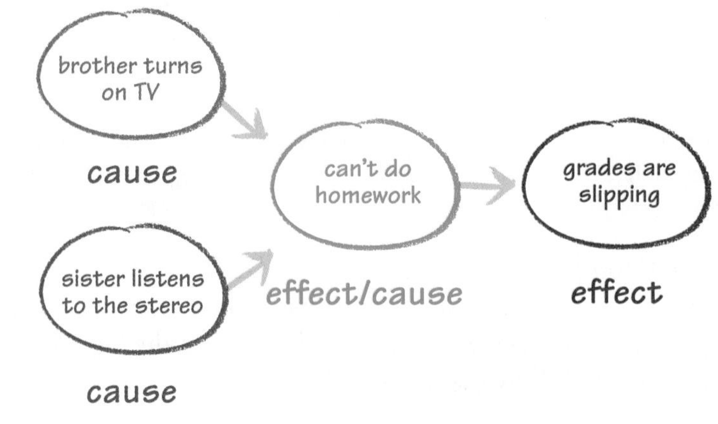

YOUR TURN 3 Finding Causes and Effects

In "I Can't Hear You!" Bob Hugel explores the causes of hearing loss. In your notebook, copy the graphic organizer that follows. Then, re-read the article on pages 87–89 and use the Thinking It Through steps on page 92 to fill in the graphic organizer. **Hint:** Look for a cause-and-effect chain in the "Hearing Loss: No Cure" section of the reading selection. Your answers to the active-reading questions on pages 87 and 88 may help you fill in the chain.

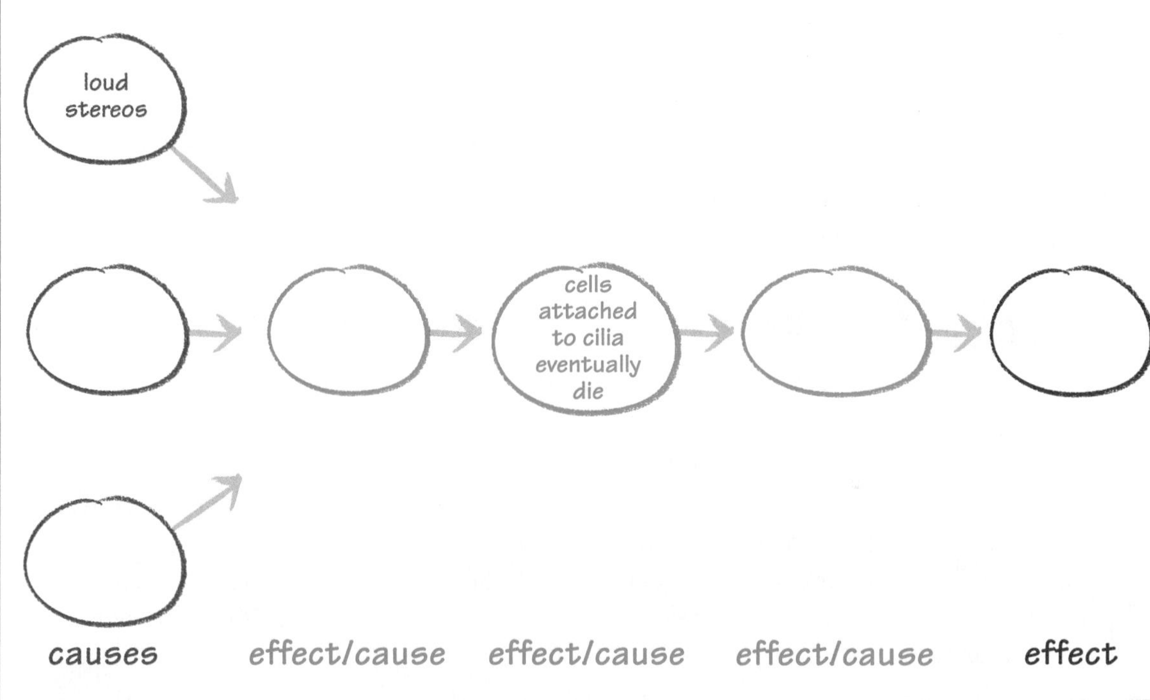

OH NO! TOO MUCH BUBBLE BATH!
UH OH!
POP!
HOW ON EARTH DO YOU DO THIS??!
THESE THINGS JUST SEEM TO HAPPEN.

MINI-LESSON **VOCABULARY**

Wordbusting (CSSD)

Cause-and-effect articles often provide new information, so you may come across words that are unfamiliar to you. **Wordbusting** combines four ways of figuring out words you do not know. The letters ***CSSD*** can help you remember the four parts of the strategy. You only need to use as many of these parts as it takes you to figure out the word's meaning.

- **Context:** Sometimes you will be able to guess the word's meaning by understanding the words, sentences, or paragraphs around it.
- **Structure:** Looking at the word's root, prefix, or suffix can help you figure out its meaning.
- **Sound:** Say the word out loud to see if it sounds familiar.
- **Dictionary:** If you can't determine the word's meaning, look it up.

THINKING IT THROUGH — Using the Wordbusting Strategy

Here is an example of Wordbusting, using a word from "I Can't Hear You."

Word: auditory

Context: "The cochlea has thousands of tiny hairlike structures called *cilia*, which pick up vibrations from the fluid and transmit them to the auditory nerve. The auditory nerve carries sounds to the brain, which interprets them."

The writer is describing the cochlea and cilia, which are parts of the ear. Then, he tells us that the auditory nerve carries sounds to the brain. Could auditory have something to do with hearing or some other part of the brain?

Structure: audi + tory

Doesn't "audi" have to do with sound?

Sound: ô′də tôr′ē

Sounds like "auditorium," which is a place where you hear things. Based on what I know, I think auditory means having to do with hearing.

PRACTICE

Figure out what the words on the right mean. Each word is underlined in "I Can't Hear You!" so you can see its context. Write down the steps of CSSD that you actually use to define each word, starting with *C* (context) each time. Use the example above as a model.

1. pulsating (page 87)
2. shrill (page 87)
3. impaired (page 87)
4. susceptible (page 88)
5. amplified (page 88)

MINI-LESSON **TEST TAKING**

Answering Comparison-Contrast Questions

Cause and effect is one kind of text structure writers use to organize information. Another is comparison and contrast. Comparison-and-contrast writing looks at how two or more things are alike and how they are different. To answer reading test questions that require you to recognize or explain similarities or differences between subjects, look closely at the text structure and use a graphic organizer.

Writers use two common structures when comparing and contrasting. Both are based on the use of *points of comparison.* The **points of comparison** are the important points that the writer focuses on when comparing or contrasting two subjects. In a comparison of polar bears and grizzly bears, for example, the points of comparison may be physical characteristics, habitat, and diet.

- **Point-by-point** explanations alternate between the two subjects, looking at the same point of comparison in each. A point-by-point comparison of grizzly bears and polar bears would be organized as follows:

Points	Subject
1. Physical Characteristics	polar bears grizzly bears
2. Habitat	polar bears grizzly bears
3. Diet	polar bears grizzly bears

- **Block structure** focuses on all the points of comparison for one subject at a time. A block comparison of polar bears and grizzly bears would be organized by subject.

Subject	Points
1. Polar Bears	physical characteristics habitat diet
2. Grizzly Bears	physical characteristics habitat diet

Expect to see **clue words** in both point-by-point structure and block structure. The clue words *both* and *neither* help you find similarities. Clue words such as *but* and *however* help you pinpoint differences.

As you read a comparison-and-contrast piece, identify its structure so you can keep track of similarities and differences between the subjects. A graphic organizer such as the Venn diagram, which uses intersecting circles to show relationships, will help you keep track of the information. Venn diagrams are especially useful for organizing ideas arranged in block structure.

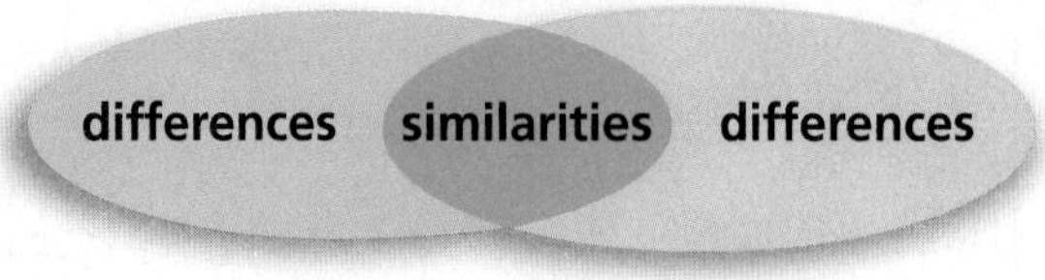

Suppose the passage below and the question following it appeared on a reading test. How would you approach the question?

Dolphins and porpoises are two different species that are often confused with one another because they have many similarities; however, there are some important distinctions that separate them. Dolphins and porpoises are both toothed whales with torpedo-shaped bodies. They both breathe through blowholes on the tops of their heads. Dolphins have a beaked head and sharp, pointed teeth, but porpoises have a rounded head with no beak and flat teeth. Both eat fish, squid, and shrimp, and both hunt using echolocation, which means they bounce sounds off objects to find food. Dolphins can be found in all the oceans of the world, usually in coastal areas. Porpoises are found only in temperate coastal waters.

What is a major difference between dolphins and porpoises?

A. One uses sight to find food; the other uses sound.

B. One lives in deep water; the other lives in coastal waters.

C. One has a beaked head; the other has a rounded head.

D. One is a sort of whale; the other is a fish.

THINKING IT THROUGH

Answering a Comparison-and-Contrast Question

STEP 1 Identify what the question is asking.

It is asking for differences, so I'll look for contrasts in the passage.

STEP 2 Decide what structure the passage uses. If it uses point-by-point structure, look for clue words to help you pinpoint differences. If the passage uses block structure, a Venn diagram can help you identify differences.

The passage uses point-by-point structure. It discusses dolphins' and porpoises' physical characteristics, their diets, and their habitats. The clue word but points out a difference in their physical characteristics.

STEP 3 Compare your answer to the answer choices available.

A. No—The passage says they both use echolocation to find food.

B. No—They can live in different oceans, but both live in coastal areas.

C. Yes— I used the clue word but to see that dolphins have a beak and porpoises do not.

D. No—The clue word both tells me that this is not the answer.

Writing a Cause-and-Effect Essay

WHAT'S AHEAD?

In this workshop you will write a cause-and-effect essay. You will also learn how to

- **evaluate a cause-and-effect topic**
- **provide evidence to support causes and effects**
- **identify false cause-and-effect statements**
- **replace passive verbs with active verbs**
- **use colons and semicolons correctly**

"What causes a rainbow?" "What will happen if we cut off my doll's hair?" "Why do I have to eat vegetables?" If you baby-sit or have little brothers and sisters, these questions are probably familiar to you. Asking questions about causes and effects seems to be part of growing up. When children learn answers to their questions, they often come to know the world better.

In this workshop you will have the opportunity to explain causes or effects to an audience of fourth- or fifth-graders. The people in your audience will be older than the ones who might want to know why they must eat vegetables, but you can still help them learn something new by sharing your knowledge of cause and effect.

Prewriting

Choose a Topic

Pick a Winner So many cause-and-effect issues affect you daily that it may be hard to choose just one for your essay. Try finding a topic by asking questions about subjects that interest you. Here are some examples.

Nature: What causes a tidal wave? What will happen if we continue to pollute the ocean?

Health: Why is exercise healthy? What causes a heart attack?

School: If the school day were lengthened, what would happen?

You might also get ideas from resources such as science magazines, TV newsmagazines, your history class, and Internet news groups.

. . . And This One Is Just Right Not every question will lead to a suitable topic for a cause-and-effect essay. Before you choose a topic, evaluate it carefully to see how broad it is. For instance, suppose you are interested in health and medicine and have asked yourself the question, "What makes people sick?" Such a topic would be impossible to cover in an essay because it is much too broad. Focus your question more narrowly: "What causes juvenile diabetes?" **Choose a topic that allows you to discuss at least two causes or effects but no more than three causes or effects.**

KEY CONCEPT

Your paper should be about either causes *or* effects. If you are writing about *why* something happened, then you are focusing on causes. If your paper looks at the *results* of something, it is about effects.

Here is how one student went about thinking of possible topics, evaluating those topics, and choosing one.

Possible Topics	What I Think About the Topic
Why do students drop out of extracurricular activities?	This is too broad. There are probably as many causes as there are students.
✓ If I don't get enough sleep, what will happen?	I'm interested in this topic; if I find that there are too many effects, then I will discuss the most important ones.
What will happen if I skip lunch today?	This is too narrow. I can think of only one immediate effect.

Consider Your Audience and Purpose

Meet Them Halfway You are writing to inform fourth- or fifth-graders about a cause-and-effect relationship. When you *inform,* your purpose is to make something as clear as possible. Remember that your audience is younger, less knowledgeable, and less experienced than you are. To help your audience learn, you need to present your ideas in a way they will understand easily. As you consider your audience's needs, think about the following points.

- A younger audience may not know anything about your topic. Give some background information about the general subject before you write about the causes or effects.
- Younger children learn best if you start with examples or ideas they already understand. Find a way to connect the new information with something they may already know.

Words to Fit Ideas You have a pretty good idea of what you want to say in your essay, but *how* will you say it? What words will you use to express your ideas? Your audience and purpose help determine your *voice* and your *style.*

Watch Your Voice Everyone knows that the words you write on paper or on a computer screen do not talk, so how can writing have a voice? Your writing **voice** is communicated partly by the words you choose and by the rhythm and sound of your language. Your voice is your personal style of talking to your reader.

To help fourth- and fifth-graders learn from your paper, aim for a friendly and informative voice. Remember, they have a smaller vocabulary than you do. Use easy words and define any that you think they may not know.

Write in Style In an e-mail to a friend, you might use contractions, slang, or sentence fragments. When you write an essay for a test, however, you use a more formal style. **Style** is a writer's way of adapting language to suit different occasions. The ingredients that make up your style are your choice of words, the kinds of sentences you write, and your *tone.* **Tone** reveals the writer's attitude and feelings toward the audience and the subject. A writer's tone may be humorous, serious, angry, sarcastic—or many other feelings.

Reference Note

For more on **style,** see page 844 in the Quick Reference Handbook.

YOUR TURN 4 Choosing a Topic and Considering Your Audience and Purpose

List possible topics for your cause-and-effect essay in a chart like the one on page 98. Evaluate each topic, and choose one. Then, consider your audience and purpose by answering these questions.

- What connections can you make to new information?
- What background information and definitions will you need to include in your essay?
- Will your tone be serious, humorous, or something else?
- Will you choose a formal or informal writing style?

Gather Information

Just the Facts (and Other Support) "I want to stay up and watch the next program. Why do I have to go to bed now?"

"Because I said so!"

Have you ever had a conversation like this? If so, you know that an "I said so" answer is not very satisfying. You must support each cause or each effect that you discuss in the body of your essay.

Support Provide logical support in your essay by including **facts, examples,** and **expert opinions.**

Reference Note

For more on **types of evidence,** see page 217.

- Facts can be checked and proved true.
- Examples give a particular instance of a general idea.
- Expert opinions state what an expert in the field has said about the subject.

Sometimes you will need to **elaborate** on your support through explanation or further facts or examples. Here is an example.

> **Effect:** Lack of sleep makes it easier to get sick.
>
> **Support (fact):** Sleep gives the body time to fix itself.
>
> **Elaboration:** If your body is not given time to fix itself, it becomes too weak to fight sickness.

TIP The encyclopedia is a reference that will help you develop ideas before you begin writing. Reference materials are available for writing and revising (such as Part 3 of this book) and for proofreading (such as the dictionary). Ask your teacher or librarian to direct you to helpful **reference materials** and **resources.**

Finding Information For some topics you can rely on your knowledge and experience for information about causes or effects. However, for many topics you will need to do some research. As you have seen, you need two kinds of information for your essay: the *causes* or *effects* related to the topic and *support* to explain the causes or effects. Where can you find the information you need?

- **Books, magazines, and encyclopedias.** Look for books or magazines that relate to the general topic. For example, if you are writing about something in nature, look in science books and magazines. You can look up any topic in the encyclopedia.
- **Internet searches.** There may be Web sites devoted to your topic. Type the topic into a search engine and check the sites.
- **People.** People who are experts on your topic can give you information or help you find places to look. Ask a teacher or someone who works in a field related to your topic to help you locate information.

YOUR TURN 5 Gathering Information

Gather information and support for your cause-and-effect essay. As you gather information, ask yourself these questions:

- What are the causes or effects related to my topic?
- What facts, examples, or expert opinions will best support my cause-and-effect explanations?

State Your Main Idea

What's Your Point? You now need to think about the main idea of your paper. Your **main idea,** or **thesis, statement** will be a brief announcement of the cause-and-effect relationship you will discuss in your essay. Here are examples of main idea statements.

Focus on causes: Two factors cause students to stay up too late and lose sleep.

Focus on effects: Losing sleep can affect your grades and your health.

TIP When writing a main idea statement, link causes and effects with clue words and phrases such as these:

causes

affects

results from (results in)

leads to

because

makes you (makes us, makes them, makes it)

YOUR TURN 6 Writing a Main Idea Statement

To write your main idea statement, use the information you gathered to figure out how the causes or the effects relate to your topic. Write a general statement that tells what the cause-and-effect relationship is and whether you are focusing on causes or on effects.

Organize Information

First Things First Once you have gathered information and written a main idea statement, you need an organizational plan. A good essay will have **coherence**—that is, one idea will flow logically to the next. To achieve coherence, think about **progression,** or order, of your ideas. You might plan to use **order of importance,** starting with the least important cause or effect (or support) and saving the most important one until last, so the reader will remember it. A graphic organizer such as the one on the next page will help you organize your main idea, causes or effects, and support.

Main Idea Statement
Losing sleep can affect your grades and your health.

Effect 1
It is difficult to pay attention in school.

Support (expert opinion)
Sleep researchers say that when you lose too much sleep, your brain does not work as well as it should.

Elaboration
When you cannot think clearly, it is hard to pay attention and do well in school.

Effect 2
It is easier to get sick.

Support (fact)
While you sleep, your body fixes itself.

Elaboration
If you lose too much sleep, your body does not fight sickness as well as it should.

YOUR TURN 7 Organizing Information

Organize your main idea statement, causes or effects, support, and elaboration in a graphic organizer like the one above. First, write your main idea statement. Below the main idea, write each cause or effect (you will have two or three) that you will discuss. Then, list your support and elaboration for each cause or effect.

MINI-LESSON **CRITICAL THINKING**

Identifying False Cause-and-Effect Statements

"Because I rode my bike to school, I had a flat tire." Most people would agree that this sentence does not express a true cause-and-effect relationship. Sometimes, though, it takes serious thought to tell the difference between a **false cause-and-effect relationship** and one that is reasonable. Do not assume that just because one thing happens after another, the first thing caused the second to happen. A **reasonable cause-and-effect relationship** exists only if there is a logical connection between two events. Reasonable relationships can be supported with evidence.

Use your common sense when you read cause-and-effect statements. Consider whether the statement sounds true according to your experience; then ask yourself how you could prove the statement.

False cause and effect: My family went out to dinner, and we all ordered the same food. In the middle of the night I became ill. The restaurant must have served bad food that made me sick.

[This *could* be true, but I was the only one who was sick. It is more likely that something else, like a virus, made me sick.]

Reasonable cause and effect: When my family and I went on vacation, I forgot to feed my fish; as a result, they died.

[Fish need food to live, so this is a clear cause-and-effect relationship.]

PRACTICE

On a piece of paper, write *F* for each situation that has a false cause and effect. Write *R* for cause-and-effect statements that are reasonable. Also, write a brief explanation of your answers.

1. Ross wore a new pair of jeans today. He was in a very good mood and talked to a lot of people. The new jeans made him happy and popular.
2. Whenever Margo comes to my house, her eyes itch and start to water. Margo sneezes all the time she is here. We have three cats that live in the house. Margo may be allergic to cats.
3. Madeline, our star soccer player, always wears her lucky red socks to play soccer. Today she forgot her red socks, and we lost the game. When Madeline wears her red socks, the team wins.
4. Pilar eats well and gets plenty of rest. She also exercises every day. Pilar is the star of the track team. Proper nutrition, rest, and exercise make her a good athlete.
5. James just moved to our town. He is in my homeroom class, and I know that he gets good grades. Moving to a new town causes you to get good grades.

Cause-and-Effect Essay

Framework | **Directions and Explanations**

Introduction
- Attention-grabbing beginning
- Main idea statement
- Definitions and/or Background information

Grab your readers' attention right away with an **interesting beginning**. A young audience will pay closer attention if you start with ideas that are familiar to them. Also, include a **main idea statement** that clearly states the cause-and-effect relationship you will be discussing in your essay. Provide **definitions** and **background information** about the topic.

Body
- Cause or Effect 1
  Support with elaboration
- Cause or Effect 2
  Support with elaboration

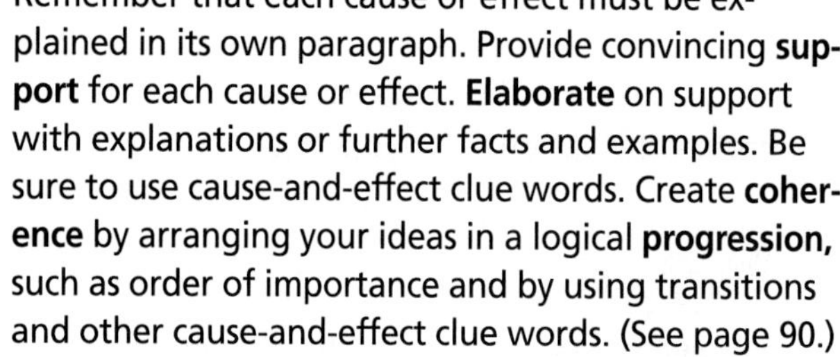

Remember that each cause or effect must be explained in its own paragraph. Provide convincing **support** for each cause or effect. **Elaborate** on support with explanations or further facts and examples. Be sure to use cause-and-effect clue words. Create **coherence** by arranging your ideas in a logical **progression,** such as order of importance and by using transitions and other cause-and-effect clue words. (See page 90.)

Conclusion
- Summary of causes or effects
  and/or
- Restatement of main idea

Remind readers of the main points in your essay, or **restate your main idea** in a new way. (You may decide to do both.)

YOUR TURN 8 Writing Your Cause-and-Effect Essay

Now it is your turn to write a cause-and-effect essay. As you write, keep your audience in mind, include a clear main idea statement, and support each cause or effect. Also, refer to the Writer's Model on page 105 and the framework above.

A Writer's Model

The final draft below closely follows the framework for a cause-and-effect essay.

Get to Sleep!

Do you always bargain for a later bedtime? Do you sneak a flashlight under the covers and read until midnight? These habits may cause you to lose sleep. Losing sleep can affect both your grades and your health. Most people between the ages of nine and twelve need nine hours of sleep every night. Teenagers need even more sleep, at least ten hours. Being tired may make you feel slow and cranky, but the effects go even deeper than how you feel. The effects of losing sleep go right to your brain and immune system—the system that keeps your body healthy.

Attention-grabbing beginning

Main idea statement

Background information

Definition

One effect of not getting enough sleep is falling grades. Sleep researchers say that when you are tired, it is harder to learn. For example, sitting through math class with your eyes drooping and head bobbing is a sign that your brain is busy trying to keep you awake. When you later look at your homework, you have a hard time thinking back to what your teacher told you.

Effect 1

Support (expert opinion)

Elaboration (example)

Lack of sleep affects not only your grades, but also your health. Sleep is important for your whole body. As you sleep, your body is fixing itself. You are growing fast, and sleep is the time your body takes to make sure everything is okay. Your whole body needs this resting time in order to run well when you are awake. Without enough rest, your body loses the energy that helps it fight germs and other things that make you sick. When you do not get enough sleep, your body suffers.

Effect 2

Support (fact)

Elaboration (fact)

You may think that you will get to stay up later as you get older, but you may need even more sleep in your teen years than you are getting now. So, if you want to do well in school and stay healthy, get to sleep!

Restatement of main idea

A Student's Model

When you write a cause-and-effect essay for a younger audience, remember to elaborate clearly on the causes or effects. Below is the body of an essay by Julie Clift, which she wrote when she was an eighth-grader in Satellite Beach, Florida. Notice that Julie clearly explains the effects of participating in team sports.

Effect 1 | Support (fact) | Elaboration (example)

. . . One effect of being in team sports is that you gain skills that help you cooperate, or work well with others. By working with an athletic team, you are exposed to working with and meeting many kids. For example, if you decide to join a school sport such as soccer, you will meet other kids who share the same interests as you do. Not only will this result in an increased number of friends, but now you will have buddies who will come home with you after school to play a fun game of soccer. By working with these kids, you learn how to be friendly and get along better with other teammates.

Support (fact) | Elaboration (examples)

Working with a team teaches you how to use all of the different members' strengths so that each of the team's members plays the position in which they are strongest. If you are fast, you can dribble down the field, kick the ball, and watch it zoom into the net for a goal. On the other hand, if you are more aggressive, then you could add to the team by booting the ball high in the air, which clears the ball away from the other team.

Effect 2 | Elaboration (analogy)

Another effect of participating in a team sport is that it teaches you how to motivate, or cheer on, yourself and your teammates. Have you ever heard the expression "a chain is only as strong as its weakest link"? Well, if one teammate is not doing his best on the field, then he is weakening the whole team. If you can say positive comments to get him going again, now your weakest link is stronger than he was before. You do not have to wear a uniform and have pompoms to be a cheerleader; you can encourage your teammates by supporting them and encouraging them to do their best. . . .

Evaluate and Revise Content, Organization, and Style

Give Your Essay the Old "One, Two" When you read over your own draft or respond to someone else's, you should read it twice: once for clear content and organization, and once for style.

First Reading: Content and Organization Use this chart to evaluate and revise your cause-and-effect essay so that your explanations are clear and interesting.

Quick guide

Guidelines for Self-Evaluation and Peer Evaluation

Evaluation Questions	Tips	Revision Techniques
1 Does the introduction include a main idea statement that identifies the cause-and-effect relationship?	**Underline** the cause-and-effect statement in the first paragraph. Ask whether the causes or effects are clearly stated.	**Add** a clear statement of the cause-and-effect relationship, if needed. Tell whether you will focus on causes or on effects.
2 Will the essay make sense to a younger audience?	**Put question marks** next to words the audience may not know or in places where background information may be helpful.	If necessary, **elaborate** with definitions or examples that will make the explanation clearer.
3 Does each paragraph discuss one cause or one effect? Does the support follow the cause or effect? Do transitions help ideas flow together coherently?	**Put a check** by the cause or effect in each paragraph. Mark transitions with **stars.**	**Rearrange** the causes or effects and the support so each paragraph contains one cause or effect followed by its support. Add transitions if needed.
4 Does the essay include enough logical support for each cause or effect?	With a colored marker, **highlight** the part of the essay that gives logical support.	**Add** a fact, an example, or an expert opinion to support each cause-and-effect statement. **Delete** statements of cause or effect that cannot be supported.
5 Does the conclusion summarize the essay's main points or restate its main idea?	**Put a star** by each of the main points mentioned in the conclusion or by the restatement.	Are there causes or effects that are not summarized? If necessary, **add** them or **add** a restatement.

ONE WRITER'S REVISIONS Here are some examples of how the writer of the essay on page 105 revised his essay.

rearrange

You are growing fast, and sleep is the time your body takes to make sure everything is okay. Lack of sleep affects not only your grades, but also your health. Sleep is important for your whole body. As you sleep, your body is fixing itself. Your whole body needs this resting time in order to run well when you are awake. ~~That is why people who sleep more are better athletes and more successful students than people who get less sleep.~~

delete

PEER REVIEW

As you evaluate a peer's cause-and-effect essay, ask yourself these questions:

- What cause or effect does the writer explain especially well?
- How could this essay be clearer for a younger audience?

Responding to the Revision Process

1. Why did the writer move the first sentence of the paragraph?
2. Why did the writer delete the last sentence from the paragraph?

Second Reading: Style Now, look at your sentences and focus on *how* you say the things you do. There are many ways to improve sentences, but this workshop will focus on replacing the passive voice with the active voice. **Passive voice** expresses an action done *to* the subject. **Active voice** expresses an action done *by* the subject. For example, the sentence *The movie was seen by Sam* is in the passive voice. The sentence *Sam saw the movie* is in the active voice.

When you evaluate your essay for style, ask yourself whether your writing includes many sentences in which the action is done *to* the subject, instead of *by* the subject. Draw a line through each sentence in which the subject receives the action. (Hint: To locate passive-voice subjects, look for forms of *be* used as helping verbs.) Then, rewrite some or all of the sentences, using the active voice.

Sentences

Active Voice

The purpose of cause-and-effect writing is to show *who* or *what* caused something. Writing in the active voice keeps the cause-and-effect relationships clear. Passive voice calls attention away from the action, which can make a cause-and-effect relationship unclear.

Examples:

Passive voice: The water was spilled by Elena. [The passive voice draws attention away from the action.]

Active voice: Elena spilled the water.

You can quickly identify passive voice in your writing by looking for *be* verbs. Passive-voice verbs are made up of a form of *be* followed by a verb form usually ending in *–ed.*

TIP Forms of *be* include *am, are, be, been, being, is, was,* and *were.*

ONE WRITER'S REVISIONS

These habits may cause you to lose sleep. ~~Both your grades and your health can be affected by losing sleep.~~ *Losing sleep can affect both your grades and your health.*

Responding to the Revision Process

How did rewriting the sentence in the active voice improve it? Try to think of a different way to revise this sentence.

Reference Note

For more information and practice on **active** and **passive voice,** see page 520.

YOUR TURN 9 Evaluating and Revising Your Cause-and-Effect Essay

- Use the guidelines on page 107 to evaluate and revise the content and organization of your cause-and-effect essay.
- Then, use the Focus on Sentences above to see if you need to change any passive-voice verbs to active-voice verbs.
- If a peer evaluated your essay, carefully consider his or her comments as you revise.

Publishing

Proofread Your Essay

A Last Look Now that you have made your revisions, look at your paper one more time. Errors in your essay will distract any reader from the message you have spent so much time creating, and errors could be especially confusing for younger audiences. Ask a friend to read your essay to catch mistakes you may have missed.

Grammar Link

Using Colons and Semicolons

When you write your cause-and-effect essay, you may find yourself needing to make a list, or you may want to tie together two sentences that have related ideas. In these situations you will need to know the difference between a colon and a semicolon.

A colon introduces a list of items. The words to the left of the colon should be an independent clause—a complete sentence. The expressions *as follows* and *the following* are clue words that a colon should be used.

Example:
Many students lose sleep for two reasons: busy schedules and early classes.

[The two items in the list are schedules and classes.]

A semicolon connects sentences that contain closely related ideas. A semicolon takes the place of a comma and a conjunction that links two separate sentences. A semicolon is like a "super-comma" because it can hold two independent clauses together all by itself, without a conjunction.

Example:
Angelina gets plenty of sleep, and she eats breakfast, too.

Angelina gets plenty of sleep; she eats breakfast, too.

PRACTICE

Write *C* on your paper for sentences that use a colon or semicolon correctly. Then, correctly rewrite the sentences that include errors.

1. I went to the store to pick up three items; cheese, milk, and bread.
2. On the way home I ran into Clarissa; she should be home soon.
3. In the living room I saw three people; Jason, Malik, and Juan.
4. They had three ideas about what to do tonight: play cards, shop, or watch TV.
5. I would rather play soccer; or go to a movie.

For more information and practice on **semicolons,** see page 649. For more information and practice on **colons,** see page 652.

Designing Your Writing

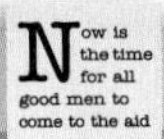

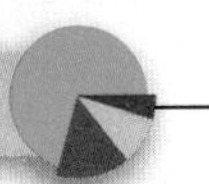

Using Visuals Illustrations make your writing clearer for any audience, but younger audiences particularly enjoy any pictures that accompany writing. Charts, graphs, drawings, or photographs will enhance your cause-and-effect essay for a younger audience.

If you have numerical information in your cause-and-effect essay, a chart or graph is the clearest way to present it. See page 113 for more about the uses of various charts and graphs. If there is no numerical information in your essay, you may want to draw pictures or take photographs that illustrate the causes or effects in your essay. For example, if your essay is about the effects of littering in a local park, you could take pictures of littered areas.

COMPUTER TIP

You can use a computer to add visuals to your paper. Many word-processing programs allow you to create graphics such as pie charts, bar graphs, and line graphs. If you are using drawings or photographs and there is a digital scanner available, you may want to convert the pictures into computer graphics.

Publish Your Essay

Go Public Share your knowledge of causes and effects. How can you make your essay available to fourth- or fifth-graders?

- Create a class newspaper or brochure about causes and effects and send it to a fourth- or fifth-grade class.
- Visit a class and give an oral presentation of your paper.

Reflect on Your Essay

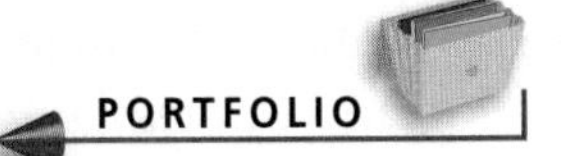

Building Your Portfolio Take time to reflect on your essay. Think about what you wrote and how you wrote it.

- What is the strongest support for a cause or effect in your essay? Why do you think it is the strongest?
- Examine your portfolio of writing. Look for the strengths and weaknesses in the pieces. What do you think caused the strengths? What caused the weakness? How would you develop the strengths and improve the weaknesses?

YOUR TURN 10 Proofreading, Publishing, and Reflecting on Your Essay

- Correct grammar, usage, and mechanics errors.
- Publish your essay for a fourth- or fifth-grade audience.
- Answer the Reflect on Your Essay questions above. Record your responses in a learning log or include them in your portfolio.

When a Documentary Changes the World

Several decades ago, CBS aired Edward R. Murrow's *Harvest of Shame.* This hard-hitting TV documentary led to legislation that improved the lives of migrant farm workers, who travel from place to place to harvest crops.

Murrow followed the workers for a season, showing viewers what life was like for these workers. One woman interviewed had been working in the fields since she was eight years old. She had worked ten hours that day and earned only one dollar. She had fourteen children to feed.

Murrow also interviewed government officials and farmers. Some of the officials wanted to change the situation of the migrant, but explained the difficulties of getting legislation passed.

Media critics say that this documentary triggered changes in federal policy toward migrant workers. What made the documentary so effective in influencing and informing viewers?

- **A timely topic.** CBS aired the program on Thanksgiving Day, forcing viewers to connect the food they ate with the migrant workers who had harvested it.
- **Powerful images and interviews.** Part of what gives images and interviews power is their arrangement. For example, an image of cattle being shipped was placed next to an image of workers jammed into trucks. This **juxtaposition,** or side-by-side arrangement, forced the audience to see that the workers were treated like cattle.
- **A bias, or point of view.** Bias can reflect the producer's **purpose.** Even informative documentaries include a bias, although it may be hidden. The producers revealed their bias indirectly through the selection and arrangement of images and interviews. Clearly, they intended to influence, not just inform. Murrow revealed his bias directly by urging viewers to help pass legislation to improve conditions for migrant workers.

YOUR TURN 11 Evaluate a Documentary

Write a one-paragraph evaluation of a documentary. Tell what you think the producer's **purpose** was and kind of **effect** you think the documentary could have. Support your response, considering each of the elements discussed above.

Analyzing Graphics

WHAT'S AHEAD?

In this workshop you will examine charts and graphs. You will also learn how to

- **read and understand graphics**
- **understand the purposes of pie charts and bar graphs**

Words, words, words! Do you ever get tired of so many words? What happened to pictures? How about some numbers? Not everything needs to be explained with words. Numbers can give strong support for cause-and-effect essays. Pictures often make ideas clearer. Because cause-and-effect writings often include numbers as support, graphics can help the reader visualize information.

Understanding Graphics

You have probably seen graphics many places—on the backs of cereal cartons, in commercials, and even on signs in your school. **Graphics,** such as charts and graphs, are a great way to present numerical information. Presenting such information visually often makes it easier for readers to understand.

Follow the Clues Every graphic gives clues that will help you understand its meaning. Some graphics may not have all of these clues, but even one or two can help you analyze a graphic.

- The **title** gives the graphic's topic or main idea.
- **Labels** identify each of the different parts shown in the graphic. In a bar graph (see next page) or line graph, labels identify the two categories of numbers plotted on the graph.
- The **legend** explains special symbols, codes, and colors.
- The **source** (in small type near the graphic) tells where the information shown in the graphic came from and the year in which that information was published.

What Works? Two common types of graphics are pie charts and bar graphs. Each is best suited to a particular purpose.

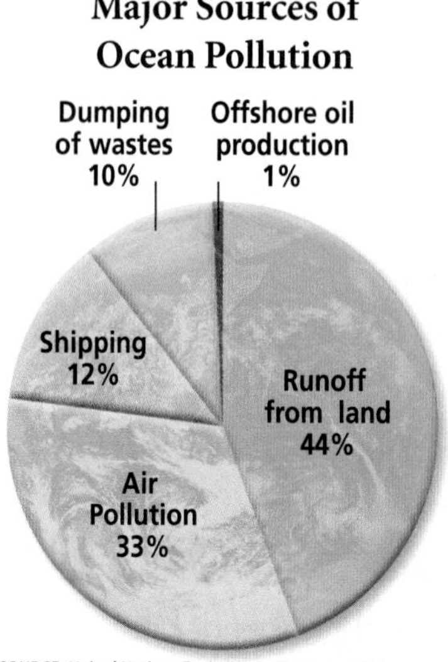

SOURCE: United Nations Environment Program, 1990

Pie charts identify the parts of a whole and each part's relative size. Pie charts are best for showing percentages. Can you identify the title, labels, and source in the pie chart to the left?

Bar graphs show comparison between quantities and can represent two sets of numbers relating to the same topic. To read a bar graph, match the label for each bar to the number that bar reaches. What two sets of numbers does each bar in the graph below represent?

YOUR TURN 12 Analyzing Graphics

Use the graphics above to answer the following questions.

- What causes are represented in the pie chart? Write a sentence or two explaining the information given in the chart.
- What point about an environmental issue does the bar graph help to make? In a sentence or two, explain how it helps make this point.

Choices

Choose one of the following activities to complete.

▶ CREATIVE WRITING

1. One Thing Leads to Another Write a **humorous story** or **poem** that uses a false cause-and-effect relationship. For example, you may write about a case of mistaken identity and the funny effects that follow. Share your story or poem with the class.

▶ JOURNALISM

2. Team Up Work with a group to write a **news article** about causes and effects. Brainstorm recent events to choose a story. Then, work together to gather information, organize, write, and revise the story. Collect stories written by other groups, and publish them in a **class newspaper.**

▶ CROSSING THE CURRICULUM: HISTORY

3. Tell It Like It Was Explore the causes or effects of a historical event. Write an **essay, narrative,** or **letter** explaining how certain historical events led to specific results. You will probably have to do some research to make sure your facts are right. Be sure to use at least one print and one non-print source. Notice how your sources differ in the treatment of the event or in the viewpoints expressed on it.

▶ CAREERS

4. What's Really Going On? Imagine you are a political analyst. Identify a political event in your city or school, and research its causes or effects. For instance, find out what caused your school to stop (or start) sponsoring a school carnival. Write a **letter of request** for information to the city or school board. Then, write a **report** explaining the causes and effects of the event.

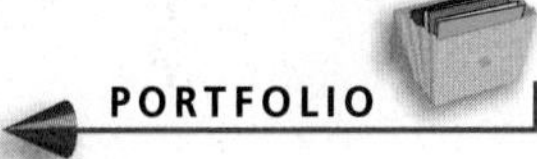

▶ CAREERS

5. What Is Your Inspiration? What causes good writing? What are the effects of writing? Invite a local newspaper reporter to give an in-class presentation. Ask the reporter to share the challenges and rewards of everyday writing. Also, ask about strategies that he or she uses. Then, write a **summary** of the presentation.

CHAPTER 4

Analyzing a Book

Reading Workshop

Reading a Book Review

Writing Workshop

Writing a Book Review

Speaking and Listening

Holding a Panel Discussion

Speaking and Listening

Producing a Scene from a Book

Informational Text

Exposition

Have you ever wondered why your favorite movie received a "thumbs down"? Why does the restaurant on the corner always have such a long line? What leads a consumer group to recommend one brand of computer over another? Reviews and rating systems are everywhere, telling us what to buy, where to eat, and which movies to see.

Reliable reviews and ratings are not snap judgments. They are based on the qualities important to the subject—the book, movie, restaurant, car, or computer—that is being reviewed. The most helpful reviews and rating systems do more than make recommendations, however. They give information that allows us to make decisions for ourselves.

YOUR TURN 1 Thinking About Reviews

- Make a list of five things you think could be reviewed, such as sports equipment, food, or video games.
- Then, choose one item from your list, and write down all of the qualities a reviewer should consider when deciding whether that item is good or bad. For example, a pair of in-line skates should have sturdy wheels, a comfortable fit, and good brakes. Pair up with another student, and see if you can add to each other's lists.

internetconnect
go.hrw.com
GO TO: go.hrw.com
KEYWORD: EOLang 8-4

Reading a Book Review

WHAT'S AHEAD?

In this workshop you will read a book review. You will also learn how to

- **identify the standards reviewers use to analyze nonfiction books**
- **form generalizations**

Some people never read book reviews. They are content to try their luck paying money for an unknown book or reading halfway through a dull book before giving up. For many people, though, knowing something about a book in advance is very important. They may be required to write a report using the book, or they may want to give the book as a gift. A reader who wants to avoid wasting time on the wrong book could definitely use the information gained from a book review. In this workshop you will read a review of a nonfiction book about President John F. Kennedy's assassination in 1963. The writer of the review analyzed the book according to specific qualities important in a nonfiction book.

Preparing to Read

READING FOCUS

Understanding Evaluation Standards The qualities that make a book good depend on the type of book it is. **Evaluation standards** are used to judge these qualities. As you read the following review by Russell Freedman, try to identify the evaluation standards he uses to analyze the nonfiction book *Kennedy Assassinated!*

READING SKILL

Making Inferences: Forming Generalizations A **generalization** is a statement that applies to many people or situations. As you read, you form generalizations about the people or situations you encounter. You do this by combining what you have read with what you know and then applying this information to other situations. Notice how Freedman leads readers to form generalizations in his review of *Kennedy Assassinated!*

Reading Selection

Read the following book review. In a notebook, jot down answers to the numbered active-reading questions in the shaded boxes. The underlined words will be used in the Vocabulary Mini-Lesson on page 124.

from The New York Times Book Review

That Day in Dallas

A highly personal minute-by-minute account of what happened when John F. Kennedy was shot.

KENNEDY ASSASSINATED!
The World Mourns:A Reporter's Story
By Wilborn Hampton

By Russell Freedman

WILBORN HAMPTON was an untested cub reporter at the Dallas office of United Press International when he answered the phone on November 22, 1963, and learned that shots had been fired at the motorcade carrying President and Mrs. John F. Kennedy through the streets of downtown Dallas. *Kennedy Assassinated!* is Hampton's highly personal minute-by-minute chronicle of what happened that momentous afternoon as he covered his first major news story, and as the world reacted with shock and disbelief to word of the president's death.

1. How does the reviewer hook the reader's interest?

. . . Hampton recalls these events for a generation of young readers who know the Kennedys as distant figures from American folklore and pop culture. Today's schoolchildren may have heard their parents or grandparents reminisce about the assassination, remembering exactly where they were when they heard the news, whom they were with, and what they said or felt. Hampton was at the scene, and his book, subtitled *The World Mourns: A Reporter's Story*, has the passion and immediacy of an eyewitness account.

2. Who does the reviewer think is the likely audience for the book?

Just out of college, with scarcely any reporting experience, he had been trying to stay out of the way that week while everyone else in the office was busy covering the president's visit to Texas. "But that was about to change," Hampton writes. "In fact, my whole life was about to change. . . . Certainly there was never anything in any of the journalism courses that I took in college or in my orientation at U.P.I.[1] that covered what to do in case you received such a telephone call."

Dispatched to Parkland Hospital, Hampton joined the frenzied activity as reporters and newscasters jostled[2] to find out what was

1. **U.P.I.:** United Press International, a news agency.
2. **jostled:** pushed or shoved roughly.

happening and how seriously the president had been hurt. The story shifts back and forth between Hampton's personal observations and events taking place beyond his view: the grim drama in Emergency Room One, where doctors worked frantically to save the president; the capture of Lee Harvey Oswald in a Dallas movie theater; the swearing in of Lyndon Baines Johnson as president aboard *Air Force One* as Jacqueline Kennedy looked on.

Young readers may be surprised to learn that in the low-tech 1960s, reporters still relied on typewriters, carbon paper, Teletype machines and rotary telephones. The Presidential motorcade's official press car was equipped with a single car phone, which was still a rare enough item to be considered modern technology. Hampton describes a farcical[3] scene in which two eminent journalists from competing wire services grapple on the floor of the press car for possession of that phone as the motorcade carrying the mortally wounded president speeds toward Parkland Hospital.

Hampton returns repeatedly to his own observations and reactions as a young, idealistic American. While he was leaving the hospital on his way to Dallas Police Headquarters, where Oswald was being held, he writes, "the full enormity of what had happened that day hit me like a bolt of lightning. . . . I stopped by a giant live oak tree on that vast front lawn of Parkland Hospital and cried. I leaned against it and sobbed, all the anger and grief I had suppressed during the afternoon pouring out as I muttered to myself, 'He's dead; he's really dead.'"

3. Do you think the book's writer included his own feelings in the book? How do you know?

The narrative moves along in partnership with historic news photographs that appear on almost every page. Beginning with the endpapers, a collage of news items about the assassination, the book is a skillfully orchestrated[4] blend of words and pictures. There are reproductions of Teletype transmissions and newspaper headlines and of President Kennedy's autopsy report. . . . And there are many striking full-page photographs documenting events from the Kennedys' arrival at Love Field in Dallas to the president's funeral in Washington. *Kennedy Assassinated!* is, in effect, a collaboration between Hampton and Ann Stott, the book's designer and photo researcher; it is an outstanding example of the role that design and illustration play in today's best nonfiction books for children.

4. What does this paragraph tell you about the content of the book?

Hampton's closely focused text does not discuss Kennedy's record as president, his personal life or the controversy surrounding his assassination. That is not the author's intention. His book does bring a shocking episode in American history vividly alive for a generation that was not yet born. It should, one hopes, encourage many readers to seek out other books on this and related topics.

5. Why do you think the reviewer believes that this book will interest a young audience?

---

3. **farcical:** absurd or ridiculous.

4. **orchestrated:** arranged for a good effect.

First Thoughts on Your Reading

1. **What detail about the book would most appeal to a young audience?**
2. **What is the reviewer's overall recommendation?**

Understanding Evaluation Standards

READING FOCUS

Everyone's a Critic A good book review is the result of careful reading and an analysis based on specific *evaluation standards.* **Evaluation standards** are the points used to judge anything, from a CD player to a puppy. Some standards, such as a fair price, can apply to many different things. Other standards only fit certain items. You might evaluate a symphony based on its use of violins, but that standard would not work for rap music.

While you might judge a fiction book's plot or characters, the standards for a nonfiction book are different. A nonfiction book is successful when it

- speaks to a particular **audience,** or group of readers
- uses an interesting and appealing **voice** as it gives information
- includes accurate, well-organized information, or **content**

I Spy a Critical Eye When you read a review of a nonfiction book, you must make sure the reviewer applies each evaluation standard. Ask these questions as you read.

Questions to Ask About Evaluation Standards
Audience: Does the reviewer ▪ mention a particular group of readers who will benefit from the book? ▪ discuss whether the book's language and level fit its audience?
Voice: Does the reviewer ▪ mention what tone the writer uses—friendly, serious, objective? ▪ comment on whether the writing keeps readers interested? ▪ include a quote or scene from the book to show the writer's voice?
Content: Does the reviewer ▪ describe the amount and kind of information in the book? ▪ refer to features in the book, such as photographs, charts, or facts? ▪ discuss the organization of information in the book?

YOUR TURN 2 Evaluating a Book Review

On a sheet of paper, write down quotations from "That Day in Dallas" on pages 119–120 that show where the reviewer addresses each of the three evaluation standards. To do this, answer each question in the chart on page 121.

READING SKILL

Making Inferences: Forming Generalizations

Signs of the Times If you see a group of people waving signs outside a business, you might guess that they are protesting. What makes you think that? You consider your experience (you have seen similar scenes on the news), or you read something (the signs they carry). Then you make your best guess. An educated guess based on what you know or have seen before is called an **inference.**

One type of inference is a *generalization.* A **generalization** is a statement that applies to *many* individuals or situations even though it is based on *specific* situations or people. When reading a book review, generalizations will help you connect information in the review with your own experiences.

TEXT: What you read
The writer of a book review in your school paper said he was glad someone finally wrote a computer book for young adults.

\+ **PRIOR KNOWLEDGE: What you already know**
You and your friends have complained that computer books always seem to be written for adults.

GENERALIZATION: A statement that applies to many other people or situations
Many young adults would like to read computer books written for their age group.

TIP To spot a faulty generalization, watch for clue words such as *no one, never, every,* and *always.* Sentences with these words may make statements that are too broad. You can turn many faulty generalizations into valid ones by using words such as *may, many, often,* and *some.* These words indicate that the statement does not necessarily apply every time or to every person.

The Generalization Gap A valid generalization draws upon solid information and applies to other people or situations. A **faulty generalization** is not valid because it applies an idea to *every* person or *every* situation. For example, the statement, "All young readers will be surprised to learn that in the 1960s, reporters still relied on typewriters" is a faulty generalization because some young people may *not* be surprised.

THINKING IT THROUGH

Forming Generalizations

The steps below show how a student might form a generalization based on the second paragraph of "That Day in Dallas" on page 119.

STEP 1 Look for any details that describe a certain situation or experience.	The reviewer says students' parents or grandparents may remember "exactly where they were" and "what they said or felt" when they heard the president had been killed.
STEP 2 Think about your knowledge of similar situations or experiences.	My parents told me they remember where they were and how they felt when Neil Armstrong walked on the moon. They said it was something they would never forget.
STEP 3 Add what you have read and what you know to form a generalization.	Many people remember special details about where they were and how they felt when important events took place.
STEP 4 Check that your generalization is not faulty.	I used the word "many" instead of "all" because some people might not remember those details.

YOUR TURN 3

Forming Generalizations

Use the Thinking It Through steps above to form two generalizations based on the following information from the review of *Kennedy Assassinated!*

1. ". . . Hampton joined the frenzied activity as reporters and newscasters jostled to find out what was happening. . . ." (page 119)

   "Hampton describes a farcical scene in which two eminent journalists . . . grapple . . . for possession of that phone. . . ." (page 120)

2. "Just out of college, with scarcely any reporting experience . . ." (page 119)

   "Certainly there was never anything in any of the journalism courses that I took in college . . . that covered what to do. . . ." (page 119)

MINI-LESSON **VOCABULARY**

Prefixes and Suffixes

A **prefix** is a word part that comes before the main part of a word. The prefix *un–* means "not." A **suffix** is a word part that comes after the main part of the word. The suffix *–able* means "able to." Knowledge of these two word parts helps you understand words you may read in a book review—words such as *unforgettable* or *unreadable.* Learning other word parts, such as those found in the chart below and on page 789, can help you figure out the meanings of unfamiliar words.

Prefix	Meaning	Example
dis–	lack of	disagreement
en–	cause to be	endanger
re–	back, again	replay
tele–	from a distance	telephone

Suffix	Meaning	Example
–cade	procession	cavalcade
–er	one who	painter
–ic	relating to	historic
–ship	condition, state	friendship

THINKING IT THROUGH

Using Prefixes and Suffixes

Here is how to figure out the meaning of the underlined word in this sentence: "There are reproductions of Teletype transmissions . . ."

STEP 1 Break the word into parts, and find the meaning of each part.

The prefix re– means "again."
A product is something that's made.
The suffix –ion means "result."

STEP 2 Create a definition based on what you now know.

A reproduction is "the result of making something again," or "a remake."

STEP 3 See if the definition makes sense in the original sentence.

"There are remakes of Teletype transmissions . . ." That makes sense.

PRACTICE

Use prefixes and suffixes to define these words, which are underlined in "That Day in Dallas."

1. motorcade (page 119)
2. disbelief (page 119)
3. Teletype (page 120)
4. partnership (page 120)
5. encourage (page 120)

MINI-LESSON **TEST TAKING**

Answering Inference Questions

Reading tests often ask you to identify an inference, such as a conclusion or generalization, that is supported by a passage. The inference should make sense based on the information you find in the passage. How might you choose the best answer for this test item?

> The assassination of President John F. Kennedy has been well covered since that day in 1963 when he was shot in Dallas. Hundreds of authors have written books on the assassination. Directors have filmed dozens of movies about the president's life and death. Internet users constantly create new Web sites to provide a place for people to post their thoughts on what has been called "The Great Conspiracy" and the "Crime of the Century."

You can tell from this passage that

A. John F. Kennedy was the greatest president in history

B. many people are still interested in President Kennedy's assassination

C. everyone has read books and seen movies about the assassination

D. the Kennedy assassination remains unsolved

THINKING IT THROUGH

Making Inferences

STEP 1 Identify the type of question you are being asked.

"You can tell from this passage" tells me that the answer won't be stated in the passage, but it must be supported by information in the passage.

STEP 2 Evaluate each answer choice. Ask yourself the following questions:

- Is this choice supported by information in the passage?
- Are there faulty generalization clue words, such as *all* or *every,* in the choice?

Answer A—This answer is not supported in the passage.

Answer B—"Many people" sounds like a generalization, and this answer is supported in the passage. This may be the right answer.

Answer C—This is a faulty generalization. Not everyone has done those things.

Answer D—This answer is not supported in the passage.

STEP 3 Choose the best answer choice.

Answer B is the right answer.

Writing a Book Review

WHAT'S AHEAD?

In this workshop you will write a review of a nonfiction book. You will also learn how to

- **preview a book**
- **summarize a book**
- **analyze a book's audience, voice, and content**
- **write an informed recommendation**
- **use adjective clauses to eliminate choppy sentences**
- **punctuate essential and nonessential phrases and clauses**

You have just read the best book ever. It showed the insides of worms, described how ants make complex underground tunnels, and told you everything you ever wanted to know about poisonous spiders. You reluctantly turn it in to the librarian, and he tells you he is about to pull the book from the shelves. No one else has checked it out in four years.

You wonder what you can do to keep the book in the library. One way to get information about the book to others is to write a book review. If you do a good job, other students will also want to check out and read the book. Not only could you save the book, but you could also communicate your ideas to other readers. This workshop will show you how to write a review of a nonfiction, or fact-based, book.

Prewriting

Choose a Book to Review

Pick of the Litter Suppose you were at the pet store trying to choose a dog to take home. You would examine each dog, measuring it against the qualities you want in a dog. One dog might be too big for your apartment. Another one might not be gentle enough with your little brother. You want to be sure to pick the right one.

Choosing a book to review requires careful thought, too. For this review, you will need to stick with a nonfiction book rather than a novel or a short story. Nonfiction includes books on history, science, art, computers, and biographies or autobiographies of interesting or famous people. Pick a book you have already read and enjoyed or a new one on a topic that interests you. It may help to brainstorm a list of nonfiction books you have read before.

If you are looking for a new book to read, *previewing* is a good way to see if you will be interested in a book. **To preview a book, read its jacket, glance at the table of contents, and flip through the book, looking at drawings, charts, or photos.** This will give you an idea about the contents of the book.

KEY CONCEPT

YOUR TURN 4 Choosing a Book to Review

To find a book to review, brainstorm a list of nonfiction books that you have read and enjoyed. You may also want to preview a few books on a topic that interests you. Choose a book you think you will like or that you remember liking.

Read and Take Notes

You Be the Judge In court, a judge carefully studies the facts of a case before making a decision. You should be just as thorough when reading your book. Your **purpose** for writing your review is to provide information to help others decide whether they want to read the book. Because people may read or not read this book based on your review, you should read the book more carefully and more critically than a "regular" reader would. To do this, generate specific questions to answer as you read. **Your questions should be related to the three evaluation standards on which you will judge the book—audience, voice, and content.** As you read, ask questions such as these.

KEY CONCEPT

- Audience What is the age of the audience the book seems to target? Does the information given fit this age group? Check to see if the book's words and explanations are too difficult or too easy.
- Voice What kind of a voice does the writer use? For example, is the writer emotional, or does he or she seem reserved? How does the emotion or lack of it affect the book? What language in the book supports your judgment?
- Content How is the content of the book presented? How much information does the book include? Are there enough examples,

Reference Note

For more on **evaluation standards,** see page 121.

As you think ...the author's audi... ...nd his or her voice, start to think about *your* **audience** and **voice.** You may decide to address the same audience that the author does, since this is the group that will be most interested in reading about the book. Choose a voice appropriate to that audience as well as to your purpose—to inform. If you like the author's voice, consider imitating it in your review; imitation is, after all, a form of flattery.

drawings, charts, or photos included? How is the information organized?

As you read, write notes when you find the answer to a question. One student chose to review *Anne Frank: Beyond the Diary,* a book of pictures and information about Anne Frank and her family. Below are some notes the student made as she read.

Audience: The information on the back cover of the book makes it seem as if the writers want middle school students to read it. After the first few pages, I could tell that the writers had gotten it just right for this age group because the book was easy to understand and had an interesting story about the birthday party when Anne got her diary.

YOUR TURN 5 Reading and Taking Notes for Your Review

- Prepare a list of questions before you read the book you have chosen to review. Include questions about audience, voice, and content. Some questions are suggested on page 127. Include your own questions that are specific to your book.
- Read the book, and take notes when you find answers to your questions. Keep your notes handy. You will need them later when you prepare to write your review.

Write a Summary

Short and Sweet One important part of any book review is a *summary* of the book. A **summary** is a brief restatement of the most important ideas of a work. The Mini-Lesson on the next page shows you how to write a summary of the book you chose to review.

YOUR TURN 6 Summarizing Your Book

Write a summary of the book you have chosen to review, using the steps given in the Writing Mini-Lesson on page 129. Your summary should fit into one paragraph.

MINI-LESSON **WRITING**

Summarizing

What's It All About? Suppose you just watched a great television program about tigers, and you want to e-mail a friend about it. What do you write? Explaining every fact you learned would take too long. Instead, you *summarize* the show.

In a **summary,** you explain only the most important ideas of a work. When you summarize a lengthy work, such as a book, you have to make decisions about which ideas to include and which ones to leave out. The Thinking It Through below shows the steps one student followed to create a summary for *Anne Frank: Beyond the Diary.*

THINKING IT THROUGH

Summarizing a Book

STEP 1 Identify the book's overall goal. What is the book's focus? What does it spend the most time discussing?

Anne Frank: Beyond the Diary gives information about the Franks' lives that was not included in Anne's diary. It also gives pictures to go with the diary.

STEP 2 Note any other major chapters, points, or features included in the book.

The book gives background information on World War II and Hitler. It also includes many charts and maps of Europe to show how the war progressed and how the war affected Jewish people.

STEP 3 Write a short paragraph, including only the information from Step 1 and Step 2. Avoid adding specific examples or quotes.

Anne Frank: Beyond the Diary goes beyond the information in her famous diary to provide details about the lives of the people who lived in the secret hideaway. The book includes photographs, quotations from Anne's diary, and historical information about World War II.

PRACTICE

Follow the steps above to write a summary of a book you have read recently. If you wish, you may adapt the steps for a television show and summarize a television program you have seen lately.

Analyze Your Book

Presenting Your Findings Now that you have taken notes, you probably have some ideas about how the nonfiction book you are reviewing handles the three evaluation standards of audience, voice, and content. **The next step is to present your ideas in evaluation statements.** An evaluation statement explains how well the author met each of the standards. You will write three evaluation statements—one each for audience, voice, and content. You will use the information in your notes to write these statements. The following evaluation statements were made by the student analyzing *Anne Frank: Beyond the Diary.*

KEY CONCEPT

Audience: The writers of Anne Frank: Beyond the Diary appealed to their young-adult audience by using plain language and by including lots of visuals and interesting quotes from Anne.

Voice: Because the story of Anne Frank's life is an emotional one, the writers wisely keep the captions and text unemotional.

Content: The book, which is well organized, blends facts about the war with the story of Anne's life.

YOUR TURN 7 Writing Evaluation Statements

Review the notes you took on audience, voice, and content. Then, write an evaluation statement for each of these evaluation standards.

Provide Evidence

Can I Quote You on That? Suppose a scientist being interviewed on the news claimed, "There is definitely life on Mars." The first question the reporter would ask is, "What evidence do you have?"

KEY CONCEPT

Most people want proof for any claim. **When writing your review, you must provide evidence to support your evaluation statements on audience, voice, and content.** Evidence may include facts, examples, and direct quotations from the book.

When you took notes on audience, voice, and content as you read your book, you were actually gathering evidence. If your notes do not include at least two pieces of evidence to support each of your evaluation statements, go back through the book and look for more evidence to support the evaluation statement.

Graphic organizers will help you list and organize the evidence you found. You should create a graphic organizer for each of the three standards. Notice that three pieces of evidence support the evaluation statement.

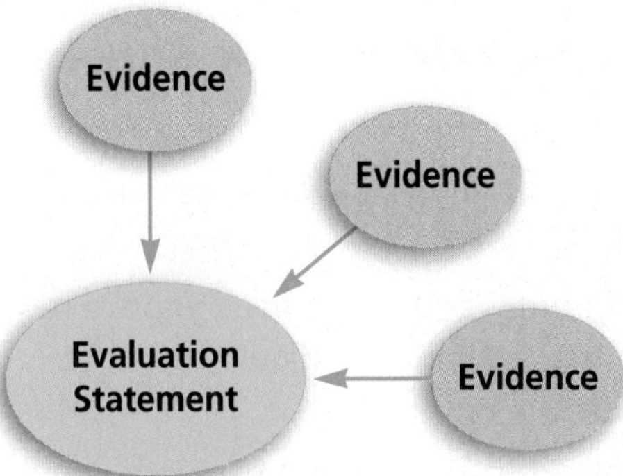

Here is how the reviewer of *Anne Frank: Beyond the Diary* filled in a graphic organizer for her evaluation statement on audience. (Notice how the quotation could have come from any teenager.)

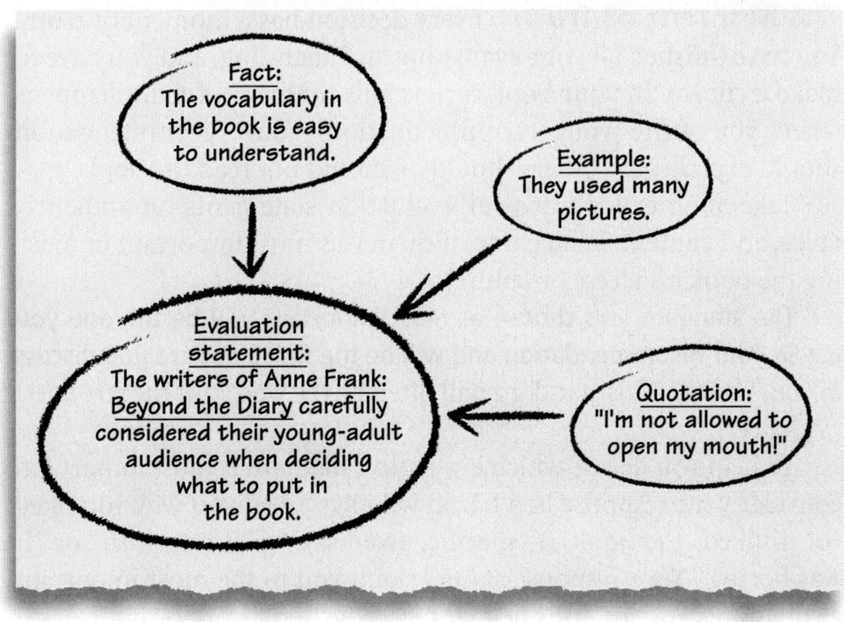

Reference Note

For more information and practice on **punctuating quotations,** see page 662.

TIP Follow these guidelines when you use quotations from a book as evidence in your review.

- Be sure to use the words exactly as they appear in the book. Place quotation marks before and after the words and punctuation you are quoting.
- If you quote only part of a sentence or paragraph, use an ellipsis (. . .) to show where you have left words out.

Example:
"All the clothes which Anne had brought with her . . . soon became much too small for her."

YOUR TURN 8 Gathering Evidence for Support

- Create three graphic organizers like the one shown on page 131.
- In the large ovals, write your evaluation statements for audience, voice, and content.
- Then, return to your notes and to the book you are reviewing, and choose evidence (facts, examples, and quotations) to support each evaluation statement.
- Fill in the small ovals with the strongest evidence you have.

Form a Recommendation

The Moment of Truth Every decision has a moment of truth. You have finished all your evaluating and analyzing, and you have to make a choice. In your book review, this moment of truth happens when you write your recommendation. Your recommendation should explain why others should or should not read the book.

Take another look at your evaluation statements on audience, voice, and content. Which one of them was most important in making the book a success or failure?

KEY CONCEPT

The standard you choose as most important will be the one you use in your recommendation and will be the first standard you discuss in your review. This standard will often be the one with the strongest evidence.

To help you decide which evaluation standard is most important, consider your response to a friend who has asked you why you liked (or disliked) the book. Be specific; avoid saying "It was great" or "It was boring." Your response should point you to the most important evaluation standard, the one that made the book work or not work.

Example: The historical photographs make this book worth reading.

This statement points to content as the most important evaluation standard.

Once you have chosen the most important evaluation standard, use it to write your recommendation. For example, if you felt the book's dull *voice* caused you to dislike the book, make a negative recommendation, using the voice as your reason. If you felt the book's great *content* made you like the book, write a positive recommendation and give content as the reason why.

Here is the recommendation made by the student who reviewed *Anne Frank: Beyond the Diary.* The student wanted to recommend the book and thought that the *audience* evaluation standard was most important.

> This book is perfect for young-adult readers who want to learn more about Anne Frank's life because it is written for our age group.

It is clear from this recommendation that the student thought the book was good, especially for that particular audience.

TIP A recommendation is like the main idea statement for your review because it explains the topic and your thoughts about it. As with a main idea statement, the body of the review must support the recommendation you make. If you think people should read the book you review, your body paragraphs should support that recommendation by giving them plenty of examples based on the notes you made as you read. If you disliked the book, the body of your review should clearly explain why the writer failed to meet the standards for audience, content, or voice. When you make either kind of recommendation, the body of your review must prove to your readers that they should believe you and take your advice.

YOUR TURN 9 Writing a Recommendation

- Decide which one of the three evaluation standards is most important for your book.
- Then, write a recommendation that tells whether other people should read the book, focusing on the most important standard.

Book Review

Framework	Directions and Explanations
Introduction ■ Hook ■ Summary ■ Recommendation	■ Pull your readers into your review with a **hook,** an interesting statement or piece of information. ■ Follow the hook with a **summary** that lets your readers know the title of the book, who wrote it, and what it is about. ■ Include a **recommendation** that focuses on the evaluation standard you think is most important.
Body ■ First evaluation statement and supporting evidence ■ Second evaluation statement and supporting evidence ■ Third evaluation statement and supporting evidence	Include at least one body paragraph for each of the three evaluation standards—audience, voice, and content. Arrange these body paragraphs in **order of importance:** Start the body of your review with the evaluation statement on the **most important standard,** followed by paragraphs on your **second** and **third most important standards.** A standard may take more than one paragraph to analyze.
Conclusion ■ Restatement of recommendation	Wrap up your review by **restating your recommendation** in different words.

YOUR TURN 10 Drafting Your Book Review

Now, it is your turn to draft a book review. As you write,

- use the ideas in your notes and graphic organizers
- refer to the framework above and to the Writer's Model on the following page

A Writer's Model

The final draft below closely follows the framework for a book review.

More Than Words: Remembering Anne Frank in Pictures

Anne Frank lived for thirteen years before she began writing her famous diary. In Ruud van der Rol and Rian Verhoeven's book Anne Frank: Beyond the Diary, the authors explain what her life was like before the war and provide pictures of her and her family. This book goes beyond the information in Anne's famous diary to provide details about the lives of the people who lived in the secret hideaway. The book includes photographs, quotations from Anne's diary, and historical information about World War II. This book is perfect for young-adult readers who want to learn more about Anne Frank's life because it is written for our age group.

The writers of Anne Frank: Beyond the Diary carefully considered the young-adult audience when deciding what to put in the book. The vocabulary is easy to understand, and the photographs are excellent. The facts in the book are balanced by photographs and quotations from Anne's diary. Readers will also identify with Anne Frank. Her comments about being a teenager could have been written by anyone: "I'm not allowed to open my mouth! . . . We aren't even allowed to have any opinions!"

Because the story of Anne Frank's life is an emotional one, the writers wisely keep the captions and text unemotional. They provide facts about her life and the war, letting the pictures and quotations carry the emotion. Next to a picture of the concentration camp Bergen-Belsen, where Anne and her sister died amidst dirt and disease, the caption simply reads, "Anne and Margot died a few weeks before the camp was liberated by the British Army." The most emotional parts of the book are not in the text, but in the photographs of Anne at different ages. Readers do not

Hook

Summary

Recommendation

First evaluation statement (audience)

Evidence (example)

Evidence (quotation)

Second evaluation statement (voice)

Evidence (fact)

Evidence (quotation)

(continued)

(continued)

need to be told anything to sense the sadness of looking at pictures of a little girl who never got to grow up.

Third evaluation statement (content)

The book, which is well organized, blends facts about the war with the story of Anne's life. Most of the book

Evidence (fact)

tells Anne's story and provides historical background in chronological order using facts, photos, and excerpts from Anne's diary. Mixing the family's life in hiding with historical events happening at the same time helps readers

Evidence (example)

see the diary in the context of the outside world. The many personal items shown in the book vividly illustrate how much Anne was like the young people who read her diary today. Readers may find comfort in seeing that the life that she led before the war was a happy one.

Restatement of recommendation

Readers will enjoy Anne Frank: Beyond the Diary. It tells the full story of Anne Frank's life in a way that is interesting and new. Best of all, young adults will find it is written just for them.

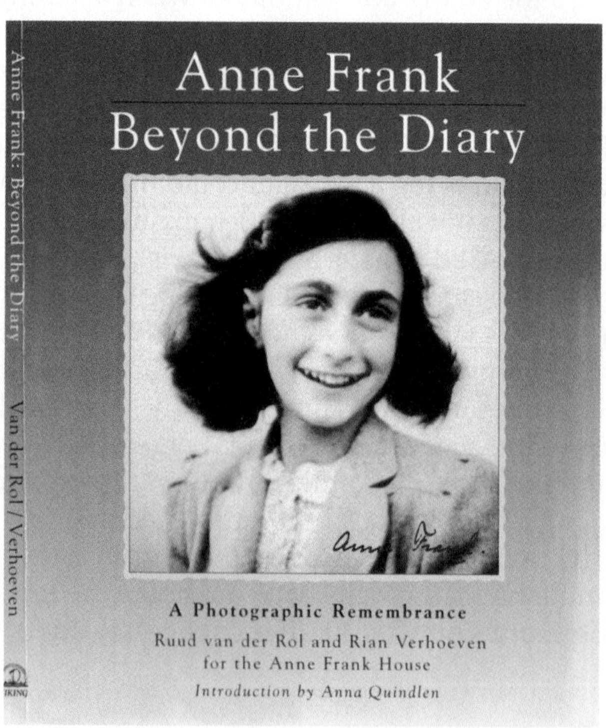

Anne Frank
Beyond the Diary
A Photographic Remembrance
Ruud van der Rol and Rian Verhoeven
for the Anne Frank House
Introduction by Anna Quindlen
Anne Frank: Beyond the Diary
Van der Rol / Verhoeven

A Student's Model

In the following excerpted review, Carolyn Paisie, an eighth-grader at Davis Drive Middle School in Apex, North Carolina, uses descriptive words and examples from the book *Cheaper by the Dozen* to get the feeling of the book across to readers.

Remembering Childhood

How would you like to be a member of a family which has twelve kids? In Frank Gilbreth, Jr., and Ernestine Carey's Cheaper by the Dozen, readers get a peek at what it was like growing up in such a family during the early 1900s. Written by two of the children, this autobiography tells what life was like in the Gilbreth household. It includes funny stories such as when all twelve children have their tonsils removed on the same day, or when Frank, Jr. is left behind at a roadside restaurant. This entertaining book will keep young-adult readers interested from the first paragraph.

The events are well organized and easy to follow. There is a moment of confusion in the middle of the book when the narrators take us back to the time before there were any kids in the family and then go forward telling about how the family got started. Even with this flashback, the story is told in an order that makes sense for the reader. . . .

Cheaper by the Dozen is an outstanding book for young adults. It is written in an easy-to-read manner, and the vocabulary is not difficult. Young-adult readers will also relate to the problems the kids had with trying to get their parents to let them make their own decisions, like when the oldest daughter, Anne, ends up cutting her own hair to convince her parents that all of the girls in the family should be allowed to have their hair "bobbed."

Everyone who likes to read about family life will enjoy this factual and entertaining book. The simplicity of the language and the humorous tone will definitely appeal to young-adult readers. . . .

Hook

Summary

Recommendation

First evaluation statement (content)

Evidence (fact)

Second evaluation statement (audience)

Evidence (example)

Restatement of recommendation

Revising

Evaluate and Revise Content, Organization, and Style

Checking It Twice As you evaluate and revise the draft of your book review, you should read it at least twice. In the first reading, focus on the content and organization of your draft. In your second reading you will focus on sentence style.

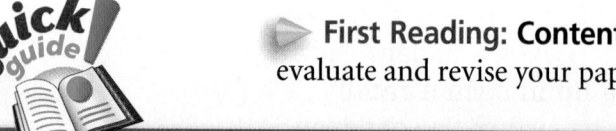

First Reading: Content and Organization Use this chart to evaluate and revise your paper or to review a peer's paper.

Guidelines for Self-Evaluation and Peer Evaluation

Evaluation Questions	Tips	Revision Techniques
1 Does the introduction hook the reader's attention?	**Put a star** next to the question, brief story, or detail that would interest the reader.	If needed, **add** a question, brief story, or detail to the beginning of the introduction.
2 Does the summary include all the important ideas contained in the book?	**Circle** the summary. Check to see if it gives a good idea of the book's contents.	**Add** information to include all important ideas in the book, or **delete** unimportant ideas.
3 Does the recommendation tell whether the reviewer thinks other people should read the book?	Ask a peer to read the recommendation and **put a plus sign** if it is positive **or a minus sign** if it is negative.	**Add** or **replace** words in the recommendation to make it clear whether or not others should read the book.
4 Does the review include evaluation statements for each of the three standards?	**Double underline** the evaluation statements for *audience, voice,* and *content.*	**Add** a paragraph that discusses any missing evaluation standards, if necessary.
5 Is there evidence to support each evaluation statement?	Use different colors to **highlight** the evidence for each evaluation statement.	If necessary, **elaborate** with examples, details, or quotations to support the evaluation statements.
6 Does the restatement of the recommendation use different words to repeat ideas in the original recommendation?	**Put a check** next to the original recommendation and the restatement.	**Revise** the restatement so that it uses different words to restate the original recommendation.

ONE WRITER'S REVISIONS This revision is an early draft of the book review on pages 135–136.

> This book goes beyond the information in Anne's famous diary to provide details about the lives of the people who lived in the secret hideaway. The book includes photographs, quotations from Anne's diary, and historical information about World War II. ~~It also shows the museum you can visit in Amsterdam.~~ This book is perfect for young-adult readers who want to learn more about Anne Frank's life because it is written for our age group.

add

delete

add

Responding to the Revision Process

1. Why do you think the writer added to the second sentence?
2. Why do you think the writer deleted a sentence from the summary?
3. Why do you think the writer added "perfect" to the recommendation in the last sentence?

PEER REVIEW

As you evaluate a peer's book review, ask yourself the following:

- Is it clear why the writer made this recommendation? Why or why not?
- Does the review make me want to read the book? Why or why not?

Second Reading: Style In your first reading, you made sure that all your ideas were included in your review. Now it is time to look at the way you used sentences to present your ideas. If you tend to write short, choppy sentences, one way to improve them is to combine sentences by using an adjective clause that describes a noun or pronoun.

When you evaluate your review, ask yourself whether your writing contains two or more short, choppy sentences next to each other. Draw a wavy line under any short sentences. Check to see whether any are next to each other. Then, revise one or more of the choppy sentences by using adjective clauses to combine information. See the Focus on Sentences on the next page for more information on how to use adjective clauses.

Sentences

Adjective Clauses

A set of two or more very short sentences can distract readers. For example, look at the following sentences.

The annex door led to a stairway. The door was hidden.

The sentences above are "choppy." They can disrupt the flow of your writing and the connections between ideas.

An *adjective clause* can fix the problem. **Adjective clauses** usually follow a noun or a pronoun and tell *which one* or *what kind.* To use an adjective clause, combine the information from one sentence with the other sentence, and add one of the words in the tip to the left if needed.

TIP Adjective clauses often start with relative pronouns such as *that, which, who, whom,* or *whose.*

The annex door, **which was hidden,** led to a stairway.

Rewriting choppy sentences by using adjective clauses will make your writing smoother and your ideas easier to understand.

Reference Note

For more information and practice on **adjective clauses,** see page 444.

ONE WRITER'S REVISIONS

The book, which is well organized, blends facts about the war with the story of Anne's life.

Responding to the Revision Process

How did using an adjective clause improve the passage above?

YOUR TURN 11 Evaluating and Revising Your Book Review

- First, evaluate and revise the content and organization of your book review, using the guidelines and tips on page 138.
- Next, use the Focus on Sentences above to see if you should use adjective clauses to eliminate choppy sentences from your draft.
- Think carefully about any peer evaluation comments as you revise.

Publishing

Proofread Your Review

The Final Touch If you proofread with a partner, you can catch more mistakes. Others will use your review to decide if they should read a book, so **edit** carefully to make sure they are influenced by information, not errors.

Grammar Link

Punctuating Essential and Nonessential Clauses

The adjective clauses you can use to revise choppy sentences come in two types: essential and nonessential. These two types of clauses are punctuated differently.

A **nonessential clause** adds information that is not needed to understand the meaning of a sentence. Use commas to set off a nonessential clause from the rest of the sentence.

Nonessential clause Miep Gies, **who gave Anne writing paper,** hid Anne's diary from the Nazis.

[The sentence would mean the same thing even without the clause about the paper.]

An **essential clause** tells *which one(s),* so it cannot be omitted without changing the basic meaning of the sentence. Do not set off an essential clause with commas.

Essential clause The photographs **that Mr. Frank took of the Secret Annex** helped me imagine Anne Frank's life there.

[The clause explains *which photographs.*]

PRACTICE

Identify the essential or nonessential clause in each sentence below. Rewrite the sentences to add commas where needed.

Example:

1. Anne's favorite window which was usually covered looked out over a huge tree.

1. Anne's favorite window, which was usually covered, looked out over a huge tree.

1. The diary entries that Anne Frank wrote made her famous.
2. Anne's father who died in 1980 dedicated his life to promoting Anne's ideas.
3. Her diary which was first published in English in 1951 has been translated into thirty-one other languages.
4. The Secret Annex which is now a museum receives 600,000 visitors a year.
5. Visitors can still see the pictures of movie stars that Anne put on the walls of her room.

For more information and practice on **essential and nonessential clauses,** see page 639.

COMPUTER TIP 

Italics are letters that are slanted. Since most word-processing software and printers can produce italic type, you can put titles of books in italics when you are working on a computer.

Substitute underlining for italics when writing by hand or with a typewriter.

Publish Your Book Review

Spread the Word Here's how to let others read your review.

- Submit your review to a Web site. Many Internet bookstores allow online visitors to review books that the bookstores sell.
- Collect your reviews in a notebook, and place it in the school library. Other students may use the notebook as a reference guide.

Designing Your Writing

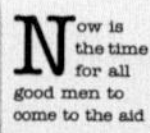

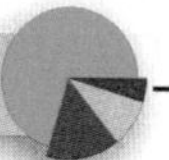

Using Pull-Quotes Many reviews include catchy sentences that have been pulled out of the review, shortened, and set in larger type. These sentences, called **pull-quotes,** catch readers' attention. Pull-quotes can act like magnets to draw readers into an article.

Choose an interesting sentence from your review. If you used a computer to write your review, use the formatting tools to put space around your pull-quote and change the size of the type.

Pull-quotes can act like magnets to readers.

PORTFOLIO

Reflect on Your Review

Building Your Portfolio Take some time to reflect on your book review—not just *what* you wrote but *how* you wrote it.

- How well did your writing communicate your evaluation of the book? Do you think your review is convincing?
- What did you learn about using evaluation standards to analyze a book? Could you use this skill in other types of writing?

YOUR TURN 12 Proofreading, Publishing, and Reflecting on Your Review

First, correct grammar, usage, and mechanics errors; then, publish your review using one of the suggestions above. Finally, answer the questions from Reflect on Your Review above. Record your responses in a learning log, or include them in your portfolio.

MINI-LESSON **TEST TAKING**

Examining Good Points and Bad Points for Tests

An essay test may ask you to discuss the good points and the bad points of an idea, an object, or a place. When you answer a good points/ bad points question, it is important to avoid emphasizing one side over the other. If the prompt to the right were on an essay test, how would you approach it?

Many books are made into movies. There are both good things and bad things about seeing a movie based on a book you have read. Write an essay for your teacher in which you explain both what is good and what is bad about seeing a movie based on a book you have read. Explain each point fully.

THINKING IT THROUGH

Writing About Good Points and Bad Points for Tests

STEP 1 Read the prompt and identify the topic, the purpose, and the audience.

The topic is seeing a movie based on a book I have read. The purpose is to discuss the good points and bad points. My audience is my teacher.

STEP 2 Make a T-chart in which you list the good points and bad points of the topic. Eliminate any points that will be weak or hard to support with examples.

Good	Bad
~~you are already familiar with the story, so the movie makes sense~~	characters may not be the way you pictured them
can "see" characters and settings	the story may change and parts may be left out
emotions may be more obvious	~~acting or music may be awful~~

STEP 3 Make a plan for writing your essay. Choose an example to help you elaborate on each point you will use in your essay.

I can restate the prompt in my introduction. I'll discuss the good points (strongest one first) in the second and third paragraphs. Then, I'll discuss the bad points (strongest one first) in the next couple of paragraphs. I'll use Anne Frank's book <u>The Diary of a Young Girl</u> and the movie based on it called <u>The Diary of Anne Frank</u> as my examples.

Here is a sample response to the prompt on page 143.

Many books have been made into movies. Sometimes the movie is better than the book and other times the book is better than the movie. Of course, viewers only know this if they have both read the book and seen the movie. There are good points and bad points to seeing a movie based on a book you have already read.

One good point about seeing a movie when you have already read the book is that seeing a movie version can bring characters to life. The character of Peter's father in Anne Frank's book The Diary of a Young Girl wasn't very interesting, but in the movie he was awful. He was ugly and loud and stole food when everyone else was asleep. It made it clearer how awful it would be to be in hiding with him.

Another good thing about seeing a movie version of a book you have read is that it can make the emotions and experiences of the characters seem much more real. I never realized how much time the people in Anne Frank's diary spent doing nothing. The movie built tension by showing the people trying to sit quietly for hours when workers and burglars who might hear them moving around were in the building below them. It also vividly showed how quickly people stuck together in a small place could get on each other's nerves.

In spite of the good points, there are some bad points to seeing a movie based on a book you have read, especially if you really liked the book. The worst thing about seeing a movie version of a book is that the movie has to cut out a lot of the story in order to tell it in two hours or so. The movie The Diary of Anne Frank cut out a lot of events, including everything that happened before Anne's family went into hiding.

Another bad point about seeing a movie based on a book you have read is that characters may be different in the movie than they were in the book. The actress who played Anne Frank in the movie seemed older and more glamorous, and she said some things that sounded more like things an adult would say.

Whether you prefer seeing the movie or reading the book, there are good points and bad points about doing both. A movie can bring a book to life, but it also can change the story and characters in negative ways.

Connections to

Literature

Create a Slide Show Comparing a Book and Its Movie

Now that you have evaluated a nonfiction book, it is time to take a closer look at fictional works. To analyze novels, movies, and other works of fiction, you must use different evaluation standards than those you used in your book review. Because the stories told in novels are often retold in movies, you can use these evaluation standards for evaluating fiction to compare the print and movie versions of the same story. In this section you will create a slide show explaining the differences and similarities between a book and its movie.

Common Denominators Fictional books and movies both have plot, characters, setting, and theme. In a book, a writer has hundreds of pages to provide details. A movie, on the other hand, has only two hours or so to cover the same material. The chart below compares how movies and books handle their four common elements.

Element	Books	Movies
Plot—the series of events in a story	■ use hundreds of pages to develop the plot ■ often have a main plot and several subplots	■ have to develop a plot quickly ■ often include only one basic plot and no subplots because viewers must be able to follow the story line easily
Characters—people or animals that take part in the action	■ describe and tell the character's life history throughout the book ■ use thoughts, dialogue, and descriptions of action to show a character's personality	■ establish characters quickly through a "defining moment" that helps viewers remember important traits ■ typically use dialogue, body language, facial expressions, and action to show a character's personality
Setting—the time and place of a story	■ often provide many details and history of each setting	■ establish each setting very quickly in one visual shot
Theme—the idea about life that a story reveals	■ often use complex themes that may not be directly told to the reader	■ lead viewers more directly to the theme by using a simpler story line ■ often hint at the theme in dialogue and by use of visual symbols

Make Your Point Choose a book and movie pair. Locate a list of good young-adult books, and take it to a video store or library with you. As you read the book and watch the movie, take notes on how each one handles the four elements of plot, characters, setting, and theme. Consult the chart on page 145 for help. You will use your notes to create a slide presentation that will show your comparison point by point.

Put It on Paper Organize the information in your notes for a slide show. Do this by using a sheet of paper to draft a slide for each of the four elements. For each element, describe any differences you found between the book and the movie made from it. If the element was presented the same way in both the book and the movie, explain their similarities.

Virtually Perfect Rewrite your slide information neatly on sheets of paper. If possible, copy these sheets onto transparency film to show to the class.

You will need to practice explaining your slides and changing from one slide to the next before you give your presentation. Include one to three slides for each of the following items: Introduction, plot, character, setting, theme, and conclusion. An explanation of these elements appears in the next column.

- **Introduction** List the title of the book and the title of the movie if it is different. Then, summarize the story's plot.
- **Plot** Compare the plots of the book and movie by considering both major and minor story events.
- **Character** Consider how the main characters look and act in the book and in the movie.
- **Setting** Consider both the time period and the locations in which the story action happens.
- **Theme** Give examples that support the themes you identify in the book and in the movie.
- **Conclusion** Use the final slide to sum up your overall comparison. Also say whether you would recommend the book, the movie, or both to the audience.

Here is an example of a slide made by a student comparing the book and movie versions of the novel *Little Women.*

Element: Theme

Book: The book stresses the importance of home and family.

Movie: The movie stresses having the courage to be true to yourself.

YOUR TURN 13 Creating a Slide Show Presentation

Follow the above steps to create a slide show. Show your slides to the class, and explain each one as you show it.

Responding to a Poem

When you write your personal response to a poem, you will determine *why* you did or did not like it, much as you did in your book review. This section will explain how to write a response to a poem.

Understanding a Poem Poetry can pack a lot of ideas into just a few words. To respond to a poem, you need to make sense of it first.

Read the following poem, "Growing Up," by Harry Behn, and consider your personal response to it.

Growing Up
By Harry Behn

When I was seven
We went for a picnic
Up to a magic
Foresty place.
I knew there were tigers
Behind every boulder,
Though I didn't meet one
Face to face.

When I was older
We went for a picnic
Up to the very same
Place as before,
And all of the trees
And the rocks were so little
They couldn't hide tigers
Or *me* any more.

You can use the following questions to help you understand a poem. To answer the questions, you may need to read the poem more than once.

- Who are the characters in the poem?
- What are the characters doing?
- Where does the poem take place?
- What does the poem describe?

Here is how one student answered these questions about "Growing Up."

- The character is the speaker, who talks about two visits to a picnic spot.
- As a child, the speaker imagines tigers behind boulders. As an adult, he describes the place as ordinary—the boulders are just rocks.
- The poem takes place in a picnic area with trees and rocks.
- The poem describes the speaker's view of the picnic area, first as a child, then as a grown-up.

Take a Message Once you have an idea about the people, places, or feelings described in the poem, you can think about its message. This message, also called the **theme,** is usually an idea about life. On the next page are one student's thoughts about the message of "Growing Up."

The poem made me think about how different things are when you are a child. Grown-ups wouldn't imagine tigers behind boulders like the seven-year-old did. I think the message about life is that our viewpoints become less magical and more ordinary as we grow up.

Getting Personal Reading a poem is like peeling an orange; it can take some work to get to the good parts. A poem that you did not like at first may become your favorite. Answer these questions to determine your personal response to a poem.

- What words, phrases, or ideas from the poem stick in your mind?
- What about the poem's message could you really understand? What effects do you think this poem might have on other readers?
- Did you like the poem? Why or why not?

Here are one student's answers.

One thing that sticks out is how the speaker believed that tigers were hiding behind the boulders. I remember feeling scared about monsters when I was little.

I can see how visiting a special childhood place later in life would change your view of it. I think most people could relate to the feelings the narrator describes, missing some of the magic of childhood.

I liked the poem. Even though I am not a "grown-up," I can see that I have changed since I was little. For example, I am no longer afraid of monsters.

Get Graphic Graphic organizers can help you get your information and ideas in order. Before writing an essay, it is helpful to make a graphic organizer like the following one to get your ideas on paper.

Introduction
- Give the name and author of the poem.
- Describe what the poem is about.

↓

Body
Explain the poem's message, giving support for your interpretation from the text of the poem.

↓

Conclusion
Describe your personal response to the poem and explain why you feel that way.

Crafting the Draft Finally, turn the ideas in your graphic organizer into a short essay. Try to refer directly to the actual text of the poem at least once. Place the reference in quotation marks, as shown in this example.

I could understand how the seven-year-old felt when he thought there were "tigers behind every boulder."

The model on the next page shows the short essay that the student wrote based on information in the graphic organizer.

A Poet Grows Up

Introduction

In the poem "Growing Up," by Harry Behn, the speaker describes two visits to the same picnic spot. In the first stanza, the speaker is only seven and thinks the place is "a magic foresty place." In the second stanza, however, the speaker is older and everything seems small and ordinary.

Body

The poem's message is that when you grow up, you lose childhood's fears but also childhood's magic. The tigers stand for a child's fear. They also stand for magic, because only by magic could a tiger show up in a park. When the grown-up speaker returns and says "And all of the trees/ And rocks were so little/ They couldn't hide tigers/ Or *me* any more," the poet is saying that childhood fears look small from a grown-up's point of view, but it is also harder to see the magic in things.

Conclusion

I liked this poem. I could understand how the seven-year-old felt when he thought there were "tigers behind every boulder." I remember being afraid of monsters under my bed. I have also grown up some, and I now know those monsters are not real—just like the tigers in this poem.

YOUR TURN 14 Responding to a Poem

- Find a poem you like. Use the questions on pages 147 and 148 to help you understand the poem and form a personal response.
- Create a graphic organizer like the one on page 148 to organize your ideas about the poem. Then, write a first draft of your response. Include at least one quote from the poem in your essay.
- Revise your draft, watching for punctuation and grammar errors. Make sure you explain your feelings about the poem and its message.
- Be prepared to deliver your response orally to your class.

Holding a Panel Discussion

WHAT'S AHEAD?

In this section you will hold a panel discussion. You will also learn how to

- **decide the issues the panel will discuss**
- **practice and present your panel discussion**

Suppose you met a character from a book. What would you say? What questions would you ask? Can you guess how he or she would answer? This activity is your chance to become a character from a book and decide for yourself what that character might do and say. You will do this through a **panel discussion** in which group members portray a book's characters.

Purposes of a Panel Discussion

In a panel discussion people talk about a specific topic. A **moderator** guides the discussion by asking questions and making sure that everyone gets to speak. The purpose of a panel discussion may simply be to provide information, or it may be to create a **forum,** a place for people to express their opinions and ideas. Either way, the goal is to allow panelists and the audience to learn about the topic.

TIP Determine your purpose as a panelist. Whether your purpose is to provide information about the character you portray or to express your ideas and opinions about that character, you should support your comments with evidence and examples from the book. Elaborate on your support to clarify how it relates to your character.

Plan a Panel Discussion of Characters

In a panel discussion of book characters, participants must act the way their characters would act and say things their characters might say. Panel members must study their characters in order to be accurate and believable. Because group members will spend time getting to know a book's characters, the group should choose a book that all members like. Once the book is chosen, members can decide which characters from it would make the most interesting panelists.

Panels usually have four to six members, including the moderator. After everyone has read the book, group members can decide which characters to portray and who will be the moderator.

Get at the Issues The panel should focus on important issues covered in the book. For example, a group discussing Anne Frank's *The Diary of a Young Girl* would include issues such as asking friends to risk their lives to help them and living with so many people in a small place. Each character will have his or her own opinion about the issues. To help identify issues, ask the following questions.

- What conflicts occur within the book? How do different characters react to these conflicts?
- What decisions do the characters have to make in the book? Could different choices be made? What would happen?

Question Everything Once the issues are identified, the group can write questions about the issues for the moderator to ask during the panel presentation. The answers to these questions should offer insight into the characters' thoughts and feelings. For example, the group discussing Anne Frank's diary came up with this question about the issue of hiding: How did it feel to ask someone to take responsibility for hiding you?

TIP As an audience member, determine your purpose for listening. If it is to learn about the book and its characters, ask yourself,

- What major ideas is the character expressing?
- What details support those ideas?
- What is the character's overall message?

If your purpose is to evaluate a panelist, ask these questions, too:

- From whose perspective does the panel member speak? Is he or she believable in that role?
- What is the panel member's purpose, and does he or she fulfill it?

Present the Panel Discussion

Once group members are familiar with the questions they will be asked and have had a chance to do any research needed, your group is ready to present your discussion to an audience. Each member of the panel has specific responsibilities.

The moderator should	Panelists should
▪ introduce panel members and ask questions	▪ stay in character at all times
▪ give everyone a chance to speak	▪ answer each question as the character would
▪ take questions from the audience at the end of the discussion	▪ get involved in the discussion

YOUR TURN 15 Presenting a Panel Discussion

Follow the above steps to form a panel discussion of characters from a book. Present the discussion to an audience, and be prepared to answer audience members' questions after the discussion.

Producing a Scene from a Book

WHAT'S AHEAD?

In this section you will produce a scene from a book. You will also learn how to

- **choose a good scene**
- **write a script**
- **organize actors and help them rehearse**

As you read a book that you really like, do you ever imagine what it would look like up on the big screen or on stage? Do you imagine famous actors in the roles of the characters?

Producing a scene does not require professional producers, directors, and actors. With the help of a few classmates, you can do it yourself. Adapting a scene from a book for performance does, however, require a good script, an understanding of the characters, and productive rehearsals.

Choose a Scene

A good script begins with the right book and the right *scene.* A **scene** is a short story, incident, or episode that occurs within the main story. Choose a book that you like and that has scenes that are already vivid in your mind. You will want to capture your audience's attention, so your scene should have an interesting plot and characters.

A good scene to use will have the following characteristics.

- three or fewer characters
- characters, conflict, and action that will make sense to someone who has not read the book
- a definite beginning and end
- manageable setting and props

When you decide on your scene, type it up or make a photocopy of those pages from the book so that you can study it and make notes without marking directly on the book.

Study the Characters

Good actors get to know the characters they will portray. How do they do this? They might jot down notes about their characters' personalities, hobbies, habits, likes, and dislikes. Actors should also have an idea about how their characters should look and dress. Below are notes made by students for a scene from Anne Frank's *The Diary of a Young Girl.*

Anne Frank	Peter Van Daan
▪ talkative, but thoughtful and smart ▪ writes in her diary all the time ▪ diary would be good prop ▪ has outgrown all her clothes, so they are a little too small	▪ shy, awkward, and studious ▪ loves his cat ▪ cat and school books would be good props ▪ wears a sweater

TIP If you choose a book that has previously been dramatized, like *The Diary of a Young Girl,* be sure to make your version unique. Do not just mimic someone else's work.

Write the Scene

A **script** includes the lines the actors speak and the stage directions that tell them how to act and move. To get from paragraphs in a book to a script, you must convert the story from paragraphs to dialogue and stage directions. You can use the following guidelines to convert your scene.

- Any words that appear in quotation marks will become dialogue in your script. Remove the quotation marks and all the *he said*'s and *she said*'s.
- You may cut dialogue if it refers to actions or characters that are not important to the scene.
- You may also add to the dialogue to make the scene move more smoothly or to include information important to the scene. Remember to stay true to the scene and the characters.

Skim through the scene for clues to help you include the **stage directions,** which are instructions that tell actors where to stand and how to say a line. Convert this information into a direction, as in the example on the following page.

Book:	. . . when I was rummaging around in the crate of books in the attic, Peter came up and began telling me what had happened.
Stage directions:	Anne is looking through a crate of books in the attic. Peter enters.

Stage directions that set the scene should appear before a character's lines. Those that briefly describe an action or emotion should be placed in parentheses after the character's name.

Anne is looking through a crate of books in the attic. Peter enters.

ANNE: *(Looking up)* Peter, what's wrong?

PETER: Well, it's like this. I don't usually talk much, since I know beforehand I'll just be tongue-tied. *(He pauses, then continues.)* I start stuttering and blushing. . . .

Rehearse

TIP You may want to **produce a videotape** of your scene instead of presenting it live. If so, select a producer to coordinate the video production, and a camera operator.

Your group will need to create a **storyboard** showing the action and camera angle for each shot in the scene. After rehearsing each shot, have the camera operator tape the scene, one shot at a time. Review the tape and reshoot the scene if necessary.

Once your script is ready and you have chosen a cast, plan a rehearsal schedule to complete these steps.

1. Actors read through the script together.
2. Actors make notes about their characters' feelings and actions.
3. Actors rehearse the scene several times. Memorizing the lines helps create a more effective scene.
4. In rehearsal, the actors work with props and practice moving and standing so that the audience can see them.
5. Actors practice the scene until it becomes completely natural.

YOUR TURN 16 Performing a Scene from a Book

Find a scene from a book that you would like to adapt for performance. Write a script, find actors, rehearse the scene with them, and perform your adaptation for an audience.

Choices

Choose one of the following activities to complete.

▶ CROSSING THE CURRICULUM: MATH

1. On a Scale from 1 to 10
One way to evaluate a product is to ask people to rate it. Choose a product, like toothpaste, corn flakes, or hair gel, that your friends, family members, or neighbors use. Ask ten to twenty people to rate the product with a system you develop, such as four stars for "the best" and no stars for "the worst." Determine the percentage of people who gave the product each rating, such as "50 percent gave it four stars." Present your findings to the class as an **oral presentation.** If possible, include visuals, such as pictures of the product or a pie chart.

▶ LITERATURE

2. A Creative Outlet Plan a creative response to a novel, short story, poem, or other work of literature. Your response—in the form of a song, dance, poem, or work of art—should make clear the most important ideas or impressions you got from the work. Share your response with others in a brief **presentation.**

▶ SPEECH

3. Y'all Come Back Now! If you have ever encountered a character in a book who calls a water fountain a "bubbler," you know that people use words differently in various parts of the country. Choose several **regional sayings or labels** to research. Find out where in the United States people use these expressions and the origin or significance of each expression. Create a **visual** (possibly a U.S. map with labels) showing regional differences, and give a **speech** explaining your findings.

▶ WRITING

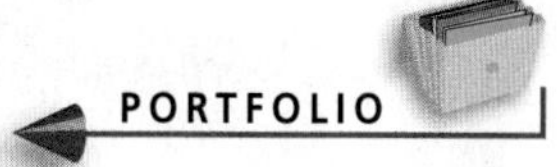

4. Please, Mr. Postman
Share your ideas about books with a friend through e-mail or regular mail. In a **letter,** tell a friend about a book you read recently that you either enjoyed or hated. Why was this book so good or so awful? Be sure to tell your friend why he or she should read or avoid the book. Keep a copy of the letter you send, and share parts of it and parts of the reply you receive with your class.

5 Reporting Your Research

Reading Workshop

Reading an Informative Web Site

Writing Workshop

Writing a Research Report

Viewing and Representing

Designing a Web Site

Informational Text

Exposition

Think of the word *investigator.* Do you see someone in a Sherlock Holmes hat slinking around with a magnifying glass? The title *investigator* applies to many people, not just famous detectives. Scientists investigate plants and animals. Journalists investigate possible news stories. You investigate when you want to know about an interesting person or event. Often, investigators publish what they have learned in informative texts such as books, articles, or Web sites.

Informative texts provide readers, viewers, or listeners with new information. You see informative texts based on research in many places—in magazines, on television, or on the Internet, for example. These research pieces help you satisfy your curiosity and learn more about your world.

YOUR TURN 1 Discovering Informative Texts

With a small group of classmates, discuss the following questions.

- How do you find information about things that interest you?
- Are some forms of information (books, videos, Web sites) easier for you to understand than others? Which ones? Why?
- Why is it sometimes difficult to understand new information? (Think about unfamiliar words and new concepts.)

internetconnect
go.hrw.com
GO TO: go.hrw.com
KEYWORD: EOLang 8-5

Reading an Informative Web Site

WHAT'S AHEAD?

In this section you will read an informative Web site. You will also learn how to

- **distinguish between fact and opinion**
- **analyze the structure of an informative Web site**

Aliens invade Earth. A gigantic ship sinks in the middle of the ocean. Huge grasshoppers roam the countryside. When movie directors need to create scenes like these, they often rely on computer animators. The following selections from an informative Web site contain information about animation and *synthespians.* **Synthespians** are characters created digitally, that is, on a computer. As you read, consider whether the information seems well organized, and watch for statements of fact and opinion.

Preparing to Read

READING SKILL

Fact and Opinion **Facts** are statements that can be proved true. A fact can always be confirmed by another source. An **opinion** is someone's belief about something. No source can prove an opinion true or false. Informative writing, such as the following Web site, presents many facts and sometimes a few opinions about a subject. As you read the Web site, consider whether each statement you read could be proved by another source.

READING FOCUS

Informative Web Site Structure A good Web site has a carefully planned **structure,** or organization. Readers navigating a Web site should be able to find the information they need quickly. Web sites help readers find information by providing **links** that allow readers to move from one section of the site to another. Notice how the following Web site is structured to help you find the information you need.

Reading Selection

Read the following selections from a Web site. As you read, write down the answers to the numbered active-reading questions in the shaded boxes. Highlighted words will be used in the Vocabulary Mini-Lesson on page 167.

1. Which of the links below would you click to see an overview of the entire NOVA site?

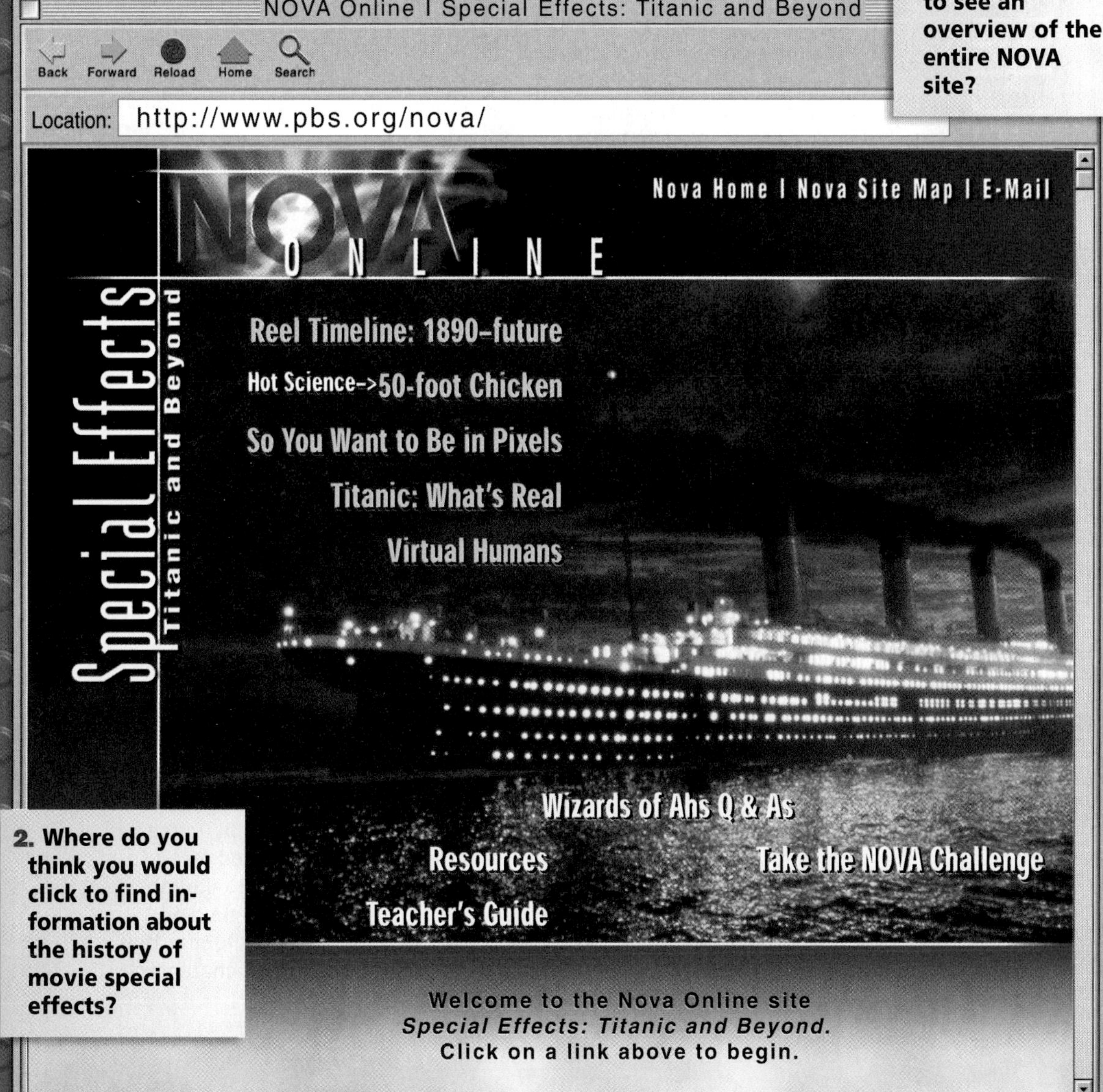

2. Where do you think you would click to find information about the history of movie special effects?

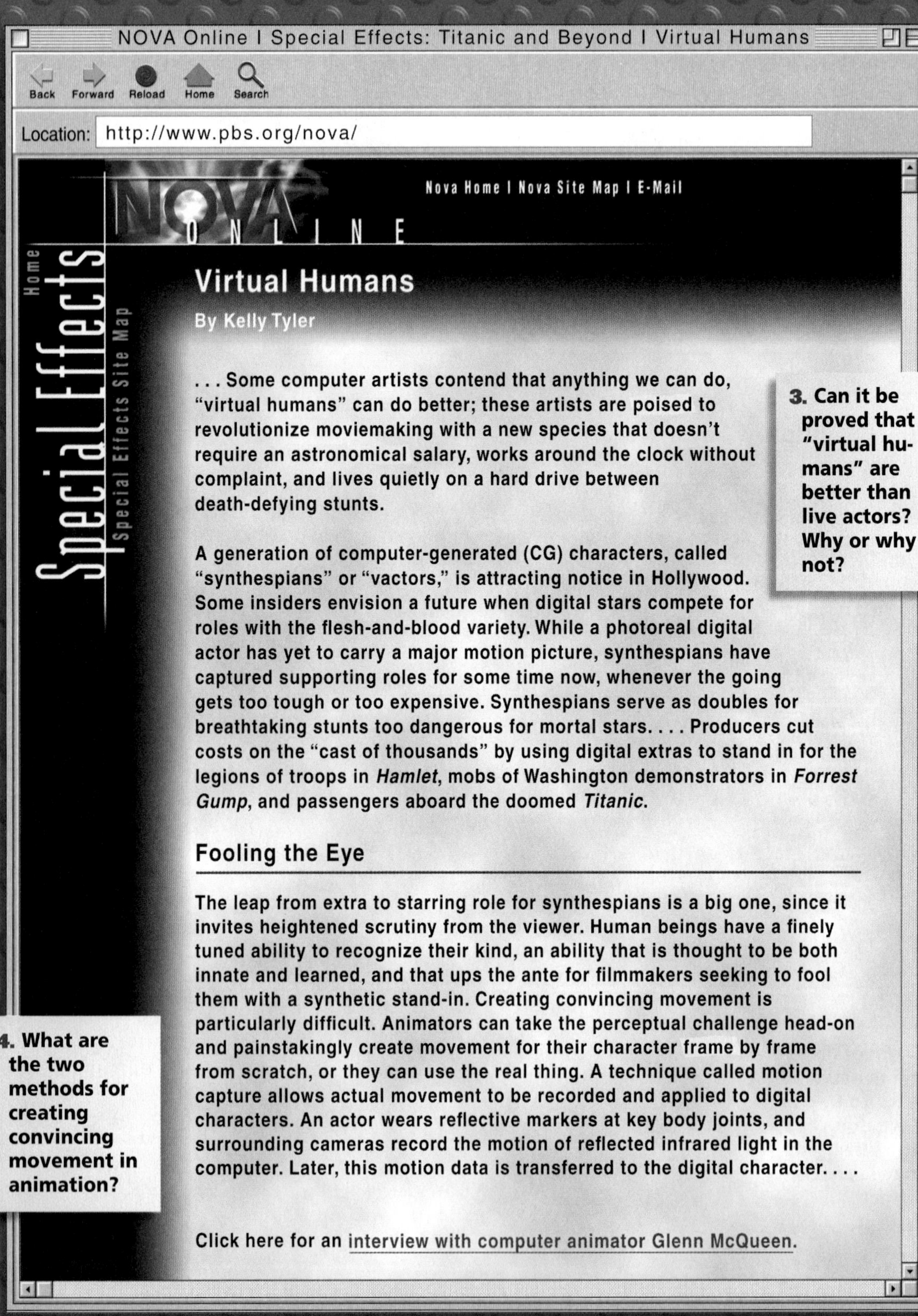

Virtual Humans

By Kelly Tyler

. . . Some computer artists contend that anything we can do, "virtual humans" can do better; these artists are poised to revolutionize moviemaking with a new species that doesn't require an astronomical salary, works around the clock without complaint, and lives quietly on a hard drive between death-defying stunts.

3. Can it be proved that "virtual humans" are better than live actors? Why or why not?

A generation of computer-generated (CG) characters, called "synthespians" or "vactors," is attracting notice in Hollywood. Some insiders envision a future when digital stars compete for roles with the flesh-and-blood variety. While a photoreal digital actor has yet to carry a major motion picture, synthespians have captured supporting roles for some time now, whenever the going gets too tough or too expensive. Synthespians serve as doubles for breathtaking stunts too dangerous for mortal stars. . . . Producers cut costs on the "cast of thousands" by using digital extras to stand in for the legions of troops in *Hamlet*, mobs of Washington demonstrators in *Forrest Gump*, and passengers aboard the doomed *Titanic*.

Fooling the Eye

The leap from extra to starring role for synthespians is a big one, since it invites heightened scrutiny from the viewer. Human beings have a finely tuned ability to recognize their kind, an ability that is thought to be both innate and learned, and that ups the ante for filmmakers seeking to fool them with a synthetic stand-in. Creating convincing movement is particularly difficult. Animators can take the perceptual challenge head-on and painstakingly create movement for their character frame by frame from scratch, or they can use the real thing. A technique called motion capture allows actual movement to be recorded and applied to digital characters. An actor wears reflective markers at key body joints, and surrounding cameras record the motion of reflected infrared light in the computer. Later, this motion data is transferred to the digital character. . . .

4. What are the two methods for creating convincing movement in animation?

Click here for an interview with computer animator Glenn McQueen.

NOVA Online | Special Effects: Titanic and Beyond | Glenn McQueen

Back Forward Reload Home Search

Location: http://www.pbs.org/nova/

5. Which link would take you from this page back to the Special Effects home page?

Nova Home | Nova Site Map | E-Mail

Special Effects

Home

Special Effects Site Map

An Interview with Computer Animator

Glenn McQueen

Glenn McQueen

NOVA: How does the animation process happen?

GM: First, the art department and director design the models, first on paper, then in the computer—think of them as being puppets in the computer. You can look at this character from any point of view. There's sort of a virtual camera that lives in the computer, and you can position that anywhere around the character and look at it from any point of view. One of the first things we do as animators is test these models to make sure that they have the flexibility to make them act. Whether the character is a grasshopper or a spaceman, you're probably going to want the elbow to bend and the wrist to bend. You want the head to twist and move up and down. It's the visual and the technical people working together, every now and then having to compromise a little bit, but to come up with the best character solution for what we're going to need in the film. . . .

NOVA: What part of a film do you contribute?

GM: Each animator is given a series of shots in the film. Every time the camera changes, it's a different shot. Hopefully, they're consecutive shots so you can keep the continuity going from one shot to the next. All the dialogue is prerecorded before the animators ever get the shots. So we listen to the dialogue again and again. We act it out. We do thumbnail sketches. We videotape ourselves acting it out. Essentially the animator is sort of a mute actor. We have to use someone else's line, but what the body does, how the character moves during that line, how many gestures, what the facial expression is, is entirely up to the animator. . . .

6. How does McQueen support the statement that an animator is "sort of a mute actor"?

First Thoughts on Your Reading

1. **Do you think that most of the statements in this Web site could be checked in other sources? What kinds of sources might you check?**
2. **Do you think this Web site is organized in a way that makes sense? Why or why not?**

READING SKILL

Fact and Opinion

Prove It! Informative writing is full of *facts.* A characteristic of reliable informative pieces is that they contain more facts than opinions. **Facts** can be proved true. Look at the examples below.

- *The moon orbits Earth.* Astronomy textbooks confirm that the moon is in orbit around our world.
- *George Washington was the first president of the United States.* Historical documents verify that George Washington was our nation's first president.
- *The boiling point of water is 100 degrees Celsius.* Experiments show that water always boils at 100 degrees Celsius at sea level.

An **opinion,** on the other hand, is a judgment about something. It cannot be proved true or false. The clues in the chart below can help you tell the difference between facts and opinions as you read.

Opinion Clues	Examples
Statements that make a judgment about the quality of something are often opinions.	*Killer Chickens from Mars* is the **best** movie to come out of Hollywood all year.
Statements containing words and phrases such as *should* or *I think* are often opinions.	Students **should** always do their homework before dinner. **I think** it is important to do your homework soon after school.

Read the paragraph on the next page, and see if you can identify the facts and opinions in it. If you are unsure whether a particular statement is a fact or an opinion, use the Thinking It Through steps that follow the paragraph to help you.

They look clumsy today. Still, the special effects of 1950s science fiction movies were truly state of the art. Many science fiction movies of that decade depicted flying saucers or alien invasions. Some movies, such as *When Worlds Collide* and *Destination Moon*, even won Academy Awards for their effects. The audiences of the 1950s were less sophisticated and more easily impressed than today's moviegoers.

THINKING IT THROUGH — Identifying Fact and Opinion

Here is how to tell whether a statement is a fact or an opinion. The statement below is from the paragraph you just read.

> Some movies, such as *When Worlds Collide* and *Destination Moon*, even won Academy Awards for their effects.

STEP 1 Answer the following questions about the statement.

- Does it express a judgment? — *No, it doesn't say whether the movies were good or not.*
- Does it use words such as *should* or *I think*? — *It doesn't use the words "should" or "I think."*
- Does it use words that have very negative or positive meanings? — *It doesn't use words that have strong negative or positive meanings.*

If you answer "Yes" to any of these questions, the statement may be an opinion.

STEP 2 Ask yourself if you can prove the statement true. If you answer "Yes," the statement is a fact. If you answer "No," it is an opinion. — *Yes. One way I can prove the statement is by looking in a movie history book. The statement is a fact.*

YOUR TURN 2 Identifying Fact and Opinion

Use the Thinking It Through steps on the previous page to identify three statements of fact and two statements of opinion in the reading selection on pages 159–161. For each statement you choose, do the following.

- First, write the statement on your paper.
- Then, write "fact" or "opinion" after the statement.
- Finally, write a sentence explaining how you can tell whether the statement is a fact or an opinion.

TIP Web sites can be excellent sources of information, but not all Web sites are trustworthy. Unreliable Web sites may contain opinions or false information expressed as facts. Some false statements, such as a claim that the earth is flat, may be easy to prove wrong. Other false statements may be harder to spot.

Whenever you use information from the Internet, consider the source and when the Web site was last updated. The most reliable Web sites are produced by universities, government agencies, mainstream news organizations, and established nonprofit groups. They also contain the most recent facts or findings.

More Reliable Source	A site about sloths produced by the San Diego Zoo
Less Reliable Source	A report on sloths posted on the Wolf Trap Elementary School Web site by a fourth-grade student
More Reliable Source	A U.S. Geological Survey site about volcanoes
Less Reliable Source	Your neighbor's Web site about volcanoes he has seen

READING FOCUS

Informative Web Site Structure

Putting the Pieces Together Good construction is an important part of what makes an item useful. You would have a hard time riding a bike held together with tape. You would also have trouble using a poorly constructed Web site. What makes a well-constructed Web site?

Reference Note

For more on **evaluating Web sites,** see page 777 in the Quick Reference Handbook.

Logical Organization Informative Web sites usually provide several types of information about a topic. In order for readers to find the exact information they need, facts, explanations, and illustrations must be presented in a way that makes sense. The creator of a Web site must organize this information into categories.

The main categories of a Web site are usually listed on the **home page,** the first page of a Web site. For example, the home page for an informative Web site about music might include categories like the ones in the diagram below.

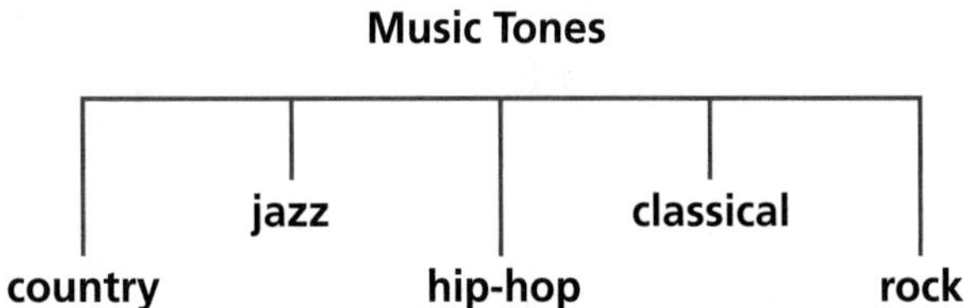

Linked Information The categories in the diagram above represent *links* on the Web site's home page. **Links** connect the pages of a Web site. When you click your mouse on a link, you go to another location. For example, if you clicked on the jazz link, you might connect to a page within the Music Tones Web site that has information about jazz artists. There you might find links to more pages within the Music Tones Web site or links to other related Web sites, such as a record company site that includes audio clips. Links usually show up as underlined words printed in a different color from the surrounding text.

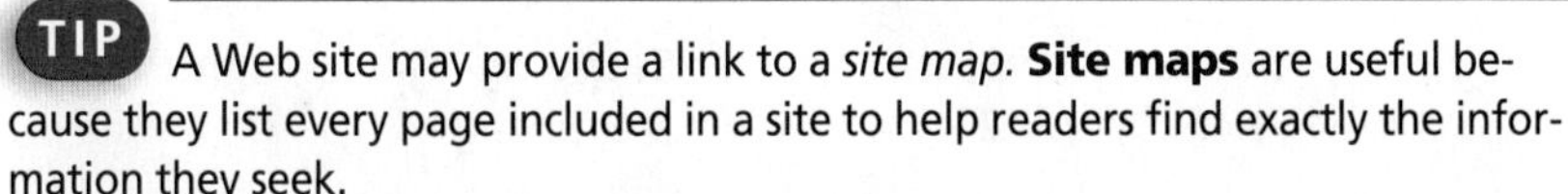

TIP A Web site may provide a link to a *site map.* **Site maps** are useful because they list every page included in a site to help readers find exactly the information they seek.

Which Way? Because a Web site is made up of links that lead to more links, two people are unlikely to read the same site in exactly the same way. When you read information on the Internet, you choose which links to follow based on your **purpose,** or on what you want to know. Because you choose your own path through a Web site, you will sometimes make "wrong turns" leading to pages that do not give you the information you are seeking. However, you can limit the number of wrong turns you take if you keep your purpose in mind as you read.

As you navigate a Web site, try to predict the type of information to which each link will lead. The flowchart on the next page shows how a student might navigate a Web site about special effects. The student's purpose is to find instructions for creating special effects with a handheld video camera.

After starting at the home page, the student

- checked the Web site's definition for special effects against her own (1 and 2)
- followed the link Lights, Camera, Action, looking for information on camera effects (3 and 4); she did not find what she wanted
- tried the home page's third link, which also sounded promising (5); this link did lead to useful information (6 and 7)

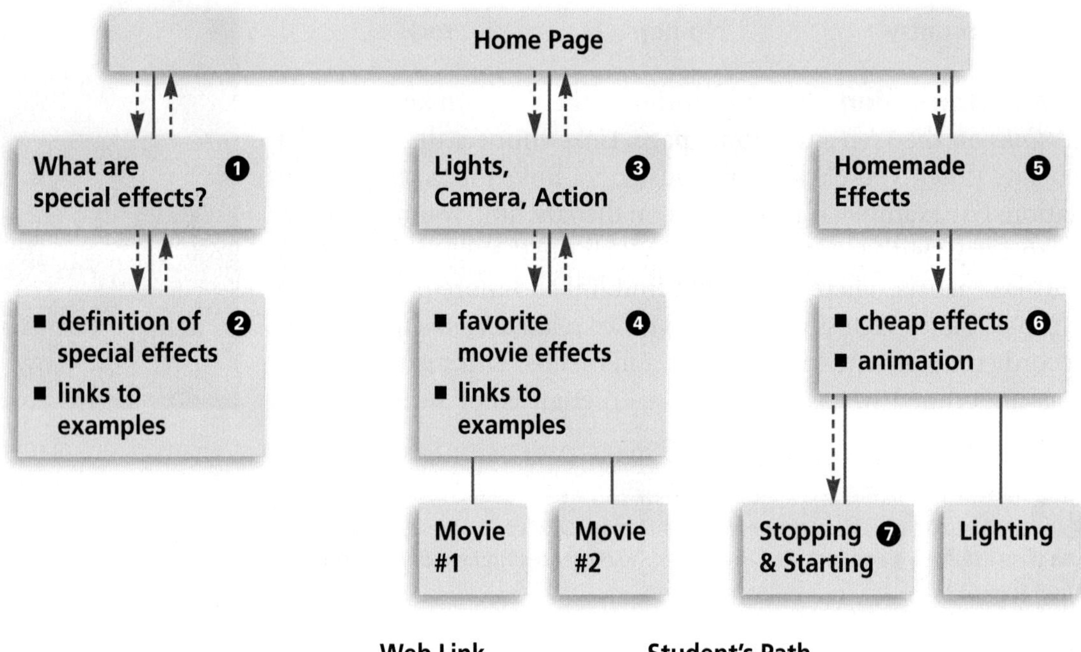

YOUR TURN 3 Creating a Flowchart of a Web Site

Use the following steps to map the organization of the special effects Web site on pages 159–161.

- Create a flowchart of the site using the example flowchart above and the links shown on the three pages of the reading selection. Show links between pages of the site by drawing lines between the boxes in your flowchart. Your completed flowchart will have three or four levels. (The example above has four levels.)
- Re-read the selection, and map the path you took through the information.

MINI-LESSON **VOCABULARY**

Words with Multiple Meanings

When you read an informative text, you may see a word that has a different meaning from the one you are used to seeing. This can make a whole passage confusing. As you read, watch for words that have **multiple meanings,** such as *lap.*

- I ran a *lap* around the track at school.
- My dog will *lap* water out of my hand.

To choose the correct meaning of a word, consider the word's part of speech and its **context,** the words and sentences around it. (For more on **parts of speech,** see page 344.)

THINKING IT THROUGH

Understanding Multiple-Meaning Words

Here is an example using the word *astronomical* from the reading selection.

STEP 1 Use a dictionary to look up all the meanings of the word. Eliminate any that are the wrong part of speech for the sentence.

(1) related to astronomy; (2) unusually [or very] large. The word is used as an adjective in the sentence. Both definitions fit the part of speech.

STEP 2 Plug each remaining meaning into the sentence in place of the word. Start with definitions that fit the context in which the word is used.

- . . . they're poised to revolutionize moviemaking with a new species that doesn't require an (related to astronomy) salary. . . .
- . . . they're poised to revolutionize moviemaking with a new species that doesn't require an (unusually large) salary. . . .

STEP 3 Pick the meaning that makes the most sense in the sentence.

The sentence is talking about unusually large salaries, not astronomy.

PRACTICE

Figure out the meaning of each word to the right as it is used in the reading selection. Write the correct meaning of each word followed by its other definitions in parentheses. Finally, write a sentence after each set of definitions explaining why the meaning you chose is correct.

1. poised (page 160)
2. frame (page 160)
3. virtual (page 161)
4. thumbnail (page 161)
5. expression (page 161)

MINI-LESSON **TEST TAKING**

Fact vs. Opinion

Reading tests often ask you to identify facts and opinions in reading passages. How might you approach the following passage and question on a test?

> Movies have used special effects since film's beginnings in the late nineteenth century. In the 1895 movie *The Execution of Mary Queen of Scots*, audiences saw an actress "beheaded" on screen through an effect called a substitution shot. During substitution, the camera was stopped while a headless dummy replaced the actress. The camera was started again, making it appear that the actress had actually lost her head. The substitution shot is a crude and awkward technique, but it was exciting to audiences in 1895.

Which of the following is an OPINION expressed in this passage?

A. Present-day special effects are much better than effects created without modern technology.

B. Viewers of *The Execution of Mary Queen of Scots* saw an actress "beheaded" on screen.

C. The substitution shot is a basic and clumsy technique.

D. Movies have used special effects since the late nineteenth century.

THINKING IT THROUGH

Identifying Fact and Opinion

STEP 1 Read the question and decide whether it asks for a statement of fact or a statement of opinion.

The question asks me to find a statement of opinion. That means I should look for a statement that can't be proved.

STEP 2 Read each of the answer choices. If the question asks for a fact, cross out any statement that cannot be proved. If it asks for an opinion, cross out any statement that can be proved.

B and D are facts because you can prove that they are true by checking an almanac or film history book. I'll cross them out.

STEP 3 Re-read the answer choices that are left. Try to locate the answer choices in the passage. The choices might be worded differently than in the passage.

A talks about technology and special effects. The passage doesn't mention technology. C talks about a substitution shot, which is in the passage.

STEP 4 Choose the best answer.

C is the best answer because it is an opinion that is stated in the passage.

Writing a Research Report

WHAT'S AHEAD?

In this workshop you will write a research report. You will also learn how to

- **ask research questions**
- **find sources and take notes**
- **paraphrase ideas**
- **eliminate wordiness**
- **cite sources correctly**

"I wonder . . ." Some of the most interesting journeys ever made have started with those two words. It is natural to be filled with curiosity about the world around you. As you go through school and on to college or a career, you will frequently encounter subjects that excite your curiosity. When you come across a topic that grabs you, dig in and research!

Writing a research report is a great way to go below the surface of a topic. In this workshop you will write a research report on a topic of your choice. Your report will present information to your readers in a clear and concise way.

Prewriting

Choose a Subject

Endless Possibilities What will you research? The possibilities are truly endless. You should pick a subject you will not mind spending quite a bit of time reading, thinking, and writing about. Begin by brainstorming a list of subjects that interest you.

Below is one student's list of possible subjects to research. After brainstorming and getting his ideas on paper, he could choose two or three subjects that he wanted to consider in greater depth.

basketball	recording music	Borneo
World War II	martial arts	tropical fish

Reference Note

For more on **generating ideas,** see page 839 in the Quick Reference Handbook.

Getting Down to Business Now that you have thought of some possible subjects, evaluate the most interesting ones. Not every subject will work for a research report. **A good subject must involve research.** In other words, you will need to choose a subject that is not well-known to you. A good subject is also one that is interesting or important to many people. To help you choose the best subject, ask yourself the questions in the chart below.

KEY CONCEPT

Possible Subject: World War II	
Can I find enough facts about this subject? Where?	Yes. There are books, Web sites, videos, and other information about World War II.
Will I be able to get the information I need in time?	Yes. All of this information is available either at the school library or my neighborhood library.
Can I make this subject interesting to others?	Yes. It is an important part of history.

After evaluating his most interesting possible subjects, the student chose to write about World War II because he answered yes to all three questions about it.

Narrow Your Subject

TIP You may be able to narrow your subject based on your own prior knowledge. However, if you need to know more about your subject in order to narrow it, read an encyclopedia article or a general Web page.

Getting It into Focus If you tried to write a research report on the subject of astronomy, you would soon find you had written a book. By focusing on a narrow topic, such as asteroids in our solar system, you can write a shorter, more detailed report.

To narrow your subject, consider its individual parts. Ask yourself, "How can I break this subject into topics?" You will choose one topic to explain in your report. This topic should be broad enough that you can find information about it, but narrow enough that you could not write a whole book about it.

The student who chose to write about World War II narrowed his subject by using a cluster diagram to think about focused topics having to do with World War II. His cluster diagram is shown on the next page.

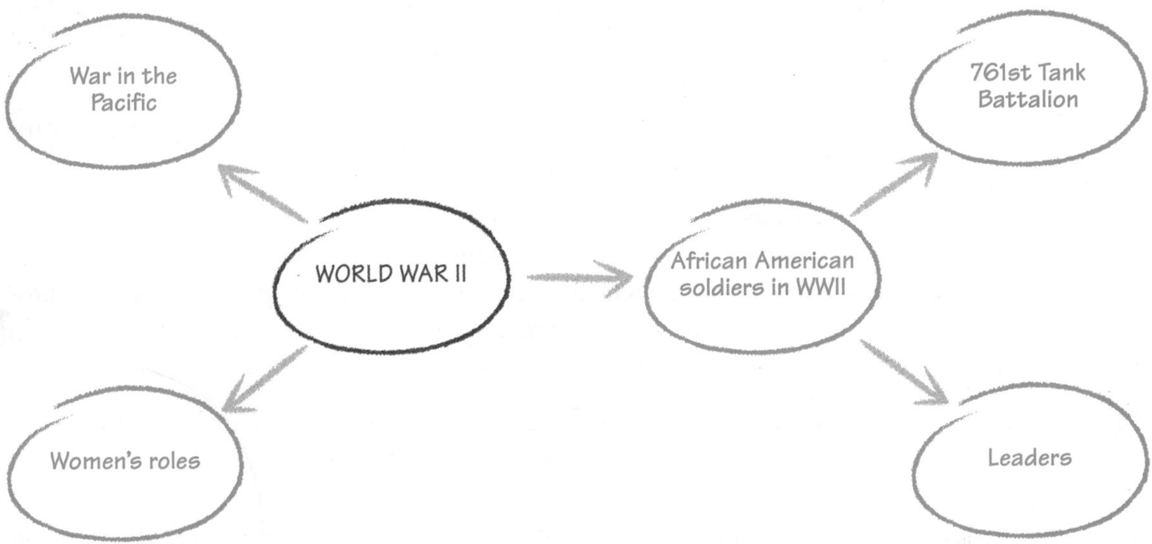

My focused topic is the 761st Tank Battalion.

YOUR TURN 4 Choosing and Narrowing a Subject

- Brainstorm a list of several possible subjects.
- Then, evaluate your most interesting ideas by answering the questions in the chart on page 170, and select a subject to research.
- Use a cluster diagram to narrow this subject into individual parts, and identify one part that you could explain well in a research report.
- Write your focused topic in the form of a statement:

  My focused topic is ____.

Reference Note

For more on **clustering** and other ways to generate ideas, see page 839 in the Quick Reference Handbook.

TIP Research reports are not built in a day! Make a schedule to budget your time. Include these six items on your schedule.

- Develop a research question and find information on your topic (allow 10% of your total time).
- Take notes (25% of total time).
- Write your main idea statement and create an outline (15%).
- Write a first draft, including your Works Cited list (25%).
- Evaluate and revise your first draft (15%).
- Proofread, rewrite if necessary, and publish your report (10%).

Think About Purpose and Audience

Getting Your Message Across Once you have chosen a focused topic, you can begin thinking about how you want to communicate your ideas.

KEY CONCEPT

Purpose The main purpose of a research report is to share what you have discovered about your topic. You will not just put together a collection of facts, though. **Instead, your research report should be a balanced mixture of information you have found and conclusions you have drawn about your topic.**

TIP Your audience should find your research report informative and truthful. To achieve a credible **voice,** write your report from the third-person point of view. That means you should report the facts objectively without using the pronoun *I*.

Audience As you write a research report, it is important to communicate clearly with your audience. For your report, imagine that your readers are about your age and not experts on your topic. You can assume that your readers will know some general information about your topic, but do not make the mistake of thinking that they will know the specifics. Ask yourself these questions to help you communicate with your audience.

- What does my audience already know about my topic?
- What does my audience need to know to understand my topic?
- What else will my audience want to know about my topic?

YOUR TURN 5 Thinking About Purpose and Audience

To help you share with an audience the information you learn, jot down answers to the questions above.

Develop a Research Question

KEY CONCEPT

Funny You Should Ask . . . If the photographer Eadweard Muybridge had never wondered whether a series of movements could be captured on film, we might not be able to watch videos today. One simple question led to an important discovery. **All research begins with a question.** In your own research, a question will give you a purpose for reading and exploring the sources you find. Your research question will guide your research, just as Muybridge's question guided his.

I Wonder . . . To develop a broad research question, you might begin with many specific questions. You can start with the *5W-How?* questions (*Who? What? When? Where? Why?* and *How?*). Write down everything you want to know about your topic, and try to write at least one question for each of the five *W*s and *How*. Here are questions the student writing about the 761st Tank Battalion asked.

> How did the 761st Tank Battalion form?
>
> Who commanded the 761st?
>
> Where did the soldiers of the 761st train and fight?
>
> How many soldiers fought with the 761st Tank Battalion?
>
> When did they begin fighting battles?
>
> What did the 761st Tank Battalion do during World War II?
>
> What kinds of discrimination did these soldiers face?

The Big Question You will need to choose one question that will guide your entire research project. This guiding question will help you keep your project focused and on track. In looking over your list of questions, you may find that you already have a question that might lead to answers for many of the others. The student writing about the 761st Tank Battalion realized that researching the question, "What did the 761st Tank Battalion do during World War II?" would probably lead him to answers for most of the other questions on his list. He chose that as his research question.

TIP Some questions can lead to a dead end in your research. "Dead-end" questions can be answered with a word or a sentence. For example, the question, "How many soldiers fought with the 761st Tank Battalion?" can be answered with a number.

An open-ended question such as, "What did the 761st Tank Battalion do during World War II?" can lead you to a paragraph, chapter, or even an entire book of information.

YOUR TURN 6 Developing a Research Question

To develop a question to guide your research, follow these steps.

- Brainstorm several questions using the *5W-How?* technique. It may help to begin by reading general information about your topic.
- Re-read your list of questions. Look for a "big picture" question that will lead to answers for many of your other questions. If your list does not contain a broad question, write one that will lead to answers for most of your questions.

Find and Evaluate Sources

TIP Another source you may consult is an expert on your topic. You might arrange an interview with that person or plan to listen to a presentation he or she is giving.

Get to the Source You can find sources of information everywhere, from your school library to your community video store. Two types of sources you can use are *primary sources* and *secondary sources.* **Primary sources** are documents and records that contain first-hand knowledge, such as maps, diaries, and letters. **Secondary sources** are interpretations of primary materials produced by others. They include encyclopedia entries, newspaper articles, and documentaries.

Searching the World Wide Web The World Wide Web can be an excellent source of information. First, though, you need to locate sites on your topic. To find useful Web sites, use a **search engine,** a Web site that helps you search for sites that have information on a specific topic. To use a search engine, you will enter a **keyword,** an important word or phrase that identifies your topic.

Basic keyword searches often find a large number of sites. Some sites will fit your purpose, but many others will not. To get sources **relevant,** or related, to your topic, you can limit your search by using the words *AND* and *NOT* or by using quotation marks. Here is how these limiters can affect the results of a search.

COMPUTER TIP

If you don't find the information you need with the first keyword you try, brainstorm other keywords. For example, if you don't find useful sites for a report about making movies using the keyword *moviemaking,* you might try *filmmaking* or *movie production.*

Search Term	Results
military segregation	Some search engines will give you sites that mention one or both of the words in the search term. You may wind up with everything from sites on age segregation in schools to the U.S. Army home page.
military AND segregation	This term will find only sites that include both the words *military* and *segregation*. These sites may provide useful information, but the listing will still have off-topic sites, such as an article on military academies admitting female students.
"military segregation"	This term will find only sites that use these two words together in this order. This search will mainly find information on the segregation of women and minorities in the military.
"military segregation" NOT women	This search will find the same sites as the search above, but will leave out those concerning women. This will provide a short list of sites about racial segregation in the military.

A Closer Look Because some sources may contain out-of-date information or mistakes, you should evaluate each of your sources. For example, even after limiting a World Wide Web search, do not automatically accept all of the information you find. The Internet is a wonderful research tool, but no one checks the accuracy of every site that is posted. To get reliable information, stick to sites created by authoritative sources. Sites with addresses ending in *.org* (non-profit organizations), *.edu* (educational institutions), and *.gov* (U.S. government agencies) are good places to start. Because you will need to investigate all aspects of your topic, though, you will probably need to look beyond these sources.

You can evaluate any source, print or nonprint, by answering the questions in the following Thinking It Through.

Reference Note

For more on **evaluating Web sites,** see page 777 in the Quick Reference Handbook.

THINKING IT THROUGH: Evaluating Sources

STEP 1 Is the source nonfiction? Do not use stories or novels as sources for a factual report.	Yes. The book <u>Black Fighting Men</u> is a nonfiction book. It has facts about African American soldiers.
STEP 2 Is the information current? Topics in rapidly changing fields require up-to-date sources. For historical topics, finding the latest information is not essential.	The book was published in 1994. Since my topic, the 761st Tank Battalion, concerns the 1940s, this information is current enough.
STEP 3 Is the information trustworthy? Whether the source is a primary or secondary source, you should be able to verify all of the facts with other sources. Avoid strongly biased sources.	Yes, my source is trustworthy. Another book about the 761st confirms some of the information in the book. The information should be reliable.

Making a List You should list any sources you might use. Formal research reports require a detailed list of sources used called a Works Cited list. You will need to list these sources in alphabetical order, using Modern Language Association, or MLA, style (as shown on the next page). Listing information about your sources now will save you the trouble of going back and finding it later.

MLA Guide for Listing Sources	
Encyclopedia article	Author (if listed). "Title of Article." Name of Encyclopedia. Year or edition. Hornsby, Alton, Jr. "Black Americans." World Book Encyclopedia. 1995.
Book	Author/Editor. Title. City: Publisher, year. Reef, Catherine. Black Fighting Men: A Proud History. New York: Twenty-First Century Books, 1994.
Magazine or newspaper article	Author. "Title of Article." Publication Name Date: page number(s). Ringle, Ken. "For Black Soldiers, an Overdue Honor; Seven Cited for Valor in World War II." The Washington Post 14 Jan. 1997: A1.
Interview or guest speaker	Speaker. Personal interview/Telephone interview/Guest speaker. Date. McConnell, E. G. Guest speaker. 15 Aug. 2000.
Television or radio program	"Title of Episode." Title of Program. Network. Station Call Letters, City. Date of broadcast. "Belated Honor." Newshour. PBS. KUSD, Vermillion. 13 Jan. 1997.
Movie or video recording	Title. Name of Director (Dir.) or Producer (Pro.). Name of Distributor, year released. African Americans in WWII: A Legacy of Patriotism and Valor. Pro. Department of Defense. OnDeck Home Entertainment, 1998.
Electronic sources	**Online** Author (if known). "Document Title." Web Site or Database Title. Date of electronic publication. Name of Sponsoring Institution. Date information was accessed <URL>. "Remarks by the President at the Presentation of United States Medals of Honor, The White House." Veterans Outlook. March/April 1997. BRAVO. 28 Nov. 1998 <http://www.bravo.org/moh20397.htm>. **CD–ROM** Author's name (if known). "Title of Article." Title of Database. Medium (CD–ROM). City of Electronic Publication: Electronic Publisher, electronic publication date. "World War II German Surrender Documents." Multimedia World History. CD–ROM. Parsippany: Bureau of Electronic Publishing, 1994.

You can list information about sources you might use on source cards like those that follow. Number each card, and record the information for each possible source you find.

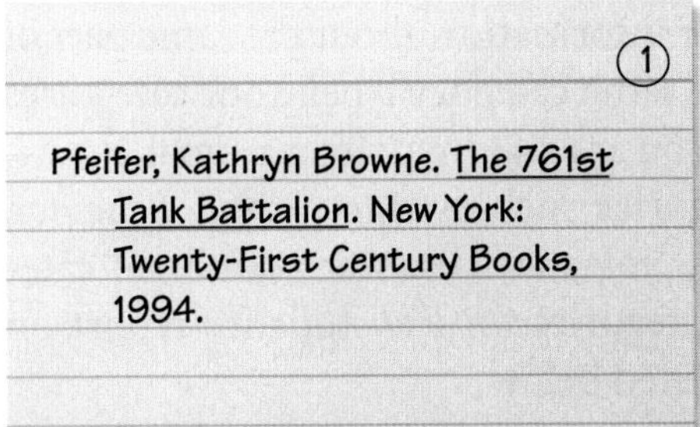

(1)

Pfeifer, Kathryn Browne. The 761st Tank Battalion. New York: Twenty-First Century Books, 1994.

(2)

"Remarks by the President at the Presentation of United States Medals of Honor, The White House." Veterans Outlook. March/April 1997. BRAVO. 28 Nov. 1998 <http://www.bravo.org/moh20397.htm>.

source number

YOUR TURN 7 Finding Sources

Start your research by finding a variety of reliable and up-to-date sources. Choose at least three different sources to use for your report, and create a source card for each using the chart on the previous page as a guide.

COMPUTER TIP

If you make your source list on a computer, italicize all items shown underlined in the examples on page 176.

Take Notes

Make a Note of It Once you have found sources, it is time to take notes. Making note cards will help you organize the information you gather as you read. To make your note cards, follow the guidelines below.

- **Take thorough notes.** Write down facts, statistics, examples, and quotations that help answer your research question. Your notes will provide the elaboration you need in each paragraph of your report. Instead of just saying "the 761st Tank Battalion performed admirably in World War II," for example, good notes should provide details about the battalion's accomplishments. How can you decide whether something is important enough to write down? Ask yourself these questions. If you can answer yes to both of them, make a note of the information.
  1. Does the information relate to my research question?
  2. Will the information interest my audience or give them a clearer understanding of my topic?

TIP Keep in mind that organizing and recording information on a **chart, map,** or **graphic** could also be helpful. For example, a map could show the locations of battles, and a time line could show the dates of the battles.

TIP As you find information, you may notice that you have additional questions about your topic. If the questions relate to your guiding research question, it is fine to go back and do more research until these questions are answered.

- **Label each note card with its source number.** Also include the page number where you found the information in case you need to find it again.
- **Label each card with a category that tells the type of information it provides.** When you find other information about the same part of your topic, you will give it the same category label. Your categories will depend on your topic. If you are researching an animal, for example, you might have categories such as *Appearance, Behavior,* and *Habitat.* As you research, you may discover additional categories of information. The categories for the student's report on the 761st Tank Battalion are listed below.

Categories:
Background (before the unit was created)
Training
Early Battles
Later Battles

Here is a sample note card.

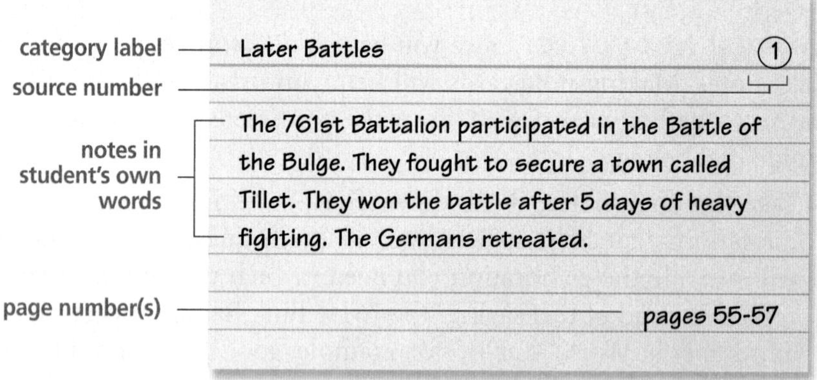

category label
source number
notes in student's own words
page number(s)
Later Battles
1
The 761st Battalion participated in the Battle of the Bulge. They fought to secure a town called Tillet. They won the battle after 5 days of heavy fighting. The Germans retreated.
pages 55-57

YOUR TURN 8 Researching Your Topic

With your research question in mind, take notes from your sources. Look for facts, statistics, examples, and quotations that will give your readers a complete picture of your topic. Label each note card with its source number and its category of information.

MINI-LESSON **WRITING**

Paraphrasing vs. Plagiarizing

When you take notes, you may **summarize** the information by writing only the important ideas, or you may **paraphrase** the information by writing all the ideas in your own words. These techniques help you avoid stealing another writer's words. Copying information word-for-word and presenting it as your own is called **plagiarism.** It is never all right to copy directly from another writer without putting the passage in quotation marks and identifying the writer.

This paragraph and the notes that follow show the difference between paraphrasing and plagiarizing.

> Many words and phrases we use have interesting origins. The term *goose bumps* dates back to the medieval era, when goose feathers were important in Britain. Farmers often plucked the geese's feathers, leaving the birds completely bare until new feathers grew. When the naked geese got cold, their skin popped out in goose bumps!

Paraphrase: The expression *goose bumps* comes from Britain. In medieval times, farmers plucked geese's feathers. When the featherless geese got cold, little bumps formed. People started calling these bumps *goose bumps*, even when they occurred on people.

Plagiarized Paragraph: The term *goose bumps* refers to the geese of Britain in the medieval era. Farmers often plucked the geese's feathers. When the naked geese got cold, they got bumps that became known as goose bumps.

PRACTICE

Write a paraphrase for each of the following passages. Note the important ideas from the passage without copying phrases word-for-word.

1. In the days before incubators, chickens could not be hatched in the winter. Spring chickens fetched the highest prices in the summer. A dishonest vendor might try to pass off an older chicken as a fresher "spring" chicken. This is the source of the phrase *no spring chicken*, meaning past one's prime.

2. Hitting your *funny bone* is anything but funny. So why the humorous name? The reason is that the bone running from the shoulder to the elbow is called the *humerus.* Someone made a play on words and called it the *funny bone.*

Write Your Main Idea Statement

KEY CONCEPT

Get to the Point The **main idea statement,** or **thesis,** of a report tells readers what the point of the paper will be. Main idea statements are usually located in the first paragraph to guide readers. **Your main idea statement should state not only the topic of your paper, but also the most important thing you learned about your topic.** To write your main idea statement, think about your research question and the answers you found. Here is how one student developed a main idea statement.

> Research question: What did the 761st Tank Battalion do during World War II?
>
> What I learned: I learned about their victories and their example of fighting bravely in spite of prejudice against them.
>
> Main idea statement: The 761st Tank Battalion proved that African American soldiers could serve their country with excellence and bravery.

YOUR TURN 9 Writing a Main Idea Statement

Write down your research question. Then, look over your notes and write down the most important thing you learned about your topic. Put these ideas together in one sentence to write the main idea statement for your research report.

TIP Choose an order to arrange your ideas. For example, you may use chronological order if your topic is historical. If you are comparing or classifying two subjects, you may want to use logical order. For other topics, order of importance may be appropriate. For more on **types of order,** see page 303.

Plan Your Report

Place Your Order The category labels on your notes will help you organize the information you have gathered. Begin by sorting your cards into groups based on their labels. Then, create an outline based on these groups, or subtopics, and on the information in your notes. To turn your organized note cards into a formal outline for your report, follow these steps.

- Number your subtopics with Roman numerals and leave several blank lines after each subtopic.

- Within each subtopic, you will probably find two or three kinds of information. Give each kind of information a capital letter, and list these items below their Roman numeral. Leave two or three blank lines after each kind of information.
- Finally, list individual facts, examples, and other details from your notes under the appropriate capital letter. Give each of these details a number. (Consider comparing and contrasting your findings from different sources to organize these details.)

Here is an example of part of a student's outline.

I. Background of African Americans in the military
   A. Limited roles
      1. Service mostly in support units
      2. Segregated from white soldiers
   B. Beginnings of change
      1. Black leaders' pressure on officials
      2. Selective Training and Service Act of 1940
      3. Creation of 761st Tank Battalion
II. Training of the 761st Tank Battalion
   A. Training at Camp Claiborne in Louisiana

TIP For now, you can set aside any information that does not easily fit into your subtopics. This information might make an interesting item for your introduction or conclusion, or you may decide not to use it at all. It is better to write a well-organized paper than try to cram in every fact you found.

YOUR TURN 10 Creating an Outline

Organize your note cards based on their labels. Then, follow the instructions on pages 180–181 to create an outline for your report. Refer to the partial outline above to help you.

TIP You can organize your ideas in an **informal outline,** a **conceptual map,** or a **time line.** For more on these and other **graphic organizers,** see page 842 in the Quick Reference Handbook.

Designing Your Writing

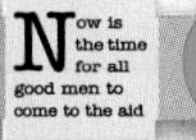

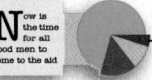

Now is the time for all good men to come to the aid

Creating Headings Using headings in your research report can make your writing easier to follow. If you use a word processor, you can type your headings in **bold type.** Otherwise, underline headings, or type or write them in all capital letters. The headings will be the major subtopics of information from your notes; these are the items numbered with Roman numerals in your outline.

Research Report

Framework	Directions and Explanations
Introduction ■ Attention-grabbing beginning ■ Main idea statement	Hook your readers' attention by contrasting what they already know about the topic with new information. You might also ask your research question or tell readers why you picked this topic. Your **main idea statement** should identify both your topic and what you are going to say about it.

Body ■ Subtopic 1 and elaboration ■ Subtopic 2 and elaboration and so on	■ Each Roman numeral in your outline will represent a subtopic. Each subtopic will be covered in its own paragraph. However, if a Roman numeral has several capital letters beneath it, you may need more than one paragraph. To create **coherence,** link ideas with transitions (see page 309). ■ **Elaborate** on each subtopic using **facts, statistics, examples, direct quotations,** and your own **conclusions.** Be sure to distinguish your own ideas from those of your sources.

Conclusion ■ Related, unanswered question or final comment	To finish your report, you may want to include a **related** and **interesting question** that your research did not answer. Another way to end is by making a **final statement about why your topic is important.**

Works Cited List ■ Alphabetical list of sources used	List the sources you used for your report in a Works Cited list or a bibliography. You can list different types of sources on a **Works Cited list.** However, a bibliography is a source list that only includes books. Use the correct format for each citation, based on the examples on page 176. Your teacher may ask you to use a separate sheet for your Works Cited list or bibliography.

A Writer's Model

The final draft below closely follows the framework for a research report.

The Brave Soldiers of the 761st

World War II brings many heroic images to mind. People may think of Rosie the Riveter or the Iwo Jima statue of six Marines. One lesser-known story, though, is the heroism of African American soldiers in World War II. The 761st Tank Battalion proved that African Americans could serve their country with excellence and bravery.

When the war began in the late 1930s, African Americans made up only a small part of the army. The armed forces were segregated, or separated, by race. Black soldiers and white soldiers trained and lived separately. African American leaders began pressuring government officials to change the unfair system. In 1940, the U.S. Congress passed the Selective Training and Service Act. The act included the words, "there shall be no discrimination against any person on account of race or color" (Pfeifer 13–14). The act led to the creation of black combat units, including the 761st Tank Battalion (Pfeifer 22).

In 1942, the 761st Tank Battalion was formed at Camp Claiborne, Louisiana (African Americans). The battalion had 27 officers, all of them white, and 313 enlisted men. Within a year a group of black officers, which included the baseball player Jackie Robinson, was assigned to the battalion (Pfeifer 22, 25). Conditions at Camp Claiborne were difficult for the soldiers. Their housing was in a swampy area near the sewage treatment plant (Pfeifer 24). Worst of all, African American soldiers had fewer rights than some German prisoners in the camp (Pfeifer 30–31). Despite these injustices, the 761st Tank Battalion worked hard to earn a reputation for excellence. In maneuvers, military exercises designed to resemble real combat situations, the soldiers of the 761st proved their readiness for battle (Pfeifer 29).

(continued)

Attention-grabbing beginning

Main idea statement

Subtopic 1: Background

Subtopic 2: Training

TIP The Writer's Model includes examples of **parenthetical citations.** Your teacher may ask you to use parenthetical citations, too. In parentheses following the information, list the author's last name (or the title) and the page number where you found the information.

(continued)

Subtopic 3: Early battles

In October 1944, the battalion joined General George S. Patton's Third Army in Europe. According to writer Catherine Reef, Patton told the soldiers, "I would never have asked for you if you weren't good. I have nothing but the best in my Army" (51). In their first battle, the 761st Tank Battalion had to cut off German escape and supply routes to Metz, France. At the town of Morville, they encountered heavy gunfire and mines. Although the Germans knocked out seven tanks, the men of the 761st prevented worse losses (Pfeifer 42–45).

Subtopic 4: Later battles

In December, the 761st Tank Battalion went to Belgium to join the Battle of the Bulge, the largest land battle of the war. The 761st fought a fierce battle for a little town called Tillet. After five days the Germans retreated (Pfeifer 51–57). The battalion pressed on through the Netherlands, France, and Germany, fighting battles along the way. One of their last accomplishments during the war was breaking through the Siegfried Line. This line protected the German border with bunkers and concrete and steel antitank structures. Finally, the 761st Tank Battalion met up with their Russian allies at the Enns River (African Americans). Two days later, the war in Europe was over.

Final comment

The soldiers of the 761st Tank Battalion battled discrimination and inequality to serve their country. In 1978, President Carter awarded them a Presidential Unit Citation for their courageous deeds (Pfeifer 10–11). The 761st Tank Battalion, one of the first African American combat units, set an example of heroism for all Americans.

TIP Research reports and their *Works Cited* lists are normally double-spaced. Because of limited space, A Writer's Model and A Student's Model are single-spaced. To see an interactive model of a double-spaced research report, go to **go.hrw.com** and enter the keyword **EOLang 8-5.**

Works Cited

African Americans in WWII: A Legacy of Patriotism and Valor. Pro. Department of Defense. OnDeck Home Entertainment, 1998.

Pfeifer, Kathryn Browne. The 761st Tank Battalion. New York: Twenty-First Century Books, 1994.

Reef, Catherine. Black Fighting Men: A Proud History. New York: Twenty-First Century Books, 1994.

A Student's Model

A research report can be about anything—even the weather. That subject interested eighth-grader Chris Janney of Edward E. Drew, Jr., Middle School in Falmouth, Virginia. The danger of hurricanes in his area led him to wonder about how hurricanes are tracked. Excerpts from his report follow.

Tracking Hurricanes

The safety of millions of families on the East Coast depends on scientists' ability to track and predict the path of a hurricane. Tracking hurricanes is a constantly changing learning experience for weather scientists. Today, scientists use four basic methods to track hurricanes. These methods include the use of satellites, radar, reconnaissance aircraft, and observations.

Attention-grabbing beginning

Main idea statement

Using satellites is one of many ways to track hurricanes. Satellites help scientists see cloud patterns. When scientists first started using satellites, they thought that if a hurricane's cloud pattern was small, the hurricane would not be a strong one. For example, Hurricane Camille in 1969 had a very small cloud pattern, so scientists thought that it would be a weak hurricane. When they flew planes into the eye, which is the center of the hurricane, they discovered that Camille was a Category 5 hurricane, the strongest hurricane possible. After Camille, they learned to judge a hurricane's strength by the position of the eye in relation to the rest of the cloud cover. They also found that by putting together satellite pictures in motion, they could estimate the track of the developing hurricane. . . .

Subtopic 1: Satellites

Radar, another method for tracking hurricanes, is used to detect rain along the coast. It tells scientists the amount of rainfall and shows the bands of rain in the hurricane. It also shows the eye and the eye wall. The eye wall is an organized band of clouds, intense rain, and strong winds surrounding the eye. Scientists use this information to show the movement of

Subtopic 2: Radar

(continued)

(continued)

hurricanes and the tornadoes that sometimes come with them.

Subtopic 3: Reconnaissance aircraft

Reconnaissance aircraft is perhaps the most exciting method for tracking hurricanes. Pilots from a special Air Force Reserve squadron actually fly directly into the eye of the hurricane in order to find out how intense the storm is. Sometimes they use a dropsonde to collect data about wind speed, direction, air pressure, and temperature. A dropsonde is a small tube with a parachute attached that is dropped into the hurricane from the plane. A radio transmitter sends data from the instruments inside the tube back to the plane.

Subtopic 4: Observation

Even with all of the technology available through radar, satellites, and aircraft, observation is still one of the methods used in tracking hurricanes. . . . Today, there are data buoys in the Gulf of Mexico and on the Atlantic and Pacific coasts that send out radio signals to scientists. These signals give information on air temperature, water temperature, wind speed, air pressure, and wave conditions. This information helps scientists predict and monitor storms during hurricane season.

Why topic is important

Satellites, Doppler radar, reconnaissance planes, and observations are all important methods of tracking hurricanes. Together, they provide scientists with the tools to predict accurately the path of a hurricane and to warn the public of its dangers.

TIP Unlike the Writer's Model, the model above does not include parenthetical citations. Be sure to ask your teacher whether you need to include parenthetical citations in your report.

YOUR TURN 11 Writing a First Draft

Now it is time to write the first draft of your research report. As you write, refer to the framework on page 182 and the Writer's Model on pages 183–184. Use the information in your notes to elaborate on your ideas.

Evaluate and Revise Content, Organization, and Style

Take Another Look When you evaluate your own report or a peer's, you should read it at least twice. During the first reading, focus on what is in the report—the content—and how that information is organized. The second time through, read each sentence and evaluate its style, using the Focus on Sentences on page 189.

First Reading: Content and Organization Use the chart below to help you evaluate and revise, or **edit,** the content and organization of your report.

Quick guide!

Guidelines for Self-Evaluation and Peer Evaluation

Evaluation Questions	Tips	Revision Techniques
1 Does the introduction contain a clear main idea statement?	**Put a star** next to the statement that tells readers the report's topic and main point.	**Add** a main idea statement or **add** the main point about the topic to the main idea statement.
2 Does each paragraph explain no more than one subtopic from your outline?	**Label** the margin of each paragraph with the subtopic it explains.	If necessary, **delete** unrelated ideas or **rearrange** the information into separate paragraphs. To create coherence, link ideas with transitions.
3 Does each paragraph include facts, statistics, examples, direct quotations, or conclusions that elaborate on the subtopic?	**Highlight** the facts and explanations in each paragraph.	**Elaborate** paragraphs that need support with facts and explanations from research notes.
4 Is there an unanswered question or final comment in the conclusion?	**Put a check mark** next to the question or final statement.	**Add** a question or final statement or **revise** the statement or question to make it clearer.
5 Does the Works Cited list include at least three sources?	**Number** the sources listed in the Works Cited list.	If needed, **add** sources to the Works Cited list, and **add** information from those sources to the report.

ONE WRITER'S REVISIONS Here is how the writer revised part of an early draft of the essay on page 183.

Within a year, a group of black officers, which included the baseball player Jackie Robinson, was assigned to the battalion. ~~After the war, Jackie Robinson became the first African American ballplayer to join a major league team.~~ Conditions at Camp Claiborne were difficult for the soldiers. *Their housing was in a swampy area near the sewage treatment plant.* Worst of all, African American soldiers had fewer rights than some German prisoners held at the camp.

Despite these injustices, the 761st Tank Battalion worked hard to earn a reputation for excellence.

delete

add

rearrange

Responding to the Revision Process

1. Why do you think the writer deleted a sentence?
2. Why do you think the writer added a sentence to the paragraph above?
3. Why did the writer move information from a later paragraph back into an earlier paragraph?

PEER REVIEW

As you evaluate a peer's research report, ask yourself these questions:

- What more do I want to know about the topic? Why?
- Is there information in one part of the report that seems to belong in another part?

Second Reading: Style During your second reading, you will look at your style, or the way you express your ideas in sentences. One way to revise your sentences is to eliminate wordiness.

When you evaluate your research report for style, ask yourself whether any sentences use more words than necessary to get a point across. As you re-read your report, put brackets around unnecessary words and word groups. Then, delete unnecessary words and revise sentences to be more concise.

Revising to Eliminate Wordiness

When you write a research report, it is easy to fall into the trap of using too many words. Note the difference in the sentences below.

Wordy Sentence It should be pointed out that only with your help can we stop fires from burning down forests.

Concise Sentence Only you can prevent forest fires.

Although research reports are formal papers, avoid using a **voice** that does not sound like you. Cross out unnecessary words or ideas that are repeated in your report. Replace phrases such as "due to the fact that" and "at the present time" with "because" and "now." Straightforward sentences are strong sentences.

ONE WRITER'S REVISIONS

~~Due to the fact that~~ the armed forces were segregated, ~~which means~~ separated by race, ~~the soldiers of different colors could not live together.~~ Black soldiers and white soldiers trained and lived separately.

Responding to the Revision Process

Do you think the passage above has been improved? Why?

YOUR TURN 12 Revising Content, Organization, and Sentence Style

Evaluate and revise the content and organization of your report using the guidelines on page 187. Then, refer to the Focus on Sentences above to eliminate wordiness in your report. Finally, if a peer evaluated your paper, carefully consider each of your peer's comments as you revise.

Publishing

Proofread Your Report

Catching Mistakes After revising for content, organization, and style, you need to **edit** your report one more time. This time, search for errors in grammar and mechanics. Errors in the final draft of your report may make readers doubt the accuracy of your research. Try to have another person help proofread your report.

Grammar Link

Source Citation Format

Most research reports include a Works Cited list. Writers list information about sources in a specific order following certain rules for punctuation. Using a standard format can help your readers find out more about your topic, and it can help your teacher check the information in your report. (See the chart on page 176.)

PRACTICE

Use the formats in the chart on page 176 to write a citation for each source listed. Punctuate each citation carefully, and add underlining or quotation marks as necessary.

Example:

1. An article in Science News magazine called Butterfly May Use Flowery Stepping-Stones, published on April 25, 1998, on page 262. The author is Mari N. Jensen.

1. *Jensen, Mari N. "Butterfly May Use Flowery Stepping-Stones." Science News 25 April 1998: 262.*

1. An article in the newspaper The Washington Post, titled City Ready to Raze Monument. The article was published on July 14, 1998, on page A4.
2. A book by Jeanette Winter called Sebastian: A Book About Bach. It was published in Orlando by Harcourt Brace and Company in 1999.
3. The television show Newstime, hosted by Angel Martinez. The ABC show was broadcast on September 25, 1997, in New Orleans on WGNO.
4. An article in Newsweek magazine called The Power of Big Ideas, published on January 11, 1999, on page 58. The author is Sharon Begley.
5. A Web page called EARTHFORCE on the Franklin Institute Online Web site. The page was published on the Web in 1998, and was accessed on March 22, 2000. The URL is <http://www.fi.edu/earth/earth.html>. No author is given. The site is sponsored and maintained by the Franklin Institute Science Museum.

For more information and practice on using **underlining (italics)** and **punctuation marks** with titles, see pages 660 and 667.

Publish Your Report

Share Your Work Now it is time to show off your work. Get it in front of your audience by trying one of these ideas.

- Use the Connections to Life on pages 195–196 to turn your report into an informative speech, and share your report with your class as a multimedia presentation.
- Use the Focus on Viewing and Representing on pages 197–200 to turn your research report into a Web site.
- With other students who wrote on topics similar to yours, create a class magazine that includes your group's reports. Your magazine could be about animals, historical figures, or arts, for example.

TIP Your teacher may ask you to create a **title page** for your report. In the middle of a separate sheet of paper, write your name, the date, your teacher's name, and any other information your teacher requests. Attach this page to the front of your report before you publish it.

Reflect on Your Report

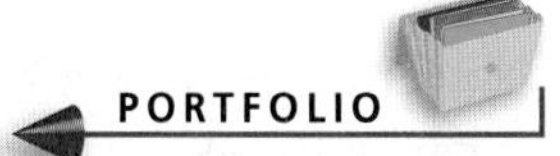

Building Your Portfolio Take a step back and think about your research report. Reflecting on what you wrote and how you wrote it can help you improve on future assignments.

- What was the most interesting part of your report? Why?
- What kinds of sources were the most useful? What sources were easiest to find? What sources could you use in the future?

Now, consider your research report in the context of your entire portfolio so far. Review the pieces in your portfolio and answer these questions.

- What writing skills have you improved between earlier pieces in your portfolio and your research report?
- What kinds of writing are included in your portfolio? What goals can you set for types of writing you would like to try in future pieces?

YOUR TURN 13 Proofreading, Publishing, and Reflecting on Your Report

- Correct grammar, usage, and mechanics errors using reference materials and resources, such as Part 3 of this book, computer grammar and spelling features, or a dictionary.
- Publish your report for your target audience.
- Answer the Reflect on Your Report questions above. Record your responses in a learning log, or include them in your portfolio.

MINI-LESSON **TEST TAKING**

Writing an Informative Essay for a Test

As you probably know by now, most writing tests do not allow you to do research. However, on many tests you will organize your ideas just as you did in writing your research report. One type of writing test you may be required to take asks you to explain why something is important to you. Like the research report, this kind of writing is informative, or **expository.** Because these test questions ask you to *clarify,* or make clear, a topic, these essays are sometimes called **clarification** essays.

Read the prompt below and think about how you would answer it. Then, study the steps in the Thinking It Through that follow the prompt.

> Change of seasons or holidays—we each have a favorite time of year, whether that time is an entire season or a special holiday. Before you begin writing, think about which season or holiday is your favorite. Then, write a letter to your classmates explaining why you prefer that time of year above all others.

THINKING IT THROUGH

Prewriting for an Informative Essay

Here is how to prewrite for an informative prompt like the one above.

STEP 1 Identify what you are supposed to write about (topic), whom you are writing for (audience), and why you are writing (purpose).

I'm going to write a letter to my classmates. The prompt says to explain why a certain season or holiday is my favorite, so my purpose is to inform, not to persuade.

STEP 2 Choose a specific topic. If you have trouble identifying a specific topic, brainstorm on a separate sheet of paper. Write as many ideas related to the general topic as you can. Then, pick one specific topic which best fits the prompt and about which you have the most to say.

Times of year I like: Hanukkah, Fourth of July, Thanksgiving, my birthday . . . I guess my birthday isn't really a holiday. I like Fourth of July best. I can probably think of many reasons why.

STEP 3 Create a conceptual map like the one on the next page. Write your topic at the top, and below it, jot down the reasons that explain why you chose it. Then, use a prewriting technique like the *5W-How?* questions to come up with support for your reasons. Finally, create a main idea statement that sums up your topic and what you have to say about it.

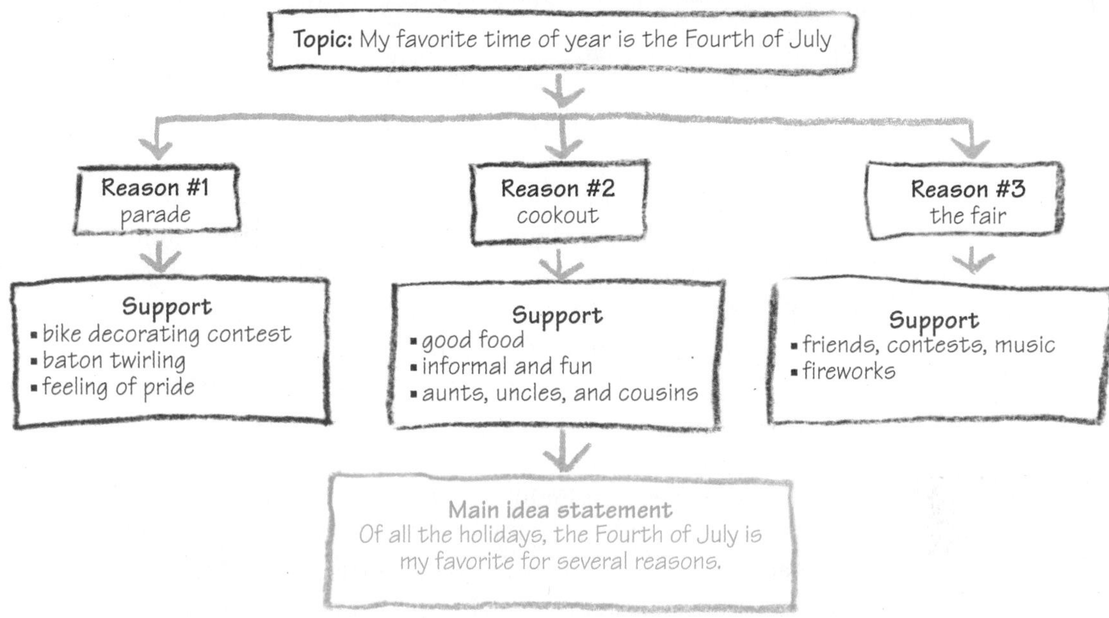

Write After you organize ideas, start writing. Follow the simple framework below.

I. Introduction. Grab your audience's attention by asking a question or telling an anecdote. Then, state your main idea.

II. Body. Each reason and its support should be in a separate paragraph. To flesh out each paragraph, use the elaboration guidelines to the right.

III. Conclusion. End by making a connection between the main idea and the body of your essay.

Elaborate Your conceptual map shows the details you generated to support your reasons. This single level of details is not enough to create a high-quality essay. You need to elaborate on your details. Try this elaboration strategy: *Feed* your essay with

F = facts or feelings
E = examples
E = explanations
D = details

Here is the essay that started with the conceptual map above.

The glow of fireworks, the smell of fried chicken, the sound of trumpets—these are the sights, smells, and sounds of a special day in midsummer, July 4. Of all the holidays, the Fourth of July is my favorite for several reasons. **Attention-grabber** **Main idea statement**

First, I love the parade. I've been participating in the parade since I competed in the tricycle-decorating contest as a three-year-old. Like all the other kids who decorated their bicycles, I **Reason #1** **Support** **Elaboration**

(continued)

(continued)

would win an award each year, which made me feel proud. These
days I help other little kids have that same feeling by helping give
Support out the awards. I still participate in the parade, too, by marching
Elaboration with my baton-twirling class. I love dressing up in my sparkling
uniform and hearing the crowd cheer as I toss my baton high in
Support the air. Whatever I do in the parade, it is always fun to walk
Elaboration through town to the beat of the music, to see the people waving
from the sidewalk, and to hear the competing sounds of the
marching band, bicycle horns, and horses' hooves clomping on
the pavement. It makes me feel good to see the whole town come
together either to march or cheer on the marchers.

Reason #2 After the parade, my family meets at the local park for a huge
Support cookout—my second reason for loving July 4th. I drink ice-cold
lemonade, stuff myself on my uncle's famous fried chicken, and
Elaboration enjoy my mom's pecan pie. Everything tastes better than usual be-
Support cause I'm hot and hungry from the long march. I love being able to
Elaboration eat outside where I don't have to say, "May I be excused," and I am
Support allowed to spit watermelon seeds. When I'm full, there are plenty of
cousins to play ball with while the adults sit under a big oak tree. It
Elaboration makes me feel good to see my family members all around.

Reason #3 Fourth of July does not end with the picnic, though. In fact, the
Support best part is yet to come. Late in the afternoon, we all head over to
the fairgrounds to meet our friends, compete in contests, and listen
Elaboration to live music. I love to run the three-legged race, inhale the smells
of popcorn and cotton candy, and hear the country music pump-
Support ing through the huge PA system. Best of all, when the sun sets, the
Elaboration sky lights up with fireworks. I relax on the grass and watch the col-
ored lights explode over my head.

Conclusion You can say what you want about the other special days. For
me, fun and games, mouthwatering food, and a great finale
make the Fourth of July my favorite holiday.

Edit and Revise To revise your essay, ask yourself, Do I need to make any part of my explanation clearer? If necessary, neatly write in additional facts, feelings, examples, explanations, or details.

Finally, use **proofreading symbols** like those on page 844 to correct errors in grammar, spelling, and punctuation.

Giving an Informative Speech Using a Web Site as a Visual

When researchers present their findings, they often do so in a **multimedia presentation,** a speech that includes visuals and gives audience members the opportunity to ask questions. While charts or overhead transparencies can be helpful visuals, Web sites can grab an audience by including sound and motion. The links on Web pages also allow a presenter to switch quickly from one page of information to another in a way that traditional videotapes or audiotapes do not. **Note:** If you do not have access to the Internet, you can still give a research presentation. Read the following section, and use visuals such as illustrations, charts, or video segments. (For more on **creating visuals,** see pages 77–80.)

Adapt Your Report Even though your report is about an interesting topic, simply reading it aloud will not keep your audience interested. You will need to adapt your report in order to use it as a short speech (under ten minutes). Follow these steps.

- Make notes about the most important points of your report. One way to organize your speech is by making one note card per category of information. Make sure you include evidence, examples, and elaboration to support and clarify your main points.
- Use your Works Cited list to tell listeners the sources for statistics, quotes, or unusual facts you use in your speech. If your audience knows where the information comes from, they will consider it more trustworthy. To credit your source, simply say something like, "According to the *World Book Encyclopedia,* the U.S. Armed Forces were segregated until 1948."

Choose a Web Site Once you have created your speech, pick a Web site to use as a visual. Ask your teacher if your school has the tools needed to allow an entire class to view a Web site. You might use an overhead projector (Liquid Crystal Display or LCD) to project the site onto a screen. You could also print and photocopy Web pages for your class.

Choose a Web site with a strong visual connection to your topic. For example, look for pictures of important people, places, or things you will mention in your speech, or for charts that show data supporting the ideas in your speech. You can use one page that addresses a key point, or several pages that illustrate ideas in your speech. If the pages you choose are only weakly connected to your ideas, though, they will confuse your audience.

Evaluate the Web Site Make sure the Web site you choose meets the following requirements.

- The words and images should be large enough to be seen from the back of the room.
- Pages should be easy to view. Avoid pages with cluttered graphics.

Note: If you cannot find a Web site that will work well with your speech, try making your own. (For more on **creating a Web site,** see pages 197–200.)

Practice Now you are ready to practice giving your speech using the Web site. Keep in mind that sites with graphics and animation may take a long time to load, creating awkward pauses in your presentation. To lessen this problem, use your Web browser's bookmark function to capture the pages you will use so they are easier to retrieve when you need them.

You can also anticipate questions an audience may ask by practicing your presentation in front of your parents or friends. Once you know what type of questions your audience may ask, you can bookmark the answers in your source materials. This will make it easier to find answers when you actually make your presentation. Just remember to bring your source materials with you on the day of your speech.

Show Time The time has come for you to give your multimedia presentation. Follow the guidelines below as you present your findings to your class.

- Speak clearly, loudly, and slowly so that everyone can hear you.
- Make eye contact with your audience. Avoid turning your back to them when you use your visual.
- Answer questions from the audience in your own words. Do not read directly from the source materials.
- If you are unable to locate an answer quickly, simply write the question down, and answer it at a later time.

(For more on **formal speaking,** see page 794 in the Quick Reference Handbook.)

TIP As you listen to and view a classmate's multimedia presentation, consider the following questions.

- How appropriate is the Web site or other visual to the speaker's topic? Does the visual fit the topic, or is it distracting or confusing?
- How effective is the Web site or other visual? Is it easy to view? Does it make ideas presented in the speech clearer? How well does the speaker handle the presentation of the visual?
- How well does the Web site or other visual fit the purpose of the presentation? Is it designed to present information or for some other purpose, such as to be creative or to persuade?

YOUR TURN 14 Giving Your Presentation

Use the information on the previous page and above to adapt your report, choose appropriate visuals, and give your own multimedia presentation.

Designing a Web Site

WHAT'S AHEAD?

In this section you will design a Web site. You will also learn how to

- **use a flowchart to map out links on your Web site**
- **create storyboards to plan your Web pages**

Are you a Web surfer, like millions of other people? The Internet has transformed communication and information delivery in our world. The technology needed to design and post a Web site is now available to more people than ever. More sites about a greater variety of subjects are being added every day. Not all Web sites are equal, though. In this workshop you will learn how to develop a well-designed, informative Web site.

What Makes a Good Site?

Effective Web sites have certain elements in common. Most have a welcome page, or home page, which provides introductory information about the topic. The home page may also include an index, sometimes called a "main menu," which links users to other pages of information about the topic. Look at page 159 for an example of a home page that has an index.

On well-designed Web pages, you may find the text, or words, broken up with empty space. Short chunks of text are easier to read than long, uninterrupted text. Effective Web pages may also contain helpful illustrations and other graphics. If you have searched the Internet before, have you ever found sites with cluttered graphics, hard-to-read text, or no empty space? If so, you may have found those sites difficult to use.

TIP Take a second look at the NOVA Web site on pages 159–161. Identify the various ways that it conveys information (text, graphics, lists, and so on).

How well do you think the Web site informs?

Designing Your Web Site

Do It Yourself Using the information you gathered for your research report, you can design your own Web site. Start by thinking about the topic and subtopics you covered in your report. You can use the outline you created for your report if you need a reminder. Each subtopic in your outline should have its own page on your site and be linked to the home page. Rather than copying your report word-for-word on your site, adapt the information using the steps below.

THINKING IT THROUGH

Presenting Information on a Web Site

STEP 1 Use your outline to identify the topic and major subtopics of your research report.

STEP 2 Think about the topic and each subtopic as a separate page in your site. (The topic will be represented by your home page.) Rewrite the information in your report so that it is in short, easy-to-read chunks with headings. This will make it easier for readers to find what they need.

Reference Note

For more on **creating headings,** see page 181.

STEP 3 Underline words or phrases that readers might not know. You can link these terms to a glossary page, which will provide definitions of terms.

Go with the Flow Once you have started to adapt the ideas and information from your research report, the next step is to create a *flowchart.* A **flowchart** is similar to an outline for the whole site. It shows each page and its links to other pages. Below is a flowchart for a Web site based on the Writer's Model on pages 183–184. Each box represents a page on the site, while the arrows represent links.

Tell Your Story Once you have planned your site, it is time to plan each individual page. Create a *storyboard* for each page of your site. A **storyboard** shows everything that will appear on a page, including text, graphics, and links to other pages. Show links by underlining the word that will serve as the link. Use empty space and chunks of information to make your pages easy to read. The storyboard examples below show one student's home page and another page on his Web site. Use these examples of storyboards to help you create your own.

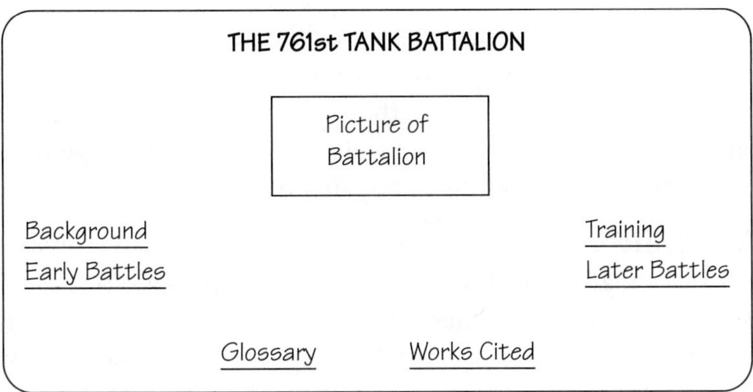

LATER BATTLES

The Battle of the Bulge

The Battle of the Bulge took place in Ardennes, near the borders of Belgium and Luxembourg. It was the largest land battle of World War II. The 761st Battalion helped capture Tillet, a little town. They lost many soldiers but eventually won the battle (Pfeifer 51–57).

The Siegfried Line

The Siegfried Line was a collection of bunkers and concrete and steel antitank structures that protected the German border. The 761st Battalion's breaking through the Siegfried Line contributed to the end of the war in Europe.

Glossary The 761st Tank Battalion home page

TIP You will need to include credits on your site for any sources you used. Create a page on your Web site that lists the same information about each source as your Works Cited list. Add parenthetical citations where you used information, too.

As you create your storyboards, focus on these elements.

- **Creating a home page:** This is the first page your readers will see, so it should be eye-catching and helpful. Your readers will use this page to find links to other pages with information about the topic.

You might include brief descriptions of what additional information readers will find on each linked page.

- **Creating and linking to other pages:** Create a separate page for each of the Roman numerals in your outline. Link your home page to each of these pages using the headings from your outline to let readers know exactly what they will find. Also, make sure you create links to explain information that may be difficult for your readers to understand without help. These might be links to a glossary that defines terms readers might not know or links to other pages that explain or illustrate complicated ideas.
- **Adding graphics:** Photographs, drawings, and diagrams can help explain your ideas. The more graphics you include on a page, though, the longer it will take that page to load. Use only graphics that you create or that are copyright-free. Using an image without permission is just as wrong as copying directly from a book.

TIP You can also create links that will let readers jump directly to the part of a long page that has the information they need, as well as to other Web sites you have found that might interest readers.

If You Build It . . . Now that you have designed a great Web site on storyboards and flowcharts, create it. There are many different software programs available to help you create your site without having to know a programming language. You can also find many tutorials and tips on building Web sites on the Internet or in books.

Try It Out After you have created your site, post it on the Internet. Before you do, though, use a Web browser to test the site. Make sure it is easy to move from one page to another. Have a friend navigate your site, trying out each link.

Even without technology, you can test the site you have designed. Have a friend look at your storyboards and try to follow the underlined links. Add or change some links if your tester has trouble getting around your site.

If you use especially helpful illustrations or graphics on your Web pages, you might use one of those pages as a visual during a research presentation. (For more on **research presentations,** see pages 195–196.)

TIP Think about your purpose for creating a Web site. How do the language, the presentation of text and graphics, and the medium itself (World Wide Web) help inform others?

YOUR TURN 15 Designing Your Web Site

Use the instructions on pages 197–200 to design a Web site. Make sure you create a Web site that is easy to read and navigate. If you have access to the Internet and the necessary software, create and post your Web site.

Choices

Choose one of the following activities to complete.

DRAMA

1. Act It Out In a group, plan and perform a **skit** (a short, funny play) that includes some of the information you discovered during your research. For example, a student who researched the immune system could have a few students play white blood cells and a few others play viruses. The students could then act out an invasion to explain the relationship.

SPEAKING AND LISTENING

2. Talk It Over With a few other classmates, discuss what you learned about conducting research as you wrote your report. Consider skills that helped you, including searching the Internet, using the library effectively, or talking to experts. Also, discuss what you would do differently if you had it to do over. Then, create a **chart** or other **visual** showing the results of your discussion. Some categories your visual might include are "best sources," "mistakes we made," and "skills we used."

CROSSING THE CURRICULUM: SOCIAL STUDIES

3. Famous Faces With one or two classmates, choose a scientist, athlete, or other notable person, and divide research duties. Work together to organize what you have learned about this person by creating a **database** that includes **records** for important parts of his or her life and career. Before you turn in your database, evaluate each record, and add more information if necessary.

CAREERS

4. The Real World Research a career that interests you by interviewing someone in that field. Check with people you know, or search the Internet or your local telephone directory to find someone in that field. You might ask what the best and worst parts of the career are or what kind of education and training are needed to enter the field. Present what you learn in a **brochure.**

CHAPTER
6
Sharing an Opinion
"ANYWAY, THAT'S WHAT I THINK!"
"WELL, IN MY OPINION..."

Reading Workshop

Reading a Persuasive Essay

Writing Workshop

Writing a Persuasive Essay

Speaking and Listening

Giving and Listening to a Persuasive Speech

Informational Text

Persuasion

"All of this for three easy payments of $19.95!" "This is the must-see movie of the year!" "Vote for Maria for student council president." Thumb through any magazine and you will find pages of product-peddling ads. Glance out of the car window and you will see larger-than-life billboards advertising everything from hospitals to movies. Flip to the editorial section of the newspaper and you will read pages jammed with writers trying to get you to believe as they do. It seems that everywhere you turn someone is using *persuasion.* What is persuasion? **Persuasion** is the art of convincing individuals to do or believe something.

YOUR TURN 1 Discovering Persuasion

Using magazines and newspapers, find two examples of persuasion. One example should be an advertisement for a product or service; the other one should be an article that tries to get you to do or believe something. Then, answer the following questions:

- What tools does the advertisement use to convince you to buy the product or service? Does it use low prices? clever slogans?
- What is the main reason the writer of the persuasive article gives in his or her effort to convince you? Does this reason make sense?
- Of the two examples, which is more convincing? Why?

Reading a Persuasive Essay

WHAT'S AHEAD?

In this workshop you will read a persuasive essay. You will also learn how to

- **recognize the logical appeals writers use to convince others**
- **identify the emotional appeals writers use to persuade readers**

What do police officers and basketball players have in common? They both wear uniforms. Uniforms can serve many functions, one of which is identification. If you need help, the man or woman in the blue uniform and badge can probably assist you. When you go to a basketball game, you know to cheer for the team that wears your school's uniform. The question is, are uniforms a good idea for students to wear every day in the classroom? As you read the persuasive essay on the next page, focus on how the writer presents her opinions on this issue.

Preparing to Read

READING SKILL

Logical Appeals Thoughtful readers use their heads when making decisions about what to do or believe. This is why persuasive writers use *logical appeals.* A writer makes a **logical appeal** by using *reasons* and *evidence* to support an opinion. In the persuasive essay on the next page, Charol Shakeshaft uses logical appeals to support her opinion about school uniforms.

READING FOCUS

Emotional Appeals Knowing that feelings and emotions can be powerful persuasive tools, some writers also use *emotional appeals.* Any time a writer tries to get the reader's emotions involved—emotions such as happiness, fear, or pity—he or she is using an **emotional appeal.** Notice that Charol Shakeshaft uses a mix of logical and emotional appeals in her effort to get readers to see things her way.

Reading Selection

Read the following essay, and write down answers to the numbered active-reading questions in the shaded boxes. Underlined words will be used in the Vocabulary Mini-Lesson on page 210.

from Newsday

Should Public School Students Wear Uniforms?

By Charol Shakeshaft

WHEN I WAS a kid in school, we didn't wear uniforms. In junior high, I argued for school uniforms, believing they would save students—especially girls—time and hassle. Thirty-five years later, as a parent of a ten-year-old, I still think uniforms would improve the quality of life for students.

Uniforms in public schools are legal, as long as the uniform does not infringe upon students' political speech or impose different standards for males and females. Although the Supreme Court has not addressed the legality of uniforms in schools, lower courts have upheld the right of public schools to require uniforms. California has gone so far as to pass a law explicitly making it legal for public schools to adopt uniform requirements, an action designed to reinforce the legality of this kind of local decision. . . .

From Seattle to Phoenix to Charleston, praise of uniform policies is profuse. One of the most often cited benefits of requiring uniforms is economic. Uniforms generally cost less than do most clothes that students want to wear. For instance, the yearly cost of uniforms in Long Beach, California, is \$70 to \$90 for a set of three. Compare that to a trip to the mall!

Uniforms also can diminish the display of material wealth among students. If expensive jackets, shoes, and outfits aren't allowed, students are relieved of anxiety over their attire. Wearing uniforms during the school day provides a time when economic privilege seems equalized.

Uniforms promote individuality. Yes, individuality. If students are judged by what they think and how they perform, rather than on how they dress,

1. What is the writer's opinion on the issue of school uniforms?

2. In the paragraph above, what reason does the writer give for having her opinion?

3. According to the writer, how can uniforms promote individuality?

they are more likely to develop and value diversity of thought. In most school districts, kids already wear uniforms by social category—jocks, . . . preppies . . .—often without articulating what values and lifestyles these uniforms represent.

Long Beach, California, offers impressive evidence that schools where students wear uniforms are safer than those where students don't. Since Long Beach adopted a uniform requirement for its 83,000 students, there have been a third fewer assault and battery cases, student fights have been cut by half, and student suspensions are down by 32 percent.

What compels me to urge school districts to adopt uniforms are the data I've collected during the past three years in nine middle and high schools on Long Island. In those schools, the girls report they spend as much as two-and-a-half hours each day selecting their clothes and "getting ready" for school. These girls describe great anxiety about their appearance, particularly their clothes, and report harassment from both males and females about how they look. I long for a safe space for girls that diminishes such pressure and decreases their anxiety. Schools that expect all students to wear the same type of dress offer support to girls in their fragile adolescent years.

4. What purpose do the numbers in the second paragraph above serve?

5. Does the paragraph above appeal more to your head or your heart? Why do you think so?

Studies tell us that nearly all parents welcome uniforms. Students are not so quick to approve of wearing the same dress as their classmates every day. However, many students who first balk at uniforms change their minds once they have tried them.

Uniforms honor the occasion of school. They help students separate what is expected in school from what they do in malls or on beaches or at movie theaters. Uniforms help create a climate that fosters learning and puts it at the center of students' lives.

First Thoughts on Your Reading

1. Regardless of whether you agree with the writer's opinion, did it make sense to you? Why or why not?
2. In what paragraph or paragraphs did the writer try to arouse feelings of fear, anger, or another emotion? Was this strategy effective? Explain.

Logical Appeals

READING SKILL

That Makes Sense The most persuasive opinions are those that speak to the reader's head, or common sense. Knowing this, persuasive writers use *logical appeals.* A **logical appeal** consists of an *opinion statement* that is supported by *reasons* and *evidence.* A persuasive writer uses logical appeals to show thoughtful readers like you that his or her opinion makes sense.

Opinion Statement An **opinion statement** states the issue and the writer's opinion on the issue. Notice that the writer of the following example states the issue and his opinion about it in the same sentence.

> We should buy products with less packaging.

Reason A **reason** answers the question *Why?* about an opinion statement. *Why* does the writer of the example above feel that people should buy products with less packaging? Here is one of the reasons he gives.

> Consuming products with less packaging would ease the burden on our overcrowded landfills.

Evidence Facts and other types of **evidence** provide important support for a reason. After reading a reason like the one above, you might ask, "What makes the writer say that? Where is the evidence?" The writer uses the following evidence (two **statistics**) to support his reason. Would his reason seem as convincing without this support?

> In a single year, people in North America dispose of over 130 million tons of garbage, up to half of which comes from packaging.

The chart on the next page lists and gives an example for some of the most common types of evidence: facts, statistics, examples, and anecdotes.

TIP Be skeptical of persuasive arguments that include poorly supported opinions, evidence that is not documented or seems illogical, or stereotypes.

Type of Evidence	Example
A **fact** is a statement that can be proved.	Last year, the PTA voted to ban backpacks from the classroom.
A **statistic** is a fact in number form.	Sixty-three percent of the students at our school have never attended a school sports event.
An **example** is a specific instance that illustrates a general idea.	General idea: You can earn money by recycling. Example: Every month, I earn a little extra money by taking our aluminum cans, bottles, and old newspapers to the recycling center.
An **anecdote** is a brief story that illustrates a general idea.	General idea: Some students worry too much about their clothes. Anecdote: My sister spent almost an hour this morning deciding what to wear to school. When she asked me if I was going to wear what I had on to school, I said "no" and changed my outfit—twice!

TIP Writers also use *expert opinions* as evidence to support their opinions. An **expert opinion** is a statement made by an authority on a subject.

Example
According to Marjorie Lamb, author of *2 Minutes a Day for a Greener Planet,* saving paper is one of the most beneficial things we can do for the environment.

Read the paragraph below, and identify the three parts of a logical appeal. If you have trouble, use the steps that follow.

> People should spend less time in front of the television, because television can be harmful to your health. A study by the federal government shows that boys and girls who watch four or more hours of television a day are more likely to be overweight than those who watch less.

THINKING IT THROUGH

Identifying the Parts of a Logical Appeal

STEP 1 Identify the opinion statement. Ask yourself "What is the writer trying to convince me to do or believe?"

The writer wants to convince me to spend less time watching TV.

STEP 2 Identify the reason. Ask yourself "Why does the writer have this opinion?"

The writer says that watching too much TV can cause health problems.

STEP 3 Find and identify the supporting evidence.

The writer uses a fact from a study as evidence.

YOUR TURN 2 Identifying the Parts of a Logical Appeal

Re-read the first paragraph of "Should Public School Students Wear Uniforms?" on page 205 and identify the writer's opinion. Then, re-read the fourth and sixth paragraphs, and identify the reasons and evidence in these two paragraphs that support that opinion.

Emotional Appeals

READING FOCUS

Have a Heart Have you ever wondered why television advertisers often use cute, cuddly looking babies to sell diapers? The answer is simple: Pulling at the audience's heartstrings can be a powerful persuasive tool. Like advertisers, persuasive writers sometimes use emotions to convince their audience. A writer who attempts to persuade readers by touching their emotions creates an **emotional appeal.**

A writer can create an emotional appeal by using evidence that speaks to the reader's heart as opposed to the reader's head. An emotional appeal arouses feelings of fear, guilt, happiness, and so on. For example, the following anecdote stirs feelings of sadness.

> When I arrived at the beach, the first thing I saw was an oil-soaked chick sadly squawking next to its mother. I picked up the frail chick and did my best to wash the black gunk from its tiny wings. I realized then it would take much time and money to clean up the mess.

TIP A convincing writer uses an emotional appeal in addition to—not instead of—a logical appeal. A logical appeal is the best foundation for a convincing essay.

TIP Another way to be persuasive is by creating an **ethical appeal.** One way to create an ethical appeal is to use evidence from sources your readers will recognize and respect, such as an encyclopedia or your principal. By doing this, you show your readers you are trustworthy.

YOUR TURN 3 Identifying Emotional Appeals

Re-read the seventh paragraph of "Should Public School Students Wear Uniforms?" What kind of evidence does the writer use? To which emotions does the evidence appeal?

MINI-LESSON **VOCABULARY**

Conceptual Maps

Persuasive essays can be great reading—especially if the topic is one that interests you. However, not knowing a word can sometimes keep you from fully understanding what the writer is saying about the topic. One way to learn an unfamiliar word is to create a *conceptual map.* A vocabulary **conceptual** (or **concept**) **map** gives a word and presents a definition, a synonym, a picture, and an original sentence for the word. A concept map is an excellent tool for studying a word's meaning.

THINKING IT THROUGH

Developing a Vocabulary Concept Map

STEP 1 Look up the word in a dictionary, and define it in your own words.

STEP 2 Write down a synonym from a dictionary or thesaurus.

STEP 3 Draw a picture that illustrates the word. (The first idea that enters your mind will probably be the easiest to remember.)

STEP 4 Write a sentence about the picture you created.

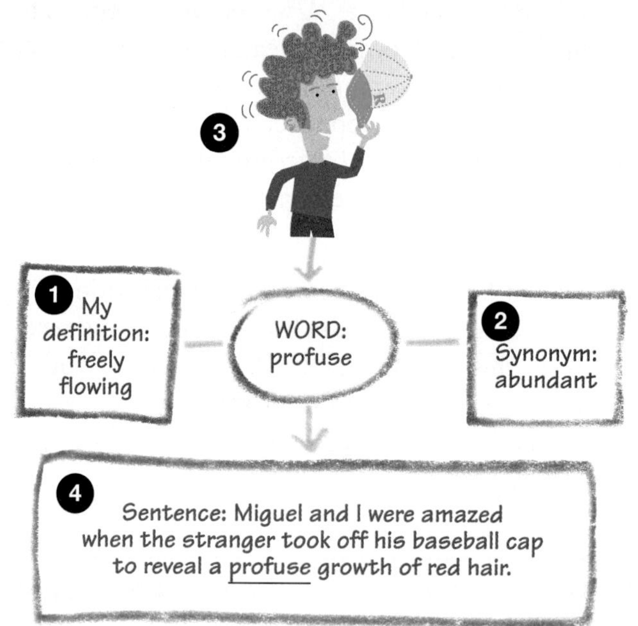

3
1 My definition: freely flowing
WORD: profuse
2 Synonym: abundant
4 Sentence: Miguel and I were amazed when the stranger took off his baseball cap to reveal a profuse growth of red hair.

PRACTICE

Using the example above, develop a vocabulary concept map for each of the following words. The words are underlined in "Should Public School Students Wear Uniforms?"

1. infringe (page 205)
2. explicitly (page 205)
3. diminish (page 205)
4. diversity (page 206)
5. compels (page 206)

MINI-LESSON **TEST TAKING**

Answering Questions About Persuasive Devices

When taking a test, you may be asked to answer test items about persuasive reading passages. To answer these kinds of test items successfully, you have to understand how the writer supports his or her opinion. How would you answer the test item following the passage below?

Washington Middle School students should be required to wear uniforms. Uniforms will help families save money. For the cost of a jacket with a popular sports team logo, a student can have a year's worth of school clothes. Parents of quickly growing middle school students will no longer feel the need to waste money on expensive clothes that their children will outgrow before the end of the school year.

The writer states, "For the cost of a jacket with a popular sports team logo, a student can have a year's worth of school clothes," in order to

A. show how clothes can affect a student's social status in a positive way

B. persuade people that students should be able to wear whatever they want

C. inform readers that uniforms will last longer than regular clothes

D. convince readers that school uniforms are cost-effective

THINKING IT THROUGH

Answering Questions About Persuasive Devices

STEP 1 Determine what the test item is asking.

The item asks why the writer states, "For the cost of a jacket with a popular sports team logo, a student can have a year's worth of school clothes."

STEP 2 Find your own answer by determining if the statement in the item is the paragraph's main idea or support for it.

The statement in the item is not the paragraph's main idea. The main idea is an opinion: Students should be required to wear uniforms. Everything else the writer says should support it. Therefore, the writer talks about the high cost of sports team logo jackets to support the opinion that uniforms should be required.

STEP 3 Find the answer choice that is the most consistent with your answer.

The writer doesn't even mention social status, so choice A isn't correct. Answer choice B is not consistent with the opinion. Answer choice C is consistent with the opinion, but the writer never mentions it. Choice D is the answer.

Writing a Persuasive Essay

WHAT'S AHEAD?

In this workshop you will write a persuasive essay. You will also learn how to

- **choose and take a stand on an issue**
- **support an opinion statement with reasons and evidence**
- **create an appropriate voice and tone**
- **add variety to sentence beginnings**
- **revise "There is/are, It is" constructions**

Do you feel that CDs should carry warnings about bad language? Do you think school lunch periods should be longer? Do you believe professional athletes have a responsibility to be good role models? You probably have strong opinions about these and many other issues. However, your opinion alone will probably not convince anyone to agree with you. After all, opinions are like umbrellas on a rainy day: Almost everyone has them! The question is, how do you make it more likely that people will agree with *your* opinion? One way is to use the tools of **persuasion** to show your readers that your point of view is the right one.

In this workshop you will write a persuasive essay that uses reasons and evidence to support an opinion. This is your chance to convince others to see things the way you do.

Prewriting

Choose and Evaluate Your Issue

KEY CONCEPT

First Things First The final goal of persuasive writing is to convince your readers to agree with your opinion on an issue that concerns you. However, before you can convince anyone, you must first choose an issue for your essay. **An issue is a subject about which people disagree,** such as whether CDs should carry warnings about potentially offensive language.

When choosing your issue, try to find one that has an impact on your life as well as the lives of others. For example, you may write an essay about the issue of year-round school. Such an issue would be a good choice for an essay because it creates strong feelings in you as well as many other people. However, the issue of whether or not you should get a raise in allowance would not be as appropriate because it only impacts you and maybe one or two others.

If you have trouble finding an issue for your essay, try reading the opinion section of your local newspaper or watching the national news. You might also think about important issues at school. What school policies would you change or adopt if you had the power? To decide if the issue you find is a good one, ask yourself the following questions:

- Is the issue debatable? In other words, will people disagree about it?
- Do I have strong feelings about the issue?
- Would other people have strong feelings about the issue?

The student in the following example brainstormed a list of possible subjects and evaluated them. Which issue do you think the student should choose? Why?

Issue	**Is the issue debatable?**	**Do I have strong feelings about the issue?**	**Would other people have strong feelings about the issue?**
banning students from wearing backpacks to class	Yes. Some people think banning them would make the school safer, but some think it would only cause students to go to class without everything they need.	Not really. I always leave my backpack in my locker.	Yes. When the principal mentioned banning them, many of my classmates complained.
starting a paper-recycling program at our school	Yes. Some people think recycling is too much trouble, but others think it is important.	Yes. I realize that what we do to the planet today affects it—and us—in the future.	Yes. Some of my friends are worried that we are destroying the planet.

TIP Instead of choosing a broad issue, such as freedom of speech, choose a narrower issue for your essay, such as starting a student-run school newspaper. Narrow issues can be handled more easily in a single essay.

YOUR TURN 4 Choosing and Evaluating Your Issue

Brainstorm a list of issues. Then, make a chart like the one on the previous page to evaluate the issues. After reviewing the chart, choose a debatable issue that is important to you and that creates strong feelings in others.

State Your Opinion

KEY CONCEPT

Choosing Sides Like a fence, an issue has two distinct sides. What side of the fence will you choose? Are you in favor of the issue you have chosen or against it? You can state your point of view about your issue in an *opinion statement.* **An opinion statement, also known as a *thesis statement,* is a statement that tells both the issue and your point of view on it.** An opinion statement acts as the main idea for your persuasive essay.

issue: starting a paper-recycling program at our school

\+ **point of view:** We need to start one.

---

opinion statement: We need to start a paper-recycling program at our school.

YOUR TURN 5 Writing Your Opinion Statement

Write an opinion statement on the issue you have chosen. Make sure that your opinion statement tells both your issue and your point of view on it.

Identify and Analyze Your Audience

To Whom It May Concern Would you ever write a note to your best friend and then post it on a bulletin board for everyone to read? Probably not. After all, in a note, you write each thought with a specific person in mind. You use words and situations you feel only that person would understand and appreciate. For the same reason, you should also write a persuasive essay with a specific group of people in mind. The specific group of people you want to persuade is called your **audience.**

The student writing about starting a paper-recycling program at school answered the following questions to identify his audience.

Which groups of people would find my issue important? My classmates and teachers would find this issue important. Parents and school employees might also be interested.

Which specific group do I want to convince? I want to convince students because they are the ones who would participate in the school's recycling program.

TIP As you begin to write your persuasive essay, be sure to write in your own **voice.** In other words, avoid trying to sound like a journalist or someone you are not. Your writing should sound like you—a serious and thoughtful you who uses standard English.

Reference Note

For more on **voice,** see the Writing Mini-Lesson on page 224.

To Know Them Is to Persuade Them Analyzing the audience you have identified is an important part of persuasion. **If you can identify what type of people make up your audience and what they care about, you can use this information to help you write a convincing essay.** The writer of the following example analyzed his audience by answering three simple questions.

KEY CONCEPT

Issue: starting a paper-recycling program at our school

Audience: my classmates

What type of people make up my audience? My classmates are all around my age. Many of them are involved in sports and other outdoor activities.

How does this group feel about the issue? I'm not sure how they will feel about starting a paper-recycling program, but I do know that most of my classmates care about the future of the environment.

What objections might this group have to my opinion? Students might not think recycling at our school will make a difference because our school is small. Also, some students might think that recycling is too much trouble.

YOUR TURN 6 Identifying and Analyzing Your Audience

- Identify the audience for your persuasive essay by thinking about which groups would have strong feelings about your issue. Then, choose the specific group you want to convince.
- Analyze your audience by answering the questions in the second example on page 215.

Evaluate and Support Reasons

The House That Logic Built A good persuasive essay is like a sturdy house: Both rely on strong support to stand. One way to build a strong persuasive essay is to speak to the reader's head, or common sense, by making a **logical appeal. A writer who makes a logical appeal uses reasons and evidence to support an opinion.**

KEY CONCEPT

Reasons When someone writes "Television shows should have strict ratings," the obvious question *Why?* comes to the reader's mind. A **reason** tells *why* a writer has a particular point of view. Reasons are essential in persuasive writing. A writer who fails to give good reasons for a point of view will also fail to convince the reader.

Where can you find reasons? Sometimes you will have plenty of convincing reasons in your mind already, especially if you chose a familiar issue. You can also research resources such as the following to find reasons.

Resources for National Issues	Resources for Local Issues
major magazines	community leaders, school leaders, or other knowledgeable people in the community
the national section of newspapers, especially the opinion section	local newspapers, especially the opinion section
national news programs	local news programs
Web sites	Web sites
books and informational videos	books, booklets, pamphlets, or informational videos created by local agencies

Reference Note

For information on **evaluating Web sites,** see page 777 in the Quick Reference Handbook.

In order to be persuasive, you should make sure that each reason you choose for your essay appeals—or is attractive—to your audience. After all, they are the ones you want to convince. In the following example, the writer listed reasons for his school to start a paper-recycling program. Then, the writer evaluated (in boxes) each reason. Notice that he chose reasons that would appeal to a specific audience, his classmates.

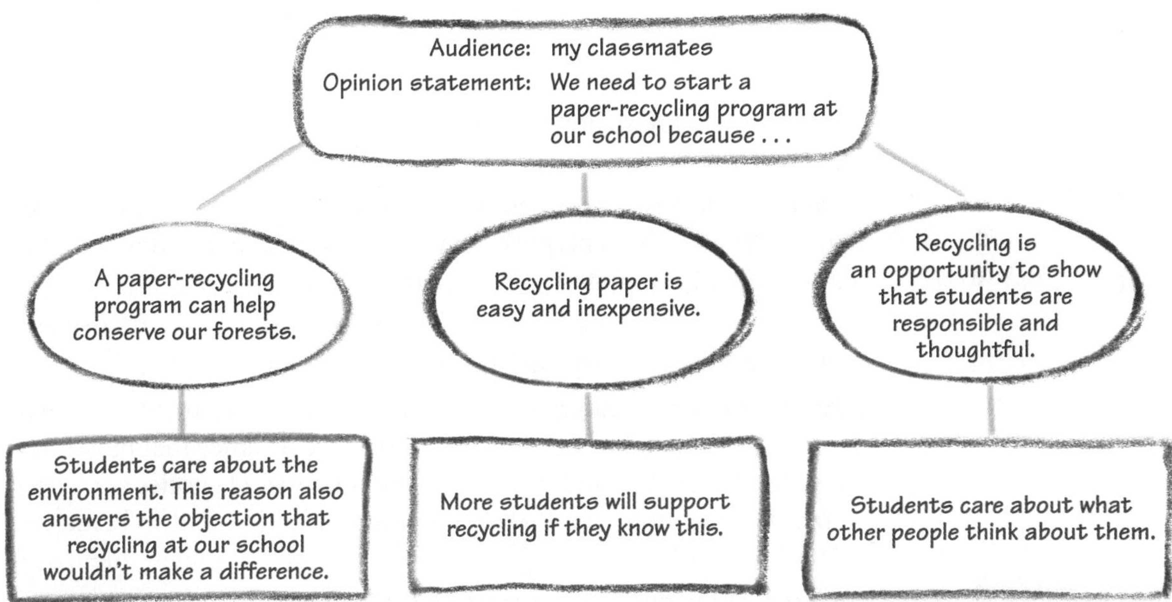

Audience: my classmates
Opinion statement: We need to start a paper-recycling program at our school because . . .
A paper-recycling program can help conserve our forests.
Recycling paper is easy and inexpensive.
Recycling is an opportunity to show that students are responsible and thoughtful.
Students care about the environment. This reason also answers the objection that recycling at our school wouldn't make a difference.
More students will support recycling if they know this.
Students care about what other people think about them.

YOUR TURN 7 Supporting and Evaluating Reasons

- Brainstorm or research a list of reasons that support your opinion on the issue you have chosen.
- Then, make a conceptual map like the one above to list and evaluate your reasons. Be sure to choose reasons that will be persuasive to your audience.

TIP Answering a possible objection the audience might raise to your opinion can be very persuasive. As you write your reasons, try to think of these objections, or **counterarguments,** and incorporate answers to them in your essay.

Evidence What does your audience have in common with a judge in a court of law? Both require strong evidence to make a decision. This is why a persuasive writer uses **evidence** in the form of *facts, statistics, examples, anecdotes,* or *expert opinions* to back up his or her reasons. Giving strong evidence to back up each of your reasons will increase the odds that the reader will judge in your favor and accept your point of view. Notice that the evidence (a **statistic**) in the following example makes the writer's reason more convincing.

> **Opinion Statement:** We should start a paper-recycling program at our school.
>
> **Reason:** A paper-recycling program can help conserve our forests.
>
> **Evidence:** We use about six tons of paper a year at our school.

Reference Note

For more on the types of **evidence,** see page 208.

Here are the major types of evidence that writers of persuasive essays typically use:

Facts A **fact** is a statement that can be proven true. For example, to say "It takes less energy to recycle aluminum than it does to produce it from raw material" is to state a fact.

Statistics A **statistic** is a fact in number form. "Almost 25 percent of our students are vegetarian" is an example of a statistic.

Anecdotes and Examples An **anecdote** is a brief story that illustrates a general idea. An **example** is a specific instance that illustrates a general idea: "Many resources about endangered species are available. For example, the Web has many interesting and informative sites."

Expert Opinions An **expert opinion** is the opinion of an authority on the subject. If you were writing about wildlife preservation, you might quote a person from a local wildlife refuge.

TIP Try using expert opinions from professional or knowledgeable people in your community. For example, if you were trying to get the lunchroom to offer vegetarian meals, you might get a doctor's opinion on the benefits of vegetarianism.

To find evidence to back up each of your reasons, try one or more of the following tips:

- Conduct a keyword search on an Internet search engine.
- Visit the library and search by subject in either the card catalog or the online catalog.
- Search newspapers and magazines for articles about your issue.
- Draw on your own experience by listing anecdotes and examples.

YOUR TURN 8 Gathering Evidence

Find at least one piece of evidence to support each of your reasons. Try to use more than one type of evidence as support.

Designing Your Writing

Using Graphics to Illustrate Support Persuasive writers often represent evidence in graphic form by using charts and graphs. Charts and graphs not only help a writer stress a point, but they also make the evidence easier to understand for the reader. The writer of the following example used a line graph to support the opinion that the study hall program at her school should be reinstated.

When the study hall program was in place, the average grade in my class rose to 90 percent. After a grading period without the study hall, the average fell to 82 percent.

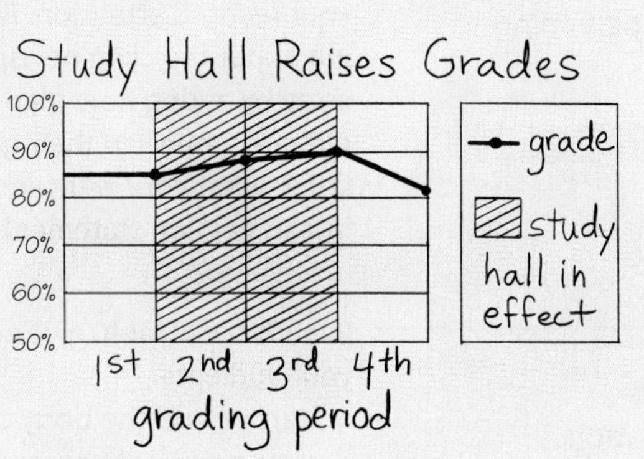

Elaborate on Your Support

Explain Yourself To avoid frustrating and confusing your readers, you should **elaborate on** your ideas. You can elaborate by

- defining a word that your readers may not know
- explaining a reason or how a piece of evidence supports a reason
- adding evidence, such as a fact, statistic, or anecdote

In the example below, the writer elaborates on his opinion by using two pieces of evidence and a sentence of explanation.

A paper-recycling program can help conserve our forests.	**Reason**
A ton of paper made from recycled material saves approximately seventeen trees.	**Evidence (fact)**
We use about six tons of paper each year at our school.	**Evidence (statistic)**
We could save over one hundred trees a year if we recycled that paper.	**Explanation**

TIP When elaborating on an idea, try using an analogy. Writers use **analogies** to explain or emphasize an idea by comparing it to something familiar.

Picking up garbage in your neighborhood is like going to the dentist for a checkup: It is not a lot of fun, but it needs to be done.

Reference Note

For more on **elaboration,** see page 311.

Persuasive Essay

Framework	Directions and Explanations
Introduction ■ Attention-grabbing beginning ■ Opinion statement	Start with an **interesting beginning,** or *lead,* to get your reader's attention. For example, if you were writing about recycling newspapers, you could open your essay by asking how many people have huge stacks of old newspapers in their garages. Let your readers know what your issue and point of view are by including an **opinion statement.**
Body ■ Reason #1 ■ Evidence and elaboration ■ Reason #2 ■ Evidence and elaboration and so on	In each paragraph, give a **reason** that will convince your audience. ■ Start or end the body of your essay with a bang by arranging your reasons according to their **order of importance.** ■ Be sure that you **logically support** your reasons by using **evidence** and that you **elaborate** on your reasons and evidence.
Conclusion ■ Restatement of opinion ■ Summary of reasons ■ Call to action or closing statement	**Restate your opinion** in different words, and **summarize your reasons** in one or two sentences. Close your essay with a **call to action** that tells your readers what you want them to do or with a strong **closing statement.**

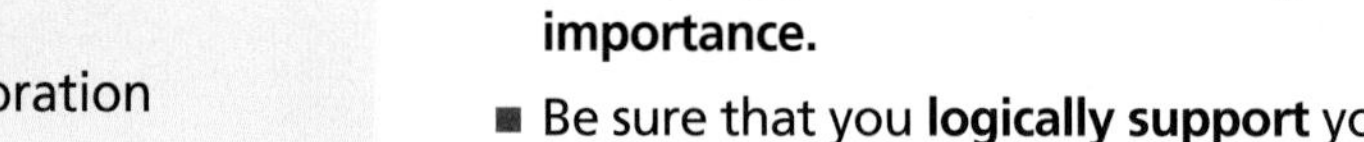

YOUR TURN 9 Drafting Your Persuasive Essay

As you write the first draft of your persuasive essay, refer to the framework above and the following Writer's Model.

A Writer's Model

The final draft below closely follows the framework for a persuasive essay.

One Hundred Trees, Please

As you probably know, the paper we use for our schoolwork and notes to our friends is made from trees. To this, some might say, "So what? Paper must be cheap, since it grows on trees." True, in a way paper *does* grow on trees and is inexpensive. However, the environmental cost of making new paper is quite high. We should start a paper-recycling program here at our school if we are truly serious about helping the environment and ourselves.

Attention-grabbing beginning

Opinion statement

A paper-recycling program can help conserve our forests—forests filled with vital oxygen-producing trees. By decreasing our demand for trees, we can make a difference right here at our school. A ton of paper made from recycled material saves approximately seventeen trees. We use about six tons of paper each year at our school. If we recycled that paper, we could save over one hundred trees a year.

Reason #1

Elaboration

Statistic

Elaboration

Recycling paper is easy and inexpensive. According to Marjorie Lamb, author of *2 Minutes a Day for a Greener Planet,* saving paper is one of the "easiest and most beneficial contributions we can make to our environment." North Lake Middle School started a paper-recycling program last year, and it has been a great success. In each classroom the teacher has a box for white paper. All the students have to do is throw white paper into the box and other trash into the regular trash can. The teacher's job is easy, too. At the end of the week, he or she simply sends a student to empty the box into one of the school's fifteen recycling containers. These containers, which are just trash cans marked "white paper only," cost the school only about $150. At the end of the week, the janitors take

Reason #2

Expert opinion

Anecdote

Elaboration

Fact

(continued)

(continued)

the recycling cans outside, where the city collects them at no charge. As you can see, for the cost of a few trash cans, we can start our own paper-recycling program.

Elaboration

Reason #3

A student-supported paper-recycling program could also show that we, as students, are responsible and thoughtful. A recent survey that appeared in the school newspaper revealed that 58 percent of adults see teenagers as people who are mostly interested in dating and shopping. We are interested in these things, but we also understand the importance of issues like recycling. We know that what we do now affects the world we live in tomorrow. If we were not concerned about the future, we would not have organized a carnival last year to raise money for endangered whales.

Statistic

Example

Scientists estimate that, in prehistoric times, forests covered about 60 percent of the earth's surface. Today, about 30 percent of the earth is covered with forests. Part of this problem is caused by our demand for new paper. I am not asking everyone to stop using paper. We need to use paper. What I *am* asking is that we do our part to help our environment and ourselves by starting a paper-recycling program. It will not only make a difference, but it is also easy, inexpensive, and a good opportunity for us to show that we care about the future of our planet. We can make a difference but only if we take the initiative.

Restatement of opinion

Summary of reasons

Closing statement

A Student's Model

The following is part of a persuasive essay by Arlyne Torres, a student at Carr Intermediate School in Santa Ana, California.

Viewing Violence

On television today, there is an exceptional amount of violence. It seems as if no matter what show you watch there is always some sort of violence going on. Whether it is actual people engaging in violence or cartoon characters, it is all the same. The problem is that many parents do not realize the negative effect television violence might have on their children. The violence on television needs to be limited, especially in children's programming.

Attention-grabbing beginning

Opinion statement

There are many shows on television that have violence in them, such as science fiction shows, morning talk shows, police shows, and some cartoon programming. I am convinced that every kid in America has imitated a show that had violence in it at some point. I know I have. Every day I see kids imitating violent programs on my way home. There are always little kids running after each other playing cops and robbers, while singing the theme song from the latest police or cartoon show. You cannot pass by one elementary school playground without seeing kids hitting each other because they are pretending to be characters from their favorite television shows.

Reason #1

Example

Kids learn things from television. One thing they learn is to solve problems with violence. According to the American Academy of Child and Adolescent Psychiatry, children can be influenced by violence on television. Many studies show that children see violence as a way to work out their problems. Josh, a sixteen-year-old, says, "I think that kids see that on cartoons the characters usually solve their problems by resorting to violence. I guess they think that if TV characters can work out their problems by using violence, they can, too. . . ."

Reason #2

Expert opinion

MINI-LESSON WRITING

Creating an Appropriate Voice and Tone

In the same way that your speaking voice reveals your personality, so too does your writing voice. **Voice,** in writing, is the way a writer uses his or her own style to "talk" to the reader. One aspect of your writing voice is your **tone.**

When you speak, you can raise, lower, or change the sound of your voice to reveal your attitudes and feelings. In writing your **tone** must be carried by your word choice and the way you handle your subject.

The tone for an essay should fit the purpose for writing. An effective tone for a persuasive essay is reasonable rather than whiny or unreasonable. Here are some tips for creating an effective tone:

- Show your audience that you are reasonable by using strong reasons and evidence.

Reasonable tone: Many students feel that the current amount of time between classes is just right for them to relax and socialize. In fact, last week's school paper reported that 73 percent of teachers feel the same way. After all, a happy, relaxed student is probably more likely to learn than a frazzled student.

Whiny tone: Shortening the time between classes is not fair. I want time to talk to my friends between classes. The amount of time we have now is just right, so don't shorten it.

- Attack the issue rather than those who oppose your opinion.

Reasonable tone: The mayor's plan to help the homeless by banning homeless shelters makes no sense at all. This plan would actually make it harder for the homeless to get back on their feet.

Unreasonable tone: The mayor has the common sense of a rock. Living in his big mansion has probably affected his brain.

PRACTICE

Read the paragraph to the right. Which sentences would you revise to keep the tone of this paragraph reasonable and formal? Show your revisions, and explain why you would make them.

The school board is considering a ban on backpacks in schools. I think the people who want the ban lack sense. The ban would also cause problems in class. According to a survey conducted by the principal, 78 percent of teachers in our school feel that students without backpacks will be less prepared for class than students with backpacks. Also, we should be able to carry backpacks if we want. The ban is not fair. I like my backpack.

Evaluate and Revise Content, Organization, and Style

Take a Second Look Like any artist, a writer must slowly craft an essay until, after much work, it is finished. To make your essay a finished piece, read it at least twice. In the first reading, check the content and organization of the essay. When you read it a second time, brush up its style by using the Focus on Sentences on page 227.

First Reading: Content and Organization Use the following chart to edit the organization and content of your essay.

Quick guide

Guidelines for Self-Evaluation and Peer Evaluation		
Evaluation Questions	**Tips**	**Revision Techniques**
1 Does the introduction have a clear opinion statement?	**Circle** the sentence that states the issue and the writer's point of view on it.	If needed, **add** an opinion statement, or **revise** the opinion statement to make the point of view clearer.
2 Do the paragraphs progress in order of importance?	**Number** the paragraphs in order of importance.	**Rearrange** the order of paragraphs, if necessary.
3 Does the writer give reasons to support his or her opinion? Does each reason have at least one piece of evidence to support it?	**Put a star** next to each reason, and **highlight** the evidence for each reason.	**Add** a reason, or **add** a fact, statistic, anecdote, example, or expert opinion to support a reason, if needed.
4 Does the body include elaboration to clarify reasons or evidence?	**Have a friend read** the essay. Ask him or her to **put a box** around anything that does not make sense.	**Elaborate** by adding definitions or explanations of words, reasons, and evidence where needed.
5 Does the conclusion restate the writer's opinion and summarize the reasons for the writer's opinion?	**Underline** the summary of reasons and restatement of opinion.	If necessary, **revise** the conclusion to include a summary of reasons and a restatement of opinion.

ONE WRITER'S REVISIONS The following is an early draft of the essay on pages 221–222.

add — *A student-supported paper-recycling program could also show that we, as students, are responsible and thoughtful.* ^ A recent survey that appeared in the school newspaper revealed that 58 percent of adults see teenagers as people who are mostly interested in dating and shopping. We are interested in these things, but we also understand the importance of issues like recycling. ^ *We know that what we do now affects the world we live in tomorrow.* — elaborate

Responding to the Revision Process

1. What does adding a sentence to the beginning of this paragraph do?
2. Why do you think the writer added a sentence to the end of the paragraph?

PEER REVIEW

As you evaluate a peer's persuasive essay, ask yourself these questions:

- What is the writer's issue and point of view?
- What is the most convincing reason the writer presents? What makes it convincing?

Second Reading: Style Content and organization have to do with *what* you say and *where* you say it. Style, on the other hand, involves *how* you say it. The content and organization of your persuasive essay may be excellent; however, if your style is boring or lacks variety, you may end up putting the audience to sleep. One way to improve the style of your essay and keep your audience awake is to make sure that your sentences have a variety of beginnings.

When you evaluate your persuasive essay for style, ask yourself whether the sentences in the essay have a variety of beginnings. As you re-read your writing, underline the first four words of each sentence. Then, read each sentence beginning aloud to identify sentences with similar kinds of beginnings. Revise some of the sentences by moving a phrase or clause from the end of the sentence to the beginning.

Sentences

Revising to Vary Sentence Beginnings

Using a variety of beginnings is one way to keep your audience's interest. When you revise your essay, look for places where you can move a verbal phrase or adverb clause from the end of a sentence to the beginning. A **verbal phrase** contains a verbal and acts as an adjective, noun, or adverb. An **adverb clause** is a clause that modifies a verb, adjective, or adverb.

Original Sentence	Revision Strategy	Revised Sentence
Some people take showers instead of baths to save water.	Move the *verbal phrase* to the beginning.	To save water, some people take showers instead of baths.
We must change our habits if we want to preserve our natural resources.	Move the *adverb clause* to the beginning.	If we want to preserve our natural resources, we must change our habits.

ONE WRITER'S REVISIONS The following revision is from an early draft of the essay on pages 221–222.

> We use about six tons of paper each year at our school. We could save over one hundred trees a year if we recycled that paper.

Responding to the Revision Process

How does this change add variety to this part of the essay?

TIP A verbal phrase or adverb clause that introduces a sentence is generally followed by a comma.

Reference Note

For more information and practice on **phrases** and **clauses,** see pages 415 and 439.

YOUR TURN 10 Evaluating and Revising Your Persuasive Essay

Evaluate the content and organization of your essay by using the guidelines on page 225. Then, use the Focus on Sentences above to help you add variety to your sentences.

Publishing

Proofread Your Essay

Reference Note

For more on **proofreading,** see page 13.

Too Close to See Have you ever lost something important, such as a key or a homework assignment? You look and look until someone says those words that make you feel silly: "Here it is, right in front of your face." Sometimes you get so close to something—be it a set of keys or an essay—that you cannot see it clearly. That is why it is important to have someone else, such as a friend or classmate, check your essay for mistakes. He or she might be able to find mistakes in grammar, usage, and punctuation that you have overlooked.

Grammar Link

Revising "There is/are, It is" Constructions

When giving evidence, persuasive writers sometimes use a sentence that begins with "There is/are" or "It is." These sentences have *delayed* or *lost subjects.* A **delayed subject** is one that comes too late in the sentence. A **lost subject** is one that is totally missing. Delayed or lost subjects can weaken the evidence in a persuasive essay.

Delayed: *There are* many doctors who say that exercise is important. [The true subject is *doctors.* Beginning the sentence with *There* weakens its focus.]

Better: Many doctors say that exercise is important.

Lost: *It is* believed that the hole in the ozone layer is getting worse. [The subject is lost. *Who* believes the hole in the ozone layer is getting worse?]

Better: *Scientists* believe that the hole in the ozone layer is getting worse.

PRACTICE

The following sentences have lost or delayed subjects. If the sentence has no subject, try to add one that makes sense. Write the revised sentences on your own paper.

1. It is known that it takes light from the sun about eight minutes to reach the earth.
2. It is felt by 32 percent of my classmates that the proposal should be adopted.
3. There are several researchers who credit the new drug with saving lives.
4. It is believed that the world's supply of fossil fuels will not last much longer.
5. There are many people who will vote against Proposition 22.

For more on **identifying subjects,** see page 327.

Publish Your Essay

Extra, Extra, Read All About It Now that you have brainstormed, researched, written, and revised, it is time for your essay to do what it was meant to do—to persuade. Here are some ideas that will help you get your essay to your audience.

- Consider making a collection of persuasive essays for your school's library. Ask your classmates to submit their essays. Then, with the help of those who submitted essays, group the essays according to subject. For example, in one group you might have essays about environmental issues. Then, put the essays into a notebook, and make an index that lists the title, page number, and author of each essay.
- If you participate in a school publication, such as a literary magazine or a newspaper, try to get your essay published as an editorial in that publication.
- If you have a more specialized audience, such as baseball card collectors or Civil War history buffs, post your essay on a Web page that is related to your issue.

Reflect on Your Essay

Building Your Portfolio Think about what you wrote and how you wrote it by answering the following questions:

- What piece of evidence in your essay was the strongest? Why do you think so?
- How did you find supporting evidence for your essay? Do you think finding evidence will be easier the next time you write an essay? Why or why not?
- Do you think your essay could have been more convincing? Why or why not?
- Did your essay achieve your purpose for writing? In what way?

YOUR TURN 11 Proofreading and Publishing Your Essay

- Proofread your essay for grammar, mechanics, and usage mistakes.
- Publish your essay for your audience.
- Answer the Reflect on Your Essay questions. Write your responses in a learning log, or record them in your portfolio.

COMPUTER TIP

Use a spelling checker to find errors. However, because spelling checkers only show misspellings, you should also read your essay to find words often confused, such as *brake* and *break*. For more information and practice on **words often confused,** see page 698.

MINI-LESSON **TEST TAKING**

Writing a Position Paper for a Test

In a writing test, you may be asked to discuss two sides of an issue and then to recommend one side. This type of essay is called a **position paper.** How would you approach the test prompt below?

> Your principal has decided that students should complete twenty hours of community service during the school year. The two plans under consideration are assigning students a job during school hours or allowing students to choose a job and complete the hours on their own time. In a letter to your principal, discuss both options, state your position, and provide reasons to support your position.

THINKING IT THROUGH

Taking a Position

STEP 1 Identify the issue, options, purpose, and audience.

Issue: how students should complete their hours; Option 1: assigned a job and given time during school; Option 2: choose a job and complete the hours on own time; Purpose: to persuade; Audience: my principal

STEP 2 Use the memory device **MEETS** (**m**oney, **e**ffort, **e**ducation, **t**ime, **s**afety) to list the benefits of each position.

Students choose: I can complete the hours when I want; I'll get to do work that I enjoy; Principal chooses: I'll have no trouble finding a job; it won't conflict with activities outside school.

STEP 3 Use **MEETS** to list the drawbacks of each position.

Students choose: I might have less time to do my homework; Principal chooses: Students may not like the work assigned to them; students may not learn responsibility if the principal chooses the job and work schedule for them.

STEP 4 Write your essay in five paragraphs.

Introduction: Identify the issue and the two options.

Body Paragraph #1: Discuss the benefits of the first option.

Body Paragraph #2: Discuss the benefits of the second option.

Body Paragraph #3: State your position and fully explain the drawbacks of the option you did not choose.

Conclusion: Restate your position and close your essay.

Writing a Short Story That Persuades

Although pigs cannot write, they can be very persuasive—at least when they are characters in a *fable.* **Fables** are short stories that teach lessons about life.

A Fabulous Recipe Fables generally follow a formula. Using this formula helps a writer make a persuasive point in just a few paragraphs. The main ingredients of a fable are shown below.

Element	Definition	Example
Characters	usually animals that talk and act like humans	an ant who saves food all summer and a grasshopper who relaxes all summer
Conflict	the problem the characters face	In winter, the ant has food because he prepared, but the grasshopper has none.
Moral	the lesson	Be prepared.

A Lesson for Us All The most important part of a fable is its *moral.* The **moral,** or lesson, is like the opinion statement of a persuasive essay. It expresses what the writer wants readers to do or believe.

Read the following fable by Aesop, retold by Anne Terry White.

The Dog and His Shadow
by Aesop

Curly the Dog was happily trotting home. It wasn't every day that the butcher gave him a juicy bone with meat on it! The Dog was carrying it very carefully in his mouth.

On the way he had to cross a little stream. He looked down from the footbridge into the clear water. And, to his surprise, he saw another dog under the water. Yes, and that other dog also had a bone in his mouth! It seemed to Curly that it was a bigger bone than his own.

With a growl he dropped his bone in order to grab the other dog's bone too. But he had no sooner done that than the dog under the water also dropped his bone.

For a moment Curly stood looking angrily down at his shadow. He couldn't understand it. All he knew was that he had lost his bone and must now trot home without it.

MORAL: Grasp for all and lose all.

Aesop's character is a dog named Curly. The conflict is that Curly wants more than what he has. The moral is that greed will only cause unhappiness.

The steps on the next page will show you how to write a fable of your own.

THINKING IT THROUGH Planning a Modern Fable

STEP 1 Decide what lesson you want readers to learn from your fable, and write your moral.

I want people to learn that they should always try to help others. The moral could be "Those who help others will be helped when they need it."

STEP 2 Choose a conflict that will lead to your moral, and choose a setting.

Two characters will get in a bad situation. The one who has helped others will get help and the other will not. I'll set my fable in an airport to make it modern.

STEP 3 Decide what part each character will play in the lesson.

I'll use a dog and a cat. The dog will be helpful to others. The cat will always ignore people who need help.

STEP 4 Map out the plot events that will show the lesson in action.

Before getting on the plane, a passenger asks the cat for some money to use the phone, but the cat ignores him. The dog loans money to the needy passenger. The cat and the dog get off the plane, but neither has enough money to get a taxi home. Since the needy passenger is a taxi driver, he gives the dog a ride home in his taxi to thank him. The cat has to walk five miles home in the rain with his luggage.

Room for Improvement Here are a few suggestions for improving your fable.

- **Explain *why* your characters do what they do.** Giving reasons for your characters' actions helps readers see what you have in mind more clearly.
- **Rewrite your moral to fit the ending of the story better.** You may find that your story idea changed as you wrote. If your moral no longer fits the story well, it will lose some of its persuasive punch.
- **Change your characters to better fit the roles they play.** Fable writers choose characters that represent certain personality traits. A greedy character might be a vulture, or a clever character might be a fox. Choosing traditional or well-known characters will help your readers understand your lesson.

YOUR TURN 12 Writing a Modern Fable

Follow the Thinking It Through steps above to plan a persuasive modern fable. Then, write and revise your fable using the suggestions above.

Giving and Listening to a Persuasive Speech

WHAT'S AHEAD?

In this section you will give a speech. You will also learn how to

- **adapt a persuasive essay for use as a speech**
- **use visuals while delivering a speech**
- **practice a good speaking voice**
- **evaluate a persuasive speech**

One way to convince others to accept your opinion is to give a persuasive speech. Since you have already written a persuasive essay, you might be tempted to read your essay out loud directly from the page. However, to give an effective persuasive speech, you will need to do much more than read your essay to your audience; you will need to deliver the most important points of your essay in a solid presentation that will keep your audience interested in what you have to say.

Adapting Your Persuasive Essay

When giving a persuasive speech, you should be concerned with both the content of your speech and the way you deliver it. As you review your essay to find material for your speech, use these hints to help you.

- **Get and keep your audience's attention.** Begin your speech by telling a quick anecdote, asking a question, or contrasting viewpoints on your issue. Then, use a persuasive technique, such as an emotional appeal, to maintain your audience's attention.
- **Think about your audience.** Try to anticipate and give answers to the main **counterarguments** your audience may have. In other words, tailor your speech to appeal to your listeners. Every story, point, example, and visual you choose should be directed to them.
- **Adjust the tone of your speech.** Delivering your speech from a simple outline—an organized list of your main points—will help your speech sound more conversational than an essay.

Reference Note

For more on **speaking skills**, see page 794 in the Quick Reference Handbook.

For more information and practice on **identifying persuasive techniques,** see page 254.

For more on **counterarguments,** see the tip on page 217.

Reference Note

For more information on **using graphics,** see page 77.

Delivering a Persuasive Speech

Get the Picture? Since the purpose of your speech is to persuade others, your delivery, or *how* you give the speech, is critical. Even a speech with not-so-strong content can be successful if the speaker presents it well. One way to make your speech more convincing is to use visuals. Each visual you use should help the audience better understand a main point from your speech.

Visuals can be used to make logical or emotional appeals. For example, to convince adults to bicycle to their jobs to help reduce pollution, you might make a logical appeal. You could do this by creating a graph showing the increase in pollution from automobile exhaust over the last five years. The data in the graph would show your audience that your opinion makes sense.

On the other hand, you may use an emotional appeal in a visual to convince small children not to litter. By showing a picture of a smiling girl throwing away her trash, your audience will think that taking responsibility to keep the city clean can make them feel good.

When deciding which visuals to use with your persuasive speech, consider the following guidelines.

- Choose a visual that will complement or extend an important idea from your speech.
- Make words and images large enough for everyone to see.
- Keep words to a minimum to avoid clutter.
- Use an easel, if available, for graphs, charts, and other hand-held visuals; if you use video stills, be sure that a TV and VCR will be available. You can also use presentation software.
- Be sure to explain the visual to your audience.

TIP Also refer to the evaluation guidelines and other information on page 236 when planning and practicing your speech.

Be a Smooth Talker Would you be persuaded to believe someone's opinion if during the speech he or she stumbled over words several times, spoke too quietly, and generally did not have his or her act together? To ensure that your speech runs smoothly and to avoid embarrassment, keep the following suggestions in mind when practicing your speech.

- If possible, practice in front of an audience so that you can get used to speaking in front of a group.
- Use your visuals as you practice delivering your speech.
- Do not turn your back to the audience as you point to or explain a visual.

- If you plan to use special equipment that you do not have at home, such as an overhead projector, make sure it works. Then, practice using it at school.

Speak Up! A good speaking voice is another factor that can determine how persuasive you are. A speaker who can barely be heard or who speaks in a flat, uninteresting voice will have trouble getting an audience to listen to his or her opinion. The chart below shows important elements of a good speaking voice and describes how to practice using them.

Element	Explanation	Practice Tips
Pronunciation	Speak clearly and carefully so that your words are easy to understand.	After practicing your speech, ask your audience if there were words or sentences that they could not understand. Remember these trouble spots when you deliver the real speech.
Volume	Speak loudly enough so the people in the back of the room can hear you. You may want to raise and lower your voice to stress certain points or words.	Ask your audience if they can hear you. Adjust your volume accordingly.
Pitch	A flat voice can lull an audience to sleep. Varying your pitch—how high or deep your voice is—will help you keep the audience interested in your speech.	Experiment with your pitch to find an interesting balance, somewhere between too flat and too excited.
Eye contact	Make eye contact with the audience rather than looking down at your notes all the time. Eye contact will keep the audience involved.	If no one is available to watch you rehearse, practice looking at items in the room, such as lamps, tables, pictures, or chairs.
Rate	Speak slowly so your audience can keep up with what you are saying. When necessary, pause to catch your breath. You may also wish to pause after a major point or question to give the audience time to think about what you have said.	On the day of your actual speech, you will probably speak faster than you expect. Concentrate on speaking at a slow and comfortable pace.

When practicing, try to simulate the conditions of the actual day you deliver the speech. Practice using your simple outline to deliver your speech. Also, experiment with a timer or watch to ensure that you stay within a certain time if your teacher has given you a limit.

YOUR TURN 13 Delivering a Persuasive Speech

Adapt your persuasive essay for use as a persuasive speech. Then, practice and refine your speech before presenting it to your class.

Evaluating a Persuasive Speech

TIP As you listen to a classmate's persuasive speech, evaluate the speaker's **credibility.** Develop your own criteria, or use these tips: Begin by interpreting the speaker's **perspective,** or bias. What is the speaker's relationship to the topic? Does the speaker have personal motives for wanting to persuade you? Listen for the speaker's use of fact and opinion. Credible speakers use facts and other types of evidence to support an opinion. However, speakers who lack credibility fill their speeches with unsupported opinions and let their bias overwhelm the speech.

Reference Note

For more information on **listening to evaluate,** see page 807 in the Quick Reference Handbook.

For more on **distinguishing fact from opinion,** see page 779 in the Quick Reference Handbook.

To evaluate the effectiveness of an essay, you only have to consider the words on the page. However, evaluating a speech is a little more complicated. After all, a speech involves not only words but also a speaker. To help you decide if a classmate's persuasive speech is effective, answer the questions in the chart below as you listen to the speech.

Content	▪ What is the purpose of the presentation? ▪ What is the topic? What is the speaker's verbal message about the topic? Does the speaker clearly state his or her opinion? ▪ Does the speaker include convincing reasons and enough strong support for those reasons?
Use of Visuals	▪ Does the speaker use visuals that make important ideas easy to understand? ▪ Are the visuals easy to see? ▪ Does the speaker explain the visual thoroughly? ▪ Overall, do the visuals add to the effectiveness of the presentation?
Delivery	▪ Is the speaker's tone conversational? ▪ Does the speaker speak loudly and slowly enough? ▪ Does the speaker make eye contact with the audience? ▪ Do the speaker's nonverbal messages (such as gestures and facial expressions) match the verbal message?

YOUR TURN 14 Evaluating a Persuasive Speech

As students in your class deliver their speeches, use the chart above to help you evaluate each speaker's message and delivery. Then, compare your evaluations with the evaluations of one of your classmates. In what ways were your evaluations different or similar?

Choices

Choose one of the following activities to complete.

CAREER

1. Choose Me Pretend that as you are filling out an application for your dream job, you come to a writing prompt, which reads: "Briefly explain why this company should consider you for employment." Respond to this prompt by writing a short, yet convincing, **essay.**

WRITING

2. A Strong Reaction Read the editorial section of a newspaper. Look for an editorial that discusses an issue that is important to you. Then, write your own **editorial** explaining why you agree or disagree with the opinion in the editorial you read. As you write your editorial, give reasons to support your opinion. Post your editorial on a Web page or bulletin board.

CROSSING THE CURRICULUM: ART

3. A Picture Is Worth a Thousand Words Express your opinion on a current event or issue by creating a **political cartoon.** First, collect and study a few cartoons from your newspaper's editorial section. Notice that political cartoonists do not use many words; instead, they rely on techniques such as exaggeration and symbolism to express their views. After studying the cartoons, create your own. When you are done, trade with a classmate and see if he or she can tell what your opinion is.

CROSSING THE CURRICULUM: MUSIC

4. The Beat Goes On Persuade others through music by creating a **jingle** for a made-up product, such as a new cereal or toy. Jingles use repeated words, rhymes, and rhythms so the listeners will remember the product. To compose your jingle, you can use a tune you already know and write lyrics that appeal to a particular audience.

MASS MEDIA

5. Change the World Videotape a **public service announcement** for a social issue that is important to you. Decide on a message, such as "stay in school" or "preserve the rain forests." Use words, sounds, and pictures that will get your target audience to take action.

CHAPTER

7 Using Brochures

Reading Workshop

Reading a Brochure

Writing Workshop

Creating a Brochure

Viewing and Representing

Analyzing a Caricature

Informational Text

Persuasion

You and your family are spending spring break with relatives out of state. You want to do something fun, but you cannot persuade your family to leave the house, and besides, you are not familiar with the area. What can you do? One way to inform your family about area attractions—and to persuade them to take you to one of these attractions—is to hand them a *promotional brochure.* **Promotional brochures** are foldout advertisements. You can find brochures in hotel lobbies, visitor centers, and restaurants.

Whether they advertise area attractions or products and services, most promotional brochures share some common characteristics. They are designed to be easy to carry and distribute. They also share the same goal: to persuade potential customers through pictures and words.

YOUR TURN 1 Discovering Brochures

Gather a few brochures from a doctor's office, travel agency, or your school counselor's office. Then, answer the following questions.

- What product or service does each brochure advertise?
- For whom do you think each brochure was created? Explain.
- Which brochure is the most effective? What makes this brochure effective? Be specific.

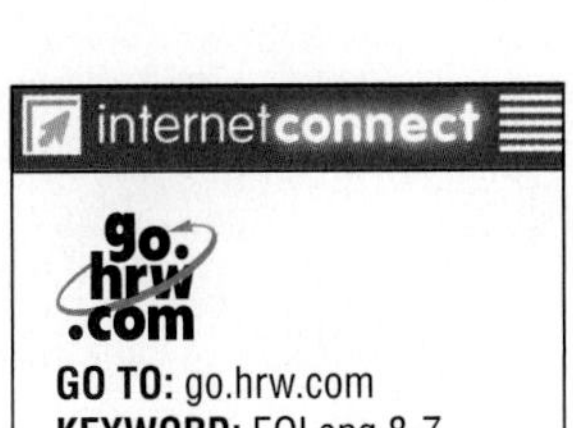

GO TO: go.hrw.com
KEYWORD: EOLang 8-7

Reading a Brochure

WHAT'S AHEAD?

In this section you will read a promotional brochure. You will also learn how to

- **analyze illustrations**
- **identify a writer's point of view**

Imagine counting an alligator's teeth or walking through a garden brimming with butterflies. These are two of the many activities mentioned in the brochure that appears on the next few pages. As you read the brochure, decide whether it is persuasive enough to convince you to visit one of the nature centers it advertises.

Preparing to Read

READING FOCUS

Illustrations Creators of promotional brochures know that in a split second, a reader decides whether to toss the brochure aside or continue reading. **Illustrations,** including drawings and photographs, have the job of catching the reader's attention and communicating information quickly. Before you read the brochure on pages 241–243, give it a brief glance. Do the illustrations capture your interest and make you want to look at the brochure more closely?

READING SKILL

Point of View Promotional brochures use more than just illustrations to be persuasive. They also present a **point of view** that clearly expresses how the writer feels—and more important, how the writer wants the reader to feel—about the subject. The point of view is expressed in the **slogan,** which is a brief, catchy saying that expresses the main idea of the advertisement. The point of view can also be found in the carefully chosen words of the text. As you read the brochure "The Wildest Places in Southwest Florida," see if you can use the slogan and the text to identify the writer's point of view—why he or she wrote this piece.

Reading Selection

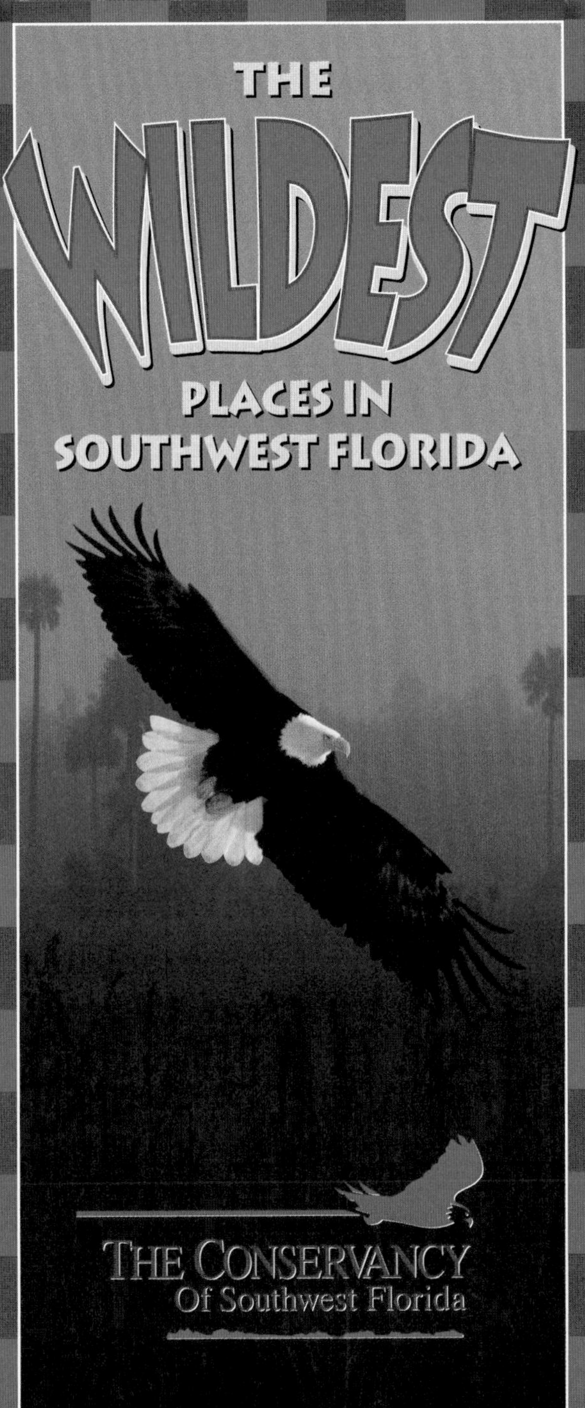

To the left is the front panel of a brochure. Read it, and then read the inside of the same brochure, which appears on the following pages. In a notebook, jot down answers to the active-reading questions in the shaded boxes. The underlined words will be used in the Vocabulary Mini-Lesson on page 248.

1. What does the slogan at the top of the brochure emphasize?

2. Why do you think the front cover uses bright colors and few words?

The Wildest Places In Naples Are At The Conservancy

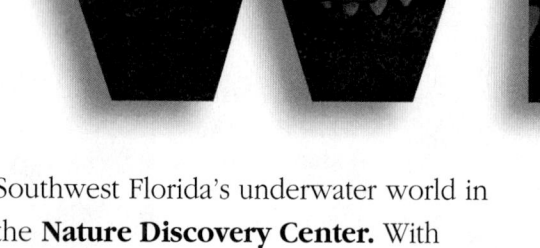

Our two nature centers offer a great way to take a walk on the *wild side!* At the **NAPLES NATURE CENTER**, touch a snake, count an alligator's teeth, and explore Southwest Florida's underwater world in the **Nature Discovery Center.** With hands-on exhibits, daily presentations and special programs, you'll discover a whole new side to Southwest Florida's *wild side!*

Next, visit a special "hospital" for native wild animals at the **Wildlife Rehabilitation Center**. Through the "O.L.W.S." video monitoring system, watch recuperating "patients" and learn why wild animal rehabilitation is so important. You can also see several of the Center's permanent residents, including bald eagles, hawks and owls.

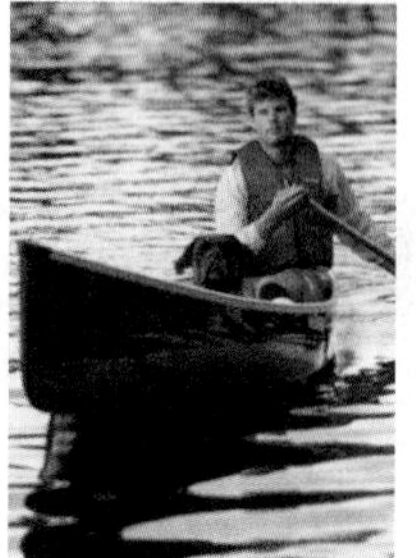

For a real walk on the *wild side*, join a naturalist-guided trail walk or take a boat ride through a mangrove forest. Or, rent a canoe or kayak and explore the *wild side* on your own!

Stop off at the **Nature Store** for guides and gear before heading off to **BRIGGS NATURE CENTER**, located in the 12,700 acre Rookery Bay National Estuarine Research Reserve.

In the **Interpretive Center**, meet some *wild side* residents of the mangrove-estuary ecosystem—a system second only to the rainforests in species diversity and productivity—then take a walk through the **Butterfly Garden**, filled with native plants that attract more than 27 species of butterflies.

Next, hike into the heart of Rookery Bay along the half-mile boardwalk or meander through the maze of mangroves during a guided boat tour, canoe trip or wilderness excursion—offered seasonally.

Guided boat trips include a bird-watching tour, a beachcombing and shelling trip to a nearby barrier island, and a backwater tour through Rookery Bay's mangrove islands.

And, guided canoe and wilderness excursions are a great way to explore more of Southwest Florida's *wild side!*

For independent adventurers, canoe and kayak rentals are also available, along with a self-guided aquatic trail. Take a walk on the *wild side* with The Conservancy.

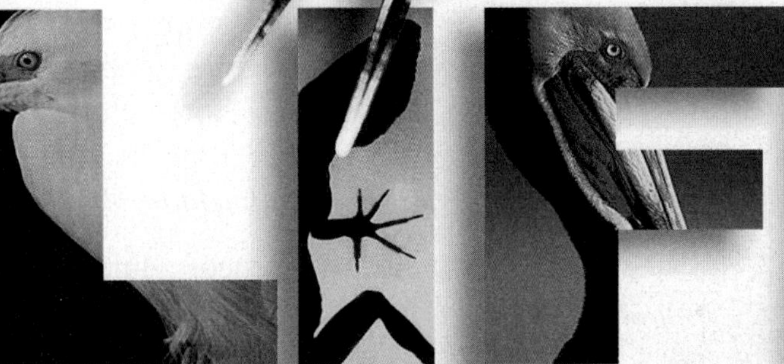

3. What effect do you think the word "wildlife" and its colorful pictures might have on readers?

4. What makes this picture eye-catching?

5. Why do you think the brochure writer repeats the *wild side* phrase?

First Thoughts on Your Reading

1. **Do the pictures of wildlife make you want to visit the places mentioned in the brochure? Why or why not?**
2. **How does the information in the brochure affect your opinion of the nature centers?**

READING FOCUS

Illustrations

A Quick Draw Think of the difficult task of a promotional brochure. It must attract readers to look at it, provide important information, and persuade—all in a limited amount of space.

Often, people pick up promotional brochures because of the brochure's secret weapon—illustrations. Carefully chosen illustrations help grab a reader's attention, but they do not stop there. Illustrations also provide information about products, places, or objects, so that the reader can *see* what the brochure is selling.

Creators of promotional brochures choose illustrations that will have an impact. They consider three important elements when choosing illustrations: *story, color,* and *medium.*

Story You see a picture of someone surfing, and suddenly you can imagine yourself in the scene, catching the perfect wave as admirers watch from the shore. Many illustrations are more than just images—they pull you into a story. If the story seems interesting, the viewer will want to know more.

The picture to the left suggests a story about a bike rider in a competition. Does he win? Is he part of a team? How did he get so good? One simple picture has drawn you into the story and made you interested. Now, imagine that this picture is part of a brochure for a stunt bike-riding clinic. The picture may prompt you to read further or even to call about enrolling. If so, the illustration has done its job.

Reference Note

For more on **elements of illustration,** see page 826 in the Quick Reference Handbook.

Color Color is an important element of illustration because different colors can set different moods and influence people in different ways. To understand how color affects people, you need to understand the two types of color: warm and cool.

Warm colors include reds, yellows, and oranges. As you might imagine, warm colors give a feeling of warmth, emotion, and interest.

Their deep intensity draws the viewer in by creating a more vivid picture. Which one of the pictures on the right interests you more?

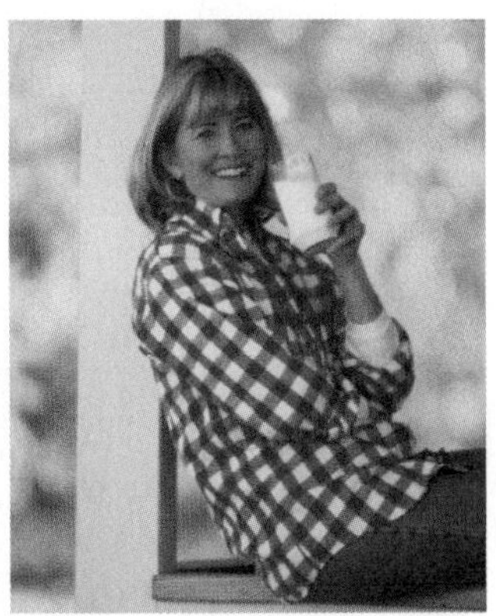

The woman on the porch is the same in both pictures. The warm colors in the second photo, however, catch the reader's eye and spark attention and interest.

Cool colors are blues, greens, and purples. They are soothing. You may think that no one would choose cool colors for a brochure since advertisers would want strong emotional reactions to their products. Imagine, however, that you had to choose between the two pictures to the right for a brochure about a walk-in health clinic.

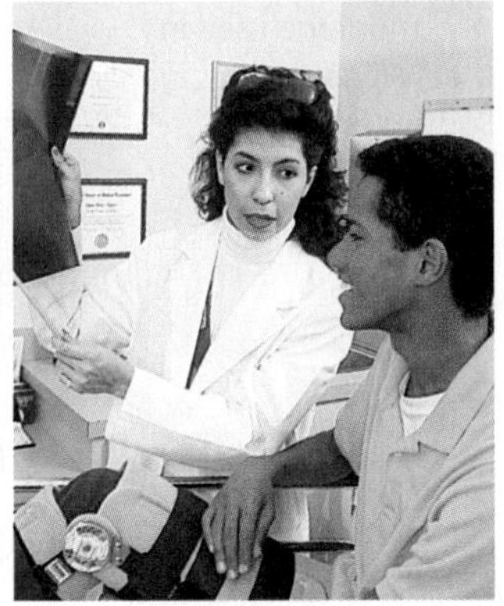

Which picture inspires a sense of calm and confidence? The cool colors of the second picture make the viewer feel relaxed and the doctor seem professional. Many doctors actually use cool colors on their office walls to promote a calm atmosphere. Look at the wall colors in your classroom and hallways. Is your school doing the same thing?

Medium If the story of Winnie-the-Pooh had used photographs instead of cute drawings, children's reactions would probably have been quite different. A real bear would be much scarier, and it would have been difficult to photograph an actual bear in many of Pooh's situations, such as getting stuck in a doorway after eating too much honey.

An advertiser creating a brochure has to decide what medium will be the most effective. Should the picture be a photograph, a pencil drawing, clip art from a computer, or some other art form? These various forms are known as **media.** Different media can serve different purposes and have different effects. The choice of one medium over another will affect the force of an illustration. Suppose you were selling a lawn mower light enough to pick up with one hand. Which would be more persuasive: a photograph of a person holding the lawn mower or a drawing of the same scene? A photograph showing a *real* person holding the *real* lawn mower would be much more effective.

TIP A **medium** is an instrument, such as a photograph, used to communicate ideas. The plural form of *medium* is *media.*

YOUR TURN 2 Analyzing Illustrations

Using the chart below, analyze the illustrations in the brochure on pages 241–243. Copy the chart onto a sheet of paper, and write the answers to the questions for the three illustrations.

Element Questions	Eagle page 241	The word *Wildlife* pages 242–243	Canoe page 242
Story What is the story in the illustration? What does the illustration make the reader want to know?			
Color Are warm or cool colors used? What effects could the colors have?			
Medium What medium has the illustrator used? Why was this medium chosen? Is the medium effective? Explain.			

TIP A **photomontage** is a picture that is made up of several smaller pictures.

? Where is a photomontage used in the "Wildest Places in Southwest Florida" brochure?

READING SKILL

Point of View

Get to the Point Brochures aim to persuade readers to buy or do something. *How* a brochure writer tries to persuade readers depends on that writer's *point of view.* The **point of view** is what the writer believes about the product, place, or service the brochure advertises. Point of view is also known as **bias.**

Readers can identify a writer's point of view by looking at the slogan and the use of positive or negative words in the brochure. (A **slogan** is a phrase or motto that summarizes the main idea of the brochure in a catchy or memorable way.) The point of view in the slogan "Take A Bite Out Of Crime®" is clear. The writer believes readers should join the fight against crime, and the slogan commands the reader to do it. Point of view is also expressed in the positive and negative words in a brochure's text. Look at the following sentence:

> The tranquil beauty of the Wildflower Nature Center takes visitors far away from the frantic pace of the city.

TIP The way a slogan sounds is just as important as what it says. Here are two slogans: "Take A Bite Out Of Crime®" and "Reduce Crime."

Which slogan is more effective? Why?

The use of *tranquil* to describe the nature center and *frantic* to describe the city shows the writer's preference for nature.

Try figuring out the point of view of the following paragraph. Examine the use of positive and negative words in the text. The steps that follow the paragraph will help you if you get stuck.

Our Stars Are Ready When You Are

Stargazing can be tricky. Sometimes the weather is uncooperative. Other times you have trouble adjusting your telescope. When you do spot a brilliant set of stars, you have no idea what they are. Highlands Planetarium has the solution. Our indoor planetarium will cradle you in comfort as you gaze at a dazzling night sky. You will not need a complicated telescope, and the weather always cooperates—just like our stars.

THINKING IT THROUGH Identifying Point of View

STEP 1 Read the slogan and the paragraph. Write down any positive or negative words.

Positive: solution, cradle, comfort, dazzling, cooperates

Negative: tricky, uncooperative, trouble, complicated

STEP 2 Look for patterns in the words.

All the negative words describe looking at the stars outside. The positive words describe seeing the stars in the planetarium.

STEP 3 What is the writer's point of view?

The writer thinks it is more comfortable and informative to look at artificial stars in a planetarium than it is to look at real stars outside.

YOUR TURN 3 Identifying Point of View

Use the Thinking It Through steps above to determine the writer's point of view in the brochure on pages 241–243.

MINI-LESSON **VOCABULARY**

Understanding Connotation and Denotation

Imagine that a friend invites you on a *difficult* hike. Would you go? What if the hike is *challenging*? Are you more interested?

The difference between these words is the **connotation,** the meaning you associate with a word. *Difficult* and *challenging* both mean "hard to do." They have the same **denotation,** or dictionary meaning. *Difficult*, however, has a more negative association than *challenging*. Connotation is an important tool in persuasion.

To understand a new word completely, whether reading it or hearing it, be aware of both the word's denotation and connotations. A dictionary will help you with the denotation, but the word's context and your own experience will help you understand its connotation.

THINKING IT THROUGH — Determining the Connotation of Words

Here is an example of determining the connotation of the word *meander* from "The Wildest Places in Southwest Florida" brochure.

STEP 1 Write down the word's definition. (Use a dictionary if needed.)	Definition: to wander without purpose
STEP 2 Consider your experiences with the word, and determine whether you associate a meaning with it.	Advertisers always try to make their products look good. Since the brochure is trying to persuade me to meander, it probably has a positive meaning.
STEP 3 Examine the word's context to see if you can get clues to its connotation.	"Meander through the maze of mangroves. . . ." I think the writer wants you to think about taking your time to enjoy the sights.
STEP 4 Revise the dictionary definition to include the connotation.	Meander: to wander without purpose, taking your time to enjoy the sights

PRACTICE

Determine the connotation of these words as they are used in "The Wildest Places in Southwest Florida" brochure. The words are underlined so you can see each word's context.

1. explore (page 242)
2. recuperating (page 242)
3. diversity (page 243)
4. excursions (page 243)
5. adventurers (page 243)

MINI-LESSON **TEST TAKING**

Answering Questions about a Writer's Point of View

A strong sales pitch has a clear point of view that explains why a product is worth buying. In informative writing, however, the writer usually tries to downplay his or her bias and focuses on presenting the facts. Still, even informative writers have a point of view, and a careful reader can often figure out what that point of view is. How would you approach the following passage and the question that follows it?

> The Ad Council uses public service announcements to build awareness of pressing social issues facing the United States. The Ad Council began as the War Advertising Council during World War II. It created its first impressive symbol in "Rosie the Riveter," who convinced women to work for the war effort. The council has had many powerful symbols and slogans since its beginnings with Rosie, including Smokey Bear and "A Mind Is A Terrible Thing To Waste.®"

What is the writer's point of view in this passage?

A. The Ad Council uses public service announcements to make money.

B. The Ad Council's work has little impact.

C. The Ad Council creates powerful ads that address social problems.

D. Rosie the Riveter is not an effective symbol anymore.

THINKING IT THROUGH

Identifying Point of View

STEP 1 Determine whether the writer uses more positive words or more negative words.

The writer uses several positive words, including impressive, convinced, and powerful, to describe the Ad Council's work.

STEP 2 Try to answer the question in your own words.

The writer's point of view seems to be that the Ad Council creates effective ads.

STEP 3 Look for the choice that best matches your own answer.

Answer A may be true, but there is no information in the passage to support it.

Answer B cannot be right. The passage calls the Ad Council's work "powerful."

Answer C is close to what I guessed. It might be the right answer.

Answer D is not correct because the author never says anything negative about Rosie the Riveter. Answer C is the right answer.

Creating a Brochure

WHAT'S AHEAD?

In this workshop you will create a promotional brochure. You will also learn how to

- **identify the wants and needs of your target market**
- **write a catchy slogan**
- **identify persuasive techniques**
- **choose illustrations effectively**
- **punctuate a series of adjectives**

The ancient Babylonians hung signs outside of their stores. Tenth-century European shopkeepers hired town criers. By the nineteenth century, business owners around the world used printed posters, newspaper advertisements, and brochures. Over the centuries, business-minded people have done—and continue to do—all of these things with one purpose in mind: to convince customers to buy products or services.

This workshop will give you the opportunity to participate in the age-old art of advertising by creating a promotional brochure for a product or service. Creating a promotional brochure allows you to be a writer, an artist, and a salesperson all at the same time.

Prewriting

Choose a Product or Service

Did Somebody Say Fund-raiser? You have plenty of soap, dozens of sponges, a huge stack of towels, and half a dozen helpers. Your car wash is all set up, but where are the cars? If your club, team, or school raises money through a fund-raiser, consider using that activity as the subject of your brochure. Then, you can use your brochure to advertise your fund-raiser and help ensure that you will have customers.

If a fund-raising activity does not interest you, consider creating an advertising brochure for a new product or service that you invent, such as

- a new video game
- a computer tutoring service
- a different style of clothing
- a dog-walking service

What's in a Name? Would you buy a juice called Prune-Berry Surprise? If the product were called Super Berry Blast, would you reconsider? The name of your product or service is one of the most important decisions you will make. Keep your product's name short, simple, and as descriptive as possible.

Provide Details

Sweat the Small Stuff Once you choose your product or service, think about some of its important qualities or details. For a product, important qualities may include color, size, cost, value, or key features. Important details for a service might include a location and hours. One student decided to create a baby-sitting service as a fund-raiser for her school band. She used a **cluster diagram** to help her brainstorm the following details about her service.

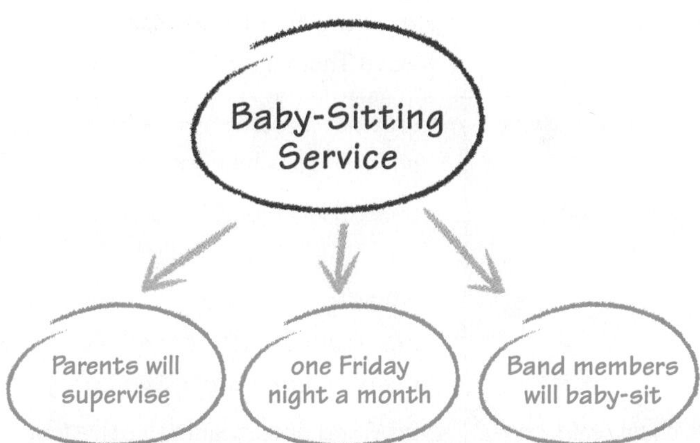

YOUR TURN 4 Choosing Your Product or Service and Brainstorming Details

Decide on a product or service for your brochure. You may advertise a fund-raising activity or invent a new product or service. Then, choose a name, and brainstorm some important qualities or details of your product or service.

Consider Your Target Market

KEY CONCEPT

Right on Target **The people who will buy or use your product or service are your target market.** The more you know about your target market, the better you can tailor your brochure to attract that market's attention.

To determine your target market and to brainstorm a list of its wants and needs, ask yourself these questions.

- Who will use my product or service?
- Why would these people want or need my product or service?

The student writing a brochure for the baby-sitting service knew right away that her target market would be parents. Not every parent would use the service, however. The student narrowed the target market to those parents with children under age ten. She then thought about the wants and needs of these parents.

TIP A **target market** for a brochure is similar to the **audience** for other types of writing.

TIP Be sure to adjust your **voice,** or the sound of your writing, so that it appeals to your target market. One way to do this is by using words that will have a positive impact on your target market. Which of these examples is more appropriate for a brochure aimed at parents?

- "We'll show your kids a good time for a low price."
- "The members and parents of the Eagle Marching Band provide safe, fun, and affordable childcare."

Get What You Want Now think about the ways your product or service will meet each of the wants and needs of your target market. One student created the list below to show the ways her baby-sitting service meets the wants and needs of her target market.

Wants and Needs	How Baby-Sitting Service Meets Them
▪ to have a night away from children	▪ provides a convenient place to leave children for the evening
▪ to know their children will be safe	▪ provides teenager and adult supervision
▪ to pay a reasonable price	▪ costs only $8 per child with a family maximum of $24 regardless of how many children are in the family
▪ to let their children have fun	▪ provides entertaining activities for children

YOUR TURN 5 Considering Your Target Market

Determine your target market, and brainstorm its wants and needs. Then, create a chart like the one above to identify ways your product or service will meet the wants and needs of your target market.

Write a Slogan

Attention Shoppers! Look around when you are at the mall and notice how many people are wearing T-shirts with advertisements on them. Advertisers know the importance of logos and **slogans,** or catchy phrases. **A good slogan provides a quick, attention-grabbing message**—usually short enough to fit on the front of a T-shirt.

Most slogans focus on one thing the target market needs or wants. Consider the slogan "Milk. It Does A Body Good.®" This slogan appeals to the need for good health and nutrition. The slogan "A Mind Is A Terrible Thing To Waste®" appeals to the need to help students continue their education. Both of these slogans could have focused on other wants or needs, but the writer had to choose one.

To attract attention and be remembered, slogans must be catchy. Advertising writers choose words carefully and arrange them to create the biggest impact. If the milk campaign had used the slogan "Milk Is Good For You," would it have been as effective? When you write your slogan, try rearranging and replacing words until you get a memorable, catchy phrase. You can also use one of the following techniques.

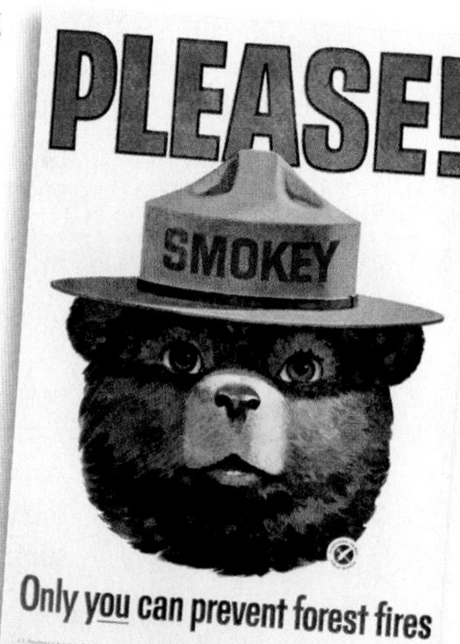

- rhyme, or words with the same vowel sounds

  Give A Hoot. Don't Pollute.

  —USDA Forest Service

- repetition, or words that are used more than once

  Army. Be All You Can Be.®

  —U.S. Army

- alliteration, or words with the same initial consonant sounds

  Loose Lips Might Sink Ships.

  —The War Advertising Council

Before you start choosing words for your slogan, think about *how* you intend to persuade your target market. Is there an emotion associated with your product or service? Would the words of a celebrity help you make sales? The mini-lesson on page 254 will explain the important persuasive techniques you can apply to your slogan. Later, you will decide which technique will work best for your target market.

MINI-LESSON **CRITICAL THINKING**

Identifying Persuasive Techniques

Baiting the Hook The secret to catching fish is the right bait. Writing slogans is similar to fishing. You have to know both the fish (your target market) and the right bait *(persuasive technique)* to use.

Persuasive techniques are methods advertisers use to convince a target market to buy something. These techniques use specific appeals based on the target market's needs or wants. Each technique is designed to convince the reader to do or buy something for a certain reason, such as buying certain clothes so that others will admire your taste.

Below is a chart of some common persuasive techniques.

Common Persuasive Techniques		
Bandwagon	Appeal urges you to do or believe something because everyone else does.	*Two million visitors have been awed by our butterfly exhibit.*
Testimonial	Appeal uses famous people to endorse a product or idea.	*Actress Andrea Star brings her children to the nature museum.*
Emotional Appeals	Appeals use words or images that target the audience's positive or negative emotions.	*Without your support, the museum may be forced to close its doors.*
"Plain Folks"	Appeal uses "ordinary" people—not famous or rich ones—to sell a product. You are supposed to trust these people because they are like you.	*Parents rave about how excited children get about science while at the museum.*
Snob Appeal	Appeal suggests that you can be like the wealthy, well-dressed people who support this product or idea.	*Donate $5,000 and gain exclusive entry to the museum's private lunchroom.*

PRACTICE

Identify the persuasive technique used in each sentence that follows.

1. Our watches adorn the most fashionable wrists in town.
2. Visit the country everyone is talking about—Brazil.
3. The Food Bank needs your help to make sure everyone has a meal for Thanksgiving.
4. Vana Lariat, nationally renowned rodeo star, wears Bart's Boots.
5. Mama Sue's Restaurant: Where good folks gather for good food.

The Complete Picture A jigsaw puzzle will not make a complete picture if some pieces are missing. To come up with a memorable, catchy slogan, you must put all the pieces together, including

- your product or service
- your target market
- one of the target market's wants or needs
- a persuasive technique
- a clever or catchy method of expressing it all

The Thinking It Through below will take you through this process step by step.

TIP Keep in mind that the slogan will be placed on the front panel of your brochure. It should introduce your service or product and be as interesting and catchy as possible.

THINKING IT THROUGH: Writing a Slogan

STEP 1 List the product or service and your target market.

My service is a baby-sitting service. My target market is parents with children under ten.

STEP 2 Review the wants and needs of your target market, and choose one as the focus of your slogan.

I will focus on parents' need to have a night away from their children.

STEP 3 Choose a persuasive technique.

A positive emotional appeal about the ease and convenience of our service would work well.

STEP 4 Decide on the piece of information that will make that persuasive technique work.

I think the fact that our service is in the neighborhood is very important.

STEP 5 Write the first draft of your slogan. Keep revising your slogan, adding catchy phrasing, rhyme, repetition, or alliteration.

A quality baby sitter can be found nearby!

↓

A quality baby sitter is just around the corner!

↓

A better baby sitter is just around the corner!

YOUR TURN 6 Writing Your Slogan

Write your slogan, using the steps in the Thinking It Through on the previous page. Remember to revise your slogan as many times as necessary to make it catchy and memorable.

Provide Reasons to Buy

Rhyme and Reason Baby-sit any three-year-old, and you will notice how many times he or she asks "Why?" Readers who pick up your brochure will also want to know "why" before they decide to buy what you are selling. You will give reasons to buy your product or service on the inside pages of the brochure. **Reasons should clearly explain how your product or service meets your target market's wants and needs.** By writing the notes below, the student making a brochure for the baby-sitting service discovered how her service would meet another one of the target market's needs.

KEY CONCEPT

TIP Use skills from other classes to develop reasons. For example, use math to explain a discount, or make a comparison to a historical event or person to grab attention.

Want or need: to let their children have fun

Reason to use my service: We provide fun activities.

Details to use in brochure:

- We offer a whole evening of activities.
- Children will play board games, indoor sports, and work on arts and crafts projects.
- Near the end of the evening, we show a G-rated movie to settle the children down.

YOUR TURN 7 Providing Reasons to Buy

Brainstorm reasons your target market should buy your product or service. Use the chart you created for Your Turn 5 to make sure each reason responds to one of your target audience's wants or needs. Then, list some details that you can use to persuade your target market.

Call Your Market to Action

The Keys to Success The back panel of your brochure should "close the deal." In other words, you will provide a quick list of key information about your product or service. With this last piece in place, people in your target market should know exactly what you are selling and how they can buy it.

KEY CONCEPT

The back panel gives a basic list of key information about your product or service. This information should include the specific information your market needs to know about your product or service.

Key Information for a Brochure's Back Panel			
For a product:	▪ Size ▪ Color	▪ Warranties ▪ Price	▪ Important features
For a service:	▪ Hours ▪ Location	▪ Price ▪ Guarantee	▪ Other important information

Calling All Customers After the key information, a brochure should have a *call to action.* The **call to action** gives information about where to find the product or service and urges the customer to buy it with a message such as "Buy a Tomboy toboggan today by calling 555-0150!"

YOUR TURN 8 Writing Key Information and a Call to Action

Use the chart above to identify key information to list on your brochure's back panel. Then, tell your readers what to do next by writing a call to action.

Choose Illustrations

Show and Tell Show and tell is not just for kindergarten. Brochures also show and tell through a partnership between words and pictures. The medium for these illustrations can take many forms, including photographs, drawings, computer-generated

Reference Note

For more on **medium,** see page 245.

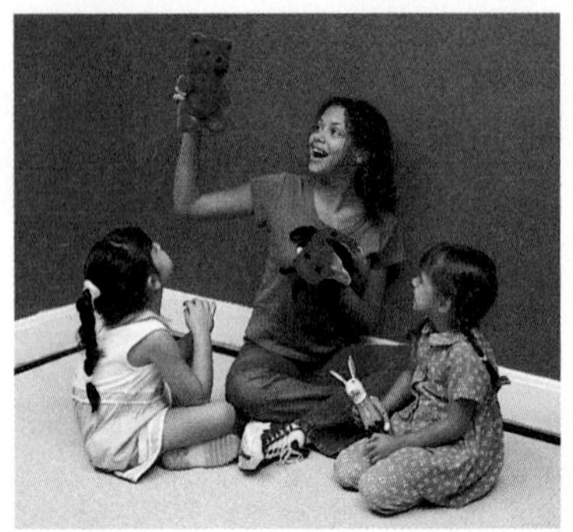

art, maps, or sketches. The photograph in the margin was chosen by the student creating the brochure for the baby-sitting service.

This picture is effective because it addresses one of the audience's wants or needs: It makes parents feel that their children will have a good time with the baby sitters. The picture might also make them curious about what the children are doing. They will be interested enough to read the brochure and learn more about the baby-sitting service.

KEY CONCEPT

Choose illustrations that will encourage your target market to read your brochure. Answering the following questions will help you choose persuasive illustrations.

- **What story do I want to tell?** Choose a picture that involves the reader in a story. The story should make the reader want to know more about the product or service.
- **What feelings should the colors in the illustration convey?** Make sure the colors communicate the right feelings. Warm, vibrant colors communicate warmth and happiness. Cool colors convey professionalism and calmness.
- **What medium should I use?** The choice of medium will depend on what you are trying to sell. A child's art drawing is a good medium to advertise arts and crafts, but a photograph might be better than a drawing to advertise a beautiful vacation resort. Consider all alternatives before drawing, photographing, painting, or computer-generating your illustrations.

Reference Note

For more on **illustrations,** see page 244.

Design Your Brochure

Inside and Out Brochures come in all shapes and sizes. A common form is the basic bi-fold brochure. This brochure format has three parts.

- The **front panel** includes the product or service name, a slogan, and an illustration.
- The **inside spread** includes the paragraphs explaining reasons to buy the product or service and some illustrations.
- The **back panel** gives the key information and the call to action.

Designing Your Writing

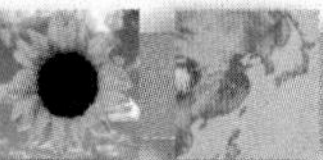

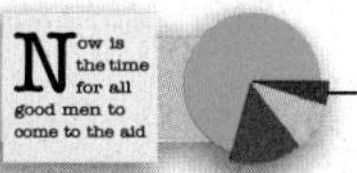

Brochure Layout Before you begin writing your brochure, you should have a good idea of the basic layout.

Your brochure will have three parts—the inside spread on one side of the paper and the front and back panels on the other side of the paper.

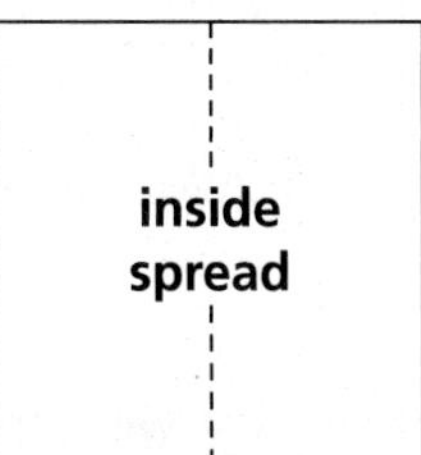

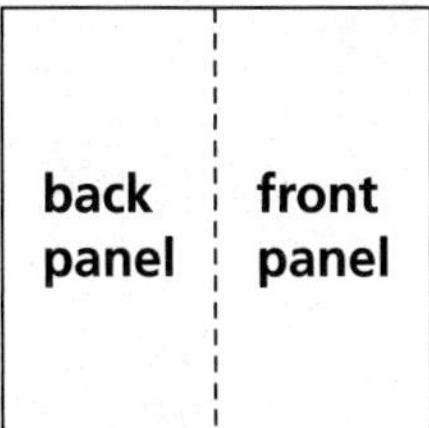

Look at the inside of the brochure first. Place all of your text on the page, leaving room for illustrations. Spread out your illustrations, and make sure one illustration is bigger than all the others. Experiment with fonts (designs and sizes of type) to make everything fit. You can use two columns, or you can run the lines across the spread.

You must design and treat the other side of your brochure differently. The left side will be the back panel of the brochure, and the right side will be the front panel. The reader will not see these two panels together once the brochure is folded, so you must make them separate columns. Leave plenty of space between the columns so that you have room to fold your brochure in half.

COMPUTER TIP

Set up the page layout on computer software to show that your paper will be a custom size—$8\frac{1}{2} \times 8\frac{1}{2}$ inches. You can still print on ordinary $8\frac{1}{2}$- × 11-inch paper, but you will have to cut off the extra white space to make your brochure square.

Reference Note

For more on **font,** see page 759 in the Quick Reference Handbook.

YOUR TURN 9 Choosing Illustrations and Designing Your Brochure

- To decide what kinds of illustrations to use in your brochure, review the information on story, color, and medium on pages 244–245.
- Find or create illustrations that match the story, colors, and medium you chose.
- Use the Designing Your Writing above and the brochure on pages 241–243 to decide where to place illustrations and text in your brochure.

Writing

Framework

Front Panel

- Name of Product or Service
- Slogan and Illustration

Inside Spread

- Reasons and Details
- Illustrations

Directions and Explanations

- Use a catchy **slogan** that readers will remember.
- Make sure each of your **reasons** explains how the reader will benefit from your product or service.

A Writer's Model

A better baby sitter is just around the corner!

The Eagle Marching Band

presents

Parents' Night Out Baby-Sitting Service

Get away for an evening.

Parents, when was the last time you had a night to yourselves? Finding a reliable sitter can be impossible or can cost a fortune. Why does having fun have to be so much trouble?

It doesn't! With Parents' Night Out, *a better baby sitter is just around the corner!* The members and parents of the Eagle Marching Band provide safe, fun, and affordable childcare.

Know your children are safe.

- Experienced parents supervise the teenage staff at all times.
- We know how to feed and diaper babies.
- All of our staff have taken and passed a baby-sitting course.

Promotional Brochure

Inside Spread, Cont.
- Reasons and Details
- Illustrations

Back Panel
- Key Information
- Call to Action

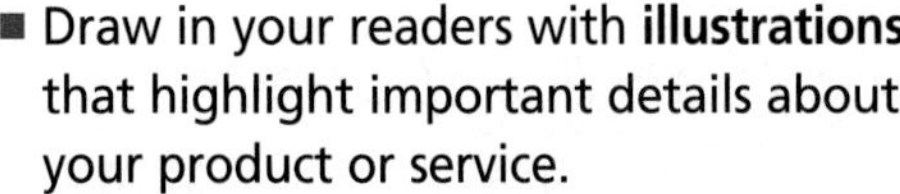

- Draw in your readers with **illustrations** that highlight important details about your product or service.

- Provide **key information** that answers common questions readers might have about your product or service.

Let us entertain your children while you have fun, too.

While you enjoy your evening out, we offer your children a whole evening of structured activities, including

- board games
- indoor sports
- arts and crafts projects
- G-rated videos

Best of all, pay only $8 per child with a $24 family maximum!

Parents' Night Out Quick Facts

Where: Highlands Community Center
When: Third Friday of each month
Hours: 6:00–10:00 P.M.
Sponsored by: The Eagle Marching Band
Cost: $8 per child/$24 family maximum

Call now!
It's the better baby sitter!

Make your reservations by calling the Community Center at 555-0187.

Highlands Community Center is located at the corner of Oak and Main Streets.

All proceeds go to support the Eagle Marching Band trip to New York City to perform in the Thanksgiving Day Parade.

A Student's Model

Anthony Falso, a student at Linton Middle School in Penn Hills, Pennsylvania, created a brochure for a lawn-mowing service. The front and one inside panel of his brochure are shown below.

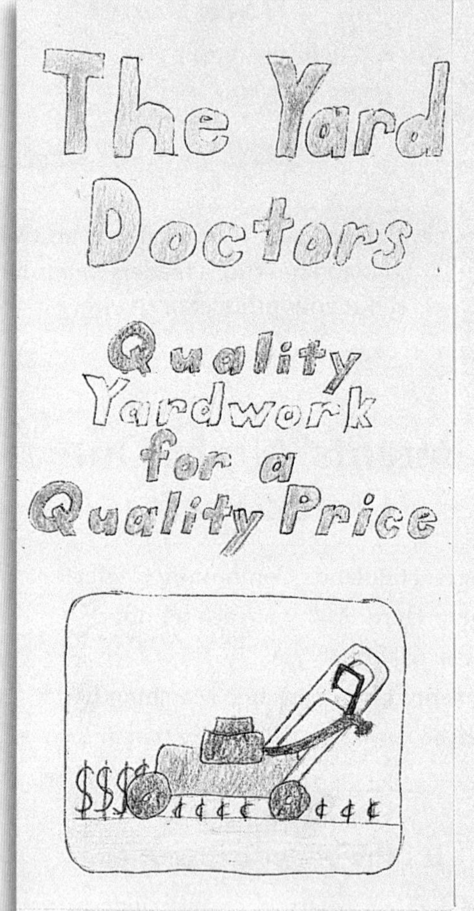

The Quality Price

Our prices are unbeatable! No yard costs more than $30! If you already have a yardworker, we will guarantee a lower price. All our tools are gas powered. You will not have to worry about your electric bill. We are very affordable.

Others	Ours
$ $ $ $ $	¢ ¢ ¢ ¢ ¢ ¢ ¢

Our prices are chump change compared to others.

YOUR TURN 10 Drafting Your Brochure

Create a draft of your brochure. Refer to the framework and the Writer's Model on pages 260–261 as you write. For now, you may sketch your illustrations.

Evaluate and Revise Content, Organization, and Style

Packing a Punch A dull brochure will not attract its target market. After you have written a draft, evaluate and revise your brochure to make it interesting and effective. Read your brochure twice, focusing first on content and organization. Use the guidelines below to help you. In the second reading, pay attention to the wording of your brochure, using the Focus on Word Choice on page 265.

First Reading: Content and Organization Use this chart to evaluate and revise your brochure so it packs a persuasive punch.

Quick guide

Guidelines for Self-Evaluation and Peer Evaluation

Evaluation Questions	Tips	Revision Techniques
1 Is the slogan short, catchy, and memorable?	**Say the slogan out loud** to a friend. Ask the friend to repeat it to see if the slogan is easy to remember.	If needed, **rearrange** or rewrite the slogan's words to make them easier to remember. **Add** repeated words or sounds.
2 Do the illustrations make readers want to read the text?	**Put stars** next to attention-getting illustrations and **circles** next to uninteresting ones.	**Delete** uninteresting images and **add** images that interest the reader, if necessary.
3 Does the brochure give convincing reasons and clear details?	**Underline** the reasons to buy the product or service and **put a check mark** by the details supporting the reasons.	If needed, **add** reasons or **elaborate** on the reasons provided with more details.
4 Does the key information tell everything the reader needs to know about the product or service?	**Highlight** pieces of key information on the back of the brochure.	**Add** to the key information, if necessary.
5 Does the brochure include a clear call to action?	**Draw a wavy line** under the part of the brochure that calls the reader to action.	**Add** a call to action that tells the reader exactly how to buy the brochure's product or service.

ONE WRITER'S REVISIONS This revision is an early draft of the brochure on pages 260–261.

Where: Highlands Community Center

add ^ *When: Third Friday of each month*

Hours: 6:00–10:00 P.M.

Sponsored by: The Eagle Marching Band

Cost: $8 per child / $24 family maximum

add ^ *Call now!*

It's the better baby sitter!

add Make your reservations by calling the community center ^ *at 555-0187.*

Responding to the Revision Process

1. Why do you think the writer added information to the key information?
2. Why do you think the writer added "Call now!" and a telephone number?

PEER REVIEW

As you evaluate a peer's brochure, ask yourself these questions:

- Who is the target market for this brochure?
- How did the writer attempt to convince the target market to buy the product or service?

Second Reading: Style Style involves the way you express your ideas in writing and should be appropriate to your purpose. One way to ensure that your writing style fits your purpose is to pay close attention to the words you use. In persuasive writing, every word should help make your message more convincing. When you use words with emotional impact, you add persuasion to ordinary sentences. Changing just a few words to make a stronger emotional appeal can help your brochure become a strong selling tool.

When you evaluate your brochure for style, ask yourself whether your writing includes words that have a strong emotional impact. As you re-read your advertisement, circle words that create an emotional response. If the brochure contains only a few emotional words, delete some ordinary words and replace them with ones that will draw a more intense response.

Emotional Language

Emotions such as joy, anger, pride, and envy can help you sell your product or service. You can tap into the persuasive power of these emotional appeals by understanding the emotional impact that words carry. Consider these two sentences:

> Parents are **pleased** with the new baby-sitting service.
>
> Parents are **thrilled** with the new baby-sitting service.

The words *pleased* and *thrilled* basically mean the same thing: to be happy. *Thrilled,* however, has a stronger emotional appeal. The reader of this brochure would recognize that burst of excitement of being *thrilled* as opposed to just being *pleased.* Choosing the right word can make a difference in the way your reader will understand and respond to your writing.

When you write a brochure, take advantage of the emotion a word carries. Emotion sells, and selling is the job of your brochure.

ONE WRITER'S REVISIONS

Finding a reliable sitter can be ~~difficult~~ *impossible* or can cost a ~~lot.~~ *fortune.*

Responding to the Revision Process

How did replacing *difficult* and *lot* improve the sentence above?

YOUR TURN 11 Evaluating and Revising Your Brochure

- First, evaluate and revise the content and organization of your brochure, using the guidelines on page 263.
- Next, use the Focus on Word Choice above to improve the emotional impact of your brochure.
- If a peer evaluated your brochure, think carefully about each of your peer's comments as you revise.

Publishing

Proofread Your Brochure

Mirror, Mirror Proofreading is like looking in a mirror. Both help you get ready to face the public. Your friends might overlook socks that do not match, but potential customers will not overlook mistakes in your brochure. Proofread your brochure carefully, and **edit** to fix any problems.

Grammar Link

Using Commas Between Adjectives

Because adjectives help create a vivid description, sentences in brochures often use several adjectives at a time. Incorrect punctuation can make a description fuzzy or confusing. Follow these rules to punctuate groups of adjectives properly.

When two or more adjectives appear before a noun, use a comma to separate the adjectives.

Our skateboard is a *fast, safe, popular* model for beginners.

When the last adjective and the noun are considered a unit, do not use a comma before the last adjective.

The watch has a *wide, stylish leather* band.

In the example above, no comma is used between *stylish* and *leather* because the words *leather* and *band* are considered a unit. Try using this test. Insert the word *and* between the adjectives. If *and* makes sense, use a comma. In the example, *and* makes sense between *wide* and *stylish*. *And* does not make sense between *stylish* and *leather*.

PRACTICE

For each of the following sentences, insert commas where they are needed.

Example:

1. Mama Sue's restaurant offers tasty inexpensive attractive meals.

*1. Mama Sue's restaurant offers tasty**,** inexpensive**,** attractive meals.*

1. Take a leisurely informative carriage ride through the historic district.
2. Our huge gentle Belgian horses pull the carriages.
3. Our comfortable authentic carriage seats eight people.
4. Your guides are trained friendly student volunteers.
5. You will enjoy the relaxing scenic ride through the heart of the historic district.

For more information and practice on **using commas with adjectives,** see page 636.

Publish Your Brochure

Going All Out for Business Your brochure is useless until it finds its way into your customers' hands. Think about the best way to reach those customers. Make copies of your brochure, and try one of these ideas:

- If your brochure is part of a fund-raising activity, ask other students to be responsible for distributing a minimum number of brochures to friends, family, neighbors, and potential customers they know.
- Send a letter of request or make a phone call to ask an area hotel, restaurant, or other public place if you can include a stack of your brochures in its brochure rack.
- If you created a new product or service for your brochure, get together with some classmates who did the same thing. Create a display of these brochures in your classroom.

COMPUTER TIP

Brochures with columns often look best when the lines of text are *justified.* **Justified text** is aligned on both sides. Use word-processing features to justify the text in your brochure to make it look as neat as possible.

Reference Note

For more on **alignment,** see page 757 in the Quick Reference Handbook.

PORTFOLIO

Reflect on Your Brochure

Building Your Portfolio Take time to reflect on your **writing portfolio**—everything you have written so far this year, including your brochure. Jot down answers to the following questions, and include your responses in your portfolio.

- How well did you achieve your purpose in creating your brochure? Explain.
- While creating your brochure, what skills did you learn that will help you improve on future writing projects? Be specific.
- What are your strengths and weaknesses as a writer? What makes you say so? Point to specific works in your portfolio.
- What goals can you set for yourself to help you grow as a writer? Explain how you intend to reach your goals.

YOUR TURN 12 Proofreading, Publishing, and Reflecting on Your Brochure

- Correct grammar, usage, and mechanics errors.
- Publish your brochure for your target market.
- Answer the Reflect on Your Brochure questions above. Record your responses in a learning log, or include them in your portfolio.

Comparing Local and National Ads

You turn on the television and see a couple of teenagers laughing and doing flips on a trampoline. Then, the screen goes blank except for the logo for a brand of jeans, and the commercial is over.

The American Way You may wonder what the jeans ad was all about. It did not talk about the jeans or why people should buy them. In fact, you did not even know it was a jeans ad until the end.

National advertisements often use commercials like the one for jeans to make viewers associate a product with a feeling or emotion. The purpose of the advertisement is to get the target market—young adults—to think that if they wear the jeans displayed in the ad, they will be as happy as the actors appear to be.

The Local Scene Compare the national jeans ad to this description of a local ad for a store having a clothing sale. The local commercial shows the store owner standing in his store. He gives you the details—prices, discounts, and the brands he sells. Clearly, this local ad, unlike the national ad, wants you to know exactly what the store has to offer.

You can see that these two types of advertisements have different goals. As you analyze an ad, consider the following purposes it could have.

Purposes of Local Ads
to explain where a product can be purchased
to encourage support of local businesses
to reveal a product's features and price

Purposes of National Ads
to increase awareness of a brand name
to associate a product or brand with a specific feeling, need, or an admired celebrity

YOUR TURN 13 Finding Ads with Different Purposes

Find an example of a local ad and a national ad. Cut out a magazine or newspaper ad, or write a summary of a television or radio ad. Answer these questions on the back of each ad or summary.

- What is the main purpose of this ad?
- Is this ad local or national? How can you tell?

Analyzing a Caricature

WHAT'S AHEAD?

In this section you will analyze a caricature. You will also learn about

- **the history of caricature**
- **elements of caricature**

What if you wanted to persuade people not to litter? You might create a brochure with a picture of a creek filled with aluminum cans and food wrappers. You might also include a drawing of a litterer tossing cups, cans, and wrappers into the creek. Then, you might give this litterbug monstrous, buglike eyes and add an extra set of arms. This drawing would be a *caricature.*

What Is a Caricature?

A **caricature** is an image, picture, cartoon, or description that expresses the creator's point of view by exaggerating or distorting the characteristics of the subject. Caricature uses exaggeration and symbols to create a "truthful misrepresentation"—a picture that does not quite look like its subject but that still says something true about the subject. For example, the distorted, monstrous features make the person in the caricature to the right look unlike any real person. However, if you feel littering is a monstrous act, then the drawing may seem truthful.

A History of Making Fun People have long used caricature to criticize, persuade, and amuse others. This art form gained widespread popularity, however, in late fifteenth-century Europe. Around 1440, the German printer Johannes Gutenberg developed an efficient printing process. This new process meant art could be reproduced in inexpensive and convenient media, such as handbills and pamphlets. These media, like brochures, were easy to hide from disapproving eyes. Therefore, people felt freer to use art, in the form of caricature, to criticize authorities. Some caricaturists aim to influence their audiences by pointing out their subjects' failings; others simply aim to entertain.

TIP By showing the litterbug stepping on a flower, the caricaturist is using a *symbol.* A **symbol** is an object that stands for another thing or idea. The flower might represent the earth.

TIP William Hogarth, who lived in Britain in the 1700s, was one of the most famous early caricaturists. Hogarth developed an early version of today's comic strips by using a linked series of illustrations to tell a story. Today's funny papers are not all caricature, though. Many cartoons are meant just to be funny and not criticize or persuade.

Analyzing Caricature

The first reason for analyzing caricature is to understand completely its elements—to "get it." The second reason is to figure out the artist's purpose. The following Thinking It Through shows how one reader analyzed details of the caricature on page 269 in order to figure out its message and purpose.

THINKING IT THROUGH Analyzing Caricature

STEP 1 What things or features does the caricature exaggerate? What is the effect of these exaggerations?

It exaggerates the ugliness of littering by giving the litterer buglike features. The effect is to make the behavior of littering seem monstrous.

STEP 2 Does the caricature include any symbols? Look for objects around the subject. What might these objects represent?

The flower might represent nature or the earth.

STEP 3 Does the caricature tell a story? Are any actions that point out causes or effects shown?

The litterbug is stepping on a flower. This action shows what litter can do to the environment.

STEP 4 What was the artist's purpose in creating the caricature?

The artist wanted to convince others not to litter.

Collection of the Jonson Gallery of the University of New Mexico Art Museum, Albuquerque, Gift of Mrs. Jerome Frank.

YOUR TURN 14 Analyzing Caricature

The photograph at left shows American businessman John D. Rockefeller. Below it is a caricature of him. Through his companies, the Standard Oil Trust and the Standard Oil Company, Rockefeller controlled the refinement and distribution of most oil in the United States. Many people were critical of Standard Oil's exclusive control, or *monopoly,* over the oil business; the Supreme Court ultimately broke up the Standard Oil Company in 1911. Use the Thinking It Through questions above to analyze the caricature.

CHAPTER

Choices

Choose one of the following activities to complete.

CAREERS

1. A Firm Yes Would you like to be a writer, artist, or researcher for an advertising firm? If so, collaborate with a classmate who has a similar interest, and write a **letter of request** to an advertising firm to find out more. In the letter, ask questions about the educational requirements and the day-to-day demands of the job(s). Be sure to ask clear, specific questions. (For more on **letters of request,** see page 838 in the Quick Reference Handbook.)

CROSSING THE CURRICULUM: SOCIAL STUDIES

2. Extra! Extra! Visit the library and research old newspapers. Examine the differences between ads in the early 1900s and today's newspaper ads. Select one product category, such as clothes or cars. Write a **journal entry** that discusses the differences and similarities between old and new ads.

CROSSING THE CURRICULUM: ART

3. T-shirt Wisdom T-shirts often have slogans that offer a humorous philosophy on life. Create your own bit of T-shirt wisdom with a **slogan** and some **art.** Check into having your design printed on a T-shirt.

CROSSING THE CURRICULUM: SCIENCE

4. Save the Whales **Problem solve** to help an endangered species avoid extinction. Identify an endangered species and research why the animals are in trouble. Use this research to find a possible solution to their problem. Then, write a **paper** or create a **brochure** explaining what can be done to help them. Share your findings with your science teacher or with a classmate.

SPEECH

5. Teacher of the Year Choose your favorite teacher, and write a short **presentation** about why he or she should be chosen to be teacher of the year. Give your presentation aloud, or write it in brochure form and send it to your teacher as a thank you.

PART 2

Sentences and Paragraphs

CHAPTER

Writing Effective Sentences

Writing Clear Sentences

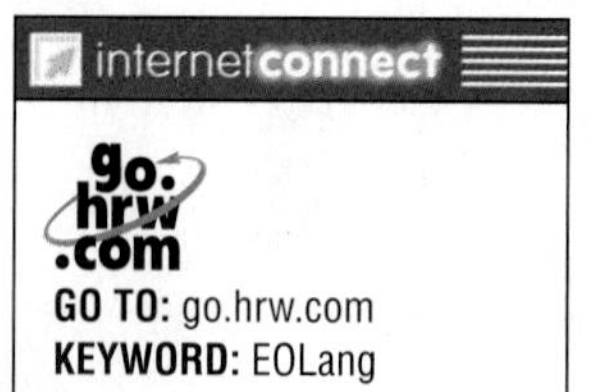

No matter who your audience is, you want your writing to be clear and understandable. One of the easiest ways to make your writing clear is to use complete sentences. A ***complete sentence*** is a word group that

- has a subject
- has a verb
- expresses a complete thought

EXAMPLES The Great Wall of China was begun in 214 B.C.

It spans 1,450 miles and is twenty-five feet high.

Be careful not to fall!

Each of the previous examples meets all the requirements of a sentence. At first glance, the third example may not appear to have a subject. The subject, *you,* is understood in the sentence even though it is not stated: "(You) be careful not to fall!"

Two stumbling blocks to the development of clear sentences are *sentence fragments* and *run-on sentences.* Once you learn how to recognize fragments and run-ons, you can revise them to create clear, complete sentences.

Sentence Fragments

A ***sentence fragment*** is a group of words that has been capitalized and punctuated as if it were a complete sentence. Like a fragment of a painting or photograph, a sentence fragment can be confusing because it fails to give the whole picture.

FRAGMENT Commanded the Continental army in the Revolutionary War. [The subject is missing. *Who* commanded the Continental army during the Revolutionary War?]

SENTENCE George Washington commanded the Continental army in the Revolutionary War.

FRAGMENT On December 25, 1776, Washington his troops across the icy Delaware River into Trenton, New Jersey. [The verb is missing. *What did Washington do* on December 25, 1776?]

SENTENCE On December 25, 1776, Washington led his troops across the icy Delaware River into Trenton, New Jersey.

FRAGMENT Even though the Continental army captured a British outpost at Trenton in 1776. [This group of words has a subject and a verb, but it does not express a complete thought.]

SENTENCE Even though the Continental army captured a British outpost at Trenton in 1776, it would still face many challenges.

NOTE Often, sentence fragments are the result of writing in a hurry or being a little careless. For example, you might accidentally chop off part of a sentence by putting in a period and a capital letter too soon.

EXAMPLE Raphael had finished his homework. Before his mother came home from the grocery store. [The second word group is a fragment and belongs with the sentence before it.]

You can correct the sentence fragment by combining it with or attaching it to the sentence with which it belongs.

EXAMPLE Raphael had finished his homework **before his mother came home from the grocery store.**

Exercise 1 Identifying Sentence Fragments

Use this simple three-part test to find out which of the following word groups are sentence fragments and which are complete sentences.

1. Does the group of words have a subject?
2. Does it have a verb?
3. Does it express a complete thought?

If the group of words is a complete sentence, write *S*. If it is a fragment, write *F*.

1. Eleanor Roosevelt was First Lady of the United States from 1933 to 1945.
2. Raised by her grandmother because both of her parents had died by the time she was ten.
3. Wrote a popular newspaper column entitled "My Day."
4. As First Lady, worked for the rights of the poor and underprivileged.
5. Because she felt strongly about the struggles of children and minorities.
6. Eleanor Roosevelt traveled all over the world.
7. Press conferences at which she discussed important issues.
8. Important role in forming the United Nations.
9. Chairperson of the United Nations Commission on Human Rights.
10. After a long life of public service, died in 1962.

Exercise 2 Finding and Revising Sentence Fragments

Some of the following groups of words are sentence fragments. Revise each fragment by (1) adding a subject, (2) adding a verb, or (3) attaching the fragment to a complete sentence. You may need to change the punctuation and capitalization, too. If the word group is already a complete sentence, write *S*.

EXAMPLE 1. Before the sun rose.
1. *We awoke before the sun rose.*

1. Felt tired because we did not get much sleep the night before.
2. A bear growling in the bushes outside the tent at 2:00 A.M.
3. Because we had left food on the fire.
4. Came from the bushes and circled the campfire.

5. Our eyes grew large as the bear stood up and revealed its teeth.
6. When my friend let out a screeching yell.
7. Put my hand over his mouth.
8. Then growled at us menacingly.
9. We stood still.
10. Dropping to all fours, ran back into the forest.

Run-on Sentences

If you run together two complete sentences as if they were one sentence, you create a ***run-on sentence.*** Run-ons are often confusing because the reader cannot tell where one idea ends and another one begins.

RUN-ON Margaret Bourke-White was a famous photographer she worked for *Life* magazine during World War II.

CORRECT Margaret Bourke-White was a famous photographer**. S**he worked for *Life* magazine during World War II.

RUN-ON Bourke-White traveled all over the world taking photographs in Africa and other foreign countries won her fame and respect.

CORRECT Bourke-White traveled all over the world**. T**aking photographs in Africa and other foreign countries won her fame and respect.

To spot run-ons, try reading your writing aloud. A natural, distinct pause in your voice usually marks the end of one thought and the beginning of another. If you pause at a place where you have no end punctuation, you may have found a run-on sentence. Take care not to use just a comma between two sentences. If you do, you will create a run-on sentence.

RUN-ON Our dog finally came home late last night, she was dirty and hungry.

CORRECT Our dog finally came home late last night**. S**he was dirty and hungry.

HELP

A run-on sentence that has two sentences joined with just a comma is called a **comma splice.**

Reference Note

For more on **commas,** see page 633.

Revising Run-on Sentences

Here are two ways you can revise run-on sentences.

1. You can make two sentences.

RUN-ON Kite building is an ancient art the Chinese made the first kites around three thousand years ago.

CORRECT Kite building is an ancient art**. T**he Chinese made the first kites around three thousand years ago.

2. You can use a comma and a coordinating conjunction such as *and, but,* or *or.*

RUN-ON The Chinese sometimes used kites in religious ceremonies, they usually used them for sport.

CORRECT The Chinese sometimes used kites in religious ceremonies**, but** they usually used them for sport.

Exercise 3 Identifying and Revising Run-on Sentences

Decide which of the following groups of words are run-ons. Then, revise each run-on by (1) making it into two separate sentences or (2) using a comma and a coordinating conjunction. If the group of words is already correct, write *C.*

1. The Louvre is the largest museum in the world it is also one of the oldest.
2. The first works of art in the Louvre were bought by the kings of France each ruler added more treasures.
3. King Francis I was a great supporter of the arts he bought the *Mona Lisa.*
4. As other French rulers made additions, the collections of fine works of art grew.
5. The Louvre is now a state-owned museum, its new pieces are either bought by the museum or received as gifts.
6. Each year, about one and a half million people from all over the world come to see the artwork at the Louvre.
7. The buildings of the Louvre form a rectangle there are courtyards and gardens inside the rectangle.
8. The Louvre covers about forty acres, it has about eight miles of gallery space.
9. Over one million works of art are exhibited in the Louvre.

10. Many of the buildings of the Louvre have been expanded and modernized, this photograph shows how the Louvre looks today.

Review A **Revising Sentence Fragments and Run-on Sentences**

The following paragraph is confusing because it contains some sentence fragments and run-on sentences. First, identify the fragments and run-ons. Then, revise each fragment and run-on to make the paragraph clearer.

The 1956 movie Godzilla about a huge reptile. Godzilla looks like a dinosaur he breathes fire like a dragon. He comes up out of the ocean. After an atomic bomb wakes him up. Godzilla can melt steel with his atomic breath he is big enough to knock down huge buildings. In the original film he destroys the city of Tokyo he gets killed at the end.

COMPUTER TIP

Use a word-processing program when you revise your draft for sentence fragments, run-on sentences, or style. The cut and paste commands make it easy for you to move words or phrases within a sentence and to move sentences within your draft.

Combining Sentences

Would you enjoy reading a book that contains only one simple character facing ordinary, uncomplicated situations? Of course not. To hold your attention, a writer must include a *variety* of characters who encounter many different and interesting situations. A writer must also *vary sentence length and structure* to keep the reader's interest. Consider the following example in which the author mainly uses short, choppy sentences:

```
   The Persians landed at Marathon in
490 B.C. The Persians invaded Greece.
The mighty Persians outnumbered the small
Greek army. The Greeks defeated the
Persians. The Greek commander sent
Phidippides (fī•dip'i•dēz') to Athens to
spread the good news. Phidippides was his
fastest runner. Phidippides ran the
entire way. Phidippides proudly announced
the Greek victory. Then, he died. We get
the term "marathon" from Phidippides's
run. Phidippides's run was historic.
```

Now read the revised version. To make the paragraph more interesting, the writer combined some of the short, choppy sentences into longer, smoother ones. Notice how the ***sentence combining strategies*** listed to the right of the paragraph have helped to eliminate some repeated words and ideas. Explanations of these strategies appear on the following pages.

Strategy	Revised paragraph
Using conjunction	The Persians landed at Marathon in 490 B.C. and invaded Greece.
Inserting clause	Although the mighty Persians outnumbered the small Greek army, the Greeks defeated the Persians. The Greek commander sent
Inserting phrase	Phidippides, his fastest runner, to Athens to spread
Inserting phrase	the good news. After running the entire way, Phidippides proudly announced the Greek victory. Then, he died. We get the term
Inserting word	"marathon" from Phidippides's historic run.

Combining by Inserting Words

One way to combine short sentences is to pull a key word from one sentence and insert it into another sentence. Sometimes you will need to change the form of the key word before you can insert it.

Inserting Without a Change

ORIGINAL Louis Armstrong was a famous musician. He was a jazz musician.

COMBINED Louis Armstrong was a famous **jazz** musician.

Inserting with a Change

ORIGINAL Armstrong was an easygoing person. He was a friend to many people.

COMBINED Armstrong was an easygoing, **friendly** person.

Exercise 4 Combining Sentences by Inserting Words

Combine each of the following sentence pairs by taking the italicized word from the second sentence and inserting it into the first sentence. Some sentences have hints in parentheses for changing the forms of words.

EXAMPLE **1.** Young Louis Armstrong first showed his talent on the streets of New Orleans. His talent was for *music.* (Add *–al.*)

1. Young Louis Armstrong first showed his musical talent on the streets of New Orleans.

1. Louis Armstrong had a deep voice. His voice was *rough.*

2. He became a jazz musician. He received *acclaim* for his music. (Add *–ed* and change *a* to *an.*)

3. Louis Armstrong sang jazz. His jazz singing was *brilliant.* (Add *–ly.*)

4. Louis started playing at a New Orleans nightspot. He played *cornet.*

5. He became famous as a solo trumpet player. He was famous on an *international* level. (Add *–ly.*)

Combining by Inserting Phrases

A ***phrase*** is a group of words that acts as a single part of speech and that does not have both a subject and a verb.

TIPS & TRICKS

You can often move a key word from one sentence to another by adding certain endings. The endings *–ed* and *–ing* can turn some verbs into words that act like adjectives or nouns. Adding *–ly* can turn some adjectives into adverbs and some nouns into adjectives.

EXAMPLES

relieve: The reliev**ed** student sighed.

sing: A sing**ing** canary flew overhead.

fortunate: Fortunate**ly,** we were finished.

cost: The cost**ly** necklace gleamed.

You can combine sentences by taking a phrase from one sentence and inserting it into the other sentence.

ORIGINAL Brown bears gather in groups. They gather around the banks of rivers.

COMBINED Brown bears gather in groups **around the banks of rivers.**

Reference Note

For more about **using commas with introductory phrases,** see page 644. For more information and practice on **using commas with appositive phrases,** see page 641.

Sometimes you will need to put commas after or around the phrase you are inserting. For example, if the prepositional phrase above appeared at the beginning of the sentence, it would be followed by a comma because the phrase consists of two smaller phrases. However, a single short prepositional phrase usually does not require a comma. Also, ask yourself whether the phrase renames or describes a noun or pronoun in the sentence. If it does, it is an ***appositive phrase,*** and you may need to use a comma or commas to set off the phrase from the rest of the sentence.

ORIGINAL Alaska is home to the big brown bears. The big brown bears are the largest kind of bear.

COMBINED Alaska is home to the big brown bears**, the largest kind of bear.** [The phrase in boldface type describes the noun *bears.*]

ORIGINAL The brown bear eats fish caught from the stream. The brown bear is a skilled and patient hunter.

COMBINED The brown bear, **a skilled and patient hunter,** eats fish caught from the stream. [The phrase in boldface type renames the noun *bear.*]

Reference Note

For more information and practice on **verb forms using *–ing, –ed,* or *to,*** see page 421.

Another way to combine sentences is to change the verb in a sentence to make a new phrase. You change the verb by adding *–ing* or *–ed* or by putting the word *to* in front of it. You can then use the new phrase to modify a noun, verb, or pronoun in another sentence.

ORIGINAL The bear prepares his winter retreat. He digs a burrow in a bank.

COMBINED **Digging a burrow in a bank,** the bear prepares his winter retreat. [The phrase in boldface type modifies the noun *bear.*]

ORIGINAL Bears dig in the ground. This is how they find roots and sweet bulbs.

COMBINED Bears dig in the ground **to find roots and sweet bulbs.** [The phrase in boldface type modifies the verb *dig.*]

NOTE When you combine sentences, be sure to keep the compound elements **parallel,** or matching in form. In other words, use the same kind of word or phrase in each of the compound elements.

ORIGINAL Julie likes **fishing** in a mountain stream. Julie also likes **to swim** in a cool mountain stream.

NOT PARALLEL Julie likes **fishing** and **to swim** in a mountain stream. [*Fishing* is a gerund; *to swim* is an infinitive.]

PARALLEL Julie likes **fishing** and **swimming** in a cool mountain stream. [*Fishing* and *swimming* are both gerunds.]

Exercise 5 Combining Sentences by Inserting Phrases

Combine each pair of sentences by taking the italicized words from the second sentence and inserting them into the first sentence. The hints in parentheses tell you how to change the forms of words. Add commas where needed.

EXAMPLE **1.** The Empire State Building was completed in 1931. It *towers above New York City at a height of 1,454 feet.* (Change *towers* to *towering.*)

1. Towering above New York City at a height of 1,454 feet, the Empire State Building was completed in 1931.

1. The Empire State Building was constructed in one year and forty-five days. The Empire State Building was *once the tallest building in the world.*

2. The building cost over twenty-four million dollars to complete. The building was *a gigantic structure.*

3. The building is a popular tourist attraction. It *weighs 365 million tons and contains 102 floors.* (Change *weighs* to *weighing* and *contains* to *containing.*)

4. The building was the site of a tragic event. The event occurred *in 1945.*

5. An Army B-25 cargo plane crashed into the seventy-ninth floor, killing fourteen people. The plane *flew through heavy fog.* (Change *flew* to *flying.*)

Combining by Using *And, But,* or *Or*

You can also combine sentences by using the coordinating conjunctions *and, but,* or *or.* With one of these connecting words, you can form a *compound subject,* a *compound verb,* or a *compound sentence.*

TIPS & TRICKS

When you form a compound subject, make sure that it agrees with the verb in number.

ORIGINAL
Tasmania is in Australia. Queensland is in Australia.

REVISED
Tasmania and Queensland are in Australia. [The plural subject takes the verb *are.*]

Reference Note

For more information and practice on **subject and verb agreement,** see page 476.

Compound Subjects and Verbs

Sometimes two sentences with different subjects have the same verb. You can combine the sentences by linking the two subjects with *and* or *or.* When you do this, you create a ***compound subject.***

ORIGINAL Kangaroos carry their young in pouches. Koalas carry their young in pouches.

COMBINED **Kangaroos and koalas** carry their young in pouches.

If two sentences with different verbs have the same subject, you can link the verbs with *and, but,* or *or* to form a ***compound verb.***

ORIGINAL Kangaroos can hop on their hind legs. They can walk on all four legs.

COMBINED Kangaroos can **hop** on their hind legs **or walk** on all four legs.

Exercise 6 Combining by Forming Compound Subjects and Compound Verbs

Combine each of the following sentence pairs by forming a compound subject or a compound verb. Make sure your new subjects and verbs agree in number.

1. Alligators are among the largest living reptiles. Crocodiles are among the largest living reptiles.
2. To hunt, the crocodile submerges itself in water. It waits for prey to swim near.
3. Crocodiles have strong tails. They are excellent swimmers.
4. Crocodiles have sharp, piercing teeth. Alligators have sharp, piercing teeth.
5. Crocodiles feed mostly on small animals such as turtles and fish. Crocodiles can live up to one hundred years.

Compound Sentences

Sometimes you may want to combine two sentences that express equally important ideas. You can connect the two sentences by using a comma and the coordinating conjunction *and, but,* or *or.* When you link sentences in this way, you create a ***compound sentence.***

ORIGINAL Many nations throughout the world use the metric system. The United States still uses the old system of measurement.

COMBINED Many nations throughout the world use the metric system**,** **but** the United States still uses the old system of measurement.

TIPS & TRICKS

Before you create a compound sentence out of two simple sentences, make sure the thoughts in the sentences are closely related to each other. If you combine two sentences that are not closely related, you will confuse your reader.

UNRELATED
Kim chopped the vegetables, and I like soup.

RELATED
Kim chopped the vegetables, and I stirred the soup.

Exercise 7 Combining Sentences by Forming a Compound Sentence

The sentences in each of the following pairs are closely related. Make each pair into a compound sentence by adding a comma and the coordinating conjunction *and, but,* or *or.*

EXAMPLE **1.** The kilogram is the basic unit of weight in the metric system. The meter is the basic unit of length.

1. The kilogram is the basic unit of weight in the metric system, and the meter is the basic unit of length.

1. The metric system was developed in France. It became popular in many countries.
2. We can keep the old system of measurement. We can switch to the metric system.
3. The old system of measurement has more than twenty basic units of measurement. The metric system has only seven.
4. A meter equals ten decimeters. A decimeter equals ten centimeters.
5. Counting by tens is second nature to most people. Many people still find the metric system difficult to learn.

Combining by Using a Subordinate Clause

A ***clause*** is a group of words that contains a verb and its subject. An ***independent clause*** can stand alone as a sentence. A ***subordinate*** (or ***dependent***) ***clause*** cannot stand alone as a sentence because it fails to express a complete thought.

INDEPENDENT CLAUSE In the 1850s, Elizabeth Cady Stanton was a civil rights activist. [This clause can stand alone as a sentence.]

SUBORDINATE CLAUSE Who fought to win women of all states the right to vote in federal elections. [This clause cannot stand alone as a sentence.]

Reference Note

For more information and practice on **complex sentences,** see page 465.

If two simple sentences are closely related but unequal in importance, you can combine them by using a subordinate clause. Just turn the less important idea into a subordinate clause and attach it to the other sentence. The result is a ***complex sentence.*** The subordinate clause will give additional information about an idea expressed in the rest of the sentence.

ORIGINAL Many women could not cast a vote in a federal election. The Nineteenth Amendment was ratified in 1920.

COMBINED Many women could not cast a vote in a federal election **until the Nineteenth Amendment was ratified in 1920.**

Clauses Beginning with *Who, Which,* or *That*

You can make a short sentence into a subordinate clause by inserting *who, which,* or *that* in place of the subject.

ORIGINAL The Aztecs were an American Indian people. They once ruled a mighty empire in Mexico.

COMBINED The Aztecs were an American Indian people **who once ruled a mighty empire in Mexico.**

Reference Note

For more about **commas after subordinate clauses,** see page 645.

Clauses Beginning with Words of Time or Place

You can also make a subordinate clause by adding a word that indicates time or place, such as *after, before, since, where, wherever, when, whenever,* or *while.* You may need to add, delete, or change some words to insert the clause into another sentence.

ORIGINAL The Aztecs built the capital city of Tenochtitlán. They moved into Mexico in the twelfth century.

COMBINED The Aztecs built the capital city of Tenochtitlán **after they moved into Mexico in the twelfth century.**

ORIGINAL The capital city of the Aztec empire was in central Mexico. Mexico City stands in that spot today.

COMBINED The capital city of the Aztec empire was in central Mexico, **where Mexico City stands today.**

Exercise 8 Combining Sentences by Using a Subordinate Clause

Combine each of the following sentence pairs by making the second sentence into a subordinate clause and attaching it to the first sentence. The hint in parentheses will tell you what word to use at the beginning of the clause. To make a smooth combination, you may need to delete one or more words in the second sentence of each pair.

1. The Aztecs practiced a religion. It affected every part of their lives. (Use *that.*)
2. Aztec craft workers made drums and rattles. Drums and rattles were their main musical instruments. (Use a comma and *which.*)
3. Aztec cities had huge temples. The people held religious ceremonies there. (Use *where.*)
4. Their empire was destroyed by the Spanish. The Spanish conquered it in 1521. (Use a comma and *who.*)
5. There was very little left of the Aztec civilization. The Spanish invaders tore down most of the Aztec buildings. (Use *after.*)

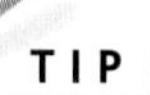

STYLE TIP

Varying sentence beginnings by moving a phrase or clause to the beginning of a sentence can make your writing more interesting. If you put a time or place clause at the beginning of a sentence, you will need to put a comma after the clause.

ORIGINAL
The Aztec empire grew. Aztec warriors conquered nearby territories.

COMBINED
When Aztec warriors conquered nearby territories, the Aztec empire grew.

Review B Revising a Paragraph by Combining Sentences

The following paragraph sounds choppy because it has too many short sentences. Use the methods you have learned in this section to combine some of the sentences. You will notice the improvement when you finish.

In 1814, a man acquired some land. This land was located around Tuxedo Lake in the state of New York. In 1886, the area became an exclusive neighborhood for the wealthy. Eventually, the word *tuxedo* was given to a style of clothing. This style of clothing was worn by many of the men of Tuxedo Park. These men were fashionable. However, most of these men probably did not know something. They probably did not know that the word *tuxedo* actually came from the American Indian word *p'tuksit.* This word means "he has a rounded foot." American Indians used this word to describe wolves. Wolves were plentiful around the lake. Of course, now you can see how funny the English language can be. Just picture the men of Tuxedo Park at a formal party. Picture them dining and dancing. Most of these men probably did not know that their tuxedo jackets were really "wolf" jackets.

Improving Sentence Style

You have learned how to improve choppy sentences by combining them into longer, smoother sentences. Now, you will learn how to improve *stringy* and *wordy sentences* by making them shorter and more precise.

Revising Stringy Sentences

Stringy sentences just ramble on and on. They have too many independent clauses, or complete thoughts, strung together with coordinating conjunctions such as *and* or *but.* If you read a stringy sentence out loud, you may run out of breath.

Mary McLeod Bethune dreamed of being a teacher, and she attended a college in Chicago, and she won a scholarship for her hard work, and Bethune eventually became a teacher, and she earned the respect of educators and presidents.

As you can see, stringy sentences are confusing because they do not show how the ideas fit together. To fix a stringy sentence, you can

- break the sentence into two or more sentences
- turn some of the independent clauses into phrases or subordinate clauses

Now read the revised version of the stringy sentence. Notice how the writer turned two of the independent clauses into subordinate clauses.

> Mary McLeod Bethune dreamed of being a teacher. She attended a college in Chicago after she won a scholarship for her hard work. Bethune eventually became a teacher who earned the respect of educators and presidents.

NOTE When you revise a stringy sentence, you may decide to keep *and* or *but* between two closely related independent clauses. If you do leave the sentence in compound form, be sure to use a comma before the *and* or *but* to show a pause between the two complete thoughts.

ORIGINAL Mary McLeod Bethune went on to found Bethune Cookman College and she also directed the Division of Negro Affairs under President Franklin Delano Roosevelt.

REVISED Mary McLeod Bethune went on to found Bethune Cookman College**, and** she also directed the Division of Negro Affairs under President Franklin Delano Roosevelt.

Exercise 9 Revising Stringy Sentences

Some of the following sentences are stringy and need revision. First, identify the stringy sentences. Then, revise them by using the methods you have learned. If a numbered item needs no revision, write *C* for correct.

1. Harriet Ross grew up as a slave in Maryland, and she worked on a plantation there, but in 1844 she married John Tubman, and he was a freed slave.

2. Harriet Tubman did not believe that people should be slaves, and she decided to escape, and late one night she began her dangerous trip to the North.
3. She made the long journey to Philadelphia, Pennsylvania, by traveling at night.
4. New friends told her about the Underground Railroad, and it was a secret group of people, and they helped runaway slaves get to the North.
5. Tubman decided she would rescue more slaves from the South, and she used the North Star as her guide, and she led groups of slaves along the road to freedom, and she made nineteen trips in twelve years.
6. The slaves hid during the day and continued their journey at night.
7. Tubman never learned to read or write, but she was a powerful speaker, and she spoke at many antislavery meetings.
8. The Civil War broke out, and Tubman volunteered to help the Union army, and she served as a cook and a nurse and later she became a spy.
9. The war ended, and Tubman settled in Auburn, New York, and she started a home for elderly black men and women.
10. The people of Auburn built Freedom Park in memory of Tubman.

Revising Wordy Sentences

STYLE  TIP

Extra words and phrases tend to make writing sound awkward and unnatural. As you revise your writing, try reading your sentences aloud to check for wordiness or a stringy style. If a sentence sounds like a mouthful to you, chances are it is stringy, wordy, or both.

Sometimes you may use more words than you really need. Extra words do not make writing sound better. They just get in the reader's way. You can revise ***wordy sentences*** in three different ways.

1. Replace a group of words with one word.

WORDY	I did not get to school on time **due to the fact that** I missed the bus.
REVISED	I did not get to school on time **because** I missed the bus.
WORDY	Juan opened his birthday gift **with a great eagerness.**
REVISED	Juan **eagerly** opened his birthday gift.

2. Replace a clause with a phrase.

WORDY **When the play had come to an end,** we walked to a restaurant and treated ourselves to pizza.

REVISED **After the play,** we walked to a restaurant and treated ourselves to pizza.

WORDY I ordered a slice with mushrooms, **which are my favorite topping.**

REVISED I ordered a slice with mushrooms, **my favorite topping.**

3. Take out a whole group of unnecessary words.

WORDY **What I mean to say is that** Carlos did not go to the movie with us.

REVISED Carlos did not go to the movie with us.

WORDY We all liked the movie because it had some very funny scenes **that were the kinds of scenes that make you laugh.**

REVISED We all liked the movie because it had some very funny scenes.

Exercise 10 Revising Wordy Sentences

Decide which of the following sentences are wordy and need revision. Then, revise each of the wordy sentences. You can (1) replace a phrase with one word, (2) replace a clause with a phrase, or (3) take out unnecessary words. If the sentence is effective as it is, write *C.*

1. Most wasps are helpful to humanity because of the fact that they eat harmful insects.
2. What I want to say is that wasps do far more good than harm.
3. Social wasps are the type that live together as groups and work as a team to build their nests.
4. Social wasps make their nests from old wood and tough plant fibers.
5. They chew and chew the wood and fiber until the mixture becomes pasty and mushy.
6. The mixture becomes a material that is called wasp paper.
7. According to some historians, the Chinese invented paper after watching wasps make it.

8. A wasp colony lasts only through the summer.
9. The queen wasp, being the only member of the colony to survive the winter, comes out of hibernation in the spring.
10. The queens start new colonies by means of building nests and laying eggs.

Review C Revising Stringy and Wordy Sentences

The following paragraph is hard to read because it contains stringy and wordy sentences. First, identify the stringy and wordy sentences. Then, revise them to improve the style of the paragraph.

On October 31, 1938, an amazing event took place that was very surprising. Many families were gathered around their radios, and they were listening to music, and then they heard that Martians had invaded Earth. Actually, the fact is that the news report was a radio version of H. G. Wells's novel <u>The War of the Worlds</u>. Orson Welles, who was the producer of this famous hoax, made the show very realistic. Thousands of Americans were frightened and upset, and many people jumped in their cars to escape from the aliens, and some people even reported seeing the Martians and their spaceships.

"Yeeeeeeeeeeeeha!"

Review D Applying Sentence Revision Strategies

Using the skills you have learned throughout this chapter, revise the following paragraph to revise fragments, run-ons, and stringy and wordy sentences. Try to combine at least five sentences so that the revised paragraph includes compound and complex sentences.

A wealthy and rich kingdom was emerging in southeast Africa this was in the twelfth century. Was located between the Zambezi and Limpopo rivers. The land was rich, and the land was fertile. Stone buildings were common structures here, and the largest and biggest of the stone buildings was called the "Great Zimbabwe," and this was the most impressive building. The word *Zimbabwe* means "dwelling of the chief." This was the home of the king. Massive walls were built around the king's home. These walls were in the shape of a circle that was round. They were thirty-two feet high. They were eight hundred feet around. Visitors came to the city. Visitors had to walk through a passage. They did this to reach the chief's home. The passage was situated in a location between the two circular walls. Passed through the circular walls. They saw a magnificent building. It was in the center of the circle's circumference. This building was the "Great Zimbabwe." This building was cone-shaped. The present-day country of Zimbabwe. Gets its name from this building.

CHAPTER

Learning About Paragraphs

What Is a Paragraph?

A ***paragraph*** is a group of sentences that relates one main idea. Usually, a paragraph is part of a longer piece of writing; however, before you learn to write a multiparagraph essay, you must first understand the characteristics of individual paragraphs.

Why Use Paragraphs?

What would happen if cars were not equipped with turn signals? Obviously, more accidents would occur. Turn signals are designed to inform one driver when another driver plans to turn or change lanes. In the same way, paragraphs also serve as signals: They tell the reader when the writer is switching to a new main idea. Without paragraphs, main ideas would run into each other, confusing the reader. So remember, as a writer, you are in the driver's seat—be courteous and signal when you switch to a new main idea by creating a new paragraph.

What Are the Parts of a Paragraph?

Paragraphs usually contain a *main idea,* a *topic sentence,* and *supporting sentences.* In addition, some paragraphs end with a *clincher sentence.*

The Main Idea

Have you ever met some of your friends for a game of baseball? Even if you do not have enough players, you always have a pitcher and a catcher. Without a pitcher and a catcher, you do not have a baseball game.

Paragraphs are like that, too. They may not have a topic sentence and a clincher sentence, but they must have a main idea. Without a main idea, you do not have a paragraph.

The ***main idea*** is the topic around which the entire paragraph is organized. Look back at the paragraph under the heading "Why Use Paragraphs?" on page 294. What is the main idea? It is that paragraphs are similar to turn signals. The other sentences in the paragraph give specific details about the characteristics that make turn signals and paragraphs similar.

PEANUTS reprinted by permission of United Feature Syndicate, Inc.

The Topic Sentence

The ***topic sentence*** states the main idea of the paragraph. It can occur anywhere in the paragraph, but it is usually the first or second sentence.

However, a topic sentence can come later in the paragraph, or even at the end. A topic sentence that comes later in a paragraph can often pull the ideas together and help the reader see how they are related. Sometimes the topic sentence summarizes, as in the following paragraph.

> The first skateboard was probably constructed in the 1930s. This skateboard was a homemade contraption consisting of a two-by-four and the metal wheels from a roller skate. Eventually in 1958, Bill Richards and his son Mark made a deal with the Chicago Roller Skate Company to produce skateboards, and the modern skateboard was born. Today, skateboarding is a sport enjoyed across the country. From garage hobby to national sport, skateboarding has certainly come a long way.

TIPS & TRICKS

You should generally use a topic sentence when writing a paragraph. A topic sentence will ensure that the reader will understand your main idea.

Many paragraphs have no topic sentence. This is especially true of narrative paragraphs that tell about a series of events. The reader has to add the details together to figure out what the main idea is. Look at the following paragraph. What is the main idea?

> When the coyote had finished drinking, it trotted a few paces, to above the steppingstones, and began to eat something. All at once it looked up, directly at me. For a moment it stood still. Then it had turned and almost instantly vanished, back into the shadows that underlay the trees. From behind the trees, a big black hawklike bird with a red head flapped out and away. Up in the lake, the herons took wing. They, too, circled away from me, angled upriver.
>
> Colin Fletcher, *The Secret Worlds of Colin Fletcher*

Each sentence in the previous paragraph describes a separate action. However, if you put them all together, they suggest the main idea: Colin Fletcher disturbed the animals and they fled.

Exercise 1 Identifying Main Ideas and Topic Sentences

Throughout your school career, you will be asked to read something and figure out what the main idea is. Sharpen your skills by identifying the main ideas in the following paragraphs. If the paragraph has a topic sentence, tell what it is. If there is not a topic sentence, summarize the main idea in your own words.

> **1.** In the sun's family of planets, the earth is unique in its possession of oceans. Indeed, it is remarkable that oceans exist at all. They do only because the largest part of the earth has a surface temperature in the small range within which water remains a liquid: in short, between 32° F (below which, under ordinary conditions, water freezes) and 212° F (when it boils and becomes a gas).
>
> Leonard Engel, *The Sea*

2. I arrived in San Francisco, leaner than usual, fairly unkempt, and with no luggage. Mother took one look and said, "Is the rationing that bad at your father's? You'd better have some food to stick to all those bones." She, as she called it, turned to, and soon I sat at a clothed table with bowls of food, expressly cooked for me.

Maya Angelou, *I Know Why the Caged Bird Sings*

3. Although living with a disability can be difficult, many disabled people lead independent lives. Gemma is one of those people. Left legally blind and deaf at age nine from an operation to remove a brain tumor, Gemma had to learn to overcome her disabilities. With the help of a cane, a hearing aid, and a magnifying glass to help her read, Gemma is able to be self-sufficient. She lives in an apartment by herself. She has a job, and she attends classes to learn new computer skills.

Supporting Sentences

In addition to a main idea and a topic sentence, effective paragraphs also have supporting sentences. ***Supporting sentences*** give specific details that explain or prove the main idea. These sentences may use sensory details, facts, or examples.

Sensory Details

When you use words that appeal to one or more of your five senses—sight, hearing, touch, taste, and smell—you are using ***sensory details.*** Vivid sensory details help your reader form a clear image of the subject.

Notice the sensory details in the paragraph on the next page from an article titled "Sweet Temptation." For example, in the first three sentences, you can "see" the rows of apple trees swaying in the wind on a hot Kentucky day. What other sensory details can you find?

My earliest childhood memory is of the swaying limbs of Golden Delicious apple trees. Rows of them stood next to a dirt road that separated our orchard from the front yard. The Kentucky summer sky hung hot behind those high twigs, their leaves leathery green on top, soft as down underneath. The apples, little bigger than shooter marbles then, played hide-and-seek with a child's eyes.

Frank Browning, "Sweet Temptation," *Reader's Digest*

Facts

Reference Note

For more about **facts** and **opinions,** see page 162.

A ***fact*** is a statement that can be proved true by direct observation or by checking a reliable reference source. For example, if you say that Washington, D.C., is the capital of the United States, you state a fact that can be proved. However, if you say that Washington, D.C., is the best city in the world, you state an opinion. Opinions cannot be proved.

Look at how the facts in the following paragraph support the main idea that a volcano was erupting. Many of the facts are statistics, or numbers. In the first sentence, for example, facts include the date and time of the boom, as well as the height of the peak. Can you find other facts? How might they be proved?

Those who camped overnight on March 28 atop 3,926-foot-high Mitchell Peak were wakened about 2:00 A.M. by a loud boom and whistling sounds. In the brilliant moonlight they watched a great plume of steam rise from the crater. Another eruption at 3:45 A.M. blew ash three miles into the sky and was followed by three quakes registering 4.0 on the Richter intensity scale. Later observers learned the volcano had blown out a second crater. Three small mudflows, not lava, dribbled a thousand feet down the slope. The east and south slopes turned gray from the ash projected by gases roiling from the magma far below the surface.

Marian T. Place, *Mount St. Helens: A Sleeping Volcano Awakes*

Examples

Examples are a third kind of supporting idea. They are specific instances or illustrations of a general idea. Soccer and football are examples of team sports played with a ball. Getting grounded is an example of what might happen if you disobey your parents. In the following paragraph the author gives examples of how people in Japan make use of limited space.

> If anyone on earth knows how to get the most out of cramped quarters, it is the Japanese. . . . A typical Japanese washing machine is so light and small it can be moved easily with one hand from one room to another. Many Japanese sleep on quilted mattresses called futons . . . [which] can be rolled up after use. . . . Aisles in many shops are so narrow that a visitor needs a shoehorn to move around in them. . . . Pizzas are the size of apple pies; coffee isn't served in mugs but in delicate cups; [and] newspapers have only between four and a dozen pages.
>
> John Langone, *In the Shogun's Shadow*

Exercise 2 **Collecting Supporting Details**

Have you ever collected baseball cards, seashells, or stamps? You search and choose only the ones you think are best. Now you are going to collect supporting details for topic sentences. Think of at least two details to support each of the following main ideas. For each idea, a type of support—sensory details, facts, or examples—is suggested.

1. Staying healthy is partly under your control. (facts)
2. When I walk around my neighborhood (or city), there is always something going on. (sensory details)
3. No one in my class is just like me. (examples)

The Clincher Sentence

Not only does a good paragraph contain a main idea, a topic sentence, and supporting details, but it may also end with a clincher sentence. A ***clincher sentence,*** also known as a ***concluding***

STYLE TIP

You do not need to include a clincher sentence in every paragraph. If you do, you may disrupt the rhythm of your composition. Consider adding a clincher sentence to the last body paragraph of your composition.

sentence, pulls together the preceding sentences by emphasizing the main idea. Ending with a clincher sentence is an effective way to ensure that the reader gets the overall point of the paragraph. Notice how the author of the following paragraph uses a clincher sentence to bring the paragraph to a close.

> What most people don't realize is that [shark attacks] almost never happen. In a particularly bad year, as many as one hundred people may be attacked by sharks. Of those attacks, a small minority—15 percent at most—prove fatal. Far more people are killed by bees, poisonous snakes, and elephants, as well as bathtub falls and lightning strikes. It's much more dangerous to drive to the beach than to venture into the water once you get there.
>
> Michael D. Lemonick, "Under Attack," *Time*

HELP To complete Exercise 3, look for the main idea of the paragraph. Once you have determined the main idea, consider the supporting details. How can you bring the main idea and supporting details together in one sentence?

Exercise 3 Developing a Clincher Sentence

Provide a clincher sentence for each of the following paragraphs. Remember that a good clincher sentence brings the paragraph to a close by emphasizing the main idea.

1. Without the inventiveness of Thomas Edison, we would be without many of the devices that make our lives more enjoyable. Everyone knows, of course, that he invented the light bulb. The usefulness of this invention needs no explanation. However, many do not know that Edison invented other things as well. Edison not only invented the movie camera, but he also invented the phonograph.

2. As a student, you should find out what kind of study environment is right for you because the wrong study conditions can lead to poor grades. Some students must have a quiet environment in which to study. The noise of the TV or radio, the whirring of a fan, or the movement of people can cause these students to lose concentration.

```
As a result, they often have ineffective
study sessions. However, some students
actually seem to need what is called "back-
ground noise." In other words, these
students need to hear the hum of the TV or
radio in the background to study effectively.
```

What Makes a Good Paragraph?

Although a paragraph may have a main idea, a topic sentence, and supporting sentences, the reader may still not understand it fully. What may be missing is *unity, coherence,* or *elaboration.*

Unity

When a paragraph has ***unity,*** all the sentences relate to the main idea. For example, in a paragraph explaining the origin of baseball, every sentence should give some information about baseball's beginnings. Including a sentence about this year's best team would ruin the paragraph's unity. That sentence is not about the paragraph's main idea—how baseball began.

As you read the following paragraph, notice how each sentence is directly connected to the main idea: how sailors once believed in mermaids.

> Another monster that was equally dreaded by sailors was the beautiful mermaid. Like the sirens, mermaids were thought to be half woman and half fish. Such creatures were said to carry a mirror in one hand and a comb in the other, and from time to time they would run the comb through their long sea-green hair. Most sailors were convinced that it was very bad luck to see a mermaid. At best, it meant that someone aboard their ship would die soon afterward. At worst, it meant that a terrific storm would arise, the ship would sink, and many of the crew would drown.
>
> William Wise, "Strange and Terrible Monsters of the Deep," *Boys' Life*

Exercise 4 Identifying Sentences That Destroy Unity

In each of the following paragraphs, one sentence should make you say, "What is *that* doing there?" Find the sentence that destroys the unity of each paragraph. Remember that in a unified paragraph, all details are directly related to the main idea.

1. The disappearance of Amelia Earhart remains a mystery. Earhart, who was the first woman pilot to fly across the Atlantic Ocean, crashed into the Pacific Ocean while attempting to fly around the world. She was born in Atchison, Kansas, in 1897. Some searchers believe that she survived the crash into the Pacific, because radio distress calls were received. An intensive search for the source of the signals was made. Searchers were not able to find her, however. Finally, the distress signals ceased. In spite of continued searches by airplane and ship, no clue about what became of Amelia Earhart has yet been found.

2. After being a city dweller for almost twelve years, I was forced to move to the country. At the time, I hated the idea of living in the "wide-open spaces." After all, what could a teenager do on a farm located fifteen miles from the nearest town? Farming, once commonplace, seems to be in danger of extinction as more people take jobs in large cities. The simple pleasures of the city were miles away. Casual jaunts to the arcade were out of the question. A simple stroll to the mall—once fifteen minutes away by foot—was quite impossible. I felt as if I would never again have fun. But one day, as I explored deep into the quiet woods behind our house, I realized something important: Those wide-open spaces I had once hated held countless possibilities.

Coherence

In addition to having unity, a paragraph also needs to be coherent. A coherent paragraph is one in which all of the sentences logically fit together. When a paragraph has ***coherence,*** the reader can easily see how all of the details are connected. You can use two methods to create coherence in your writing. First, you can order details in a way that makes sense to the reader. Second, you can show how the details are connected by using appropriate transitional words.

Order of Details

Organizing your details in a specific order is one way to be sure your paragraph is clear and coherent. Use one of the four patterns listed below.

Chronological order	presents details in the order in which they occur
Spatial order	presents details according to their location in space
Order of importance	arranges details from the least to most important, or the reverse
Logical order	groups related details together

Chronological Order When you put ideas in **chronological order,** you arrange them in the order in which they occur.

- **Using chronological order to write a narrative** A narrative can be a fictional account of an event. For example, a novel is a fictional narrative. However, a narrative can also be an account of a factual event. Your history book is filled with narratives that actually happened, such as the story of the Revolutionary War. All narratives, whether fiction or fact, have one thing in common: They use chronological order to explain a series of related events. As you read the paragraph on the next page, notice that Nancy Mohr uses chronological order to relate a factual narrative.

In 1482, the duke of Milan commissioned Leonardo da Vinci to create the biggest horse statue ever. Made to honor the duke's father, it was to be twenty-four feet high. Leonardo spent years sketching a great charger, eventually sculpting a full-sized model in clay and leaving notes about how to cast it—the bronze would weigh eighty tons! But then a French army threatened and the metal was needed for cannon. When Milan fell to the French in 1499, French archers used the clay horse for target practice. For more than four centuries it was lost to history until Leonardo's sketches were rediscovered in Spain in 1966.

Nancy Mohr, "A Long Shot Pays Off," *Smithsonian*

- **Using chronological order to explain a process** Many writers use chronological order to explain a process, such as how to do something or how something occurs. Explaining a process using chronological order often involves explaining how something develops over time. For instance, a writer might explain how erosion helped form the Grand Canyon over millions of years. Explaining a process using chronological order can also involve telling the reader how to complete a certain task step by step. For example, notice how the writer of the following paragraph uses chronological order to explain how to teach a dog commands.

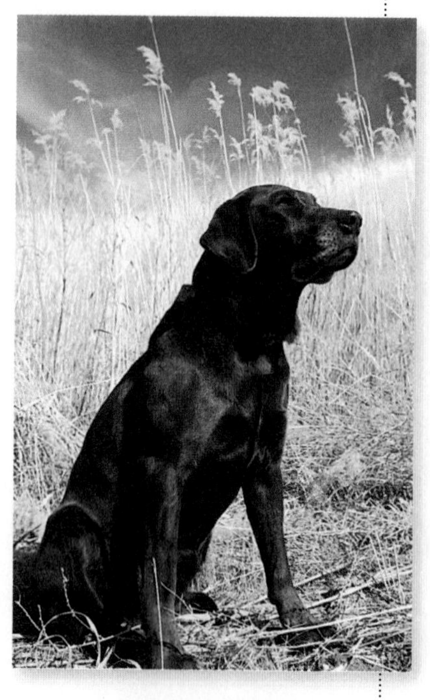

For the command "Sit," hold the leash in your right hand and gently press on the dog's hindquarters with your left hand. At the same time, say "Sit." When he or she is in the correct position, stroke and praise your dog. When your dog will sit on command without having to be pushed, he or she is ready to learn "Stay." Move a couple of feet in front of the dog, still holding on to the leash. If the dog tries to follow, you say "No" firmly and repeat the word "Stay." Repeat this process, moving farther away from the dog each time. . . .

Pam Jameson, *Responsible Pet Care*

- **Using chronological order to explain causes and effects** Chronological order is often used to explain a *cause-and-effect chain.* A ***cause-and-effect chain*** occurs when an initial cause triggers an effect which itself becomes a cause, and so on. Think of a cause-and-effect chain in terms of a row of carefully arranged dominoes. If you push the first domino in the row (cause), it will fall into the second domino and make it fall (effect/cause). The second domino will make the third domino fall, and so on with a series of causes and effects until the final domino topples (the final effect). Notice in the following paragraph that the first "domino" (the hot weather) begins a chain of related causes and effects.

> Bees create their own air conditioning. When the weather becomes especially hot and the temperature inside the hive threatens to melt the wax, one group of bees stations itself at the entrance to the colony while another remains inside. Both groups then flap their wings simultaneously, sometimes at a rate of four hundred flaps per second. Thus they create a cross-draft that pulls the hot air out of the hive and draws the cooler air in.
>
> David Louis, *2201 Fascinating Facts*

Cause (When the weather becomes especially hot)
Effect/Cause (one group of bees stations itself)
Effect/Cause (a cross-draft)
Effect (draws the cooler air in)

Exercise 5 Using Chronological Order to Develop Paragraphs

Follow the directions for each item, making sure to arrange supporting details in chronological (time) order.

1. Choose one of the topics listed below and list at least five details that would need to be included in a paragraph about it.
   a. the Boston Tea Party
   b. my happiest moment
2. List at least five steps to explain the process involved in completing each task.
   a. how to make a sandwich
   b. how to use the Web or library to find a book on dogs

3. Pick one of the following topics and list a chronological chain of causes and effects.
   a. not getting enough exercise
   b. being tardy for class

Spatial Order *Spatial order* is often used in descriptive paragraphs because it helps the reader visualize the subject. The following writer describes her room by moving from the left wall to the right wall, allowing the reader to see how the details fit together in space.

> My apartment is so small that it will no longer hold all of my possessions. Every day when I come home from school, I am shocked by the clutter. The wall to my immediate left is completely obscured by art and movie posters that have become so numerous they often overlap, hiding even each other. Along the adjoining wall is my sound system: CDs and tapes are stacked several feet high on two long tables. The big couch that runs across the back of the room is always piled so high with schoolbooks and magazines that a guest usually ends up sitting on the floor. To my right is a large sliding glass door that opens onto a balcony—at least it used to, before it was permanently blocked by my tennis gear, golf clubs, and ten-speed bike. Even the tiny closet next to the front door is bursting with clothes—both clean and dirty. I think the time has come for me to move.
>
> Jean Wyrick, *Steps to Writing Well*

Exercise 6 Using Spatial Order to Develop Paragraphs

How would you describe your room, your favorite store, or the inside of your locker? Choose one of the following subjects and list at least six supporting details to describe the subject. Then, arrange the details in spatial order.

1. an amusement park or city park

2. the inside of your dream house or apartment
3. your school on the first or last day of the school year

Order of Importance Another way to organize writing is to arrange supporting details according to their ***order of importance.*** As a writer, you might decide to begin a paragraph with the supporting detail that "packs the most punch" and end with a weaker idea. For example, in a paragraph about the effects of air pollution, you might choose to begin by explaining that air pollution can lead to disease and death in humans. Then, you might decide to end the paragraph by stating that air pollution can also cause eye irritation, nausea, and headaches. However, you can also do the opposite by beginning your paragraph with a less forceful idea and ending it with a stronger one, as in the following paragraph.

> Daniel "Chappie" James, Jr., lived by the "Eleventh Commandment" created by his mother, Lillie: "Thou shalt never quit." Although segregation, prejudice, and the narrow-mindedness of both whites and blacks placed obstacles in his path, James never gave up. He had a distinguished military career as one of the original Tuskegee Airmen and as a combat pilot in Korea and Vietnam, and was an inspirational speaker during times of great turmoil in America. In 1975, he became America's first African American four-star general.
>
> "Never Give Up," *Cobblestone*

TIPS & TRICKS

It is important to remember your options when you are writing. To help remember the four orders that give your writing coherence, think about making your writing "SLIC." *SLIC* stands for ***S****patial order,* ***L****ogical order, order of* ***I****mportance,* and ***C****hronological order.*

Exercise 7 Using Order of Importance to Develop Paragraphs

Choose one of the following topics and list at least three supporting details for each. Then, arrange these details according to how important they are. You may choose to order the details from least important to most important, or the reverse.

1. the qualities that make a good friend
2. the reasons we should take care of the environment
3. what would happen in your perfect day

Logical Order *Logical order* involves arranging supporting details into related groups. A logical pattern of organization can help the reader understand the connection between details. For example, a writer of an informative paragraph about wolves might decide to group details about their diet in the first three to five sentences. Then, she might group details about their social behavior in the last several sentences.

When you *compare* or *contrast* two things, you use logical order to group similarities and differences. For example, the following paragraph contrasts butterflies and moths by using a logical order. Notice how related details about moths and butterflies are grouped together. Details about when they fly, how they hold their wings, and what their antennae look like are each grouped together and discussed separately. Also, notice the pattern the authors use: A statement about butterflies is always paired with a contrasting statement about moths. This pattern makes the paragraph easier to understand.

Old World swallowtail butterfly

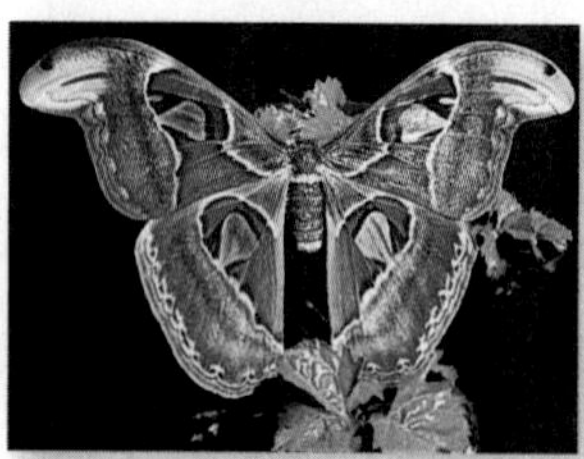

Atlas moth

> There are three main differences between butterflies and moths. Butterflies are out by day while moths usually fly at night, but this is not an infallible guide since some moths fly by day. Second, moths spread their wings sideways at rest, whereas butterflies hold them together over their backs, though again there are exceptions. Third, the butterfly's antennae are long and slender, whereas a moth's are shorter and feathery.
>
> Gerald Durrell with Lee Durrell, *The Amateur Naturalist*

Exercise 8 Using Logical Order to Develop Paragraphs

Ordering supporting details ideas into related groups can help the reader better understand your topic. Choose one of the following topics and list four to six details about it. Then, order those details into related groups.

1. the difference between elementary school and middle school
2. things to consider when shopping for school clothes
3. good pets and bad pets

Transitional Words and Phrases

The second way to create coherence is to use transitional words and phrases. ***Transitional words and phrases*** can help create coherence by showing how related details are connected. The following chart lists some common transitions.

Transitional Words and Phrases		
Chronological Order		
Showing Time		
after	finally	soon
at last	first	then
at once	later	thereafter
before	meanwhile	when
eventually	next	while
Showing Cause-and-Effect Relationships		
as a result	for	so
because	for this reason	so that
consequently	since	therefore
Spatial Order		
above	beneath	inside
across	beside	into
among	beyond	near
around	by	next to
before	down	over
behind	here	there
below	in	under
Order of Importance		
first	mainly	then
last	more important	to begin with

(continued)

(continued)

Logical Order		
Comparing Ideas		
also	just as	moreover
and	like	similarly
another	likewise	too
Contrasting Ideas		
although	in spite of	on the other hand
but	instead	still
however	nevertheless	yet

In the following paragraph, notice how the underlined transitions help create coherence by showing how ideas are related to one another.

STYLE TIP

Think about what kind of connection each transitional word or phrase in this paragraph makes between ideas. What do the transitions tell you about how the piece is organized? In your own writing, try to use transitions that will give readers clues about the pattern of organization you have chosen.

In ancient times, it was a very expensive process to dye cloth or any other material. With no chemical dyes or synthetic products, artisans had to make dyes from products found in nature. For this reason, explorers in the Americas must have been quite excited when they discovered that the natives knew how to make a dye extract . . . from a common tree, known as the *brasil.* European merchants soon developed a great trade in brasil wood. The Portuguese, who, as a result of the treaty of Tordesillas, laid claim to the land where these trees grew, named the area *Terra de Brasil* or "Land of Red-dye-wood." Soon cartographers and others began to refer to the land as *Brasil.* Speakers of English later adopted the name and the way it was pronounced. However, because an *s* between two vowels sounds like a *z* in Portuguese, English changed the spelling of *Brasil* to *Brazil.*

"Word Stories: Brazil," *Calliope*

Exercise 9 Identifying Transitional Words and Phrases

Can you find the words and phrases that connect the writer's details? Make a list of all the transitional words and phrases you can find in this paragraph about bartering in ancient times.

In the days before the invention of paper money and strip malls, people had to trade for goods and services. However, one could imagine the problems this system produced. For example, say that Kino, a fisherman living in ancient times, realizes he needs a new coat to keep him warm at sea. How does he get it? First, he takes twenty fish from his basket so that he can trade for the coat. Then, he makes the day's journey to the coat-maker's shop. When he arrives, an unforeseen problem arises that makes Kino shiver: The coat-maker hates fish but loves carrots. As a result, the coatmaker will supply Kino with a coat for ten bushels of carrots. Consequently, Kino walks about the region—in the cold, as luck would have it—and finally finds a carrot farmer willing to take the fish. Kino at last returns to the coatmaker and trades the carrots for the coat. However, after all of this, another problem that distresses Kino arises: The long journey has completely worn out Kino's shoes, and, unfortunately, the shoemaker likes neither fish nor carrots.

Elaboration

Have you ever seen a mosaic? A mosaic begins as an outline of a picture or design. The artist then ***elaborates*** on, or works out in greater detail, the outline by inlaying small, colorful bits of colored stones or glass into mortar, which is like cement. What once was only a simple outline grows into a detailed picture.

Writing a paragraph is much like producing a mosaic. You begin with a main idea and a few supporting details. Then, piece by piece, you craft the paragraph by adding more details and explanation. If you, as the writer, fail to elaborate on your main idea, the reader is left with an unclear picture of the subject. Notice that the following paragraph contains a main idea and a few supporting details but fails to paint a complete picture. Could you clearly and accurately describe a hyena to someone else based on what you read in this paragraph?

> The spotted hyena is an able hunter. It has powerful jaws and sharp teeth. The spotted hyena has strong, short hind legs. Hunting in large packs allows the spotted hyena to overwhelm much larger prey. Only the fittest, smartest, and strongest survive in the wild.

Now consider the following paragraph. Notice the many different types of additions and changes the writer made to create a thorough and vivid description of a hyena.

Definition	The spotted hyena, a meat-
	eating mammal that roams the
Adjective	plains of Africa, is a fierce and
	able hunter. The spotted hyena is
Comparison	similar to a gray wolf in some
	ways: It has powerful jaws and
Contrast	sharp teeth. However, unlike the
	wolf, the spotted hyena has
Adjective	strong, stubby hind legs. Hunting
	in large packs allows the spotted
	hyena to overwhelm much larger
Example	prey, such as the gazelle, a
Fact	deerlike animal. The moment a
	gazelle becomes separated from
	the herd, the pack quickly moves
Sensory details	in for the kill. Hovering around
	the prey in an ever-tightening
	circle, the menacing group sounds
	a shrill, piercing cry before
	setting upon its victim. Only the
	fittest, smartest, and strongest
	survive in the wild.

The following is a list of strategies that will help you elaborate on, or further explain, your main ideas.

- Use highly **descriptive words,** including vivid adjectives and adverbs and precise verbs and nouns.
- Give a detailed **definition** of the subject or detail.
- Provide an **example** that illustrates your point.
- Use **comparison** to explain how what you are describing is similar to something else. *Metaphors* and *similes* are types of comparisons.
- Use **contrast** to explain how what you are describing is different from something else.
- Include a **fact** to support your main idea.
- Use a **statistic** to support your main idea. Statistics are facts in numerical form.
- Use **sensory details,** descriptive language that appeals to one or more of the five senses.
- Use **cause and effect** to explain how one thing causes another, or how one thing results from another.

Reference Note

For more on **metaphors** and **similes,** see page 41.

Exercise 10 Elaborating Details

Using the strategies for elaboration listed above, rewrite the following paragraph by adding more detail. Remember to create a clear, well-defined "word picture" for the reader. Be ready to explain the elaboration strategies you used and why you used them.

My day is filled with activity. I wake up very early, eat breakfast, and go to school. Once in the classroom, I am on a very tight schedule. Each class has its own routine. I am glad when the lunch bell finally rings because I finally have time to relax. However, all too soon lunch is over and I am in the classroom for the rest of the afternoon. When school is out, I go home, eat, do my homework, and go to bed. The next day, I do it all again.

What Are the Types of Paragraphs?

The following chart lists the four types of paragraphs.

Types of Paragraphs	
Narrative	used to tell a story or relate a sequence of events
Expository	used to inform or explain, often by including facts, definitions, or instructions on how to do something
Descriptive	used to describe a person, place, thing, or idea; often used to express or entertain
Persuasive	used to influence others to agree with the writer's opinion or to take action

The type of paragraph you choose to write will depend on whether your *purpose* for writing is to *inform* or *explain, influence* or *persuade, express,* or *entertain.* For example, if your purpose is to influence the audience, you would most likely write a persuasive paragraph.

Narrative Paragraphs

A ***narrative paragraph*** uses chronological order to tell a story or relate a sequence of events. Consider the following narrative paragraph about a mystery involving the early American settlement of Roanoke.

> In 1587, Sir Walter Raleigh, an ambitious English adventurer, launched a second colony at Roanoke. The original location of the colony was to be in the Chesapeake Bay area, but unexpected winds caused the ships to veer off course and land at Roanoke Island. Upon their arrival, 118 men and women, under the leadership of John White, built shelters and began to fish and hunt for game. The
>
> *(continued)*

(continued)
colonists seemed to thrive in their new home. However, between 1587 and 1590, something mysterious happened to the settlers. When a ship from England arrived at Roanoke in 1590, all of the colonists were gone without a trace. The only clue to the whereabouts of the colonists was a curious inscription etched on a tree: the word "Croatoan." Since Croatoan was the name of a nearby island, the ship set sail for it. Once there, the sailors sang English songs in a vain attempt to signal them, but no one responded. After an extensive search, the ship returned to England. The fate of the original settlers of Roanoke remains a mystery to this day.

The Granger Collection, New York.

Expository Paragraphs

The word *expository* is related to the word *expose,* a verb that means "to allow to be seen, or to reveal." For example, newspaper reporters try to *expose* the truth. When writing an ***expository paragraph,*** the writer seeks to reveal information about a subject. An expository paragraph can list facts, show cause and effect, compare and contrast, or explain instructions. The following paragraph compares the settlements established at Roanoke and Jamestown.

Some early American settlements were in poor locations. Roanoke, for example, was on an island that proved hard to reach. Rough ocean currents and storms made the voyage difficult for ships to bring much-needed supplies. The site for a later colony, Jamestown, also had problems. Jamestown sat on a marshy, disease-ridden piece of land. Because of its location, Jamestown's settlers had to endure increased incidents of illness as well as a salty water supply. However, despite the negatives, Roanoke and Jamestown shared one important advantage: The semihidden location of both colonies aided against surprise attacks.

Descriptive Paragraphs

A ***descriptive paragraph*** creates an accurate picture of the subject by including sensory details and adjectives. In the following paragraph, Esther Forbes describes Colonial Boston. Notice how she paints a "picture" by appealing to the senses of sight and hearing.

> Boston slowly opened its eyes, stretched, and woke. The sun struck in horizontally from the east, flashing upon weather vanes—brass cocks and arrows, here a glass-eyed Indian, there a copper grasshopper—and the bells in the steeples cling-clanged, telling the people it was time to be up and about.
>
> Esther Forbes, *Johnny Tremain*

Persuasive Paragraphs

Should your town or city have a curfew for teenagers? Should school lunch periods be longer? Who was the better president: Washington or Lincoln? A ***persuasive paragraph*** seeks to convince the reader to agree with an opinion or to take a certain course of action. Study the following excerpt from Patrick Henry's famous "Give me liberty or give me death" speech. In this speech, Henry uses an emotional appeal to convince his audience to arm the Virginia militia for war against England.

Reference Note

For more on **emotional appeals,** see page 209.

> The battle is not won by the strong alone. It is won by the alert, the active, the brave. Besides, we have no choice. Even if we were cowardly enough to desire it, it is now too late to back down from the conflict. There is no retreat but in submission and slavery! Our chains are forged! Their clanking may be heard on the plains of Boston. The war is inevitable—and let it come! I repeat, let it come!
>
> Patrick Henry, *Sketches of the Life and Character of Patrick Henry*

Exercise 11 Identifying Types of Paragraphs

Using newspapers, magazines, books, or Web sites, find an example of each of the four types of paragraphs. Identify each paragraph as *narrative, expository, descriptive,* or *persuasive.* Then, answer the following questions.

1. What is the writer trying to influence his audience to do or believe in the persuasive paragraph? Support your response.
2. List two or three of the sensory details you found in the descriptive paragraph.
3. What was the main idea of the expository paragraph?
4. List, in order, the main supporting details of the narrative paragraph.

How Are Paragraphs Used in Longer Pieces of Writing?

By now, you know that a paragraph is a group of sentences that communicates one distinct idea. However, a paragraph usually does not stand on its own. Instead, most writing is composed of several paragraphs that relate to one topic.

To help you learn when to begin a new paragraph, study the following tips. Begin a new paragraph when

- you express a new main idea
- you explain a different part or aspect of your subject
- the setting—time or location—of your piece changes
- a different character or person speaks (as in dialogue)
- you provide another kind of support for your opinion

Exercise 12 Dividing a Composition into Paragraphs

The paragraph indentations have been removed from the article on the next page. With a small group of classmates, read the selection and discuss where to start and end paragraphs. Be prepared to explain your answers. Be aware that there may be more than one way to divide the selection.

In the winter of 1692, several young women in Salem, Massachusetts, were stricken with seizures. The community attributed the seizures to demonic possession. Most people there believed in the Devil's existence and ability to possess humans. They also believed that the Devil empowered human agents, called witches, to cause this possession. Members of the village community pressed the possessed females to name those responsible for their afflictions. Once the young women began identifying witches in their midst, hundreds of residents of Salem and other towns came forward to testify that they too were victims of witchcraft. They claimed witches had used supernatural powers to kill their children, sicken their farm animals, and otherwise harm their families and property. Witchcraft accusations and trials had taken place in New England many times prior to 1692. What made the Salem trials so unusual was the number of people involved. In a matter of months, over two hundred persons were named as witches. At least fifty-nine were tried, thirty-one convicted, and nineteen hanged. As in earlier times, older women were the main targets. For a long time, many historians considered the Salem outbreak a bizarre and irrational event and argued that the young women were mentally disturbed. Other accusers, most of whom were adult men, were thought either to have been carried away with the hysteria of the moment or to have deliberately accused people they resented. The older women who were convicted and executed as witches were simply viewed as convenient targets. Recent historians have challenged this view of the trials, emphasizing how the trials were rooted in the social and cultural climate of New England. The religious, economic, and family life of New England's settlers all fostered an environment in which witchcraft fears flourished and accusations were an accepted way of dealing with personal conflict and community tensions.

Dr. Carol Karlsen

Review A Writing a Narrative Paragraph

A narrative paragraph is used to tell a story or relate a sequence of events. The subject of a narrative paragraph can be real or fictional. Write a narrative paragraph on one of the following topics. Remember to arrange your details in chronological order.

- an eventful birthday or other special occasion
- your favorite year in school so far
- the funniest thing that ever happened to you

Review B Writing an Expository Paragraph

The purpose of an expository paragraph is to reveal information about a subject. Use an expository paragraph either to explain a topic of your choice or to explain a process.

Review C Writing a Descriptive Paragraph

Write a descriptive paragraph about one of the following topics. Do not forget to appeal to the reader's senses. Also, be sure to create coherence by putting your ideas in spatial order.

- your bedroom
- your favorite place
- a beautiful sunset
- a friend or relative

Review D Writing a Persuasive Paragraph

Write a persuasive paragraph on a topic of your choice. Remember that the goal of a persuasive paragraph is to convince the reader to agree with you. To convince the reader, use reasons to support your opinion. If you have trouble finding a topic, answer one of the following questions.

- What school policy would you change or enact if you could?
- What is your opinion on an issue you have seen on the news or read about in the newspaper?
- Who is the greatest historical figure of all time?

TIPS & TRICKS

When you are writing, try using a cluster diagram to brainstorm supporting details about your topic. Simply draw a circle in the center of a piece of paper and write your topic within it. Then, draw three more circles around your topic, labeling them "sensory details," "facts," and "examples." Use lines to connect these *detail circles* to your *topic circle.* Then, connect three more circles to each of your *detail circles* and try to think of a detail to put in each circle. Look at the model below.

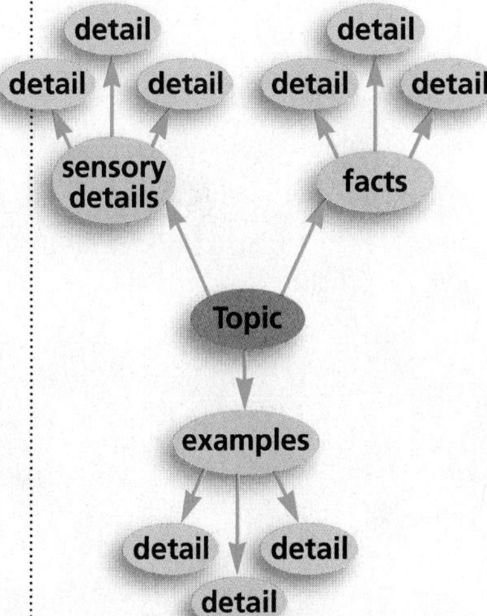

Grammar, Usage, and Mechanics

Grammar

Usage

Mechanics

CHAPTER

The Sentence

Subject and Predicate, Kinds of Sentences

Diagnostic Preview

A. Identifying Sentences and Sentence Fragments

Identify each group of words as a *sentence* or a *sentence fragment.* If the word group is a sentence fragment, correct it by adding the words necessary to make a complete sentence.

EXAMPLES **1.** Do you like the U.S. Postal Service's special postage stamps?

1. sentence

2. When my parents buy stamps.

2. sentence fragment—When my parents buy stamps, they ask for new commemorative ones.

1. Commemorative stamps are issued to give recognition to someone or something special.
2. Stamps with pictures of animals or famous people.
3. A block of four different, colorful stamps that commemorate Earth Day.
4. Because all four of the winning designs for the Earth Day 1995 stamps were created by young people.
5. I like "Love" stamps and holiday stamps.

B. Identifying Subjects and Predicates

Classify each italicized group of words as the *complete subject* or the *complete predicate* of the sentence. Then, identify the simple subject or the verb in each italicized word group.

EXAMPLES 1. *Anyone searching for the highest mountains* must look on land and in the sea.

1. complete subject; simple subject—Anyone

2. Not all mountains *are easy to see.*

2. complete predicate; verb—are

6. *Much of the earth's surface* is mountainous.
7. *Can* you *name the world's highest mountain*?
8. *Mount Everest in the Himalayas* claims that title.
9. In fact, *seven of the world's highest mountains* are in the Himalayan mountain range.
10. Mount Everest *towers to a height of 29,028 feet above sea level.*
11. *The Alps in Europe, the Rockies in North America, and the Andes in South America* are other high mountain ranges.
12. High mountains *also have been discovered under the ocean.*
13. Down the middle of the Atlantic Ocean floor runs *the earth's longest continuous mountain range.*
14. The peaks of some undersea mountains *rise above the surface of the water and form islands.*
15. *The islands of Hawaii* are actually the peaks of submerged mountains in the Pacific Ocean.

C. Classifying Sentences

Classify each of the following sentences as *declarative, interrogative, imperative,* or *exclamatory.* Then, write the last word of each sentence and provide appropriate end punctuation.

EXAMPLE 1. Write your name and the date on your paper

1. imperative—paper.

16. Juana plans to study architecture after she graduates
17. Isn't this the right answer to the question
18. How confused we are
19. Bring me the map of Paraguay, please
20. I can't right now, Andy, because I am carrying two boxes

GRAMMAR

The Sentence

In casual conversation, people often leave out parts of sentences. In your writing at school, however, it is almost always best to use complete sentences. They help make your meaning clear to the reader.

10a. A *sentence* is a word group that contains a subject and a verb and that expresses a complete thought.

A sentence begins with a capital letter and ends with a period, a question mark, or an exclamation point.

EXAMPLES **S**ean was chosen captain of his soccer team**.**

Have you ever seen a Broadway musical**?**

What a thrilling adventure we had**!**

Stop**!** [The understood subject is *you.*]

Reference Note

For more about the **understood subject,** see page 339.

A ***sentence fragment*** is a word group that looks like a sentence but does not contain both a subject and a verb or does not express a complete thought.

Reference Note

For more information about **correcting sentence fragments,** see page 275.

SENTENCE FRAGMENT Was a well-known ragtime pianist. [This group of words has a verb (*Was*), but the subject is missing. *Who* was a well-known ragtime pianist?]

SENTENCE **Scott Joplin** was a well-known ragtime pianist.

SENTENCE FRAGMENT A butterfly with bright blue wings and long antennae. [This group of words has a subject (*butterfly*), but the verb is missing. *What* did the butterfly do?]

SENTENCE A butterfly with bright blue wings and long antennae **landed.**

SENTENCE FRAGMENT Even though she had worked a long time. [This group of words has a subject (*she*) and a verb (*had worked*), but it does not express a complete thought. *What happened* even though she had worked a long time?]

SENTENCE **Louise Nevelson had not completed the sculpture** even though she had worked on it a long time.

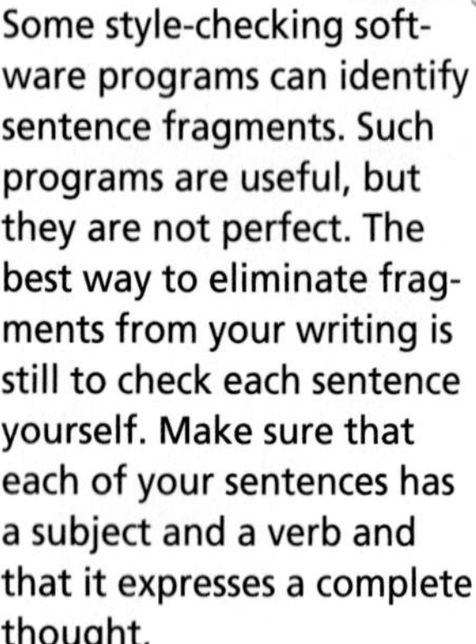

COMPUTER TIP

Some style-checking software programs can identify sentence fragments. Such programs are useful, but they are not perfect. The best way to eliminate fragments from your writing is still to check each sentence yourself. Make sure that each of your sentences has a subject and a verb and that it expresses a complete thought.

Exercise 1 Identifying Sentences and Sentence Fragments

Tell whether each of the following groups of words is a *sentence* or a *sentence fragment.*

EXAMPLES

1. Can you name the famous American woman in the picture below?

   1. sentence

2. A woman who made history.

   2. sentence fragment

1. One of the best-known women in American history is Sacagawea.
2. A member of the Lemhi band of the Shoshone.
3. She is famous for her role as interpreter for the Lewis and Clark expedition.
4. Which was seeking the Northwest Passage.
5. In 1800, the Lemhis had encountered a war party of the Hidatsa.
6. Who captured some of the Lemhis, including Sacagawea.
7. Later, with Charbonneau, her French Canadian husband, and their two-month-old son.
8. Sacagawea joined the Lewis and Clark expedition in what is now North Dakota.
9. Her knowledge of many languages enabled the explorers to communicate with various peoples.
10. Sacagawea also searched for plants that were safe to eat.
11. And once saved valuable instruments during a storm.
12. As they traveled farther.
13. The explorers came across the Lemhis.
14. From whom Sacagawea had been separated years before.

The Granger Collection, New York.

GRAMMAR

15. The Lemhis helped the explorers.
16. By giving them guidance.
17. After they returned from the expedition.
18. Clark encouraged Sacagawea and Charbonneau to settle in St. Louis.
19. However, the couple moved back to Sacagawea's native land.
20. Where this famous woman died in 1812.

Exercise 2 Identifying Sentences and Revising Sentence Fragments

Tell whether each of the following groups of words is a *sentence* or a *sentence fragment.* If the word group is a sentence, add a capital letter and end punctuation. If the word group is a sentence fragment, correct it by adding words that will make it a complete sentence, and then add a capital letter and end punctuation.

EXAMPLES
1. classes in mountain climbing will begin soon
1. sentence—Classes in mountain climbing will begin soon.

2. living alone in the mountains
2. sentence fragment—Living alone in the mountains, the couple make their own furniture and clothes.

1. after he caught the baseball with both hands
2. doing the multiplication tables
3. a long, narrow passage with a hidden trapdoor at each end
4. after waiting for six hours
5. the gymnasium is open
6. last night there were about six television commercials every half-hour
7. instead of calling the doctor this morning about her sore throat
8. are you careful about turning off unnecessary lights
9. beneath the tall ceiling of the church
10. in the back of the storeroom stands a stack of boxes

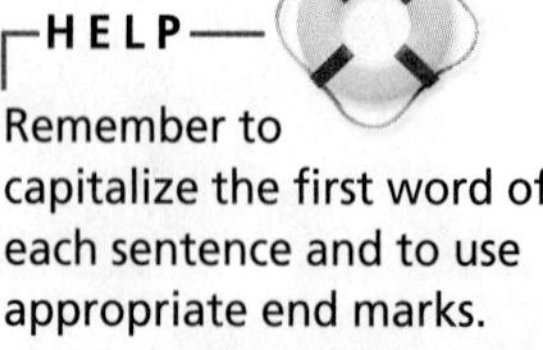
HELP
Remember to capitalize the first word of each sentence and to use appropriate end marks.

Exercise 3 Writing Interesting Sentences

Revise each sentence fragment by adding words to make an interesting sentence.

EXAMPLE
1. at the last minute
1. At the last minute, his parachute opened.

1. on the last day of summer
2. found only in the country
3. a graceful ballerina
4. burning out of control
5. the old building by the lake
6. the duck-billed platypus
7. three days after Thanksgiving
8. until I finish my work
9. singing loudly in the woods
10. in the final quarter of the game

The Subject and the Predicate

Sentences consist of two basic parts: *subjects* and *predicates.*

The Subject

10b. A *subject* tells *whom* or *what* the sentence is about.

EXAMPLES **Aunt Louise** found a beautiful antique lamp at the garage sale.

The kitten with the white paws is called Boots.

Where are **your mittens,** Kris?

How surprised **we** were!

To find the subject, ask *who* or *what* is doing something or *about whom* or *what* something is being said.

EXAMPLES Laughing and running down the street were **two small boys.** [Who were laughing and running down the street? Two small boys were.]

A sealed envelope rested near the edge of the desk. [What rested near the edge of the desk? A sealed envelope rested there.]

Are **Dalmatians** very good watchdogs? [About what is something being said? Something is being said about Dalmatians.]

Can **horses and cattle** swim? [What can swim? Horses and cattle can swim.]

TIPS & TRICKS

To find the subject in a question, turn the question into a statement. Then, ask *who* or *what* is doing something or *about whom* or *what* something is being said.

QUESTION
Did they win the race?

STATEMENT
They did win the race.
[Who did win? *They* did. *They* is the subject.]

GRAMMAR

The ***complete subject*** consists of all the words that tell *whom* or *what* the sentence is about. The simple subject is part of the complete subject.

10c. The *simple subject* is the main word or word group that tells *whom* or *what* the sentence is about.

EXAMPLES The dangerous **trip** over the mountains took four days. [The complete subject is *The dangerous trip over the mountains.*]

Someone in this room is about to get a big surprise! [The complete subject is *Someone in this room.*]

In the last forty years, **he** has missed seeing only one home game. [The complete subject is *he.*]

Pacing back and forth in the cage was a hungry **tiger.** [The complete subject is *a hungry tiger.*]

Joey arrived late for the dance. [The complete subject is *Joey.*]

As you can see in the following examples, the simple subject may consist of more than one word.

EXAMPLES **Stamp collecting** is my father's favorite hobby.

Containing over eighty million items, the **Library of Congress** is the nation's largest single library.

Madeleine Albright was appointed secretary of state.

Accepting the award was **Leo Kolar.**

The simple subjects in the four preceding examples are all compound nouns.

The subject of a sentence is never in a prepositional phrase.

EXAMPLES **Several** of the players hit home runs. [Who hit home runs? *Several* hit home runs. *Players* is part of the prepositional phrase *of the players.*]

At the end of our street is a **bus stop.** [What is? *Bus stop* is. *End* and *street* are parts of the prepositional phrases *At the end* and *of our street.*]

NOTE In this book, the term *subject* generally refers to the simple subject unless otherwise noted.

Reference Note

For more information about **compound nouns,** see page 346.

Reference Note

For more information about **prepositional phrases,** see page 416.

TIPS & TRICKS

Sometimes crossing out the prepositional phrases in a sentence can help you find the subject.

EXAMPLE
The girl ~~in the red boots~~ is Marlene.

Exercise 4 Identifying Complete Subjects and Simple Subjects

Identify the *complete subject* and the *simple subject* in each of the following sentences.

EXAMPLE 1. My favorite teams compete in the Caribbean Baseball Leagues.

1. complete subject—My favorite teams; simple subject—teams

1. People throughout Latin America enjoy going out to a ballgame.
2. The all-American sport of baseball has been very popular there for a long time.
3. In fact, fans in countries such as Cuba, Panama, and Venezuela go wild over the game.
4. As a result, the Caribbean Baseball Leagues were formed more than fifty years ago.
5. Each year the teams in Latin America play toward a season championship.
6. That championship is known as the Caribbean World Series.
7. A total of more than one hundred players compete in the series.
8. Many talented Latin American players are recruited by professional United States teams each year.
9. The list of these players includes such baseball greats as José Canseco, Ramón Martinez, and Fernando Valenzuela.
10. In addition, a number of U.S. players train in the Latin American winter leagues.

The Predicate

10d. The *predicate* of a sentence tells something about the subject.

The ***complete predicate*** consists of a verb and all the words that describe the verb and complete its meaning.

EXAMPLES Marco's brother **delivers pizzas.**

Under a large bush sat the tiny rabbit.

Does this copier **staple and fold documents**?

How talented you **are**!

Sometimes the complete predicate appears at the beginning of a sentence. In the following examples, vertical lines separate the complete subjects from the complete predicates.

EXAMPLES

comp. pred.	comp. subj.
On the tiny branch perched	a chickadee.
Covering the side of the hill were	wildflowers.

Part of the predicate may appear on one side of the subject and the rest on the other side.

EXAMPLES

pred.	comp. subj.	pred.
Before winter	many birds	**fly south.**
Yesterday	the movie star	**signed autographs.**

10e. The *simple predicate,* or *verb,* is the main word or word group that tells something about the subject.

Reference Note

For more about **verb phrases,** see page 372.

A simple predicate may be a one-word verb, or it may be a ***verb phrase*** (a main verb and one or more helping verbs).

EXAMPLES

comp. subj.	comp. pred.
These books	**are** available in the media center.
Our English class	**is reading** the novel *Frankenstein.*
The musicians	**have been rehearsing** since noon.

NOTE In this book, the term *verb* generally refers to the simple predicate.

The words *not* (*–n't*) and *never,* which are frequently used with verbs, are not part of a verb phrase. Both of these words are adverbs.

EXAMPLES She **did** not **believe** me.

They **have**n't **left** yet.

The two cousins **had** never **met.**

I **will** never **eat** there again!

Exercise 5 Identifying Complete Predicates and Verbs

Identify the complete predicate and the verb in each of the following sentences.

EXAMPLE 1. A ton and a half of groceries may seem like a big order for a family of five.

1. complete predicate—may seem like a big order for a family of five; verb—may seem

HELP—Keep in mind that parts of the complete predicate may come before and after the complete subject.

1. Such a big order is possible in the village of Pang.
2. This small village is near the Arctic Circle.
3. Once a year the people of Pang receive their groceries.
4. A supply ship can visit Pang only during a short time each summer.
5. In spring, families order their year's supply of groceries by mail.
6. A few months later the huge order is delivered to Pang.
7. The people store the groceries in their homes.
8. Frozen food is kept outdoors.
9. Too costly for most residents is the airfreight charge for a grocery shipment to Pang.
10. Villagers also must hunt and fish for much of their food.

Exercise 6 Identifying Simple Predicates

Identify the simple predicate in each of the following sentences.

EXAMPLE 1. Samuel Pepys was an English government worker.

1. was

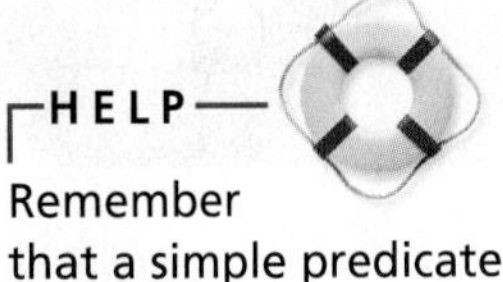

Remember that a simple predicate can be a one-word verb or a verb phrase.

1. Between 1660 and 1669, Samuel Pepys kept a diary.
2. He wrote the diary in a secret shorthand.
3. This secret shorthand was finally decoded after many years of hard work.
4. In 1825, *The Diary of Samuel Pepys* was published.
5. The diary presents a personal look at life in England during the seventeenth century.
6. In many entries Pepys told about his family and friends.
7. Some of these accounts are quite humorous.
8. In other entries Pepys described very serious events.
9. For example, in entries during 1666, Pepys gave a detailed account of the Great Fire of London.
10. What other events might be described in the diary?

GRAMMAR

Link to Literature

Review A Identifying Subjects and Verbs

Identify the subject and the verb in each of the following sentences.

EXAMPLE **1.** In Greek mythology, Medusa was a horrible monster.

1. subject—Medusa; verb—was

1. On Medusa's head grew snakes instead of hair.
2. According to Greek myth, a glance at Medusa would turn a mortal into stone.
3. However, one proud mortal, named Perseus, went in search of Medusa.

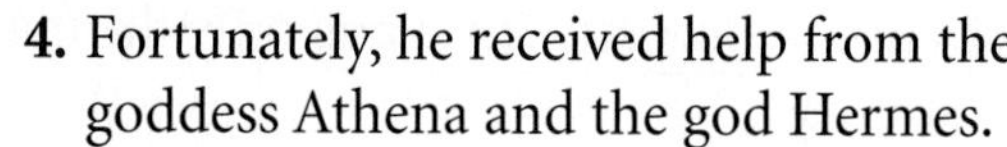

4. Fortunately, he received help from the goddess Athena and the god Hermes.
5. From Athena, Perseus accepted a shiny shield.
6. With Hermes as his guide, Perseus soon found Medusa.
7. He knew about Medusa's power.
8. Therefore, he did not look directly at her.
9. Instead, he watched her reflection in the shiny shield.
10. The picture on the left shows Perseus's victory over the evil Medusa.

Review B Identifying Complete Subjects and Complete Predicates

Copy the following sentences. Separate the complete subject from the complete predicate with a vertical line.

EXAMPLE **1.** Legends and folk tales have been repeated and enjoyed throughout the Americas.

1. Legends and folk tales | have been repeated and enjoyed throughout the Americas.

1. The Chorotega people lived in Nicoya, Costa Rica, hundreds of years ago.

2. One Chorotega folk tale tells the story of the Chorotegan treasure and praises Princess Nosara for protecting it from the Chirenos.
3. Chireno warriors landed, according to the story, on the Nicoya Peninsula and attacked the Chorotegas.
4. The Chorotegas were surprised but reacted quickly.
5. Princess Nosara grabbed the treasure and ran to her friend's house for help.
6. Nosara and he took a bow and some arrows and fled into the woods.
7. The couple ran from the enemy all night and at last reached a river.
8. The brave girl dashed into the mountains alone, hid the treasure, and returned to the river.
9. Chireno warriors attacked shortly after her return, however, and killed the princess and her friend.
10. The murderous warriors searched for the treasure but never found it.

GRAMMAR

Review C Identifying Complete Subjects and Complete Predicates

Copy each of the following sentences. Underline the complete subject once and the complete predicate twice.

EXAMPLE 1. The word *acrostic* comes from the Greek word for "line of verse."

1. The word acrostic comes from the Greek word for "line of verse."

HELP— Remember that the subject may come between parts of the predicate.

1. Are you familiar with acrostics?
2. Counting the letters of your name starts the fun.
3. Ruled paper with enough lines for the letters is needed.
4. One letter of your name goes on each line of the paper.
5. Sometimes the names of people and places are used.
6. The letters are the starting points for lines of poetry or prose.
7. Ink or pencil may be used to do the writing.
8. Complete sentences on each line are not necessary.
9. Have you noticed what the first letters of the eight preceding sentences spell?
10. Acrostics and other writing help you express yourself.

GRAMMAR

HELP—
Remember to capitalize the first word of each sentence and to use appropriate end marks. Even though two sentences are given for the example, you need to write only one for each item.

Review D Writing Sentences

Add words to each of the following subjects and verbs to make detailed, complete sentences.

EXAMPLE **1.** kite flew

1. The kite that we made from balsa wood and paper flew very high.

or

A large green-and-purple kite just flew into our backyard.

1. tent collapsed
2. rabbits hop
3. had neighbors gone
4. hours passed
5. shirt was
6. piñatas will be fastened
7. horses ran
8. cars compete
9. Africa contains
10. is Japan

HELP—
Remember to capitalize the first word of each sentence and to use appropriate end marks.

Review E Writing Sentences

Some of the following word groups are complete subjects, and some are complete predicates. Write each word group, adding the part needed to make a sentence. Then, underline the subject once and the verb twice.

EXAMPLE **1.** had been marching for five hours

1. The members of the band had been marching for five hours.

1. should not be left alone
2. the vacant lot down the street
3. danced across the floor
4. looked mysteriously at us
5. their best player
6. the famous movie star
7. is going to the game
8. one of the Jackson twins
9. could have been left on the bus
10. the neighborhood watch group

The Compound Subject

10f. A *compound subject* consists of two or more connected subjects that have the same verb.

The most common connecting words are *and* and *or.*

EXAMPLES **Keshia** and **Todd** worked a jigsaw puzzle.

Either **Carmen** or **Ernesto** will videotape the ceremony tomorrow.

Among the guest speakers were an **astronaut,** an **engineer,** and a **journalist.**

Exercise 7 Identifying Compound Subjects and Their Verbs

Identify the *compound subject* and the *verb* in each of the following sentences.

EXAMPLE 1. Festivals and celebrations are happy times throughout the world.

1. compound subject—Festivals, celebrations; verb—are

1. Children and nature are honored with their own festivals in Japan.
2. Among Japanese nature festivals are the Cherry Blossom Festival and the Chrysanthemum Festival.
3. Fierce dragons and even huge ships fly in the sky during Singapore's Kite Festival.
4. Elaborate masks and costumes are an important part of the Carnival Lamayote in Haiti.
5. Flowers or other small gifts are presented to teachers during Teacher's Day in the Czech Republic.
6. Brave knights and their ladies return each year to the medieval festival at Ribeauvillé, France.
7. During Sweden's Midsommar (midsummer) Festival, maypoles and buildings bloom with fresh flowers.
8. Wrestling and pole climbing attract crowds to the Tatar Festival of the Plow in Russia.
9. Games, dances, and feasts highlight the Green Corn Dance of the Seminole Indians in the Florida Everglades.
10. In Munich, Germany, floats and bandwagons add color to the Oktoberfest Parade.

GRAMMAR

The Compound Verb

10g. A *compound verb* consists of two or more verbs that have the same subject.

A connecting word—usually *and, or,* or *but*—is used between the verbs.

EXAMPLES The dog **barked** and **growled** at the stranger.

The man **was convicted** but later **was found** innocent of the crime.

Some plants **sprout, bloom,** and **wither** quickly.

You **can leave** now or **wait** for the others.

Notice in the last sentence that the helping verb *can* is not repeated before *wait.* In compound verbs, the helping verb may or may not be repeated before the second verb if the helper is the same for both verbs.

STYLE TIP

You can use compound subjects and verbs to combine sentences and reduce wordiness in your writing.

WORDY
Anne Brontë wrote under a male pen name. Charlotte Brontë wrote under a male pen name. Emily Brontë wrote under a male pen name.

REVISED
Anne, Charlotte, and Emily Brontë wrote under male pen names.

Exercise 8 Identifying Subjects and Compound Verbs

Identify the *subject* and the *compound verb* in each of the following sentences.

EXAMPLE 1. The hikers loaded their backpacks and studied the map of the mountain trails.
1. subject—hikers; compound verb—loaded, studied

1. Linda wrote her essay and practiced the piano last night.
2. Miami is the largest city in southern Florida and has been a popular resort area since the 1920s.
3. According to Greek mythology, Arachne angered Athena and was turned into a spider.
4. Martina Arroyo has sung in major American opera halls and has made appearances abroad.
5. This year the Wildcats won seven games and lost five.
6. During special sales, shoppers arrive early at the mall and search for bargains.
7. Maria Montessori studied medicine in Italy and developed new methods for teaching children.
8. Jim Rice autographed baseballs and made a short speech.
9. General Lee won many battles but lost the war.
10. In the summer many students go to music camps or take music lessons.

Both the subject and the verb of a sentence may be compound. In such a sentence, each subject goes with each verb.

EXAMPLE The **guide** (S) and the **hikers** (S) **sat** (V) inside and **waited** (V) for the storm to pass. [The guide sat and waited, and the hikers sat and waited.]

NOTE There are times when a sentence may contain more than one subject or verb without containing a compound subject or a compound verb.

EXAMPLES **Noah** (S) **entered** (V) the race, and **he** (S) **won.** (V) [compound sentence]

When **you** (S) **go** (V) to the store, **you** (S) **can get** (V) more milk. [complex sentence]

The **puppies** (S) **ran** (V) to the fence, and **they** (S) **barked** (V) at the mail carrier **who** (S) **was** (V) outside. [compound-complex sentence]

Reference Note

For more about **compound, complex,** and **compound-complex sentences,** see Chapter 16.

Exercise 9 Identifying Compound Subjects and Compound Verbs

Identify the subjects and the verbs in each of the following sentences.

EXAMPLE 1. Aaron Neville and his brothers, pictured here, have often performed at the New Orleans Jazz and Heritage Festival.

1. subjects—Aaron Neville, brothers; verb—have performed

1. Aaron, Art, Charles, and Cyril are the Neville Brothers.
2. The four brothers play different instruments and have their own individual styles.

GRAMMAR

3. They formed their act and performed together in 1977.
4. Before then, the brothers performed and toured separately.
5. New Orleans is their hometown and has greatly influenced their music.
6. They grew up hearing music at home and found it everywhere.
7. New Orleans gospel sounds and jazz rhythms fill many of the brothers' songs.
8. The four brothers have strong opinions and often sing about social issues.
9. *Yellow Moon* and *Brother's Keeper* are two of their most popular albums.
10. The children and grandchildren of the Neville Brothers have now joined in this family's musical tradition.

HELP

Some sentences in Review F contain compound subjects, compound verbs, or both.

Review F Identifying Subjects and Verbs

Identify the subjects and verbs in each of the following sentences. If a sentence has an understood subject, write *(you)*.

EXAMPLES
1. Valerie and Tranh have been best friends since third grade.
   1. subjects—Valerie, Tranh; verb—have been
2. Pass the potatoes, please.
   2. subject—(you); verb—pass

1. The train to Baltimore must have left the station at exactly 12:03 P.M.
2. To my surprise, out of my backpack spilled the golf balls.
3. Is Emily or her sister taking a computer animation class this summer?
4. On the hiking trail we spotted two brown bear cubs.
5. For Vietnamese noodles, James and I always go to Kim Phung Restaurant.
6. Have you met Marisa and her younger brother?
7. Please gather the birthday cards and hand them to me.
8. In the garage were stacked old boxes, hundreds of magazines, and rusty cans of paint.
9. Rows of wheat and corn sprouted and grew in the rich soil.
10. Last night Hector and the varsity team played well but lost the game anyway.

Classifying Sentences by Purpose

A sentence may be classified, depending on its purpose, as *declarative, imperative, interrogative,* or *exclamatory.*

10h. A *declarative sentence* makes a statement and ends with a period.

EXAMPLES Miriam Colón founded the Puerto Rican Traveling Theatre.

Curiosity is the beginning of knowledge.

Lani wondered why the sky looks blue.

10i. An *imperative sentence* gives a command or makes a request. Most imperative sentences end with a period. A strong command ends with an exclamation point.

EXAMPLES John, please close the door. [request]

Do your homework each night. [mild request]

Stop her! [strong command]

The subject of an imperative sentence is always *you.* Often the *you* is not stated. In such cases, *you* is called the ***understood subject.***

EXAMPLES [You] Do your homework each night.

[You] Stop her!

John, [you] please close the door. [*John* is a noun of direct address identifying the person spoken to in the sentence. The understood subject is still *you.*]

10j. An *interrogative sentence* asks a question and ends with a question mark.

EXAMPLES What do you know about glaciers?

Was the game exciting?

How do diamonds form?

10k. An *exclamatory sentence* shows excitement or strong feeling and ends with an exclamation point.

EXAMPLES What a sight the sunset is!

How thoughtful Tim was to rake the leaves!

Sarah won the VCR!

Reference Note

A sentence may also be classified according to its structure. For information about **classifying sentences by structure,** see Chapter 16.

Reference Note

For information about **punctuating nouns of direct address,** see page 642.

STYLE  **TIP**

Many people overuse exclamation points. In your own writing, save the exclamation point for sentences that really do express strong emotion. When overused, this punctuation mark loses its impact.

GRAMMAR

Exercise 10 Classifying Sentences

Write the final word of each sentence, and add appropriate punctuation. Then, classify each sentence according to its purpose.

EXAMPLE **1.** Do you know what the word *Hopi* means

1. means?—interrogative

1. It means "good, peaceful," I believe
2. The Hopi live primarily in northeastern Arizona
3. Have you been to Arizona
4. Wow, the Grand Canyon is awesome
5. You must go see it
6. Meteor Crater is interesting, too
7. The fall of that meteor would have been something to see
8. Have you seen western movies with red cliffs in them
9. They may have been filmed near Sedona, Arizona
10. How exciting it is to visit new places

Review G Writing a Variety of Sentences

Write your own sentences according to the following guidelines. Use different subjects and verbs for each sentence.

EXAMPLE **1.** Write an interrogative sentence with a single subject and a single verb.

1. Is Danielle bringing dessert?

1. Write a declarative sentence with a compound subject.
2. Write an imperative sentence with a compound verb.
3. Write a declarative sentence with a single subject and a single verb.
4. Write an interrogative sentence with a compound subject.
5. Write an interrogative sentence with a compound verb.
6. Write an exclamatory sentence with a single subject and a single verb.
7. Write an imperative sentence with a single verb.
8. Write a declarative sentence with a compound verb.
9. Write an exclamatory sentence with a compound verb.
10. Write a declarative sentence with a compound subject and a compound verb.

Chapter Review

A. Identifying Sentences and Sentence Fragments

Identify each group of words as a *sentence* or a *sentence fragment.* If the word group is a sentence fragment, correct it by adding words to make a complete sentence.

1. Where can the lion live with the lamb?
2. Just as Miguel entered the Korean restaurant.
3. My stepbrother helped me with this.
4. With their songs, whales can communicate throughout the oceans.
5. My sister in college is studying all night.
6. Excited by the news that Grandfather was to come soon.
7. Where the horses are stabled.
8. Deep in the forest a broken-down cabin sheltered us.
9. Jesse Owens, who won four gold medals in the 1936 Olympics.
10. The many-colored lights delighted the viewers.

B. Identifying Subjects and Predicates

Identify each italicized group of words as the *complete subject* or the *complete predicate* of the sentence. Then, identify the simple subject or the verb in each word group.

11. Mr. Adams *gave me his old croquet set.*
12. Why did *that large, new boat* sink on such a clear day?
13. *Trees and bushes all over the neighborhood* had been torn out by the storm.
14. Walking to school, Bill *was splashed by a passing car.*
15. *My old bicycle with the drop-style handlebars* is rusting away in the garage now.
16. *The creek behind my house* rises during the summer rains.
17. Sandy's little sister *bravely dived off the high board at the community pool.*
18. *Fridays and other test days* always seem long to me.

19. My cousins and I *played basketball and walked over to the mall yesterday.*
20. *Does* Max *want another serving of spaghetti*?

C. Classifying Sentences

Identify each of the following sentences as *declarative, interrogative, imperative,* or *exclamatory.* Then, write the last word of each sentence and give the correct end punctuation.

21. The sea horse is a very unusual kind of fish
22. What a beautiful butterfly that is
23. Can you believe that most polar bears don't hibernate
24. Daniel, find out how many miles per hour a rabbit can hop
25. Some jack rabbits can hop forty miles per hour
26. That is not as fast as a cheetah can run, though
27. The cheetah is the fastest land animal on earth
28. How fast can a cheetah run
29. A cheetah can run at a top speed of fifty to seventy miles per hour
30. Wow, they could break the speed limit in some places

D. Identifying Subjects and Verbs

Identify the subject and the verb in each of the following sentences. If a sentence contains a *compound subject* or a *compound verb,* write both words that make up the compound.

31. Charles de Gaulle was a famous French general and statesman.
32. Lille, de Gaulle's birthplace, is a city in northern France.
33. Young de Gaulle served and fought in the French Army before and during World War I.
34. As a soldier, he was loyal and courageous.
35. In World War II, he and the Free French Forces led French resistance against the occupying Germans.
36. After World War II, de Gaulle hoped to retire from public life.
37. However, he returned to politics in 1958.
38. The French people twice elected him president.
39. A political crisis and low public support led to his resignation in 1969.
40. Controversial at home and abroad, de Gaulle died in 1970.

Writing Application

Using Subjects and Predicates in a Paragraph

Writing Complete Sentences Your best friend is on vacation, and you are pet-sitting. Write a paragraph about your experiences taking care of your friend's pet.

Prewriting You can write about a pet you know or one that is unfamiliar to you. Jot down notes about the pet you choose. Then, think about what you might do or what might happen while you are taking care of the pet.

Writing As you write your first draft, think about how to organize your notes and your thoughts. Tell about your experiences in a logical order, and use complete sentences. Your tone can be humorous or serious.

Revising Read through your paragraph to be sure that each sentence has a subject and a predicate. Does your paragraph tell about your experience in an interesting way? Add, delete, or rearrange details to make your paragraph more entertaining or informative.

Publishing Read over your paragraph once more, correcting errors in punctuation, spelling, and capitalization. Ask a classmate to read the paragraph, and use the completed paragraph as a basis of a class discussion. With your teacher's permission you may also want to post it on your class bulletin board or Web page, if available.

CHAPTER

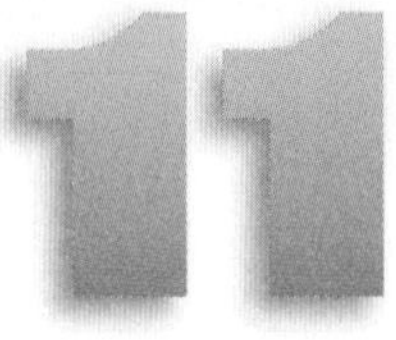

Parts of Speech Overview

Noun, Pronoun, Adjective

Diagnostic Preview

A. Identifying Nouns, Pronouns, and Adjectives

Tell whether each italicized word or word group in the following sentences is used as a *noun*, a *pronoun*, or an *adjective*.

EXAMPLE **1.** *Each* student is required to take a foreign *language.*

1. Each—adjective; language—noun

1. *That* drummer is the *best* performer.
2. That *German shepherd* puppy is a sweet-natured and *lively* rascal.
3. *Everybody* says that *high school* will be more work but more fun, too.
4. *This* is the greatest year the junior varsity volleyball *team* has ever had.
5. *Who* can tell me whose bicycle *this* is?
6. Jenna prepared a special breakfast for her parents and *herself* this *morning.*
7. This is their fault because *they* ignored all the *danger* signals.
8. *We* received word that they aren't in *danger.*
9. *Each* of these clubs decorated a float for the Cinco de Mayo *parade.*
10. The runner *Carl Lewis* won several Olympic *medals.*

B. Identifying Nouns, Pronouns, and Adjectives

Tell whether each italicized word or word group in the following paragraph is used as a *noun*, a *pronoun*, or an *adjective*.

EXAMPLES The **[1]** *president* travels in a **[2]** *reserved* jet known as Air Force One.

1. *president—noun*
2. *reserved—adjective*

[11] *American* presidents have used many different types of transportation. President Thomas Jefferson's way of getting to his first inauguration was **[12]** *simple.* **[13]** *He* walked there and then walked home after taking the **[14]** *oath* of office. President Zachary Taylor proudly rode the **[15]** *same* horse throughout the **[16]** *Mexican War* and later during his term of office. James Monroe had the **[17]** *honor* of being the first president to ride aboard a steamship. In 1899, William McKinley became the **[18]** *first* president to ride in an automobile. President Theodore Roosevelt, **[19]** *who* is remembered for his love of adventure, rode in a submarine in 1905. Probably **[20]** *nobody* was surprised when the president himself took over the controls.

The Noun

11a. A *noun* is a word or word group that is used to name a person, a place, a thing, or an idea.

Persons	Alice Walker, Dr. Lacy, women, team
Places	forest, town, Canada, Grand Rapids
Things	jewelry, rain, pets, *Skylab,* Eiffel Tower
Ideas	fairness, care, loyalty, idealism, beauty

Exercise 1 Identifying Nouns

Identify all the nouns in each of the following sentences.

EXAMPLE **1.** Many American Indian leaders have been known for their courage and wisdom.

1. *leaders, courage, wisdom*

1. Chief Joseph of the Nez Perce was a wise leader.
2. He was an educated man; he wrote that his people believed in speaking only the truth.
3. In this photograph, Satanta, a Kiowa chief, wears a silver medal with the profile of President James Buchanan on it.
4. Satanta wore the medal during a famous council for peace at Medicine Lodge Creek in Kansas.
5. In a moving speech, Satanta described the love that his people had for the Great Plains and the buffalo.
6. *The Autobiography of Black Hawk* is an interesting book by the Sauk chief who fought for land in the Mississippi Valley.
7. Sitting Bull and his warriors soundly defeated General George Custer and his troops at the Battle of the Little Bighorn.
8. After years of leading the Sioux in war, Sitting Bull toured with Buffalo Bill and his Wild West Show.
9. Red Cloud of the Oglala Sioux and Dull Knife of the Cheyennes were other powerful leaders.
10. Chief Washakie received praise for his leadership of the Shoshones, and he was also a noted singer and craftsman.

Compound Nouns

11b. A *compound noun* is made up of two or more words used together as a single noun.

The parts of a compound noun may be written as one word, as separate words, or as a hyphenated word.

One Word	basketball, filmmaker, drugstore, doghouse, grasshopper, grandson, Passover, Greenland, Iceland
Separate Words	fire drill, chain reaction, *The Call of the Wild,* Thomas A. Edison, House of Representatives, North Americans
Hyphenated Word	self-control, cross-references, fund-raiser, eighteen-year-olds, mother-in-law, out-of-doors, president-elect

NOTE When you are not sure how to write a compound noun, look it up in a dictionary.

Exercise 2 Identifying Compound Nouns

Identify the compound noun in each of the following sentences.

EXAMPLE **1.** Did you know that the most famous alphabet used by people with visual impairments was invented by a fifteen-year-old?

1. fifteen-year-old

1. Louis Braille was born in 1809 in France.
2. His father was a saddlemaker who often let Louis play with pieces of leather.
3. In 1812, when the three-year-old tried to punch a hole in a piece of leather, the tool slipped and injured his left eye.
4. Infection from the wound spread to both eyes, and Louis completely lost his eyesight.
5. Louis left for Paris in 1819 to attend the National Institute for the Blind.
6. By 1824, Louis made real his daydream to develop an alphabet for the blind.
7. His first version used both dots and dashes, but that system had drawbacks.
8. As a young teacher at the National Institute for Blind Children, Braille perfected an alphabet of raised dots.
9. Now a machine called a braillewriter is used.
10. Braille died in 1852, and although his alphabet is widely appreciated and used now, it never was during his lifetime.

GRAMMAR

Common Nouns and Proper Nouns

11c. A *common noun* names any one of a group of persons, places, things, or ideas.

A common noun generally does not begin with a capital letter.

Reference Note

For information on **capitalizing proper nouns,** see page 606.

11d. A *proper noun* names a particular person, place, thing, or idea.

A proper noun begins with a capital letter.

Common Nouns	Proper Nouns
poem	"The Raven," *I Am Joaquín*
country	Spain, Ivory Coast
athlete	Joe Montana, Zina Garrison-Jackson
ship	*Mayflower,* U.S.S. *Constitution*
newspaper	*The New York Times, USA Today*
river	Rio de la Plata, Ohio River
street	Market Street, University Avenue
day	Friday, Independence Day
city	Los Angeles, New Delhi, Houston
organization	National Forensic League, Girl Scouts of America

Exercise 3 Identifying Nouns

Identify the nouns in each of the following sentences, and label them *common* or *proper.*

EXAMPLE **1.** I went camping in Cibola National Forest during the summer.

1. Cibola National Forest—proper; summer—common

1. Are there forests near your home?
2. Forests exist in many shapes, sizes, and kinds.
3. Boreal forests grow in regions that have cold winters and short springs.
4. The boreal forests in Canada contain mostly evergreens, which grow well in cold climates.
5. Rain forests, however, are usually located in tropical regions.

6. However, one rain forest is found on a peninsula in the northwestern state of Washington.
7. This rain forest is able to grow in a northern climate because the area is extremely damp.
8. Forests throughout most areas of the United States have both evergreens, such as pines and cedars, and deciduous trees, such as oaks, beeches, and maples.
9. Pacific coastal forests extend from central California to Alaska.
10. One type of tree that grows in these forests is the famous redwood, the tallest tree in the world.

Concrete Nouns and Abstract Nouns

11e. A *concrete noun* names a person, place, or thing that can be perceived by one or more of the senses (sight, hearing, taste, touch, and smell).

11f. An *abstract noun* names an idea, a feeling, a quality, or a characteristic.

Concrete Nouns	hummingbird, telephone, teacher, popcorn, ocean, Golden Gate Bridge, Jesse Jackson
Abstract Nouns	knowledge, patriotism, love, humor, self-confidence, beauty, competition, Zen Buddhism

Collective Nouns

11g. A *collective noun* is a word that names a group.

People	Animals	Things
audience	brood	batch
chorus	flock	bundle
committee	herd	cluster
crew	litter	collection
faculty	pack	fleet
family	pride	set

HELP

Nouns that are not collective have to be made plural to name a group. The singular form of a collective noun names a group.

Review A Identifying and Classifying Nouns

Identify the nouns in each of the following sentences. Classify each noun as *common* or *proper* and as *concrete* or *abstract.* Also tell whether a noun is *collective.*

EXAMPLE **1.** I went with a group of students to see the monument that commemorates Abraham Lincoln.

1. group—common, concrete, collective; students—common, concrete; monument—common, concrete; Abraham Lincoln—proper, concrete

1. Each day huge crowds visit the Lincoln Memorial, which is in Washington, D.C.

2. The memorial is in a beautiful setting not far from two other presidential monuments and the capitol.

3. The Lincoln Memorial is separated from the Jefferson Memorial by the Tidal Basin.

4. Between the memorial and the Washington Monument are two long, shallow pools.

5. The Lincoln Memorial was designed by a noted architect of the time, Henry Bacon.

6. The memorial is styled to look like a Greek temple and has thirty-six columns, one for each state in the union at the time of the death of Lincoln.

7. As you can see in the photograph, the inside of the Lincoln Memorial is a large marble hall.

8. The gigantic statue of Lincoln, designed by the sculptor Daniel Chester French, was carved from blocks of white marble.

9. The statue of Lincoln depicts him sitting in a large armchair as if in deep meditation.
10. In the lower lobby of the memorial, a set of murals by Jules Guerin shows allegories of Emancipation and Reunion.

The Pronoun

11h. A *pronoun* is a word used in place of one or more nouns or pronouns.

EXAMPLES When Kelly saw the signal, Kelly pointed the signal out to Enrique.

When Kelly saw the signal, **she** pointed **it** out to Enrique.

Lee and Pat went fishing. Lee caught three bass, and Pat caught three bass.

Lee and Pat went fishing. **Each** caught three bass.

The word that a pronoun stands for is called its ***antecedent.***

EXAMPLES Elena read the **book** [antecedent] and returned **it** [pronoun] to the library.

The **models** [antecedent] bought **themselves** [pronoun] new dresses.

Catherine [antecedent] told **her** [pronoun] father **she** [pronoun] would be late.

Sometimes the antecedent is not stated.

EXAMPLES **Who** [pronoun] invented the telephone?

No one [pronoun] could solve the riddle.

I [pronoun] thought **you** [pronoun] said that **everybody** [pronoun] would help.

Exercise 4 Identifying Pronouns

Identify the pronoun or pronouns in each of the following sentences. After each pronoun, write the antecedent to which the pronoun refers. If a pronoun does not refer to a specific antecedent, write *unidentified.*

Reference Note

For more about **pronouns,** see Chapter 19: Using Pronouns Correctly.

Reference Note

For more about choosing **pronouns that agree with their antecedents,** see page 493.

HELP

When you use a pronoun, be sure that its antecedent is clear. If two or more nouns in the sentence could be the antecedent, the reader may not be able to tell what the sentence means. Rewording the sentence to change the position of the pronoun can make the meaning clearer.

EXAMPLES

Sara called Nicole while she was cooking dinner. [Who was cooking dinner, Sara or Nicole?]

While Sara was cooking dinner, **she** called Nicole. [The pronoun *she* now clearly refers to *Sara.*]

While Nicole was cooking dinner, Sara called **her.** [The pronoun *her* now clearly refers to *Nicole.*]

HELP

In Exercise 4, the antecedent may appear before or after the pronoun, or even in a previous sentence.

EXAMPLE 1. When the luggage cart fell on its side, the bags and their contents scattered everywhere.

1. *its—cart; their—bags*

1. The passengers scrambled to find their luggage and even got down on hands and knees to pick up their belongings.
2. In no time, the travelers found themselves quibbling.
3. One person shouted, "The brown bag belongs to me!"
4. "It has my name on it," somebody replied.
5. "Are you sure the blue socks are yours?" asked another traveler.
6. "I have a pair just like them."
7. A young couple asked, "Who owns a pink and yellow shirt?"
8. "This isn't our shirt."
9. "Those are the birthday presents I bought for a friend of mine!" yelled an angry man in a blue suit.
10. As a crowd of people gathered, some just laughed, but several offered to help.

Personal Pronouns

11i. A *personal pronoun* refers to the one speaking (*first person*), the one spoken to (*second person*), or the one spoken about (*third person*).

Personal Pronouns	
First Person	I, me, my, mine, we, us, our, ours
Second Person	you, your, yours
Third Person	he, him, his, she, her, hers, it, its, they, them, their, theirs

EXAMPLES Last spring, **I** visited **my** relatives. [first person]

Did **you** say that this pen is **yours**? [second person]

The coach gathered the players around **her** and gave **them** a pep talk. [third person]

Reference Note

For more about **possessive forms of pronouns,** see page 545.

NOTE In this book, the words *my, your, his, her, its,* and *their* are called pronouns. Some authorities prefer to call these words adjectives. Follow your teacher's instructions regarding possessive forms.

Reflexive and Intensive Pronouns

11j. A *reflexive pronoun* refers to the subject and functions as a complement or an object of a preposition.

11k. An *intensive pronoun* emphasizes a noun or another pronoun.

Notice that reflexive and intensive pronouns have the same form.

Reflexive and Intensive Pronouns	
First Person	myself, ourselves
Second Person	yourself, yourselves
Third Person	himself, herself, itself, themselves

REFLEXIVE The rescuers did not consider **themselves** heroes. [direct object]

Juan wrote **himself** a note. [indirect object]

She is **herself** again. [predicate nominative]

I don't feel like **myself.** [object of the preposition]

INTENSIVE Amelia designed the costumes **herself.**

I **myself** sold more than fifty tickets.

Exercise 5 Identifying Pronouns and Antecedents

Identify the pronoun or pronouns in each of the following sentences as *personal, reflexive,* or *intensive.* After each pronoun, write the antecedent to which the pronoun refers. If a pronoun does not refer to a specific antecedent, write *unidentified.*

EXAMPLE 1. Italian explorer Marco Polo traveled to China, where he and Emperor Kublai Khan became friends.

1. he—personal—Marco Polo

1. The British explorer Sir Richard Burton himself wrote many books about his adventures in Africa.
2. We watched the movie about Robert O'Hara Burke's trip across Australia in the 1800s.
3. Queen Isabella of Spain herself gave approval for the famous voyages of Christopher Columbus.

Reference Note

For more about **complements,** see Chapter 13. For more about the **objects of prepositions,** see page 388.

TIPS & TRICKS

If you are not sure whether a pronoun is reflexive or intensive, try omitting the pronoun. If the basic meaning of the sentence stays the same, the pronoun is intensive. If the meaning changes, the pronoun is reflexive.

EXAMPLES
Rachel painted the fence herself.

Rachel painted the fence. [Without *herself,* the meaning stays the same. The pronoun is intensive.]

They treated themselves to a picnic.

They treated to a picnic. [Without *themselves,* the sentence doesn't make sense. The pronoun is reflexive.]

HELP

In Exercise 5, the antecedent may appear before or after the pronoun, or even in a previous sentence.

GRAMMAR

4. Matthew Henson prided himself on being part of the first expedition to reach the North Pole.
5. He wrote *A Negro Explorer at the North Pole,* a book about his expeditions with Commander Robert E. Peary.
6. I myself just read about the Dutch explorer Abel Tasman's voyages on the South Seas.
7. Lewis and Clark surely considered themselves lucky to have Sacagawea, a Shoshone woman, as their guide.
8. President Thomas Jefferson sent them to explore the land west of the Mississippi River.
9. Do you think the Spanish explorer Francisco Coronado really pictured himself finding the Seven Cities of Gold?
10. Our teacher told us about Samuel de Champlain's founding of the colony of Quebec.

Demonstrative Pronouns

11l. A *demonstrative pronoun* points out a person, a place, a thing, or an idea.

Demonstrative Pronouns			
this	that	these	those

EXAMPLES **This** is the most valuable baseball card I have, but **that** is also valuable.

These are the names of **those** who volunteered.

Reference Note

For more about **demonstrative adjectives,** see page 360.

NOTE When the words *this, that, these,* and *those* are used to modify a noun or a pronoun, they are considered adjectives, not pronouns.

EXAMPLE **This** card is my favorite.

Interrogative Pronouns

11m. An *interrogative pronoun* introduces a question.

Interrogative Pronouns				
what	which	who	whom	whose

EXAMPLES **What** is the largest planet in our solar system?

Who scored the most points in the game?

NOTE When the words *what, which,* and *whose* are used to modify a noun or a pronoun, they are considered adjectives, not pronouns.

EXAMPLE **Which** player scored the most points?

Relative Pronouns

11n. A *relative pronoun* introduces a subordinate clause.

Common Relative Pronouns				
that	which	who	whom	whose

EXAMPLES The Bactrian camel, **which** has two humps, is native to central Asia.

Ray Charles is a performer **who** has had many hit recordings.

Reference Note

For information on **relative pronouns** and **subordinate clauses,** see Chapter 15.

Exercise 6 Identifying Demonstrative, Interrogative, and Relative Pronouns

Identify the demonstrative, interrogative, and relative pronouns in each of the following sentences.

EXAMPLE 1. Which of you has heard of *The Mustangs of Las Colinas,* a sculpture that is located in Irving, Texas?

1. Which—interrogative; that—relative

1. The nine mustangs that make up the work appear to gallop across Williams Square in the Las Colinas Urban Center.
2. The Mustang Sculpture Exhibit, which is housed in a building near the statue, provides more information.
3. The horses, whose images are cast in bronze, form the world's largest equestrian (horse) sculpture.
4. That is an amazing sight!
5. What is the name of the sculptor who created the mustangs?
6. Robert Glen, who was born in Kenya, is the artist whom you mean.

GRAMMAR

7. This is a picture of the sculpture, which is made up of bronze horses that are larger than life-size.
8. Looking at the sculpture, you can imagine the amount of time that Glen has spent studying wildlife.
9. Who told me mustangs are descended from horses brought to the Americas by the Spanish?
10. Horses like these roamed wild over Texas and other western states in the 1800s.

Indefinite Pronouns

Reference Note

For more about the **agreement of indefinite pronouns and their antecedents,** see page 494.

11o. An *indefinite pronoun* refers to a person, a place, a thing, or an idea that may or may not be specifically named.

Common Indefinite Pronouns				
all	both	everything	neither	other
another	each	few	nobody	several
any	each other	many	none	some
anybody	either	more	no one	somebody
anyone	everybody	most	nothing	someone
anything	everyone	much	one	something

EXAMPLES **Everyone** completed the test before the bell rang.

Neither of the actors knew what costume the **other** was planning to wear.

Many words that can be used as indefinite pronouns can also be used as adjectives.

ADJECTIVE Look in **both** cabinets. [*Both* is an adjective modifying *cabinets.*]

PRONOUN **Both** contain winter clothing. [*Both* is an indefinite pronoun.]

ADJECTIVE **Each** player took **one** cap. [*Each* is an adjective modifying *player; one* is an adjective modifying *cap.*]

PRONOUN **Each** of the players took **one** of the caps. [*Each* and *one* are indefinite pronouns.]

WE HAD DREAMS OF GREATNESS.
WE WERE GOING TO WIN THE KENTUCKY DERBY.
WE WERE GOING TO TAKE THE TRIPLE CROWN.
WE WERE GOING TO HAVE A FANTASTIC YEAR.
YOU BLEW IT!
WHAT HAPPENED TO 'WE' ALL OF A SUDDEN?

BERRY'S WORLD reprinted by permission of Newspaper Enterprise Association, Inc.

Exercise 7 Using Indefinite Pronouns

Write an indefinite pronoun for the blank in each of the following sentences. Use a different pronoun for each blank.

EXAMPLE 1. We hope ____ in the Science Club knows about the meeting.
1. *everyone*

1. ____ of the members are working on their science fair projects.
2. ____ of these reports on pollution levels in Smith's Pond are by Aba and Benito.
3. They need ____ of the science students to help collect and test water.
4. Kwan, Lucy, and William have taken ____ of the pictures through a telescope.
5. They have developed and printed ____ of their pictures themselves.
6. Zane has found that bacteria will grow in ____ of the mouthwash.
7. ____ Zane decides to do is unusual.
8. Shannon has offered to draw ____ of the illustrations for posters.
9. We hope that ____ misses the fair.
10. Last year ____ went well.

GRAMMAR

Review B Identifying Kinds of Pronouns

Identify each pronoun in the following sentences as *personal, reflexive, intensive, demonstrative, interrogative, relative,* or *indefinite.*

EXAMPLE **1.** Can you name some of the many famous Hispanic entertainers who have their stars on Hollywood's Walk of Fame?

1. *you—personal; some—indefinite; who—relative; their—personal*

1. This is Tito Puente himself at the ceremony to install his star.
2. Many refer to him as the "King of Latin Music" or the "King of Salsa."
3. Who is the woman kneeling beside him?
4. She is Celia Cruz, a famous Cuban salsa singer, and as you can see for yourself, both of them are very happy and proud.

5. Everybody has heard of some of the entertainers honored with bronze stars on Hollywood Boulevard.
6. A musician whose name you might recognize appeared on the old *I Love Lucy* TV show, which is still shown.
7. Of course, that was Desi Arnaz, who was a Cuban bandleader.
8. Can you name some Hispanic singers who have stars on the Walk of Fame?
9. All of the following singers have their stars there: Julio Iglesias, Tony Orlando, Ritchie Valens, and José Feliciano.
10. The actors José Ferrer, Cesar Romero, and Ricardo Montalbán—all of them have stars.

The Adjective

11p. An *adjective* is a word used to modify a noun or a pronoun.

To ***modify*** a word means to describe the word or to make its meaning more definite. An adjective modifies a word by telling *what kind, which one, how much,* or *how many.*

What Kind?	Which One?	How Much? or How Many?
stone house	**another** one	**seven** rings
rushing river	**next** customer	**more** money
Irish linen	**first** day	**some** water
eager clerk	**those** people	**several** others
tired dog	**that** dress	**many** books
secret message	**these** mangoes	**larger** share

Exercise 8 **Using Appropriate Adjectives**

Revise the following sentences, replacing the italicized questions with adjectives that answer them. Do not use the same adjective more than once.

EXAMPLE **1.** They sold *how many?* tickets for the *which one?* show.
1. They sold fifty tickets for the first show.

1. Even though we had already run *how many?* laps around the track, we still had to run *how many?* more.
2. *Which one?* weekend, *how many?* hikers went on a *what kind?* trip to the *what kind?* park.
3. We rode in a *what kind?* van that carried *how many?* people and drove *how many?* miles to the game.
4. There was *how much?* time left when I started to answer the *which one?* question on the test.
5. During the *what kind?* afternoon we washed more than *how many?* cars and earned *how many?* dollars.
6. The recipe calls for *what kind?* flour and *how many?* eggs.
7. The *what kind?* paint livened up the *what kind?* room.
8. There were *how many?* rabbits hopping around in our *what kind?* yard this morning.
9. *How many?* musicians in the band are in *which one?* grade.
10. *Which one?* books on *which one?* table have *what kind?* stories for the *what kind?* children.

Articles

The most frequently used adjectives are *a, an,* and *the.* These adjectives are called ***articles.*** The adjectives *a* and *an* are called ***indefinite articles*** because they refer to any member of a general

STYLE TIP

You can make your writing more lively and interesting by using specific adjectives. Avoid overused adjectives such as *good, nice,* and *big.* Instead, use specific, vivid adjectives to make your descriptions come alive.

DULL
The small man was accompanied by two big dogs.

VIVID
The short, slim man was accompanied by two massive dogs.

COMPUTER TIP

Some word-processing programs have thesauruses. You can use an electronic thesaurus to help you find specific, descriptive adjectives to use in your writing. To make sure an adjective has the connotation you intend, look up the word in a dictionary.

GRAMMAR

group. *A* is used before a word beginning with a consonant sound. *An* is used before a word beginning with a vowel sound.

EXAMPLES How is **a** gerbil different from **a** hamster?

Uncle Bill wears **a** uniform to work. [The article *a* is used because *uniform* begins with a consonant sound.]

An accident stalled traffic for **an** hour. [The article *an* is used before *hour* because *hour* begins with a vowel sound.]

Reference Note

For more on using **adjectives,** see Chapter 20: Using Modifiers Correctly.

The adjective *the* is called the ***definite article*** because it refers to someone or something in particular.

EXAMPLES **The** astronaut appeared calm aboard **the** shuttle.

The key would not open **the** lock.

Demonstrative Adjectives

This, that, these, and *those* can be used both as adjectives and as pronouns. When they modify nouns or pronouns, they are called ***demonstrative adjectives.*** When they take the place of nouns or pronouns, they are called ***demonstrative pronouns.***

Reference Note

For more about **demonstrative pronouns,** see page 354.

ADJECTIVE Did Jessica win **this** trophy or **that** one?

PRONOUN Did Jessica win **this** or **that?**

ADJECTIVE **These** flags are much more colorful than **those** banners are.

PRONOUN **These** are much more colorful than **those** are.

Adjectives in Sentences

An adjective may come before or after the word it modifies.

EXAMPLES **Each** one of us brought **used** books for the auction.

The blouse, once **bright,** now looks **faded.**

These rare coins are extremely **valuable.**

NOTE An adjective that follows a linking verb and modifies the subject of the sentence is called a ***predicate adjective.***

Reference Note

For more about **predicate adjectives,** see page 407.

Exercise 9 Identifying Adjectives and the Words They Modify

Identify the adjectives and the words they modify in each of the following sentences. Do not include the articles *a*, *an*, and *the*.

EXAMPLE 1. Many people considered the old man unlucky.
1. Many—people; old—man; unlucky—man

1. For eighty-four days, Santiago, an elderly Cuban fisherman, had not caught a single fish.
2. Despite his bad luck, he remained hopeful.
3. On the eighty-fifth day, he caught a ten-pound albacore.
4. Soon after this catch, he hooked a huge marlin.
5. For nearly two days, the courageous fisherman struggled with the mighty fish and finally harpooned it.
6. Exhausted but happy, Santiago sailed toward shore.
7. Within an hour, however, his bad luck returned.
8. What happened to the weary fisherman and his big catch?
9. Does the story have a happy ending?
10. You can find the answers in the classic novel *The Old Man and the Sea.*

Link to Literature

GRAMMAR

Exercise 10 Revising Sentences

In each of the following sentences, add specific, vivid adjectives to modify the nouns.

EXAMPLE 1. The children took a nap.
1. The five grumpy children took a long nap.

1. Did Carolyn give a cat to her aunt?
2. Cesar donated books and jeans for the sale.
3. We watched the parade pass under our window.
4. The outfielder caught the baseball and made a throw to the catcher.
5. A dancer leaped across the stage.
6. Quickly, the hikers took shelter in the cabin.
7. The actor played the role of a detective.
8. Trapped, neither of the explorers could find a way out of the cave.
9. A lawyer questioned the witness.
10. Later, the knight fought the dragon and saved the village.

GRAMMAR

Proper Adjectives

Reference Note

For more information about **capitalizing proper adjectives,** see page 616.

A ***proper adjective*** is formed from a proper noun and begins with a capital letter.

Proper Nouns	Proper Adjectives
Canada	**Canadian** citizen
China	**Chinese** calendar
Islam	**Islamic** law
Carter	**Carter** administration
New Jersey	**New Jersey** coast

Some proper nouns do not change spelling when they are used as adjectives.

PROPER NOUN Seattle
PROPER ADJECTIVE **Seattle** skyline

HELP—
Some sentences in Exercise 11 contain more than one proper adjective.

Exercise 11 Identifying Proper Adjectives

Identify the proper adjectives and the words they modify in the following sentences.

EXAMPLE 1. In recent years many American tourists have visited the Great Wall of China.
1. *American—tourists*

1. Early Spanish explorers built forts along the Florida coast.
2. The professor of African literature gave a lecture on the novels of Camara Laye, a writer who was born in Guinea.
3. Which Arthurian legend have you chosen for your report?
4. The program about the Egyptian ruins was narrated by a British scientist and a French anthropologist.
5. Aeolus was the god of the winds in ancient Greek mythology.
6. The society of Victorian England was the subject of many British novels in the late 1800s.
7. During the press conference last night, the president commented on the Bosnian situation.
8. A friend who is Japanese gave me a kimono from Tokyo.
9. We saw a display of Appalachian crafts in the public library.
10. Marian McPartland, a jazz pianist from New York City, played several Scott Joplin songs.

Review C Identifying Adjectives

Identify the adjectives in each of the following sentences. Do not include the articles *a, an,* and *the.*

EXAMPLE 1. Have you heard of the Heidi Festival, a popular event in the small town of New Glarus, Wisconsin?

1. popular, small

1. For geography class, I wrote a short paper about New Glarus.
2. It was founded by adventurous Swiss settlers in 1845, and people call it Little Switzerland.
3. As you can see in these photographs, colorful reminders of that Swiss heritage are everywhere.
4. The special emblems of the cantons, or states, of Switzerland are on street signs and buildings.
5. Many of the women make beautiful lace, and there is even an embroidery factory.
6. Dairying is big business, too, and the townsfolk make delicious cheeses.
7. In a historical village, visitors can see reconstructed buildings, such as a schoolhouse, a blacksmith shop, a church, and the cheese factory shown here.
8. In this village, pioneer tools and belongings are on display.
9. New Glarus also has a museum in a mountain lodge, or *chalet.*
10. Someday, I hope to see a summer festival, such as the Heidi Festival.

HELP 

If an adjective is capitalized as part of a name, as in *New York* and *White House*, consider it part of the proper noun and not a separate adjective.

Determining Parts of Speech

The way that a word is used in a sentence determines what part of speech the word is. Some words may be used as nouns or as adjectives.

NOUN	How often do you watch **television**?
ADJECTIVE	What is your favorite **television** program?
NOUN	Return these books to the **library.**
ADJECTIVE	These **library** books are overdue.
NOUN	Would you like to have a cookout this **Labor Day**?
ADJECTIVE	Our annual **Labor Day** cookout is always a wonderful event.

Some words may be used as pronouns or adjectives.

PRONOUN	**That** is not a dragonfly; it's a damsel fly.
ADJECTIVE	**That** insect is not a dragonfly; it's a damsel fly.
PRONOUN	**Some** have gone to their dressing rooms.
ADJECTIVE	**Some** actors have gone to their dressing rooms.
PRONOUN	**Whose** are these?
ADJECTIVE	**Whose** gloves are these?

Exercise 12 Identifying Nouns, Pronouns, and Adjectives

Tell whether the italicized word in each of the following sentences is used as a *noun,* a *pronoun,* or an *adjective.*

EXAMPLE **1.** The robin carried *some* twigs to its nest.
1. adjective

1. This new *computer* program makes printers work twice as fast.
2. The program runs on this *computer.*
3. The *football* hit the ground and bounced right into his arms.
4. Are you going to the *football* game?
5. The book is much better than the *movie.*
6. The *movie* star rode at the front of the parade.
7. We'll start painting *that* section next.
8. *That* must be an interesting job.
9. *One* of the trees still has all its leaves.
10. The raccoon carried *one* baby at a time back to the nest.
11. The next race is scheduled for *Tuesday* night.
12. According to some surveys, *Tuesday* is the best day to get work done.

13. *Which* stars make up Orion's belt?
14. *Which* of the otters caught the first fish?
15. *All* mammals are vertebrates.
16. Matt has already memorized *all* of his lines in the play.
17. The only *mystery* is how it ended up in a box in the back of the closet.
18. The next guest speaker is a famous *mystery* writer.
19. If you lose *any* of the pieces, we won't be able to complete the puzzle.
20. Amazing things can be found by turning over almost *any* rock.

GRAMMAR

Review D Identifying Nouns, Pronouns, and Adjectives

Tell whether each italicized word in the following sentences is used as a *noun,* a *pronoun,* or an *adjective.*

EXAMPLE 1. Remember, don't let *anyone* tell you that the age of exploration is over.

1. *pronoun*

1. Two brothers, Lawrence and Lorne Blair, went on an amazing *adventure* that began in 1973.
2. For ten years they traveled among the nearly fourteen thousand *islands* of Indonesia.
3. *Each* of them returned with remarkable tales about the lands, animals, and people they had seen.
4. Their *adventure* story began when some pirates guided them through the Spice Islands.
5. There, the brothers located *one* of the world's rarest and most beautiful animals—the greater bird of paradise.
6. Another *island* animal that the brothers encountered was the frightening Komodo dragon.
7. *Some* Komodo dragons are eleven feet long and weigh more than five hundred pounds.
8. *Each* day brought startling discoveries, such as flying frogs and flying snakes.
9. On *one* island, Borneo, they found a group of people thought to be extinct.
10. To *some,* the brothers' stay with the cannibals of West New Guinea is the strangest part of their trip.

GRAMMAR

HELP— You may want to go through Review E three times: First, look for nouns, then for pronouns, and finally for adjectives.

Review E Identifying Nouns, Pronouns, and Adjectives

Identify each *noun, pronoun,* and *adjective* in the following sentences. Do not include the articles *a, an,* and *the.*

EXAMPLE **1.** Charles Drew was an American doctor.

1. Charles Drew—noun; American—adjective; doctor—noun

1. Charles Drew developed innovative techniques that are used in the separation and preservation of blood.
2. During World War II, Dr. Drew himself was the director of donation efforts for the American Red Cross.
3. He established blood-bank programs.
4. His research saved numerous lives during the war.
5. Dr. Drew set up centers in which blood could be stored.
6. The British government asked him to develop a storage system in England.
7. Shortly before the beginning of World War II, Dr. Drew became a professor of surgery at Howard University.
8. After the war, he was appointed chief surgeon at Freedman's Hospital.
9. This physician and researcher made important contributions to medical science.
10. Many people who have needed blood owe their lives to his methods.

Review F Writing Sentences with Nouns, Pronouns, and Adjectives

Write two sentences with each of the following words. Use each word as two different parts of speech—*noun* and *adjective* or *pronoun* and *adjective.* Write the part of speech of the word after each sentence.

EXAMPLE **1.** this

1. This bicycle is mine.—adjective
This cannot be the right answer.—pronoun

1. game
2. some
3. American
4. right
5. that
6. green
7. more
8. Saturday
9. what
10. water

Chapter Review

A. Identifying Nouns, Pronouns, and Adjectives

Identify each italicized word or word group as a *noun, pronoun* or *adjective*.

1. I don't feel happy when the dark *sky* threatens *rain*.
2. My little sister, *afraid* of *thunder* and lightning, hid under the bed.
3. Inger's mother gave *each* of us a glass of *cold* milk.
4. One by one, *each* husky ventured out into the *cold*.
5. *Who* went to the movie on *Saturday* night?
6. When the famous *performer* came to town, we went to *his* concert.
7. The house across the street has been up for *sale* since *Tuesday*.
8. *Michelangelo Buonarroti* painted many *large* murals in the Sistine Chapel.
9. *That* jacket doesn't belong to *anyone*.
10. *That* is an *Aleut* mask.
11. Give me *some* iced *lemonade*, please.
12. *Somebody* said that there would be no more *discount* movie tickets.
13. I got a *discount* on *our* tickets, though.
14. *Mr. Taylor* donated the *sports* equipment for the new middle school in our town.
15. In high school, Uncle Todd excelled in *track* and several other *sports*.
16. *Everyone* liked one painting or the *other*.
17. Juana went to the *mall* by *herself*.
18. Hobbies take up so *much* time that they often become *work*.
19. My aunt's very busy *work* schedule often takes *her* out of town for several days at a time.
20. This parakeet screeches if *it* doesn't get *enough* food.

B. Identifying Pronouns

Identify the pronoun or pronouns in each of the following sentences as *personal, reflexive, intensive, demonstrative, interrogative, relative,* or *indefinite.*

21. Our teacher and Ms. de la Garza said they would be at the meeting.

22. The members of the cast checked themselves in the dressing-room mirrors.

23. Mr. O'Shaughnessy himself said the quiz might be postponed.

24. The late Senator Duddington was a giving, generous, and warm human being, wasn't he?

25. Which of the science classes is she taking next year?

26. The chimpanzee taught itself to use a remote control.

27. A friend of mine said you had won several of the events at the 4-H competition.

28. Did Sally paint the apartment herself?

29. The zebras took the same path that they had always taken across the veldt.

30. Darryl answered the phone himself.

31. Is Queen Elizabeth I remembered because she was a great leader of England?

32. Kimiko wrote herself a note.

33. These are the books that I mentioned earlier.

34. The choice was hard, as both were excellent students.

35. Almost everything my grandfather did was motivated by concern for the family.

36. The council member whom the reporter wants to interview is out of town today.

37. Who may I say is calling?

38. Somebody has given Benno the Dalmatian a bath.

39. According to Sanjay, either of the two movies is worth seeing.

40. We found ourselves in an awkward situation.

Writing Application

Writing a Movie Review

Using Nouns, Pronouns, and Adjectives Write a paragraph about a movie you have recently seen and enjoyed. Be sure to use at least ten each of nouns, pronouns, and adjectives.

Prewriting You could write about a movie you have seen that is very popular or one that is less well-known but that you enjoyed. Write down some thoughts about the movie—what you especially liked, what you think worked, and what you think didn't work. Read some short newspaper movie reviews for an idea of the kind of style you might use.

Writing Think about how to organize your notes and your ideas. Write down your impressions of the movie in a logical order, starting with your overall opinion, then going into a little more detail about the story, and concluding with a short summary.

Revising Does your paragraph give your opinion of the movie in an interesting way? Add, delete, or rearrange details to make your paragraph more entertaining or informative. Read through your paragraph to make sure that you have used at least ten each of nouns, pronouns, and adjectives.

Publishing Check for errors in grammar, punctuation, and spelling. Then, ask a classmate to read the paragraph, and post the completed paragraph on the class bulletin board or Web page, if available.

CHAPTER

Parts of Speech Overview

Verb, Adverb, Preposition, Conjunction, Interjection

Diagnostic Preview

A. Identifying Different Parts of Speech

Identify each italicized word or word group in the following sentences as a *verb,* an *adverb,* a *preposition,* or a *conjunction.* For each verb, indicate whether it is an *action verb* or a *linking verb.*

HELP—
Keep in mind that correlative conjunctions can be made up of more than one word.

EXAMPLE 1. You probably know that Christopher Columbus was a famous explorer, *but* do you know anything *of* his personal life?

1. *but—conjunction; of—preposition*

1. I *have discovered* some interesting facts *about* Christopher Columbus.
2. He was born *into* a hard-working Italian family and *learned* how to sail as a boy.
3. He *became*, in fact, *not only* a master sailor *but also* a map maker.
4. Although he had *barely* any formal education, he *studied* both Portuguese and Spanish.
5. The writings *of* ancient scholars about astronomy and geography *especially* interested him.

6. Columbus *apparently* also *had* keen powers of observation.
7. These *served* him *well* on his expeditions.
8. On his voyages to find a sea route *to* the East Indies, Columbus *was* a determined, optimistic leader.
9. He let *neither* doubters *nor* hardships interfere *with* his plans.
10. Many people mistakenly think that Columbus was poor when he died in 1506, *but* he was actually *quite* wealthy.

B. Identifying Different Parts of Speech

Identify each italicized word or word group in the following sentences as a *verb,* an *adverb,* a *preposition,* a *conjunction,* or an *interjection.*

EXAMPLE **1.** I *am reading* a book *about* baseball cards.
1. am reading—verb; about—preposition

11. We *watched* as the skywriter *carefully* spelled out the words "Marry me, Diane."
12. *Both* the dog *and* the cat *are* dirty and need baths.
13. *Whoops*! I dropped my ring *under* the counter.
14. *Today* we studied the contributions that ancient North Africans made *to* mathematics.
15. Clever replies *never* occur to me until it is *too* late.
16. Sandy *does* not *have* enough granola *for* breakfast.
17. The girl *tried* climbing the rock face again *in spite of* her previous difficulty.
18. *Well,* I really want to see *either* Key West *or* the Everglades when we go to Florida next summer.
19. How *did* the other team *win so* easily?
20. The beans with rice *tasted* good, *for* we were hungry after a long day of yardwork.

HELP
Keep in mind that verbs, correlative conjunctions, and some prepositions can be made up of more than one word.

The Verb

12a. A *verb* is a word used to express action or a state of being.

In this book, verbs are classified in three ways—(1) as *helping* or *main verbs,* (2) as *action* or *linking verbs,* and (3) as *transitive* or *intransitive verbs.*

Helping Verbs and Main Verbs

A ***helping verb*** helps the ***main verb*** express action or a state of being. Together, a main verb and at least one helping verb (also called an ***auxiliary verb***) make up a ***verb phrase.***

The following sentences contain verb phrases.

EXAMPLES Seiji Ozawa **will conduct** many outstanding orchestras. [The main verb is *conduct*.]

He **has been praised** for his fine conducting. [The main verb is *praised.*]

His recordings **should be heard** by anyone interested in classical music. [The main verb is *heard.*]

He **will be leading** the orchestra tonight. [The main verb is *leading.*]

Commonly Used Helping Verbs			
Forms of *Be*	am are be	been being is	was were
Forms of *Do*	do	does	did
Forms of *Have*	had	has	have
Other Helping Verbs	can could may	might must shall	should will would

NOTE Some helping verbs may also be used as main verbs.

EXAMPLES Did he **do** his homework?

She will **be** here soon.

We do not **have** enough time, but we **have** a plan.

Sometimes a verb phrase is interrupted by another part of speech. In most cases, the interrupter is an adverb. In a question, however, the subject often interrupts a verb phrase.

EXAMPLES The newspaper **has** finally **arrived.**

Because of the fog, we **did** not [*or* **did**n't] **have** a clear view of the mountains.

Will the boy in the blue jacket **write** his report on Lucy Stone, the suffragist?

Notice in the second example that the word *not* is not included in the verb phrase. *Not* (as well as its contraction, –*n't*) is an adverb and is never part of a verb phrase.

Reference Note

For information about **contractions** such as –*n't*, see page 487.

GRAMMAR

Exercise 1 Identifying Verb Phrases

Identify the verb phrases in the following sentences. Then, underline each helping verb.

EXAMPLE **1.** Many people are earning a living at unusual jobs.

1. *are earning*

1. Even today people can find positions as shepherds, inventors, and candlestick makers.
2. It might seem strange, but these people have decided that ordinary jobs have become too boring for them.
3. Some people have been working as messengers.
4. You may have seen them when they were wearing clown makeup or costumes such as gorilla suits.
5. Other people have been finding work as mimes.
6. They can be seen performing at circuses, fairs, and festivals.
7. Chimney sweeps still do clean chimney flues for people.
8. Some chimney sweeps may even wear the traditional, old-time clothes of the trade.
9. With a little imagination, anyone can find an unusual job.
10. What unusual jobs can you name?

HELP

Some sentences in Exercise 1 contain more than one verb phrase.

Action Verbs

An ***action verb*** is a verb that expresses either physical or mental activity.

Physical Activity	laugh, paint, leap, sneeze, play

EXAMPLES Langston Hughes **wrote** volumes of poetry.

A distinguished cinematographer, James Wong Howe, **arrived.**

COMPUTER TIP

Some word-processing programs come with built-in thesauruses. You can use a computer thesaurus to help you find fresh, lively action verbs to make your writing more interesting. Always make sure the verb you select has the precise meaning you wish to express.

Mental Activity	understand, wish, trust, realize, dream

EXAMPLES The scientist **studied** the ant colony.

Mario **knew** the answer to every question on the test.

GRAMMAR

Exercise 2 Identifying Action Verbs

Link to Literature

Identify the action verb or verbs in each of the following sentences.

EXAMPLE 1. Joseph Bruchac writes and publishes poems and stories.

1. writes, publishes

1. Bruchac, of Slovak and Abenaki heritage, tells personal histories also.
2. He and his wife Carol own and run Greenfield Review Press.
3. The press publishes the work of American Indian writers.
4. Bruchac himself wrote more than fifty books for adults and children.
5. One of his books, *Lasting Echoes,* tells the history of American Indians.
6. Bruchac subtitled the book, "An Oral History of Native American People."
7. *Lasting Echoes* describes the importance of the land to the American Indian.
8. Bruchac shares the stories he wishes he had heard as a child.
9. American Indians narrate their own experiences and ideas.
10. Bruchac believes their stories should be told and remembered.

Linking Verbs

A ***linking verb*** connects the subject to a word or word group that identifies or describes the subject. The noun, pronoun, or adjective that is connected to the subject by a linking verb completes the meaning of the verb.

EXAMPLES Tranh **is** one of the finalists. [Tranh = one]

Marie Curie **became** a famous scientist. [Marie Curie = scientist]

Wild animals **remain** free on the great animal reserves in Africa. [free animals]

The watermelon **looks** ripe. [ripe watermelon]

Commonly Used Linking Verbs				
Forms of *Be*	am	be	being	was
	are	been	is	were
Other Verbs	appear	grow	seem	stay
	become	look	smell	taste
	feel	remain	sound	turn

NOTE The forms of the verb *be* are not always used as helping verbs or linking verbs. When followed by a word or word group that tells *when* or *where,* a form of *be* is a ***state-of-being verb.***

EXAMPLE Your roller skates **are** in the attic.

Exercise 3 Using Linking Verbs

Supply a linking verb for each blank in the following sentences. Try to use a different verb in each blank. Then, identify the words that each verb links.

EXAMPLE **1.** Judith Jamison ____ calm during the première of the dance.

1. Judith Jamison remained calm during the première of the dance.

Judith Jamison—calm

1. The first day ____ long.
2. Your suggestion ____ good to me.
3. Our room ____ festive after we decorated it for the party.
4. The orange ____ a little too sweet.
5. In the novel the main character ____ a doctor, and he returns home to set up a clinic.
6. Before a storm the air ____ wet and heavy.
7. Did she ____ happy about living in Florida?

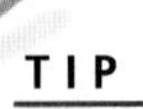

STYLE TIP

Overusing the linking verb *be* can make your writing dull and lifeless. When possible, replace a dull *be* verb with a verb that expresses action.

BE VERB
Edgar Allan Poe **was** a writer of poems and frightening short stories.

ACTION VERB
Edgar Allan Poe **wrote** poems and frightening short stories.

COMPUTER TIP

The overuse of *be* verbs is a problem that a computer can help you solve. Use the computer's search function to find and highlight each occurrence of *am, are, is, was, were, be, been,* and *being.* For each such use, decide whether the *be* verb is needed or whether it could be replaced with an action verb for greater variety.

8. The diver ____ more confident with each dive she made.
9. They ____ quiet as the theater lights dimmed.
10. The lilacs in the garden ____ lovely.

GRAMMAR

TIPS & TRICKS

Try the following test to determine whether a verb is a linking verb or an action verb. Substitute a form of *be* for the verb. If the sentence still makes sense, the verb is probably a linking verb. If not, the verb is most likely an action verb.

EXAMPLES
Mona felt sleepy.
Mona was sleepy. [The sentence still makes sense. Here, *felt* is a linking verb.]
Mona felt the soft fabric.
Mona is the soft fabric. [This sentence does not make sense. Here, *felt* is an action verb.]

Most linking verbs, not including the forms of *be* and *seem*, may also be used as action verbs. Whether a verb is used to link words or to express action depends on its meaning in a sentence.

LINKING Those plums **appeared** ripe.
ACTION Those plums **appeared** on our back porch.

LINKING The soup **tasted** good.
ACTION I **tasted** the soup.

LINKING She **had grown** tired of playing.
ACTION She **had grown** into the new coat.

Exercise 4 Verbs and Their Subjects

Identify the verb and its subject in each of the following sentences. If the verb is a linking verb, identify also the word or words that the verb links to its subject.

EXAMPLES
1. People enjoy the International Championship Chili Cook-off in Terlingua, Texas.
1. enjoy, People
2. The event, first held in 1967, is extremely popular.
2. is, event—popular

1. Chili cook-offs throughout the Southwest attract fans.
2. Real fans grow hungry at the mention of chili peppers and chili powder.
3. These are important ingredients in Mexican cooking.
4. Chili cooks start with their favorite chili powder.
5. Basic chili powder consists of ground, dried chilies and other spices.
6. The most common chili is chili con carne.
7. This is a thick, spicy meat stew, often with beans in it.
8. Chili varies from somewhat spicy to fiery hot.
9. You also find many recipes for chili without meat.
10. Regardless of the other ingredients in a batch of chili, the chili powder smells wonderful to chili fans.

Exercise 5 Identifying Verbs

Identify the verb or verbs in each of the following sentences. If the verb is a linking verb, identify also the words that the verb links.

EXAMPLES 1. Do you know Tomás Herrera?
1. Do know

2. He is a friend of mine who lives next door to me.
2. is, He—friend; lives

1. Tomás is a young musician.
2. He likes all kinds of music and practices many hours each week.
3. His parents are proud of his talent and discipline.
4. One afternoon Tomás became restless.
5. The notes sounded wrong, and none of his music seemed right to him.
6. He wrote some notes on several sheets of music paper.
7. After a little careful revision, he formed the notes into an original harmony.
8. That night he performed his song for some of his friends.
9. Cristina exclaimed, "Tomás, that was excellent!"
10. "Is that really your first original song?"

Review A Identifying Helping and Main Verbs and Action and Linking Verbs

Identify each verb or verb phrase in the following sentences as an *action verb* or a *linking verb*. For each verb phrase, underline the main verb twice and each helping verb once.

EXAMPLE 1. Who were the Vikings, and where did they live?
1. were—linking verb; did live—action verb

1. The Vikings were Norsemen who roamed the seas from A.D. 700 to 1100.
2. The term *Vikings* applies to all Scandinavian sailors of this period, whether they were Norwegians, Swedes, or Danes.
3. People in other countries considered the Vikings the terror of Europe.
4. Vikings worshiped such fierce gods as Thor and Odin.
5. Viking warriors were hopeful that they would die in battle.

HELP— Some sentences in Review A contain more than one verb.

GRAMMAR

6. They believed that if they died in battle, they would go to Valhalla.
7. In Valhalla, they could always enjoy battles and banquets.
8. Each day, the warriors in Valhalla would go out to the battlefield and would receive many wounds.
9. Then, in spite of their injuries, at the end of the day they would all meet back at the banquet hall.
10. Their wounds would promptly heal, and they could boast about their great bravery in battle.

Review B Identifying Helping and Main Verbs and Action and Linking Verbs

HELP
Some sentences in Review B contain more than one verb.

Identify each verb or verb phrase in the following sentences as an *action verb* or a *linking verb.* For each verb phrase, underline the main verb twice and each helping verb once.

EXAMPLES
1. Have you heard of Mary McLeod Bethune?
1. Have heard—action verb
2. She dedicated her life to young people.
2. dedicated—action verb

1. Mary McLeod Bethune is a major figure in American history.
2. Bethune taught school after she had completed her education in South Carolina.
3. In 1904, she moved to Florida and opened a school of her own.
4. This school eventually became Bethune-Cookman College, and Mary Bethune served as its president.
5. In 1930, Bethune was invited to a presidential conference on child health and protection.
6. Then, during Franklin Roosevelt's administration, she and others founded the National Youth Administration.
7. Her outstanding efforts impressed President Roosevelt, and he established an office for minority affairs.
8. This office gave money to serious students so that they could continue their education.
9. In 1945, Bethune was an observer at the conference that organized the United Nations.
10. Throughout her long life, Bethune remained interested in education, and her efforts earned her national recognition.

Transitive and Intransitive Verbs

A ***transitive verb*** is a verb that expresses an action directed toward a person, place, thing, or idea.

EXAMPLES Joel **held** the baby. [The action of *held* is directed toward *baby*.]

Loretta **brought** flowers. [The action of *brought* is directed toward *flowers*.]

Did Grandpa **sharpen** the ax this morning? [The action of *Did sharpen* is directed toward *ax*.]

With transitive verbs, the action passes from the doer—the subject—to the receiver of the action. Words that receive the action of transitive verbs are called ***objects.***

Reference Note

For more about **objects** and their uses in sentences, see page 401.

EXAMPLES Our scout troop made a **quilt.** [*Quilt* is the object of the verb *made*.]

The voters elected **him.** [*Him* is the object of the verb *elected*.]

How quickly the dog chased the **cat!** [*Cat* is the object of the verb *chased*.]

An ***intransitive verb*** expresses action (or tells something about the subject) without the action passing to a receiver, or object.

EXAMPLES **Did**n't Samuel Ramey **sing** beautifully in the opera *Don Giovanni*?

The Evans twins **played** quietly indoors the whole day.

How long **have** you **been painting,** Mary?

A verb may be transitive in one sentence and intransitive in another.

EXAMPLES Janet **swam** ten laps. [transitive]
Janet **swam** well. [intransitive]

The teacher **read** a poem. [transitive]
The teacher **read** aloud. [intransitive]

NOTE Because linking verbs do not have objects, they are classified as intransitive verbs.

GRAMMAR

HELP

In the example for Exercise 6, the object of the transitive verb *know* is *it.*

Exercise 6 Identifying Transitive Verbs and Intransitive Verbs

Identify each italicized verb as *transitive* or *intransitive*. Be prepared to identify the object of each transitive verb.

EXAMPLE 1. Whether you *know* it or not, many cowboys in the United States were African Americans.

1. *transitive*

1. During the years following the Civil War, thousands of African American cowboys *rode* the cattle trails north from Texas.
2. They *worked* alongside Mexican, American Indian, and European American trail hands.
3. All the members of a cattle drive *slept* on the same hard, sometimes rocky ground.
4. They *ate* the same food and did the same hard jobs.
5. When the day was done, they *enjoyed* each other's company as they swapped stories.
6. Often they also *sang* around the campfire.
7. After long weeks on the trail, they finally *reached* their destinations with their herds.
8. Then they *celebrated* by having rodeos, parades, and shooting contests.
9. Nat Love, one of the most famous African American cowboys, *wrote* about his experiences on the range.
10. In his book, Love *recalls* many of the times that he and the other cowboys looked out for one another, regardless of skin color.

Exercise 7 Writing Sentences with Transitive Verbs and Intransitive Verbs

For each of the verbs on the following page, write two sentences. In the first sentence, use the verb as a *transitive* verb and underline its object. In the second, use the verb as an *intransitive* verb. You may use different tenses of the verb.

EXAMPLE 1. read

1. *For tomorrow, read the chapter that begins on page 441. (transitive)*

I think I'll read this evening instead of watching television. (intransitive)

1. win	**3.** play	**5.** freeze	**7.** jump	**9.** paint
2. move	**4.** run	**6.** build	**8.** cook	**10.** help

GRAMMAR

The Adverb

12b. An *adverb* is a word that modifies a verb, an adjective, or another adverb.

Just as an adjective makes the meaning of a noun or pronoun more definite, an adverb makes the meaning of a verb, an adjective, or another adverb more definite. An adverb tells *where, when, how,* or *to what extent* (*how much or how long*).

Reference Note

For information on **adjectives,** see page 358.

Where?	When?
They said the forest fire started **here.**	Louis **promptly** rounded up suspects.
The couple was married **nearby.**	**Then** several suspects were questioned.
How?	**To What Extent?**
The accident occurred **suddenly.**	Ms. Kwan was **quite** proud of the girls' debate team.
The prime minister spoke **carefully.**	She has **scarcely** begun the math lesson.

Adverbs Modifying Verbs

Adverbs may come before or after the words they modify.

EXAMPLES **Slowly** the man crawled **down.** [The adverb *Slowly* tells *how* the man crawled, and the adverb *down* tells *where* he crawled.]

I **seldom** see you **nowadays.** [The adverb *seldom* tells *to what extent* I see you, and the adverb *nowadays* tells *when* I see you.]

Adverbs may come between the parts of verb phrases.

EXAMPLES Keisha has **already** completed her part of the project. [The adverb interrupts and modifies *has completed.*]

Many students did **not** understand the directions. [The adverb interrupts and modifies *did understand.*]

Adverbs are sometimes used to ask questions.

EXAMPLES **Where** are you going?

How did you do on the test?

Exercise 8 Identifying Adverbs That Modify Verbs

Identify the adverbs and the verbs they modify in the following sentences.

EXAMPLE **1.** How can I quickly learn to take better pictures?

1. How—can learn; quickly—can learn

1. You can listen carefully to advice from experienced photographers, who usually like to share their knowledge.
2. Nobody always takes perfect pictures, but some tips can help you now.
3. To begin with, you should never move when you are taking pictures.
4. You should stand still and hold your camera firmly.
5. Some photographers suggest that you move your feet apart and put one foot forward to help maintain your balance.
6. Many beginners do not stand near the subject when they take pictures.
7. As a result, subjects frequently are lost in the background, and the photographers later wonder what happened to their careful compositions.
8. A good photographer automatically thinks about what will be in a picture and consequently avoids disappointment with the result.
9. Nowadays, many cameras have built-in light meters, but you should still check the lighting.
10. You may already have heard the advice to stand with your back to the sun when taking pictures, and that tip is often a good one.

Adverb or Adjective?

Many adverbs end in *–ly*. Many of these adverbs are formed by adding *–ly* to adjectives.

Adjective	+	–ly	=	Adverb
bright	+	–ly	=	brightly
loud	+	–ly	=	loudly

However, some words ending in *–ly* can be used as adjectives.

EXAMPLES	friendly	monthly	lonely
	likely	timely	only

Adverbs Modifying Adjectives

EXAMPLES An **unusually** fast starter, Karen won the race. [The adverb *unusually* modifies the adjective *fast,* telling *how fast* the starter was.]

Our committee is **especially** busy at this time of year. [The adverb *especially* modifies the adjective *busy,* telling *to what extent* the committee is busy.]

Exercise 9 Identifying Adverbs That Modify Adjectives

Identify the adverbs and the adjectives they modify in the following sentences.

EXAMPLE 1. Because so many bicycles have been stolen, the principal hired a guard.

1. so—many

1. The team is extremely proud of its record.
2. Frogs may look quite harmless, but some are poisonous.
3. The class was unusually quiet today.
4. The Mardi Gras celebration in New Orleans is very loud and remarkably colorful.
5. The coach said we were too careless during the play.
6. I waited nearly two hours to get tickets to that show.
7. When the kittens are with their mother, they look thoroughly contented.

TIPS & TRICKS

If you are not sure whether a word is an adjective or an adverb, ask yourself what the word modifies. If it modifies a noun or a pronoun, it is an adjective.

EXAMPLE

She gave us the **daily** report. [*Daily* modifies the noun *report* and so is used as an adjective.]

If a word modifies a verb, an adjective, or an adverb, then it's an adverb.

EXAMPLE

Alicia **recently** won the spelling bee. [The adverb *recently* modifies the verb *won.*]

HELP

A sentence in Exercise 9 contains more than one adverb that modifies an adjective.

GRAMMAR

GRAMMAR

8. Weekends are especially hectic for me when all of my teachers assign homework.
9. Those fajitas seem much spicier than these.
10. The exchange student from Norway is surprisingly fluent in English.

STYLE TIP

The adverb *very* is often overused. In your writing, try to replace *very* with more descriptive adverbs. You can also revise a sentence so that other words carry more of the descriptive meaning.

EXAMPLE
Vikram Seth's novel *A Suitable Boy* is very long.

REVISED
Vikram Seth's novel *A Suitable Boy* is **extremely** long.

or

Vikram Seth's novel *A Suitable Boy* is **1,349 pages** long and **weighs four pounds.**

Exercise 10 Choosing Adverbs to Modify Adjectives

The adverb *very* is used far too often to modify adjectives. Choose an adverb other than *very* to modify each adjective below. Use a different adverb with each adjective.

EXAMPLE **1.** strong
1. incredibly strong

1. cheerful	**4.** messy	**7.** heavy	**9.** calm
2. sour	**5.** honest	**8.** long	**10.** graceful
3. wide	**6.** timid		

Adverbs Modifying Other Adverbs

EXAMPLES Elena finished the problem **more** quickly than I did. [The adverb *more* modifies the adverb *quickly,* telling *how quickly* Elena finished the problem.]

Our guest left **quite** abruptly. [The adverb *quite* modifies the adverb *abruptly,* telling *to what extent* our guest left abruptly.]

Exercise 11 Identifying Adverbs That Modify Other Adverbs

Identify each adverb that modifies another adverb in the following sentences. Then, write the adverb that it modifies.

EXAMPLE **1.** Condors are quite definitely among the largest living birds.
1. quite—definitely

1. The California condor and the Andean condor are almost entirely extinct.
2. So very few California condors exist today that they are rarely seen outside captivity.
3. Andean condors are slightly more numerous, and more of them can still be seen in the wild.

4. You can see from these photographs why some people think that condors are most assuredly the ugliest birds.
5. However, once in the air, condors soar so gracefully that they can look beautiful.
6. Condors fly amazingly gracefully considering that some weigh more than fifteen pounds.
7. The heads of the Andean and California condors differ quite distinctly.
8. The California condor in the photograph on the right has a head that is very handsomely shaped compared to that of the Andean condor.
9. The Andean condor's head has a large fleshy caruncle protruding quite noticeably above the beak.
10. The extinction of condors is happening especially quickly, so the time left to observe them may be sadly short.

GRAMMAR

Review C **Identifying Adverbs**

Identify the adverbs in each of the following sentences. After each adverb, write the word that the adverb modifies.

EXAMPLE 1. Sherlock Holmes solved the case very quickly.
1. *very—quickly; quickly—solved*

HELP—Some sentences in Review C have more than one adverb.

1. I have been a fan of mystery stories since I was quite young.
2. Some stories are incredibly exciting from start to finish.
3. Others build suspense very slowly.
4. If I like a story, I almost never put it down until I finish it.
5. In many cases, I can scarcely prevent myself from peeking at the last chapter to see the ending.
6. I never start reading a mystery story if I have homework because then it is more tempting to read than to study.
7. My favorite detectives are ones who cleverly match wits with equally clever villains.
8. I especially like detectives who carefully hunt for clues.

9. The clues that they uncover are almost always found in unexpected, spooky places.
10. It's amazing how detectives can use these clues to solve the most complicated cases.

The Preposition

12c. A *preposition* is a word that shows the relationship of a noun or pronoun, called the *object of the preposition,* to another word.

Notice how a change in the preposition changes the relationship between *package* and *tree* in each of the following examples.

EXAMPLES The package **under** the tree is mine.
The package **near** the tree is mine.
The package **next to** the tree is mine.
The package **in front of** the tree is mine.

STYLE TIP

In formal writing, many people consider it best to avoid ending a sentence with a preposition. However, this practice is becoming more accepted in casual speech and informal writing. You should follow your teacher's instructions on sentences ending with prepositions.

NOTE As a general rule, the object of the preposition follows the preposition.

EXAMPLE Melissa is writing **about** her **stay in** the **hospital.** [*Stay* is the object of the preposition *about*; *hospital* is the object of the preposition *in*.]

Sometimes, however, the object of the preposition comes before the preposition.

EXAMPLE **What** I'm most concerned **about** is your safety. [*What* is the object of the preposition *about*.]

Commonly Used Prepositions

aboard	along	at	but (meaning *except*)
about	along with	before	
above	amid	below	by
according to	among	beneath	down
across	around	beside	during
after	aside from	besides	except
against	as of	between	for

Commonly Used Prepositions			
from	near	over	until
in	next to	past	unto
in addition to	of	since	up
in front of	off	through	upon
inside	on	throughout	with
in spite of	on account of	to	within
instead of		toward	without
into	out	under	
like	out of	underneath	

NOTE Prepositions that consist of more than one word, such as *in front of*, are called ***compound prepositions.***

Exercise 12 Identifying Prepositions

Identify each preposition in the following sentences. Be sure to include all parts of any compound prepositions you find.

EXAMPLE 1. Throughout the centuries people have read about the legend of Romulus and Remus.

1. Throughout, about, of

1. According to legend, Mars, the god of war in Roman mythology, was the father of the twin brothers Romulus and Remus.
2. When the twins were infants, an evil ruler had them placed in a basket and cast into the Tiber River.
3. Fortunately, they safely drifted to the bank of the river.
4. There they were rescued by a wolf.
5. Later they were found by a shepherd and his wife.
6. When the twins were adults, they tried building a city on the site where they had been rescued.
7. Instead of working together, however, the twins fought against each other.
8. During the quarrel Romulus killed Remus.
9. Then, the legend continues, Romulus founded the city of Rome in approximately 753 B.C.
10. Out of hundreds of legends about the founding of Rome, this one has remained among the best known.

GRAMMAR

The Prepositional Phrase

Reference Note

For more information about **prepositional phrases,** see page 416.

All together, the preposition, the object of the preposition, and any modifiers of the object are called a ***prepositional phrase.***

EXAMPLE The tired tourists climbed **onto the crowded bus.** [The prepositional phrase consists of the preposition *onto,* its object *bus,* and two adjectives modifying the object—*the* and *crowded.*]

Reference Note

For more about **infinitives,** see page 508.

NOTE Be careful not to confuse a prepositional phrase that begins with *to* (*to town, to her club*) with an infinitive that begins with *to* (*to run, to be seen*). Remember: A prepositional phrase has a noun or a pronoun as an object.

Exercise 13 Identifying Prepositional Phrases

Identify the prepositional phrase or phrases in each of the following sentences. Then, underline each preposition.

EXAMPLE 1. Walt Whitman wrote the very moving poem "O Captain! My Captain!" about President Abraham Lincoln.

1. *about Abraham Lincoln*

1. In Whitman's poem, the captain directs his ship toward a safe harbor.
2. The captain represents Abraham Lincoln, and the ship is the ship of state.
3. The captain has just sailed his ship through stormy weather.
4. This voyage across rough seas symbolizes the Civil War.
5. On the shore, people joyfully celebrate the ship's safe arrival.
6. One of the ship's crew addresses his captain, "O Captain! My Captain! rise up and hear the bells."
7. Sadly, everyone except the captain can hear the rejoicing.
8. The speaker in the poem says that the captain "has no pulse nor will."
9. The captain has died during the voyage, just as Lincoln died at the end of the Civil War.
10. According to many people, "O Captain! My Captain!" is one of Whitman's finest poems.

Adverb or Preposition?

Some words may be used as both prepositions and adverbs. To tell an adverb from a preposition, remember that a preposition always has a noun or pronoun as an object.

ADVERB The plane circled **above.**
PREPOSITION The plane circled **above** the field.

ADVERB Please go **inside** soon.
PREPOSITION Please go **inside** the house soon.

Exercise 14 Writing Sentences with Adverbs and Prepositions

Use each of the following words in two sentences, first as an adverb and then as a preposition. Underline the given word.

EXAMPLE **1.** along

1. Do you have to bring your little brother along?
Wildflowers were blooming along the riverbank.

1. off **3.** below **5.** down **7.** on **9.** around
2. across **4.** outside **6.** under **8.** about **10.** near

The Conjunction

12d. A *conjunction* is a word used to join words or groups of words.

Coordinating conjunctions join words or groups of words that are used in the same way.

Coordinating Conjunctions						
and	but	for	nor	or	so	yet

EXAMPLES Theo **or** Tyler [two nouns]

quickly **but** carefully [two adverbs]

through a forest **and** across a river [two prepositional phrases]

Cocker spaniels make good pets, **but** they require a lot of grooming. [two clauses]

You can remember the coordinating conjuctions as FANBOYS.
For
And
Nor
But
Or
Yet
So

GRAMMAR

STYLE TIP

The coordinating conjunction *so* is often overused. For variety, reword a sentence to avoid using *so*.

EXAMPLE
You are new, **so** you might get lost.

REVISED
Because you are new, you might get lost.

NOTE When *for* is used as a conjunction, it connects clauses. On all other occasions, *for* is used as a preposition.

CONJUNCTION We wrote to the tourist bureau, **for** we wanted information on places to visit.

PREPOSITION We waited patiently **for** a reply.

Correlative conjunctions are pairs of conjunctions that join words or word groups that are used in the same way.

Correlative Conjunctions		
both . . . and	either . . . or	neither . . . nor
whether . . . or	not only . . . but also	

EXAMPLES **Both** horses **and** cattle were brought to North America by the Spanish. [The correlative conjunction joins two nouns.]

The student council will meet **not only** on Tuesday **but also** on Thursday. [The correlative conjunction joins two prepositional phrases.]

I don't know **whether** to walk **or** to ride my bike to the grocery store. [The correlative conjunction joins two infinitive phrases.]

Either help me set the table now, **or** wash the dishes later. [The correlative conjunction joins two clauses.]

Reference Note

A third kind of conjunction—the ***subordinating conjunction***—is discussed on page 448.

Exercise 15 Identifying Coordinating and Correlative Conjunctions

Identify each of the conjunctions in the following sentences as *coordinating* or *correlative.* Be prepared to tell what words or word groups the conjunctions join.

EXAMPLE 1. The man and women in the picture on the next page are wearing African clothes.
1. *and—coordinating*

HELP

In the example, the conjunction *and* joins the nouns *man* and *women.*

1. African clothing is fashionable today for both men and women in the United States.

2. People wear not only clothes of African design but also Western-style clothes made of African materials.
3. American women have worn modified African headdresses for years, but nowadays men are wearing African headgear, too.
4. Men and women sometimes wear *kufi* hats, which originated with Muslims.
5. Both women's dresses and women's coats are especially adaptable to African fashions.
6. Many women wear African jewelry or scarves.
7. Clothes made of such materials as *kente* cloth from Ghana, *ashioke* cloth from Nigeria, and *dogon* cloth from Mali have become quite popular.
8. These fabrics are decorated either with brightly colored printed designs or with stripes.
9. African-inspired clothes usually fit in whether you are at work or at play.
10. African styles are popular, for they show appreciation of ancient cultures.

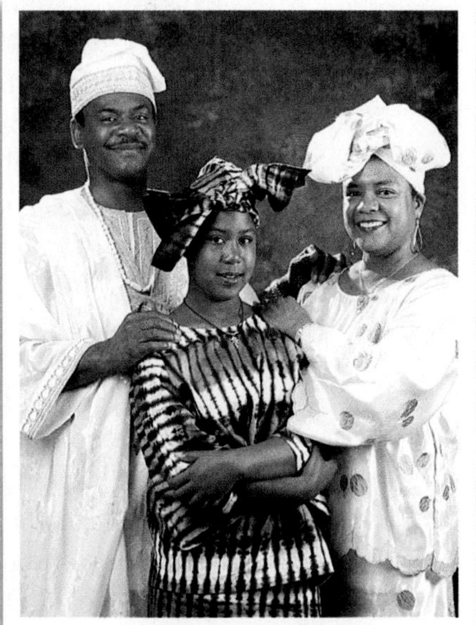

The Interjection

12e. An *interjection* is a word used to express emotion.

An interjection has no grammatical relation to other words in the sentence. Usually an interjection is followed by an exclamation point. Sometimes an interjection is set off by a comma or commas.

EXAMPLES **Oh!** You surprised me.

Wow! Am I tired!

Aha, you've discovered the secret.

Could you**,** **well,** be quiet, please?

NOTE Interjections are common in informal writing and speaking situations. However, interjections are rarely used in formal situations, except as part of written dialogue.

GRAMMAR

Exercise 16 **Identifying Interjections**

Some fairy-tale characters are meeting to discuss their image. They are worried that the familiar fairy tales make them look stupid or silly. Identify the ten interjections used in the following dialogue. Then, try to guess who the four fairy-tale speakers are.

EXAMPLE 1. "Hooray! We're finally getting a chance to tell our side of the stories!"

1. *Hooray*

1. "Beans! It's not fair what they say. I knew I was taking a giant step that day."
2. "Well, it's not fair what they say about us, either. Don't you think Papa and Mama saw that little blond girl snooping around our house?"
3. "Yeah! Don't you think I intended to buy magic beans?"
4. "You guys don't have it as bad as I do. Ugh! How dumb do people think I am? Of course I'd know my own grandmother when I saw her."
5. "Sure! I think your cloak was over your eyes, but how about me? I didn't go near those three pigs."
6. "What! Next you'll probably tell me that I didn't see your brother at Grandmother's house."
7. "Humph! I don't know what you really saw. It's difficult to tell sometimes in the woods."
8. "Aw, let's not argue. We've got to put our best feet forward—all the way up the beanstalk if need be."
9. "Yes! I want to give people the real story about that kid who broke my bed."
10. "Great! I'm ready to squeal on those three little pigs!"

Determining Parts of Speech

12f. The way a word is used in a sentence determines what part of speech it is.

The same word may be used as different parts of speech.

PRONOUN **Each** was painted blue.
ADJECTIVE **Each** ornament was painted blue.

ADVERB The raccoon climbed **down.**
PREPOSITION The raccoon climbed **down** the hill.

NOUN The crew has spotted **land.**
VERB The crew can **land** here safely.

INTERJECTION **Well,** he seems healthy.
ADJECTIVE He seems **well.**

Review D Identifying Parts of Speech

Identify the part of speech of the italicized word in each sentence. Be prepared to explain your answers.

EXAMPLES
1. The *ship* entered the harbor slowly.
   1. noun
2. Did they *ship* the package to Dee and Seth?
   2. verb

1. The English test was easy *for* him.
2. He didn't go to the movies, *for* he wanted to practice on the drums.
3. It was a steep *climb,* but we made it to the top of the hill.
4. Kimiko and I *climb* the stairs for exercise.
5. *Some* volunteered to sell tickets.
6. We donated *some* clothes to the rummage sale.
7. Looking for shells, the girl strolled *along* the shore.
8. When we went sailing, Raúl and Manuel came *along.*
9. I lost *my* book report!
10. *My*! This is not a good day!

HELP— You may want to review Chapter 11 before working on Review D.

Review E Identifying Parts of Speech

Identify the part of speech of each italicized word or word group in the following paragraphs.

EXAMPLES Dancing **[1]** *may be* easy for **[2]** *some,* but I have **[3]** *always* had **[4]** *two* left **[5]** *feet.*

1. verb *3. adverb* *5. noun*
2. pronoun *4. adjective*

[1] *Yesterday* after [2] *school,* one of my friends [3] *tried* to teach [4] *me* some new dance steps. [5] *Well,* I was [6] *so* embarrassed I could have hidden [7] *in* the [8] *closet.* My feet [9] *seem* to have [10] *minds* of [11] *their* own [12] *and* do [13] *not* do what I want them to.

HELP— You may want to review Chapter 11 before working on Review E.

"You're [14] *too* tense when you dance, [15] *or* you're trying too hard. [16] *You* [17] *should relax* more," my friend told me.

[18] "*What*! [19] *How* can I relax?" I groaned. [20] "*No one* [21] *can relax* when his body goes [22] *left* and his feet go right!" At that point, I [23] *decided* to give up dancing, but I know I'll try [24] *again* [25] *another* day.

GRAMMAR

Review F Using Different Parts of Speech

Complete the following poem by adding words that are the parts of speech called for in the blank spaces.

EXAMPLES Why **[1]** (__verb__) Robin all alone?
[2] (__adverb__) have all the others gone?

1. *Why sits Robin all alone?*
2. *Where have all the others gone?*

[1] (interjection), Robin thought her day was just fine.
She [2] (__verb__) to the concert, and there wasn't a line.

Then when she got in [3] (conjunction) sat herself down,
People were leaving [4] (preposition) rows all around.

You can see that Robin looks [5] (__adverb__) dejected;
She thinks that she [6] (__verb__) rejected.

If only she could have the chairs as her friends—
[7] (interjection)!—she'd have friends without end.

She sat [8] (__adverb__) and worried and pondered.
Was the problem with her [9] (conjunction) the others?
she wondered.

Then she [10] (__verb__) at her ticket and saw she was late,
So she imagined the concert, and it was just great!

Chapter Review

A. Identifying Verbs, Adverbs, Prepositions, Conjunctions, and Interjections

Label the italicized word or word group in each of the following sentences as an *action verb,* a *linking verb,* an *adverb,* a *preposition,* a *conjunction,* or an *interjection.*

1. Rosie hit a home run *and* tied up the score.
2. *Wow,* that's the best meal I've eaten in a long time!
3. School *can be* fun sometimes.
4. Neither Carlos nor Jan wanted to go *very* far into the water.
5. That dog looks mean *in spite of* his wagging tail.
6. *Have* you ever *celebrated* Cinco de Mayo?
7. If Ken will *not* help us finish the project, then he cannot share in the rewards.
8. My older sister was a cheerleader *during* her senior year.
9. The road that runs *near* the railroad tracks is usually crowded.
10. Several of my friends *enjoy* the music of Quincy Jones.
11. No one could do much to help, *for* the damage had already been done.
12. *Where* have you been putting the corrected papers?
13. *Oh,* I didn't know he had already volunteered.
14. Jodie *was taking* in the wash for her mother.
15. Surely Ms. Kwan *does*n't *expect* us to finish our art projects by today.
16. May I have a glass of milk and a club sandwich *without* onions?
17. James *became* impatient, but he waited quietly.
18. My uncle *always* brings us interesting presents when he visits during Hanukkah.
19. The car swerved suddenly to avoid the dog, *yet* the driver remained in control.
20. The rose *smells* lovely.

GRAMMAR

HELP
Keep in mind that correlative conjunctions and some prepositions have more than one word.

B. Identifying Different Parts of Speech

Identify each italicized word or word group in the following sentences as a *verb,* an *adverb,* a *preposition,* or a *conjunction.*

21. I *read* an interesting article *about* the great Italian composer Giuseppe Verdi.

22. Born near Parma in 1813, the son of a grocer, he *studied* music locally *but* was rejected by the prestigious Milan Conservatory.

23. *However,* he persevered, *and* when he was twenty-six, his first opera was accepted by the famous La Scala opera house.

24. *Shortly* afterward, personal tragedy hit him hard, and he *nearly* gave up.

25. The success *of* his next opera, Nabucco, *inspired* him to continue.

26. Verdi, an Italian patriot, *soon* became a symbol of Italy's struggle *for* unity.

27. He was admired *not only* for his operas, *but also* for his political career.

28. In fact, he was *eventually* elected a senator *in* the new parliament of united Italy.

29. At the same time, he *was becoming* famous for operatic masterpieces such as La Traviata, Rigoletto, and Aida.

30. Giuseppe Verdi was *so* admired by his fellow Italians that a period of national mourning *was declared* following his death in 1901.

HELP
You may want to review Chapter 11 before working on Part C.

C. Identifying Parts of Speech

Identify the part of speech of the italicized word in each sentence. Be prepared to explain your answers.

31. *Some* even made it to the top before noon.

32. They bought *some* tomatoes and peppers in the market.

33. The lion cubs waited their turn, *for* an adult lion was drinking at the water hole.

34. These large tires are made especially *for* that kind of mountain bicycle.

35. Every morning, Fran goes out for a *run.*

36. My doctor recommended that I *run* in moderation.

37. I wanted to nap, *so* I went home early.
38. The dogs were *so* excited that one of them knocked over the coat rack.
39. I enjoyed walking *along* Ipanema Beach in Rio.
40. Come *along*, it's time to go!

Writing Application

Using Verbs in a Story

Action Verbs Your little sister likes for you to tell her exciting stories, but you've run out of new ones. To get ideas for new stories, you think about events you've read about or seen. Write a summary of an exciting incident from a book, a movie, or a television show. Use action verbs that are fresh and lively.

Prewriting Think about books that you've read recently or movies and television shows that you've seen. Choose an exciting incident from one of these works, and write what you remember about that incident.

Writing As you write your first draft, think about how you're presenting the information. When telling a story, you should usually use chronological order. This method would be easiest for your young reader to follow. Try to use fresh, lively action verbs.

Revising Imagine that you are a young child hearing the story for the first time. Look over your summary, and ask yourself if the verbs used in the story would help you picture what happened.

Publishing Make sure that each verb you use is in the correct form and tense. Also, check to make sure that any pronouns, conjunctions, adverbs, and interjections are used correctly. Proofread your story for errors in usage, spelling, and punctuation. Then, with your teacher's permission, share your story with the class by reading it aloud or posting the completed story on a class bulletin board.

Complements

Direct and Indirect Objects, Subject Complements

Diagnostic Preview

Identifying Complements

Identify each italicized word in the following paragraphs as a *direct object,* an *indirect object,* a *predicate nominative,* or a *predicate adjective.*

EXAMPLES I enjoy [**1**] *cooking* but it can be hard [**2**] *work.*

1. *cooking—direct object*
2. *work—predicate nominative*

My dad has been giving [**1**] *me* cooking [**2**] *lessons* since last summer. At first, I was [**3**] *reluctant* to tell the guys because some of them think that cooking is a girl's [**4**] *job.* Dad told me to remind them that we guys eat [**5**] *meals* just as often as girls do. He also said that cooking is an excellent [**6**] *way* for us to do our share of the work around the house.

When I began, I could hardly boil [**7**] *water* without fouling up, but Dad remained [**8**] *patient* and showed [**9**] *me* the correct and easiest ways to do things. For example, did you know that water will boil faster if it has a little [**10**] *salt* in it or that corn-starch can be an excellent thickening [**11**] *agent* in everything from batter to gravy?

My first attempts tasted [**12**] *awful,* but gradually I've become a fairly good [**13**] *cook.* My best main dish is chicken [**14**] *stew.* Although stew doesn't require the highest [**15**] *grade* of chicken, a good baking hen will give [16] *it* a much better taste. I am always very [17] *careful* about choosing the vegetables, too. Maybe I am too [18] *picky,* but I use only the best [19] *ingredients.* I know, though, that when I serve my [20] *family* my stew, they say it is their favorite dish.

Recognizing Complements

13a. A *complement* is a word or a word group that completes the meaning of a verb.

Every sentence has at least one subject and verb. Often a verb also needs a complement to make the sentence complete.

	S V
INCOMPLETE	Marlene brought [*what?*]
	S V C
COMPLETE	Marlene brought **sandwiches.**
	S V
INCOMPLETE	Carlos thanked [*whom?*]
	S V C
COMPLETE	Carlos thanked **her.**
	S V
INCOMPLETE	We were [*what?*]
	S V C
COMPLETE	We were **hungry.**

As you can see, a complement may be a noun, a pronoun, or an adjective.

EXAMPLES My uncle sent **me** a **postcard.** [The pronoun *me* and the noun *postcard* complete the meaning of the verb by telling *what* was sent and *to whom* it was sent.]

The Ephron sisters are **writers.** [The noun *writers* completes the meaning of the verb *are* by identifying the sisters.]

This story is **exciting.** [The adjective *exciting* completes the meaning of the verb *is* by describing the story.]

GRAMMAR

Reference Note

For information on **adverbs,** see page 381. For information on **prepositional phrases,** see page 388.

TIPS & TRICKS

If you have trouble finding the complement in a sentence, try this trick. Cross out all the prepositional phrases first. Then, look for the subject, verb, and complement in the rest of the sentence.

EXAMPLE

Juanita wrote the letter ~~on a sheet of plain notebook paper.~~ [The subject is *Juanita.* The verb is *wrote. Sheet* and *paper* cannot be complements because they are both in prepositional phrases. The complement is *letter.*]

An adverb is never a complement.

ADVERB The dog is **outside.** [*Outside* modifies the verb by telling where the dog is.]

COMPLEMENT The dog is **friendly.** [The adjective *friendly* modifies the subject by telling what kind of dog.]

A complement is never part of a prepositional phrase.

OBJECT OF PREPOSITION Ben is studying for his geography **test.** [*Test* is the object of the preposition *for.*]

COMPLEMENT Ben is studying his geography **notes.**

Exercise 1 Identifying Subjects, Verbs, and Complements

Identify the subject, verb, and complement in each of the following sentences.

EXAMPLE
1. William Shakespeare was one of the owners of the Globe Theatre.
   1. *William Shakespeare—subject; was—verb; one—complement*

1. During Shakespeare's time, plays were a common form of entertainment in England.
2. A great many people watched plays at the most popular playhouse in London—the Globe Theatre.
3. Richard and Cuthbert Burbage built the Globe in 1599.
4. In this drawing, you can see many of the differences between the Globe and most modern theaters.

The Granger Collection, New York

5. The Globe Theatre was a building with eight sides.
6. The building enclosed a spacious inner courtyard.
7. The stage was a raised platform at one end of the courtyard.
8. Some of the audience watched the play from seats around the courtyard.
9. Many playgoers, however, did not have seats during a performance.
10. These people filled the courtyard in front of the stage.

Exercise 2 **Writing Sentences with Complements**

Write ten sentences by adding a different complement to each of the following subject-verb pairs.

		Subject	Verb
EXAMPLE	1.	kittens	like
	1.	*The kittens like cream.*	

	Subject	Verb
1.	men	asked
2.	days	are
3.	Pam	sent
4.	runner	seemed
5.	weather	will be
6.	girls	climbed
7.	letter	contained
8.	elephant	is
9.	neighbors	kept
10.	dog	wants

Objects of Verbs

Direct objects and ***indirect objects*** complete the meaning of transitive verbs.

Direct Objects

13b. A *direct object* is a noun, pronoun, or word group that tells who or what receives the action of the verb.

A direct object answers the question "Whom?" or "What?" after a transitive verb.

EXAMPLES Our history class built a **model** of the Alamo. [The noun *model* receives the action of the verb *built* and tells *what* the class built.]

Has the freeze destroyed **some** of the crops? [The pronoun *some* receives the action of the verb *Has destroyed* and tells *what* the freeze has destroyed.]

Mr. Ito greets **whoever comes into the shop.** [The noun clause *whoever comes into the shop* receives the action of the verb *greets* and tells *whom* Mr. Ito greets.]

Reference Note

For more information about **transitive verbs,** see page 379.

TIPS & TRICKS

To find the direct object in a sentence, say the verb and then ask "What?" or "Whom?"

EXAMPLE

In his free time, Eduardo writes mystery stories. [Writes what? Stories.] *Stories* is the direct object.

Reference Note

For more about **noun clauses,** see page 450.

Reference Note

For more about **linking verbs,** see page 374.

GRAMMAR

NOTE A direct object can never complete the meaning of a linking verb because a linking verb does not express action.

LINKING VERB William Wordsworth **became** poet laureate of England in 1843. [The verb *became* does not express action. Therefore, it has no direct object.]

Reference Note

For more information about **prepositional phrases,** see page 388.

A direct object is never part of a prepositional phrase.

EXAMPLE He walked for hours in the English countryside. [*Hours* is not a direct object of the verb *walked*. It is the object of the preposition *for. Countryside* is not a direct object either. It is the object of the preposition *in*. The sentence has no direct object.]

NOTE A direct object may be compound.

EXAMPLES Mrs. Neiman planted **tulips** and **daffodils.**

The man wore a white **beard,** a red **suit,** and black **boots.**

HELP—
One sentence in Exercise 3 contains a compound direct object.

Exercise 3 Identifying Verbs and Direct Objects

Identify the verb and its direct object in each of the following sentences.

EXAMPLE 1. Volunteers distributed food and water to the flood victims.
1. *distributed—food, water*

1. On the plains of the American West, the Cheyenne hunted buffalo for food and clothing.
2. We watched a performance of Lorraine Hansberry's *A Raisin in the Sun.*
3. During most of its history, the United States has welcomed refugees from other countries.
4. The leading man wore a hat with a large plume.
5. Are you recycling bottles and cans?
6. After the game, the coach answered questions from the sports reporters.
7. Did you see her performance on television?
8. The researchers followed the birds' migration from Mexico to Canada.

9. Mayor Fiorello La Guardia governed New York City during the Depression.
10. Have the movie theaters announced the special discount for teenagers yet?

Indirect Objects

13c. An *indirect object* is a noun, pronoun, or word group that sometimes appears in sentences containing direct objects.

An indirect object tells *to whom* or *to what* or *for whom* or *for what* the action of the verb is done.

EXAMPLES Luke showed the **class** his collection of comic books. [The noun *class* tells *to whom* Luke showed his collection.]

Sarita bought **us** a chess set. [The pronoun *us* tells *for whom* Sarita bought a chess set.]

Dad gave **whatever needed fixing** his full attention. [The noun clause *whatever needed fixing* tells *to what* Dad gave his attention.]

NOTE Linking verbs do not have indirect objects.

LINKING VERB Her mother **was** a collector of rare books. [The linking verb *was* does not express action, so it cannot have an indirect object.]

An indirect object, like a direct object, is never in a prepositional phrase. A noun or pronoun that follows *to* or *for* is the object of the preposition, not an indirect object.

OBJECT OF PREPOSITION He gave some flowers to his **sister.** [*Sister* is the object of the preposition *to*.]

INDIRECT OBJECT He gave his **sister** some flowers.

NOTE Like a direct object, an indirect object may be compound.

EXAMPLES Uncle Alphonso bought my **brother** and **me** an aquarium.

Tanya sent **Kim, Raymond,** and **him** invitations.

TIPS & TRICKS

A sentence with an indirect object will always have a direct object, too. What are the direct objects in the examples following Rule 13c?

Reference Note

For more about **noun clauses,** see page 450.

HELP

An indirect object usually comes between a verb and a direct object.

GRAMMAR

HELP—
Not every sentence in Exercise 4 has an indirect object.

Exercise 4 Identifying Direct Objects and Indirect Objects

Identify the direct objects and the indirect objects in the following sentences.

EXAMPLE 1. They gave us their solemn promise.
1. *promise—direct object; us—indirect object*

1. They sent me on a wild-goose chase.
2. Gloria mailed the company a check yesterday.
3. The speaker showed the audience the slides of Zimbabwe.
4. Juan would not deliberately tell you and me a lie.
5. The coach praised the students for their school spirit.
6. I sent my cousins some embroidered pillows for their new apartment in New York.
7. The art teacher displayed the students' paintings.
8. Sue's parents shipped her the books and the magazines.
9. Carly, Mary Ellen, and Doreen taught themselves the importance of hard work.
10. In most foreign countries, United States citizens must carry their passports for identification.

HELP—
Not every sentence in Review A has an indirect object.

Review A Identifying Direct Objects and Indirect Objects

Identify the direct objects and the indirect objects in each of the following sentences.

EXAMPLE 1. The spring rodeo gives our town an exciting weekend.
1. *weekend—direct object; town—indirect object*

1. This year Mrs. Perez taught our class many interesting facts about rodeos.
2. She told us stories about the earliest rodeos, which were held more than a hundred years ago.
3. The word *rodeo* means "roundup" in Spanish.
4. Mrs. Perez also showed us drawings and pictures of some well-known rodeo performers.
5. The Choctaw roper Clyde Burk especially caught the interest of our class.
6. The Rodeo Cowboys Association awarded Burk four world championships during his career.
7. For years, Burk entertained audiences with his roping skill.

8. He also trained some of the best rodeo horses available.
9. The picture on the previous page shows Clyde Burk on his horse Baldy.
10. Burk often gave Baldy credit for their success.

Subject Complements

13d. A *subject complement* is a word or word group that completes the meaning of a linking verb and that identifies or describes the subject.

EXAMPLES Alice Eng is a dedicated **teacher.** [The noun *teacher* completes the meaning of the linking verb *is* and identifies the subject *Alice Eng.*]

The lemonade tastes **sour.** [*Sour* completes the meaning of the linking verb *tastes* and describes the subject *lemonade*.]

The new pliers were **what she wanted.** [The noun clause *what she wanted* completes the meaning of the linking verb *were* and identifies the subject *pliers*.]

There are two kinds of subject complements—the *predicate nominative* and the *predicate adjective.*

Predicate Nominatives

13e. A *predicate nominative* is a word or word group that is in the predicate and that identifies the subject or refers to it.

A predicate nominative may be a noun, a pronoun, or a word group that functions as a noun. A predicate nominative completes the meaning of a linking verb.

EXAMPLES Mr. Richards became **mayor** of a small town in Ohio. [The noun *mayor* identifies the subject *Mr. Richards.*]

My aunt's niece is **she.** [The pronoun *she* identifies *niece.*]

Is the winner **whoever gets the most votes**? [The noun clause *whoever gets the most votes* identifies the subject *winner.*]

GRAMMAR

Reference Note

For more about **linking verbs,** see page 374.

Reference Note

For more about **noun clauses,** see page 450.

TIPS & TRICKS

To find the subject complement in an interrogative sentence, rearrange the sentence to make a statement.

EXAMPLE
Was the dog muddy?
The dog was **muddy.**

To find the subject complement in an imperative sentence, insert the understood subject *you.*

EXAMPLE
Stay still.
(You) stay **still.**

Predicate nominatives do not appear in prepositional phrases.

EXAMPLE Sophia is **one** of my closest friends. [*One* is the predicate nominative. *Friends* is the object of the preposition *of,* not the predicate nominative.]

NOTE Predicate nominatives may be compound.

EXAMPLE Hernando de Soto was a **soldier** and a **diplomat.**

Exercise 5 Identifying Predicate Nominatives

Identify the predicate nominatives in each of the following sentences.

EXAMPLE 1. Botany, a branch of biology, is the study of plants.
1. study

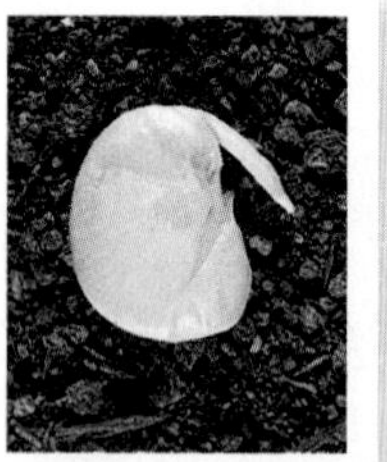

1. Horticulture is the art or science of growing flowers, fruits, vegetables, and other plants.
2. Through germination, a seed becomes a plant.
3. The developing plant is a seedling.
4. Growing plants is a pleasure for many people.
5. With light and moisture, seedlings will become healthy plants.
6. Nasturtiums are flowers that can be eaten.
7. Rain is a welcome sight for gardeners.
8. *Helio,* from the Greek language, is a word meaning "sun."
9. Some flowers that turn to the sun, like sunflowers, are heliotropes.
10. Some other flowers always remain shade lovers.

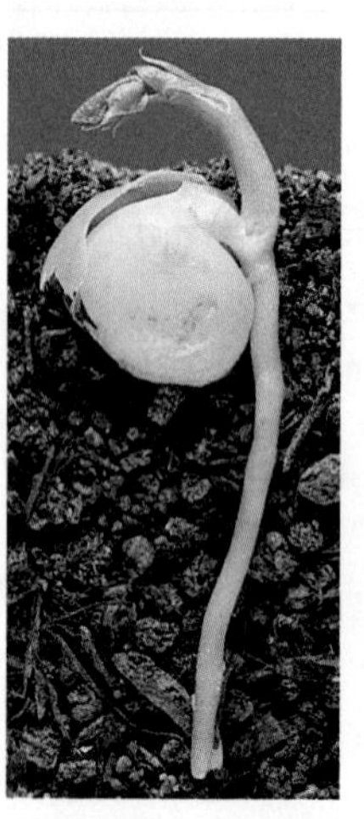

Predicate Adjectives

13f. A *predicate adjective* is an adjective that is in the predicate and that describes the subject.

A predicate adjective completes the meaning of a linking verb.

EXAMPLES A nuclear reactor is very **powerful.** [The adjective *powerful* completes the meaning of the linking verb *is* and describes the subject *reactor.*]

This chili tastes **spicy.** [The adjective *spicy* completes the meaning of the linking verb *tastes* and describes the subject *chili.*]

How **cheerful** the baby is! [The adjective *cheerful* completes the meaning of the verb *is* and describes the subject *baby.*]

NOTE Predicate adjectives may be compound.

EXAMPLE A computer can be **fun, helpful,** and sometimes **frustrating.**

Exercise 6 Identifying Predicate Adjectives

Identify the predicate adjective or adjectives in each of the following sentences.

EXAMPLE **1.** San Francisco's Chinatown is large and colorful.

1. large, colorful

1. The great stone dogs that guard the entrance to Chinatown look a bit frightening.
2. The streets there are crowded and full of bustling activity.
3. The special foods and beverages at the tearooms and restaurants smell wonderful.
4. To an outsider, the mixture of Chinese and English languages can sound both mysterious and intriguing.
5. The art at the Chinese Culture Center is impressive.
6. The Chinese Historical Society of America is fascinating.
7. Taking a walking tour of Chinatown is tiring.
8. Chinatown appears huge, and it is; it covers about sixteen square blocks.
9. To be in the midst of it feels exciting.
10. After a while, the surroundings become familiar.

STYLE TIP

Overusing the linking verb *be* can make writing dull and lifeless. As you review your writing, you may get the feeling that nothing is happening, that nobody is doing anything. That feeling is one sign that your writing may contain too many *be* verbs. Wherever possible, replace a dull *be* verb with a verb that expresses action.

BE VERB
A secret hope **was** in his heart.

ACTION VERB
A secret hope **surged** in his heart.

Some verbs, such as *look, grow,* and *feel,* may be used as either linking verbs or action verbs.

LINKING VERB The gardener **grew** tired. [*Grew* is a linking verb; it links the predicate adjective *tired* to the subject *gardener.*]

ACTION VERB The gardener **grew** carrots. [*Grew* is an action verb; it is followed by the direct object *carrots,* which tells what the gardener grew.]

Review B Identifying Linking Verbs and Subject Complements

Identify the linking verb and the subject complement in each of the following sentences. Then, identify each complement as a *predicate nominative* or a *predicate adjective.*

EXAMPLE **1.** The raincoat looked too short for me.
1. looked; short—predicate adjective

1. The package from Aunt Janice felt light.
2. I am the one who called you yesterday.
3. Many public buildings in the East are proof of I. M. Pei's architectural skill.
4. The downtown mall appeared especially busy today.
5. Sally Ride sounded excited and confident during the television interview.
6. The actress playing the lead is she.
7. These questions seem easier to me than the ones on the last two tests.
8. The singer's clothing became a symbol that her fans imitated.
9. Some poems, such as "The Bells" and "The Raven," are delightfully rhythmical.
10. While the mountain lion looked around for food, the fawn remained perfectly still.

Review C Identifying Subject Complements

Each of the following sentences has at least one subject complement. Identify each complement as a *predicate nominative* or a *predicate adjective.*

EXAMPLE **1.** All the food at the Spanish Club dinner was terrific.
1. terrific—predicate adjective

1. Of the Mexican foods brought to the dinner, the tacos and Juan's fajitas were the most popular dishes.
2. The *ensalada campesina,* or peasant salad of Chile, which contained chickpeas, was Rosalinda's contribution.
3. The Ecuadorean tamales not only looked good but also tasted great.
4. The baked fish fillets from Bolivia were spicy and quite appetizing.
5. Peru is famous for its soups, and the shrimp soup was a winner.
6. The noodles with mushroom sauce are a specialty of Paraguay.
7. The Spanish cauliflower with garlic and onions was a treat but seemed too exotic for some students.
8. However, the pan of *hallacas,* the national cornmeal dish of Venezuela, was soon empty.
9. *Arroz con coco,* or coconut rice, from Puerto Rico quickly became the most requested dessert.
10. After dinner, all of us certainly felt full and much more knowledgeable about foods from Spanish-speaking countries.

GRAMMAR

Review D Identifying Complements

For each of the following sentences, identify each italicized complement as a *direct object,* an *indirect object,* a *predicate nominative,* or a *predicate adjective.*

EXAMPLE 1. Because they want artistic *freedom,* many people from other countries become United States *citizens.*

1. *freedom—direct object; citizens—predicate nominative*

1. Gilberto Zaldivar's story is a good *example.*
2. Zaldivar was an *accountant* and a community theater *producer* in Havana, Cuba, in 1961.
3. He became *unhappy* and *frustrated* with the Cuban government's control over the arts.
4. He left his *job* and his *homeland* and started a new *life* in New York City.
5. The change brought *Zaldivar* many *opportunities.*
6. It also gave *audiences* in the United States a new entertainment *experience.*

7. Zaldivar was a *cofounder* of the Repertorio Español in 1968.
8. This company quickly established a *reputation* as the country's best Spanish-language theater troupe.
9. Their productions were *fresh* and *unfamiliar* to audiences.
10. Throughout the years, the company has performed numerous Spanish *classics* as well as new plays.

Review E Writing Sentences with Complements

Write sentences according to the following guidelines. Underline each direct object, indirect object, predicate nominative, or predicate adjective that you write.

EXAMPLE 1. Write a sentence with a three-part compound predicate adjective.

1. The fire is warm, cheery, and fragrant.

1. Write a sentence with a direct object.
2. Write a sentence with a predicate nominative.
3. Write a sentence with a predicate adjective.
4. Write a sentence with an indirect object and a direct object.
5. Write a sentence without a complement.
6. Write a sentence with a compound indirect object and a direct object.
7. Write a sentence with a compound predicate nominative.
8. Write a sentence with a compound direct object.
9. Write a sentence with a compound predicate adjective.
10. Write a sentence with a three-part compound direct object.

Chapter Review

A. Identifying Direct Objects and Indirect Objects

Identify the direct objects and the indirect objects in the following sentences.

1. The coach awarded her a varsity letter.
2. My pen pal from Guatemala visited me last summer.
3. Did you hear the news?
4. The car stalled, and we couldn't restart it.
5. Dad told him and me stories about growing up in Idaho.
6. I bought a CD of Italian folk songs for her birthday.
7. We called the dogs and gave them their food.
8. Timmy, could you give the baby his bath?
9. Our dog and cat need rabies vaccinations.
10. Anita proudly mounted the dais, and the principal gave her the gold medal.

B. Identifying Subject Complements

Each of the following sentences has at least one subject complement. Write each complement, and identify it as a *predicate nominative* or a *predicate adjective.*

11. Enid Blyton has always been one of the most popular children's authors.
12. All of the astronauts look confident.
13. The entrance to the cave looks a bit narrow to me.
14. That soil seems awfully dry.
15. Angela has become a very good runner.
16. The breeze from the sea feels fresh and cool.
17. James Joyce was a novelist and a short-story writer.
18. History is the study of the past.
19. The cast members seem happy and excited about the good reviews in today's newspapers.
20. You should be careful; that rope is frayed.

GRAMMAR

C. Identifying Complements

Identify each of the italicized words or word groups in the following sentences as a *direct object,* an *indirect object,* a *predicate nominative,* or a *predicate adjective.*

21. Pilar caught the *ball* and threw it to first base.

22. Your cousin seems *nice.*

23. I'm not the *one* who did that.

24. The sun grew *hotter* as the day went on.

25. Mrs. Sato gave *me* a passing grade.

26. Peter Sellers was *famous* for comedy.

27. Amy's two cousins are both truck *drivers.*

28. Have you bought your *tickets* yet?

29. Did James ride his new *bike* to school today?

30. The angry customer sent the *manager* a letter of complaint.

31. The nurse gave *Linda* a flu shot.

32. Josh often looks *tired* on Monday mornings.

33. With his calloused hands he cannot feel the *texture* of velvet.

34. My sister's room is always *neater* than mine.

35. Heather, who is new at our school, is the nicest *girl* I know.

36. The Algonquians used *toboggans* to haul goods over snow and ice.

37. Dave, throw *Eric* a screen pass.

38. When left to dry in the sun, certain kinds of plums become *prunes.*

39. Dr. Charles Drew gave *science* a better way to process and store blood.

40. Ms. Rosada will be our Spanish *teacher* this fall.

Writing Application
Using Objects in a Letter

Direct and Indirect Objects Imagine that you have just returned from an interesting and enjoyable shopping trip. Write a letter to a friend telling about what happened on this trip. Use direct objects and indirect objects in your letter.

Prewriting You may want to write about an actual shopping trip that you have made recently, perhaps to a shopping mall or a flea market. Otherwise, you can make up a shopping trip to another country or even another planet. Make a list of what you did, what you saw, and what you bought for whom.

Writing As you write your first draft, think about describing your shopping trip in a way that will interest your friend. Use vivid action verbs and specific direct objects and indirect objects. Be sure to tell when and where your trip took place.

Revising Read over your paragraph. Does it clearly tell why the shopping trip was so interesting and enjoyable? If not, you may want to add or change some details. Be sure that your paragraph follows a consistent and sensible order.

Reference Note

For more information about **organizing ideas in a paragraph,** see Chapter 9.

Publishing Proofread your paragraph for errors in grammar, punctuation, and spelling. If you wrote about real places that are near your home, you can use a telephone book to check the spelling of names of stores, shopping malls, or shopping centers. With your teacher's permission, you may want to gather your class's letters together in a binder and create a Smart Shoppers' Guide.

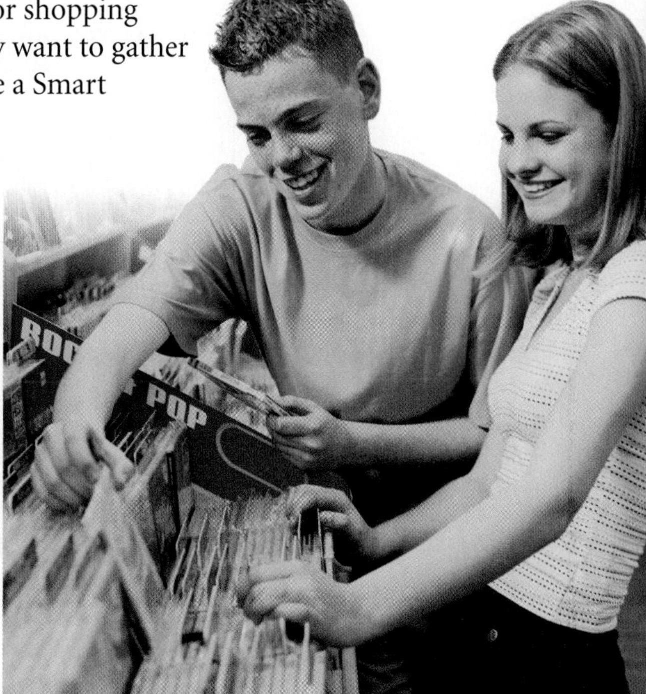

The Phrase

Prepositional, Verbal, and Appositive Phrases

Diagnostic Preview

Identifying Prepositional, Verbal, and Appositive Phrases

Identify each italicized phrase in the following paragraphs as a *prepositional, participial, gerund, infinitive,* or *appositive phrase.* You need not separately identify a prepositional phrase that is part of a larger phrase.

EXAMPLES After [**1**] *giving me my allowance,* my father said [**2**] *not to spend it all in one place.*

1. *giving me my allowance—gerund phrase*
2. *not to spend it all in one place—infinitive phrase*

Gina, [**1**] *my best friend since elementary school,* and I decided [**2**] *to go to the mall after school yesterday.* At first Gina suggested [**3**] *taking the back way* so that we could jog, but I was wearing sandals [**4**] *instead of my track shoes,* so we just walked. Along the way we saw Cathy [**5**] *sitting on her front porch* and asked her if she wanted [**6**] *to join us.* She was earning a little spending money by [**7**] *baby-sitting her neighbor's children,* though, and couldn't leave.

[**8**] *Walking up to the wide glass doors at the mall,* Gina and I looked in our purses. We both had some money and our student passes, so we stopped [**9**] *to get orange juice* while we checked

what movies were playing. None [**10**] *of the four features* looked interesting to us. However, Deven Bowers, [**11**] *a friend from school and an usher at the theater,* said that there would be a sneak preview [**12**] *of a new adventure film* later, so we told him we'd be back then.

Since stores usually do not allow customers to bring food or drinks inside, Gina and I gulped down our orange juice before [**13**] *going into our favorite dress shop.* We looked [**14**] *through most of the sale racks,* but none of the dresses, [**15**] *all of them formal or evening gowns,* appealed to us. A salesclerk asked if we were shopping [**16**] *for something special.* After [**17**] *checking with Gina,* I told the clerk we were just looking, and we left.

We walked past a couple of shops—[**18**] *the health food store and a toy store*—and went into Music World. [**19**] *Seeing several CDs by my favorite group,* I picked out one. By the time we walked out of Music World, I'd spent all my money, so we never did get [**20**] *to go to the movie that day.*

What Is a Phrase?

14a. A *phrase* is a group of related words that is used as a single part of speech and that does not contain both a verb and its subject.

PREPOSITIONAL PHRASE	a message **from the other members of the debate team**
PARTICIPIAL PHRASE	monkeys **swinging through the dense jungle**
INFINITIVE PHRASE	asking **to go with them on their Antarctic expedition**
APPOSITIVE PHRASE	a painting by van Gogh, **the famous Dutch painter**

NOTE A group of words that has both a verb and its subject is called a ***clause.***

EXAMPLES Leta is watching television. [*Leta* is the subject of the verb *is watching.*]

before the train arrived [*Train* is the subject of the verb *arrived.*]

Reference Note

For more about **clauses,** see Chapter 15.

The Prepositional Phrase

14b. A *prepositional phrase* includes a preposition, a noun or pronoun called *the object of the preposition,* and any modifiers of that object.

EXAMPLES The Seine River flows **through Paris.** [The noun *Paris* is the object of the preposition *through.*]

The car **in front of us** slid **into an icy snowbank.** [The pronoun *us* is the object of the compound preposition *in front of.* The noun *snowbank* is the object of the preposition *into.*]

Reference Note

For a list of commonly used **prepositions,** see page 386.

STYLE TIP

Sometimes you can combine two short, choppy sentences by taking a prepositional phrase from one sentence and inserting it into the other.

CHOPPY
That day Lettie received a package. It was from her grandmother.

REVISED
That day Lettie received a package **from her grandmother.**

CRANKSHAFT copyright 1996 Mediagraphics. Reprinted with permission of Universal Press Syndicate. All rights reserved.

Any modifier that comes between a preposition and its object is part of the prepositional phrase.

EXAMPLE **During the stormy night,** the black horse ran off. [The adjectives *the* and *stormy* modify the object *night.*]

An object of the preposition may be compound.

EXAMPLE The dish is filled **with raw carrots and celery.** [Both *carrots* and *celery* are objects of the preposition *with.*]

NOTE Be careful not to confuse a prepositional phrase with an infinitive. A prepositional phrase always has an object that is a noun or a pronoun. An infinitive is a verb form that usually begins with *to.*

PREPOSITIONAL PHRASE When we went **to Florida,** we saw the old Spanish fort in St. Augustine.

INFINITIVE When we were in Florida, we went **to see** the old Spanish fort in St. Augustine.

Reference Note

For more information about **infinitives,** see page 428.

Exercise 1 **Identifying Prepositional Phrases**

Identify the prepositional phrase or phrases in each of the following sentences.

EXAMPLE **1.** Do you recognize the man in this picture?
1. in this picture

1. Hubert "Geese" Ausbie was well known for both his sunny smile and his athletic skill during his career.
2. For twenty-five years, Ausbie played on one of the most popular teams in basketball's history.
3. He was a star with the Globetrotters.
4. The team, which was started in 1927, is famous for its humorous performances.
5. Ausbie discovered that ability must come before showmanship.
6. The combination of skill and humor is what appeals to Globetrotter fans throughout the world.
7. Ausbie, a native of Oklahoma, sharpened his skill on the basketball team at Philander Smith College in Little Rock, Arkansas.
8. In 1961, while he was still in college, he joined the Globetrotters.
9. When he retired from the Globetrotters, Ausbie formed a traveling museum of his many souvenirs.
10. His collection includes the autographs of two presidents and boxing gloves from Muhammad Ali.

The Adjective Phrase

14c. A prepositional phrase that modifies a noun or a pronoun is called an *adjective phrase.*

An adjective phrase tells *what kind* or *which one.*

EXAMPLES Wang Wei was a talented painter **of landscapes.** [The prepositional phrase *of landscapes* modifies the noun *painter,* telling what kind of painter.]

Mrs. O'Meara is the one **on the left.** [The prepositional phrase *on the left* modifies the pronoun *one,* telling which one Mrs. O'Meara is.]

An adjective phrase usually follows the word it modifies. That word may be the object of another prepositional phrase.

EXAMPLES Sicily is an island **off the coast of Italy.** [The phrase *of Italy* modifies *coast,* which is the object of the preposition *off.*]

Rena took notes **on her experiment for science class.** [The phrase *for science class* modifies *experiment,* which is the object of the preposition *on.*]

More than one adjective phrase may modify the same word.

EXAMPLE The glass **of juice on the counter** is for Alise. [The phrases *of juice* and *on the counter* modify the noun *glass.*]

Exercise 2 Identifying Adjective Phrases

Most of the following sentences contain at least one adjective phrase. Identify each adjective phrase and the word it modifies. If a sentence contains no adjective phrase, write *none.*

EXAMPLE **1.** Megan read a book on the origins of words.
1. on the origins—book; of words—origins

1. Mike's sister Tanya, a real terror with a whale of a temper, shouts "Beans!" whenever something goes wrong.
2. Some words for the expression of anger have Latin origins.
3. Many of us in English class wanted to discuss how people express their annoyance.
4. Imagine what would happen if everybody with a bad temper had a bad day simultaneously.
5. We agreed that the best thing to do is to avoid people with chips on their shoulders.
6. Perhaps, whenever they feel bad, those people should use printed signs to warn others.
7. Happenings of little importance can cause some people to get angry.
8. A misunderstanding over some innocent remark may cause trouble.
9. The offended person often creates the real problem in communication.
10. We decided that we had better maintain our own senses of good will and humor.

14 d

GRAMMAR

The Adverb Phrase

14d. A prepositional phrase that modifies a verb, an adjective, or an adverb is called an *adverb phrase.*

An adverb phrase tells *how, when, where, why,* or *to what extent* (*how long, how many, how much,* or *how far*).

EXAMPLES The snow fell **throughout the day.** [The phrase modifies the verb *fell,* telling *when* the snow fell.]

Are you good **at soccer**? [The phrase modifies the adjective *good,* telling *how* you are good.]

Elaine speaks French well **for a beginner.** [The phrase modifies the adverb *well,* telling to *what extent* Elaine speaks French well.]

Mr. Ortiz has taught school **for sixteen years.** [The phrase modifies the verb phrase *has taught,* telling *how long* Mr. Ortiz has taught.]

An adverb phrase may come before or after the word it modifies.

EXAMPLES The sportswriter interviewed the coach **before the game.**

Before the game the sportswriter interviewed the coach. [In each sentence, the phrase modifies the verb *interviewed.*]

More than one adverb phrase may modify the same word.

EXAMPLES **Over the weekend,** the family went **to two different museums.** [Both phrases modify the verb *went.*]

On April 24, 1990, the Hubble Space Telescope was launched **into space.** [Both phrases modify the verb phrase *was launched.*]

TIPS & TRICKS

If you are not sure whether a prepositional phrase is an adjective phrase or an adverb phrase, remember that an adjective phrase almost always follows the word it modifies. If you can move the phrase without changing the meaning of the sentence, the phrase is probably an adverb phrase.

Exercise 3 Identifying Adverb Phrases

Identify the adverb phrase in each of the following sentences. Then, give the word or words it modifies.

EXAMPLE 1. The new restaurant was built over a river.

1. over a river—was built

1. The Bali Hai Restaurant has opened across the road.

GRAMMAR

2. The food is fantastic beyond belief.
3. Almost everyone has gone to the new place.
4. At the Bali Hai you can eat exotic food.
5. Off the river blows a cool breeze.
6. Customers enjoy themselves in the friendly atmosphere.
7. People appear happy with the service.
8. For three weeks the Bali Hai has been crowded.
9. When we went there, we were seated on the patio.
10. None of the items on the menu are too expensive for most people.

Review A Identifying Adjective Phrases and Adverb Phrases

Identify each prepositional phrase in the following sentences. Then, tell whether each phrase is an *adjective phrase* or an *adverb phrase.* Be prepared to tell which word or expression each phrase modifies.

HELP In the example for Review A, the phrase *Through old journals* modifies the verb phrase *have learned* and *about the pioneers* modifies the pronoun *much.*

EXAMPLE 1. Through old journals, we have learned much about the pioneers.

1. *Through old journals—adverb phrase; about the pioneers—adjective phrase*

1. Few of us appreciate the determination of the pioneers who traveled west.
2. The word *travel* comes from the French word *travailler,* which means "to work," and the pioneers definitely worked hard.
3. A typical day's journey began before dawn.
4. On the trip west, people rode in wagons like these.
5. During the day the wagon train traveled slowly over the mountains and across plains and deserts.
6. At dusk, the horses were unhitched from the wagons, and tents were pitched around campfires.

Worthington Whittredge, *Encampment on the Plains.* Autry Museum of Western Heritage, Los Angeles.

7. The travelers often established a temporary camp in a valley for protection from the harsh winter weather.
8. Life in these camps was hard—food was often scarce, and many people never recovered from the hardships.
9. The pioneers who did survive by sheer determination usually continued their journey.
10. When the journey ended, these people worked hard to make homes for their families.

Verbals and Verbal Phrases

A ***verbal*** is a word that is formed from a verb but is used as a noun, an adjective, or an adverb. There are three kinds of verbals: the *participle,* the *gerund,* and the *infinitive.*

The Participle

14e. A *participle* is a verb form that can be used as an adjective.

(1) Present participles end in *–ing.*

EXAMPLES The **smiling** child waved. [*Smiling,* a form of the verb *smile,* modifies the noun *child.*]

The horses **trotting** past were not frightened by the crowd. [*Trotting,* a form of the verb *trot,* modifies the noun *horses.*]

(2) Most past participles end in *–d* or *–ed.* Some past participles are irregularly formed.

EXAMPLES The police officers searched the **abandoned** warehouse. [*Abandoned,* a form of the verb *abandon,* modifies the noun *warehouse.*]

This plate, **bought** at a flea market, is a valuable antique. [*Bought,* a form of the verb *buy,* modifies the noun *plate.*]

Chosen for her leadership abilities, Dawn was an effective team captain. [*Chosen,* a form of the verb *choose,* modifies the noun *Dawn.*]

Reference Note

For a list of **irregular past participles,** see page 510.

Reference Note

For information on **verb phrases,** see page 372.

GRAMMAR

Do not confuse a participle used as an adjective with a participle used as part of a verb phrase.

ADJECTIVE **Planning** their trip, the class learned how to read a road map.

VERB PHRASE While they **were planning** their trip, the class learned how to read a road map.

ADJECTIVE Most of the treasure **buried** by the pirates has never been found.

VERB PHRASE Most of the treasure that **was buried** by the pirates has never been found.

Exercise 4 Identifying Participles

Identify the participles used as adjectives in the following sentences. Give the noun or pronoun each participle modifies. Be prepared to identify the participle as a *present participle* or a *past participle.*

HELP In the example for Exercise 4, both *whistling* and *chugging* are present participles.

EXAMPLE **1.** We heard the train whistling and chugging in the distance.

1. whistling—train; chugging—train

1. Records, cracked and warped, were in the old trunk in the attic.
2. Shouting loudly, Carmen warned the pedestrian to look out for the car.
3. Spoken in haste, the angry words could not be taken back.
4. The papers, aged and yellowed, were in the bottom drawer.
5. For centuries the ruins remained there, waiting for discovery.
6. Carefully decorated, the piñata glittered in the sunlight.
7. The charging bull thundered across the field of red and orange poppies.
8. Cheering and clapping, the spectators greeted their team.
9. The children, fidgeting noisily, waited eagerly for recess.
10. Recently released, the movie is not yet in local theaters.

The Participial Phrase

Reference Note

For more information about **complements,** see Chapter 13. For more about **modifiers,** see Chapter 20.

14f. A *participial phrase* consists of a participle and any modifiers or complements the participle has. The entire phrase is used as an adjective.

A participle may be modified by an adverb or an adverb phrase and may also have a complement, usually a direct object.

EXAMPLES **Seeing itself in the mirror,** the duck seemed quite bewildered. [The participial phrase modifies the noun *duck.* The pronoun *itself* is the direct object of the present participle *Seeing.* The adverb phrase *in the mirror* modifies the present participle *Seeing.*]

After a while, we heard the duck **quacking noisily at its own image.** [The participial phrase modifies the noun *duck.* The adverb *noisily* and the adverb phrase *at its own image* modify the present participle *quacking.*]

Then, **disgusted with the other duck,** it pecked the mirror. [The participial phrase modifies the pronoun *it.* The adverb phrase *with the other duck* modifies the past participle *disgusted.*]

A participial phrase should be placed as close as possible to the word it modifies. Otherwise, the phrase may appear to modify another word and the sentence may not make sense.

MISPLACED Slithering through the grass, I saw a snake trimming the hedges this morning.

CORRECTED **Trimming the hedges this morning,** I saw a snake **slithering through the grass.**

Reference Note

For more about **misplaced participial phrases,** see page 572.

Exercise 5 Identifying Participial Phrases

Identify the participial phrases in the following sentences. Give the word or words that each phrase modifies.

EXAMPLE 1. Myths are wonderful stories passed on from generation to generation.

1. passed on from generation to generation—stories

1. Noted for her beauty, Venus was sought by many gods as a wife.
2. Bathed in radiant light, Venus brought love and joy wherever she went.
3. Jupiter, knowing her charms, nevertheless married her to Vulcan, the ugliest of the gods.
4. Mars, known to the Greeks as Ares, was the god of war.
5. Terrified by Ares' power, many Greeks did not like to worship him.
6. They saw both land and people destroyed by him.

GRAMMAR

7. Observing his grim path, they said that Ares left blood, devastation, and grief behind him.
8. The Romans, having great respect for Mars, made him one of their three chief deities.
9. They imagined him dressed in shining armor.
10. Mars, supposedly the father of the founders of Rome, has a planet named after him.

STYLE TIP

Sometimes you can use a participial phrase to combine short, choppy sentences.

CHOPPY
The treasure was buried by the pirates. The treasure has never been found.

REVISED
The treasure **buried by the pirates** has never been found.

Exercise 6 Writing Sentences with Participial Phrases

Use each of the following participial phrases in a sentence of your own. Place each phrase as close as possible to the noun or pronoun that it modifies.

EXAMPLE **1.** standing in line

1. Standing in line, we waited twenty minutes for the store to open.

1. waiting for the bus in the rain
2. broken in three places
3. planning the escape
4. jumping from stone to stone
5. hearing the whistle blow and feeling the train lurch
6. given to him by President Carter
7. saved over the years
8. looking down from the top of the Ferris wheel
9. hidden under the shrub
10. seeing the ocean for the first time

Review B Using Participles and Participial Phrases to Combine Sentences

You are the sports editor for the school newspaper. A new photographer just turned in several photographs from a district school track-and-field event. She also wrote captions to go under the photographs. The information is fine, but you want each caption to be a single sentence. Use participles and participial phrases to combine each set of sentences on the next page.

EXAMPLE **1.** Tamara Jackson nears the finish line in the 100-meter dash. She looks happy because she's run her best.

1. Looking happy because she's run her best, Tamara Jackson nears the finish line in the 100-meter dash.

1. In the 100-meter hurdles, Ruth Ann Garcia appears to be leading. She is known for her last-minute bursts of energy.
2. Discus thrower Zack Linquist shifts his weight to his left foot. He twists his body to the right and hurls the discus across the field.
3. Relay team member Krista Davidson reaches for the baton. She is prepared to run the last leg of the relay race.
4. In the pole vault, Dennis Nishimoto clears the crossbar. Every muscle in his body strains as he goes over the bar.
5. Julie McKay shows great promise in the broad jump. Most people favor her to win this year's event.

The Gerund

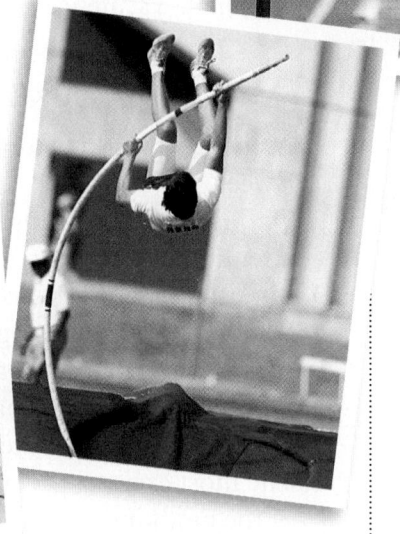

14g. A *gerund* is a verb form ending in *–ing* that is used as a noun.

SUBJECT	**Skiing** down that slope was fun.
PREDICATE NOMINATIVE	Dad's favorite pastime is **fishing** for trout and bass.
INDIRECT OBJECT	Give **sailing** a try.
DIRECT OBJECT	We enjoyed **hiking** in the Sangre de Cristo Mountains.
OBJECT OF PREPOSITION	Please sweep the front sidewalk after **mowing.**

Reference Note

For information on **subjects,** see page 327. For information on **predicate nominatives,** see page 405. For information on **indirect and direct objects,** see pages 403 and 401. For information on **objects of prepositions,** see page 388.

TIPS & TRICKS

If you are not sure whether an *–ing* word is a gerund or a participle, try this test. Substitute a pronoun for the *–ing* word. If the sentence still makes sense, the word is a gerund.

EXAMPLES

Playing tennis is good exercise.

It is good exercise. [*It* makes sense in the sentence. *Playing* is a gerund.]

We watched the dolphins playing with a ball.

We watched the dolphins it with a ball. [*It* does not make sense here. *Playing* is a participle.]

Reference Note

For more information about **complements**, see Chapter 13. For more about **modifiers,** see Chapter 20.

Do not confuse a gerund with a present participle used as part of a verb phrase or as an adjective.

EXAMPLE Pausing, the deer was sniffing the wind before **stepping** into the meadow. [*Pausing* is a participle modifying *deer,* and *sniffing* is part of the verb phrase *was sniffing. Stepping* is a gerund that serves as the object of the preposition *before.*]

Exercise 7 Identifying Gerunds

Find the gerunds in the following sentences. Identify each gerund as a *subject*, a *predicate nominative*, a *direct object*, or an *object of a preposition*. If a sentence does not contain a gerund, write *none*.

EXAMPLE **1.** Typing the paper took an hour.
1. Typing—subject

1. In the past, working took up most people's time six days a week.
2. Dr. Martin Luther King, Jr.'s powerful speaking helped draw attention to the civil rights movement.
3. My sister has always enjoyed riding horseback.
4. Why won't that dog stop barking?
5. I look forward to a rest after this tiring job is done.
6. Uncle Eli's specialty is barbecuing on the grill.
7. Nobody could stand the child's unceasing whine.
8. The most exciting part of the ceremony will be the crowning of the new king.
9. Studying usually pays off in higher scores.
10. Considering the other choices, Melinda decided on walking.

The Gerund Phrase

14h. A *gerund phrase* consists of a gerund and any modifiers or complements the gerund has. The entire phrase is used as a noun.

Because a gerund is a verb form, it may be modified by an adverb or an adverb phrase and may have a complement, usually a direct object. Also, since a gerund functions as a noun, it may be modified by an adjective or an adjective phrase.

EXAMPLES **Having a part-time job** may interfere with your schoolwork. [The gerund phrase is the subject of the sentence. The noun *job* is the direct object of the gerund *Having.* The article *a* and the adjective *part-time* modify *job.*]

The townspeople heard **the loud clanging of the fire bell.** [The gerund phrase is the direct object of the verb *heard.* The article *the,* the adjective *loud,* and the adjective phrase *of the fire bell* modify the gerund *clanging.*]

We crossed the stream by **stepping carefully from stone to stone.** [The gerund phrase is the object of the preposition *by.* The adverb *carefully* and the adverb phrases *from stone* and *to stone* modify the gerund *stepping.*]

NOTE When a noun or a pronoun comes immediately before a gerund, use the possessive form of the noun or pronoun.

EXAMPLES **Michael's** cooking is the best I've ever tasted.

The vultures didn't let anything disturb **their** feeding.

Exercise 8 Identifying Gerund Phrases

Find the gerund phrases in the following sentences. Identify each phrase as a *subject,* a *predicate nominative,* a *direct object,* or an *object of a preposition.*

EXAMPLE **1.** The rain interrupted their building the bonfire.

1. their building the bonfire—direct object

1. Angelo's pleading rarely influenced his mother's decisions.
2. The eerie sound they heard was the howling of the wolves.
3. We sat back and enjoyed the slow rocking of the boat.
4. The blue jay's screeching at the cat woke us up at dawn.
5. People supported Cesar Chavez and the United Farm Workers by boycotting grapes.
6. Our greatest victory will be winning the state championship.
7. The frantic darting of the fish indicated that a shark was nearby.
8. She is considering running for class president.
9. Ants try to protect their colonies from storms by piling up sand against the wind.
10. In his later years, Chief Quanah Parker was known for settling disputes fairly.

GRAMMAR

Exercise 9 Writing Sentences with Gerund Phrases

Use each of the following gerund phrases in a sentence of your own. Underline the gerund phrase, and identify it as a *subject,* a *predicate nominative,* a *direct object,* or an *object of a preposition.*

EXAMPLE **1.** hiking up the hill

1. Hiking up the hill took us all morning.—subject

1. getting up in the morning
2. arguing among themselves
3. refusing to board the space shuttle
4. sharpening my pencil
5. listening to the tour guide
6. walking to the video store
7. jumping into the cold water
8. figuring out puzzles
9. repairing the tires on my bicycle
10. living near a castle

The Infinitive

14i. An *infinitive* is a verb form that can be used as a noun, an adjective, or an adverb. Most infinitives begin with *to.*

NOUNS **To install** the ceiling fan took two hours. [*To install* is the subject of the sentence.]

Winona's ambition is **to become** a doctor. [*To become* is a predicate nominative referring to the subject *ambition.*]

Shina likes **to skate** but not **to ski.** [*To skate* and *to ski* are direct objects of the verb *likes.*]

ADJECTIVES The best time **to visit** Florida is December through April. [*To visit* modifies *time.*]

If you want information about computers, that is the magazine **to read.** [*To read* modifies *magazine.*]

ADVERBS The gymnasts were ready **to practice** their routines. [*To practice* modifies the adjective *ready.*]

The camel knelt at the pool **to drink.** [*To drink* modifies the verb *knelt.*]

NOTE Be careful not to confuse an infinitive with a prepositional phrase beginning with *to.* A prepositional phrase always has an object that is a noun or a pronoun. An infinitive is a verb form that usually begins with *to.*

PREPOSITIONAL PHRASE	I handed the vase **to my mother.**
INFINITIVE	Is she ready **to swim?**

Exercise 10 Identifying Infinitives

Identify the infinitive in each of the following sentences.

EXAMPLE **1.** The first time we met, June and I decided to be friends.

1. to be

1. After school, June and I like to walk home together.
2. Usually, we go to my house or her house to listen to CDs.
3. Sometimes I get up to dance to the music, but June never does.
4. I don't like to sit still when a good song is playing.
5. June finally told me that she had never learned how to dance.
6. "Do you want to learn some steps?" I asked.
7. "I want to try," she answered.
8. I decided to start with some simple steps.
9. For three weeks, we went to my house to practice.
10. Now, June is ready to go to the school dance after the game on Friday.

The Infinitive Phrase

14j. An *infinitive phrase* consists of an infinitive and any modifiers or complements the infinitive has. The entire phrase may be used as a noun, an adjective, or an adverb.

An infinitive may be modified by an adjective or an adverb; it may also have a complement.

EXAMPLES The crowd grew quiet **to hear the speaker.** [The infinitive phrase is an adverb modifying the verb *grew.* The noun *speaker* is the direct object of the infinitive *to hear.*]

Peanuts and raisins are good snacks **to take on a camping trip.** [The infinitive phrase is an adjective modifying *snacks.* The adverb phrase *on a camping trip* modifies the infinitive *to take.*]

To lift those weights takes great strength. [The infinitive phrase is a noun used as the subject of the sentence. The noun *weights* is the direct object of the infinitive *To lift.*]

Exercise 11 Identifying Infinitive Phrases

Most of the following sentences contain infinitive phrases. Identify each infinitive phrase, and tell whether it is used as a *noun,* an *adjective,* or an *adverb.* If there is no infinitive phrase in a sentence, write *none.*

EXAMPLE **1.** I told my Aunt Elise that I wanted to take better care of my bicycle.

1. to take better care of my bicycle—noun

1. Taking care of your bicycle is one way to make it last.
2. We used machine oil to lubricate the chain.
3. I learned to place a small drop of oil on each link.
4. Then she showed me the valve that is needed to fill the inner tube.
5. Using Aunt Elise's hand pump, we added some air to the back tire.
6. We were careful not to put in too much air.
7. Next, we got out wrenches to tighten some bolts.
8. My aunt said not to pull the wrench too hard.
9. Overtightening can cause as much damage to bolts as not tightening them enough.
10. When we finished, I thanked my aunt for taking the time to give me tips about taking care of my bicycle.

Exercise 12 Writing Sentences with Infinitive Phrases

Use each of the following infinitive phrases in a sentence of your own. Underline the infinitive phrase, and identify it as a *noun,* an *adjective,* or an *adverb.*

EXAMPLE **1.** to leave school early on Tuesday

1. The principal gave me permission to leave school early on Tuesday.—adjective

1. to give the right answers
2. to go to another planet
3. to run toward the zebra
4. to read the entire book over the weekend
5. to spend the night at my cousin's house
6. to wait for the meteor shower
7. to finish the posters before Kwanzaa
8. to climb the mountain with my friends
9. to close all the windows in the house
10. to sing on stage

GRAMMAR

Review C Identifying Verbals and Verbal Phrases

Each of the following sentences contains at least one verbal or verbal phrase. Identify each verbal or verbal phrase as a *gerund,* a *gerund phrase,* a *participle,* a *participial phrase,* an *infinitive,* or an *infinitive phrase.*

EXAMPLE 1. Visiting Cahokia Mounds State Historic Site in Illinois is a wonderful experience.

1. Visiting Cahokia Mounds State Historic Site in Illinois—gerund phrase

1. Cahokia was a highly developed civilization in North America more than one thousand years ago.
2. Noting the importance of Cahokia, the United Nations Educational, Scientific, and Cultural Organization (UNESCO) set aside Cahokia Mounds as a World Heritage Site.
3. After studying the site, archaeologists were able to make a sketch of the ancient city.
4. The city was destroyed long ago, but the remaining traces of it show how huge it must have been.
5. This thriving community had a population of about 20,000 sometime between A.D. 700 and A.D. 1500.
6. You can see that the people chose to build their houses mostly inside the stockade wall.

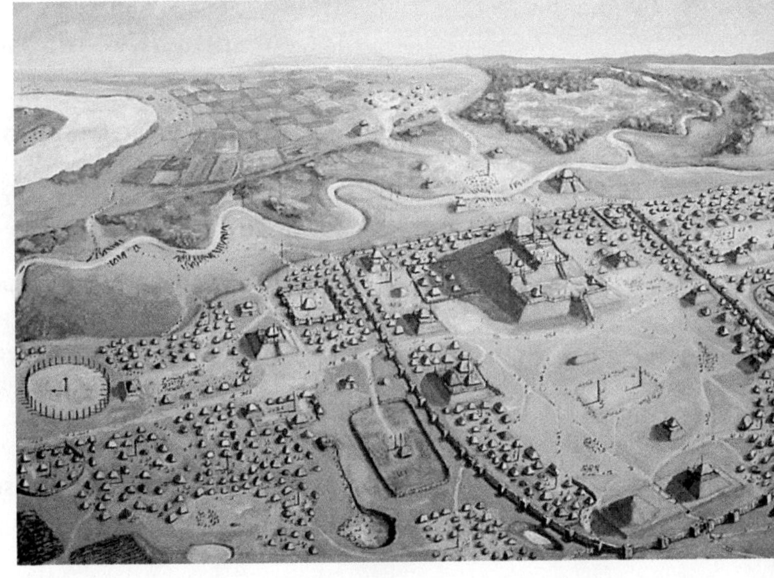

7. It's still possible to see many of the earthen mounds.
8. The historic site includes about sixty-eight preserved mounds, which were probably used for ceremonial activities.
9. Seeing the 100-foot-high Monks Mound was quite enlightening.
10. The mound was built for the city's ruler as a place to live.

Appositives and Appositive Phrases

14k. An *appositive* is a noun or a pronoun placed beside another noun or pronoun to identify or describe it.

EXAMPLES The cosmonaut **Yuri Gagarin** was the first person in space. [The noun *Yuri Gagarin* identifies the noun *cosmonaut.*]

I chose one person, **her,** to organize the volunteers. [The pronoun *her* refers to the noun *person.*]

Reference Note

For more about the use of **commas with appositives,** see page 641.

NOTE Commas are generally used with appositives that refer to proper nouns.

EXAMPLE Rachel Carson, a **biologist** and **writer,** published the book ***Silent Spring*** in 1962. [The nouns *biologist* and *writer* describe the proper noun *Rachel Carson.* The noun *Silent Spring* identifies the common noun *book.*]

14l. An *appositive phrase* consists of an appositive and its modifiers.

EXAMPLES Officer Webb, **one of the security guards,** caught the burglar. [The adjective phrase *of the security guards* modifies the appositive *one.*]

Leonardo da Vinci, **an Italian painter known for his artworks,** was also an architect, engineer, and scientist. [The article *an,* the adjective *Italian,* and the participial phrase *known for his artworks* modify the appositive *painter.*]

Appositives and appositive phrases that are not essential to the meaning of the sentence are set off by commas. If the appositive is essential to the meaning, it is generally not set off by commas.

EXAMPLES My sister**,** **Lana,** has blond hair. [The writer has only one sister. The appositive is not essential to identify the sister. Because the information is nonessential, it is set off by commas.]

My sister **Lana** has blond hair. [The writer has more than one sister. The appositive is necessary to tell which sister is meant. Because this information is essential to the meaning of the sentence, it is not set off by commas.]

Reference Note

For more on **essential and nonessential phrases,** see page 639.

STYLE  **TIP**

You can use appositives and appositive phrases to combine short, choppy sentences.

CHOPPY
Santa Fe is a major tourist center. It is the capital of New Mexico.

REVISED
Santa Fe, **the capital of New Mexico,** is a major tourist center.

Exercise 13 Identifying Appositives and Appositive Phrases

Identify the appositives and appositive phrases in the following sentences. Then, give the word or words each appositive or appositive phrase identifies or describes.

EXAMPLE **1.** My dog, the mutt with floppy ears, can do tricks.
1. the mutt with floppy ears—dog

1. Tacos, one of the most popular Mexican dishes, are served here.
2. My twin, Daniel, rode in a Mardi Gras parade.
3. Those two men, a truck driver and a sailor, helped my father push the car off the road.
4. I'll have a sandwich, tuna salad on rye bread, please.
5. Miguel has the same class, American history, this afternoon.
6. Barbara Jordan, one of my heroes, was a strong champion of both civil and human rights.
7. Shelley asked everyone where her friend Bianca had gone.
8. Somebody reported the hazard, a pile of trash containing broken bottles, to the police.
9. Be sure to bring the exact change, fifty cents.
10. They sang the song "I've Been Working on the Railroad" over and over all the way down the path.

Review D Identifying Verbals and Appositives

Find all the verbals and appositives in the following sentences. Identify each *participle, gerund, infinitive,* or *appositive.*

EXAMPLE **1.** Skating on the sidewalk, my little brother Shawn tried to do some acrobatics.
1. Skating—participle; Shawn—appositive; to do—infinitive

1. Instead of falling on the soft ground, Shawn managed to land right on the sidewalk.
2. The concrete, broken and crumbling, cut his legs.
3. We heard his piercing wail up at our house, and my mother and I rushed to see what had happened.
4. By the time we got to him, the cuts had already started bleeding, and he was struggling to get his skates off.
5. Bending down, Mom pulled off the skates and dabbed at the seeping red cuts and scrapes.
6. Shawn, a brave little boy usually, could not keep from crying.
7. Mom carried Shawn to the house, and I followed with his skates, scratched and scraped almost as badly as he was.
8. After cleaning Shawn's cuts, Mom took him to the clinic.
9. The doctor, a young intern, said that she would have to close one of the cuts with stitches.
10. When we got home, Mom said that she hoped Shawn had learned to be more careful, but knowing Shawn, I doubt it.

Review E Writing Sentences with Prepositional, Verbal, and Appositive Phrases

Write ten sentences, using one of the following phrases in each sentence. Follow the directions in parentheses.

EXAMPLE 1. to write a descriptive paragraph (*use as an infinitive phrase that is the predicate nominative in the sentence*)

1. Our assignment for tomorrow is to write a descriptive paragraph.

1. after the game (*use as an adjective phrase*)
2. instead of your good shoes (*use as an adverb phrase*)
3. in one of Shakespeare's plays (*use as an adjective phrase*)
4. going to school every day (*use as a gerund phrase that is the direct object in the sentence*)
5. living in a small town (*use as a gerund phrase that is the object of a preposition*)
6. walking through the empty lot (*use as a participial phrase*)
7. dressed in authentic costumes (*use as a participial phrase*)
8. to drive a car for the first time (*use as an infinitive phrase that is the subject of the sentence*)
9. the best athlete in our school (*use as an appositive phrase*)
10. my favorite pastime (*use as an appositive phrase*)

Chapter Review

A. Identifying Prepositional, Verbal, and Appositive Phrases

For each of the following sentences, identify the italicized phrase as a *prepositional phrase,* a *participial phrase,* a *gerund phrase,* an *infinitive phrase,* or an *appositive phrase.* Do not separately identify a prepositional phrase that is part of a larger phrase.

1. Ed likes *listening to music.*
2. The sea gulls *gliding through the air* looked like pieces of paper caught in the wind.
3. The school bus was on time *in spite of the traffic jam.*
4. Ms. Abdusalaam, *my science teacher,* got married last week.
5. There is no time left *to answer your questions.*
6. *Hoping for a new bicycle and a toy robot,* my brother couldn't sleep at all on Christmas Eve.
7. He tried *to do his best* in the race.
8. Nobody seems to be very interested in *going to the fireworks display.*
9. Have you seen my cat, *a long-haired Persian with yellow eyes*?
10. Chad said that he prefers the bike *with all-terrain tires and the wider, more comfortable seat.*
11. At the carnival, the band played songs *with a lively samba beat.*
12. Rachel talked her friends into *watching that Three Tenors video.*
13. In the United States, citizens have the right *to speak their minds.*
14. My aunt's car, *an old crate with a torn-up interior and a rattling engine,* used to belong to my grandfather.
15. The Dutch artist Jan Vermeer enjoyed *painting pictures of house interiors.*
16. Last Sunday, we all piled in the car and went *to the beach, the bowling alley, and the mall.*
17. The shark *chasing the school of fish* looked like a hammerhead.
18. Nobody wanted to read the book, *a thick hardback with a faded cover.*

19. All of the invitations *sent to the club members* had the wrong date on them.
20. Mr. Patel and Mr. Kim recruited neighborhood children *to help decorate the storefronts for Independence Day.*

B. Identifying Gerunds and Gerund Phrases

Identify the gerunds and gerund phrases in the following sentences.

21. Reaching an agreement between the parties is the goal of every negotiator.
22. Smoking has become less common in the United States.
23. The incessant raining put a damper on our holiday.
24. Relaxing at home on the weekend can be beneficial to your peace of mind.
25. When she is abroad, Aunt Ida especially enjoys meeting other travelers.
26. After a long and tiring day, swimming a lap or two can relax your muscles.
27. Cousin Mark's summer job is selling produce at the farmers' market.
28. Singing is Nina's favorite pastime.
29. Living across the street from school is convenient.
30. The only sound they heard was the barking of the seals.

C. Identifying Verbals, Verbal Phrases, Appositives, and Appositive Phrases

The following sentences contain verbals and appositives. Identify each verbal or verbal phrase as a *participle,* a *participial phrase,* a *gerund,* a *gerund phrase,* an *infinitive,* or *an infinitive phrase.* Also identify each *appositive* or *appositive phrase.*

31. The architect Bernini designed the entrance of St. Peter's Basilica in Rome.
32. We saw the raccoon escaping through the backdoor.
33. To finish what you have started is an accomplishment.
34. The honking of the car horn awoke him from his nap.
35. Gerald M. Hopkins, Jr., is the candidate to watch in the next election.

36. Waxed floors can be dangerously slippery.

37. Babs and Tim listened to the beautiful singing of the soprano.

38. Aunt Anne got her degree in zoology, the scientific study of animal life.

39. They may have paid less attention than usual because they were so eager to finish.

40. The dog's constant barking annoyed the entire neighborhood.

Writing Application

Using Prepositional Phrases in a Story

Adjective and Adverb Phrases Your class is writing and illustrating a book of original stories. The book will be given to a second-grade class during National Library Week. For the book, write a short story about a search for sunken treasure. In your story, use a variety of adjective and adverb phrases.

Prewriting Begin by thinking about stories you have read or heard about sunken treasures. Then, write down some details from these real or fictional stories. Next, use your imagination to think of a setting and some characters for your own story. Choose a point of view (first person or third person), and start writing.

Writing As you write your first draft, try to make your story exciting and interesting for second-grade readers. Since you are telling a story, arrange the events in chronological order. Remember to include details in prepositional phrases whenever possible.

Revising Read the story aloud to a friend or a younger child. Notice what reactions you get from your listener. Have you included enough details to make the story seem real? You may need to cut some details or add some information. New information often can be added easily in prepositional phrases.

Publishing Proofread your story for any errors in grammar, usage, and punctuation. Publish your story, along with any illustrations for it, in a class book. Your class may want to read the stories aloud to younger students.

CHAPTER

The Clause

Independent Clauses and Subordinate Clauses

Diagnostic Preview

Identifying Independent and Subordinate Clauses

Identify each italicized clause in the following paragraphs as an *independent clause* or a *subordinate clause.* Then, tell whether each italicized subordinate clause is used as a *noun,* an *adjective,* or an *adverb.*

EXAMPLES When my mother got a new job, **[1]** *we had to move to another town.*

1. *independent clause*

[2] *When my mother got a new job,* we had to move to another town.

2. *subordinate clause—adverb*

[**1**] *Because I didn't want to transfer to another school,* I didn't want to move. This is the fourth time [**2**] *that I have had to change schools,* and every time I've wished [**3**] *that I could just stay at my old school.* [**4**] *As soon as I make friends in a new place,* I have to move again and leave them behind. [**5**] *Then I am a stranger again at the new school.*

[**6**] *We lived in our last house for three years,* which is longer than in any other place [**7**] *since I was little.* [**8**] *Living there so long, I had a chance to meet several people* [**9**] *who became good friends of mine.* My best friends, Chris and Marty, said [**10**] *that they would write to me,* and I promised to write to them, too.

However, the friends [11] *that I've had before* had promised to write, but [12] *after a letter or two we lost touch.* [13] *Why this always happens* is a mystery to me.

I dreaded having to register at my new school [14] *after the school year had begun.* [15] *By then, everyone else would already have made friends,* and [16] *I would be an outsider,* as I knew from experience. There are always some students who bully and tease [17] *whoever is new at school* or anyone else [18] *who is different.* Back in elementary school I would get angry and upset [19] *when people picked on me.* Since then, I've learned how to fit in and make friends in spite of [20] *whatever anyone does to hassle me or make me feel uncomfortable.*

Everywhere [21] *that I've gone to school,* some students are friendly and offer to show me around. [22] *I used to be shy,* and I wouldn't take them up on their invitations. Since they didn't know [23] *whether I was shy or unfriendly,* they soon left me alone. Now, [24] *whenever someone is friendly to me at a new school or in a new neighborhood,* I fight my shyness and act friendly myself. It's still hard to get used to new places and new people, but [25] *it's much easier with a little help from new friends.*

What Is a Clause?

15a. A *clause* is a word group that contains a verb and its subject and that is used as a sentence or as part of a sentence.

Every clause has a subject and a verb. However, not every clause expresses a complete thought.

SENTENCE Writers gathered at the home of Gertrude Stein when she lived in Paris.

CLAUSE Writers [S] gathered [V] at the home of Gertrude Stein [complete thought]

CLAUSE when she [S] lived [V] in Paris [incomplete thought]

There are two kinds of clauses: the *independent clause* and the *subordinate clause.*

GRAMMAR

The Independent Clause

15b. An *independent* (or *main*) *clause* expresses a complete thought and can stand by itself as a complete sentence.

EXAMPLES

S V
The sun set an hour ago. [This entire sentence is an independent clause.]

S V
Jean Merrill wrote *The Pushcart War,* and

S V
Ronni Solbert illustrated the book. [This sentence contains two independent clauses.]

S V
After I finish studying, **I will go to the movies.** [This sentence contains one subordinate clause and one independent clause.]

HELP— Before doing Exercise 1, you may want to review subjects and verbs in Chapter 10, The Sentence.

Exercise 1 Identifying Subjects and Verbs in Independent Clauses

Identify the subject and verb in each italicized independent clause in the following sentences.

EXAMPLE 1. Before she left for college, *my sister read the comics in the newspaper every day.*
1. sister—subject; read—verb

1. *She told me* that Jump Start was her favorite.
2. Since she liked it so much, *I made a point of reading it, too.*
3. *The comic strip was created by this young man, Robb Armstrong,* who lives and works in Philadelphia.
4. *Jump Start features a police officer named Joe and his wife, Marcy,* who is a nurse.

Jump Start reprinted by permission of United Feature Syndicate, Inc.

5. If you aren't familiar with the strip, *you may not recognize Joe and Marcy standing behind their creator.*
6. Like many readers, *I like funny strips best.*
7. *Other people like more serious comics* that feature an ongoing drama.
8. *Ask your family and friends* what comics they like best.
9. *You can see* whether Jump Start is among their favorites.
10. During the holidays, *I plan to draw my own comic strip.*

The Subordinate Clause

15c. A *subordinate* (or *dependent*) *clause* does not express a complete thought and cannot stand by itself as a complete sentence.

A word such as *that, what,* or *since* often signals the beginning of a subordinate clause.

SUBORDINATE CLAUSES

that I wanted (S: I, V: wanted)

what she saw (S: she, V: saw)

since most plants die without light (S: plants, V: die)

The meaning of a subordinate clause is complete only when the clause is attached to an independent clause.

SENTENCES The store did not have the video game **that I wanted.**

The witness told the police officers **what she saw.**

Since most plants die without light, we moved our houseplants closer to the window.

Sometimes the word that begins a subordinate clause is the subject of the clause.

EXAMPLES The animals **that are in the wildlife preserve** are protected from hunters. (S: that, V: are)

Can you tell me **who wrote "America the Beautiful"**? (S: who, V: wrote)

STYLE TIP

A subordinate clause that is capitalized and punctuated as a sentence is a ***sentence fragment***. Avoid using sentence fragments in formal writing.

Reference Note

For more about **sentence fragments,** see page 324.

GRAMMAR

Exercise 2 Identifying Independent and Subordinate Clauses

Identify each of the following word groups as an *independent clause* or a *subordinate clause.*

EXAMPLE **1.** as I answered the telephone

1. subordinate clause

1. we memorized the lyrics
2. as they sat on the back porch
3. if no one is coming
4. my sister was born on Valentine's Day
5. which everyone enjoyed
6. the flood destroyed many crops
7. the singer wore a silk scarf
8. when the lights were flickering
9. since we talked to Maria
10. that the lion's cage was empty

Exercise 3 Identifying Subordinate Clauses and Their Subjects and Verbs

Identify the subordinate clause in each of the following sentences. Give the subject and the verb of each subordinate clause.

EXAMPLE **1.** My report is about the plague that spread across Europe in the fourteenth century.

1. that spread across Europe in the fourteenth century; subject—that; verb—spread

1. In 1347, trading ships arrived at the Mediterranean island of Sicily from Caffa, which was a port city on the Black Sea.
2. When the sailors went ashore, many of them carried a strange illness.
3. No medicine could save the stricken sailors, who died quickly and painfully.
4. Bubonic plague, which is the most common form of the illness, causes swelling in the legs, neck, and armpits.
5. The disease was spread by fleas, which traveled between cities in Europe on rats and other animals.
6. Millions of people became sick and died as the plague spread from Sicily across Europe.

7. On this map, you can trace how quickly the plague spread.
8. Many terrified survivors thought that the world was coming to an end.
9. No one is sure of the total number of people who died from the dreaded plague.
10. Since modern medicine offers new ways for controlling the plague, the spread of this disease is unlikely today.

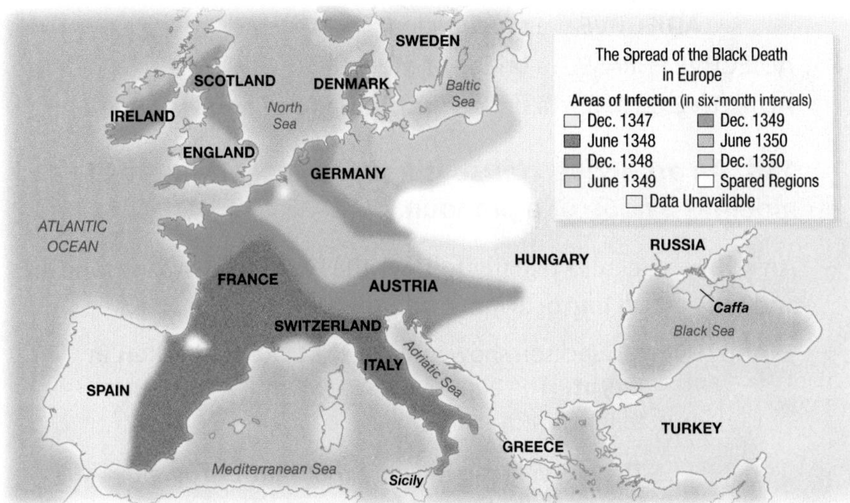

Exercise 4 Writing Sentences with Independent Clauses and Subordinate Clauses

Write a sentence by adding an independent clause to each subordinate clause. Draw one line under the subject and two lines under the verb of each clause.

EXAMPLES **1.** who came late

1. Anica is the volunteer who came late.

2. as the horn blared

2. As the horn blared, I was running out the door.

1. when the ice melts
2. if my teacher approves
3. since you insist
4. when they act silly
5. who borrowed my notes
6. as she began to shout
7. when we danced on stage
8. who gave the report
9. since I sleep soundly
10. that I bought yesterday

GRAMMAR

STYLE TIP

Adjective clauses can bring clarity and good description to your writing. Be careful, though, not to use too many adjective clauses. Overusing adjective clauses can make your writing wordy. You might want to replace some of them with adjectives or brief phrases.

WORDY
They live in the apartment building **that is made of brick** and **that is located next to the fire station.**

BETTER
They live in the **brick** apartment building **next to the fire station.**

The Adjective Clause

Like an adjective or an adjective phrase, an adjective clause may modify a noun or a pronoun.

ADJECTIVE	the **blonde** woman
ADJECTIVE PHRASE	the woman **with blonde hair**
ADJECTIVE CLAUSE	the woman **who has blonde hair**
ADJECTIVE	a **steel** bridge
ADJECTIVE PHRASE	a bridge **of steel**
ADJECTIVE CLAUSE	a bridge **that is made of steel**

15d. An *adjective clause* is a subordinate clause that modifies a noun or a pronoun.

An adjective clause usually follows the word or words it modifies and tells *which one* or *what kind.*

EXAMPLES Ms. Jackson showed slides **that she had taken in Egypt.** [The adjective clause modifies the noun *slides,* telling *which* slides.]

The brownie cap is a mushroom **that grows in lawns and other grassy areas.** [The adjective clause modifies the noun *mushroom,* telling *what kind* of mushroom.]

That one, **which is my favorite,** was bought in Kenya. [The adjective clause modifies the pronoun *one,* telling *which one.*]

Relative Pronouns

An adjective clause is usually introduced by a *relative pronoun.*

Common Relative Pronouns				
that	which	who	whom	whose

A ***relative pronoun*** relates an adjective clause to the word or words the clause modifies.

EXAMPLES Leonardo da Vinci was the artist **who painted the *Mona Lisa.*** [The relative pronoun *who* begins the adjective clause and relates it to the noun *artist.*]

Reference Note

For information on using ***who*** and ***whom*** correctly, see page 546.

The magazine, **which arrived in the mail today,** is torn. [The relative pronoun *which* begins the adjective clause and relates it to the noun *magazine.*]

NOTE The relative pronoun *that* can be used to refer both to people and to things. The relative pronoun *which* is used to refer to things only.

Reference Note

For information on **when to set off adjective clauses with commas,** see page 639.

Sometimes a relative pronoun is preceded by a preposition that is part of the adjective clause.

EXAMPLES Have you read the book **on which the movie is based**?

The actor **to whom I am referring** is Sir Alec Guinness.

In addition to relating a subordinate clause to the rest of the sentence, a relative pronoun often has a grammatical function in the subordinate clause.

EXAMPLES Is this tape the one **that is on sale**? [*That* relates the subordinate clause to the word *one* and also functions as the subject of the subordinate clause.]

The jeweler **to whom I took the broken bracelet** repaired it quickly. [*Whom* relates the subordinate clause to the word *jeweler* and functions as the object of the preposition *to*.]

Occasionally, an adjective clause is introduced by *when* or *where.* When used to introduce adjective clauses, these words are called ***relative adverbs.***

EXAMPLES This is the spot **where we caught most of the fish.**

Mrs. Itoh looks forward to Saturday afternoons, **when she works in her garden.**

In some cases, the relative pronoun or adverb can be omitted.

EXAMPLES We haven't seen the silver jewelry **[that] she brought back from Mexico.**

Do you remember the time **[when** *or* **that] the dog caught the skunk**?

A boy **[whom** *or* **that] I know** is a nationally ranked tennis player.

GRAMMAR

Exercise 5 Identifying Adjective Clauses

Identify the adjective clause in each of the following sentences. Give the relative pronoun and the word or word group to which the relative pronoun refers.

EXAMPLE **1.** Our friends have a canary that is named Neptune.
1. that is named Neptune; that—canary

1. Most proverbs are sayings that give advice.
2. Trivia questions have been organized into games that have become quite popular.
3. A black hole, which results after a star has collapsed, can trap energy and matter.
4. The school presented a special award to the student whose work had improved most.
5. Frances Perkins, who served as secretary of labor, was the first woman to hold a Cabinet position.
6. The problem that worries us right now is the pollution of underground sources of water.
7. We enjoyed the poems of Gwendolyn Brooks, who for years has been poet laureate of Illinois.
8. In *Walden,* Henry David Thoreau shared ideas that have influenced many people.
9. Athena, who ranked as an important Greek deity, protected the city of Athens.
10. A friend is a person whom you can trust.

Exercise 6 Identifying Adjective Clauses

Identify the adjective clause in each of the following sentences. Give the relative pronoun or relative adverb and the word or word group to which the pronoun refers.

EXAMPLE **1.** Crispus Attucks was an African American patriot who was killed during the Boston Massacre.
1. who was killed during the Boston Massacre; who—patriot

1. Coco Chanel is the woman for whom the perfume Chanel No. 5 is named.
2. Here is the concert hall where we heard the great cello player Pablo Casals.
3. The cello is an instrument to which I could listen for hours.

4. Ella Fitzgerald, who started singing in New York City, is famous throughout the world.
5. The English playwright Christopher Marlowe wrote of Helen of Troy, "Was this the face that launched a thousand ships?"
6. Anita was one of the sopranos who sang in the chorus.
7. In the play *My Fair Lady,* Eliza Doolittle, a poor flower seller, becomes a woman whom everyone admires.
8. The Kinderhook was the creek in which we found the shells.
9. Janet Flanner, who wrote dispatches from Paris, used the pen name Genêt.
10. The astronauts, to whom travel in the space shuttle is almost routine, must always keep in shape.

Exercise 7 Using Adjective Clauses

Add an adjective clause to each of the following sentences. Write the entire sentence. Circle the relative pronoun, underline the adjective clause once, and underline twice the word to which the pronoun refers.

EXAMPLE 1. The book is a detective story.

1. *The book (that) I read is a detective story.*

1. A new book is here.
2. My cousin likes to draw.
3. The class will go on a field trip.
4. My family traveled to my favorite state.
5. A deer and fawn were in the park.
6. Kwame and Joachim built the bookcase.
7. After the game we are going to the mall.
8. Damita won the 10K run.
9. Before the art show, there will be an international meal.
10. The author will speak tomorrow at the assembly.

The Adverb Clause

Unlike an adverb or an adverb phrase, an adverb clause has a subject and a verb.

ADVERB	He will leave **soon.**
ADVERB PHRASE	He will leave **in a few minutes.**
ADVERB CLAUSE	He will leave **when he is ready.** [*He* is the subject of the adverb clause, and *is* is the verb.]

GRAMMAR

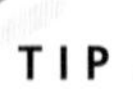

STYLE TIP

In most cases, deciding where to place an adverb clause is a matter of style, not of correctness. Both sentences below are correct.

EXAMPLES

Though she was almost unknown during her lifetime, Emily Dickinson is now known as a major American poet.

Emily Dickinson is now known as a major American poet **though she was almost unknown during her lifetime.**

15e. An *adverb clause* is a subordinate clause that modifies a verb, an adjective, or an adverb.

An adverb clause tells *where, when, how, why, to what extent,* or *under what condition.*

EXAMPLES You may sit **wherever you wish.** [The adverb clause modifies the verb *may sit,* telling *where* you may sit.]

When winter sets in, many animals hibernate. [The adverb clause modifies the verb *hibernate,* telling *when* many animals hibernate.]

Jessica and Anaba look **as though they have some exciting news for us.** [The adverb clause modifies the verb *look,* telling *how* Jessica and Anaba look.]

Happy **because he had made an A,** Tony hurried home. [The adverb clause modifies the adjective *Happy,* telling *why* Tony was happy.]

Gabrielle can type faster **than I can.** [The adverb clause modifies the adverb *faster,* telling *to what extent* Gabrielle can type faster.]

If it does not rain tomorrow, we will go to Crater Lake. [The adverb clause modifies the verb *will go,* telling *under what condition* we will go to Crater Lake.]

Reference Note

For more about using **commas** with **adverb clauses,** see page 645.

Notice that when an adverb clause begins a sentence, it is followed by a comma.

Subordinating Conjunctions

An adverb clause is introduced by a ***subordinating conjunction***—a word that shows the relationship between the adverb clause and the word or words that the clause modifies.

Common Subordinating Conjunctions			
after	as though	since	when
although	because	so that	whenever
as	before	than	where
as if	how	though	wherever
as long as	if	unless	whether
as soon as	in order that	until	while

NOTE The words *after, as, before, since,* and *until* are also commonly used as prepositions.

PREPOSITION **After** lunch we'll finish making the model airplane.

SUBORDINATING CONJUNCTION **After** you wash the dishes, I'll dry them and put them away.

Reference Note

For more information about **prepositions,** see page 386.

Exercise 8 Identifying Adverb Clauses

Identify the adverb clause in each of the following sentences. In each clause, circle the subordinating conjunction, and underline the subject once and the verb twice.

EXAMPLE **1.** Although they lived in different regions of North America, American Indian children all across the continent enjoyed playing similar kinds of games.

1. (Although) they lived in different regions of North America

1. These children once used many natural objects in games since no toy stores existed there at the time.
2. Many American Indian children played darts with large feathers as these Arapaho children are doing.
3. If you look closely at the tree, you can see the children's target, a hole in the trunk.

4. These children are throwing goose feathers attached to bones, but players also used wild turkey feathers whenever they could find them.
5. Although they played many kinds of games, American Indians in the Southwest especially liked kickball races.
6. The children made balls out of materials such as wood and tree roots before they started playing.

7. After snow had fallen, Seneca children raced small handmade "snow boats."
8. Pine cones were used in many games because they were so easy to find.
9. While some children played catch with pine cones, others had cone-throwing contests.
10. Games gave the children practice in skills they would need when they became adults.

Exercise 9 **Writing Sentences with Adverb Clauses**

Add an adverb clause to each of the following sentences. Write the entire sentence. Circle the subordinating conjunction, and underline the subject of each adverb clause once and the verb twice.

EXAMPLE 1. The movie finally ended.

1. (After) we had spent three hours in the theater, the movie finally ended.

1. Most of the members of the Drama Club auditioned for the play.
2. Erica speaks three languages.
3. We prepared moussaka, a Greek dish with lamb and egg-plant, for our Cooking Club's international supper.
4. The Goldmans have visited Acapulco several times.
5. Jill daydreams in class.
6. We students planted fifteen oak trees at our school on Arbor Day.
7. Timothy fixes computers.
8. Mr. Washington worked for a newspaper.
9. The eighth-graders in Mrs. Maranjian's class offered to decorate the gym.
10. The soccer field is closed.

The Noun Clause

15f. A *noun clause* is a subordinate clause that is used as a noun.

A noun clause may be used as a subject, as a complement (such as a predicate nominative, a direct object, or an indirect object), or as an object of a preposition.

SUBJECT	**That they were angry** was obvious to the others.
PREDICATE NOMINATIVE	Three dollars was **what Daniel offered for the trinket**.
DIRECT OBJECT	Anthony and Peter remembered **who he was.**
INDIRECT OBJECT	The hostess gives **whoever enters** a menu.
OBJECT OF A PREPOSITION	Eager to please the speaker, we listened to **whatever he said.**

Common Introductory Words for Noun Clauses

how	whatever	which	whom
that	when	who	whomever
what	whether	whoever	why

The word that introduces a noun clause often has a grammatical function within the clause.

EXAMPLES Give a free pass to **whoever asks for one.** [The introductory word *whoever* is the subject of the verb *asks.*]

Lani would not show either of us **what he wrote.** [The introductory word *what* is the direct object of the verb *wrote—he wrote what.*]

Sometimes the word that introduces a noun clause is omitted but is understood.

EXAMPLE She said **[that] the milk was sour.**

Exercise 10 Identifying Noun Clauses and Their Functions

Identify the noun clause in each of the following sentences. Then, tell whether the noun clause is used as a *subject,* a *predicate nominative,* a *direct object,* an *indirect object,* or an *object of a preposition.*

EXAMPLE **1.** We couldn't find what was making the noise.
1. what was making the noise—direct object

1. Whatever you decide will be fine with us.

Reference Note

For information about **subjects,** see page 327. For information about **complements,** see page 398. For information about **objects of prepositions,** see page 388.

TIPS & TRICKS

Notice that noun clauses and adjective clauses sometimes begin with the same words (*that, which, who, whom, whose*). To tell the difference between an adjective clause and a noun clause, you must decide how the clause functions in the sentence.

ADJECTIVE CLAUSE
Did you find any plates **that are chipped**? [*That are chipped* modifies the noun *plates.*]

NOUN CLAUSE
I can see **that this plate is chipped.** [*That this plate is chipped* tells what I can see and functions as a direct object.]

Reference Note

For information on using *who, whom, whoever,* and *whomever* correctly, see page 546.

2. No, these results are not what we had planned.
3. Do you know what happened to the rest of my sandwich?
4. Stuart is looking for whoever owns that red bicycle.
5. Checking our supplies, we discovered that we had forgotten the flour.
6. The story's worst flaw is that it doesn't have a carefully developed plot.
7. Whoever takes us to the beach is my friend for life.
8. The painter gave whatever spots had dried on the wall another coat of primer.
9. At lunch, my friends and I talked about what we should do as our service project.
10. That Coretta Scott King spoke for peace surprised no one at the conference.

HELP

Remember that the relative pronoun sometimes is omitted.

Review A Identifying Adjective, Adverb, and Noun Clauses

Identify each subordinate clause in the following sentences, and tell whether it is used as an *adjective*, an *adverb*, or a *noun*.

EXAMPLE 1. Is this the jacket that you bought?
1. that you bought—adjective

1. My aunt found the teapot that my grandfather brought back from Thailand.
2. James skied the advanced slope as if he were an expert.
3. Did anyone ask her what sort of present she would like for her birthday?
4. Eduardo can play the drums better than Alex can.
5. Have you seen the painting to which I am referring?
6. Their solution was that we work on the extra-credit project as a team.
7. Linda told Ken that Monica volunteered to help with the Special Olympics.
8. Whoever wins the student council election will have a great deal of responsibility.
9. Because the tropical storm gained strength, our flight to Belize was canceled.
10. I can't find the baseball and mitt my cousin lent me.

Review B Identifying Subordinate Clauses

Each of the following sentences contains a subordinate clause. Identify each subordinate clause as an *adjective clause,* an *adverb clause,* or a *noun clause.*

EXAMPLE **1.** The Museum of Appalachia, which is in Norris, Tennessee, is a re-created pioneer village.

1. which is in Norris, Tennessee—adjective clause

1. If you've ever wanted to step into the past, you'll like this museum.
2. You can see many pioneer crafts and tools that are still used at the museum.
3. For example, the men on the right are splitting shingles with tools that were used in their boyhood.
4. Two other men show how plowing was done before the development of modern equipment.
5. I think that the 250,000 pioneer tools and other items on display will amaze you.
6. What some visitors like to do is to tour the village's log buildings and then take a rest.
7. While they're resting, they can often listen to some mountain music.

GRAMMAR

8. Listen to all the different instruments that the musicians are playing.
9. At Homecoming, you might even meet the museum's founder, John Rice Irwin, who grew up in the Appalachian Mountains.
10. When I went to the museum's annual Homecoming, I saw the fiddler pictured on the previous page perform.

Review C Writing Sentences with Independent and Subordinate Clauses

Write your own sentences according to the following instructions. Underline the subordinate clauses.

EXAMPLE **1.** Write a sentence containing an independent clause and an adjective clause.

1. I am going to the game with Gilbert, who is my best friend.

1. Write a sentence containing an independent clause and no subordinate clause.
2. Write a sentence containing an independent clause and one subordinate clause.
3. Write a sentence containing an adjective clause that begins with a relative pronoun.
4. Write a sentence containing an adjective clause in which a preposition precedes the relative pronoun.
5. Write a sentence containing an introductory adverb clause.
6. Write a sentence containing an adverb clause and an adjective clause.
7. Write a sentence containing a noun clause used as a direct object.
8. Write a sentence containing a noun clause used as a subject.
9. Write a sentence containing a noun clause used as the object of a preposition.
10. Write a sentence containing a noun clause and either an adjective clause or an adverb clause.

Chapter Review

A. Identifying Subordinate Clauses

Identify the subordinate clause in each of the following sentences.

1. Since none of us owned bicycles, we decided to rent some.
2. The man who rented us the bikes was helpful.
3. We had bicycled six miles when Frieda's bike got a flat tire.
4. How we would repair it became a topic of heated discussion.
5. We decided to take the bike to whatever bike shop was nearest to the park.
6. The woman at the bike shop told us that she could fix the tire quickly.
7. After we had paid for the repair, we rode back to the park and bicycled for an hour.
8. Our only worry was that the man at the rental shop might not pay us back for fixing the tire.
9. When we returned our bikes, we showed the man the receipt for the repaired tire.
10. He refunded us the money we had spent to fix the tire.

B. Identifying Independent and Subordinate Clauses

Identify each italicized clause in the following sentences as an *independent clause* or a *subordinate clause.* Indicate whether each italicized subordinate clause is used as an *adjective,* an *adverb,* or a *noun.*

11. *After it had been snowing for several hours,* we took our sleds out to Sentry Hill.
12. The ring *that I lost at the beach last summer* had belonged to my great-grandmother.
13. If he doesn't get here soon, *I'm leaving.*
14. Do you know *who she is?*
15. I have not seen Sean *since the football game ended.*
16. *In the morning they gathered their belongings and left* before the sun rose.

17. Nobody knew *that Derrick had worked out the solution.*
18. *The Hopi and the Zuni built their homes out of adobe,* which is a kind of sun-dried earth.
19. My dad says never to trust strangers *who seem overly friendly.*
20. *That he had been right* became obvious as the problem grew worse.
21. Julio knew the right answer *because he looked it up.*
22. Today's assignment is to write a three-paragraph composition on *how a bill becomes law.*
23. On our vacation we visited my dad's old neighborhood, *which is now an industrial park.*
24. *Mr. Johnson told us* that in the late 1800s at least one fourth of all the cowboys in the West were African Americans.
25. Did you get the package *that your mother sent?*
26. Tranh raked up the leaves *while his father stuffed them into plastic bags.*
27. *In Israel, the tour group visited several* <u>*kibbutzim*</u>, which are communal farms.
28. We will be over *as soon as Sandy finishes his lunch.*
29. That is the man *whose dog rescued my sister.*
30. Free samples were given to *whoever asked for them.*

C. Identifying Adjective, Adverb, and Noun Clauses

Identify each subordinate clause in the following sentences. Then, tell whether each is used as an *adjective,* an *adverb,* or a *noun.*

31. When my family went to New York last summer, we visited the Theodore Roosevelt museum.
32. The museum has been established in the house where Theodore Roosevelt was born.
33. It is located on the basement floor of Roosevelt's birthplace, which is on East Twentieth Street.
34. The museum contains books, letters, and documents that tell about Roosevelt's public life.
35. There are mounted heads of animals, a stuffed lion, and zebra skins from the days when Roosevelt went big-game hunting in Africa.

36. That he had been a cowboy is obvious from the branding irons and chaps.

37. Before Roosevelt became president, he gained fame in the Spanish-American War.

38. During that war he led the Rough Riders, who made the famous charge up San Juan Hill.

39. Whoever rode with the Rough Riders shared in Roosevelt's later fame.

40. The Roosevelt Memorial Association, which established the museum, charges a nominal admission fee to visitors.

GRAMMAR

Writing Application

Writing a Specific Definition

Using Adjective Clauses Sometimes, people misunderstand each other because they aren't thinking of the same meanings for words. Write a paragraph defining one of the people or things listed below or another term that you choose. Use at least four adjective clauses. Underline those clauses.

a clean room	a loyal friend	a fun weekend
a good teacher	an ideal pet	a good-looking outfit

Prewriting First, choose a term that interests you. Then, take a few minutes to write down whatever thoughts come to mind about that term. Write specific names and details.

Writing State your definition of the term—your main idea—in a topic sentence. As you write your supporting sentences, refer to your notes for specific names and details.

Revising Read over your paragraph. Would your reader understand your definition? Would he or she agree with it? Remember that all details in your paragraph should relate to your definition. If they do not, you may need to add, cut, or revise some information.

Publishing Proofread your paragraph for errors in grammar, spelling, and punctuation. You and your classmates may enjoy comparing different definitions of the same term. You could also gather the definitions together to create a class dictionary.

Reference Note

For more information about **capitalization,** see page 602.

CHAPTER

Sentence Structure

The Four Basic Sentence Structures

Diagnostic Preview

Identifying the Four Kinds of Sentence Structure

Identify each of the following sentences as *simple, compound, complex,* or *compound-complex.*

EXAMPLE 1. When my grandmother came to visit, she taught us how to make our own holiday ornaments.

1. *complex*

1. Last year my grandmother came to stay with us from the middle of December until my brother's birthday in January.
2. While we were getting out the holiday decorations, Mom and Grandma told us all about how people used to make their own decorations.
3. Mom said that she remembered making beautiful decorations and that it used to be great fun, so we decided to try making some of our own.
4. My dad, my brother, and I drove out to the nearby woods to gather pine cones.
5. We had forgotten to ask what size to get, and since Dad had never made decorations, he didn't know.
6. We decided to play it safe and get all different sizes, especially since doing so would be easy with pine cones everywhere.

7. My brother picked up all the little hard ones, and my dad and I threw medium and big ones into the trunk of the car.
8. When Mom and Grandma saw how many we had, they laughed and said we had enough to decorate ten houses.
9. First, we sorted the cones; the little hard ones went into one pile, and the bigger ones went into another.
10. Dad and I painted the little ones silver, and Mom and Grandma painted stripes, dots, and all sorts of other designs on them.
11. Then we tied strings to the tops of the cones; later, when we put them up, they made great ornaments.
12. We painted the bigger pine cones all different colors and glued on cranberries and beads so that each cone looked like a miniature fir tree.
13. We saved some smaller ones for the dining room table, and we put most of the others all around the house.
14. My brother took some to school for a holiday party, too.
15. Besides the pine-cone decorations, we made some strings to decorate the mantel.
16. My mom got needles and a spool of heavy thread out of her sewing basket, and we strung the rest of the cranberries on six-foot lengths of the thread.
17. Mom and Grandma cut several more long pieces of thread, and we used them to make strings of popcorn like our strings of cranberries.
18. We left some of the popcorn strings white, painted the others different colors, and hung them around the living room and dining room.
19. Decorating was even more fun than usual, and I think that the whole house looked prettier, too, with all our homemade ornaments.
20. From now on, we're going to make all of our own holiday decorations every year.

GRAMMAR

What Is Sentence Structure?

The ***structure*** of a sentence refers to the kinds and the number of clauses it contains. The four kinds of sentences are *simple, compound, complex,* and *compound-complex.*

Reference Note

For information about **classifying sentences according to purpose,** see page 339.

GRAMMAR

Simple Sentences

HELP— A ***clause*** is a group of words that contains a verb and its subject and that is used as a sentence or as part of a sentence.

16a. A *simple sentence* contains one independent clause and no subordinate clauses.

EXAMPLES The hairstylist (S) gave (V) Latrice a new look.

Ernesto (S) has volunteered (V) to organize the recycling campaign.

Reference Note

For more about **clauses,** see Chapter 15.

Reference Note

For more about **compound subjects** and **compound verbs,** see pages 335 and 336. For more about the types of **phrases,** see Chapter 14.

A simple sentence may contain a compound subject, a compound verb, and any number of phrases.

EXAMPLES **Beth Heiden** (S) and **Sheila Young** (S) **won** (V) Olympic medals. [compound subject]

Lawrence (S) **caught** (V) the ball but then **dropped** (V) it. [compound verb]

The **astronomer** (S) and her **assistant** (S) **studied** (V) the meteor and **wrote** (V) reports. [compound subject and compound verb]

Both (S) of the scientists on the expedition **stood** (V) still, waiting for the jungle cat to move away. [three prepositional phrases, one participial phrase, and one infinitive phrase]

Exercise 1 Identifying Subjects and Verbs in Simple Sentences

HELP— Some sentences in Exercise 1 have compound subjects or compound verbs.

Identify the subjects and the verbs in the following simple sentences.

EXAMPLE 1. Throughout history, people have invented and used a variety of weapons.

1. people—subject; have invented, used—verbs

1. As protection from such weapons, warriors in battle needed special equipment.
2. Some warriors used shields of wood or animal hides.

3. In ancient Assyria, soldiers wore leather armor with bronze reinforcements.
4. By 1800 B.C., the Greeks had made the first metal armor out of bronze.
5. Later, the Romans manufactured strong iron armor and designed special equipment, such as shinguards.
6. Before and during the Middle Ages, European knights and foot soldiers often dressed in shirts of chain mail.
7. You can see the tiny steel links of the chains in this picture.
8. In comparison with chain mail, suits of steel armor gave better protection and therefore became more popular.
9. Helmets and shoulder pieces like these protected a knight's head and neck.
10. Over his legs and feet, a knight wore greaves and sollerets into battle.

Compound Sentences

Reference Note

For more information on **independent clauses,** see page 440.

16b. A *compound sentence* contains two or more independent clauses and no subordinate clauses.

The independent clauses are usually joined by a comma and a coordinating conjunction: *and, but, for, nor, or, so,* or *yet.*

EXAMPLES **According to legend, Betsy Ross made our first flag,** but **little evidence supports this claim.** [two independent clauses joined by the conjunction *but*]

(S: Betsy Ross; V: made; S: evidence; V: supports)

The whistle blew, the drums rolled, and **the crowd cheered.** [three independent clauses, the last two joined by the conjunction *and*]

(S: whistle; V: blew; S: drums; V: rolled; S: crowd; V: cheered)

NOTE Do not confuse a compound sentence with a simple sentence that contains a compound subject, a compound verb, or both.

SIMPLE SENTENCE **Alberto** and **Jared increased** their speed and **passed** the other runners. [compound subject and compound verb]

(S: Alberto; S: Jared; V: increased; V: passed)

COMPOUND SENTENCE **Alberto led** for half the distance, and then **Jared took** the lead. [two independent clauses]

(S: Alberto; V: led; S: Jared; V: took)

Reference Note

For more about using **semicolons** and **conjunctive adverbs** in **compound sentences,** see pages 649 and 650.

The independent clauses in a compound sentence may also be joined by a semicolon or by a semicolon, a conjunctive adverb, and a comma.

EXAMPLES Many mathematical concepts originated in North Africa**;** the ancient Egyptians used these concepts in building the pyramids.

(S: concepts; V: originated; S: Egyptians; V: used)

S V
Lynn called Marty with the good news**; however,**

S V
he was not at home.

Exercise 2 Identifying Subjects, Verbs, and Conjunctions in Compound Sentences

Each of the following sentences is a compound sentence. Identify the subject and the verb in each of the independent clauses in each sentence. Then, give any punctuation marks, coordinating conjunctions, or conjunctive adverbs that join the independent clauses.

EXAMPLE **1.** Many strange things happen backstage during a performance, but the audience usually does not know about them.

1. *things—subject; happen—verb; audience—subject; does know—verb; comma + but*

1. The director of a theater-in-the-round visited our class, and we listened to his stories for almost an hour.

2. According to him, the workers in charge of properties are usually alert and careful; however, they still make mistakes sometimes.

3. For example, in one production of *Romeo and Juliet,* the character Juliet prepared to kill herself with a dagger, but no dagger was on the stage.

4. Audiences at theaters-in-the-round can also be a problem, for they sit very close to the stage.

5. Members of the audience often set things on stage tables, or they hang their coats on the actors' coat racks.

6. Sometimes these actions are overlooked by the stagehands, and the results can be very challenging for the actors.

7. For example, the main clue in one mystery play was a scarf on the stage floor, but the audience had gathered on the stage during intermission.

8. After the intermission, the detective in the play found two scarves instead of one, yet he could not show any surprise.

9. During another mystery drama, a spectator became too involved in the play; he leaped up on the stage and tackled the villain.

10. Directors cannot always predict the reactions of the audience, nor can they always control the audience.

GRAMMAR

Exercise 3 Identifying Simple Sentences and Compound Sentences

Identify each subject and verb in the following sentences. Then, tell whether the sentence is a *simple sentence* or a *compound sentence.*

EXAMPLES
1. African American actors and actresses performed in many early Hollywood movies.
   1. *actors, actresses—subjects; performed—verb; simple sentence*
2. Hattie McDaniel, for example, made many films, and she is best known for her role in *Gone with the Wind.*
   2. *Hattie McDaniel—subject; made—verb; she—subject; is known—verb; compound sentence*

1. Over the years, African American performers have earned much acclaim and won a number of Academy Awards.
2. Hattie McDaniel won an Oscar for her role in *Gone with the Wind* in 1939.
3. Sidney Poitier acted in stage plays and made several movies early in his career.
4. Poitier won an Oscar in 1963 for *Lilies of the Field,* and he later made many other popular films.
5. McDaniel and Poitier were the first African Americans to receive Academy Awards.
6. More recently, Lou Gossett, Jr., and Denzel Washington played supporting roles as military men and won Academy Awards for their performances.
7. Another winner, Whoopi Goldberg, first gained fame as a stand-up comic; then she made several hit movies.
8. Critics praised her performance in *The Color Purple,* and in 1991, she won an Academy Award for her role in *Ghost.*
9. *The Tuskegee Airmen,* a film about African American fighter pilots during WWII, and *As Good As It Gets* brought Cuba Gooding, Jr., much attention.
10. In 1996, Gooding was nominated for an Oscar for a role as a professional football player, and he won the award for best supporting actor.

Complex Sentences

16c. A *complex sentence* contains one independent clause and at least one subordinate clause.

EXAMPLES When I watch Martha Graham's performances, I feel like studying dance.

Independent clause	I feel like studying dance
Subordinate clause	When I watch Martha Graham's performances

In *Gone with the Wind,* when Scarlett is faced with near-starvation, she vows that she never will be hungry again.

Independent clause	In *Gone with the Wind,* she vows
Subordinate clause	when Scarlett is faced with near-starvation
Subordinate clause	that she never will be hungry again

Independent clauses can be interrupted by subordinate clauses.

EXAMPLE All of the stars that we can see without a telescope are part of the Milky Way galaxy.

Independent clause	All of the stars are part of the Milky Way galaxy
Subordinate clause	that we can see without a telescope

Notice in the examples above that a subordinate clause can appear at the beginning, in the middle, or at the end of a complex sentence.

Reference Note

For more information on **independent** and **subordinate clauses,** see pages 440 and 441.

GRAMMAR

GRAMMAR

HELP—

In the first example in Exercise 4 the independent clause contains the subject *China* and the verb *is.* The subordinate clause contains the subject *which* and the verb *has.* In the second example, the independent clause contains the subject *brother* and the verb *bought.* The subordinate clause contains the subject *it* and the verb *was.*

Exercise 4 Identifying Independent Clauses and Subordinate Clauses in Complex Sentences

Identify each of the clauses in the following sentences as *independent* or *subordinate.* Be prepared to give the subject and the verb of each clause. [Hint: A sentence may have more than one subordinate clause.]

EXAMPLES

1. China, which has a population of more than one billion people, is a largely agricultural country.

1. China is a largely agricultural country—independent; which has a population of more than one billion people—subordinate

2. Although it was nearly worthless, my brother bought one of those old coins for his collection.

2. Although it was nearly worthless—subordinate; my brother bought one of those old coins for his collection—independent

1. The detective show appeared on television for several weeks before it became popular with viewers.
2. Most of the albums that my parents have from the 1970s are sitting in the corner of the basement behind the broken refrigerator.
3. Richard E. Byrd is but one of the explorers who traveled to Antarctica.
4. As studies continued, many important facts about nutrition were discovered.
5. A group of popular singers, who donated their time, recorded a song that made people aware of a famine in Ethiopia.
6. The Hawaiian ruler who wrote the famous song *"Aloha Oe"* ("Farewell to Thee") was Queen Liliuokalani.
7. After we finish our report on the history of computers, we may go to the basketball game.
8. Although few students or teachers knew about it, a group of sociologists visited our school to study the relationship between classroom environment and students' grades.
9. While the stage crew was constructing the sets, the performers continued their rehearsal, which went on into the night.
10. Although she had polio as a child, Wilma Rudolph became a top American Olympic athlete.

Compound-Complex Sentences

16d. **A *compound-complex sentence* contains two or more independent clauses and at least one subordinate clause.**

EXAMPLES

S V
Yolanda began painting only two years ago, but

S V
already she has been asked to show one of her

S V
paintings at the exhibit that is scheduled for May.

Independent clause	Yolanda began painting only two years ago
Independent clause	already she has been asked to show one of her paintings at the exhibit
Subordinate clause	that is scheduled for May

S V S V S V
When Bill left, he locked the door, but he forgot to turn off the lights.

Independent clause	he locked the door
Independent clause	he forgot to turn off the lights
Subordinate clause	When Bill left

S V S V
Emilia has several hobbies that she enjoys, but the

S S V V
one on which she spends the most time is woodcarving.

Independent clause	Emilia has several hobbies
Independent clause	the one is woodcarving
Subordinate clause	that she enjoys
Subordinate clause	on which she spends the most time

STYLE  **TIP**

When you revise your writing, pay attention to the types of sentences you use. By using a number of different sentence structures, you can make your writing clearer and more interesting.

Simple sentences are best used to express single ideas. To describe more complicated ideas and to show how the ideas fit together, use compound, complex, and compound-complex sentences.

SIMPLE SENTENCES

Yesterday I visited my friend Amy. Then I went to Willa's house. We worked on our dance steps.

COMPOUND-COMPLEX SENTENCE

After I visited my friend Amy yesterday, I went to Willa's house, and we worked on our dance steps.

COMPUTER TIP

A word processor can help you check for varied sentence structure in your writing. Make a copy of your document to work on. By inserting a return after every period, you can view the sentences in a vertical list and compare the structures of each sentence in a particular paragraph. Make any revisions on the properly formatted copy of your document.

Exercise 5 Identifying Clauses in Compound-Complex Sentences

Identify each of the clauses in the following sentences as *independent* or *subordinate.*

EXAMPLE **1.** When they returned from their vacation, they collected their mail at the post office, and they went to the supermarket.

1. When they returned from their vacation—subordinate; they collected their mail at the post office—independent; they went to the supermarket—independent

1. Before we conducted the experiment, we asked for permission to use the science lab, but the principal insisted on teacher supervision of our work.

2. Inside the old trunk in the attic, which is filled with boxes and toys, we found some dusty photo albums; and one of them contained pictures from the early 1900s.

3. We told them that their plan wouldn't work, but they wouldn't listen to us.

4. Every expedition that had attempted to explore that region had vanished without a trace, yet the young adventurer was determined to map the uncharted jungle because he couldn't resist the challenge.

5. The smoke, which steadily grew thicker and darker, billowed through the dry forest; the animals ran ahead of the fire as it spread quickly.

6. Our new neighbors, who moved in last month, have painted their house, and the children have put up a basketball hoop.

7. Because Traci, Sheila, and Tomas like to compete, they swim laps in the pool in the park, and they keep a chart of who wins each time.

8. We bought tortillas, cheese, tomatoes, and onions; and Ernesto made enchiladas, which everyone enjoyed.

9. Gabriel and Daniel earned the money that they wanted for new bikes, but then they put the money into their savings accounts instead.

10. I was glad that the school bus came early the day of the science fair; I needed extra time at school to set up my exhibit.

Review A Identifying the Four Kinds of Sentence Structure

Identify each of the following sentences as *simple, compound, complex,* or *compound-complex.*

EXAMPLE 1. If she had not practiced, my cousin Sheila could not have become a good skater.

1. complex

1. People who are learning a new sport begin by mastering basic skills.
2. After people have practiced basic skills for a while, they can progress to more difficult moves.
3. At this point a beginner may become discouraged, and the temptation to quit grows strong.
4. One of the most common problems that beginners face is lack of coordination; another is muscular aches and pains.
5. A beginner who is not careful can injure muscles, yet strenuous activity usually strengthens the muscle tissues.
6. When enough oxygen reaches the warmed-up muscles, the danger of injury lessens, and the muscles grow in size.
7. At the same time, coordination grows with confidence.
8. The hours of practice that a beginner puts in usually result in rewarding improvements.
9. As a rule, learning something new takes time and work, or it will not seem worthwhile.
10. In sports, as in most other activities, persistence and patience often pay off.

Review B Writing a Variety of Sentence Structures

Write your own original sentences according to the following instructions.

EXAMPLE 1. Write a compound sentence with two independent clauses joined by a comma and *and.*

1. My mother usually serves us spaghetti for supper once a week, and she makes the best spaghetti in the world.

1. Write a simple sentence with a compound subject.
2. Write a simple sentence with a compound verb.
3. Write a compound sentence with two independent clauses joined by a comma and *but.*

4. Write a compound sentence with two independent clauses joined by a comma and *or.*
5. Write a compound sentence with two independent clauses joined by a semicolon.
6. Write a complex sentence with one subordinate clause.
7. Write a complex sentence with two subordinate clauses.
8. Write a complex sentence with a subordinate clause at the beginning of the sentence.
9. Write a complex sentence with a subordinate clause at the end of the sentence.
10. Write a compound-complex sentence.

GRAMMAR

Chapter Review

A. Identifying Sentence Structures

Identify each of the following sentences as *simple, compound, complex,* or *compound-complex.*

1. Christina left on time, but her bus was late.
2. When the rabbit saw us, it ran into the bushes.
3. In 1967, Thurgood Marshall became the first African American on the U.S. Supreme Court.
4. You can either buy a new bicycle or fix the old one.
5. Yoko said that this would be the shortest route, but I disagree.
6. How could we tell what had really happened?
7. That seems to me like the answer to the first problem.
8. Mercedes Rodriguez of Miami, Florida, entered and won the contest.
9. Do you know who wrote this note and left it on my desk?
10. I'm not sure what you mean, but I think that I agree.
11. Nobody is worried about that, for it will never happen.
12. Whatever you decide will be fine with me.
13. Is the movie that we want to see still playing in theaters, or is it available on video?
14. Rommel knew the plan, and he assigned each unit a part.
15. Amphibians and some insects can live both on the land and in water.
16. The detectives searched for the woman who had been wearing a blue beret, but there weren't any other clues.
17. The tornado cut across the edge of the housing development yesterday morning, and seven homes were damaged.
18. By July of 1847, the Mormons had reached the Great Salt Lake valley.
19. Before the game started, all the football players ran out onto the field, and everyone cheered.
20. My father helped the family whose car had broken down on the highway.

21. My cousin sent me a present for my birthday.

22. When I jog, the dog next door often follows me.

23. Tara opened the door, but when she saw the snow, she decided to stay inside.

24. Delsin drew the picture, and I added the text.

25. Are those letters from New Jersey for me?

26. When birds fly during a rainstorm, the rain will probably last all day.

27. Eagerly, we unpacked the tent, and my uncle who had been in the army helped us set it up in the side yard.

28. The lake was filled with trout, and we caught enough fish for a delicious dinner.

29. Gordon Parks wrote *The Learning Tree* and directed the film version of the novel.

30. Alaska's flag was designed by a boy who was in the seventh grade.

B. Identifying Clauses in Compound, Complex, and Compound-Complex Sentences

Identify each clause in the sentences in the following paragraph as *independent* or *subordinate.*

[31] Jan Vermeer (pronounced yahn vuhr-MEER) was a seventeenth-century Dutch painter who used the pointillist method of painting. **[32]** With this method, the painter uses small dots, or points, of unmixed color, and the result is almost like putting gauze in front of a camera lens. **[33]** In paintings such as *The Lacemaker,* this technique gives the light a soft, blurry quality that has become the best-known characteristic of Vermeer's work. **[34]** His paintings are now world-famous, but Vermeer never left his hometown of Delft in the Netherlands. **[35]** In fact, he did not work primarily as a painter at all but spent most of his life as an art dealer and innkeeper. **[36]** Vermeer's paintings deal with many subjects, including landscapes, but they are primarily known for their scenes of house interiors. **[37]** They show young people who are talking, playing musical instruments, reading letters, and laughing, all in a relaxed and peaceful atmosphere. [**38**] Many of his subjects are caught in moments of concentration, yet the overall feeling is calm. [**39**] Perhaps his own paintings are unique because he never left his hometown and therefore did not see much of other artists' work. [**40**] Vermeer's paintings are alive with color, and they shine with a pure, serene light that is rarely found in art or life.

Writing Application

Using Sentence Variety in a Telephone Message

Sentence Structures Imagine that you have missed your ride home after school, so you have gone to a friend's house. No one is at your home now, but you know you should call and leave a message on the answering machine. Write out the message that you will leave. Use a variety of sentence structures.

Prewriting First, decide what will be in your message. You will want to tell where you are, why you are there, and why you missed your ride. You may also want to say when you will be home and whether arrangements should be made to pick you up. Make notes on all these details.

Writing Use your notes to write your first draft. As you write, remember that your message must be short but clear and informative. Think about how you can combine ideas.

Revising Read your message aloud, and listen to how it sounds. Are your explanations and plans complete? Do they sound logical? Check to be sure that you have used a variety of sentence structures.

Publishing Read over your message again, checking for errors in grammar, spelling, and punctuation. You and your classmates may want to hold a contest to determine the best of several messages. Once the best message has been chosen, you may want to post it on a class bulletin board or Web page.

Reference Note

For more information about **punctuating compound sentences,** see pages 637 and 649. For more about **using commas with subordinate clauses,** see page 644.

CHAPTER

Agreement

Subject and Verb, Pronoun and Antecedent

Diagnostic Preview

A. Identifying Verbs That Agree with Their Subjects

In each of the following sentences, if the italicized verb does not agree with its subject, write the correct form of the verb. If the sentence is already correct, write *C.*

EXAMPLES
1. The people on the bus *have* all been seated.
   1. C
2. The fish, bass and perch mostly, *has* started feeding.
   2. have

1. The swarm of bees *have* deserted its hive.
2. My spelling lessons and science homework sometimes *takes* me hours to finish.
3. Somebody who is on the council *don't* approve of the new rule.
4. Neither Danny Glover nor Morgan Freeman *stars* in tonight's movie.
5. *Doesn't* those children still take piano lessons?
6. There *is* probably a few children who don't like strawberries.
7. Most of the guests *likes* the inn's Irish soda bread.
8. Both of those varsity players *exercise* for an hour each day.
9. Evenings *is* the best time to visit her.
10. Physics or mathematics *are* the subject you should study.

B. Identifying Pronouns That Agree with Their Antecedents

In each of the following sentences, if the italicized pronoun does not agree with its antecedent, write the correct form of the pronoun. If the sentence is already correct, write *C.*

EXAMPLES
1. Either of the men could have offered *their* help.
   1. *his*
2. Both of the flowers had spread *their* petals.
   2. *C*

11. Why doesn't somebody raise *their* hand and ask Mr. Liu for directions?
12. One of the birds lost most of *their* tail feathers.
13. Joey sold *his* last ticket to Heather.
14. The old tennis court has weeds growing in *their* nets.
15. The Smithsonian's National Museum of the American Indian had closed *their* doors for the day.
16. I don't understand how chameleons sitting on a green leaf or on a bush change *their* color.
17. Alex has studied gymnastics for many years, and he is now very good at *them.*
18. These girls can choose *her* own materials from the supply room.
19. The senior class has chosen *their* theme for homecoming.
20. Island of the Blue Dolphins is my sister's favorite book, and she has read *it* three times.

Number

Number is the form a word takes to indicate whether the word is singular or plural.

17a. When a word refers to one person, place, thing, or idea, it is *singular* in number. When a word refers to more than one person, place, thing, or idea, it is *plural* in number.

Reference Note

For more about forming **plurals of nouns,** see page 694.

Singular	egg	person	fox	I	die	each
Plural	eggs	people	foxes	we	dice	all

USAGE

Oral Practice 1 Classifying Nouns and Pronouns by Number

Read the following expressions aloud. Tell whether each italicized noun or pronoun is *singular* or *plural.*

1. The *lion* yawns.
2. The *cubs* play.
3. *No one* stays.
4. The *refugees* arrive.
5. *She* wins.
6. The *play* opens.
7. *Everyone* goes.
8. *All* applaud.

Exercise 1 Classifying Nouns and Pronouns by Number

Classify each of the following words as *singular* or *plural.*

EXAMPLE 1. cat
1. singular

1. rodeos
2. book
3. they
4. I
5. many
6. igloo
7. geese
8. we
9. friends
10. it
11. lake
12. heroes
13. oxen
14. aunt
15. roof
16. year
17. children
18. those
19. mice
20. skate
21. shoes
22. bases
23. him
24. license
25. guess

Reference Note

The plurals of some nouns do not end in *s* (for example, *feet, children, moose*). For more about **irregularly formed plurals,** see page 695.

TIPS & TRICKS

Generally, nouns ending in *–s* are plural (*bands, thoughts, friends, lizards*), and verbs ending in *–s* are singular (*jumps, hears, borrows, waits*). However, verbs used with the singular pronouns *I* and *you* do not end in *–s.*

EXAMPLES
The **friends talk.**
The **friend talks.**
I talk.
You talk.

Agreement of Subject and Verb

17b. A verb should agree in number with its subject.

(1) Singular subjects take singular verbs.

EXAMPLES The **car comes** to a sudden stop. [The singular verb *comes* agrees with the singular subject *car.*]

On that route the **airplane flies** at a very low altitude. [The singular verb *flies* agrees with the singular subject *plane.*]

(2) Plural subjects take plural verbs.

EXAMPLES Many **senators oppose** the new tax bill. [The plural verb *oppose* agrees with the plural subject *senators*.]

The **dolphins leap** playfully in the channel. [The plural verb *leap* agrees with the plural subject *dolphins*.]

In a verb phrase, the first helping verb agrees in number with the subject.

EXAMPLES **He is building** a bird feeder. [The singular helping verb *is* agrees with the singular subject *He*.]

They are building a bird feeder. [The plural helping verb *are* agrees with the plural subject *They*.]

Does anyone know the answer? [The singular helping verb *Does* agrees with the singular subject *anyone*.]

Do any **students know** the answer? [The plural helping verb *Do* agrees with the plural subject *students*.]

Reference Note

For more about **helping verbs,** see page 372.

Exercise 2 Identifying Verbs That Agree in Number with Their Subjects

Choose the form of the verb in parentheses that agrees with the given subject.

EXAMPLES 1. it (*is, are*)
1. is

2. they (*does, do*)
2. do

1. this (*costs, cost*)
2. Chinese lanterns (*glows, glow*)
3. the swimmer (*dives, dive*)
4. we (*considers, consider*)
5. the men (*was, were*)
6. she (*asks, ask*)
7. these (*needs, need*)
8. those tacos (*tastes, taste*)
9. that music (*sounds, sound*)
10. lessons (*takes, take*)
11. several actors (*accepts, accept*)
12. children (*interferes, interfere*)
13. they (*says, say*)
14. counselor (*advises, advise*)
15. the woman (*leads, lead*)
16. you (*chooses, choose*)
17. mice (*approaches, approach*)
18. friends (*tries, try*)
19. the officer (*appreciates, appreciate*)
20. I (*swims, swim*)

COMPUTER TIP

Some word-processing programs can find problems in subject-verb agreement. You can use such programs to search for errors when you proofread your writing. However, such programs are not perfect. If you are not sure that an error found by the word processor is truly an error, check the relevant rule in this book.

Exercise 3 Identifying Verbs That Agree in Number with Their Subjects

Choose the correct form of the verb in parentheses in each of the following sentences.

EXAMPLE **1.** (*Do, Does*) you like soccer?
1. Do

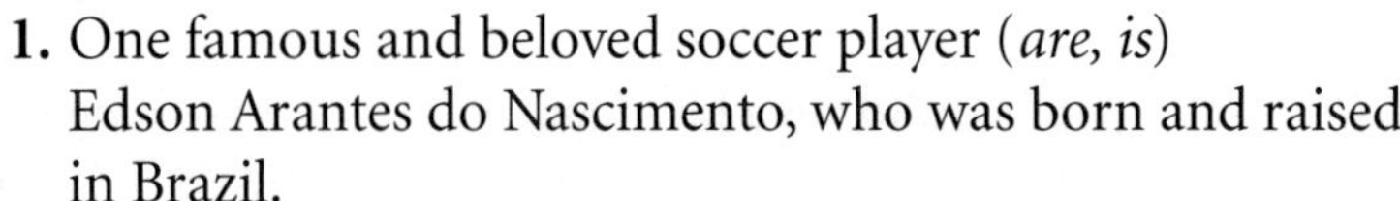

1. One famous and beloved soccer player (*are, is*) Edson Arantes do Nascimento, who was born and raised in Brazil.
2. His father (*were, was*) a soccer player, and young Edson loved to watch his father play.
3. The Brazilian fans (*call, calls*) the game *futebol.*
4. When the crowd (*cheers, cheer*), Edson's father beams.
5. Edson's mother (*keep, keeps*) her children from playing soccer whenever she can.
6. Many (*are, is*) injured while playing, and Edson's mother doesn't want her children to be among them.
7. The neighborhood children (*loves, love*) the game so much that they make a ball from a sock stuffed with paper, rags, and string and play in the dusty street.
8. The neighborhood boys (*nicknames, nickname*) Edson "Pelé," the name by which he is known when he later becomes a famous soccer player.
9. Even as a child, Pelé (*excels, excel*) at the game, and his father starts coaching him.
10. When Pelé is fifteen years old, he (*begins, begin*) to play professionally.

Problems in Agreement

Phrases and Clauses Between Subjects and Verbs

17c. The number of a subject is not changed by a phrase or clause following the subject.

EXAMPLES The **lights** on the Christmas tree **create** a festive atmosphere. [The prepositional phrase *on the Christmas tree* does not affect the number of the subject *lights.*]

The **distance** between the two posts **is** eight feet. [The prepositional phrase *between the two posts* does not affect the number of the subject *distance.*]

Karen's **brother,** who has always enjoyed bicycle repair and maintenance, **works** at the bike shop on weekends. [The adjective clause *who has always enjoyed bicycle repair and maintenance* does not affect the number of the subject *brother.*]

NOTE If the subject is the indefinite pronoun *all, any, more, most, none,* or *some,* its number may be determined by the object of a prepositional phrase that follows it.

EXAMPLES **All** of the vegetables **were** peeled. [*All* refers to the plural word *vegetables.*]

All of the salad **was** eaten. [*All* refers to the singular word *salad.*]

Exercise 4 Identifying Subjects and Verbs That Agree in Number

Identify the subject in each sentence. Then, choose the form of the verb in parentheses that agrees with the subject.

EXAMPLE 1. The houses on my block (*has, have*) two stories.
1. houses—subject; have

1. The launch of a space shuttle (*attracts, attract*) the interest of people throughout the world.
2. Our thermos, which is in the picnic basket, (*is, are*) filled with apple juice.
3. That collection of poems (*is, are*) *Where the Sidewalk Ends.*
4. People in some states (*observes, observe*) the fourth Friday in September as Native American Day.
5. The children of the world (*needs, need*) food and medicine.
6. The house on the hill (*is, are*) where my grandfather was born.
7. Koalas that live in the wild and in captivity (*eats, eat*) only eucalyptus leaves.
8. The principal of each high school (*awards, award*) certificates to honor students.
9. Stories about Hank Aaron always (*makes, make*) me want to play baseball.
10. The cucumbers in my garden (*grows, grow*) very quickly.

TIPS & TRICKS

The subject of a sentence is never in a prepositional phrase.

EXAMPLE
The **files** in this drawer **are** neat and organized. [The subject is *files. Drawer* is part of the prepositional phrase *in this drawer.*]

As well as, along with, together with, and *in addition to* are compound prepositions. Phrases beginning with compound prepositions do not affect the number of the subject or verb.

EXAMPLE
The **conductor,** as well as the musicians, **wears** formal wear at every performance. [The prepositional phrase *as well as the musicians* does not affect the number of the subject *conductor.*]

Reference Note

For a list of **common prepositions,** see page 386.

USAGE

Indefinite Pronouns

You may recall that personal pronouns refer to specific people, places, things, or ideas. Some pronouns do not refer to a definite person, place, thing, or idea and are therefore called ***indefinite pronouns.***

17d. The following indefinite pronouns are singular: *anybody, anyone, anything, each, either, everybody, everyone, everything, neither, nobody, nothing, no one, one, somebody, someone,* and *something.*

EXAMPLES **Everyone was invited** to the celebration.

Either of the answers **is** correct.

One of the tapes **belongs** to Sabrena.

Someone in the stands **has been waving** at us.

Pronouns like *each* and *one* are frequently followed by prepositional phrases. Remember that, for these pronouns, the verb agrees with the subject of the sentence, not with a word in a prepositional phrase.

17e. The following indefinite pronouns are plural: *both, few, many,* and *several.*

EXAMPLES **Both** of the apples **are** good.

Few know about the surprise.

Many of the students **walk** to school.

Several of the club's members **have** not **paid** their dues.

17f. The indefinite pronouns *all, any, more, most, none,* and *some* may be singular or plural, depending on their meaning in a sentence.

Often, the object in a prepositional phrase that follows the pronoun indicates whether the pronoun is singular or plural. Usually, if the object of the preposition is singular, the pronoun is singular. If the object is plural, the pronoun usually is plural.

EXAMPLES **All** of the fruit **looks** ripe. [*All* refers to the singular object *fruit.*]

All of the pears **look** ripe. [*All* refers to the plural object *pears.*]

TIPS & TRICKS

The words *body, one,* and *thing* are singular. The indefinite pronouns that contain these words are singular as well.

EXAMPLES

Was any**body** there?

Some**one is** inside.

Every**thing has** been done.

USAGE

HELP

Some indefinite pronouns, such as *both, each,* and *some,* can also be used as adjectives. When one of these words comes before the subject of a sentence, the verb agrees with the subject as it normally would.

Just as you would write **Children love** playing in the park.

or

The **child loves** playing in the park.

You would write **Both children love** playing in the park.

or

Each child loves playing in the park.

Reference Note

For more about **indefinite pronouns,** see page 356.

Some of the equipment **has been stored** in the garage. [*Some* refers to the singular object *equipment.*]

Some of the supplies **have been stored** in the garage. [*Some* refers to the plural object *supplies.*]

NOTE The pronouns listed in Rule 17f are not always followed by prepositional phrases.

EXAMPLES **All have** left.

Some was eaten.

In such cases, you should look at the context—the other words and sentences surrounding the pronoun—to see if the pronoun refers to a singular or a plural word.

Exercise 5 Identifying Subjects and Verbs That Agree in Number

Identify the subject in each of the following sentences. Then, choose the form of the verb in parentheses that agrees with the subject.

EXAMPLE 1. Each of the marchers (*was, were*) carrying a sign protesting apartheid.

1. Each—subject; was

1. All of my friends (*has, have*) had the chickenpox.
2. Everyone at the party (*likes, like*) the hummus dip.
3. Both of Fred's older brothers (*celebrates, celebrate*) their birthdays in July.
4. Some of the story (*is, are*) funny.
5. None of those rosebushes in my mother's garden ever (*blooms, bloom*) in February.
6. Several of those colors (*do, does*) not appeal to me.
7. Many of Mrs. Taniguchi's students (*speaks, speak*) fluent Japanese.
8. Nobody in these beginning painting classes (*has, have*) displayed work in the annual art show.
9. Most of the food here (*tastes, taste*) delicious.
10. One of Georgia O'Keeffe's paintings (*shows, show*) a ram's skull.

COMPUTER TIP

Using indefinite pronouns correctly can be tricky. To help yourself, you may want to create an indefinite pronoun guide. First, summarize the information in Rules 17d–17f and 17t. Then, choose several examples to illustrate the rules. If you use a computer, you can create a "Help" file in which to store this information.

Call up your "Help" file whenever you run into difficulty with indefinite pronouns in your writing. If you do not use a computer, keep a writing notebook.

HELP—

Some sentences in Review A have more than one verb.

USAGE

Review A **Proofreading Sentences for Subject-Verb Agreement**

Many of the following sentences contain errors in subject-verb agreement. If the verb does not agree with its subject, write the correct form of the verb. If the sentence contains no errors, write *C.*

EXAMPLES

1. One of the best-known prehistoric monuments in the world stand in a field in Britain.

   1. *stands*

2. Today everybody calls the monument Stonehenge, and thousands of people visits it each year.

   2. *visit*

1. All of the visitors to Stonehenge wants to know why the structure was built.
2. The huge rocks at Stonehenge challenges tourists and scientists alike to uncover their mysteries.
3. Most people easily recognize the monument as it looks in the photograph below.
4. However, nobody are sure how Stonehenge looked long ago.
5. Some of the archaeologists studying the site believes that Stonehenge once looked very different.
6. Few of the stones remains in their original places.
7. Many visitors to Stonehenge assume that ancient Druids built the monument.
8. Most scientists, though, says it was built many years before the Druids—perhaps four thousand years ago.

9. After seeing Stonehenge, few doubt that the stones weighs as much as fifty tons.
10. Of course, nearly everyone seem to have a theory about how these stones were set in place and what they were used for, but no one knows for sure.

Compound Subjects

17g. Subjects joined by *and* usually take a plural verb.

Most compound subjects joined by *and* name more than one person or thing and take plural verbs.

EXAMPLES **Antonia Brico** and **Sarah Caldwell are** famous conductors. [Two persons are conductors.]

Last year a **library** and a **museum were built** in our town. [Two things were built.]

Reference Note

For more about **compound subjects,** see page 335.

A compound subject that names only one person or thing takes a singular verb.

EXAMPLES The **secretary** and **treasurer** of the science club **is** Leona. [One person is both the secretary and the treasurer.]

Chicken and dumplings is a favorite Southern dish. [*Chicken and dumplings* is one dish.]

Exercise 6 Choosing Verbs That Agree in Number with Compound Subjects

Identify the compound subject in each of the following sentences as *singular* or *plural.* Then, choose the form of the verb that agrees with the compound subject.

EXAMPLE 1. Cleon and Pam (*is, are*) here.
1. *plural—are*

1. March and April (*is, are*) windy months.
2. The mechanic and shop owner (*is, are*) preparing his estimate.
3. Martina Hingis and Venus Williams (*plays, play*) in the finals today.
4. Red beans and rice (*is, are*) my favorite Cajun dish.

5. Carla and Jean (*takes, take*) dancing lessons.
6. The knives and forks (*is, are*) in the drawer.
7. English and science (*requires, require*) hours of study.
8. Our star and winner of the meet (*has, have*) just entered the gym.
9. The bread and the honey (*is, are*) in the pantry.
10. An Austrian and a German generally (*speaks, speak*) the same language.

17h. Singular subjects joined by *or* or *nor* take a singular verb. Plural subjects joined by *or* or *nor* take a plural verb.

EXAMPLES A **pen** or a **pencil is needed** for this test.

Neither **Miami** nor **Jacksonville is** the capital of Florida.

Neither the **leopards** nor the **tigers were** paying attention to the herd.

Are the **Bulldogs** or the **Mustangs** winning the game?

USAGE

Exercise 7 Choosing Verbs That Agree in Number with Compound Subjects

Choose the form of the verb in parentheses that agrees with the compound subject in each of the following sentences.

EXAMPLE 1. Neither Theo nor Erin (*has, have*) learned the Jewish folk dance *Mayim, Mayim.*

1. has

1. Either Mrs. Gomez or Mr. Ming (*delivers, deliver*) the welcome speech on the first day of school.
2. Neither our guava tree nor our fig tree (*bears, bear*) fruit if we experience a drought.
3. Tuskegee Institute or Harvard University (*offers, offer*) the best courses in Francine's field.
4. Do armadillos or anteaters (*has, have*) tubular mouths and long, sticky tongues for catching insects?
5. Either the president or the vice-president of the class (*thinks, think*) we should have a paper drive.
6. Neither Sarah's report on Booker T. Washington nor the boys' reports on Quanah Parker (*sounds, sound*) boring to me.
7. Green or royal blue (*looks, look*) nice in this bedroom.

8. Bridge or canasta (*is, are*) my favorite card game.
9. Neither my sister nor my brother (*mows, mow*) the lawn without complaining.
10. Either the tulips or the daffodils in Mrs. Green's garden (*is, are*) the first to bloom every April.

17i. When a singular subject and a plural subject are joined by *or* or *nor*, the verb agrees with the subject nearer the verb.

EXAMPLES Neither the **manager** nor the **employees want** to close the store early. [The verb agrees with the nearer subject, *employees*.]

Neither the **employees** nor the **manager wants** to close the store early. [The verb agrees with the nearer subject, *manager*.]

STYLE TIP

Whenever possible, revise sentences to avoid awkward constructions containing both singular and plural subjects. For instance, the sentences under Rule 17i could be revised in the following ways:

Both the **employees** and the **manager want** to keep the store open.

or

The **manager doesn't** want to close the store early, and **neither do** the employees.

Exercise 8 Choosing Verbs That Agree in Number with Compound Subjects

Choose the form of the verb in parentheses that agrees with the compound subject in each of the following sentences.

EXAMPLE 1. Neither Derrick nor his friends (*is, are*) going to the concert tomorrow.

1. are

1. Either Sylvia or her brothers (*scrubs, scrub*) the kitchen floor.
2. This bread or those muffins (*contains, contain*) no preservatives.
3. Either the students or the teacher (*reads, read*) aloud during the last ten minutes of each class period.
4. Heavy rain clouds or a powerful wind (*shows, show*) that a hurricane is approaching.
5. Neither the seal nor the clowns (*catches, catch*) the ball that the monkey throws into the circus ring.
6. Mr. Speck or his cousins (*teach, teaches*) Spanish in New York City.
7. Neither the horses nor the dog (*wants, want*) to go into the barn.
8. Either the boys or Lee Ann (*calls, call*) out words at the spelling bee.
9. The curtains or the bedspread (*is, are*) on sale.
10. Neither the CD players nor the computer (*belongs, belong*) to the school.

Review B Choosing Verbs That Agree in Number with Their Subjects

Choose the form of the verb in parentheses that agrees with its subject in each of the following sentences.

EXAMPLE 1. *Pan dulce* and other baked goods (*sells, sell*) well at the Mexican American bakery shown below.

1. *sell*

1. The wonderful smells at the bakery (*invites, invite*) hungry customers.
2. Children and their parents always (*enjoy, enjoys*) choosing and tasting the baked treats.
3. Display cases and large bowls (*holds, hold*) the fresh breads and pastries.
4. Rolls with powdered toppings and braided breads (*goes, go*) quickly.
5. Either an empanada or some giant biscuits (*are, is*) likely to be someone's breakfast.

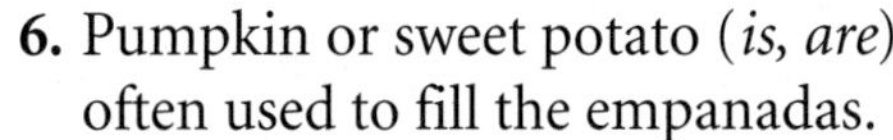

6. Pumpkin or sweet potato (*is, are*) often used to fill the empanadas.
7. Most children (*likes, like*) volcano-shaped pastries known as *volcanes.*
8. Some raisin bars or a *buñuelo* (*makes, make*) a special after-school treat.
9. Bakeries like this one (*prepares, prepare*) mainly traditional Mexican American breads.
10. Holidays and special occasions (*calls, call*) for extra-fancy baked goods.

Other Problems in Agreement

17j. When the subject follows the verb, find the subject and make sure the verb agrees with it.

The subject usually follows the verb in sentences beginning with *here* or *there* and in questions.

EXAMPLES Here **is** my **seat.**
Here **are** our **seats.**

There **is** an exciting **ride** at the fair.
There **are** exciting **rides** at the fair.

Where **is** the **bread**?
Where **are** the **loaves** of bread?

Does he know them?
Do they know him?

Exercise 9 Choosing Verbs That Agree in Number with Their Subjects

For each of the following sentences, choose the word or word group in parentheses that correctly completes the sentence.

EXAMPLE **1.** (*Here's, Here are*) the Nina Simone tapes I borrowed.
1. Here are

1. According to this map, (*there's, there are*) seven countries in Central America.
2. Where (*is, are*) the rough draft you were proofreading for me?
3. (*Has, Have*) they returned from the cafeteria yet?
4. There (*has, have*) been fewer rainy days this month than last month.
5. (*Here's, Here are*) the team's new uniforms.
6. (*There's, There are*) no reason we can't finish these math problems on time.
7. When (*is, are*) the next lunar eclipse?
8. (*Does, Do*) your parents know about the new schedule?
9. Janelle, (*here's, here are*) a question only you can answer.
10. When (*does, do*) you expect to hear from your cousin in Singapore again?

17k. The contractions *don't* and *doesn't* should agree with their subjects.

The word *don't* is a contraction for *do not.* Use *don't* with all plural subjects and with the pronouns *I* and *you.*

EXAMPLES These **gloves don't** fit.

I don't want to be late.

Don't you feel well?

HELP

The contractions *here's, there's,* and *where's* contain the verb *is* and should be used with only singular subjects.

NONSTANDARD
Here's your keys.

STANDARD
Here **are** your **keys.**

STANDARD
Here**'s** your **key.**

TIPS & TRICKS

When the subject of a sentence follows part or all of the verb, the word order is said to be ***inverted.*** To find the subject of a sentence with inverted order, restate the sentence in normal word order.

INVERTED	Here **is Eileen.**
NORMAL	**Eileen is** here.
INVERTED	**Are they** on time?
NORMAL	**They are** on time.
INVERTED	Into the woods **ran** the **deer.**
NORMAL	The **deer ran** into the woods.

Reference Note

For more information about **contractions,** see page 672.

The word *doesn't* is a contraction of *does not.* Use *doesn't* with all singular subjects except the pronouns *I* and *you.*

EXAMPLES The **music box doesn't** play.

Doesn't she like cold weather?

It doesn't matter.

STYLE TIP

Some people consider contractions informal. Therefore, it is generally best not to use them in formal writing and speech.

USAGE

Oral Practice 2 Using *Doesn't* and *Don't* with Singular Subjects

Read the following sentences aloud, emphasizing the italicized words.

1. *Don't Oktoberfest* and the *Fall Carnival* start Saturday?
2. *We don't* call meetings often.
3. *One doesn't* interrupt a speaker.
4. *They don't* play their stereo loudly.
5. *Doesn't* the television *set* work?
6. *It doesn't* look like a serious wound.
7. *She doesn't* play basketball.
8. *Fido doesn't* like his new dog food.

Exercise 10 Using *Doesn't* and *Don't* Correctly

Complete each sentence by inserting the correct contraction, *doesn't* or *don't.*

EXAMPLE 1. ____ they go to our school?

1. Don't

1. ____ anyone in the class know any interesting facts about Susan B. Anthony?
2. Kareem Abdul-Jabbar ____ play professional basketball anymore.
3. They ____ have enough people to form a softball team.
4. You ____ need to change your schedule.
5. It ____ hurt very much.
6. ____ the Japanese celebrate spring with a special festival?
7. Those snow peas ____ look crisp.
8. Hector ____ win every track meet; sometimes he places second.
9. ____ anybody know the time?
10. He ____ know the shortest route from Dallas to Peoria.

17l. A collective noun may be either singular or plural, depending on its meaning in a sentence.

The singular form of a ***collective noun*** names a group of persons, animals, or things.

Reference Note

For more about **collective nouns,** see page 349.

Common Collective Nouns			
army	club	fleet	public
assembly	committee	flock	swarm
audience	crowd	group	team
class	family	herd	troop

A collective noun is

- singular when it refers to the group as a unit
- plural when it refers to the individual parts or members of the group

EXAMPLES Tomorrow the science **class is taking** a field trip to the planetarium. [The class as a unit is taking a field trip.]

The science **class are working** on their astronomy projects. [The members of the class are working on various projects.]

The **family has moved** to Little Rock, Arkansas. [The family as a unit has moved.]

The **family have been** unable to agree on where to spend their next vacation. [The members of the family have different opinions.]

Review C **Proofreading Sentences for Subject-Verb Agreement**

Most of the following sentences contain errors in subject-verb agreement. If a sentence contains an error in agreement, write the correct form of the verb. If a sentence is already correct, write *C.*

EXAMPLE **1.** There is a man and a woman here to see you.

1. are

1. Leilani and Yoshi doesn't know how to swim.
2. Here are the vegetables for the stir-fry.
3. The Seminoles of Florida sews beautifully designed quilts and jackets.

4. Here's the sweaters I knitted for you.
5. Each of these ten-speed bicycles cost more than two hundred dollars.
6. The soccer team always celebrate each victory with a cookout at Coach Rodriguez's house.
7. The jury was arguing among themselves.
8. The flock of geese fly over the lake at dawn.
9. Doesn't that Thai dish with chopped peanuts taste good?
10. Where's the bus schedules for downtown routes?

USAGE

Review D Proofreading Sentences for Subject-Verb Agreement

Some of the following sentences contain errors in subject-verb agreement. If a sentence contains an error in agreement, write the correct form of the verb. If a sentence is already correct, write *C.*

EXAMPLE 1. Don't this neon sign light up the night with color?
1. Doesn't

1. The public have been fascinated with neon lights since they were introduced in the 1920s.
2. There's neon lights in large and small cities all over the world.
3. Times Square in New York City and Tokyo's Ginza district is two places famous for their neon lights.
4. Some of today's neon signs are very large and creative.
5. Many signs like the one shown here is used in advertising.
6. Nowadays you sometimes see neon decorations and sculptures.
7. Our science class are learning how neon lights work.
8. Neon lights is made from hollow glass tubes filled with neon gas.

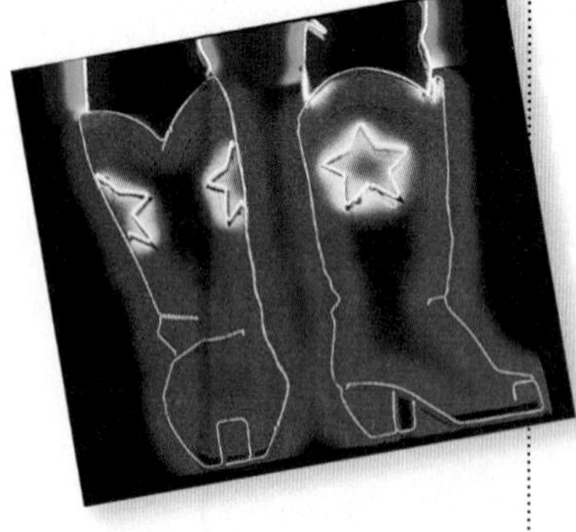

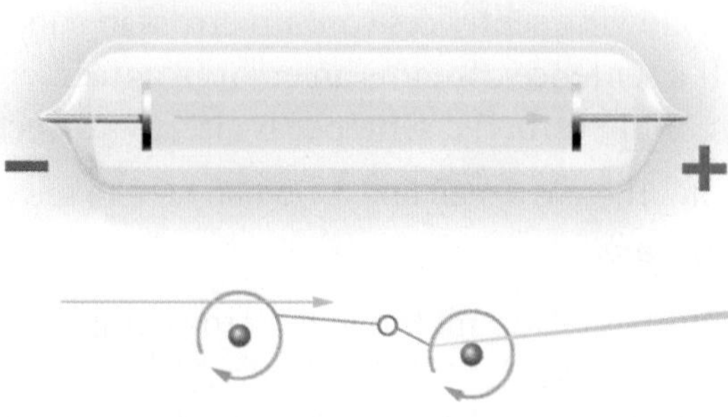

9. An electric current shot through the tube makes the gas glow.
10. The diagrams on the previous page shows the action of a neon light.

17m. **An expression of an amount (a measurement, a percentage, or a fraction, for example) may be singular or plural, depending on how it is used.**

An expression of an amount is

- singular when the amount is thought of as a unit
- plural when the amount is thought of as separate units

EXAMPLES **Three years seems** like a long time.

Two years in particular **were** difficult for the family.

A fraction or a percentage is singular when it refers to a singular word and plural when it refers to a plural word.

SINGULAR **Two thirds** of the city council **was** at the meeting.
Eighty percent of the student body **is** present.

PLURAL **Two thirds** of the council members **were** present.
Eighty percent of the students **are** present.

Expressions of measurement (such as length, weight, and area) are usually singular.

EXAMPLES **Ten feet** of yarn **is needed** for this art project.

Two gallons of that paint **covers** approximately two hundred square feet.

17n. **Some nouns that are plural in form take singular verbs.**

The following nouns take singular verbs:

civics	genetics	measles	news
economics	gymnastics	molasses	physics
electronics	mathematics	mumps	summons

EXAMPLES **Economics is** my sister's favorite subject.

The evening **news begins** at 6:00.

However, some nouns that are plural in form and that name singular objects take plural verbs.

binoculars	pants	shears
eyeglasses	pliers	shorts
Olympics	scissors	slacks

EXAMPLES Your **binoculars have** complicated controls.

The **slacks are** torn in two different spots.

The **pliers belong** in the toolbox.

17o. Even when plural in form, the title of a creative work (such as a book, song, movie, or painting) or the name of a country, city, or organization generally takes a singular verb.

EXAMPLES ***Blue Lines*** **is** an early Georgia O'Keeffe painting. [one painting]

The Souls of Black Folk **has** often **been cited** as a classic of African American literature. [one book]

"Greensleeves" is an old English folk song. [one song]

The **Netherlands has** thousands of canals. [one country]

Cedar Rapids is a manufacturing center in the Midwest. [one city]

Friends of the Earth was founded in 1969. [one organization]

17p. A verb agrees with its subject but not necessarily with a predicate nominative.

EXAMPLES The best **time** (S) to visit **is** (V) weekday **mornings.** (PN) [The verb *is* agrees with the singular subject *time,* not the plural predicate nominative *mornings.*]

Weekday **mornings** (S) **are** (V) the best **time** (PN) to visit. [The verb *are* agrees with the plural subject *mornings,* not the singular predicate nominative *time.*]

STYLE TIP

If constructions like the ones shown under Rule 17p sounds awkward to you, revise the sentence so that it does not contain a predicate nominative.

AWKWARD
The main attraction is the marching bands.

REVISED
The audience considers the marching bands the main attraction.

USAGE

Review E **Choosing Verbs That Agree in Number with Their Subjects**

Choose the form of the verb in parentheses that agrees with the subject in each of the following sentences.

EXAMPLE 1. There (*is, are*) many new students this year.
1. are

1. The audience (*loves, love*) the mime performance.
2. The story "Flowers for Algernon" (*makes, make*) me appreciate what I have.
3. Eight dollars (*is, are*) too much for that baseball card.
4. Andy's gift to Janelle (*was, were*) two roses.
5. Here (*is, are*) the letters I have been expecting.
6. The public (*differs, differ*) in their opinions on the referendum.
7. Physics (*was, were*) my sister's favorite subject.
8. The softball team usually (*practices, practice*) every Saturday morning.
9. His legacy to us (*was, were*) words of wisdom.
10. Where (*is, are*) the limericks you wrote?

Agreement of Pronoun and Antecedent

A pronoun usually refers to a noun or another pronoun called its ***antecedent.*** Whenever you use a pronoun, make sure that it agrees with its antecedent.

Reference Note

For more information about **antecedents,** see page 351.

17q. A pronoun should agree in both number and gender with its antecedent.

Some singular personal pronouns have forms that indicate gender. Masculine pronouns (*he, him, his*) refer to males. Feminine pronouns (*she, her, hers*) refer to females. Neuter pronouns (*it, its*) refer to things (neither male nor female) and sometimes to animals.

EXAMPLES **Bryan** lost **his** book.

Dawn lent **her** book to Bryan.

The **book** had Dawn's name written inside **its** cover.

STYLE TIP

Even when used correctly, the construction *his or her* sounds awkward to many people. To avoid using *his or her*, try to revise the sentence, using a plural pronoun and antecedent.

AWKWARD

Everyone in the club paid his or her dues.

Each of the mechanics uses his or her own tools.

REVISED

All of the club members paid **their** dues.

The **mechanics** use **their** own tools.

Sentences with singular antecedents joined by *or* or *nor* can sound awkward if the antecedents are of two different genders. Revise awkward sentences to avoid the problem.

AWKWARD

Ben or Maya will present his or her oral report.

REVISED

Ben will present **his** oral report, or **Maya** will present **hers.**

USAGE

The antecedent of a personal pronoun can be another kind of pronoun, such as *each, neither,* or *one.* Often, the object of a prepositional phrase that follows the antecedent indicates the gender of the pronoun.

EXAMPLES **Each** of the men put on **his** hat. [*Men,* the object of the preposition *of,* indicates that the pronoun *Each* refers to males.]

Neither of those women got what **she** ordered. [*Women,* the object of the preposition *of,* indicates that the pronoun *Neither* refers to females.]

Some singular antecedents may be either masculine or feminine. When referring to such antecedents, use both the masculine and the feminine forms.

EXAMPLES Did **someone** in this line lose **his or her** ticket?

Everybody in the class wanted to know **his or her** grade.

17r. Use a singular pronoun to refer to two or more singular antecedents joined by *or* or *nor.*

EXAMPLES **Julio or Van** will bring **his** football.

Neither the **mother nor** the **daughter** had forgotten **her** running shoes.

17s. Use a plural pronoun to refer to two or more antecedents joined by *and.*

EXAMPLES My **mother and father** send **their** regards.

My **dog and cat** never share **their** food.

17t. Some indefinite pronouns are plural, some are singular, and some may be either.

(1) Use a singular pronoun to refer to *anybody, anyone, anything, each, either, everybody, everyone, everything, neither, nobody, no one, nothing, one, somebody, someone,* and *something.*

EXAMPLES **Anyone** who has finished **his or her** sketch should show it to the teacher.

Each of the birds built **its** own nest.

(2) The following indefinite pronouns are plural: *both, few, many,* and *several.*

EXAMPLES **Several** of the ice sculptures are melting. How can we save **them**?

Were **both** of the concerts canceled, or were **they** just rescheduled?

(3) The indefinite pronouns *all, any, more, most, none,* and *some* may be singular or plural, depending on their meaning in a sentence.

These pronouns are singular when they refer to a singular word and plural when they refer to a plural word.

EXAMPLES **Some** of the test is hard, isn't **it**? [*Some* refers to the singular noun *test.*]

Some of the questions are easy. I'll do **them** first. [*Some* refers to the plural noun *questions.*]

All of the casserole looks burned, doesn't **it**?
All of the potatoes look burned, don't **they**?

Was **any** of the music original, or had you heard **it** all before?
Were **any** of the songs original, or were **they** covers of old hits?

Exercise 11 Proofreading for Pronoun-Antecedent Agreement

Many of the following sentences contain errors in pronoun-antecedent agreement. If the sentence contains an error in agreement, write the antecedent and the correct form of the pronoun. If the sentence is already correct, write *C.*

EXAMPLE **1.** Everyone in my English class will give their oral report on Friday.

1. Everyone—his or her

1. Either Don or Buddy will be the first to give their report on literary devices.
2. Several others volunteered to give theirs first.
3. Everybody else in class wanted to put off giving their report as long as possible.

Reference Note

For information on the correct usage and spelling of the pronouns ***its, their,*** and ***your,*** see pages 590, 594, and 596.

4. Last year my friend Sandy and I figured out that waiting to give our reports was worse than actually giving them.
5. I am surprised that more people did not volunteer to give his or her reports first.
6. Someone else will be third to give their report; then I will give mine.
7. Some of the students will show slides or play music with his or her reports.
8. Our teacher, Mrs. Goldenburg, says that anyone who is nervous about giving their report should try rehearsing it in front of a mirror.
9. Most of us think that giving a report later will leave more time to work on them.
10. While they may put off giving his or her reports till later, I would rather do mine as soon as possible.

USAGE

Exercise 12 Identifying Antecedents and Writing Pronouns That Agree with Them

Complete the following sentences with pronouns that agree with their antecedents. Identify each antecedent.

EXAMPLE 1. Ann Marie and Margaret wore ____ cheerleader uniforms.

1. *their—Ann Marie and Margaret*

1. The trees lost several of ____ branches in the storm.
2. Each of the early Spanish missions in North America took pride in ____ church bell.
3. Anthony, do you know whether anyone else has turned in ____ paper yet?
4. Many in the mob raised ____ voices in protest.
5. The creek and the pond lost much of ____ water during the drought.
6. One of my uncles always wears ____ belt buckle off to one side.
7. No one should be made to feel that ____ is worth less than someone else.
8. One of the dogs had gotten out of ____ collar.
9. A few of our neighbors have decided to fence ____ backyards.
10. Lucinda and Val looked forward to ____ chance to play basketball during the district playoffs.

Review F Proofreading for Pronoun-Antecedent Agreement

Many of the following sentences contain errors in pronoun-antecedent agreement. If a sentence contains an error in agreement, write the antecedent and the correct form of the pronoun. If the sentence is already correct, write *C.*

EXAMPLE 1. Each of the president's Cabinet officers gave their advice about what to do.

1. *Each—his or her*

1. All of the nation's presidents have had his own Cabinets, or groups of advisors.
2. Shortly after taking office, presidents appoint the members of their Cabinets.
3. Everyone appointed to the Cabinet is an expert in their field.
4. George Washington and John Adams met regularly with his advisors.
5. Neither had more than five people in their Cabinet.
6. The Cabinet received its name from James Madison, the fourth president.
7. Congress and the president have used their power over the years to create new government agencies.
8. In 1979, Shirley M. Hufstedler took their place on the Cabinet as the first secretary of education.
9. Neither President Reagan nor President Bush created a new post in their Cabinet.
10. The room where it meets now has more than fifteen chairs around their large table.

17u. Either a singular or a plural pronoun may be used to refer to a collective noun, depending on the meaning of the sentence.

Reference Note

For a list of **collective nouns,** see page 349.

EXAMPLES The first **group** will give **its** presentation next Friday. [The group as a unit will give the presentation.]

The **group** shared **their** ideas for topics. [The members of the group had various ideas.]

The **committee** has given **its** full approval. [The committee as a unit has given approval.]

After a brief debate, the **committee** recorded **their** final votes. [The committee members recorded their individual votes.]

USAGE

17v. An expression of an amount may take a singular or plural pronoun, depending on how the expression is used.

EXAMPLES **Ten dollars** is all I need. I think I can earn **it** over the weekend. [The amount is thought of as a unit.]

Where are the **two dollars** that were on the counter? Have **they** been taken? [The amount is thought of as individual pieces or parts.]

17w. Some nouns that are plural in form take singular pronouns.

(1) The following nouns take singular pronouns:

civics	gymnastics	mumps
economics	mathematics	news
electronics	measles	physics
genetics	molasses	summons

EXAMPLES Stacy enjoys **physics** even though **it** is a difficult subject.

I spilled the **molasses** and had to clean **it** up.

(2) The following nouns take plural pronouns:

binoculars	pants	shorts
eyeglasses	pliers	shears
Olympics	scissors	slacks

EXAMPLES Jason removed his **eyeglasses** and placed **them** on the table.

Please hand me the **scissors** when you are finished with **them.**

Reference Note

For information on using **italics** and **quotation marks with titles,** see pages 660 and 667.

17x. Use a singular pronoun to refer to the title of a creative work (such as a book, song, movie, or painting).

EXAMPLES After reading **"Neighbors,"** I recommended **it** to Juanita. [one story]

Terms of Endearment is my mom's favorite movie, and she has seen **it** six times. [one movie]

USAGE

17y. **Use a singular pronoun to refer to the name of a country, city, or organization.**

EXAMPLES The **Philippines** is located in the southwest Pacific Ocean; **it** consists of thousands of islands. [one country]

The **Knights of Pythias** expects **its** members to maintain high moral standards. [one organization]

Exercise 13 Choosing Pronouns That Agree in Number with Their Antecedents

In each of the following sentences, identify the antecedent for the pronouns in parentheses. Then, choose the form of the pronoun that agrees with the antecedent.

EXAMPLE **1.** I looked for my binoculars until I remembered that I had lent (*it, them*) to my sister.

1. binoculars—them

1. The chess club decided that (*it, they*) would each bring two cans of food for the food drive.
2. *Cats* is one of Joan's favorite musicals, and she is very excited that (*it, they*) will be performed in town soon.
3. Lourdes is a famous town in France; (*it, they*) may attract as many as two million visitors each year.
4. Next, I carefully measured out three cups of water and poured (*it, them*) into the bowl.
5. Once Janette started paying close attention to the news, she found (*it, them*) fascinating.
6. The flock of ducks flapping (*its, their*) wings gracefully overhead made very little noise.
7. When he got paid for mowing lawns, Jason's little brother put the four dollars in separate places so that he wouldn't spend (*it, them*) all at once.
8. The Bear Backers is what our high school booster club calls (*itself, themselves*).
9. When you are finished, be sure to put the scissors back where you found (*it, them*).
10. Before the measles was finally controlled with an effective vaccine, (*it, they*) often caused dangerous epidemics in the United States.

USAGE

Review G Proofreading Sentences for Subject-Verb and Pronoun-Antecedent Agreement

Most of the following sentences contain errors in pronoun-antecedent agreement or subject-verb agreement. Identify each error in agreement, and give the correct pronoun or verb. If a sentence is already correct, write *C.*

EXAMPLE 1. Ray Bradbury, shown below, is a favorite writer of many young people because he makes science fun for him or her.

1. *him or her—them*

1. One reason for his stories' popularity are that they are usually about people, not things.
2. There is some science fiction writers who care more about the gadgets they can imagine than the characters who use them.
3. Bradbury tries to show that a person is more important than the technology that affects them.
4. If you have not read his most famous book, *The Martian Chronicles,* you should read them right away.
5. In one of his short stories, children on Venus sees the sun only once every seven years.
6. One girl, who grew up on earth, remembers what the heat of the sun is like.
7. Some of the other children make fun of her, and they lock her in a closet.
8. When the rain stops and the sun comes out, each of the other children have fun outside.
9. After the rain starts again, all of the children feel bad about what he or she did to their classmate.
10. Even though the story is set in the future and on another planet, human emotions, as opposed to technology, is the focus of the story.

Chapter Review

A. Identifying Verbs That Agree with Their Subjects

For each of the following sentences, if the italicized verb does not agree with its subject, rewrite the sentence, using the correct form of the verb. If the sentence is already correct, write *C.*

1. When *is* Bill's parents coming to pick us up?
2. Mr. Epstein said that it *don't* look like rain today.
3. Neither of the bar mitzvahs *have* been scheduled yet.
4. Everyone who wears eyeglasses *is* having vision tests today.
5. My baseball bat and my catcher's mitt *was* in my room.
6. Neither Esteban nor Tina *have* tried out for the play yet.
7. All of our guests *have* been to Fort Worth's Japanese garden.
8. *Don't* the team captain plan to put her into the game soon?
9. One of the men *have* decided that he will get his car washed.
10. The Bill of Rights *give* the American citizens the right to worship where they please.

B. Identifying Pronouns That Agree with Their Antecedents

For each of the following sentences, if the italicized pronoun does not agree with its antecedent, rewrite the sentence, using the correct form of the pronoun.

11. Each of the boys brought *their* permission slip.
12. One of the does was accompanied by *their* fawn.
13. Have all of the winners taken *his or her* science projects home?
14. Everyone going to the concert should bring *their* own food.
15. Many of the buildings had yellow ribbons on *its* windows.
16. Neither Stephanie nor Marilyn had brought *their* book bag.
17. Every dog had a numbered tag hanging from *their* collar.
18. Someone in the Boy Scout troop camped near poison ivy and has gotten it all over *themselves.*
19. Only a few workers had brought tools with *him or her.*
20. One of the contest winners had *their* picture taken.

C. Proofreading a Paragraph for Subject-Verb Agreement

Some of the following sentences contain errors in subject-verb agreement. If a sentence contains an error in agreement, write the correct form of the verb. If a sentence is already correct, write *C.*

[21] People in Switzerland has four national languages. **[22]** German is spoken by most Swiss, but French and Italian, as well as the old Latin dialect Romansh, has equal status. **[23]** Not many speakers of Romansh exists, but the Romansh language, which is also called Grishun, has semiofficial national status. **[24]** Romansh, along with German, are spoken in the mountains of eastern Switzerland. **[25]** In the Western cities of Geneva and Lausanne, French are the language of most inhabitants. **[26]** To the north, the people in Bern, the capital, and in the famous banking centers of Basel and Zürich, speak German. **[27]** Visitors in search of an Italian lifestyle enjoys the Italian-speaking city of Lugano, in the south. **[28]** One of Switzerland's larger cities are actually divided between two languages. **[29]** Truly bilingual, the city is called Biel on the German-speaking side and Bienne on the French-speaking side. **[30]** Communication between the two sides are no problem, because everybody in Biel/Bienne grows up speaking both languages!

D. Proofreading Sentences for Pronoun-Antecedent Agreement

Many of the following sentences contain errors in pronoun-antecedent agreement. If a sentence contains an error in agreement, write the antecedent and the correct form of the pronoun. If a sentence is already correct, write *C.*

31. If you see either Maggie or Melanie, will you please tell them I won't be able to stay after school?

32. Tom and Mike meet every Friday with his teammates to discuss strategy.

33. The museum's portrait gallery now has more than ten portraits on their walls.

34. Each club has their own service project.

35. One of the women in the acting class designs her own costumes.

36. Linda or Rosa will donate their time to the project.

37. One of the parrots escaped from their cage.

38. Did either George or Patrick forget to bring their birth certificate?

39. People who film an animal in its natural habitat face many problems.

40. All of the students shouted his or her approval.

Writing Application

Using Correct Agreement in a Report

Agreement with Collective Nouns You are on the committee in charge of organizing your school's participation in the local Thanksgiving Day parade. Write about the committee's plans in a brief report, which you will read at the next student council meeting. Use at least five collective nouns in your report.

Prewriting Write down the names of some clubs or organizations that might be in the parade. Think about collective nouns to use in your report.

Writing Use your notes to help you write your first draft. Begin with a main-idea statement that tells other student council members what progress your committee has made. Then, tell about some of the groups that have asked to be in the parade and what those groups are planning to do.

Revising As you read your report, ask yourself these questions: Is it clear what kind of participation is planned? Have I included important details? Do the committee's plans sound logical? Revise any parts of the report that are unclear.

Publishing Proofread your report for any errors in grammar, spelling, and punctuation. Make sure that you have used five collective nouns and that the verbs and pronouns you use agree with them. Your class may wish to have each student present his or her report. Then, vote on which parade proposal is most entertaining.

Reference Note

You may want to refer to the list of **collective nouns** on page 349.

CHAPTER

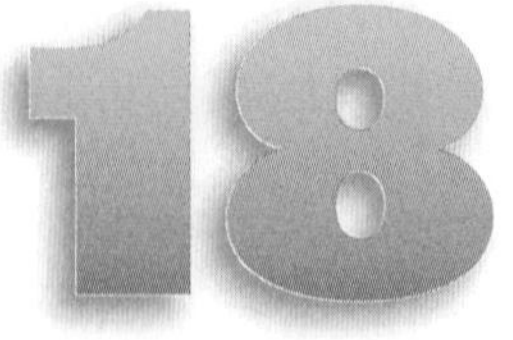

Using Verbs Correctly

Principal Parts, Regular and Irregular Verbs, Tense, Voice

Diagnostic Preview

A. Using Correct Forms of Irregular Verbs

Give the correct form (past, past participle, or present participle) of the verb in parentheses in each of the following sentences.

EXAMPLES
1. The deer (*run*) right in front of our car.
   1. ran
2. Her dog has (*run*) away from home.
   2. run

1. Eileen (*buy*) several boxes decorated with Amish designs.
2. Joan had been (*hit*) the ball hard all day.
3. I shouldn't have (*eat*) that last handful of sunflower seeds.
4. The water was (*rush*) over the rocks.
5. When the medicine finally began to work, his fever (*break*).
6. That phone has (*ring*) every five minutes since I got home.
7. If that had happened to me, I would have (*freeze*) with fear.
8. Through the murky depths, the whales (*sing*) to one another.
9. We knew that it would start to rain soon because the crickets had (*begin*) chirping.
10. The waiter (*bring*) us couscous, a popular North African dish.

B. Choosing the Forms of *Lie* and *Lay, Sit* and *Set,* and *Rise* and *Raise*

Choose the correct verb in parentheses in each of the following sentences.

EXAMPLES **1.** My cat (*lies, lays*) around the house all day.

1. lies

2. Did any contestants (*rise, raise*) their hands?

2. raise

11. The drawbridge had (*risen, raised*) before we sailed out into the bay.
12. (*Sit, Set*) that down in the chair, will you?
13. The treasure had (*lay, lain*) at the bottom of the sea for more than four hundred years.
14. Nashota read a folk tale about Coyote, the trickster, as we (*sat, set*) on the porch.
15. To avoid stepping on a snake, look on the other side of any logs (*lying, laying*) in the path.

USAGE

C. Making Tenses of Verbs Consistent

For each of the following sentences, write the italicized verb in the correct tense.

EXAMPLES **1.** My father looked at his watch and *decides* that it was time to leave.

1. decided

2. Alejandra *calls* three times, but no one answered the phone.

2. called

16. Marjorie's sister refused to give us a ride in her car, and then she *asks* us to lend her some money for gas.
17. He says he is sorry, but he *didn't* mean it.
18. In that forest, the pine trees grow close together and *had* straight trunks.
19. When the show ended, we *get* up to leave, but the crowd had already blocked the aisles.
20. Several mechanics worked on my aunt's car before one of them finally *finds* the problem.

USAGE

D. Identifying Active and Passive Voice

Tell whether the verb in each of the following sentences is in *active voice* or *passive voice.*

EXAMPLES
1. This colorful woven sash was imported from Guatemala.
   1. passive voice
2. On vacation last year, we traveled by train to Prague and Budapest.
   2. active voice

21. We were told about the contest by our favorite teacher.
22. Water rushed through the ravine and into the pool below.
23. The gate to the factory was left open all weekend.
24. A crystal glass was set too close to the edge of the coffee table.
25. The silly puppy is chasing its tail again.

The Principal Parts of a Verb

The four basic forms of a verb are called the ***principal parts*** of the verb.

18a. The four principal parts of a verb are the *base form,* the *present participle,* the *past,* and the *past participle.*

The words *is* and *have* are included in the following chart because helping verbs are used with the present participle and past participle to form some tenses.

Base Form	Present Participle	Past	Past Participle
work	[is] working	worked	[have] worked
sing	[is] singing	sang	[have] sung

EXAMPLES I **sing** in the school Glee Club.

We **are singing** at the music festival tonight.

Mahalia Jackson **sang** spirituals at Carnegie Hall.

We **have sung** all over the state.

NOTE Some teachers refer to the base form as the *infinitive*. Follow your teacher's directions in labeling this form.

Regular Verbs

18b. A *regular verb* forms its past and past participle by adding *–d* or *–ed* to the base form.

Base Form	Present Participle	Past	Past Participle
use	[is] using	used	[have] used
suppose	[is] supposing	supposed	[have] supposed
attack	[is] attacking	attacked	[have] attacked
drown	[is] drowning	drowned	[have] drowned

Avoid the following common errors when forming the past or past participle of regular verbs:

1. leaving off the *–d* or *–ed* ending

NONSTANDARD She use to work in the library.
STANDARD She **used** to work in the library.

NONSTANDARD Who was suppose to bring the decorations?
STANDARD Who was **supposed** to bring the decorations?

2. adding unnecessary letters

NONSTANDARD A swarm of bees attackted us in the orange grove.
STANDARD A swarm of bees **attacked** us in the orange grove.

NONSTANDARD Several people nearly drownded in the flood.
STANDARD Several people nearly **drowned** in the flood.

Oral Practice 1 Using the Past and Past Participle Forms of Regular Verbs

Read each of the following sentences aloud, stressing the italicized verbs.

1. She *has crossed* this street many times on the way to school.
2. The raccoon *visited* our camp every morning last summer.

HELP—
Most regular verbs that end in e drop the e before adding *–ing*. Some regular verbs double the final consonant before adding *–ing* or *–ed*.

Reference Note
For more information on correctly **adding suffixes,** see page 691.

USAGE

Reference Note
For a discussion of **standard and nonstandard English,** see page 583.

STYLE  TIP
A few regular verbs have alternative past forms ending in *t*. For example, the past form of burn is *burned* or *burnt*. Both forms are correct.

3. Ryan and Annie *repaired* the engine in less than an hour.
4. Scientists *have discovered* that birds use the sun as a compass.
5. Some people say that Stone Age surgeons in Peru *operated* on the human brain.
6. Alexandra and Anthony *have baked* Bavarian pretzels for the party.
7. The actors *jumped* across the stage to catch the falling door.
8. Sylvia *has used* her computer every day this week.

Exercise 1 Using Past and Past Participle Forms of Regular Verbs

Give the correct past or past participle form of the verb in parentheses in each of the following sentences.

EXAMPLE **1.** My aunt has (*live*) in New York State for many years.
1. lived

1. As a child, she (*enjoy*) living on one of the Shetland Islands, off the coast of Scotland.
2. Several months before her sixth birthday, she (*ask*) for a Shetland pony and got one.
3. Back then, her family (*raise*) sheep and had a Shetland sheepdog, a dog like a small collie.
4. Last year for my birthday, my aunt (*knit*) me a fine, soft sweater out of Shetland wool.
5. Recently she (*wish*) that she could go back to Scotland to visit her old home.
6. A new art museum that features the work of Mexican artists has (*open*) downtown.
7. Since reading about it, Dolores and Dario have (*apply*) for jobs there.
8. For a long time the works of Diego Rivera and José Clemente Orozco have (*fascinate*) them.
9. On Monday, the gallery manager (*call*) them.
10. They (*start*) work yesterday and will work at the museum for the rest of the summer.

Irregular Verbs

18c. An *irregular verb* forms its past and past participle in some other way than by adding *–d* or *–ed* to the base form.

An irregular verb forms its past and past participle in one of the following ways:

- changing vowels
- changing consonants
- changing vowels *and* consonants
- making no changes

Base Form	Past	Past Participle
ring	rang	[have] rung
make	made	[have] made
bring	brought	[have] brought
burst	burst	[have] burst

NOTE Since most English verbs are regular, people sometimes try to make irregular verbs follow the regular pattern. However, such words as *throwed, knowed, shrinked,* or *choosed* are considered nonstandard.

Avoid the following common errors when forming the past or past participle of an irregular verb:

1. using the past form with a helping verb

NONSTANDARD Carlos has went to the shopping mall.
STANDARD Carlos **went** to the shopping mall.
or
STANDARD Carlos **has gone** to the shopping mall.

2. using the past participle form without a helping verb

NONSTANDARD I seen all of her movies.
STANDARD I **have seen** all of her movies.

3. adding *–d* or *–ed* to the base form

NONSTANDARD The right fielder throwed the ball to the shortstop.
STANDARD The right fielder **threw** the ball to the shortstop.

HELP

When you are not sure whether a verb is regular or irregular, check a dictionary. Entries for irregular verbs generally list the principal parts.

Reference Note

For information on **using the dictionary,** see "The Dictionary" in the Quick Reference Handbook.

USAGE

STYLE TIP

Using the standard forms of verbs is important in almost all of the writing that you do for school. Your readers expect standard usage in essays and reports.

On the other hand, readers expect the dialogue in plays and short stories to sound natural. For dialogue to sound natural, it must reflect the speech patterns of real people, and real people speak in all sorts of nonstandard ways.

NONSTANDARD (DIALOGUE)
"I seen it, but I don't no way believe it!" exclaimed Jimmy.

STANDARD
Jimmy said he could not believe what he had seen.

You may want to discuss the use of nonstandard verb forms with your teacher. Together you can decide when and where such forms can be used appropriately in your writing.

Common Irregular Verbs

Base Form	Present Participle	Past	Past Participle
become	[is] becoming	became	[have] become
begin	[is] beginning	began	[have] begun
bite	[is] biting	bit	[have] bitten *or* bit
blow	[is] blowing	blew	[have] blown
break	[is] breaking	broke	[have] broken
bring	[is] bringing	brought	[have] brought
build	[is] building	built	[have] built
burst	[is] bursting	burst	[have] burst
buy	[is] buying	bought	[have] bought
catch	[is] catching	caught	[have] caught
choose	[is] choosing	chose	[have] chosen
come	[is] coming	came	[have] come
cost	[is] costing	cost	[have] cost
cut	[is] cutting	cut	[have] cut
do	[is] doing	did	[have] done
draw	[is] drawing	drew	[have] drawn
drink	[is] drinking	drank	[have] drunk
drive	[is] driving	drove	[have] driven
eat	[is] eating	ate	[have] eaten
fall	[is] falling	fell	[have] fallen
feel	[is] feeling	felt	[have] felt
fight	[is] fighting	fought	[have] fought
find	[is] finding	found	[have] found
fly	[is] flying	flew	[have] flown
forgive	[is] forgiving	forgave	[have] forgiven
freeze	[is] freezing	froze	[have] frozen
get	[is] getting	got	[have] got *or* gotten
give	[is] giving	gave	[have] given
go	[is] going	went	[have] gone
grow	[is] growing	grew	[have] grown

Common Irregular Verbs			
Base Form	**Present Participle**	**Past**	**Past Participle**
have	[is] having	had	[have] had
hear	[is] hearing	heard	[have] heard
hide	[is] hiding	hid	[have] hidden *or* hid
hit	[is] hitting	hit	[have] hit
hold	[is] holding	held	[have] held
hurt	[is] hurting	hurt	[have] hurt
keep	[is] keeping	kept	[have] kept
know	[is] knowing	knew	[have] known
lay	[is] laying	laid	[have] laid
lead	[is] leading	led	[have] led
leave	[is] leaving	left	[have] left
lend	[is] lending	lent	[have] lent
let	[is] letting	let	[have] let
lie	[is] lying	lay	[have] lain
light	[is] lighting	lighted *or* lit	[have] lighted *or* lit
lose	[is] losing	lost	[have] lost
make	[is] making	made	[have] made
meet	[is] meeting	met	[have] met
pay	[is] paying	paid	[have] paid
put	[is] putting	put	[have] put
read	[is] reading	read	[have] read
ride	[is] riding	rode	[have] ridden
ring	[is] ringing	rang	[have] rung
rise	[is] rising	rose	[have] risen
run	[is] running	ran	[have] run
say	[is] saying	said	[have] said
see	[is] seeing	saw	[have] seen
seek	[is] seeking	sought	[have] sought
sell	[is] selling	sold	[have] sold

(continued)

(continued)

Common Irregular Verbs

Base Form	Present Participle	Past	Past Participle
send	[is] sending	sent	[have] sent
set	[is] setting	set	[have] set
shake	[is] shaking	shook	[have] shaken
sing	[is] singing	sang	[have] sung
sink	[is] sinking	sank *or* sunk	[have] sunk
sit	[is] sitting	sat	[have] sat
speak	[is] speaking	spoke	[have] spoken
spend	[is] spending	spent	[have] spent
spin	[is] spinning	spun	[have] spun
spread	[is] spreading	spread	[have] spread
stand	[is] standing	stood	[have] stood
steal	[is] stealing	stole	[have] stolen
swim	[is] swimming	swam	[have] swum
swing	[is] swinging	swung	[have] swung
take	[is] taking	took	[have] taken
teach	[is] teaching	taught	[have] taught
tear	[is] tearing	tore	[have] torn
tell	[is] telling	told	[have] told
think	[is] thinking	thought	[have] thought
throw	[is] throwing	threw	[have] thrown
wear	[is] wearing	wore	[have] worn
win	[is] winning	won	[have] won

The verb *be* is probably the most common irregular verb.

The Principal Parts of *Be*

Base Form	Present Participle	Past	Past Participle
be	[is] being	was, were	[have] been

Oral Practice 2 Using the Past and Past Participle Forms of Irregular Verbs

Read each of the following sentences aloud, stressing the italicized verb.

1. Ray Charles *has written* many popular songs.
2. Leigh *did* everything the instructions said.
3. She *knew* the best route to take.
4. Maria Tallchief *chose* a career as a dancer.
5. He *ate* chicken salad on whole-wheat bread for lunch.
6. The monkey *had stolen* the food from its brother.
7. Felipe and Tonya *sang* a duet in the talent show.
8. The shy turtle *came* closer to me to reach the lettuce I was holding.

USAGE

Exercise 2 Using the Past and Past Participle Forms of Irregular Verbs

Give the correct past or past participle form of the verb in parentheses in each of the following sentences.

EXAMPLE 1. Nobody knew why he (*do*) that.
1. did

1. Did you say that the telephone (*ring*) while I was in the shower?
2. The outfielder (*throw*) the ball to home plate.
3. Diana Nyad (*swim*) sixty miles—from the Bahamas all the way to Florida.
4. Uncle Olaf has (*ride*) his new snowmobile up to Gunther's ski lodge.
5. The librarian has (*choose*) a book by Jose Aruego.
6. I'm afraid that the bean seedlings and the herbs in the garden have (*freeze*).
7. After she finished the race, she (*drink*) two glasses of water.
8. He (*tell*) me that *waffle, coleslaw,* and *cookie* are words that came from Dutch.
9. We had (*drive*) all night to attend my stepsister's college graduation ceremony.
10. Marianne (*sit*) quietly throughout the discussion.

Exercise 3 Using the Past and Past Participle Forms of Irregular Verbs

Give the correct past or past participle form of the irregular verb in parentheses in each of the following sentences.

EXAMPLE **1.** Have you (*read*) about the Underground Railroad?
1. read

1. Mr. Tucker, our new history teacher, (*write*) the words *Underground Railroad* on the chalkboard.
2. Then he (*draw*) black lines on a map to show us where the Underground Railroad ran.
3. What strange tracks this railroad must have (*have*)!
4. The lines even (*go*) into the Atlantic Ocean.
5. As you may imagine, this map (*leave*) the class very confused.
6. Then Mr. Tucker explained that no one actually (*ride*) on an underground railroad.
7. The railroad was really a secret network to help slaves who had (*run*) away.
8. Between 1830 and 1860, thousands of slaves (*get*) their freedom by traveling along the routes marked on this map.
9. The name *Underground Railroad* (*come*) from the use of railroad terms as code words.
10. Mr. Tucker (*say*) that hiding places were called "stations" and that people who helped slaves were called "conductors."

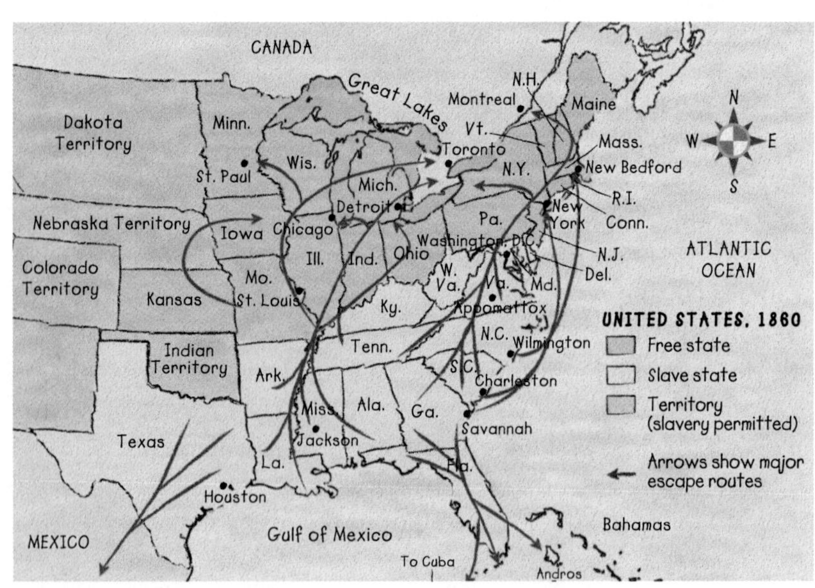

Review A Proofreading Sentences for Correct Regular and Irregular Verb Forms

Many of the following sentences contain incorrect verb forms. If a sentence has an incorrect verb form, write the correct form. If the sentence is already correct, write *C.*

EXAMPLE 1. I had spoke to my parents last week about this restaurant.

1. *had spoken*

1. My big brother Mark drived us there in Mom's car.
2. We sitted down, and the waiter brought our menus.
3. When we arrived at the restaurant, I runned ahead of everyone else and told the hostess we needed five seats.
4. Have you ever drunk water with lemon slices in the glasses?
5. Dad chose the ravioli.
6. My little sister Emilia taked two helpings of salad.
7. The waiter bringed out our dinners on a huge tray.
8. Mark given me a taste of his eggplant parmigiana.
9. Emilia stealed a bite of my lasagna.
10. Dad telled the waiter that the food was delicious.

USAGE

Review B Proofreading Sentences for Correct Verb Forms

Some of the following sentences contain incorrect verb forms. If a sentence has an incorrect verb form, write the correct form. If the sentence is already correct, write *C.*

EXAMPLE 1. I thinked I had a copy of *A Journey to the Center of the Earth.*

1. *thought*

1. During the 1800s, Jules Verne wrote many scientific adventure tales.
2. Back then, readers founded his stories amazing.
3. Some people believe that he seen into the future.
4. For example, in some of his novels he telled about space exploration and boats that traveled underwater.
5. These books fascinated readers in the days before space travel and submarines!
6. Verne lead a quiet life but had incredible adventures in his imagination.

7. He writed some wonderful stories.
8. Some inventors of modern rockets have said that they read Verne's stories.
9. Some of his books, such as *Twenty Thousand Leagues Under the Sea,* been made into great movies.
10. People have gave Verne the title "Father of Modern Science Fiction."

Verb Tense

HELP
Changing the form of a verb to show tense is called **inflection.**

18d. The *tense* of a verb indicates the time of the action or state of being expressed by the verb.

The six tenses are *present, past, future, present perfect, past perfect,* and *future perfect.* These tenses are formed from the principal parts of verbs.

Each of the six tenses has its own uses. The time line below shows how the six tenses are related to one another.

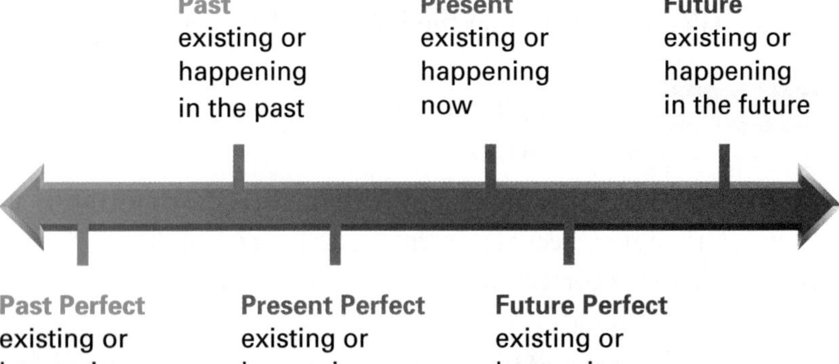

Past
existing or happening in the past
Present
existing or happening now
Future
existing or happening in the future
Past Perfect
existing or happening before a specific time in the past
Present Perfect
existing or happening sometime before now; may be continuing now
Future Perfect
existing or happening before a specific time in the future

EXAMPLES Melissa **has saved** [present perfect] her money, and now she **has** [present] enough for a guitar.

The scouts **had hiked** [past perfect] five miles before they **stopped** [past] for lunch.

The executive **will have seen** [future perfect] the report by next week and **will make** [future] a decision.

HELP
You have learned that verbs express tense. Verbs also express mood. The ***indicative mood*** expresses a fact, an opinion, or a question. The ***imperative mood*** expresses a direct command or request. The ***subjunctive mood*** expresses a suggestion, a necessity, a condition contrary to fact, or a wish.

EXAMPLES

This **is** the largest carrot I **have** ever **seen!** [indicative mood]

Please **bring** me my camera. [imperative mood]

If that **were** my garden, I would never have to buy vegetables at the store. [subjunctive mood]

Listing the different forms of a verb in the six tenses is called ***conjugating*** a verb.

Conjugation of the Verb *Write*	
Singular	**Plural**
Present Tense	
I write	we write
you write	you write
he, she, *or* it writes	they write
Past Tense	
I wrote	we wrote
you wrote	you wrote
he, she, *or* it wrote	they wrote
Future Tense	
I will (shall) write	we will (shall) write
you will (shall) write	you will (shall) write
he, she, *or* it will (shall) write	they will (shall) write
Present Perfect Tense	
I have written	we have written
you have written	you have written
he, she, *or* it has written	they have written
Past Perfect Tense	
I had written	we had written
you had written	you had written
he, she, *or* it had written	they had written
Future Perfect Tense	
I will (shall) have written	we will (shall) have written
you will (shall) have written	you will (shall) have written
he, she, *or* it will (shall) have written	they will (shall) have written

STYLE TIP

In the past, careful speakers and writers of English used *shall* and *will* in different ways. Now, however, *shall* can be used almost interchangeably with *will*.

Each of the six tenses has an additional form called the ***progressive form,*** which expresses continuing action or state of being. It consists of the appropriate tense of the verb *be* plus the present participle of a verb. The progressive is not a separate tense but rather another form of each of the six tenses.

Present Progressive	am, are, is writing
Past Progressive	was, were writing
Future Progressive	will, shall be writing
Present Perfect Progressive	has, have been writing
Past Perfect Progressive	had been writing
Future Perfect Progressive	will, shall have been writing

Only the present and the past tenses have another form, called the ***emphatic form,*** which is used to show emphasis. In the present tense, the emphatic form consists of the helping verb *do* or *does* and the base form of the verb. In the past tense, the emphatic form consists of the verb *did* and the base form of a verb.

Present Emphatic	do, does write
Past Emphatic	did write

USAGE

STYLE TIP

The emphatic form is also used in questions and negative statements. These uses do not place any special emphasis on the verb.

QUESTION
Why **do** bears hibernate?

NEGATIVE STATEMENT
If the car **does**n't [does not] start, check the battery.

Consistency of Tense

18e. Do not change needlessly from one tense to another.

When describing events that occur at the same time, use verbs in the same tense.

INCONSISTENT	When we were comfortable, we begin to do our homework. [*Were* is past tense, and *begin* is present tense.]
CONSISTENT	When we **are** comfortable, we **begin** to do our homework. [Both *are* and *begin* are present tense.]
CONSISTENT	When we **were** comfortable, we **began** to do our homework. [Both *were* and *began* are past tense.]
INCONSISTENT	Suddenly the great door opened, and an uninvited guest comes into the dining hall. [*Opened* is past tense, and *comes* is present tense.]
CONSISTENT	Suddenly the great door **opens,** and an uninvited guest **comes** into the dining hall. [Both *opens* and *comes* are present tense.]

CONSISTENT Suddenly the great door **opened,** and an uninvited guest **came** into the dining hall. [Both *opened* and *came* are past tense.]

When describing events that occur at different times, use verbs in different tenses to show the order of events.

EXAMPLE Lisa **plays** basketball now, but last year she **was** on the volleyball team. [Lisa's basketball playing is occurring in the present, so *plays* is correct. Her volleyball playing occurred at a time in the past, so the past tense, *was,* is correct.]

Susana **won** the regional spelling bee; next week she **will compete** in the state tournament. [Susana won the spelling contest sometime in the past, so the past tense, *won,* is correct. The state spelling tournament will occur in the future, so *will compete* is correct.]

COMPUTER TIP

Most word-processing programs can help you check your writing for correct verb forms. For example, a spellchecker will highlight misspelled verb forms such as *drownded* or *costed.* Style-checking software might point out inconsistent verb tenses or highlight questionable uses of problem verbs such as *lie* and *lay* and *rise* and *raise.*

Remember, though, that the computer is just a tool to help you improve your writing. As a writer, you are responsible for making all the style and content choices that affect your writing.

Exercise 4 Proofreading a Paragraph to Make the Verb Tense Consistent

Read the following paragraph, and decide whether to rewrite it in the present or past tense. Then, change verb forms to correct any unnecessary changes in tense.

EXAMPLE **[1]** At my grandparents' house, I wake up before anyone else and quietly grabbed the fishing pole and head for the pond.

1. *At my grandparents' house, I wake up before anyone else and quietly grab the fishing pole and head for the pond.*

or

At my grandparents' house, I woke up before anyone else and quietly grabbed the fishing pole and headed for the pond.

HELP

The paragraph in Exercise 4 may correctly be rewritten in the present or the past tense, as long as you are consistent.

[1] Across the water, I saw the ripples. **[2]** "I hope the fish are cooperative," I say to myself. **[3]** I threw my lure near where I see the ripples and reeled in the line. **[4]** The fish are not biting. **[5]** I saw more ripples and throw the line in the water again. **[6]** "I have a strike!" I shout to the trees around me. **[7]** As I reeled in the line, a beautiful trout jumps out of the water and spit out the hook. **[8]** Gloomily, I walk back to the house. **[9]** Grandpa was sitting at the kitchen table with a bowl of hot oatmeal for me. **[10]** I say,"Oh well, maybe tomorrow we'll have fresh trout for breakfast."

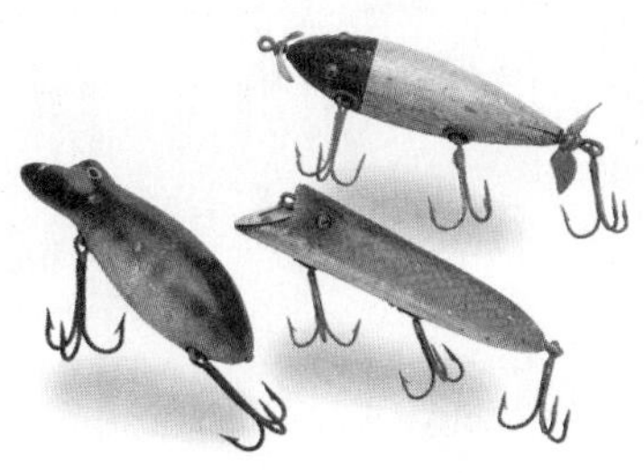

Active Voice and Passive Voice

18f. A verb in the *active voice* expresses an action done by its subject. A verb in the *passive voice* expresses an action done to its subject.

Compare the following sentences:

ACTIVE VOICE The school librarian **has formed** a book club.
PASSIVE VOICE A book club **has been formed** by the school librarian.

ACTIVE VOICE A happy clown **delivered** the balloons.
PASSIVE VOICE The balloons **were delivered** by a happy clown.

ACTIVE VOICE The illustrator **had used** watercolors.
PASSIVE VOICE Watercolors **had been used** by the illustrator.

ACTIVE VOICE Someone **broke** the shop window last night.
PASSIVE VOICE The shop window **was broken** by someone last night.

Notice that the object of the active sentence becomes the subject of the passive sentence. The subject of the active sentence is now expressed in a prepositional phrase. This prepositional phrase can be omitted.

PASSIVE VOICE The show window **was broken** last night.

In a passive sentence, the verb phrase always includes a form of *be* and the past participle of the main verb. Other helping verbs may also be included.

ACTIVE VOICE Mrs. Edwin **fixed** the computer.
PASSIVE VOICE The computer **was fixed** by Mrs. Edwin.

ACTIVE VOICE Lucinda **had planted** those marigolds.
PASSIVE VOICE Those marigolds **had been planted** by Lucinda.

The passive voice emphasizes the person or thing receiving the action. The passive voice is useful when you do not know who performed the action or when you do not want to reveal the performer of the action.

STYLE TIP

Overusing the passive voice makes your writing sound weak and awkward. In general, use the active voice to help make your writing direct and forceful.

WEAK
Shingles were torn from the roof by the high winds.

FORCEFUL
The high winds **tore** shingles from the roof.

Reference Note

For more about **helping verbs,** see page 372.

USAGE

EXAMPLES These flowers **were left** on the doorstep sometime this afternoon. [The performer is unknown.]

"A large donation **was given** anonymously," said Mrs. Neal. [The speaker does not want to reveal the performer of the action.]

Exercise 5 Identifying Active and Passive Voice

Tell whether each verb in the following sentences is in *active voice* or *passive voice.*

EXAMPLE **1.** Jared's birthday dinner was paid for by his uncle.

1. passive voice

1. Trees were being blown over by the wind.
2. The streetlights made long, scary shadows on the sidewalk.
3. The cave was explored by the science class.
4. The Gettysburg Address was written by Abraham Lincoln.
5. Marion considered the book an inspiration.
6. The cake had been eaten by the time Sandy arrived.
7. Kenny's fans cheered him on to victory.
8. The snow drifted over the fence and across the road.
9. The swelling on Kehl's arm was caused by a bee sting.
10. Bob and Judy were setting out birdseed for the cardinals and chickadees.

Special Problems with Verbs

Sit and *Set*

The verb *sit* means "to rest in an upright, seated position" or "to be in a place." *Sit* seldom takes an object. The verb *set* means "to put (something) in a place." *Set* usually takes an object. Notice that *set* has the same form for the base form, past, and past participle.

Reference Note

For information on **objects of verbs,** see page 401.

Base Form	Present Participle	Past	Past Participle
sit	[is] sitting	sat	[have] sat
set	[is] setting	set	[have] set

HELP You may know that the word *set* has more meanings than the one given on page 521. Check in a dictionary to see if the meaning you intend requires an object.

EXAMPLE

The sun **sets** in the West. [Here, *set* does not take an object.]

USAGE

EXAMPLES Let's **sit** under the tree. [no object]

Let's **set** our backpacks under the tree. [Let's set what? *Backpacks* is the object.]

The tourists **sat** on the bench. [no object]

The tourists **set** their suitcases on the bench. [The tourists set what? *Suitcases* is the object.]

We **had** just **sat** down when the telephone rang. [no object]

We **had** just **set** our books down when the telephone rang. [We had set what? *Books* is the object.]

Oral Practice 3 Using the Forms of *Sit* and *Set*

Read the following sentences aloud, stressing each italicized verb.

1. *Sit* down here, please.
2. The dog is *sitting* on the porch.
3. Our teacher *set* a deadline for our term projects.
4. Some mornings I *sit* on the steps and watch the sun rise.
5. I have always *sat* in the front row.
6. Please *set* the carton down inside the doorway.
7. Where have I *set* my book on judo?
8. After I had *set* the mop in the closet, I *sat* down to rest.

Exercise 6 Choosing the Forms of *Sit* and *Set*

Choose the correct verb in parentheses in each of the following sentences. If the verb you choose is a form of *set,* identify its object.

EXAMPLE 1. Please (*sit, set*) the serving platter on the table.

1. set; object—platter

1. Has he (*sat, set*) anything down here?
2. The kitten cautiously (*sat, set*) down beside the Great Dane.
3. Jamyce (*sat, set*) her notebook down on the kitchen counter.
4. I had been (*sitting, setting*) there all day.
5. (*Sit, Set*) the fine crystal in the china cabinet.
6. The referee is (*sitting, setting*) the ball on the fifty-yard line.
7. Aaron will (*sit, set*) the table for our Passover celebration.
8. Let's (*sit, set*) that aside until later.

9. Alex had to (*sit, set*) and catch his breath after joining in the Greek chain dance.
10. They had (*sat, set*) there for fifteen minutes without saying a word to each other.

Lie and *Lay*

The verb *lie* means "to rest," "to recline," or "to be in a place." *Lie* does not take an object. The verb *lay* means "to put (something) in a place." *Lay* usually takes an object.

Base Form	Present Participle	Past	Past Participle
lie	[is] lying	lay	[have] lain
lay	[is] laying	laid	[have] laid

EXAMPLES The napkins **are lying** next to the plates. [no object]

The servers **are laying** extra napkins beside every plate for the barbecue. [The servers are laying what? *Napkins* is the object.]

The soldiers **lay** very still while the enemy passed. [no object]

The soldiers **laid** a trap for the enemy. [The soldiers laid what? *Trap* is the object.]

Rip Van Winkle **had lain** asleep for twenty years. [no object]

Rip Van Winkle **had laid** his gun on the ground. [Rip Van Winkle had laid what? *Gun* is the object.]

HELP

The verb *lie* can also mean "to tell an untruth." Used in this way, *lie* still does not take an object.

EXAMPLE
Don't **lie** to her, Beth.

The past and past participle forms of this meaning of *lie* are *lied* and *[have] lied.*

USAGE

Oral Practice 4 Using the Forms of *Lie* and *Lay*

Read the following sentences aloud, stressing each italicized word.

1. Don't *lie* in the sun until you put on some sunscreen.
2. You should not *lay* your papers on the couch.
3. The lion had been *lying* in wait for an hour.
4. The senator *laid* her notes aside after her speech.
5. I have *lain* awake, listening to Spanish flamenco music on the radio.

6. She has *laid* her books on the desk.
7. At bedtime, Toshiro *lies* down on a futon.
8. The exhausted swimmer *lay* helpless on the sand.

Exercise 7 Using the Forms of *Lie* and *Lay*

Complete each of the following sentences by supplying the correct form of *lie* or *lay.* If the verb you use is a form of *lay,* identify its object.

EXAMPLE 1. Leo ____ the disk next to the computer.
1. *laid; object—disk*

1. After the race, Michael Andretti ____ his helmet on the car.
2. My dad was ____ down when I asked him for my allowance.
3. We ____ down the picnic blanket.
4. Have you ever ____ on a water bed?
5. Rammel had ____ his keys beside his wallet.
6. These days, my cat often ____ on the front porch.
7. Amy is ____ the coats on the bed in the guest room.
8. Yesterday that alligator ____ in the sun all day.
9. Lim Sing's great-grandfather ____ the glasses on the table.
10. The newspaper had ____ in the yard until the sun faded it.

Exercise 8 Using Forms of *Lie* and *Lay* and *Sit* and *Set*

Give the correct form of *lie* or *lay* or *sit* or *set* for each of the following sentences.

EXAMPLE 1. Does anybody ____ in bed late on the farm?
1. *lie*

1. The family ____ down to breakfast every day at 6:00 A.M.
2. One morning as they ____ around the table, they heard a terrible racket.
3. Lily, one of the cats, had ____ out on a hunting expedition.
4. By mistake, she jumped a snake that ____ asleep under a holly bush.
5. The harmless, black snake struck at Lily, who yowled and then ____ back, growling.
6. The hens, who were ____ eggs, began to squawk and flap their wings.
7. Lily seemed dazed, so the family brought her into the house and ____ her on a pillow.

8. They ____ a pan of water near her, and then Lily rolled off the pillow into the pan.
9. She was frightened and would not ____ still to be dried.
10. Long after the family ____ down to sleep, they could hear Lily pacing through the rooms.

Rise and *Raise*

The verb *rise* means "to go up" or "to get up." *Rise* does not take an object. The verb *raise* means "to lift up" or "to cause (something) to rise." *Raise* usually takes an object.

Base Form	Present Participle	Past	Past Participle
rise	[is] rising	rose	[have] risen
raise	[is] raising	raised	[have] raised

EXAMPLES My neighbors **rise** very early in the morning. [no object]

Every morning they **raise** their shades to let the sunlight in. [They raise what? *Shades* is the object.]

Sparks **rose** from the flames of the campfire. [no object]

The breeze **raised** sparks high into the air. [The breeze raised what? *Sparks* is the object.]

The senators **have risen** from their seats to show respect for the chief justice. [no object]

The senators **have raised** a number of issues. [The senators have raised what? *Number* is the object.]

HELP—You may know that the verb *raise* has more meanings than the one given here.

EXAMPLE
The Nelsons **raise** geese. [*Raise* does not mean "lift up" here, but it still takes an object.]

USAGE

Oral Practice 5 Using the Forms of *Rise* and *Raise*

Read each of the following sentences aloud, stressing the italicized verb.

1. The reporters *rise* when the president enters the room.
2. Students *raise* their hands to be recognized.
3. They *have raised* the curtain for the first act of the play.
4. Alex Haley *rose* to fame with his book *Roots.*
5. The sun *was rising* over the mountains.

6. The old Asian elephant slowly *rose* to its feet.
7. Who *had risen* first?
8. Two of the builders *raised* the cement block and set it in place.

Exercise 9 Choosing the Forms of *Rise* and *Raise*

Choose the correct verb in parentheses in each of the following sentences. If the verb you choose is a form of *raise*, identify its object.

EXAMPLE 1. Please (*raise, rise*) your hand when you want to speak.
1. raise; object—hand

1. The steam was (*rising, raising*) from the pot of soup.
2. That discovery (*rises, raises*) an interesting question about the Algonquian people of Canada.
3. The child's fever (*rose, raised*) during the night.
4. The sun (*rises, raises*) later each morning.
5. The student body's interest in this subject has (*risen, raised*) to new heights.
6. We must (*rise, raise*) the flag before school begins.
7. The children (*rise, raise*) the blinds to get a better look at the unusual visitor.
8. The kite has (*risen, raised*) above the power lines.
9. My father will (*rise, raise*) my allowance if I pull the weeds.
10. The art dealer (*rose, raised*) the price of the painting by Frida Kahlo.

Exercise 10 Using the Forms of *Rise* and *Raise*

Complete each of the following sentences by supplying the correct past or past participle form of *rise* or *raise*.

EXAMPLE 1. Have you ever ____ before dawn?
1. risen

1. We girls ____ early to start our hike to Lookout Mountain.
2. From our position at the foot of the mountain, it looked as though it ____ straight up to the skies.
3. However, we had not ____ at daybreak just to look at the high peak.
4. We ____ our supply packs to our backs and started the long climb up the mountain.

USAGE

5. With every step we took, it seemed that the peak ____ that much higher.
6. Finally, after several hours, we reached the summit and ____ a special flag that we had brought for the occasion.
7. When our friends at the foot of the mountain saw that we had ____ the flag, they knew that all of us had reached the top safely.
8. They ____ their arms and shouted.
9. Our friends' shouts ____ from the valley below.
10. Then we felt glad that we had ____ early enough to climb to the top of Lookout Mountain.

Review C Choosing the Forms of *Sit* and *Set*, *Lie* and *Lay*, and *Rise* and *Raise*

Choose the correct verb in parentheses in each of the following sentences. Be prepared to explain your choices.

EXAMPLE 1. The audience (*sat, set*) near the stage.
1. *sat*

HELP The meaning of the verb in the example is "to be in a seated position." Therefore, *sat* is the correct answer.

1. To study solar energy, our class (*sit, set*) a solar panel outside the window of our classroom.
2. Since I have grown taller, I have (*rose, raised*) the seat on my bicycle.
3. Didn't Mr. DeLemos (*lay, laid*) the foundation for the new Vietnamese Community Center building?
4. (*Sit, Set*) the groceries on the table while I start dinner.
5. The water level of the stream has not (*risen, raised*) since last summer.
6. Will you (*lie, lay*) the grass mats on the sand so that we can lie on them?
7. We (*sat, set*) under a beach umbrella so that we would not get sunburned.
8. When the sun rises, I often (*sit, set*) aside my covers and get up early to play before school.
9. He (*lay, laid*) his collection of Isaac Bashevis Singer stories on the table.
10. The crane operator (*rose, raised*) the steel beam and carefully set it in place.

Review D Proofreading for Correct Verb Forms

Most of the following sentences contain an incorrect form of the verb *sit, set, lie, lay, rise,* or *raise.* If the sentence has an incorrect verb form, write the correct form. If the sentence is already correct, write *C.*

EXAMPLES **1.** We rose early for our journey to Havasu Canyon.

1. C

2. I laid awake for hours thinking about the trip.

2. lay

1. I sat our bags in the car, and we headed for Havasu Canyon.

2. The canyon, which lies in northern Arizona, is home of the Havasupai Indian Reservation.

3. At the canyon rim, a Havasupai guide helped me onto a horse and rose the stirrups so that I could reach them.

4. After we rode horses eight miles to the canyon floor, I set for a while because I was tired.

5. However, I knew I must sit a good example for my younger brother and not complain.

6. As you can see, the trail we took is fairly narrow and lays along the side of a steep, rocky wall.

7. The sun raised high and hot as we rode through this beautiful canyon.

8. After we reached the village of Supai, I lay down to rest.

9. Still, I quickly raised my hand to join the next tour to Havasu Falls.

10. When we arrived, I was ready to lay under the spray of the waterfall shown below.

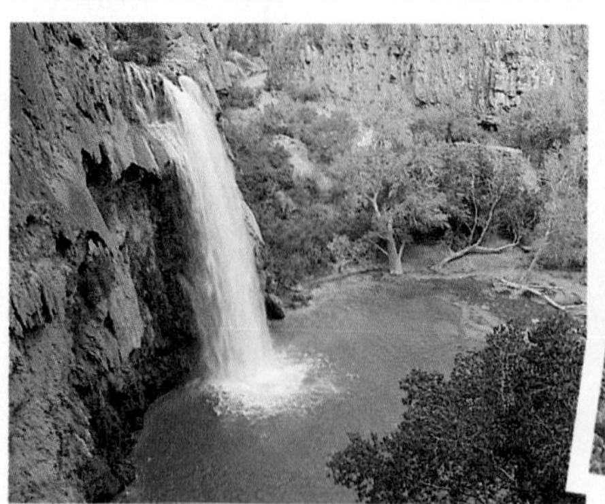

Review E Choosing Correct Verb Forms

Each of the following sentences has at least one pair of verbs in parentheses. Choose the correct verb from each pair.

EXAMPLE 1. Josh (*catched, caught*) seven fish this morning.
1. caught

1. Aretha Franklin has (*sang, sung*) professionally for more than forty years.
2. Have you (*began, begun*) your Scottish bagpipe lessons yet?
3. Cindy Nicholas was the first woman who (*swam, swum*) the English Channel both ways.
4. When the baby sitter (*rose, raised*) her voice, the children (*knew, knowed*) it was time to behave.
5. After we had (*saw, seen*) all of the exhibits at the county fair, we (*ate, eat*) a light snack and then (*went, gone*) home.
6. The egg (*burst, bursted*) in the microwave oven.
7. He (*lay, laid*) his lunch money on his desk.
8. The loud noise (*breaked, broke*) my concentration.
9. We (*sat, set*) through the movie three times because it was so funny.
10. We had (*rode, ridden*) halfway across the desert when I began to wish that I had (*brought, brung*) more water.

Review F Identifying Correct Irregular Verb Forms

Each of the following sentences has a pair of verbs in parentheses. Choose the correct verb from each pair.

EXAMPLE 1. Have you ever (*saw, seen*) an animal using a tool?
1. seen

1. I had (*thought, thinked*) that only humans use tools.
2. However, scientists have (*spended, spent*) many hours watching wild animals make and use tools.
3. Chimpanzees have been (*seen, saw*) using twigs to catch insects.
4. They (*taken, took*) sticks and poked them into termite holes, and termites climbed onto the sticks.
5. In that way, they (*caught, catched*) termites.
6. I have been (*telled, told*) that some finches use twigs to dig insects out of cracks in tree bark.

USAGE

7. Sea otters have (*broke, broken*) open shellfish by banging them against rocks.
8. You may have (*knew, known*) that song thrushes also use that trick to get snails out of their shells.
9. Some animals have (*builded, built*) things, using their gluelike body fluids to hold objects together.
10. For example, scientists and others have watched as tailor ants (*spread, spreaded*) their sticky film on leaves to hold them together.

USAGE

Review G Proofreading Sentences for Correct Use of Past and Past Participles of Common Irregular Verbs

Some of the following sentences contain incorrect forms of common irregular verbs. If the sentence has an incorrect verb form, write the correct form. If the sentence is already correct, write *C.*

EXAMPLE **1.** The city of Guadalajara, Mexico, beginned in 1530.
1. began

1. Guadalajara now has grew into the second-largest city in Mexico, with a population of over three and a half million people.
2. Many people from the United States have choosed to retire in Guadalajara.
3. The city was builded in the Valley of Atemajac, where it attracted many settlers.
4. The area surrounding the city is part of Mexico's central plateau, where horse and cattle ranches have kept thriving.
5. People from many different places have finded Guadalajara's architecture charming.
6. The city is filled with art and flowers and history; it also has lended itself to modern technology.
7. Until recently no one thinked of Guadalajara as another "Silicon Valley," but it is becoming an electronics center.
8. Fortunately, the city has taken care to preserve and protect the historic downtown district and its six distinct plazas.
9. The jacaranda trees and bougainvillea that bloom everywhere have stealed many people's hearts.
10. The mariachi singers rightly have singed the praises of the city through the years.

Chapter Review

A. Using the Present Participle, Past, and Past Participle Forms of Verbs

Give the correct form (present participle, past, or past participle) of the verb in parentheses in each of the following sentences.

1. The cat is (*lie*) down in front of the warm fire.
2. Since the storm began, the water has (*rise*) four feet.
3. Yolanda (*set*) the dictionary on the little table.
4. I have been (*write*) you a letter.
5. Two runners on our track team have (*break*) the school record for the mile run.
6. When the manager unlocked the door, a mob of shoppers (*burst*) into the store to take advantage of the sale.
7. Every morning last semester, the same cadet (*raise*) the flag.
8. The witness said that she (*see*) the blue truck run the red light.
9. Look in the oven to see if the cake has (*rise*) yet.
10. Everyone should be in class after the bell has (*ring*).
11. Sitting Bull (*name*) his son Crowfoot.
12. Jeanette carefully (*lay*) her coat across the back of the chair.
13. By late December the pond has usually (*freeze*) solid.
14. Several of us (*choose*) to visit the Amish community in Pennsylvania.
15. Dana will be (*run*) five laps around the track.
16. Jan was late, so she (*decide*) to run the rest of the way.
17. The man at the gate (*take*) our tickets and said that we were just in time.
18. When he comes back from Philadelphia, Father is (*bring*) me a scale model of the Liberty Bell.
19. After Sarah told me about the book of Yiddish folk tales, I (*buy*) a copy.
20. In 1926, Gertrude Ederle, the first woman to swim across the English Channel, (*swim*) from France to England in 14 hours and 39 minutes.

USAGE

B. Proofreading a Paragraph for Correct Verb Forms

Most of the following sentences contain incorrect verb forms. If the sentence has an incorrect verb form, write the correct form. If the sentence is already correct, write *C.*

[21] Born in India, Ravi Arimilli spended most of his childhood years in Louisiana. **[22]** As a youngster, he begun playing tennis. **[23]** After starting college, he winned a spot on the Louisiana State University tennis team. **[24]** Arimilli founded that tennis was too limiting, so he studied electrical engineering instead. **[25]** After college, he choosed to work at IBM's office in Austin, Texas, because it put him in the middle of exciting computer projects. **[26]** Arimilli has brung talent and imagination to his job at IBM. **[27]** By 1998, he and his team had received eighteen patents for inventions, and Arimilli had been elected to the prestigious IBM Academy. **[28]** Arimilli has never care about those things too much, though. **[29]** Having what he calls an "I love me" wall in his office, covered with awards, would not rise his self-esteem. **[30]** Ravi Arimilli has always been more interested in making computer history than in just making a name for himself.

C. Identifying Active and Passive Voice

Tell whether each verb in the following sentences is in *active voice* or *passive voice.*

31. Priscilla drew a quick sketch of the view from the terrace.
32. The ball was thrown too far to the left.
33. Mr. Bernstein gave each student a thesaurus.
34. Last night, we all worked on Dad's car.
35. Pedro or Carlie was given a raise last month.
36. The wart hogs were chased away by hyenas.
37. Houses are being painted all along the street.
38. The Empress Josephine requested a watch set in a bracelet.
39. Mom was amazed by the message.
40. Three of us asked the governor for his autograph.

Writing Application

Using Verb Forms in a Poem

Verb Tense You have decided to enter a local poetry contest. The theme of the contest is "Modern Adventures." Write a short narrative poem (a poem that tells a story) about a modern adventure. In your poem, use at least ten verbs from the list of Common Irregular Verbs on pages 510–512.

Prewriting First, you will need to pick an adventure story to tell. You could tell a true story or an imaginary one. After you select a story, jot down some specific details that you want to include in your poem.

Writing As you write your rough draft, try to express the excitement of the adventure. You may want to divide your poem into rhymed stanzas. Each stanza could tell a different event of your story.

Revising Ask a friend to read your poem. Is the adventure story easy to follow? Is it interesting? If not, you may want to add, delete, or revise some details. If your poem is a ballad or other traditional type of poem, be sure that the rhythm and rhyme follow that poetic form. Does your poem contain enough sensory details? Make sure that you have not changed needlessly from one tense to another.

Reference Note

For more about **sensory details,** see page 297.

Publishing Use your textbook to check the spelling of the irregular verbs in your poem. Be sure that you have used ten irregular verbs from the list. Read over your poem again, checking for errors in capitalization, spelling, and punctuation. With your teacher's permission, post the poem on the class bulletin board or Web page, if one is available.

CHAPTER

Using Pronouns Correctly

Case Forms of Pronouns; Special Pronoun Problems

Diagnostic Preview

A. Proofreading for Correct Forms of Pronouns

Most of the following sentences contain at least one pronoun that has been used incorrectly. Identify each incorrect pronoun, and then give the correct form. If the sentence is already correct, write *C.*

EXAMPLE 1. The teacher told Derek and I a funny story.
1. *I—me*

1. To who did you and Marie send flowers?
2. As everyone expected, the winners of the science fair were Felicia and he.
3. That television announcer's voice always irritates my father and I.
4. Us teammates have to stick together, right?
5. Aunt Ida bought we boys some boiled peanuts.
6. After the regional track meet, Coach Johnson said he was proud of Ling and I.
7. Is he the person who we met at Dan's party?

8. We split the pizza between he and I.
9. My grandmother and me enjoy the English custom of having afternoon tea.
10. The little boy asked Neil and him for help.
11. May Kim and I sit next to Terrence and he?
12. Invite she and the new girl in our class to the party.
13. Did Gisela know that it was I who called?
14. The best drummers in the high school band are themselves.
15. Ali's mother and my father said that us boys could go on the field trip.

USAGE

B. Identifying Correct Forms of Personal Pronouns

Choose the correct pronoun from the pair in parentheses in each of the following sentences.

EXAMPLE 1. Mrs. Lang gave (*we, us*) third-period students a list of good books for summer reading.

1. us

16. Beth and (*I, me*) plan to read the first five books that are on Mrs. Lang's list soon.
17. We asked (*she, her*) for some more information about the books she recommended.
18. (*She, Her*) said that *The Man Who Was Poe* is by Avi.
19. The author of *The True Confessions of Charlotte Doyle* is also (*he, him*).
20. We probably will like Avi's books because (*they, them*) combine fiction and history.
21. Both of (*we, us*) want to read *Where the Lilies Bloom* by Vera and Bill Cleaver, too.
22. Together, the two of (*they, them*) have written sixteen books for young readers.
23. The first book (*I, me*) am going to read is *Jacob Have I Loved* by Katherine Paterson.
24. Beth said that *A Gathering of Days* by Joan W. Blos will be the first book for (*she, her*).
25. Mrs. Lang told Beth and (*I, me*) that our summer reading project is a good idea.

Case

Case is the form that a noun or a pronoun takes to show its relationship to other words in a sentence. In English, there are three cases: *nominative, objective,* and *possessive.*

The form of a noun is the same for both the nominative case and the objective case. For example, a noun used as a subject (nominative case) will have the same form when used as an indirect object (objective case).

NOMINATIVE CASE The **singer** received a standing ovation. [subject]

OBJECTIVE CASE The audience gave the **singer** a standing ovation. [indirect object]

Reference Note

For more information about **possessive forms of nouns,** see page 669.

A noun changes its form in the possessive case, usually by adding an apostrophe and an *s.*

POSSESSIVE CASE Many of the **singer's** fans waited outside the theater.

Unlike nouns, most personal pronouns have different forms for all three cases. In the following example, the pronouns in boldface type all refer to the same person. They have three different forms because of their different uses.

EXAMPLE **I** [nominative] remembered to bring **my** [possessive] homework with **me** [objective].

Personal Pronouns		
Nominative Case	**Objective Case**	**Possessive Case**
Singular		
I	me	my, mine
you	you	your, yours
he, she, it	him, her, it	his, her, hers, its
Plural		
we	us	our, ours
you	you	your, yours
they	them	their, theirs

NOTE Some teachers prefer to call possessive pronouns such as *my, your,* and *our* adjectives. Follow your teacher's directions when labeling possessive forms.

Exercise 1 Identifying Personal Pronouns and Their Cases

Each of the following sentences contains at least one personal pronoun. Identify each pronoun and give its case.

EXAMPLE **1.** Uncle Theo gave us this book about rock stars of the 1950s and 1960s.

1. us—objective

1. Why don't we sit down and look through the book with Clarence and him?

2. We want to see what pictures our book has of the great American rock singers.

3. I also look forward to reading more about them!

4. The contributions they made to rock-and-roll affected popular music all over the world.

5. The stars in the pictures on this page look so different from the performers we have today.

6. That's Chuck Berry doing his famous "duckwalk."

7. These three women were known as the Supremes, and they had twelve number-one songs.

8. The woman in the middle may look familiar; she is Diana Ross.

9. Fans also liked the male vocal group the Four Tops and other groups like them.

10. Of course, we can't forget Little Richard, known for his wild piano playing.

The Nominative Case

TIPS & TRICKS

To help you choose the correct pronoun in a compound subject, try each form of the pronoun separately.

EXAMPLE
Candida and (*me, I*) like to dance. [*Me like to dance* or *I like to dance*?]

ANSWER
Candida and **I** like to dance.

USAGE

Reference Note

For more about **finding the subject of a verb,** see page 327.

Nominative case pronouns—*I, you, he, she, it, we,* and *they*—are used as subjects of verbs and as predicate nominatives.

19a. The subject of a verb should be in the nominative case.

EXAMPLES **I** like classical music. [*I* is the subject of *like.*]

Did he and **she** sell tickets? [*He* and *she* are the subjects of *Did sell.*]

They called while **we** were away. [*They* is the subject of *called. We* is the subject of *were.*]

Oral Practice 1 Using Pronouns as Subjects

Read the following sentences aloud, stressing the italicized pronouns.

1. *He* and *she* collect autographs.
2. My grandmother and *I* are painting the boat.
3. Both *they* and *we* were frightened.
4. Did Alicia or *she* answer the phone?
5. *We* are giving a fashion show.
6. *You* and *I* will stay behind.
7. Were *he* and *she* on the Old Spanish Trail?
8. My parents and *they* are good friends.

Exercise 2 Choosing Personal Pronouns Used as Subjects

Choose appropriate personal pronouns for the blanks in the following sentences. Use a variety of pronouns, but do not use *you* or *it.*

EXAMPLE 1. ____ and ____ will have a debate.
1. We, they

1. Yesterday she and ____ went shopping.
2. Our cousins and ____ are ready for the race.
3. Neither ____ nor J. B. saw the zydeco band perform in concert last night.
4. ____ and Lim Sing have copies of the book.
5. When are ____ and ____ coming?

6. Everyone remembers when ____ won the big game.
7. Someone said that ____ and ____ are finalists.
8. Did you or ____ ride in the hot-air balloon?
9. Both ____ and ____ enjoyed the stories about African American cowboys in the Old West.
10. Has ____ or Eduardo seen that movie?

19b. A *predicate nominative* should be in the nominative case.

A ***predicate nominative*** is a noun or a pronoun that is in the predicate and that identifies or refers to the subject of the verb. A personal pronoun used as a predicate nominative follows a linking verb, usually a form of the verb *be* (*am, is, are, was, were, be,* or *been*).

EXAMPLES The last one to leave was **he.** [*He* follows the linking verb *was* and identifies the subject *one.*]

Do you think the culprits may have been **they**? [*They* follows the linking verb *may have been* and identifies the subject *culprits.*]

TIPS & TRICKS

To help you choose the correct form of a pronoun used as a predicate nominative, remember that the pronoun could just as well be used as the subject in the sentence.

EXAMPLE

The group leaders will be **he** and **I.** [predicate nominatives]

He and **I** will be the group leaders. [subjects]

USAGE

Exercise 3 Identifying Personal Pronouns Used as Predicate Nominatives

Identify the correct personal pronoun in parentheses in each of the following sentences.

EXAMPLE 1. It was (*I, me*) at the door.
1. I

1. We hoped it was (*her, she*).
2. That stranger thinks I am (*she, her*).
3. Luckily, it was not (*them, they*) in the accident.
4. If the singer had been (*her, she*), I would have gone to the concert.
5. Everyone believed it was (*we, us*).
6. It might have been (*him, he*), but I'm not sure.
7. Our opponents could have been (*them, they*).
8. I thought it was (*they, them*) from whom you bought the woven Navajo blanket.
9. It could have been (*she, her*) that he called.
10. Was the person who brought flowers Claudia or (*she, her*)?

Reference Note

For more about **predicate nominatives,** see page 405.

STYLE TIP

Grammatically incorrect expressions such as *It's me, That's her,* and *It was them* are often used in informal situations. In formal speaking and writing, however, such expressions should be avoided.

Review A Identifying Personal Pronouns in the Nominative Case

Each of the following sentences contains a pair of personal pronouns in parentheses. Choose the correct pronoun from each pair.

EXAMPLE 1. (*We, Us*) think of Leonardo da Vinci mostly as an artist.

1. We

1. (*Me, I*) think you probably have seen some paintings by this Italian Renaissance master.
2. (*Him, He*) painted two works that are particularly famous.
3. The *Mona Lisa* and *The Last Supper* are (*they, them*).
4. In science class (*we, us*) were surprised by what our teacher said about Leonardo da Vinci.
5. (*Her, She*) said that he was also a brilliant inventor.
6. My friend Jill and (*me, I*) were amazed to hear that Leonardo designed a flying machine that looked like a helicopter.
7. Look at the propellers on the flying machine that (*he, him*) drew in 1488.
8. (*Me, I*) was also impressed by his drawing of a spring-driven car.
9. The designer of the diving bell and the battle tank was (*him, he*), too.
10. Scientists have studied Leonardo's work, and (*them, they*) have made models of many of his drawings.

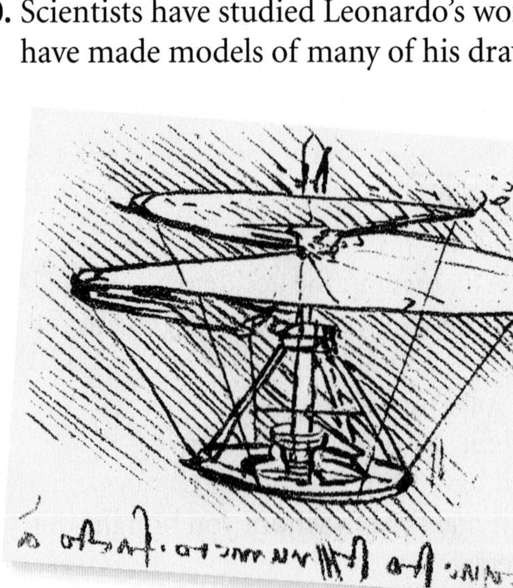

USAGE

The Objective Case

Objective case pronouns—*me, you, him, her, it, us,* and *them*—are used as direct objects, indirect objects, and objects of prepositions.

19c. A *direct object* should be in the objective case.

A ***direct object*** is a noun, pronoun, or word group that tells *who* or *what* receives the action of the verb.

EXAMPLES Evan surprised **them.** [*Them* tells *whom* Evan surprised.]

Uncle Ramón took **me** to the rodeo. [*Me* tells *whom* Uncle Ramón took.]

The ranger guided **us** to the camp. [*Us* tells *whom* the ranger guided.]

Did the class elect **you** and **me** to be the student council representatives? [*You* and *me* tell *whom* the class elected.]

Reference Note

For more about **direct objects,** see page 401.

Exercise 4 Choosing Pronouns Used as Direct Objects

Choose appropriate pronouns for the blanks in the following sentences. Use a variety of pronouns, but do not use *you* or *it.*

EXAMPLE **1.** The teacher helped ____ with the assignment.

1. us

1. The feisty little dog chased Adam and ____ for almost three blocks.
2. They asked Ms. Shore and ____ for permission.
3. Rita said that she can usually find Alberto, Tina, and ____ at your house.
4. Did you know Jarvis and ____?
5. The tour guide directed ____ to New York City's Little Italy neighborhood.
6. Aunt Aggie took ____ and ____ to the zoo.
7. Rochelle told my sister and ____ about last weekend's Freddie Jackson concert.
8. Should we call Mark and ____ and tell them the good news about the play?
9. Do you remember ____ and ____?
10. All five judges have chosen ____ and ____ as the winners of the essay contest.

TIPS & TRICKS

To help you choose the correct pronoun in a compound direct object, try each form of the pronoun separately in the sentence.

EXAMPLE
We met Tara and (*she, her*) at the video arcade. [*We met she* or *We met her*?]

ANSWER
We met Tara and **her** at the video arcade.

USAGE

TIPS & TRICKS

To help you choose the correct pronoun in a compound indirect object, try each form of the pronoun separately in the sentence.

EXAMPLE
Our neighbor gave Kristen and (*I, me*) a job for the summer. [*Our neighbor gave I a job* or *Our neighbor gave me a job*?]

ANSWER
Our neighbor gave Kristen and **me** a job for the summer.

Reference Note

For more about **indirect objects,** see page 403.

STYLE TIP

Just as there are good manners in behavior, there are also good manners in language. In English it is considered polite to put first-person pronouns (*I, me, mine, we, us, ours*) last in compound constructions.

EXAMPLE
Mr. Griffith lent **Juan and me** [not *me and Juan*] some magazines.

19d. An *indirect object* should be in the objective case.

Indirect objects often appear in sentences containing direct objects. An indirect object tells *to whom or what* or *for whom or what* the action of the verb is done. An indirect object usually comes between an action verb and its direct object.

EXAMPLES Coach Mendez gave **them** a pep talk. [*Them* tells *to whom* Coach Mendez gave a pep talk.]

His mother built **him** a footlocker. [*Him* tells *for whom* his mother built a footlocker.]

The science teacher gave **us** posters of the solar system. [*Us* tells *to whom* the teacher gave posters.]

NOTE Indirect objects do not follow prepositions. If a preposition such as *to* or *for* precedes an object, the object is an object of the preposition.

Oral Practice 2 Using Pronouns as Direct Objects and Indirect Objects

Read the following sentences aloud, stressing the italicized pronouns.

1. The hot lentil soup burned Ahmad and *me.*
2. Li showed Raúl and *her* the new kite.
3. The stray dog followed *her* and *him* all the way to school.
4. Did you expect *us* or *them*?
5. The doctor gave *her* and *me* flu shots.
6. Carol helped Sarah and *him* with their chores.
7. Have you seen the Romanos or *them*?
8. After supper Mrs. Karras gave *us* some baklava for dessert.

Exercise 5 Using Personal Pronouns as Indirect Objects

Fill in the blank with the correct personal pronoun for each of the following sentences.

EXAMPLE 1. My sister likes humorous poetry, so I lent ____ a copy of *Parents Keep Out: Elderly Poems for Youngerly Readers* by Ogden Nash.

1. her

1. She's happy because the book has given ____ many reasons to laugh.
2. When our family is all together, my sister reads ____ Ogden Nash poems.
3. Our uncle asked to borrow the book, but instead Sabrina bought ____ a copy of *You Can't Get There from Here.*
4. My uncle seeks me out and says, "Let me read ____ this poem. It's a really funny one!"
5. The family was curious about Ogden Nash's life, so I gave ____ some biographical information about him.
6. My literature book tells ____ his life span, which was 1902–1971.
7. He left ____ great humorous writings in movies, plays, and poems to enjoy.
8. Sabrina asked ____ questions about Nash's childhood.
9. I provided ____ the information that he was born in Rye, New York, and grew up in cities along the East Coast.
10. Nash's creative works still bring ____ much enjoyment.

19e. An *object of a preposition* should be in the objective case.

A noun or a pronoun that follows a preposition is called the ***object of a preposition.*** Together, the preposition, its object, and any modifiers of that object make a ***prepositional phrase.***

EXAMPLES	to **Lee**	in an **hour**	like red **clay**
	without **me**	near **her**	except **them**
	for **him**	by **us**	next to **us**

A pronoun used as the object of a preposition should be in the objective case.

EXAMPLES When did you mail the package to **them**? [*Them* is the object of the preposition *to.*]

Are you still planning to go to the movies with **us**? [*Us* is the object of the preposition *with.*]

The reward money was divided equally between **him** and **her.** [*Him* and *her* are the objects of the preposition *between.*]

Reference Note

For a list of **prepositions,** see page 386. For more about **prepositional phrases,** see page 416.

TIPS & TRICKS

To determine the correct pronoun form when the object of a preposition is compound, use each pronoun separately in the prepositional phrase.

EXAMPLE

Grandma sent a package to (*she, her*) and (*I, me*).
[*To she* or *to her*? *To I* or *to me*?]

Grandma sent a package to **her** and **me.**

USAGE

Oral Practice 3 Using Pronouns as Objects of Prepositions

Read the following sentences aloud, stressing the italicized words.

1. The safari continued *without her* and *me.*
2. Everyone *except us* saw the Navajo rugs.
3. We stood *beside* their families and *them* during the ceremony.
4. Do you have any suggestions *for* Jalene or *me*?
5. The clowns talked *to* Claire and *him.*
6. Please give this *to* either your father or *her.*
7. With the help *of* Juan and *her,* we built a fire and set up camp.
8. There was a contest *between us* and *them.*

Exercise 6 Choosing Pronouns Used as Objects of Prepositions

Choose appropriate pronouns for the blanks in the following sentences. Use a variety of pronouns, but do not use *you* or *it.*

EXAMPLE **1.** We could not find all of ____.
1. them

1. The teacher read to André and ____ a saying by Confucius about friendship.
2. I made an appointment for ____ and you.
3. There are some seats behind Lusita and ____.
4. No one except Patrice and ____ was studying.
5. I couldn't have done it without you and ____.
6. Why didn't you speak to Christie and ____?
7. Our team has played basketball against the Jets and ____.
8. I was near you and ____ during the parade.
9. Just between you and ____, I think our chances are good.
10. Did you go with ____ to the Herb Harvest Fall Festival at the Ozark Folk Center?
11. The referee called fouls on ____ and me.
12. Maggie is off fishing with ____.
13. Without you and ____ in the group, meetings have been dull.
14. They assigned the same lab equipment to them and ____.
15. The duke sneered haughtily at ____ and me.
16. The player tried to dodge between Sheridan and ____.
17. Uncle Vic will get the details from Sofia and ____ later.
18. I will talk about the next formation with ____.

19 f

19. The letter you wrote to ____ and me was very funny.
20. The curious duck circled around Jade and ____.

The Possessive Case

19f. The personal pronouns in the possessive case—*my, mine, your, yours, his, her, hers, its, our, ours, their, theirs*—are used to show ownership or possession.

(1) The possessive pronouns *mine, yours, his, hers, its, ours,* and *theirs* are used as parts of a sentence in the same ways in which pronouns in the nominative and the objective cases are used.

SUBJECT	Your car and **mine** need tuneups.
PREDICATE NOMINATIVE	This jacket is **hers.**
DIRECT OBJECT	We painted **ours** yesterday.
INDIRECT OBJECT	Ali gave **theirs** her complete attention.
OBJECT OF A PREPOSITION	Next to **yours,** my bonsai crabapple tree looks puny.

(2) The possessive pronouns *my, your, his, her, its, our,* and *their* are used before nouns to show ownership or possession.

EXAMPLES **My** CD player is on the desk.

Do you know **their** phone number?

NOTE Some authorities prefer to call these words possessive adjectives. Follow your teacher's instructions regarding these possessive forms.

Special Pronoun Problems

Who and *Whom*

Nominative Case	who	whoever
Objective Case	whom	whomever

USAGE

Reference Note

For information about **subordinate clauses,** see page 441.

STYLE TIP

In informal English, the use of *whom* is becoming less common. In fact, when you are speaking informally, you may begin any question with *who* regardless of the grammar of the sentence. In formal English, however, you should distinguish between *who* and *whom.*

USAGE

19g. The use of *who* or *whom* in a subordinate clause depends on how the pronoun functions in the clause.

When you are choosing between *who* and *whom* in a subordinate clause, follow these steps.

STEP 1 Find the subordinate clause.

STEP 2 Decide how the pronoun is used in the clause—as a subject, predicate nominative, object of the verb, or object of a preposition.

STEP 3 Determine the case of the pronoun according to the rules of standard English.

STEP 4 Select the correct form of the pronoun.

EXAMPLE Do you know (*who, whom*) they are?

STEP 1 The subordinate clause is (*who, whom*) *they are.*

STEP 2 The subject is *they,* the verb is *are,* and the pronoun is the predicate nominative: *they are* (*who, whom*).

STEP 3 A pronoun used as a predicate nominative should be in the nominative case.

STEP 4 The nominative form is *who.*

ANSWER Do you know **who** they are?

EXAMPLE Mayor Neiman, (*who, whom*) I have met, is intelligent.

STEP 1 The subordinate clause is (*who, whom*) *I have met.*

STEP 2 The subject is *I,* and the verb is *have met.* The pronoun is the direct object of the verb: *I have met* (*who, whom*).

STEP 3 A pronoun used as a direct object should be in the objective case.

STEP 4 The objective form is *whom.*

ANSWER Mayor Neiman, **whom** I have met, is intelligent.

Oral Practice 4 Using *Who* and *Whom* Correctly

Read the following sentences aloud, stressing the italicized pronouns.

1. Our team needs a pitcher *who* can throw curve balls.
2. For *whom* do the gauchos in Argentina work?
3. They work for ranch owners *who* often live far away.
4. Dr. Martin Luther King, Jr., is a man *whom* we honor.
5. He told me *who* the author is.
6. The boy, *who* was new in town, was lost.

7. Is he the new student to *whom* this locker belongs?
8. *Whom* did they suggest for the job?

Appositives

19h. A pronoun used as an appositive is in the same case as the word to which it refers.

Reference Note

For more information about **appositives,** see page 432.

An ***appositive*** is a noun or pronoun placed next to another noun or pronoun to identify or describe it.

EXAMPLES The runners—**he, she,** and **I**—warmed up on the track. [The pronouns are in the nominative case because they are used as appositives of the subject, *runners.*]

Every student except two, **him** and **her,** joined the archaeological dig. [The pronouns are in the objective case because they are used as appositives of *two,* the object of the preposition *except.*]

The drama coach introduced the actors, Laura and **me.** [The pronoun is in the objective case because it is used as an appositive of the direct object, *actors.*]

Sometimes a pronoun is followed directly by an appositive. To help you choose which pronoun to use before an appositive, omit the appositive and try each form of the pronoun separately.

EXAMPLE (*We, Us*) cheerleaders practice after school. [*Cheerleaders* is the appositive identifying the pronoun.]

We practice after school.

Us practice after school.

ANSWER **We** cheerleaders practice after school.

EXAMPLE The coach threw a party for (*we, us*) players. [*Players* is the appositive identifying the pronoun.]

The coach threw a party for *we.*

The coach threw a party for *us.*

ANSWER The coach threw a party for **us** players.

"So, then . . . Would that be 'us the people' or 'we the people?'"

Reflexive Pronouns

Reflexive pronouns such as *himself* and *themselves* can be used as objects. Do not use the nonstandard forms *hisself* and *theirselfs* or *theirselves* in place of *himself* and *themselves.*

Reference Note

For more about **reflexive pronouns,** see page 353.

NONSTANDARD	The mayor voted for hisself in May's election.
STANDARD	The mayor voted for **himself** in May's election.

NONSTANDARD	The girls bought theirselves some comic books.
STANDARD	The girls bought **themselves** some comic books.

COMPUTER TIP

A computer may be able to help you find pronoun problems in your writing. For example, if you sometimes use *who* and *whom* incorrectly, you can use the search feature to highlight all the uses of *who* and *whom.* Then, examine how each of these pronouns is used. If you have used an incorrect form, replace it with the correct form.

USAGE

Exercise 7 Identifying Correct Forms of Pronouns

Choose the correct pronoun in parentheses in each of the following sentences.

EXAMPLE **1.** Mrs. Johnson said she was proud of (*we, us*) band members.

1. us

1. (*Who, Whom*) selected the new team captain?
2. They asked (*themselves, theirselves*) where the money from the fund-raiser could be.
3. The head nurse gave several volunteers—the Mullaneys, Alice, and (*she, her*)—a tour of the new hospital wing.
4. Did you know that (*we, us*) girls are going to the concert tomorrow night?
5. From (*who, whom*) did you order the food?
6. Two runners, Jill and (*she, her*), finished in record time.
7. We are not sure (*who, whom*) the next president of the honor club will be.
8. (*We, Us*) members of the band hope to cut a demo tape soon.
9. (*Who, Whom*) shall we invite?
10. Robert took two helpings for (*hisself, himself*).

Review B Identifying Correct Forms of Pronouns

Identify the correct pronoun in parentheses in each of the following sentences. Then, tell whether the pronoun is used as a *subject,* a *predicate nominative,* a *direct object,* an *indirect object,* or an *object of a preposition.*

EXAMPLE **1.** Say hello to (*she, her*) and Anna.

1. her—object of a preposition

1. Tulips surround (*we, us*) during May in Holland, Michigan.
2. The audience clapped for Rudy and (*he, him*).
3. The best singer in the choir is (*she, her*).

4. The officer gave (*we, us*) girls a ride home.
5. I wrote a story about Grandpa and (*he, him*) last week.
6. Daniel and (*me, I*) read a book about Pelé, the soccer player.
7. Last year's winner was (*he, him*).
8. To (*who, whom*) did you send invitations?
9. Please tell me (*who, whom*) the girl in the yellow dress is.
10. (*We, Us*) sisters could help Dad with the dishes.

Review C Identifying Personal Pronouns and Their Uses

Each of the following sentences contains at least one personal pronoun. Identify each personal pronoun, and tell whether it is used as a *subject,* a *predicate nominative,* a *direct object,* an *indirect object,* or an *object of a preposition.*

EXAMPLE **1.** I enjoy watching Edward James Olmos in movies and television shows because he always plays such interesting characters.

1. I—subject; he—subject

1. The cowboy in this picture from the movie *The Ballad of Gregorio Cortez* is he.
2. In the movie he plays an innocent man hunted by Texas Rangers.
3. The film will give you a good idea of Olmos's acting talents.
4. After I saw him in this movie, I wanted to know more about him.
5. A librarian gave me a book of modern biographies.
6. I read that Olmos's father came from Mexico but that the actor was born in Los Angeles.
7. Growing up, Olmos faced the problems of poverty and gang violence, but he overcame them.
8. Before becoming a successful actor, he played baseball, sang in a band, and moved furniture.
9. In 1978, Olmos's role in the play *Zoot Suit* gave him the big break he needed in show business.
10. Later, the movie *Stand and Deliver,* in which he played math teacher Jaime Escalante, earned him widespread praise.

Review D Selecting Pronouns to Complete Sentences Correctly

Choose the correct pronoun in parentheses in each of the following sentences. Then, tell whether each is used as a *subject,* a *predicate nominative,* a *direct object,* an *indirect object,* an *object of a preposition,* or an *appositive.*

EXAMPLE **1.** Ms. Lee gave the debaters, (*they, them*) and us, name tags.

1. them—appositive

1. The two winners, Sean and (*she, her*), received scholarships.
2. Will Marc and (*she, her*) run the concession stand this season?
3. Ms. Lozano asked them to carry the equipment for you and (*I, me*).
4. Did they buy (*theirselves, themselves*) new shoes?
5. The lighting crew for the production was Manuel and (*I, me*).
6. They treat (*whoever, whomever*) they hire very well.
7. They met Jenna and (*he, him*) at the airport.
8. I think that the people who were costumed as pirates are (*they, them*).
9. (*Us, We*) sophomores raised the most money for charity.
10. Coach Escobar congratulated the two starting forwards, Angela and (*I, me*).

USAGE

Chapter Review

A. Identifying Correct Forms of Pronouns

For each of the following sentences, identify the correct pronoun in parentheses.

1. Just between you and (*I, me*), I think he's wrong.
2. I don't know (*who, whom*) I'll invite to the dance.
3. We saw (*they, them*) and the Andersons at a Mardi Gras parade in New Orleans.
4. The winners in the contest were Amelia and (*I, me*).
5. The wasp flew in the window and stung (*he, him*) on the arm.
6. Edward and (*she, her*) will give reports this morning.
7. The two scouts who have earned the most merit badges are Angelo and (*he, him*).
8. Several people in my neighborhood helped (*we, us*) boys clear the empty lot and measure out a baseball diamond.
9. Nina sits behind Alex and (*I, me*) on the bus every morning.
10. My father and (*he, him*) are planning to go into business together.
11. We thought that we'd be facing (*they, them*) in the finals, but they were eliminated in an earlier round.
12. May I sit next to Terrance and (*he, him*)?
13. The tour guide showed Kimberly and (*she, her*) some Japanese *raku* pottery.
14. My aunt once gave (*me, I*) two dolls made from corn husks.
15. Did you know that it was (*I, me*) who called?
16. Corey's stepmother and my father said that (*we, us*) boys could go on the field trip.
17. Our friends asked (*we, us*) if we had ever been to San Francisco's Chinatown.
18. Invite (*she, her*) and the new girl in our class to the party.
19. Do you know (*who, whom*) received the award?
20. The soloists in the band—Terry and (*I, me*)—finally got our chance to perform.

USAGE

B. Proofreading Sentences for Correct Forms of Personal Pronouns

Most of the following sentences contain at least one pronoun that has been used incorrectly. Write each incorrect pronoun in the following sentences, and then write its correct form. If the sentence is already correct, write *C.*

21. The police officer told Pedro and him to move their bikes.
22. She was the counselor who I talked to last Friday.
23. He seemed eager to tell Sue and I how bad the movie was.
24. Danny and me like to make fajitas for the whole family.
25. Us students are enjoying the field trip to Rancho La Cima.
26. They gave the award to Maria and me.
27. The antics of the sea otters entertained we onlookers.
28. After the ceremony, Dad told Tim and I how proud he was.
29. The authors of the piece were Amanda and him.
30. Ms. Christensen told Leonora and I the fable of the fox and the grapes.

C. Identifying Personal Pronouns and Their Uses

Each of the following sentences contains at least one personal pronoun. Identify each personal pronoun, and tell whether it is used as a *subject,* a *predicate nominative,* a *direct object,* an *indirect object,* or an *object of a preposition.*

31. Of the three applicants, the most promising is she.
32. With a sigh, the teacher handed him the letter.
33. She felt much better after taking vitamins and spending the afternoon in bed.
34. The albatross flew slowly over them.
35. Hello? Yes, this is he.
36. We are the best soccer players in the district.
37. When Winston Churchill was prime minister of Britain, the Canadian photographer Yousuf Karsh photographed him.
38. Half-hearted supporters are they.
39. The waiter gave us a complimentary serving of quesadillas.
40. The poster fell on her.

Writing Application

Using Pronouns in a Letter

Nominative and Objective Case A national magazine has asked its readers to send in letters telling about the people they respect the most. You decide to enter the contest. Write a letter to the magazine, telling about the person you most respect. You want your writing to appeal to many people, so be sure the pronouns you use are correct according to the rules of standard English.

Prewriting Begin by thinking about a person you respect. The person could be someone you know, such as a family member, a teacher, or a friend; or it could be someone you have heard or read about (perhaps an author or a scientist). Choose one person as the topic of your letter. Then, make some notes about why you respect that person.

Writing As you write your first draft, include only the most convincing details from your list. Think about how you want to group these details and how they will fit in your letter. Throughout your letter, use personal pronouns so that you do not keep repeating names.

Revising As you read over your letter, imagine that you are a magazine editor. Ask yourself these questions:

- Is it clear why you respect the person?
- Have you supported all opinions with facts?

Mark any places where more information would be helpful. Delete any unnecessary information.

Publishing Proofread your letter for any errors in grammar, usage, and mechanics. Check to be sure that all pronouns are in the correct case. You and your classmates could display your letters on a class bulletin board or Web page, if available. You might also want to send a copy of your letter to the person you described.

CHAPTER

Using Modifiers Correctly

Comparison and Placement

Diagnostic Preview

A. Using the Correct Forms of Modifiers

Most of the following sentences contain an error in the use of modifiers. Identify each error; then, revise the sentence, using the correct form of the modifier. If a sentence is already correct, write *C*.

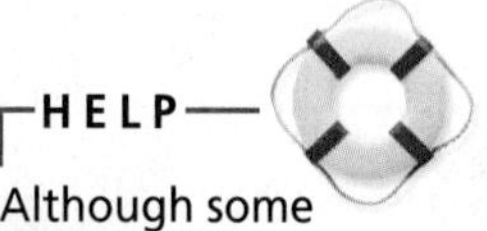

HELP— Although some of the sentences in the Diagnostic Preview can be correctly revised in more than one way, you need to give only one revision for each sentence.

EXAMPLE **1.** I didn't want to live nowhere else.

1. didn't . . . nowhere—I didn't want to live anywhere else.

1. The wonderfullest place in the whole world is my grandmother's house.
2. We lived there until we got an apartment of our own.
3. Since her house is bigger than any house in the neighborhood, we all had plenty of room.
4. Grandma was glad to have us stay, because my dad can fix things so that they're gooder than new.
5. He plastered and painted the walls in one bedroom so that I wouldn't have to share a room no more with my sister.
6. I don't know which was best—having so much space of my own or having privacy from my sister.
7. My grandmother can sew better than anybody can.

8. She taught my sister and me how to make the beautifullest clothes.
9. She has three sewing machines, and I like her oldest one better.
10. We started with the more simpler kinds of stitches.
11. After we could do those, Grandma showed us fancier stitches and sewing tricks.
12. For instance, she taught us to wrap thread behind buttons we sew on, so that they will be more easier to button.
13. We learned how to make skirts, blouses, and all sorts of other things, and now there isn't hardly anything we can't make.
14. I was sad when we left Grandma's house, but I like our new apartment more better than I thought I would.
15. Luckily, we moved to a place near my grandmother's, and after school I can go over there or go home—whichever I want to do most.

USAGE

B. Correcting Misplaced and Dangling Modifiers

The following sentences each contain a misplaced or a dangling modifier. Revise each sentence so that it is clear and correct.

EXAMPLE 1. The cook will win a new oven that makes the best bread.

1. *The cook that makes the best bread will win a new oven.*

16. Our math teacher told us that she had been a nurse yesterday.
17. We read a story written by Jade Snow Wong in class.
18. Destroyed by fire, the man looked at the charred house.
19. After missing the school bus, my mother gave me a ride.
20. The fox escaped from the hounds pursuing it with a crafty maneuver into the hollow tree.
21. Walking through the park, the squirrels chattered and scurried along the path.
22. Tearing away his umbrella, Mr. Pérez became completely drenched.
23. The squid fascinated the students preserved in formaldehyde.
24. Keeping track of the race with binoculars, the blue car with a yellow roof pulled into the lead.
25. Piling up in snowdrifts, our house was warm and toasty.

What Is a Modifier?

Reference Note

For more information on **adjectives,** see page 358. For more on **adverbs,** see page 381.

A ***modifier*** is a word or word group that makes the meaning of another word or word group more specific. Two parts of speech are used as modifiers: adjectives and adverbs. ***Adjectives*** modify nouns and pronouns. ***Adverbs*** modify verbs, adjectives, and other adverbs.

ADJECTIVE Ramona makes **beautiful** weavings.

ADVERB Ramona weaves **beautifully.**

Adjective or Adverb?

Many adverbs end in *–ly,* but not all of them do. A few common adjectives also end in *–ly.* Therefore, you cannot tell whether a word is an adjective or an adverb simply by looking for the *–ly* ending.

ADJECTIVES **lovely** dress **likely** outcome

silly story **daily** exercise

To decide whether a word is an adjective or adverb, determine how the word is used in the sentence.

Adjectives	Adverbs
Greyhounds are **fast** dogs.	Greyhounds run **fast.**
Matt is my **second** cousin.	Matt came in **second.**
They took a **late** flight.	Their flight arrived **late.**

20a. If a word in the predicate modifies the subject of the verb, use the adjective form. If it modifies the verb, use the adverb form.

ADJECTIVE His movements were **awkward.** [*Awkward* modifies the noun *movements.*]

ADVERB He moved **awkwardly.** [*Awkwardly* modifies the verb *moved.*]

ADJECTIVE The **speedy** train moved down the tracks. [*Speedy* modifies the noun *train.*]

ADVERB The train moved **speedily** down the tracks. [*Speedily* modifies the verb *moved.*]

USAGE

In many cases, linking verbs are followed by a predicate adjective.

Common Linking Verbs		
appear	grow	smell
be (am, is, are, *etc.*)	look	sound
become	remain	stay
feel	seem	taste

EXAMPLES That performance was **powerful.** [The predicate adjective *powerful* follows the linking verb *was* and describes the subject *performance.*]

The ground looks **muddy.** [The predicate adjective *muddy* follows the linking verb *looks* and describes the subject *ground.*]

NOTE Some verbs can be used as either linking verbs or action verbs. As action verbs they may be modified by adverbs.

ADJECTIVE When we asked whether to turn right or left, Greg looked **blank.** [*Blank* modifies the noun *Greg.*]

ADVERB Greg looked **blankly** at the sign. [*Blankly* modifies the action verb *looked.*]

Reference Note

For more about **linking verbs,** see page 374.

Exercise 1 Identifying Adjectives and Adverbs

Identify the italicized word in each of the following sentences as either an adjective or an adverb.

EXAMPLE **1.** They had been *best* friends since second grade.
1. best—adjective

1. Does Mike's flight leave *early*?
2. Carolina was the *last* player on the field.
3. I can *hardly* hear the lead actor's monologue.
4. If we walk *fast,* we can make it to the gate on time.
5. The woven tapestry of *vivid* colors was lovely.
6. Have you met Kelly and her *younger* brother?
7. The *daily* news program begins in half an hour.
8. In the garage were stacked old boxes and *rusty* cans of paint.
9. Adrian and his sister boarded the airplane *last.*
10. Please hand me the small box on the *third* shelf.

Reference Note

For more about ***good*** and ***well,*** see page 587.

USAGE

Good and *Well*

Good is an adjective. It should be used to modify a noun or a pronoun. Use *well* to modify a verb.

EXAMPLES Whitney Houston's voice sounded very **good** to me. [*Good* modifies the noun *voice.*]

Whitney Houston sang the national anthem very **well.** [*Well* modifies the verb *sang.*]

Good should not be used to modify a verb.

NONSTANDARD Paula does good in all her school subjects.
STANDARD Paula does **well** in all her school subjects. [*Well* modifies the verb *does.*]

NONSTANDARD The mariachi band can play good.
STANDARD The mariachi band can play **well.** [*Well* modifies the verb *can play.*]

Well may be used either as an adjective or as an adverb. As an adjective, *well* has two meanings: "in good health" or "satisfactory."

EXAMPLES Rammel is **well** today. [Meaning "in good health," *well* modifies the noun *Rammel.*]

All is **well.** [Meaning "satisfactory," *well* modifies the pronoun *All.*]

NOTE *Feel good* and *feel well* mean different things. *Feel good* means "to feel happy or pleased." *Feel well* means "to feel healthy."

EXAMPLES I felt **good** [*happy*] when I got an A.

He did not feel **well** [*healthy*] after lunch.

Oral Practice 1 Using *Well* Correctly

Read the following sentences aloud, stressing the modifier *well.*

1. Everyone did *well* on the test.
2. We work *well* together.
3. Do you sing as *well* as your sister does?
4. I can't water-ski very *well.*
5. How *well* can you write?
6. All went *well* for the Korean gymnastics team.

7. Our class pictures turned out *well.*
8. The freshman goalie can block as *well* as the senior.

Exercise 2 Using *Good* and *Well* Correctly

Use *good* or *well* to complete each of the following sentences correctly.

EXAMPLE **1.** We danced ____ at the recital.
1. well

1. Melba did not run as ____ during the second race.
2. The casserole looked ____ to us.
3. How ____ does she play the part?
4. Everyone could hear the huge Swiss alphorn very ____ when the man played it.
5. He certainly appears ____ in spite of his illness.
6. I gave them directions as ____ as I could.
7. The children behaved very ____.
8. Bagels with cream cheese always taste ____ to him.
9. The debate did not go as ____ as we had hoped.
10. How ____ the pool looks on such a hot day!

USAGE

Comparison of Modifiers

The two kinds of modifiers—adjectives and adverbs—may be used to compare things. In making comparisons, adjectives and adverbs take different forms. The specific form that is used depends upon how many syllables the modifier has and how many things are being compared.

ADJECTIVES This building is **tall.** [no comparison]
This building is **taller** than that one. [one compared with another]
This building is the **tallest** one in the world. [one compared with many others]

ADVERBS I ski **frequently.** [no comparison]
I ski **more frequently** than she does. [one compared with another]
Of the three of us, I ski **most frequently.** [one compared with two others]

20b. **The three degrees of comparison are the positive, the comparative, and the superlative.**

Positive	Comparative	Superlative
sharp	sharper	sharpest
quickly	more quickly	most quickly
bad	worse	worst

Regular Comparison

(1) Most one-syllable modifiers form the comparative degree by adding *–er* and the superlative degree by adding *–est.*

Positive	Comparative	Superlative
meek	meeker	meekest
cold	colder	coldest
dry	drier	driest

(2) Two-syllable modifiers form the comparative degree by adding *–er* or using *more* and form the superlative degree by adding *–est* or using *most.*

Positive	Comparative	Superlative
simple	simpler	simplest
easy	easier	easiest
often	more often	most often

(3) Modifiers that have three or more syllables form the comparative degree by using *more* and the superlative degree by using *most.*

Positive	Comparative	Superlative
delicate	more delicate	most delicate
creative	more creative	most creative
carefully	more carefully	most carefully

STYLE TIP

Most two-syllable modifiers can correctly form the comparative and superlative degrees using either the suffixes *–er* and *–est* or the words *more* and *most.* If adding *–er* or *–est* sounds awkward, use *more* or *most.*

AWKWARD
specialer

BETTER
more special

USAGE

(4) To show a decrease in the qualities they express, modifiers form the comparative degree by using *less* and the superlative degree by using *least*.

Positive	Comparative	Superlative
safe	less safe	least safe
expensive	less expensive	least expensive
often	less often	least often
gracefully	less gracefully	least gracefully
heartily	less heartily	least heartily

Exercise 3 Forming the Degrees of Comparison of Modifiers

Give the forms for the comparative and superlative degrees of the following modifiers.

EXAMPLE **1.** rich

1. richer, less rich; richest, least rich

1. sure
2. cautiously
3. early
4. thankful
5. possible
6. clean
7. heavy
8. confident
9. seriously
10. loyal

Irregular Comparison

20c. The comparative and superlative degrees of some modifiers are not formed by the usual methods.

Positive	Comparative	Superlative
good	better	best
bad	worse	worst
well	better	best
many	more	most
much	more	most
little	less	least
far	farther *or* further	farthest *or* furthest

TIPS & TRICKS

The word *little* also has regular comparative and superlative forms: *littler, littlest.* These forms are used to describe physical size (the **littlest** bunny). The forms *less* and *least* are used to describe an amount (**less** time).

Exercise 4 Using Comparative and Superlative Forms of Adjectives

Using the chart about skyscrapers that is provided below, give the correct form of an adjective for each of the following sentences.

EXAMPLE 1. The Empire State Building is ____ than the John Hancock Center.

1. taller

1. One Liberty Place, built in 1987, is the ____ of all the buildings listed.
2. The Sears Tower has the ____ stories of all the buildings listed in the chart below.
3. The Amoco Building, now known as the Aon Center, is four years ____ than the John Hancock Center.
4. The Chrysler Building is the ____ of all the buildings.
5. The Sears Tower has ten ____ stories than the John Hancock Center.
6. The Pittsburgh Plate Glass skyscraper has the ____ number of stories of all the buildings listed.
7. New York has ____ skyscrapers on the list than Chicago has.

SKYSCRAPERS IN THE UNITED STATES

Building	Height	Year Completed
Sears Tower, Chicago, IL	110 stories (1,454 feet)	1974
Empire State Building, New York City, NY	102 stories (1,250 feet)	1931
John Hancock Center, Chicago, IL	100 stories (1,127 feet)	1969
Amoco Building, Chicago, IL	83 stories (1,136 feet)	1973
Chrysler Building, New York City, NY	77 stories (1,046 feet)	1930
One Liberty Place, Philadelphia, PA	61 stories (945 feet)	1987
Pittsburgh Plate Glass, Pittsburgh, PA	40 stories (635 feet)	1984

8. Chicago's Sears Tower, at 1,454 feet, is the ____ building listed on the chart.
9. It would be fun to compare some of the ____ well-known buildings, too.
10. Although the Pittsburgh Plate Glass tower has the ____ stories of all the skyscrapers listed on the previous page, Pittsburgh residents think it is the most beautiful.

Review A **Forming the Comparative and Superlative Degrees of Modifiers**

Give the comparative and superlative forms of the following modifiers.

EXAMPLES 1. wasteful

1. *more wasteful, less wasteful; most wasteful, least wasteful*

2. *young*

2. *younger, less young; youngest, least young*

1. sheepish	6. quick	11. furious	16. hot
2. simply	7. weary	12. enthusiastic	17. good
3. much	8. easily	13. suddenly	18. well
4. surely	9. many	14. frequently	19. bad
5. gracious	10. tasty	15. generous	20. old

TIPS & TRICKS

Here's a way to remember which form of a modifier to use. When comparing *two* things, use *–er* (the *two*-letter ending). When comparing *three* or more things, use *–est* (the *three*-letter ending).

Use of Comparative and Superlative Forms

20d. Use the comparative degree when comparing two things. Use the superlative degree when comparing more than two.

COMPARATIVE The second problem is **harder** than the first.
Luisa can perform the gymnastic routine **more gracefully** than I.
Of the two tape players, this one costs **less.**

SUPERLATIVE Crater Lake is the **deepest** lake in the United States.
This is the **most valuable** coin in my collection.
Of the three dogs, that one barks the **least.**

STYLE TIP

In everyday speech, you may hear and use expressions such as *Put your best foot forward* and *May the best team win.* Such uses of the superlative are acceptable in informal situations. However, in your writing for school and other formal situations, you should follow Rule 20d.

Avoid the common mistake of using the superlative degree to compare two things.

NONSTANDARD	Of the two plans, this is the best one.
STANDARD	Of the two plans, this is the **better** one.
NONSTANDARD	Felicia is the youngest of the two girls.
STANDARD	Felicia is the **younger** of the two girls.

USAGE

Review B Proofreading for Correct Use of Comparative and Superlative Forms

Some of the following sentences contain incorrect comparative and superlative forms. For each incorrect form, give the correct form. If a sentence is already correct, write *C*.

EXAMPLE **1.** Julie and I spend the most time preparing for Cinco de Mayo than any other girls on our block.

1. the most—more

1. Julie works even more hard than I do to prepare for the holiday.
2. I get exciteder about the parade and festivals, though.
3. I think Cinco de Mayo is the better holiday of the year.
4. At least it's the more lively one in our neighborhood.
5. Cinco de Mayo celebrates Mexico's most important victory over Napoleon III of France.
6. Of all the speakers each year, the mayor always gives the more stirring speech about the history of the day.
7. For me, the better part of the holiday is singing and dancing in the parade.
8. I get to wear the beautifulest dresses you've ever seen.
9. They're even more lovely than the ones worn by the girls in this picture.
10. Although these white dresses are certainly pretty, they are less colorful than mine.

20e. Include the word *other* or *else* when comparing one member of a group with the rest of the group.

NONSTANDARD Jupiter is larger than any planet in the solar system. [Jupiter is one of the planets in the solar system and cannot be larger than itself.]

STANDARD Jupiter is larger than any **other** planet in the solar system.

NONSTANDARD Roland can type faster than anyone in his computer class. [Roland is one of the students in his computer class and cannot type faster than himself.]

STANDARD Roland can type faster than anyone **else** in his computer class.

Exercise 5 Using Comparisons Correctly in Sentences

Write *other* or *else* to complete the meaning of each of the following sentences.

EXAMPLE 1. No one ____ knows how much I love music.
1. else

1. Several of my relatives think there are no ____ careers from which to choose.
2. I'd rather be a performer, playing the guitar or some ____ musical instrument.
3. A friend of mine plays the tenor saxophone better than anyone ____ I've heard.
4. Stringed instruments appeal to me more than ____ kinds of instruments, such as brass.
5. There are lutes, dulcimers, violins, cellos, sitars, harps, and many ____ ancient strings.
6. Everyone ____ in my family expects me to become a music teacher.
7. What ____ could be as much fun as teaching music?
8. The sound of acoustic music appeals to me more than anything ____.
9. Voice, strings, drums, and ____ ancient ways of making music interest me.
10. While I take guitar lessons, I will research the history of guitars and ____ stringed instruments.

USAGE

20f. Avoid using double comparisons.

A ***double comparison*** is the use of both *–er* and *more* (or *less*) or both *–est* and *most* (or *least*) to form a degree of comparison. For each degree, comparisons should be formed in only one of these two ways, not both.

NONSTANDARD The Asian elephant is more smaller than the African elephant.
STANDARD The Asian elephant is **smaller** than the African elephant.

NONSTANDARD Ribbon Falls, in Yosemite National Park, is the most beautifulest waterfall I have ever seen.
STANDARD Ribbon Falls, in Yosemite National Park, is the **most beautiful** waterfall I have ever seen.

Review C Revising for Correct Comparative and Superlative Forms

Most of the following sentences contain incorrect forms of comparison. Revise each incorrect sentence, using the correct form. If a sentence is already correct, write *C.*

EXAMPLES
1. It's the most homeliest dog in the world.
1. It's the homeliest dog in the world.

2. Which of these three is the more expensive?
2. Which of these three is the most expensive?

1. The pitcher is worse at bat than any member of the team.
2. The most largest ancient cliff dwellings in Arizona are in Navajo National Monument.
3. That modern sculpture is the most strangest I've ever seen.
4. After watching the two kittens for a few minutes, Rudy chose to adopt the most playful one.
5. This morning was more sunnier than this afternoon.
6. Your cough sounds worser today.
7. The music on this album is better for dancing than the music on that one.
8. New York City has a larger population than any city in the United States.
9. Karl likes German sauerkraut more better than Korean kimchi.
10. She was the most talented singer in the show.

The Double Negative

20g. **Avoid using double negatives.**

A ***double negative*** is the use of two negative words to express one negative idea.

Common Negative Words			
barely	never	none	nothing
hardly	no	no one	nowhere
neither	nobody	not (*or* –n't)	scarcely

Many negative words are used as modifiers.

NONSTANDARD We don't have no extra chairs.
STANDARD We have **no** extra chairs.
STANDARD We do**n't** have **any** extra chairs.

NONSTANDARD He couldn't hardly talk.
STANDARD He **could hardly** talk.

Exercise 6 Proofreading to Correct Double Negatives

Revise each of the following sentences to correct the double negative.

EXAMPLE 1. We don't hardly have time to relax.
1. We hardly have time to relax.

1. Alejandro hasn't never been to Tennessee.
2. Because of the strong wind and heavy rain, we couldn't scarcely find our way home.
3. He never had no problem with public speaking.
4. The athletes don't hardly have a break between events.
5. The authorities don't allow no passenger cars on Michigan's popular Mackinac Island.
6. By the time I had made spring rolls for everyone else, I didn't have nothing left for me.
7. I never listen to no one who gossips.
8. Your answer doesn't make no difference to me.
9. The goalie doesn't have no excuse.
10. Don't never use both *not* and *scarcely* together.

HELP Although some sentences in Exercise 6 can be correctly revised in more than one way, you need to give only one revision for each sentence.

HELP

Although some sentences in Reviews D and E can be correctly revised in more than one way, you need to give only one revision for each sentence.

USAGE

Review D Using Modifiers Correctly

Most of the following sentences contain errors in the use of modifiers. Revise each incorrect sentence to correct the error. If a sentence is already correct, write *C*.

EXAMPLE **1.** We don't never stay after school.

1. We never stay after school.

1. Which did you like best—the book or the movie?
2. Gina has more ideas for the festival than anyone.
3. The Suez Canal is more longer than the Panama Canal.
4. I can't hardly reason with her.
5. Jean and Dominic work good as a team.
6. Ben's bruise looks worse today than it did yesterday.
7. They haven't said nothing to us about it.
8. Of the two singers, Mariah Carey has the best voice.
9. Which has better sound, your stereo or mine?
10. The cast performed extremely good.

Review E Proofreading for Correct Use of Modifiers

Most of the following sentences contain errors in the use of modifiers. If a sentence contains an error, give the correct form of the modifier. If a sentence is already correct, write *C*.

EXAMPLE **1.** Of the three programs, the one on Japanese plays was the more interesting.

1. more—most

1. Before the program, I didn't hardly know anything about Japanese theater.
2. I learned that Japanese theater is much more old than theater in many other countries.
3. *Noh* and *kabuki* are the two most best-known kinds of Japanese drama.
4. Dating from the Middle Ages, *noh* is different from any form of Japanese theater.

5. *Noh* plays, which are narrated in an ancient language, are performed more slowly than *kabuki* plays.
6. *Noh* plays are seen less oftener than the more modern and dramatic *kabuki* plays.
7. In the West, we don't have no theater like Japan's *bugaku* for the Imperial Court.
8. I was more interested in Japan's puppet theater, the *bunraku,* than anyone in my class.
9. Puppet theater performers have a more harder job than other theater performers.
10. I didn't never know that it takes three people to operate one *bunraku* puppet.

Placement of Modifiers

Notice how the meaning of the following sentence changes when the position of the phrase *from Canada* changes.

EXAMPLE The professor **from Canada** gave a televised lecture on famous writers. [The phrase modifies *professor.*]

The professor gave a televised lecture on famous writers **from Canada.** [The phrase modifies *writers.*]

The professor gave a televised lecture **from Canada** on famous writers. [The phrase modifies *gave.*]

20h. Place modifying words, phrases, and clauses as near as possible to the words they modify.

A modifier that seems to modify the wrong word in a sentence is called a ***misplaced modifier.***

MISPLACED My aunt has almost seen all of the documentaries directed by Camille Billops.

CORRECT My aunt has seen **almost** all of the documentaries directed by Camille Billops.

A modifier that does not clearly modify another word or word group in a sentence is called a ***dangling modifier.***

DANGLING While vacationing in Mexico, snorkeling in the bay was the most fun.

CORRECT **While vacationing in Mexico,** we had the most fun snorkeling in the bay.

Exercise 7 Correcting Misplaced Modifiers and Dangling Modifiers

Revise each of the following sentences to correct the misplaced or dangling modifier in italics.

EXAMPLE 1. *Surprised,* the finish line was only fifty yards away!
1. *I was surprised that the finish line was only fifty yards away!*

HELP — Although some sentences in Exercise 7 can be correctly revised in more than one way, you need to give only one revision for each sentence.

USAGE

1. Both Dr. Albert Sabin and Dr. Jonas Salk succeeded in *almost* developing polio vaccines at the same time.
2. Kristi Yamaguchi won a gold medal in the 1992 Olympics *for figure skating.*
3. *Looking out the airplane window,* the volcano seemed ready to erupt.
4. *As a new student,* the teacher introduced me to my classmates.
5. *Before eating supper,* your hands must be washed.
6. Bessie Coleman dreamed of starting a flying school for African Americans, *who was the first U.S. woman to earn an international pilot's license.*
7. *Hot and tired,* cold water was what the team needed.
8. Did you look for the black-and-white photographs taken by Grandfather *in that old shoe box*?
9. My uncle got a service dog from Canine Assistants *that could open cabinets, pull a wheelchair, and go for help.*
10. *Thrilled,* my sister's face lit up with excitement.

Prepositional Phrases

A ***prepositional phrase*** consists of a preposition, a noun or pronoun called the ***object of the preposition,*** and any modifiers of that object.

A prepositional phrase used as an adjective should generally be placed directly after the word it modifies.

MISPLACED This book describes Nat Turner's struggle for freedom by Judith Berry Griffin.

CORRECT This book **by Judith Berry Griffin** describes Nat Turner's struggle for freedom.

Reference Note

For more information about **prepositions,** see page 386. For more about **prepositional phrases,** see pages 388 and 416.

A prepositional phrase used as an adverb should be placed near the word it modifies.

MISPLACED Spanish explorers discovered gold along the river that runs near my house during the 1500s. [Did the river run near my house during the 1500s?]

CORRECT **During the 1500s,** Spanish explorers discovered gold along the river that now runs near my house.

CORRECT Spanish explorers discovered gold **during the 1500s** along the river that now runs near my house.

Avoid placing a prepositional phrase in a position where it can modify either of two words. Place the phrase so that it clearly modifies the word you intend it to modify.

MISPLACED Emily said before sunset it might get colder. [Does the phrase modify *said* or *might get*?]

CORRECT Emily said it might get colder **before sunset.** [The phrase modifies *might get.*]

CORRECT **Before sunset** Emily said it might get colder. [The phrase modifies *said.*]

Exercise 8 Correcting Misplaced Prepositional Phrases

Find the misplaced prepositional phrases in the following sentences. Then, revise each sentence, placing the phrase near the word it modifies.

EXAMPLE **1.** I read that a satellite was launched in the news today.

1. I read in the news today that a satellite was launched.

1. The nature photographer told us about filming a herd of water buffalo in class today.
2. The quick steps of the Texas clog-dancing teams amazed us on the wooden stage.
3. The robotic mannequins drew a huge crowd in the futuristic window display.
4. Many people watched the Fourth of July fireworks in their cars.
5. We saw several capuchin monkeys on vacation in Costa Rica.
6. My aunt promised me on Saturday she will take me to the symphony.
7. There is one gymnast who can tumble as well as vault on our gymnastics team.

TIPS & TRICKS

To find misplaced prepositional phrases in a piece of your own writing, try this method: Look at each sentence, and circle each prepositional phrase. Then, draw an arrow from the circled phrase to the word it modifies.

Is the phrase near the word it modifies? If the phrase is used as an adjective, does it come right after the word it modifies? If not, move the misplaced phrase to the correct spot in your sentence.

HELP

Although some sentences in Exercise 8 can be correctly revised in more than one way, you need to give only one revision for each sentence.

8. That man bought the rare painting of Pocahontas with the briefcase.
9. The model posed gracefully in front of the statue in the designer gown.
10. We saw the trapeze artist swinging dangerously through our field binoculars.

Participial Phrases

A ***participial phrase*** consists of a verb form—either a present participle or a past participle—and any modifiers or complements the participle has. A participial phrase modifies a noun or a pronoun.

Like a prepositional phrase, a participial phrase should be placed as close as possible to the word it modifies.

MISPLACED Bandits chased the stagecoach yelling wildly. [Was the stagecoach yelling wildly?]

CORRECT **Yelling wildly,** bandits chased the stagecoach.

MISPLACED The vase was lying on the floor broken into several pieces. [Was the floor broken into pieces?]

CORRECT The vase, **broken into several pieces,** was lying on the floor.

To correct a dangling participial phrase, supply a word that the phrase can modify, or change the phrase to a clause.

DANGLING Jogging down the sidewalk, my ankle was sprained. [Was my ankle jogging down the sidewalk?]

CORRECT Jogging down the sidewalk, **I** sprained my ankle.

CORRECT I sprained my ankle **while I was** jogging down the sidewalk.

DANGLING Dressed in warm clothing, the cold was no problem. [Was the cold dressed in warm clothing?]

CORRECT Dressed in warm clothing, **we** had no problem with the cold.

CORRECT **Since we were** dressed in warm clothing, the cold was no problem.

USAGE

Reference Note

For more information on **participial phrases,** see page 422. For guidelines on using **commas with participial phrases,** see page 639.

COMPUTER TIP

A computer can help you find and correct problems with modifiers. A spell-checker can easily find nonstandard forms such as *baddest, expensiver,* and *mostest.* However, you will need to examine the placement of phrase and clause modifiers yourself.

Exercise 9 Correcting Misplaced and Dangling Participial Phrases

Revise each incorrect sentence to eliminate the misplaced or dangling modifier. You may need to add, delete, or rearrange words. If a sentence is already correct, write *C.*

EXAMPLE 1. Dressed in our clown costumes, the police officer waved and smiled.

1. Seeing us dressed in our clown costumes, the police officer waved and smiled.

or

Dressed in our clown costumes, we saw the police officer wave and smile.

1. Standing on the dock, the boat didn't look safe to the sailors.
2. Pat found a secret passage exploring the old house.
3. Having brought in plenty of firewood, the cabin soon warmed up, and we fell asleep.
4. Wanting to see more of Mexico City, our vacation grew from one to two weeks.
5. Questioned by reporters, the governor's view on the matter became clear.
6. Suffering from cramps, Ali's chance of winning was slight.
7. Reading a book, my cat crawled into my lap.
8. The old suit hanging in the closet would make the perfect costume for the play.
9. Balancing precariously on the high wire, the tricks that the tightrope walker performed were amazing.
10. Exhausted after hiking in the Florida Everglades, a tall, cool glass of water was a welcome sight.

HELP— Although some of the sentences in Exercise 9 can be correctly revised in more than one way, you need to give only one answer for each sentence.

USAGE

Adjective Clauses

An ***adjective clause*** is a subordinate clause that modifies a noun or a pronoun. Most adjective clauses begin with a relative pronoun—*that, which, who, whom,* or *whose.*

Like an adjective phrase, an adjective clause should be placed directly after the word it modifies.

MISPLACED The book was about insects that we read. [Did we read the insects?]

CORRECT The book **that we read** was about insects.

Reference Note

For more information on **adjective clauses,** see page 444. For more about **using commas with adjective clauses,** see page 639.

MISPLACED	A little boy walked up to Jenny who was lost. [Who was lost, the little boy or Jenny?]
CORRECT	A little boy **who was lost** walked up to Jenny.
MISPLACED	His parents traded an old television for a new CD player which they no longer wanted. [Did his parents no longer want a new CD player?]
CORRECT	His parents traded an old television, **which they no longer wanted,** for a new CD player.

HELP

Although some of the sentences in Exercise 10 can be correctly revised in more than one way, you need to give only one answer for each sentence.

USAGE

Exercise 10 Correcting Misplaced Adjective Clauses

Find the misplaced adjective clauses in the following sentences. Then, revise each sentence, placing the clause near the word it modifies.

EXAMPLE **1.** I retyped the first draft on clean paper, which I had corrected.

1. I retyped the first draft, which I had corrected, on clean paper.

or

After I corrected the first draft, I retyped it on clean paper.

1. The boy is from my school that won the contest.
2. We tiptoed over the ice in our heavy boots, which had begun to crack.
3. The jade sculpture was by a famous Chinese artist that my cousin broke.
4. We sometimes play soccer in one of the parks on nice days that are near the school.
5. Did the telethon achieve its goal that was on for more than thirty-six hours?
6. Nisei Week is in August, which is celebrated by Japanese Americans in Los Angeles.
7. The friendly man said hello to my mother, whose name I can't remember.
8. The sweater belongs to my best friend that has a V-shaped neck.
9. My married sister has the flu who lives in Ohio.
10. That documentary was filmed in several countries, which will be broadcast in the fall.

Review F Proofreading for Misplaced Modifiers and Dangling Modifiers

Most sentences in the following paragraph contain misplaced or dangling modifiers. They may be words, prepositional phrases, participial phrases, or adjective clauses. Revise each sentence that contains a misplaced or dangling modifier. If a sentence is already correct, write *C*.

EXAMPLE **1.** Living in cold and treeless areas, snow houses are built by some Native Arctic people.

1. Living in cold and treeless areas, some Native Arctic people build snow houses.

[**1**] You've probably seen pictures of houses on television built of snow. [**2**] Knowing that these houses are called igloos, other facts about them may be new to you. [**3**] At one time, the word *igloo,* which means "shelter," applied to all types of houses.[**4**] However, *igloo* has come to mean houses now built of snow. [**5**] For igloos, large blocks of snow are stacked together, which are used only during the winter. [**6**] Adapting to their environment long ago, snow houses provided protection against the bitter cold. [**7**] Looking at the drawing below, the three steps in the building of an igloo are shown. [**8**] First, blocks are carefully cut by the builders of snow. [**9**] Arranged in a circle about ten feet across, the builders slant the blocks inward. [**10**] The finished igloo that you see is dome shaped and has a hole at the top.

HELP Although some of the sentences in Review F can be correctly revised in more than one way, you need to give only one answer for each sentence.

USAGE

USAGE

Review G **Using Modifiers Correctly**

In each of the following sentences, a modifier is used incorrectly. The mistake may result from (1) a misuse of *good* or *well,* (2) an incorrect comparison, (3) the use of a double negative, or (4) a misplaced or dangling modifier. Revise each sentence so that it is clear and correct.

EXAMPLE **1.** That was the more entertaining concert I have ever seen.

1. That was the most entertaining concert I have ever seen.

1. During last night's charity concert, the singing group was protected from being swarmed by guards.

2. The group played before an extremely enthusiastic crowd performing most of their old hits as well as several new tunes.

3. Years ago the singers wore strange costumes and makeup so that fans couldn't hardly tell what their faces looked like.

4. Bored, these gimmicks no longer appealed to the group's fans after a while.

5. The band finally chose the most simply tailored look of the two they had considered.

6. Enthusiastic about the group's new look, a change in its performance style was barely noticed by the fans.

7. Few fans could tell the first time they appeared in public after changing their style how nervous the singers were.

8. "That was the most scariest performance of my career," one singer remarked.

9. Cheering heartily, the singers' fears were relieved.

10. Both the concert and the picnic did exceptionally good at raising funds.

Chapter Review

A. Using the Correct Forms of Modifiers

The following sentences contain errors in the use of modifiers. Rewrite each sentence to correct the errors.

1. Of all the characters in the movie, I think the gardener is the most funniest.
2. Alan thinks that this dessert tastes more good than the others.
3. I couldn't hardly believe that she said that.
4. Yolanda is the tallest of the twins.
5. The house on Drury Avenue is the one we like the bestest.
6. The book doesn't cost much, but I don't have no money.
7. They offer so many combinations that I don't know which one I like more.
8. The movie made me curiouser about the Muslim period in Spanish history.
9. There's nothing I like more better to eat for supper than barbecued chicken.
10. Why doesn't the teacher ask questions that are more easier?

B. Correcting Misplaced and Dangling Modifiers

Each of the following sentences contains a misplaced or dangling modifier in italics. Rewrite each sentence so that it is clear and correct.

11. *Searching for hours,* the missing retainer could not be found.
12. The library has several books about dinosaurs *in our school.*
13. *Sleeping soundly,* Harry woke his father when supper was ready.
14. The book is not in the library *that I wanted to read.*
15. Aunt Lucia found a coupon for free recipes *in a magazine.*
16. *Alarmed,* a sudden gust of wind swept through the camp and battered our tent.
17. *Left alone for the first time in his life,* the night seemed long and scary.

18. *After eating all their food,* we put the cats outside.
19. *Floating across the sky,* we could see shapes in the clouds.
20. *Sitting in the bleachers,* the outfielder caught the ball right in front of us.

C. Using Comparisons Correctly in Sentences

Write the following sentences, and complete the meaning of each sentence by using *other* or *else.*

21. Sharon sings better than anyone.
22. Rather than watch TV, I think I'll read *Adventures of Huckleberry Finn* or some book.
23. New York City has more inhabitants than any U.S. city.
24. Everyone in my class thinks my Spanish is better than I do.
25. The sun is brighter than anything in our solar system.
26. Riding a bike down a breezy lane in early summer is more fun than anything.
27. Marcy likes New Orleans better than any city in the United States.
28. Sharon would rather play kettledrums than any percussion instrument in the orchestra.
29. No one knows how much I miss Mexico.
30. The tulips Marcia and I planted last fall bloomed sooner than any flowers in our garden.

D. Proofreading a Paragraph for Correct Use of Modifiers and Comparative and Superlative Forms

Some of the sentences in the following paragraph contain incorrect uses and forms of modifiers. Write each sentence, giving the correct form or forms where needed. If a sentence is already correct, write *C.*

[31] Before reading an article on African American actors, I didn't hardly know anything about Sidney Poitier. **[32]** In his time, he was one of the popularest male leads in Hollywood. **[33]** His background is one of the most interesting things about him. **[34]** Born to poor tomato growers, south Florida and the Bahamas were where he was raised. **[35]** Poitier worked at some of the most hard jobs you can imagine before making his Broadway debut in

1946. **[36]** In 1963, his performance in the film *Lilies of the Field* won him an Academy Award as better actor. **[37]** In many ways, 1967 has been his successfullest year so far. **[38]** *In the Heat of the Night; To Sir, With Love;* and *Guess Who's Coming to Dinner* all came out that year, and they were some of the world's favoritest movies. **[39]** Still a Bahamian citizen, Poitier was appointed ambassador to Japan in 1997 by the Bahamian government. **[40]** The life of Sidney Poitier is certainly different from that of any movie star.

Writing Application

Using Modifiers in a Letter

Placement of Modifiers You have just received a letter from a favorite aunt who is a professional athlete. She wants to hear about your sports activities and any sports events you've been to or seen on TV. Write a letter to your aunt, telling her about your activities. Place modifying phrases and clauses correctly.

Prewriting You'll first need to choose a sports activity or event to write about. You may write about your own experiences in a school or community sport, or you may use your imagination. Before you begin writing, make notes about the activity or event you find most interesting.

Writing As you write your first draft, try to include specific details that will interest your aunt. Be sure to use the proper form for a personal letter.

Revising Read your finished letter. Is it interesting and lively? If not, revise it by adding more adjectives, adverbs, and action verbs to improve your descriptions.

Publishing Underline the prepositional phrases, participial phrases, and adjective clauses. Check to see that they are correctly placed near the words they modify. Check your letter for errors in spelling and punctuation. You and your classmates may want to post the letter on a class bulletin board or Web page.

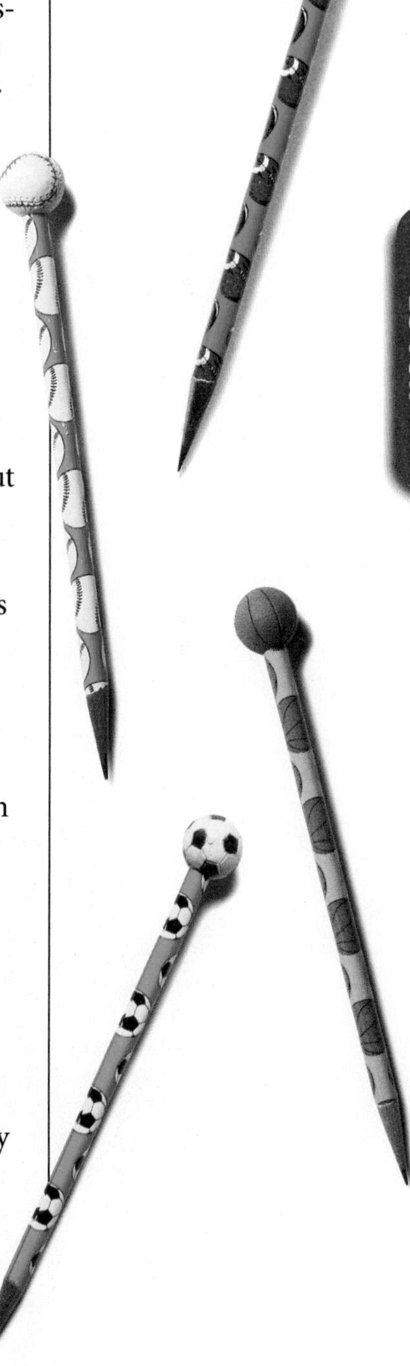

A Glossary of Usage

Common Usage Problems

Diagnostic Preview

Identifying and Correcting Errors in Usage

One sentence in each of the following sets contains an error in formal, standard usage. Choose the letter of the sentence that contains an error. Then, revise the sentence, using formal, standard English.

EXAMPLE
1. **a.** The chicken tastes bad.
   b. Where is the book about pandas at?
   c. There was agreement among the five dancers.

1. b. Where is the book about pandas?

1. **a.** Bring your notes when you come over.
   b. The glass dish busted.
   c. He could have danced.
2. **a.** Jennifer drew an apple.
   b. The cold affects that kind of plant.
   c. We are already to go.
3. **a.** Manuel says that he feels alright today.
   b. She went everywhere.
   c. We have fewer chairs than we need.

4. **a.** They danced good at the party.
   b. If I had sung, you would have laughed.
   c. You ought to help.

5. **a.** It's cold.
   b. Samuel made it hisself.
   c. Its knob is broken.

6. **a.** Teach me a song from the musical.
   b. That story is rather interesting.
   c. Who's dog is that?

7. **a.** Mr. Barnes is here for the meeting.
   b. I know why he left.
   c. Those kind of bikes are expensive.

8. **a.** These taste like oranges.
   b. Sing as she does.
   c. Whose in charge here?

9. **a.** Please come inside the house.
   b. I am real happy.
   c. The reason she laughed was that your dog looked funny.

10. **a.** I looked for the book, but someone must of misplaced it.
    b. Your forehand has improved somewhat.
    c. He sings better than I do.

11. **a.** Your coat is beautiful.
    b. You're a fast runner.
    c. I cannot leave without I wash the dishes first.

12. **a.** She is the student who plays the violin.
    b. We have only a short way to go.
    c. We read that a new store is opening in that there mall.

13. **a.** I use to read mysteries.
    b. Set that crate down over here.
    c. This hat is old.

14. **a.** I gave you them books.
    b. They bought themselves new shirts.
    c. There is the cat.

15. **a.** Sit down anywhere that looks comfortable.
    b. They're smiling.
    c. There soccer team is good.

USAGE

16. **a.** Gail did not feel well.
    b. Have a orange.
    c. You invited everyone except Cai.

17. **a.** I ate an apple with breakfast this morning.
    b. Sunscreen lessens the affects of the sun's rays.
    c. We already read the book in class.

18. **a.** Your answers are all right.
    b. They went nowheres.
    c. He looks as if he has lost something.

19. **a.** Nancy's ankle was hurt bad.
    b. The funds were divided among the three cities.
    c. The pipe burst.

20. **a.** I cannot hardly dance.
    b. Warm days make me feel good.
    c. It's pretty.

21. **a.** He must be somewhere.
    b. I can scarcely ride this bike.
    c. The reason I like him is because he is kind.

22. **a.** We have less shelves than we need.
    b. Those kinds of shirts are warm.
    c. This morning I could have slept longer.

23. **a.** Latoya doesn't put her books on the couch.
    b. Learn how to play this game.
    c. Do like he does.

24. **a.** They are inside the house.
    b. I could of eaten the entire sandwich.
    c. He placed the chair next to the table himself.

25. **a.** Their my cats.
    b. Do you need those books?
    c. Did you accept the apology?

About the Glossary

This chapter provides a compact glossary of common problems in English usage. A ***glossary*** is an alphabetical list of special terms or expressions with definitions, explanations, and examples. You'll notice that some examples in this glossary are labeled *nonstandard, standard, formal,* or *informal.*

The label ***nonstandard*** identifies usage that is suitable only in the most casual speaking situations and in writing that attempts to re-create casual speech. ***Standard*** English is language that is grammatically correct and appropriate in formal and informal situations. ***Formal*** identifies usage that is appropriate in serious speaking and writing situations (such as in speeches and in compositions for school). The label ***informal*** indicates standard usage common in conversation and in everyday writing such as personal letters. In doing the exercises in this chapter, be sure to use only standard English.

Reference Note

For a list of **words often confused,** see page 698. Use the index at the end of the book to find discussions of other usage problems.

Formal	Informal
angry	steamed
unpleasant	yucky
agreeable	cool
very impressive	totally awesome
accelerate	step on it

USAGE

a, an Use *a* before words beginning with a consonant sound. Use *an* before words beginning with a vowel sound.

EXAMPLES He did not consider himself **a** hero.

Market Avenue is **a** one-way street. [*One-way* begins with a consonant sound.]

An oryx is a large antelope.

We waited in line for **an** hour. [*Hour* begins with a vowel sound.]

accept, except *Accept* is a verb that means "to receive." *Except* may be either a verb or a preposition. As a verb, *except* means "to leave out" or "to exclude"; as a preposition, *except* means "other than" or "excluding."

Reference Note

For more about **verbs,** see page 504. For more about **prepositions,** see page 386.

EXAMPLES I **accept** your apology.

Children were **excepted** from the admission fee.

Mark has told all his friends **except** Trenell.

Reference Note

For more about **nouns,** see page 345.

affect, effect *Affect* is a verb meaning "to influence." *Effect* used as a verb means "to bring about." Used as a noun, *effect* means "the result of some action."

EXAMPLES The bad punt did not **affect** the outcome of the game.

The government's reforms **effected** great changes.

Read more about the **effects** of pollution.

ain't Avoid using this word in speaking and writing; it is nonstandard English.

all ready, already *All ready* means "completely prepared." *Already* means "previously."

EXAMPLES The mechanic checked the engine parts to make sure they were **all ready** for assembly.

We have **already** served the refreshments.

USAGE

Reference Note

For more information about **adjectives,** see page 358. For more about **adverbs,** see page 381.

all right Used as an adjective, *all right* means "unhurt" or "satisfactory." Used as an adverb, *all right* means "well enough." *All right* should be written as two words.

EXAMPLES Linda fell off the horse, but she is **all right.** [adjective]

Your work is **all right.** [adjective]

You did **all right** at the track meet. [adverb]

STYLE  **TIP**

Many writers overuse *a lot.* Whenever you run across *a lot* as you revise your own writing, try to replace it with a more exact word or phrase.

EXAMPLE

The Spaniards explored a lot of North America and South America.

The Spaniards explored **vast areas** [or **thousands of square miles**] of North America and South America.

a lot *A lot* should always be written as two words.

EXAMPLE Her family donated **a lot** of money to the Red Cross.

among See **between, among.**

anyways, anywheres, everywheres, nowheres, somewheres Use these words without a final *s.*

EXAMPLE I did not go **anywhere** [not *anywheres*] yesterday.

as See **like, as.**

as if See **like, as if, as though.**

at Do not use *at* after *where.*

NONSTANDARD Where is your saxophone at?

STANDARD Where is your saxophone?

bad, badly *Bad* is an adjective. *Badly* is an adverb.

EXAMPLES The fish smells **bad.** [*Bad* modifies the noun *fish.*]

The parrot recited the poem **badly.** [*Badly* modifies the verb *recited.*]

STYLE TIP

In informal usage the expression "feel badly" has become acceptable, even though it is ungrammatical English.

INFORMAL
Marcia felt badly about her low grade.

FORMAL
Marcia felt **bad** about her low grade.

Exercise 1 Identifying Correct Usage

Choose the correct word or word group from the pair given in parentheses in each of the following sentences.

EXAMPLE 1. Korea has been in the news (*alot, a lot*) in recent years.
1. *a lot*

1. South Korea occupies the lower half of (*a, an*) peninsula between China and Japan.
2. According to an old Korean saying, you are never out of sight of mountains (*anywheres, anywhere*) in Korea.
3. The 1988 Olympic games in Seoul had a truly dramatic (*affect, effect*) on Korea's world image.
4. I looked on a map of Asia to find out where Korea's Lotte World (*is, is at*).
5. This cultural and athletic showcase is (*a, an*) attraction to visitors in Seoul.
6. Many Koreans come to the United States to join family members who (*all ready, already*) live here.
7. In Korea some girls practice on their neighborhood swings so that they won't perform (*bad, badly*) in swinging contests during *Tano,* a spring festival.
8. Most boys hope they do (*allright, all right*) in *Tano* wrestling matches.
9. In 1446, King Sejong the Great required the Korean people to use a new alphabet, which scholars and government officials readily (*accepted, excepted*).
10. Even if you (*ain't, aren't*) interested in dancing, you'd probably enjoy watching the lively Korean folk dancers shown here.

USAGE

USAGE

because See **reason . . . because.**

between, among Use *between* when referring to two things at a time, even when they are part of a group containing more than two.

EXAMPLES In homeroom, Carlos sits **between** Bob and me.

Some players practice **between** innings. [Although a game has more than two innings, the practice occurs only between any two of them.]

Use *among* when referring to a group rather than to separate individuals.

EXAMPLES We saved ten dollars **among** the three of us. [As a group the three saved ten dollars.]

There was disagreement **among** the fans about the coach's decision. [The fans are thought of as a group.]

bring, take *Bring* means "to come carrying something." *Take* means "to go carrying something." Think of *bring* as related to *come* and of *take* as related to *go.*

EXAMPLES **Bring** your skateboard when you come to my house this weekend.

Please **take** these letters with you to the post office when you go.

bust, busted Avoid using these words as verbs. Use a form of *burst* or *break* or *catch* or *arrest.*

EXAMPLES The bubbles **burst** [not *busted*] when they touched the ceiling.

The officer **arrested** [not *busted*] the thief.

Reference Note

For more about **helping verbs,** see page 372.

could of Do not write *of* with the helping verb *could.* Write *could have.* Also avoid *ought to of, should of, would of, might of,* and *must of.*

EXAMPLE Reva **could have** [not *could of*] played the piano.

Of is also unnecessary with *had.*

EXAMPLE If I **had** [not *had of*] seen her, I would have said hello.

doesn't, don't *Doesn't* is the contraction of *does not. Don't* is the contraction of *do not.* Use *doesn't,* not *don't,* with *he, she, it, this, that,* and singular nouns.

EXAMPLES He **doesn't** [not *don't*] know how to swim.

The price **doesn't** [not *don't*] include tax.

effect See **affect, effect.**

everywheres See **anyways,** etc.

except See **accept, except.**

fewer, less *Fewer* is used with plural words. *Less* is used with singular words. *Fewer* tells "how many"; *less* tells "how much."

EXAMPLES Do **fewer** plants grow in the tundra than in the desert?

Do desert plants require **less** water?

good, well *Good* is an adjective. Do not use *good* as an adverb. Instead, use *well.*

NONSTANDARD Nancy sang good at the audition.
STANDARD Nancy sang **well** at the audition.

Although *well* is usually an adverb, *well* may also be used as an adjective to mean "healthy."

EXAMPLE He didn't look **well** after eating the entire quiche all by himself.

NOTE *Feel good* and *feel well* mean different things. *Feel good* means "to feel happy or pleased." *Feel well* means "to feel healthy."

EXAMPLES I felt **good** [happy] when I got an A on my report.

Chris stayed home because he did not feel **well** [healthy] yesterday.

had of See **could of.**

had ought, hadn't ought The verb *ought* should not be used with *had.*

NONSTANDARD Eric had ought to help us; he hadn't ought to have missed our meeting yesterday.

TIPS & TRICKS

Use *fewer* with things that can be counted. Use *less* with things that cannot be counted.

EXAMPLE
Yolanda has (*fewer, less*) pets than Kristi does.

ASK
Can you count pets? [yes]

ANSWER
Yolanda has **fewer** pets than Kristi does.

Reference Note

For more about the **differences between *good* and *well,*** see page 558.

STANDARD Eric **ought to** help us; he **oughtn't to have** missed our meeting yesterday.

or

Eric **should** help us; he **shouldn't have** missed our meeting yesterday.

Reference Note

For more about **double negatives,** see page 567.

hardly, scarcely The words *hardly* and *scarcely* convey negative meanings. They should not be used with another negative word to express a single negative idea.

EXAMPLES I **can** [not *can't*] **hardly** read your handwriting.

We **had** [not *hadn't*] **scarcely** enough food.

USAGE

Exercise 2 Identifying Correct Usage

Choose the correct word or word group from the pair given in parentheses in each sentence.

EXAMPLE 1. When you come to my house, (*bring, take*) that interesting book about U.S. presidents.

1. *bring*

1. Theodore Roosevelt must have felt (*good, well*) about having the teddy bear named for him.
2. The letter *S* in Harry S. Truman's name (*don't, doesn't*) stand for anything.
3. William Henry Harrison served as president (*fewer, less*) days than any other president.
4. Herbert Hoover (*could of, could have*) kept his presidential salary, but he gave it to charity.
5. A president who (*doesn't, don't*) throw the first ball of the baseball season breaks a tradition started in 1910.
6. Theodore Roosevelt and his cousin Franklin Roosevelt were presidents of the United States; (*between, among*) them, they served a total of twenty years in office.
7. Abraham Lincoln's ability to write (*well, good*) helped him succeed in politics.
8. Woodrow Wilson believed that countries (*had ought, ought*) to work together in the League of Nations.
9. I (*can hardly, can't hardly*) imagine a president training horses, but Ulysses S. Grant did.
10. When Zachary Taylor went to the White House in 1849, he (*brought, took*) his old war horse with him.

Review A Correcting Errors in Usage

Each of the following sentences contains at least one error in usage. Identify each error, and write the correct word or words.

EXAMPLE 1. Between the various American Indian peoples, there were alot of stories about mythological figures.

1. Between—Among; alot—a lot

1. The Creek people believed that goblins, giants, and dwarfs effected their lives bad.
2. The Micmacs believed that a enormous being named Glooskap created humans and animals everywheres.
3. This picture shows how humans busted into life because of Glooskap's magic.
4. The other animals don't appear to think that Glooskap's new creations are allright.
5. The Tehuelche people of South America tell the story of Elal, a hero who brought fire to where the people were at.
6. When the Mayas heard the thunderous approach of their god Chac, they knew he was taking rain to their dry fields.
7. The Pawnee people, who lived on the plains, couldn't hardly help noticing where the stars were.
8. They told stories about Morning Star, who fought really good and defeated star monsters.
9. One sad Tewa story is about Deer Hunter, who had ought to have excepted the death of his wife, White Corn Maiden.
10. Her death busted poor Deer Hunter's heart, causing him to disobey the laws of his people.

Michael McCurdy, wood engraving.

USAGE

he, she, it, they Do not use an unnecessary pronoun after a noun. This error is called the ***double subject.***

NONSTANDARD Annika Sorenstam she is my favorite golfer.
STANDARD Annika Sorenstam is my favorite golfer.

hisself *Hisself* is nonstandard English. Use *himself.*

EXAMPLE Ira bought **himself** [not *hisself*] a new silk tie.

how come In informal situations, *how come* is often used instead of *why.* In formal situations, *why* should be used.

INFORMAL	How come Nori's not here yet?
FORMAL	**Why** is Nori not here yet?

TIPS & TRICKS

When you are proofreading your own writing, find each use of *its* and *it's* and try substituting *it is* or *it has.* If the sentence sounds right with the substitution, the contraction *it's* is probably correct. If not, the possessive form *its* is probably correct.

EXAMPLE

Tourists flock to the island because it's so beautiful. [Does "Tourists flock to the island because *it is* so beautiful" make sense? Yes. *It's* is correct.]

its, it's *Its* is a personal pronoun in the possessive form. *It's* is a contraction of *it is* or *it has.*

EXAMPLES **Its** handle is broken. [possessive pronoun]

It's a hot day. [contraction of *it is*]

It's been a good trip. [contraction of *it has*]

kind, sort, type The words *this, that, these,* and *those* should agree in number with the words *kind, sort,* and *type.*

EXAMPLES Whitney likes **this kind** of music.

Those kinds of math problems are easy.

kind of, sort of In informal situations, *kind of* and *sort of* are often used to mean "somewhat" or "rather." In formal English, *somewhat* or *rather* is preferred.

INFORMAL	He seemed kind of embarrassed.
FORMAL	He seemed **somewhat** embarrassed.

Reference Note

For more about **possessive pronouns,** see page 545. For more about **contractions,** see page 672.

learn, teach *Learn* means "to acquire knowledge." *Teach* means "to instruct" or "to show how."

EXAMPLES I am **learning** how to type.

My father is **teaching** me how to type.

leave, let *Leave* means "to go away" or "to depart from." *Let* means "to allow" or "to permit."

NONSTANDARD	Leave her go to the concert.
STANDARD	**Let** her go to the concert.
STANDARD	Let's **leave** on time for the concert.

less See **fewer, less.**

lie, lay See page 523.

Reference Note

For more about **clauses,** see Chapter 15.

like, as In informal situations, the preposition *like* is often used instead of the conjunction *as* to introduce a clause. In formal situations, *as* is preferred.

EXAMPLE I looked up several words in my dictionary, **as** [not *like*] our teacher had suggested.

like, as if, as though In many informal situations, the preposition *like* is used for the compound subordinating conjunction *as if* or *as though.* In formal situations, *as if* or *as though* is preferred.

EXAMPLES They behaved **as if** [not *like*] they hadn't heard him.

You looked **as though** [not *like*] you knew the answer.

Exercise 3 Identifying Correct Usage

For each of the following sentences, choose from the pair in parentheses the word or word group that is correct according to the rules of formal, standard English.

EXAMPLE 1. I'd like to know (*how come, why*) folk tales about animals that play tricks have always been popular.

1. *why*

1. People all over the world enjoy stories about a creature that outsmarts (*it's, its*) enemies.
2. (*These kind, These kinds*) of stories are often referred to as trickster tales.
3. In the tales of American Indians of the Southwest, the trickster (*Coyote, Coyote he*) causes disorder and confusion.
4. In one story, Coyote (*kind of, somewhat*) playfully scatters stars across the sky.
5. In South American tales, the trickster known as Fox talks (*like, as though*) he is clever, but he really isn't.
6. Fox doesn't even understand (*how come, why*) a vulture beats him in a tree-sitting contest.
7. Our teacher (*learned, taught*) us about Brer Rabbit, a famous trickster in African American folklore.
8. Brer Rabbit gets (*himself, hisself*) into trouble by trying to trick Brer Fox.
9. In a tale from India, a monkey and a (*crocodile, crocodile they*) play tricks on each other.
10. Just (*as, like*) Aesop's tortoise defeats the hare, Toad wins a race against Donkey in a Jamaican tale.

Exercise 4 Proofreading for Standard Usage

Proofread the sentences on the following page, changing any nonstandard or informal English to formal, standard English.

USAGE

EXAMPLE 1. Mr. Arlen had ought to be careful when he operates a crane like the one shown here.

1. Mr. Arlen ought to be careful when he operates a crane like the one shown here.

1. Mr. Arlen hisself owns and operates the crane.
2. He learned Tony how to operate the crane.
3. Those kind of machines are quite complicated but fun, Mr. Arlen says.
4. Tony he is young and learns new things very quickly.
5. He says the boom needs plenty of room in which to do it's work.
6. The reason how come he looks high, low, and around is that the boom and the cab can move in a full circle.
7. Pulleys for the boom lines make the boom kind of like an arm that lifts and lowers things.
8. As Mr. Arlen says, leave the crane do the heavy lifting.
9. Crane operators they can't be too careful.
10. Its fun to watch the cranes at work unloading ships.

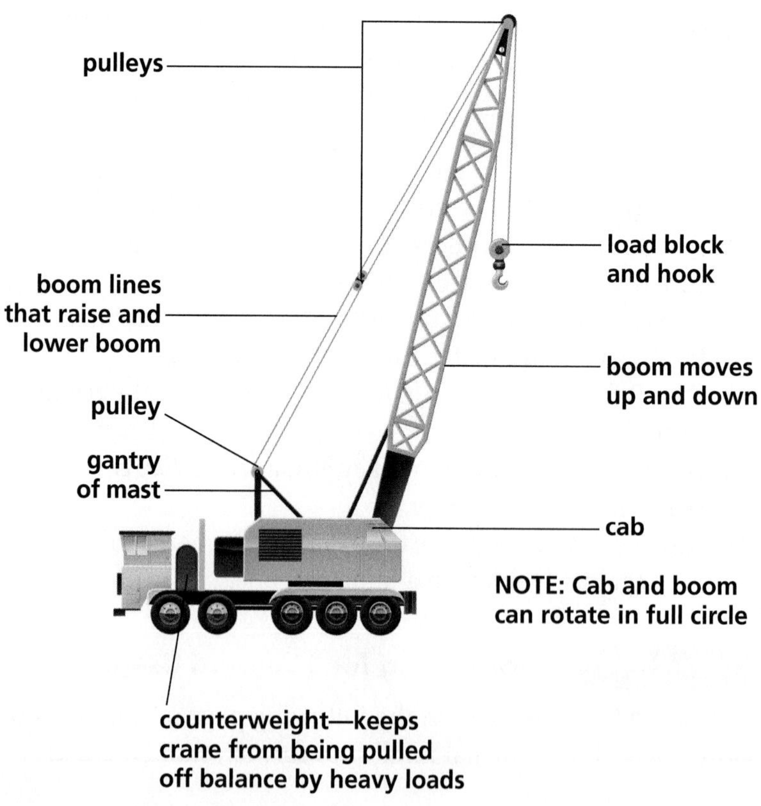

USAGE

might of, must of See **could of.**

nowheres See **anyways,** etc.

of Do not use *of* after other prepositions such as *inside, off,* and *outside.*

EXAMPLES He quickly walked **off** [not *off of*] the stage.

She waited **outside** [not *outside of*] the school.

What is **inside** [not *inside of*] this cabinet?

ought to of See **could of.**

real In informal situations, *real* is often used as an adverb meaning "very" or "extremely." In formal situations, *very* or *extremely* is preferred.

INFORMAL My mother is expecting a real important telephone call.
FORMAL My mother is expecting a **very** important telephone call.

reason . . . because In informal situations, *reason . . . because* is often used instead of *reason . . . that.* However, in formal situations, you should use *reason . . . that.*

INFORMAL The reason I did well on the test was because I had studied hard.
FORMAL The **reason** I did well on the test was **that** I had studied hard.

HELP—You can also revise your sentence to avoid using *reason.*

EXAMPLE
I did well on the test **because** I had studied hard.

rise, raise See page 525.

scarcely, hardly See **hardly, scarcely.**

should of See **could of.**

sit, set See page 521.

some, somewhat Do not use *some* for the adverb *somewhat.*

NONSTANDARD My fever has gone down some.
STANDARD My fever has gone down **somewhat.**

somewheres See **anywheres,** etc.

sort See **kind, sort, type.**

sort of See **kind of, sort of.**

take See **bring, take.**

USAGE

teach See **learn, teach.**

than, then *Than* is a subordinating conjunction; *then* is an adverb telling *when.*

EXAMPLES Great Danes are larger **than** Dobermans are.

I finished my reading. **Then** I wrote some letters.

that See **who, which, that.**

that there See **this here, that there.**

COMPUTER TIP

A word-processing program can help you find and correct usage errors in your own writing. For instance, if you tend to confuse the words *their, there,* and *they're,* you can use the search feature to find those words in your writing. Then, check each one to make sure you have used the correct spelling.

their, there, they're *Their* is the possessive form of *they. There* is used to mean "at that place" or to begin a sentence. *They're* is a contraction of *they are.*

EXAMPLES **Their** team won the game. [*Their* tells whose team.]

We are planning to go **there** during spring vacation. [*There* tells *at what place.*]

There were twenty people at the party. [*There* is used to begin the sentence but does not add to the meaning of the sentence.]

They're the best players on the team. [*They're* is a contraction of *they are.*]

theirself, theirselves *Theirself* and *theirselves* are nonstandard English. Use *themselves.*

EXAMPLE They cooked **themselves** [not *theirself* or *theirselves*] a special dinner.

them *Them* should not be used as an adjective. Use *those.*

EXAMPLE Please put **those** [not *them*] cans in the recycling bin.

this here, that there The words *here* and *there* are not necessary after *this* and *that.*

EXAMPLE Do you like **this** [not *this here*] shirt or **that** [not *that there*] one?

this kind, sort, type See **kind,** etc.

try and In informal situations, *try and* is often used instead of *try to.* In formal situations, *try to* should be used.

INFORMAL Try and be on time for the party.

FORMAL **Try to** be on time for the party.

Exercise 5 Identifying Correct Usage

For each of the following sentences, choose from the pair in parentheses the word or word group that is correct according to the rules of formal, standard English.

EXAMPLE 1. Athletes find the physical and mental challenges of their sports (*real, very*) exciting.

1. *very*

1. Yosemite Park Ranger Mark Wellman discovered new strengths (*inside of, inside*) himself when he climbed El Capitan, a rock formation in Yosemite National Park.
2. Wellman, paralyzed from the waist down, was anxious to (*try and, try to*) climb the 3,595-foot rock.
3. In this picture, Wellman strains (*somewhat, some*) as he climbs the granite peak.
4. The reason Wellman was strong enough for the climb is (*because, that*) he had trained for a year.
5. Like Wellman, many other people are able to swim, hike, cycle, and canoe in spite of (*there, their*) disabilities.
6. (*Them, Those*) newer, lighter, easier-to-use wheelchairs have helped many people enjoy a wider variety of sports activities.
7. Nowadays, national and state parks offer more services for physically challenged people (*than, then*) they used to offer.
8. (*This here, This*) magazine article lists dozens of sports organizations for athletes who have disabilities.
9. You (*might of, might have*) heard of the National Wheelchair Basketball Association, which sponsors teams and organizes tournaments.
10. Other athletes pride (*themselves, theirselves*) on being able to play wheelchair tennis.

use to, used to, suppose to, supposed to Do not leave off the *d* when you write *used to* or *supposed to*.

EXAMPLE We **used to** [not *use to*] live in Phoenix, Arizona.

I was **supposed to** [not *suppose to*] be home by dinner.

way, ways Use *way*, not *ways*, in referring to a distance.

EXAMPLE They still had a long **way** [not *ways*] to go.

USAGE

USAGE

well See **good, well.**

when, where Do not use *when* or *where* incorrectly in writing a definition.

NONSTANDARD An infomercial is where a TV program is actually a long advertisement.

STANDARD An infomercial is a TV program that is actually a long advertisement.

where Do not use *where* for *that.*

EXAMPLE I read **that** [not *where*] Sue won the tournament.

Reference Note

For more about **relative pronouns,** see page 355.

who, which, that The relative pronoun *who* refers to people only; *which* refers to things only; *that* refers to either people or things.

EXAMPLES Kim is the only one **who** got the right answer. [person]

My bike, **which** has ten speeds, is for sale. [thing]

He is the one person **that** can help you. [person]

This is the ring **that** I want to buy. [thing]

who's, whose *Who's* is the contraction of *who is* or *who has. Whose* is used as the possessive form of *who* or as an interrogative pronoun.

EXAMPLES I wonder **who's** keeping score.

Who's been using my computer?

Do you know **whose** baseball glove this is?

Whose is this?

without, unless Do not use the preposition *without* in place of the subordinating conjunction *unless.*

EXAMPLE My mother said that I can't go to the game **unless** [not *without*] I finish my homework first.

would of See **could of.**

your, you're *Your* is the possessive form of *you. You're* is the contraction of *you are.*

EXAMPLES **Your** dinner is on the table.

You're one of my closest friends.

Exercise 6 Identifying Correct Usage

Choose the correct word or word group from the pair given in parentheses in each sentence.

EXAMPLE 1. Roseanne (*use, used*) to know the names of all thirty-three state birds.

1. *used*

1. I read (*where, that*) some states have the same state birds.
2. The mockingbird, (*which, who*) mimics other birds, is the state bird of Texas, Mississippi, Arkansas, Tennessee, and Florida.
3. "Mimicking" is (*when a person or an animal imitates another, imitating another person or an animal*).
4. (*Your, You're*) probably familiar with New Mexico's state bird, the roadrunner, from cartoons.
5. My grandfather, (*who's, whose*) a fisherman, often hears the loud calls of Minnesota's state bird, the common loon.
6. The bluebird, the state bird of Missouri and New York, (*use, used*) to come around our house.
7. The bird on a baseball player's cap can represent both a state and a team quite (*good, well*).
8. (*Without, Unless*) I'm mistaken, you can guess what state claims the Baltimore oriole.
9. It travels a long (*way, ways*) between its summer and winter homes.
10. Would you (*of, have*) guessed that the cardinal is the official bird of the most states?

Review B Correcting Errors in Usage

Most of the following sentences contain an error in the use of formal, standard English. If a sentence contains an error, identify the error and write the correct form. If a sentence is already correct, write *C*.

EXAMPLE 1. It was the pirate Jean Laffite which established an early settlement on Texas's Galveston Island.

1. *which—who (or that)*

1. Since ancient times, pirates they have terrorized sailors on all the world's seas.
2. Bands of pirates use to build fortified hide-outs from which they attacked ships.

USAGE

3. I once read where the Roman general Julius Caesar was captured by pirates.
4. My history teacher learned my class about the pirates who disrupted shipping along the North African coast.
5. As you may have seen in movies, these pirates preyed upon African, European, and American ships.
6. During the 1600s and 1700s, pirates lived off of the South American coast.
7. One of these pirates, Captain William Kidd, was a real dangerous cutthroat on the Caribbean Sea.
8. You may be surprised to learn that some fearsome pirates were women.
9. Anne Bonny and Mary Read attacked and robbed alot of ships on the Caribbean.
10. You may think that piracy is a thing of the past, but its still going on in some parts of the world.

Review C Revising Sentences by Correcting Errors in Usage

Revise the sentences in the following paragraph to correct each error in the use of formal, standard English.

EXAMPLE **[1]** Our vacation along the Pan American Highway was real interesting.

1. *real—very (or extremely)*

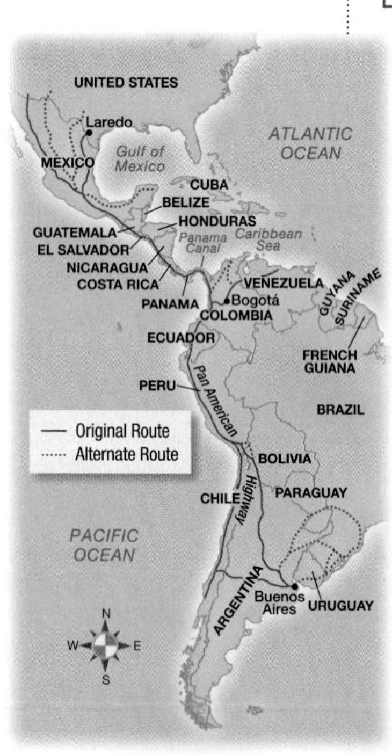

[1] My parents were already to leave as soon as school was out. [2] Mom and Dad had planned the trip themselves so that we'd see alot of country. [3] The Pan American Highway, as the map at left shows, runs among North America and South America. [4] Like a long bridge, this here highway connects the two continents. [5] Like you can see, Laredo, Texas, is one of the terminals for the highway. [6] That's how come we went to Laredo first. [7] I enjoyed visiting the towns and seeing the countryside deep inside of Mexico. [8] If you follow along on the map, you'll notice that we than drove through Central America. [9] We crossed the Panama Canal to get to Colombia; their we enjoyed touring the capital, Bogotá. [10] We couldn't of stayed in Venezuela and Chile any longer because both Mom and Dad had to get back to work.

Chapter Review

A. Identifying Correct Usage

Identify the correct word or expression of the italicized pair in parentheses in each sentence.

1. Aunt Mary felt (*good, well*) about winning the contest.
2. Mr. Yglesias always believed that people (*had ought, ought*) to look after their families.
3. A parrot that (*don't, doesn't*) talk may be a bored parrot.
4. (*They're, Their*) the cyclists I was talking about.
5. Trent bought (*hisself, himself*) a CD player.
6. An ability to speak (*well, good*) can help a person go far in life.
7. Mount Everest is higher (*then, than*) Mont Blanc.
8. He (*used to, use to*) be a track-and-field star, believe it or not.
9. I read in a magazine (*where, that*) a new treatment for acne is being developed.
10. (*Your, You're*) probably the calmest person I've ever met.

B. Identifying and Correcting Errors in Usage

One sentence in each of the following sets contains an error in usage. Choose the letter of the sentence that contains an error. Then, correctly write the sentence, using formal, standard English.

11. **a.** I rode a unicycle.
    b. Everyone came except Michael.
    c. What are the side affects of this medicine?
12. **a.** We had already been there.
    b. She feels alright now.
    c. We looked everywhere for him.
13. **a.** He behaved bad.
    b. She felt bad about being late.
    c. There is no talking between classes.
14. **a.** I know how come she left.
    b. It's windy.
    c. He likes this kind of movie.

USAGE

15. a. She looks as though she is exhausted.
    b. Meet me outside of the building.
    c. He wrote the letter and mailed it.

16. a. I just bought those shoes.
    b. This here ride is broken.
    c. Try to relax.

17. a. Tariq is real sad.
    b. Let's study now and go outside later.
    c. They're new in school.

18. a. Take the report when you go.
    b. She might have gone.
    c. Mr. Bennigan he is my English teacher.

19. a. We worked for an hour.
    b. She accepted your invitation.
    c. They can't hardly see the sign.

20. a. You should have told me.
    b. Less sugar is needed.
    c. It's pedal is stuck.

C. Proofreading a Paragraph for Correct Usage

Each sentence in the following paragraph contains at least one error in formal, standard usage. Rewrite each sentence to correct the error.

[21] Between soccer fans worldwide, the name Zinedine Zidane became famous after the World Cup soccer match in July 1998. **[22]** Zidane is the player which led the French team to victory over Brazil by scoring two goals with his head. **[23]** Not many people would of predicted such an impressive future for the son of a poor Algerian immigrant. **[24]** In some ways, this French success story don't seem different from many American success stories. **[25]** As a boy, Zidane learned himself to play soccer on the mean streets of his neighborhood in Marseille, France's second largest city. **[26]** One reason Zidane made his professional debut at the age of sixteen was because of his amazing ability to dribble. **[27]** Like others have done, he followed his dream out of poverty. **[28]** In 1994 Zidane he made his debut with the French national team by scoring two goals after only

USAGE

seventeen minutes of play. [**29**] By 1996, Zidane's "magic feet" had taken him to a real promising deal with the big Italian soccer club Juventus. [**30**] Two years later came the World Cup victory and his two "headers," so it was like he achieved his greatest success with his head, not with his feet!

Writing Application

Using Formal, Standard English in a Speech

USAGE

Formal, Standard English A local radio station is sponsoring a speech contest for Earth Day. To enter, contestants must write a speech about an environmental issue. Write a three-minute speech for the contest. Use only formal English in your speech.

Prewriting You will need to choose a specific topic about the environment. You may wish to discuss one of the following subjects: local recycling efforts, pollution, endangered animals, or rain forests. When you have selected a topic, jot down some notes about it. List not only facts and information you have read or heard about the topic but also your feelings about it. Then, make an informal outline of what you want to say.

Writing Use your notes from the prewriting activities as you write the first draft of your speech. Make the main point of your speech very clear in a thesis statement early in your speech. Then, discuss each supporting point in a paragraph or two. Restate your main point in your conclusion. Time your speech to be sure it is no longer than three minutes.

Revising Ask a friend to listen to your speech and to time it. Is the speech clear, informative, and persuasive? Did your listener hear any informal English? If your speech is too long, you will need to cut or revise some information.

Publishing Review the rules and guidelines of standard English given in this chapter. Make any necessary corrections in usage. Publish your speech by presenting it to your class. If Earth Day is near, you could offer to read your speech at an Earth Day event.

Capital Letters
Rules for Capitalization

Diagnostic Preview

A. Proofreading Sentences for Correct Capitalization

Proofread the following sentences, correcting all errors in the use of capital and lowercase letters.

EXAMPLE 1. The shubert Theater is located at 222 West Forty-Fourth Street in New York City.
1. *Shubert; Forty-fourth*

1. the planet mars was named for the roman God of war.
2. In History class we memorized the Capitals of all the states.
3. Uncle Dave owns one of the first honda Motorcycles that were sold in north America.
4. my cousin gave me a terrific book, *rules of the game.*
5. Rajiv Gandhi, who was then the prime minister of India, visited Washington, d.c., in June of 1985.
6. The Indus river flows from the Himalayas to the Arabian sea.
7. The writings and television appearances of dr. Carl Sagan increased public interest in Science.
8. In the afternoons i help Mrs. Parkhurst deliver the *Evening Independent,* a local Newspaper.
9. Many people I know have moved to the south and west recently.
10. The Writers Ernest Hemingway, an american, and Robert Service, a canadian, served in the red cross during World war I.
11. Could you please tell me how to get to ventura hall on highway 21 and riverside road?
12. For father's day, let's buy Dad a new power saw.

13. In 1978, the president of egypt and the prime minister of israel shared the nobel peace prize.
14. After we read "fire and ice" by Robert Frost, i wanted to read more of the Poet's work.
15. The knight knelt, saying "o, noble sir, have mercy."

B. Proofreading Sentences for Correct Capitalization

Proofread the following sentences, correcting all errors in the use of capital and lowercase letters.

EXAMPLE 1. The national park service celebrated its seventy-fifth Anniversary in 1991.
1. National Park Service; anniversary

16. The national park service was set up as a Bureau of the department of the interior on august 15, 1916.
17. However, the beginnings of today's park system go back to 1872, when congress established Yellowstone national park in idaho, montana, and wyoming.
18. In 1906, president Theodore Roosevelt signed the Antiquities act, which authorized the president to declare spanish missions and ancient american indian villages to be monuments.
19. Of the more than three hundred areas now under the Agency's protection, the one located farthest North is Noatak national preserve in northern Alaska.
20. Farthest east is the Buck Island National Monument on st. Croix, in the u.s. Virgin islands.
21. One park is both the farthest South and the farthest west: the national park of american Samoa, in the South pacific.
22. Continuing to expand its services to visitors, the national park service in 1991 began compiling a computerized directory of the 3,500,000 civil war Soldiers.
23. The Directory, installed at all twenty-eight civil war sites, is maintained by the national park service.
24. Almost 11,000,000 people visit those Sites each year.
25. Historians estimate that more than one third of all americans have Relatives who fought in the civil War, and the question visitors ask most often is, "did my Great-great-grandfather fight here?"

MECHANICS

Using Capital Letters Correctly

Capital letters are used to

- mark the beginnings of sentences
- distinguish proper nouns from common nouns
- indicate other words that deserve special attention

22a. Capitalize the first word in every sentence.

EXAMPLES **M**ore and more people are discovering the benefits of exercise.

Daily workouts at the gymnasium or on the running track strengthen the heart.

Regular exercise has many other benefits. **F**or instance, it can help you sleep well at night.

Reference Note

For more information about **using capital letters in quotations,** see page 663.

Capitalize the first word of a directly quoted sentence.

EXAMPLES "**O**ne of the hamsters looks sick," said Felipe.

Gwen asked, "**H**ow long did you study for the test?"

NOTE Capitalize the first word of a sentence fragment used in dialogue.

EXAMPLE "**N**ot now," Vanessa replied. "**M**aybe later."

When quoting only part of a sentence, capitalize the first word of the quotation only if the person you are quoting capitalized it or if it is the first word in your sentence.

EXAMPLES According to the speaker in the poem "My Last Duchess," the Duchess looks "**a**s if she were alive." [*As* is not capitalized in the original poem, nor does it begin this sentence.]

What does the speaker mean when he says his last Duchess was "**T**oo easily impressed"? [*Too* is capitalized in the original poem.]

"**T**he white mule / She rode with round the terrace" is another important image from the poem. [Although *the* is not capitalized in the poem, it is capitalized here because it begins this sentence.]

MECHANICS

Traditionally, the first word in a line of poetry is capitalized.

EXAMPLES **H**old fast to dreams
For if dreams die
Life is a broken-winged bird
That cannot fly.

Langston Hughes, "Dreams"

NOTE Some modern poets and writers do not follow this style. When you quote from a writer's work, use capital letters as the writer uses them.

22b. Capitalize the pronoun *I*.

Reference Note

For more about **pronouns,** see page 351.

EXAMPLES They took my lover's tallness off to war,
Left me lamenting. Now **I** cannot guess
What **I** can use an empty heart-cup for.

Gwendolyn Brooks, "The Sonnet-Ballad"

22c. Capitalize the interjection *O*.

Reference Note

For more about **interjections,** see page 391.

The interjection *O* is most often used on solemn or formal occasions. It is usually followed by a word in direct address.

EXAMPLES **O** our Mother the Earth, **O** our Father the Sky,
Your children are we, and with tired backs
We bring you the gifts you love.

a traditional song of the Tewa people

Protect us in the battle, **O** great Athena!

The interjection *oh* requires a capital letter at the beginning of a sentence. Otherwise, *oh* usually is not capitalized.

EXAMPLES **O**h, I wish I could tell you how lonely I felt.

Rudolfo A. Anaya, *Tortuga*

We felt tired but, **o**h, so victorious.

22d. Capitalize the first word in both the salutation and the closing of a letter.

Reference Note

For information on **using colons and commas with salutations and letter closings,** see pages 653 and 646.

EXAMPLES **D**ear Lauren, **S**incerely yours,

Dear Mr. Chuen: **Y**ours truly,

Notice that people's names and titles are also capitalized in salutations.

MECHANICS

Exercise 1 Correcting Sentences by Capitalizing Words

Most of the following sentences contain errors in capitalization. If there are errors in the use of capitals, identify the word or words that should be changed. Then, write the word or words correctly. If a sentence is already correct, write *C.*

EXAMPLE 1. save us, o Poseidon, on this stormy sea.
1. save—Save; o—O

1. If i need a ride, i will give you a call.
2. Loretta is spending her vacation in Maine, but Oh, how she would like to visit Paris.
3. Ana exclaimed, "oh no, I left my backpack on the bus!"
4. Please accept these gifts, o Lord.
5. Have I told you that Tara and Sandra teach aerobics at the community center?
6. this is the hottest day yet this year.
7. My wish, o Great Spirit, is to be one with the universe.
8. Han said, "no, but thanks."
9. Ms. Garibay said, "don't forget to put away the art supplies and clean up your work area."
10. The letter begins with "dear Ms. Catalano."

22e. Capitalize proper nouns.

A ***common noun*** names one of a group of persons, places, things, or ideas. A ***proper noun*** names a particular person, place, thing, or idea.

A common noun is generally not capitalized unless it begins a sentence or is part of a title. Proper nouns are capitalized.

Common Nouns	Proper Nouns
athlete	**S**heryl **S**woopes
river	**N**ile
month	**F**ebruary

Some proper nouns consist of more than one word. In these names, short prepositions (those of fewer than five letters) and articles (*a, an, the*) are generally not capitalized.

EXAMPLES Statue **o**f Liberty Alexander **t**he Great

MECHANICS

Reference Note

For more about **common and proper nouns,** see page 348.

COMPUTER TIP 

If you use a computer, you may be able to use your spellchecker to help you capitalize people's names and other proper nouns correctly. Each time you use a new proper noun in your writing, make sure you have spelled and capitalized it correctly. Then, add the word to your computer's dictionary or spellchecker.

(1) Capitalize the names of persons and animals.

Given Names	**A**lice	**F**ranklin	**C**hristy
Surnames	**W**alker	**C**hang-**D**iaz	**S**andoz
Animals	**T**rigger	**S**ocks	**R**over

NOTE For names containing more than one part, capitalization may vary.

EXAMPLES **D**e **L**a **G**arza **F**itz**G**erald **v**an **G**ogh

de **H**oyos **F**itzgerald **V**an der **M**eer

Capitalize initials in names and abbreviations that come before or after names.

EXAMPLES **H. G.** Wells Isabel Robinson, **M.D.**

Ms. Levine Gary Stamos, **S**r.

(2) Capitalize geographical names.

Type of Name	Examples	
Towns, Cities	**J**amestown **M**anor	**S**an **D**iego **S**t. **P**aul
Counties, States	**C**ook **C**ounty **B**edford **C**ounty	**T**ennessee **N**ew **H**ampshire
Countries	**G**ermany	**N**ew **Z**ealand
Islands	**W**ake **I**sland	**I**sle of **W**ight
Bodies of Water	**L**ake **E**rie **K**entucky **R**iver	**T**ampa **B**ay **I**ndian **O**cean
Forests, Parks	**T**ahoe **N**ational **F**orest	**C**himney **R**ock **P**ark
Streets, Highways	**M**adison **A**venue **W**est **F**ourth **S**treet	**R**oute 44 **I**nterstate 75

HELP — Always check the spelling of a name containing more than one part with the person whose name it is, or look up the name in a reference source.

Reference Note

For more information about **capitalizing titles used with names,** see page 619. For information on **punctuating abbreviations** that come before or after names, see page 631.

Reference Note

Abbreviations of the names of states are capitalized. See page 631 for more about using and punctuating such abbreviations.

Reference Note

In addresses, abbreviations such as *St., Blvd., Ave., Dr.,* and *Ln.* are capitalized. For information about **punctuating abbreviations,** see page 631.

NOTE In a hyphenated street number, the second part of the number is not capitalized.

EXAMPLE East Seventy-**e**ighth Street

Type of Name	Examples	
Mountains	**M**ount **W**ashington **S**awtooth **R**ange	**B**ig **H**orn **M**ountains **E**mory **P**eak
Continents	**A**ustralia **N**orth **A**merica	**A**sia **A**frica
Regions	the **W**est **C**oast the **N**orth	the **B**alkans the **M**idwest
Other Geographical Names	**M**alay **P**eninsula **S**eneca **R**ocks **S**uez **C**anal	**P**ainted **D**esert **B**ering **S**trait **D**ismal **S**wamp

STYLE TIP

Words such as *north, east,* and *southwest* are not capitalized when they indicate direction.

EXAMPLES

flying **s**outh for the winter

northeast of Atlanta

However, these words are capitalized when they name a particular place.

EXAMPLES

states in the **S**outhwest

driving in the **E**ast

MECHANICS

Exercise 2 Proofreading for Correct Capitalization

Most of the following sentences contain an error in capitalization. Identify and correct each word or words that should be capitalized. If a sentence is already correct, write *C*.

EXAMPLE **1.** If you like horses, you would enjoy reading mary O'Hara's books.

1. Mary

Link to Literature

1. Ms. O'Hara was born in New jersey in 1885.
2. She began writing as a child with a short story she titled "Lonely Laurie" and continued writing the rest of her life.
3. Her books about horses are loved even by people who live in the heart of a city, such as on Thirty-third street in New York City.
4. O'Hara's first book, *My Friend Flicka,* introduced a boy named kennie, who loves horses.
5. Kennie lives in wyoming, where Mary O'Hara also lived while she was writing the story.
6. The filly Flicka is given to Kennie, and he learns to take care of her.

7. Other characters in the story include Kennie's mother, Nell; father, Rob; and brother, howard.
8. O'Hara's second book, *Thunderhead,* continues the story of life on the mcLaughlins' ranch.
9. *Green Grass of Wyoming* is O'Hara's third and final book about Kennie and his life in the west.
10. O'Hara moved to california, where she wrote screenplays for movies and composed music.

(3) Capitalize the names of planets, stars, constellations, and other heavenly bodies.

EXAMPLES **J**upiter **S**irius the **B**ig **D**ipper

NOTE The word *earth* is not capitalized unless it is used along with the names of other heavenly bodies that are capitalized. The words *sun* and *moon* are generally not capitalized.

EXAMPLES Is **E**arth located in the galaxy called the **M**ilky **W**ay?

The **e**arth is not the only planet that has a **m**oon.

(4) Capitalize the names of teams, organizations, institutions, and government bodies.

Type of Name	Examples
Teams	**D**etroit **P**istons **K**arr **C**ougars **S**eattle **S**eahawks
Organizations	**A**frican **S**tudies **A**ssociation **L**eague of **W**omen **V**oters **A**merican **G**eographical **S**ociety
Institutions	**S**t. **J**ude **C**hildren's **R**esearch **H**ospital **H**illcrest **J**unior **H**igh **S**chool **A**ntioch **C**ollege
Government Bodies	**A**ir **N**ational **G**uard **D**epartment of **A**griculture **L**ouisiana **S**tate **S**enate

STYLE TIP

The names of organizations, businesses, and government bodies are often abbreviated to a series of capital letters.

EXAMPLES

American Telephone & Telegraph	**AT&T**
National Science Foundation	**NSF**

Reference Note

For more information about **abbreviations,** see page 631.

MECHANICS

STYLE TIP

The word *party* in the name of a political party may or may not be capitalized. Either way is correct.

EXAMPLE
Democratic **p**arty or
Democratic **P**arty

However, within a particular piece of writing, be consistent in your use of capitals.

Do not capitalize such words as *democratic, republican,* and *socialist* when they refer to principles or forms of government. Capitalize these words when they refer to a specific political party.

EXAMPLES a **d**emocratic country

the **R**epublican candidate

(5) Capitalize the names of historical events and periods, special events, holidays, and other calendar items.

Type of Name	Examples
Historical Events	**B**attle of **B**unker **H**ill **W**orld **W**ar II **Y**alta **C**onference
Historical Periods	**G**reat **D**epression **A**ge of **R**eason **M**iddle **A**ges
Special Events	**W**orld **S**eries **O**lympic **G**ames **O**klahoma **S**tate **F**air
Holidays	**F**ather's **D**ay **K**wanzaa **V**eterans **D**ay
Other Calendar Items	**H**ispanic **H**eritage **M**onth **F**riday **O**ctober

NOTE The name of a season is usually not capitalized unless it is part of a proper name.

EXAMPLES the last day of **s**ummer

the Oak Ridge **W**inter Carnival

(6) Capitalize the names of nationalities, races, and peoples.

EXAMPLES **G**reek **H**ispanic **C**aucasian

African **A**merican **A**sian **L**akota **S**ioux

MECHANICS

(7) Capitalize the names of religions and their followers, holy days and celebrations, sacred writings, and specific deities.

Type of Name	Examples	
Religions and Followers	**C**hristianity	**M**uslim
	Zen **B**uddhism	**A**mish
Holy Days and Celebrations	**A**sh **W**ednesday	**R**amadan
	Easter	**Y**om **K**ippur
Sacred Writings	**K**oran	the **B**ible
	the **T**orah	**N**ew **T**estament
Specific Deities	**G**od	**H**oly **S**pirit
	Brahma	**J**ehovah

NOTE The words *god* and *goddess* are not capitalized when they refer to deities of ancient mythology. However, the names of specific mythological gods and goddesses are capitalized.

EXAMPLE **D**iana, the Greek **g**oddess of the hunt, is the subject of my report.

(8) Capitalize the names of buildings and other structures.

EXAMPLES **W**orld **T**rade **C**enter **G**olden **G**ate **B**ridge

Shubert **T**heater **F**airmont **H**otel

Hoover **D**am **T**ower of **L**ondon

Do not capitalize words such as *hotel, theater, church,* and *school* unless they are part of a proper name.

EXAMPLES a new **s**chool

Rocky Mount Junior High **S**chool

Review A Correcting Capitalization Errors

Most of the sentences on the following page contain errors in capitalization. Identify each word that should be capitalized. Then, write the word or words correctly. If a sentence is already correct, write *C.*

STYLE TIP

The words *black* and *white* may or may not be capitalized when they refer to races. Either way is correct. However, within a particular piece of writing, be consistent in your use of capitals.

COMPUTER TIP

If you use a word processor when you write, the spellchecker might be able to help you find errors in capitalization. Spellcheckers are not perfect, though. When the spellchecker questions a certain word, you will need to decide whether it should be capitalized or not, depending on how you have used it in your sentence.

EXAMPLE 1. Towering over the surrounding countryside, the san esteban mission is visible for miles.

1. san esteban mission—San Esteban Mission

1. The mission sits atop a sandstone mesa in valencia county, new mexico.
2. Near San Esteban is the Pueblo village of acoma, which is fifty-four miles west-southwest of albuquerque.
3. Almost one thousand years old, acoma is believed to be the oldest continuously inhabited community in the united states.
4. In the seventeenth and eighteenth centuries, the spanish established dozens of missions in new mexico to promote catholicism.
5. The main purpose of the missions was to spread Christianity among the native peoples, but the outposts also served political and military purposes.
6. This photo of San esteban, which was built between 1629 and 1651, shows the type of mission architecture that developed in that region of the united states.

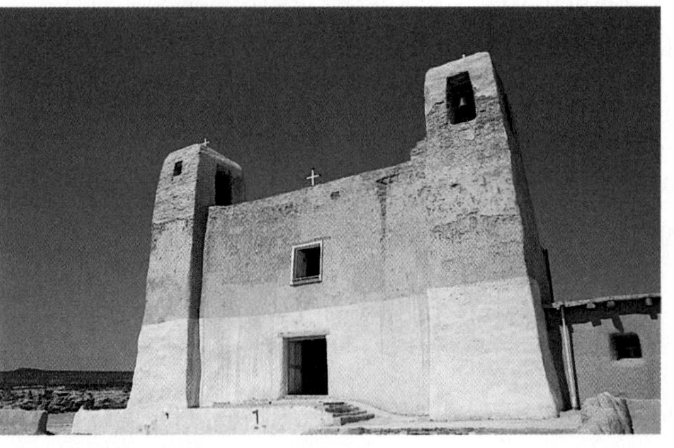

7. Adobe, a sandy clay commonly used in construction throughout the southwest, covers all the outside surfaces of the building.
8. The building's design is based on the designs of churches in central mexico.
9. Those churches, in turn, are regional variations of church buildings in spain.
10. Thus, san esteban, like other new mexican missions, combines various elements of three main cultures: american indian, mexican, and spanish.

(9) Capitalize the names of monuments, memorials, and awards.

Type of Name	Examples
Monuments and Memorials	the **G**reat **S**phinx **S**tatue of **L**iberty **C**ivil **R**ights **M**emorial **W**ashington **M**onument
Awards	**A**cademy **A**ward **N**obel **P**rize **N**ewbery **M**edal **P**urple **H**eart

(10) Capitalize the names of trains, ships, aircraft, and spacecraft.

Type of Name	Examples
Trains	***S**ilver **R**ocket* ***O**rient **E**xpress*
Ships	USS ***O**lympia* ***M**ayflower*
Aircraft	***S**pruce **G**oose* ***S**ilver **D**art*
Spacecraft	***M**ir* ***C**olumbia*

Reference Note

For information on using **italics for names,** see page 660.

(11) Capitalize the names of businesses and the brand names of business products.

BUSINESSES **A**pple **C**omputer, **I**nc.® **A**merican **A**irlines®

International **B**usiness **M**achines® **N**ational **B**roadcasting **C**ompany®

BRAND NAMES **N**ike® shoes **W**rangler® jeans

HELP

Notice that the names of the types of products are not capitalized.

EXAMPLES
Nike **s**hoes
Wrangler **j**eans

MECHANICS

Review B Common Nouns and Proper Nouns

For each proper noun, give a corresponding common noun. For each common noun, give a proper noun.

EXAMPLES **1.** Independence Hall
1. building

2. city
2. San Francisco

1. mountain range
2. Oprah Winfrey
3. historical event
4. river
5. aircraft
6. Ethiopia
7. Lincoln Memorial
8. spacecraft
9. cereal
10. Environmental Protection Agency
11. ocean
12. William Shakespeare
13. national forest
14. Newbery Medal
15. television set
16. Seattle
17. bottled fruit juice
18. computer
19. Leonardo da Vinci
20. ship

Review C Using Capital Letters Correctly

Correct each of the following expressions, using capital letters as needed.

EXAMPLES **1.** a member of the peace corps
1. a member of the Peace Corps

2. received an academy award
2. received an Academy Award

1. decisions of the united states supreme court
2. the apaches of the southwest
3. hoover dam
4. tomb of the unknown soldier
5. 512 west twenty-fourth street
6. pictures of saturn sent by *voyager 2*
7. in hawaii on maui island
8. the great lakes
9. monday, april 29
10. the stone age

MECHANICS

Review D **Correcting Capitalization Errors**

Each of the following sentences contains at least one error in capitalization. Identify the word or words that should be capitalized. Then, write each word correctly.

EXAMPLE 1. Imagine how many flowers it must take to cover just one of the floats in the rose parade!

1. *rose parade—Rose Parade*

1. I don't have plans for new year's eve yet, but i know where i'll be on new year's day.
2. watching the rose parade on TV is a new year's day tradition in my family.
3. The parade takes place each year in pasadena, california, which is northeast of los angeles.
4. The parade is sponsored by the pasadena tournament of roses association.
5. Did you know that the name *pasadena* comes from an ojibwa expression meaning "valley town"?
6. That's a fitting name for a town overlooking a valley at the base of the san gabriel mountains.
7. After the parade, we watch the rose bowl game, which is played in pasadena's brookside park.
8. The oldest postseason college football game in the united states, the rose bowl traditionally pits the winner of the big ten conference against the winner of the pacific ten conference.
9. New year's day is nearly always bitterly cold in cleveland, Ohio, where we live.
10. By the end of the game, we feel as though we've started the new year off with a minivacation in california.

MECHANICS

Review E Correcting Sentences by Capitalizing Words

Each of the following sentences contains errors in capitalization. Identify the word or words that should be capitalized. Then, write each word correctly.

EXAMPLE 1. our class visited abraham lincoln's home in springfield, illinois.

1. *our—Our; abraham lincoln's—Abraham Lincoln's; springfield—Springfield; illinois—Illinois*

1. the federal aviation administration regulates airlines only in the united states and not throughout the world.
2. when she was a child, ethel waters lived in chester, pennsylvania.
3. the sacred muslim city of mecca is located in saudi arabia.
4. in chicago, the sears tower and the museum of science and industry attract many tourists.
5. we watched the florida marlins win the world series in 1997.
6. the valentine's day dance is always the highlight of the winter.
7. several of my friends bought new adidas® shoes at the big sporting goods sale in the mall.
8. the local food pantry is sponsored and operated by protestants, catholics, and jews.
9. the second-place winners will receive polaroid cameras.
10. jane bryant quinn writes a magazine column on money management.

MECHANICS

Reference Note

For more about **proper adjectives,** see page 362.

22f. Capitalize proper adjectives.

A ***proper adjective*** is formed from a proper noun and is capitalized.

Proper Noun	Proper Adjective
China	Chinese doctor
Rome	Roman army
Islam	Islamic culture
King Arthur	Arthurian legend

Exercise 3 Correcting Sentences by Capitalizing Proper Adjectives

Capitalize the proper adjectives in each of the following sentences.

EXAMPLE 1. A finnish architect, Eliel Saarinen, designed a number of buildings in the detroit area.

1. *Finnish, Detroit*

1. The alaskan wilderness is noted for its majestic beauty.
2. The syrian and israeli leaders met in Geneva.
3. The european cities I plan to visit someday are Paris and Vienna.
4. Our american literature book includes hopi poems and cheyenne legends.
5. The south american rain forests contain many kinds of plants and animals.
6. Maria has watched two shakespearean plays on television.
7. Did you see the exhibit of african art at the library?
8. Our program will feature irish and scottish folk songs.
9. Where do the amish people live?
10. My family almost always sits down together for a sunday meal.

22g. Do not capitalize the names of school subjects, except course names followed by numerals and languages.

EXAMPLES You must pass **A**rt I before taking **A**rt II.

I have tests in **E**nglish, **L**atin, and **m**ath.

Exercise 4 Using Capital Letters Correctly

Correct each of the following expressions, using capital letters and lowercase letters as needed.

EXAMPLE 1. taking japanese and history 201

1. *taking Japanese and History 201*

1. a lesson in spanish
2. report for english II
3. a syllabus for Home Economics
4. problems in geometry I
5. studying german, Chemistry, and government II
6. problems for algebra 101
7. ready for computer III

8. choosing between french and Civics
9. taking history 4
10. in english and drama

Review F Correcting Sentences by Capitalizing Proper Nouns and Proper Adjectives

Capitalize the proper nouns and proper adjectives in each of the following sentences.

EXAMPLE **1.** The natchez trace developed from a series of trails made long before hernando de soto explored the area in 1540.

1. Natchez Trace; Hernando de Soto

1. As this map shows, the natchez trace linked the present-day cities of natchez, mississippi, and nashville, tennessee.

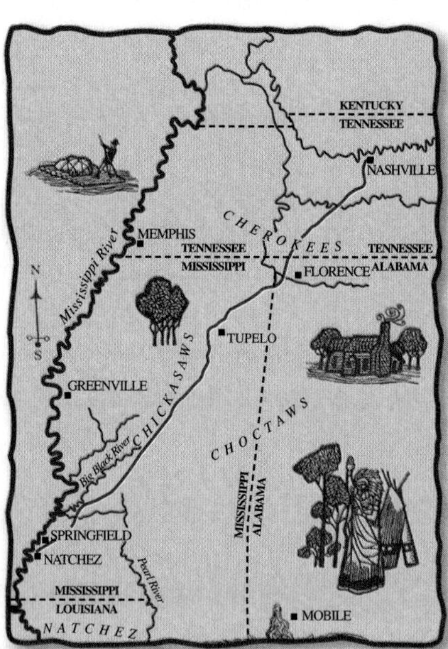

2. From natchez, the 450-mile route ran northeast between the big black river and the pearl river.
3. Turning east a few miles north of tupelo, it crossed the tennessee river near muscle shoals, alabama, and then headed into tennessee.
4. Among the peoples living along the trail were the natchez, the chickasaw, the choctaw, and the cherokee.
5. Finding no gold or silver in the area, the spanish explorers turned their attention to what is now the u.s. southwest.
6. At the conclusion of the french and indian war (1754–1763), france was forced to give most of its territory east of the mississippi river to great britain.
7. Near the time of the louisiana purchase of 1803, the natchez trace was improved for use by mail and military wagons traveling to the west.

MECHANICS

8. Traffic along the trail increased steadily until the 1830s, when regular steamboat service provided a less dangerous, more comfortable means of travel on the mississippi river.
9. Today a modern highway named the natchez trace parkway follows the general route of the ancient path.
10. In an effort to reclaim history, volunteers with the natchez trace trail conference are carving out a hiking trail the entire length of the parkway.

22h. Capitalize titles.

(1) Capitalize a person's title when the title comes before the person's name.

EXAMPLES There will be a short address by **G**overnor Halsey.

Report to **L**ieutenant Engstrom, please.

Does **M**s. Tam know **D**r. Politi?

This is the church in which the **R**everend Henry Ward Beecher preached.

Generally, a title used alone or following a person's name is not capitalized, especially if the title is preceded by *a, an,* or *the.*

EXAMPLES An **a**ttorney for the defense made a brief statement.

Is he the **r**abbi at the new synagogue?

Katie Dobbs, **c**hair of the entertainment committee, gave the status report.

However, a title used alone in direct address is usually capitalized.

EXAMPLES Is the patient resting comfortably, **N**urse?

What is your name, **S**ir [*or* **s**ir]?

(2) Capitalize a word showing a family relationship when the word is used before or in place of a person's name, unless the word follows a possessive noun or pronoun.

EXAMPLES I received a letter from **A**unt Christina and **U**ncle Garth.

When will **M**om and **D**ad be home?

Angela's **m**other and my **a**unt Daphne coach the girls' softball team.

Reference Note

For information about **abbreviating titles,** see page 631.

STYLE TIP

Titles used alone or following a person's name may be capitalized for clarity or special emphasis.

EXAMPLES

The **A**ttorney **G**eneral has served our state with distinction.

Ben Cayetano, **G**overnor of **H**awaii, delivered the keynote speech.

(3) Capitalize the first and last words and all important words in titles and subtitles.

Unimportant words in titles include

- prepositions of fewer than five letters (such as *at, of, for, from,* and *with*)
- coordinating conjunctions (*and, but, for, nor, or, so, yet*)
- articles (*a, an, the*)

Reference Note

For a list of **prepositions,** see page 386. For information about **coordinating conjunctions** and **articles,** see pages 389 and 359.

Type of Name	Examples
Books	*Dust Tracks on a Road* *River Notes: The Dance of the Herons*
Magazines	*Sports Illustrated* *Entertainment Weekly* *Woman's Day*
Newspapers	*The Boston Globe* *St. Petersburg Times*
Poems	"Refugee Ship" "With Eyes at the Back of Our Heads"
Short Stories	"The Tell-Tale Heart" "My Wonder Horse" "Gorilla, My Love"
Historical Documents	Mayflower Compact Emancipation Proclamation Monroe Doctrine
Movies	*The Wizard of Oz* *Casablanca*
Television Series	*Touched by an Angel* *FBI: The Untold Stories* *Family Matters*

Type of Name	Examples
Works of Art	***T**he **B**allet **C**lass* ***B**ird in **S**pace*
Musical Works	***M**oonlight **S**onata* "**U**nforgettable" ***T**he **M**agic **F**lute* "**O**n **T**op of **O**ld **S**moky"
Plays	***I N**ever **S**ang for **M**y **F**ather* ***B**arefoot in the **P**ark* ***T**he **M**usic **M**an*
Comic Strips	***H**agar the **H**orrible* ***G**arfield*
Videos	***M**ariah **C**arey at **M**adison **S**quare **G**arden* ***I**t's a **W**onderful **L**ife*
Video Games	***S**onic the **H**edgehog* ***S**tar **W**ars: **S**hadow of the **E**mpire*
CDs and Audiotapes	***S**gt. **P**epper's **L**onely **H**earts **C**lub **B**and* ***T**o the **F**aithful **D**eparted*

Reference Note

For information on using **italics with titles,** see page 660. For information on using **quotation marks with titles,** see page 667.

Capitalize the titles of chapters and other parts of books.

EXAMPLES José has already read **C**hapter 11, "**T**he **T**ropical **R**ain **F**orest."

The book's first section, titled "**L**egends of **B**aseball," includes a fun trivia quiz.

NOTE Capitalize an article (*a, an,* or *the*) at the beginning of a title or subtitle only if it is the first word of the official title or subtitle.

EXAMPLES Does your uncle subscribe to **t**he *Los Angeles Times?*

I read an interesting story in ***T**he New Yorker.*

HELP

The official title of a book is found on the title page. The official title of a newspaper or other periodical is found on the masthead, which usually appears on the editorial page or the table of contents.

MECHANICS

Exercise 5 Correcting Capitalization Errors

Most of the following sentences contain at least one error in capitalization. If there are errors in the use of capitals, identify the word or words that should be capitalized. Then, write the word or words correctly. If a sentence is already correct, write *C.*

EXAMPLE 1. My uncle Kevin recommended "love must not be forgotten," a short story by Zhang Jie.

1. *"love must not be forgotten"—"Love Must Not Be Forgotten"*

1. During president Woodrow Wilson's term, sheep grazed on the front lawn of the White House.
2. When my aunt Inez visited Mexico, she met grandmother Villa's brothers and sisters for the first time.
3. All of these pronunciations are correct according to *the american heritage dictionary.*
4. Well, mom, have you met dr. Brinson?
5. Did you hear commissioner of education smathers's speech recommending a longer school day?
6. Was Carrie Fisher in *return of the jedi*?
7. After the secretary read the minutes, the treasurer reported on the club's budget.
8. Elizabeth Speare wrote *calico captive.*
9. My older brother subscribes to *field and stream.*
10. The first politician to make a shuttle flight was senator Jake Garn of Utah.

MECHANICS

Review G Correcting Capitalization Errors

Each of the following sentences contains errors in capitalization. Identify the word or words that should be capitalized. Then, write the word or words correctly.

EXAMPLE 1. My cousin's class went on a field trip to the science museum of virginia, which is in richmond.

1. *science museum of virginia—Science Museum of Virginia; richmond—Richmond*

1. The andersons hosted an exchange student from argentina last year.
2. Did you know that the king ranch in texas is larger than rhode island?

3. At rand community college, ms. epstein is taking three courses: computer programming I, japanese, and english.
4. The sixth day of the week, friday, is named for the norse goddess of love, frigg.
5. The christian holiday of christmas and the jewish holiday of hanukkah are both celebrated in december.
6. My uncle ronald was stationed in the south pacific when he was an ensign.
7. The liberty bell, which is on display in independence hall in philadelphia, was rung to proclaim the boston tea party and to announce the first public reading of the declaration of independence.
8. Is your mother still teaching an art appreciation class at the swen parson gallery?
9. In the 1920s, zora neale hurston and countee cullen were both active in the literary movement known as the harlem renaissance.
10. I walk to the eagle supermarket each sunday to buy a copy of the *miami herald* and a quart of tropicana® orange juice.

Review H Proofreading Sentences for Correct Capitalization

Each of the following sentences contains at least one error in capitalization. Identify each word that should be changed. Then, write the word or words correctly.

EXAMPLE 1. Osaka, one of the largest Cities in japan, lies on the Southern coast of honshu island.

1. Cities—cities; japan—Japan; Southern—southern; honshu island—Honshu Island

1. president Roosevelt's saturday talks from the white house were broadcast on the radio.
2. In History class, we learned about these suffragists: elizabeth cady stanton, susan b. anthony, and lucretia c. mott.
3. In April the cherry blossom festival will be celebrated with a Parade through the heart of the City.
4. The 1996 olympics were held in atlanta.
5. The rio grande, a major river of north america, forms the Southwestern border of Texas.
6. jane addams, an American Social Reformer who cofounded hull house in chicago, was awarded the 1931 nobel peace prize.

MECHANICS

7. Many of the countries of europe are smaller than some states in our country.
8. In the southeast, William Least Heat-Moon began the journey that he tells about in his book *blue highways.*
9. Can we have a surprise Birthday party for uncle Victor, mom?
10. The panama canal connects the atlantic ocean and the pacific ocean.

Review I Proofreading Sentences for Correct Capitalization

Each of the following sentences contains at least one error in capitalization. Identify each word that should be changed. Then, write the word or words correctly.

EXAMPLE **1.** The south african vocal group Ladysmith Black Mambazo sings without instrumental accompaniment.

1. south african—South African

1. Ladysmith's music is based on the work songs of black south african miners.
2. In a sense, their music is the south African version of the american blues, which grew out of the work songs of enslaved Africans.
3. In 1985, ladysmith was featured on two songs on paul simon's album *graceland.*
4. Those two songs, "homeless" and "diamonds on the soles of her shoes," helped to make the album an enormous hit; it even won a grammy award.
5. To promote the album, Ladysmith and simon toured the United states, europe, and south America.
6. Most of Ladysmith's songs are in the performers' native language, zulu.
7. Even people who don't understand the Lyrics enjoy the music's power and beauty.
8. Ladysmith has also appeared in a Hollywood movie, in the music Video *moonwalker,* and on the television shows *Sesame street* and the *Tonight show.*
9. The group's exposure to american music is reflected in two songs on its 1990 album, *two worlds, one heart.*
10. One song is a gospel number, and the other adds elements of Rap music to ladysmith's distinctive sound.

MECHANICS

Chapter Review

A. Proofreading Sentences for Correct Capitalization

Each of the following sentences contains at least one error in capitalization. Rewrite the sentences to correct the errors by changing capital letters to lowercase letters or lowercase letters to capital letters.

1. The Maxwells enjoyed visiting the southwest, particularly the alamo in San Antonio.
2. Is dr. Powell's office at Twenty-first street and Oak drive?
3. On labor day we went to Three Trees State Park.
4. Our junior high school had a much more successful carnival than Lakeside junior high school had.
5. Did you know that the german folk tale "cinderella," which is included in *grimm's fairy tales,* is similar to a tale from ninth-century china?
6. Arthur's cousin joined the Peace corps and lived in a small village on the west coast of africa.
7. No fish live in the Great salt lake in Utah.
8. Save money by shopping at Al's discount city.
9. We have studied Japanese Culture and the shinto religion.
10. This semester I have English, American History, and Spanish in the morning, and Industrial Arts I in the afternoon.
11. On saturday and sunday, my mother and i are going to a family reunion in the town where she grew up.
12. The Robinsons live near route 41, not far from Memorial parkway on the South side of town.
13. At our Wednesday Night meeting, the reverend Terry DeWitt gave a talk on the beliefs of Lutherans.
14. We salute you, o Caesar!
15. Was Thursday named after the Norse God Thor?
16. Awe-struck, the tourists paused to admire the sphinx.
17. Dale Evans and Roy Rogers sang the song "Happy trails to you" at the end of their television programs.
18. Thurgood Marshall was the first african american appointed to the Supreme court.

MECHANICS

19. My Uncle won a purple heart during the Vietnam war.

20. The American revolution took place toward the end of the Age of Enlightenment, in the 1700s.

B. Proofreading a Paragraph for Correct Capitalization

Each sentence in the following word groups contains at least one error in capitalization. Write the correct form of each word that contains an error.

[**21**] For a couple of years, i have had a pen pal named Habib who lives in tunisia, an Arabic Country in africa, on the Mediterranean sea. [**22**] Habib was born in the city of kairouan, a muslim holy city famous for its carpets. [**23**] He now lives in the Capital city, Tunis, on the Northeastern coast. [**24**] He is going to a Secondary School in the Capital. [**25**] not far from his home are the ruins of carthage, which in ancient times was a Great Power led by the famous general Hannibal. [**26**] After many centuries, Carthage was defeated by the romans and became a roman colony. [**27**] Greeks, Romans, Carthaginians, normans, turks—Tunisia has seen them all in its 3,000-year history. [**28**] Along with all that history, there are beautiful beaches near Habib's home, along the mediterranean coast, where he goes swimming and water-skiing during his free time. [**29**] In his last letter he told me about going camel-trekking in the sahara, in the South. [**30**] It's a long way to go, but someday i want to visit Habib in tunisia.

C. Using Capital Letters Correctly

Each of the following word groups contains at least one error in capitalization. Rewrite each expression to correct all the errors in capitalization.

31. the governor of the bank of mexico

32. 211 fourteenth street

33. the himalayan peaks

34. the middle ages

35. thursday, january 28

36. emperor marcus aurelius

37. lake powell

MECHANICS

38. the united states department of the treasury
39. mount washington
40. a general motors executive

Writing Application

Using Capital Letters in an Essay

Correct Capitalization Your class is putting together a booklet of biographical sketches on the most-admired people in your community. Each student in your class will contribute one biography. Write a short essay about someone you admire. The person can be a friend, a family member, or someone you have never met. In your essay, use capital letters and lowercase letters correctly to help your readers understand precisely what you mean.

Prewriting Write a list of people you admire. Then, read over your list, and choose the person you admire most. Jot down information about his or her background, personality traits, and major achievements. In the case of someone you know, you may wish to interview him or her to gather additional information. Finally, organize your information in an outline.

Writing Begin your essay with a sentence or two that catches your audience's attention and identifies your subject. Using your notes and outline, write your first draft. In your conclusion, sum up the points you have made, or restate the main idea.

Revising Re-read your paper to make sure you have clearly shown why you admire this person. Did you give enough information about him or her, and is the information correct? Add, delete, or rearrange information to make your essay clearer and more interesting.

Publishing Read over your essay again, correcting any errors in grammar, punctuation, and spelling. Pay special attention to your use of capital letters and lowercase letters. Photocopy or print out your essay. With your classmates, create a booklet of your compositions. You may also wish to include photographs or sketches of the people about whom you have written. Invite other classes, friends, neighbors, and family members to read your booklet.

Punctuation

End Marks, Commas, Semicolons, and Colons

Diagnostic Preview

Correcting Sentences by Adding End Marks, Commas, Semicolons, and Colons

Rewrite the following paragraphs, inserting periods, question marks, exclamation points, commas, semicolons, and colons where they are needed.

EXAMPLE **[1]** Did I ever tell you how our washing machine which usually behaves itself once turned into a foaming monster

1. Did I ever tell you how our washing machine, which usually behaves itself, once turned into a foaming monster?

[**1**] "Oh no The basement is full of soapsuds" my youngest sister Sheila yelled [**2**] When I heard her I could tell how upset she was [**3**] Her voice had that tense strained tone that I know so well [**4**] To see what had alarmed her I ran down to the basement [**5**] Imagine the following scene The washing machine the floor and much of my sister were completely hidden in a thick foamy flow of bubbles [**6**] I made my way gingerly across the slippery floor fought through the foam and turned off the washing machine

[**7**] Doing so of course merely stopped the flow [**8**] Sheila and I now had to clean up the mess for we didn't want Mom and Dad to see it when they got home [**9**] We mopped up soapsuds we sponged water off the floor and we dried the outside of the

washing machine [10] After nearly an hour of steady effort at the task we were satisfied with our work and decided to try the washer

[11] Everything would have been fine if the machine had still worked however it would not even start [12] Can you imagine how upset we both were then [13] Thinking things over we decided to call a repair shop

[14] We frantically telephoned Mrs Hodges who runs the appliance repair business nearest to our town [15] We told her the problem and asked her to come to 21 Crestview Drive Ellenville as soon as possible

[16] When she arrived a few minutes after 4 00 Mrs Hodges inspected the machine asked us a few questions and said that we had no real problem [17] The wires had become damp they would dry out if we waited a day or two before we tried to use the machine again

[18] Surprised and relieved we thanked Mrs Hodges and started toward the stairs to show her the way out [19] She stopped us however and asked if we knew what had caused the problem with the suds [20] We didn't want to admit our ignorance but our hesitation gave us away [21] Well Mrs Hodges suggested that from then on we measure the soap instead of just pouring it into the machine

[22] Looking at the empty box of laundry powder I realized what had happened [23] It was I believe the first time Sheila had used the washing machine by herself she hadn't followed the instructions on the box

[24] This incident occurred on November 10 1999 and we have never forgotten it [25] Whenever we do the laundry now we remember the lesson we learned the day the washer overflowed

STYLE TIP

As you speak, the tone and pitch of your voice, the pauses in your speech, and the gestures and expressions you use all help make your meaning clear. In writing, marks of punctuation, such as end marks and commas, show readers where these nonverbal cues occur.

Punctuation alone won't clarify the meaning of a confusing sentence, however. If you have trouble punctuating a sentence, check to see whether rewording it would help express your meaning more clearly.

End Marks

An ***end mark*** is a mark of punctuation placed at the end of a sentence. The three kinds of end marks are the *period*, the *question mark*, and the *exclamation point.*

23a. Use a period at the end of a statement (or declarative sentence).

EXAMPLES One of the figure skaters was Tara Lipinski**.**

A small brown bird flitted from branch to branch**.**

Reference Note

For information about **how sentences are classified according to purpose,** see page 339.

23b. Use a question mark at the end of a question (an interrogative sentence).

EXAMPLE Did Gordon Parks write *The Learning Tree*?

23c. Use an exclamation point at the end of an exclamation (an exclamatory sentence).

EXAMPLE That's the biggest salad I've ever seen!

Reference Note

For more information about **interjections,** see page 391.

NOTE Interjections that express a strong emotion may be set off from the rest of the sentence with an exclamation point.

EXAMPLE Wow! What a view that is!

23d. Use a period or an exclamation point at the end of a request or a command (an imperative sentence).

EXAMPLES Please give me the scissors. [a request]
Give me the scissors! [a command]

Exercise 1 Using End Marks

HELP—
The paragraphs in Exercise 1 contain a total of ten sentences.

In the following paragraphs, sentences have been run together without end marks. Identify the last word of every sentence, and supply the proper end mark.

EXAMPLE 1. A visit to New Salem reveals that life in Lincoln's time was harder than it is today
1. today.

In New Salem Park, Illinois, you can find a reproduction of the little village of New Salem, just as it was when Abraham Lincoln lived there Can you imagine what life was like in Abraham Lincoln's time

The cabin of the Onstat family is not a reproduction but is the original cabin where Lincoln spent many hours In that cabin, on that very floor, young Abe studied with Isaac Onstat The cabin had only one room

Across the way hangs a big kettle once used by Mr. Waddell for boiling wool Mr. Waddell, the hatter of the village, made hats of wool and fur

Do any of you think that you'd like to go back to those days What endurance those people must have had Could we manage to live as they did

MECHANICS

Abbreviations

An ***abbreviation*** is a shortened form of a word or phrase.

23e. Many abbreviations are followed by a period.

Notice how periods are used with abbreviations in the following examples.

Types of Abbreviations	Examples		
Initials	Pearl S. Buck W.E.B. DuBois T. S. Eliot		I. M. Pei H. D. (Hilda Doolittle)
Titles Used with Names	Mr. Jr.	Mrs. Sr.	Ms. Dr.
States	N.Y. Mass.	La. N. Dak.	Mo. Wis.

NOTE A two-letter state abbreviation without periods is used only when it is followed by a ZIP Code. Both letters of the abbreviation are then capitalized.

EXAMPLE Austin, **TX** 78741-4144

Types of Abbreviations	Examples			
Times	A.M. (*ante meridiem,* used with times from midnight to noon) P.M. (*post meridiem,* used with times from noon to midnight) B.C. (before Christ) A.D. (*anno Domini,* "in the year of the Lord")			
Addresses	St.	Ave.	Dr.	P.O. Box
Organizations and Companies	Co.	Inc.	Corp.	Ltd.

STYLE TIP

Leave a space between two initials in a person's name. Do not leave a space between three or more initials.

STYLE TIP

The abbreviations *A.D.* and *B.C.* need special attention. Place *A.D.* before a numeral and *B.C.* after a numeral.

EXAMPLES
124 **B.C.** **A.D.** 720

For centuries expressed in words, place both *A.D.* and *B.C.* after the century.

EXAMPLES
seventh century **B.C.**
fourth century **A.D.**

HELP

A few acronyms, such as *radar, laser,* and *sonar,* are now considered common nouns. They do not need to be spelled out on first use and are no longer capitalized. When you are not sure whether an acronym should be capitalized, look it up in a recent dictionary.

An ***acronym*** is a word formed from the first (or first few) letters of a series of words. Acronyms are written without periods. If you are not sure that your readers will know what an acronym stands for, add the complete term in parentheses the first time you use the acronym.

EXAMPLES Our school will have a fund-raising drive for **UNICEF.**

The **VISTA** (Volunteers in Service to America) program provides many services to our community.

NOTE Abbreviations for government agencies and some widely used abbreviations are written as acronyms. Each letter of the abbreviation is capitalized.

EXAMPLES	FDA	CIA	NIMH
	PBS	YWCA	NBA
	URL	CD-ROM	VCR

STYLE TIP

Abbreviations are useful and appropriate in informal writing and in charts, tables, and footnotes. Only rarely should abbreviations be used in formal writing.

Abbreviations for units of measure are usually written without periods. However, you should use a period with the abbreviation *in.* (for *inch* or *inches*) to prevent confusing it with the word *in.*

EXAMPLES	cm	kg	ml	oz
	lb	ft	yd	mi

NOTE When an abbreviation with a period ends a sentence, another period is not needed. However, a question mark or an exclamation point is used if it is needed.

EXAMPLES My dog's name is T. J**.**

Why did you name your dog T. J**.?**

HELP

Use a period as a decimal point in numbers.

EXAMPLES

19**.**76 $7**.**25 **.**5 miles

Review A Correcting Sentences by Adding Periods, Question Marks, and Exclamation Points

Write the following sentences, adding periods, question marks, and exclamation points where they are needed.

EXAMPLE **1.** Look at the beautiful costume the Japanese actor on the next page is wearing

1. Look at the beautiful costume the Japanese actor on the next page is wearing!

MECHANICS

1. The picture reminds me of our visit to Little Tokyo last year
2. Have you ever heard of Little Tokyo
3. It is a Japanese neighborhood in Los Angeles, Calif, bordered by First St, Third St, Alameda St, and Los Angeles St

4. Some friends of ours who live in Los Angeles, Mr and Mrs Albert B Cook, Sr, and their son, Al, Jr, introduced us to the area
5. They met our 11:30 AM. flight from Atlanta, Ga, and took us to a $9.95 lunch buffet at a restaurant in the Japanese Plaza Village
6. Later we stopped at a bakery for *mochigashi,* which are Japanese pastries, and then we visited the Japanese American Cultural and Community Center on San Pedro St
7. Outside the center is a striking abstract sculpture by Isamu Noguchi, who created the stone sculpture garden at the UNESCO headquarters in Paris, France
8. Next door is the Japan America Theater, which stages a wide variety of works by both Eastern and Western artists
9. Soon, it was time to head for the Cooks' home, at 6311 Oleander Blvd, where we spent the night
10. What a great afternoon we had exploring Japanese culture

Commas

A ***comma*** is generally used to separate words or groups of words so that the meaning of a sentence is clear.

Items in a Series

23f. Use commas to separate items in a series.

Words, phrases, and clauses in a series are usually separated by commas to show the reader where one item in the series ends and the next item begins.

Words in a Series
Barbecue, *hammock*, *canoe*, and *moccasin* are four of the words that the English language owes to American Indians. [nouns]
Always stop, look, and listen before crossing railroad tracks. [verbs]
In the early morning, the lake looked cold, gray, and calm. [adjectives]

Phrases in a Series
Checking his shoelaces, fastening his helmet strap, and positioning his kneepads, Toshio prepared for the skateboarding competition. [participial phrases]
We found seaweed in the water, on the sand, under the rocks, and even in our shoes. [prepositional phrases]
Clearing the table, washing the dishes, and putting everything away took almost an hour. [gerund phrases]

Clauses in a Series
We didn't know where we were going, how we would get there, or when we would arrive. [subordinate clauses]
The lights dimmed, the curtain rose, and the orchestra began to play. [short independent clauses]

Reference Note

For more about **phrases,** see Chapter 14. For more about **clauses,** see Chapter 15.

NOTE Independent clauses in a series can be separated by commas only if the clauses are short. Independent clauses that are long or that contain commas are usually separated by semicolons.

Reference Note

For more information about **semicolons,** see page 649.

STYLE TIP

Including a comma before the conjunction in a series is not incorrect, so some writers prefer always to use a comma there. Follow your teacher's instructions on this point.

In your reading, you will find that some writers omit the comma before a conjunction such as *and, or,* or *nor* when it joins the last two items of a series. However, such a comma is sometimes necessary to make the meaning of a sentence clear. Notice how the comma affects the meaning in the following examples.

UNCLEAR Luanne, Zack and I are going riding. [Is Luanne being addressed, or is she going riding?]

CLEAR Luanne, Zack, and I are going riding. [Three people are going riding.]

MECHANICS

If all the items in a series are joined by *and*, *or*, or *nor*, do not use commas to separate them.

EXAMPLES I voted for Corey **and** Mona **and** Ethan in the student council officers election.

For your report you may want to read Jean Toomer's *Cane* **or** Ralph Ellison's *Invisible Man* **or** Richard Wright's *Native Son.*

Exercise 2 Correcting Sentences by Adding Commas

Rewrite each of the following sentences, inserting commas where they are needed.

EXAMPLE **1.** On their expedition, the explorers took with them 117 pounds of potatoes 116 pounds of beef and 100 pounds of fresh vegetables.

1. On their expedition, the explorers took with them 117 pounds of potatoes, 116 pounds of beef, and 100 pounds of fresh vegetables.

1. Carlos and Anna and I made a piñata filled it with small toys and hung it from a large tree.
2. I sanded the boards Ignacio primed them and Paul painted them.
3. Last week I read the novel *The Lucky Stone* the short story "Flowers for Algernon" and the poem "Legacy II."
4. Most flutes used by professional musicians are made of sterling silver fourteen-carat gold or platinum.
5. We know what we will write about where we will find sources and how we will organize our reports.
6. Squanto became an interpreter for the Pilgrims showed them how to plant corn and stayed with them throughout his life.
7. Sylvia Porter wrote several books about how to earn money and how to spend it borrow it and save it.
8. Joe looked for the cat under the bed on the sofa in the bathtub and inside the empty cardboard box.
9. The San Joaquin kit fox the ocelot the Florida panther and the red wolf are only some of the endangered mammals in North America.
10. I want to visit Thailand Nepal China and Japan.

23g. Use commas to separate two or more adjectives preceding a noun.

EXAMPLES Jack Russell terriers are small, energetic dogs.

These intelligent, loyal, playful pets always enjoy a challenge.

When the final adjective in a series is thought of as part of the noun, do not use a comma before that adjective.

EXAMPLE A skillful, enthusiastic dog trainer can teach a Jack Russell to perform many exciting tricks. [No comma is used between *enthusiastic* and *dog* because the words *dog* and *trainer* make up a compound noun.]

A comma should never be used between an adjective and the noun immediately following it.

INCORRECT The cute, clever, terrier who stars in TV's *Wishbone* is really named Soccer.

CORRECT The cute, clever terrier who stars in TV's *Wishbone* is really named Soccer.

TIPS & TRICKS

If you are not sure whether the final adjective and the noun make up a compound noun, use this test. Insert the word *and* between the adjectives. If *and* makes sense, use a comma. In the example on the right, *and* makes sense between *skillful* and *enthusiastic. And* does not make sense between *enthusiastic* and *dog.*

Another test you can use is to switch the order of the adjectives. If you can switch them and the sentence still makes sense, use a comma.

Reference Note

For more information about **compound nouns,** see page 346.

MECHANICS

Exercise 3 Correcting Sentences by Adding Commas

Write the following sentences, adding commas where they are needed.

EXAMPLE 1. A squat dark wood-burning stove stood in one corner.

1. A squat, dark wood-burning stove stood in one corner.

1. They made a clubhouse in the empty unused storage shed.
2. This book describes the harsh isolated lives of pioneer women in Kansas.
3. What a lovely haunting melody that song has!
4. Katie Couric's upbeat intelligent approach to interviewing makes her an effective television anchor.
5. The delicate colorful wings of the hummingbird vibrate as many as two hundred times each second.
6. The hot unrelenting wind blew across the desert.
7. The movie is about a bright active girl who is badly injured while riding a horse.

8. Jade Snow Wong's strong focused determination led to her success as an author.
9. What is the quickest easiest most scenic way to get to Juneau?
10. Lupe likes to read true stories about daring adventurous mountain climbers.

Compound Sentences

23h. Use a comma before a coordinating conjunction (*and, but, for, nor, or, so,* or *yet*) when it joins independent clauses in a compound sentence.

EXAMPLES I enjoyed *The King and I*, **but** *Oklahoma!* is still my favorite musical.

Oscar Hammerstein wrote the words, **and** Richard Rodgers wrote the music.

The musical comedy began as an American musical form, **yet** its popularity has spread throughout the world.

When the independent clauses are very short, the comma before *and*, *but*, or *or* is sometimes omitted.

EXAMPLE I'm tired but I can't sleep.

The cat can stay inside or it can go out.

A comma is almost always used before *nor, for, so,* or *yet* when it joins independent clauses.

EXAMPLES We will not give up, **nor** will we fail.

Everyone seemed excited, **for** it was time to begin.

No one else was there, **so** we left.

The water was cold, **yet** it looked inviting.

NOTE Do not confuse a compound sentence with a simple sentence that has a compound verb. A simple sentence has only one independent clause.

SIMPLE SENTENCE WITH COMPOUND VERB	Margo likes golf but doesn't enjoy archery.
COMPOUND SENTENCE	Margo likes golf, but she doesn't enjoy archery. [two independent clauses]

STYLE TIP

The word *so* is often overused. If possible, try to reword a sentence to avoid using *so*.

EXAMPLE
It was late, so we went home.

REVISED
Because it was late, we went home.

STYLE TIP

For clarity, some writers prefer always to use the comma before a conjunction joining independent clauses. Follow your teacher's instructions on this point.

Reference Note

For more information about **compound sentences,** see page 462. For more about **compound verbs,** see page 336.

Reference Note

For more information about **semicolons,** see page 649.

NOTE When the independent clauses in a compound sentence contain commas, a semicolon may be needed before the coordinating conjunction.

EXAMPLE Our class will read Chapter 4, Chapter 7, and Chapter 9**;** and Larry, Dana, and Louis will present reports on them.

Exercise 4 Correcting Compound Sentences by Adding Commas

For each of the following sentences, write the two words that should be separated by a comma, and add the comma. If a sentence is already correct, write *C.*

EXAMPLE **1.** Have you read this article or do you want me to tell you about it?

1. article, or

1. Human beings must study to become architects yet some animals build amazing structures by instinct.
2. The male gardener bower bird builds a complex structure and carefully decorates it to attract a mate.
3. This bird constructs a dome-shaped garden in a small tree and underneath the tree he lays a carpet of moss covered with brilliant tropical flowers.
4. Then he gathers twigs and arranges them in a three-foot-wide circle around the display.
5. Tailor ants might be called the ant world's high-rise workers for they gather leaves and sew them around tree twigs to make nests like the one shown on the left.
6. These nests are built in tropical trees and the nests may be one hundred feet or more above the ground.
7. Adult tailor ants don't secrete the silk used to weave the leaves together but they squeeze it from their larvae.
8. The female European water spider builds a waterproof nest under water and she stocks the nest with air bubbles.
9. This air supply is very important for it allows the spider to hunt underwater.
10. The water spider lays her eggs in the waterproof nest and they hatch there.

MECHANICS

Interrupters

23i. Use commas to set off an expression that interrupts a sentence.

Two commas are used to set off an interrupting expression—one before and one after the expression.

EXAMPLES Mr. Agoya, born and raised in Mexico, moved to California at the age of twenty-four.

The applications, by the way, were mailed three days ago.

Some expressions that are used as interrupters can also come at the beginning or the end of a sentence. In such cases, only one comma is needed.

EXAMPLES Born and raised in Mexico, Mr. Agoya moved to California at the age of twenty-four.

The applications were mailed three days ago, by the way.

Reference Note

For more about **commas after introductory elements,** see page 644.

(1) Use commas to set off nonessential participial phrases and nonessential subordinate clauses.

A ***nonessential*** (or ***nonrestrictive***) phrase or clause adds information that is not needed to understand the basic meaning of the sentence. Such a phrase or clause can be omitted without changing the main idea of the sentence.

Reference Note

For more information on **participial phrases,** see page 422. For more about **subordinate clauses,** see page 441.

NONESSENTIAL PHRASES This small turtle**, crossing the street slowly,** was in danger. [The main idea of the sentence remains *This small turtle was in danger.*]

Harvard College**, founded in 1636,** is the oldest college in the United States. [The main idea of the sentence remains *Harvard College is the oldest college in the United States.*]

NONESSENTIAL CLAUSES Kareem Abdul-Jabbar**, who retired from professional basketball,** holds several NBA records. [The main idea of the sentence remains *Kareem Abdul-Jabbar holds several NBA records.*]

Joshua eventually overcame his acrophobia**, which is the abnormal fear of being in high places.** [The main idea of the sentence remains *Joshua eventually overcame his acrophobia.*]

Do not use commas to set off an ***essential*** (or ***restrictive***) phrase or clause. Since such a phrase or clause tells *which one(s)*, it cannot be omitted without changing the meaning of the sentence.

ESSENTIAL PHRASES All farmers **growing the new hybrid corn** should have a good harvest. [Without the essential phrase, the sentence says *All farmers should have a good harvest.*]

The theories **developed by Einstein** have changed the way people think about the universe. [Without the essential phrase, the sentence says *The theories have changed the way people think about the universe.*]

ESSENTIAL CLAUSES The map **that we were using** did not show your street. [Without the essential clause, the sentence says *The map did not show your street.*]

Often, someone **who does a good deed** gains more than the person **for whom the deed is done.** [Without the essential clauses, the sentence says *Often someone gains more than the person.*]

TIPS & TRICKS

A clause beginning with *that* is usually essential.

EXAMPLE
A prize will be awarded to the contestant **that** spills the least water. [Omitting the clause *that spills the least water* changes the basic meaning of the sentence.]

MECHANICS

Exercise 5 Using Commas in Sentences Containing Nonessential Phrases and Clauses

Write the following sentences, adding commas to set off the nonessential phrases and clauses. If a sentence is already correct, write *C.*

EXAMPLE **1.** My favorite performer is Gloria Estefan who was the lead singer with the Miami Sound Machine.
1. My favorite performer is Gloria Estefan, who was the lead singer with the Miami Sound Machine.

1. Estefan badly injured in a bus accident in 1990 made a remarkable comeback the following year.
2. The accident which occurred on March 20, 1990 shattered one of her vertebrae and almost severed her spinal cord.
3. The months of physical therapy required after the accident were painful for the singer.
4. Less than a year later performing in public for the first time since the accident she sang on the American Music Awards telecast January 28, 1991.
5. On March 1 of that year launching a yearlong tour of Japan, Europe, and the United States she and the band gave a concert in Miami.

6. Estefan who was born in Cuba came to the United States when she was two years old.
7. Her family fleeing the Cuban Revolution settled in Miami where she now lives with her husband and their children.
8. The album that was released to mark Estefan's successful comeback is titled *Into the Light.*
9. It contains twelve songs including the first one written by the singer after the accident.
10. Appropriately, that song inspired by a fragment that her husband wrote as Gloria was being taken to surgery is titled "Coming Out of the Dark."

(2) Use commas to set off nonessential appositives and nonessential appositive phrases.

A ***nonessential appositive*** or ***appositive phrase*** provides information that is unnecessary to the meaning of the sentence.

EXAMPLES My best friend**, Nancy,** is studying ballet.

We're out of our most popular flavor**, vanilla.**

Sara**, my cousin,** has won a dance scholarship.

The Rio Grande**, one of the major rivers of North America,** forms the border between Texas and Mexico.

Reference Note

For more information about **appositives,** see page 432.

MECHANICS

An ***essential appositive*** adds information that makes the noun or pronoun it identifies more specific. Do not set off an essential appositive.

EXAMPLES The blues singer **Bessie Smith** wrote the song **"Backwater Blues."** [The appositive *Bessie Smith* tells which blues singer. The appositive *"Backwater Blues"* tells which song.]

Exercise 6 Using Commas in Sentences to Set Off Nonessential Appositives and Appositive Phrases

Rewrite the sentences that require commas, inserting the commas. If a sentence is already correct, write *C.*

EXAMPLE **1.** The dog a boxer is named Branford.

1. The dog, a boxer, is named Branford.

1. Katy Jurado the actress has appeared in many fine films.
2. The composer Mozart wrote five short piano pieces when he was only six years old.
3. Harper Lee the author of *To Kill a Mockingbird* is from Alabama.
4. The card game canasta is descended from mah-jongg an ancient Chinese game.
5. Jupiter the fifth planet from the sun is so large that all the other planets in our solar system could fit inside it.
6. The main character in many of Agatha Christie's mystery novels is the detective Hercule Poirot.
7. The writing of Elizabeth Bowen an Irish novelist shows her keen, witty observations of life.
8. Charlemagne the king of the Franks in the eighth and ninth centuries became emperor of the Holy Roman Empire.
9. Chuck Yeager an American pilot broke the sound barrier in 1947.
10. Effie Tybrec a Sioux artist from South Dakota decorates plain sneakers with elaborate beadwork.

MECHANICS

(3) Use commas to set off words of direct address.

EXAMPLES **Mrs. Clarkson,** this package is addressed to you.

Do you know**,** **Odessa,** when the next bus is due?

I'd like to go now**,** **Jeff.**

Exercise 7 Using Commas in Sentences to Set Off Words of Direct Address

Write the following sentences, adding commas to set off words of direct address.

EXAMPLE **1.** Are you hungry Jan or have you had lunch?

1. Are you hungry, Jan, or have you had lunch?

1. Ms. Wu will you schedule me for the computer lab tomorrow?
2. Have you signed up for a baseball team yet Aaron?
3. Your time was good in the hurdles Juanita but I know you can do better.
4. Wear sturdy shoes girls; those hills are hard on the feet!
5. Run Susan; the bus is pulling out!
6. Felipe you might like to enter your drawings in the contest.

7. It won't be long until your birthday Angela and then you will know what's in the package.
8. Coach Garcia do we really have to do twenty laps?
9. Which do you like better Sally rhymed or unrhymed poetry?
10. All right boys and girls let's pick up the litter in the schoolyard.

(4) Use commas to set off parenthetical expressions.

A ***parenthetical expression*** is a remark that adds information or shows a relationship between ideas.

EXAMPLES The president said**, of course,** that he was deeply disappointed.

In my opinion, the movie was too violent.

Commonly Used Parenthetical Expressions		
after all	generally speaking	of course
at any rate	I believe (hope, suppose, think)	on the contrary
by the way		on the other hand
for example	in my opinion	however
for instance	nevertheless	therefore

Some of the above expressions are not always used as interrupters. Use commas only when the expressions are parenthetical.

EXAMPLES Sidney**, I think,** volunteers at the senior center. [parenthetical]

I think Sidney volunteers at the senior center. [not parenthetical]

Traveling by boat may take longer**, however.** [parenthetical]

However you go, it will be a delightful trip. [not parenthetical]

Exercise 8 Using Commas in Sentences to Set Off Parenthetical Expressions

Write each of the following sentences, using a comma or commas to set off the parenthetical expression.

EXAMPLE 1. Mathematics I'm afraid is my hardest subject.
1. Mathematics, I'm afraid, is my hardest subject.

MECHANICS

1. The review of course covered material from the entire chapter.
2. Your subject should I think be limited further.
3. *Cilantro* is the Spanish name for the herb coriander by the way.
4. Flying however will be more expensive than driving there in the car.
5. After all their hard work paid off.
6. In my opinion we need to put ice in the picnic cooler.
7. Rabat is the capital of Morocco I believe.
8. Cooking the rice slowly therefore will make it taste better.
9. Motorcycles generally speaking are very noisy.
10. On the other hand they get better gas mileage than cars.

Introductory Words, Phrases, and Clauses

23j. Use a comma after certain introductory elements.

(1) Use a comma to set off a mild exclamation such as *well, oh,* or *why* at the beginning of a sentence. Other introductory words, such as *yes* and *no,* are also set off with commas.

EXAMPLES **Well,** I think we should ask for help.

Yes, I understand the problem.

(2) Use a comma after an introductory phrase or clause.

Prepositional Phrases

A comma is used after an introductory prepositional phrase if the phrase is long or if two or more phrases appear together.

EXAMPLES **In the darkening attic room,** the girls searched for the box of old photos.

At night in the desert, the temperature falls rapidly.

If the introductory prepositional phrase is short, a comma may or may not be used.

EXAMPLE **In the morning,** we'll tour the Caddo burial mounds.

In the morning we'll tour the Caddo burial mounds.

Verbal Phrases

A comma is used after a participial phrase or an infinitive phrase that introduces a sentence.

MECHANICS

PARTICIPIAL PHRASE	**Signaling the referee for a timeout,** the coach gathered her players for a pep talk.
INFINITIVE PHRASE	**To keep your bones strong,** be sure to get regular exercise and eat foods rich in calcium.

NOTE Sometimes an infinitive phrase at the beginning of a sentence is the subject of the sentence. In such a case, the infinitive should not be followed by a comma.

EXAMPLE **To become a museum curator** is Shanda's dream.

Adverb Clauses

An adverb clause may be placed at various places in a sentence. When it begins a sentence, the adverb clause is followed by a comma.

EXAMPLES **When March came,** the huge ice floe began to melt and break up.

Because I had a sore throat, I could not audition for the school play.

Reference Note

For more information on **prepositional phrases,** see page 416. For more information about **verbal phrases,** see page 421. For more about **adverb clauses,** see page 447.

MECHANICS

Exercise 9 Using Commas in Sentences with Introductory Phrases or Clauses

If a sentence needs a comma, write the word or numeral the comma should follow, and add the comma. If a sentence is already correct, write *C.*

EXAMPLE 1. Patented in 1883 Matzeliger's lasting machine, which attached the sole of a shoe to its upper part, revolutionized the shoe industry.

1. 1883,

1. Issued in 1991 this stamp honoring inventor Jan Matzeliger is part of the U.S. Postal Service's Black Heritage Stamp series.
2. Since the Postal Service began issuing the series in 1978 the stamps have become popular collectors' items.
3. Originally picturing only government officials or national symbols U.S. stamps now feature a wide variety of people, items, and events.
4. As stamps become more varied stamp collecting becomes even more popular.

5. Because stamps portray our country's culture they fascinate many people.
6. In the United States alone more than twenty million people enjoy stamp collecting.
7. To attract collectors the Postal Service produces limited numbers of special stamps.
8. To find a valuable, rare stamp is the dream of many a collector.
9. To keep their collections from becoming too bulky many collectors concentrate on a single topic.
10. With their treasures safely stored in albums collectors enjoy examining their first stamps as well as their most recent ones.

MECHANICS

HELP

A comma does not separate a month from a day (*April 14*), a house number from a street name (*522 Candler Lane*), or a state abbreviation from a ZIP Code (*PA 17404-8202*). A comma also does not separate a month from a year if no day is given (*June 2001*).

Conventional Situations

23k. Use commas in certain conventional situations.

(1) Use commas to separate items in dates and addresses.

EXAMPLES The United States officially observed Martin Luther King, Jr., Day for the first time on January 20**,** 1986.

Each year the Kentucky Derby is held in Louisville**,** Kentucky**,** on the first Saturday in May.

I think Passover begins on Wednesday**,** April 14**,** this year.

The company's new mailing address is 522 Candler Lane**,** York**,** PA 17404-8202.

Notice that a comma separates the last item in a date or in an address from the words that follow it.

Reference Note

For more about **writing personal letters,** see "Writing" in the Quick Reference Handbook.

(2) Use a comma after the salutation of a personal letter and after the closing of any letter.

EXAMPLES Dear Aunt Margaret**,** Yours truly**,**

Exercise 10 Correcting Dates, Addresses, and Parts of a Letter by Adding Commas

Write the following items, inserting commas as needed.

EXAMPLE 1. Friday October 2 1998

1. Friday, October 2, 1998

1. 11687 Montana Avenue Los Angeles CA 90049-4673
2. Dresser Road at North First Street in Lynchburg Virginia
3. from December 1 2001 to March 15 2002
4. Dear Joanne
5. Sincerely yours
6. at 4020 Keeley Drive Antioch Tennessee until May 2002
7. Best regards
8. Thursday September 14 1967
9. North Tenth Street at Nolana Loop in McAllen Texas
10. Yours truly

Review B Proofreading a Letter for Correct Use of End Marks and Commas

Copy the following letter, adding any needed commas and end marks.

EXAMPLE **[1]** You're the greatest Aunt Lucy

1. You're the greatest, Aunt Lucy!

[1] 1113 Collins St
[2] Fort Worth TX 76106-9299
[3] September 16 2001

[4] Dear Aunt Lucy

[5] What a great time I had at your house last week **[6]** Your two dogs Buffy and Pepper certainly kept me entertained **[7]** I've really missed taking them for walks and playing fetch **[8]** When summer vacation begins I could come visit again **[9]** Anyway thank you very much for inviting me.

[10] Sincerely

James

HELP

Use a comma in numerals of more than three digits. Place the comma between groups of three digits, counting from the right. If a number includes a decimal, count starting from the left of the decimal.

EXAMPLES
18,408
1,000,000 grains
$4,967.50

HELP

If a preposition is used between items of an address, a comma is not necessary.

EXAMPLE
He lives at 144 Smith Street **in** Moline, Illinois.

Review C Correcting Sentences by Adding Periods, Question Marks, Exclamation Points, and Commas

Write the following sentences, adding periods, question marks, exclamation points, and commas where they are needed. If a sentence is already correct, write *C.*

EXAMPLE **1.** I moved from Canton Ohio to Waco Texas in 1999
1. I moved from Canton, Ohio, to Waco, Texas, in 1999.

1. At the corner of Twelfth St and Park Ave I ran into a friend
2. Have you ever made the long tiring climb to the head of the Statue of Liberty Alan
3. Oh by the way remind Geraldine to tell you what happened yesterday
4. To prepare for her role in that movie the star observed lawyers at work
5. Must turtles crocodiles alligators frogs and dolphins breathe air in order to survive
6. His new address is 141 Park Dr Hartford CT 06101-1347
7. Junko Tabei one of a team of Japanese women reached the summit of Mount Everest in 1975
8. Students who are late must bring a note from home.
9. Did the twenty-first century begin officially on January 1 2000 or on January 1 2001 Sarah
10. What a great fireworks display that was

Review D Correcting a Paragraph by Adding Periods, Question Marks, Exclamation Points, and Commas

Write the following paragraph, adding periods, question marks, exclamation points, and commas where they are needed.

EXAMPLE **[1]** Have you ever played chess
1. Have you ever played chess?

[**1**] To beginners and experts alike chess is a complex demanding game [**2**] It requires mental discipline intense concentration and dedication to long hours of practice [**3**] Displaying those qualities the Raging Rooks of Harlem tied for first place at the National

MECHANICS

Junior High Chess Championship which was held in Dearborn Mich [4] Sixty teams competing with the Rooks came from all across the U S [5] The thirteen- and fourteen-year-old Rooks attended New York City's Public School 43 [6] When they returned to New York after the tournament they were greeted by Mayor David Dinkins [7] Becoming media celebrities they appeared on television and were interviewed by local newspapers and national news services [8] Imagine how proud of them their friends and families must have been [9] The Rooks' coach Maurice Ashley wasn't surprised that the team did so well in the tournament [10] After all Ashley the first African American grandmaster has guided two Harlem schools P.S. 43 and Mott Hall Intermediate School to national championship tournaments.

Semicolons

A ***semicolon*** is used primarily to join independent clauses that are closely related in meaning.

23l. Use a semicolon between independent clauses in a sentence when they are not joined by *and, but, for, nor, or, so,* or *yet.*

EXAMPLES On our first trip to Houston, I wanted to see the Astrodome**;** my little brother wanted to visit the Johnson Space Center.

Our parents settled the argument for us**;** they took us to both places.

Use a semicolon between independent clauses only when the ideas in the clauses are closely related.

INCORRECT I called Leon; did you notice how windy it is?

CORRECT I called Leon**. D**id you notice how windy it is?

I called Leon**;** he will be here in ten minutes.

NOTE Very short independent clauses in a series may be separated by commas instead of semicolons.

EXAMPLE The leaves whispered**,** the brook gurgled**,** the sun beamed brightly.

TIPS & TRICKS

Notice that a semicolon looks like a combination of a period and a comma. In fact, you can think of a semicolon as part period and part comma. A semicolon signals a pause in thought and is stronger than a comma but not as strong as a period.

MECHANICS

COMPUTER TIP 

A computer can help you check your writing for the correct punctuation of conjunctive adverbs and transitional expressions. Use a computer's search function to find semicolons. Then, look at each conjunctive adverb or transitional expression carefully to see how it is used. Does it join clauses? Does it interrupt a clause? Add or delete commas and semicolons as needed, using the rules in this chapter.

23m. Use a semicolon between independent clauses that are joined by a conjunctive adverb or a transitional expression.

A ***conjunctive adverb*** or a ***transitional expression*** shows how the independent clauses that it joins are related.

EXAMPLES English was Lou's hardest subject**; accordingly,** he gave it more time than any other subject.

The popular names of certain animals are misleading**; for example,** the koala bear is not a bear.

Commonly Used Conjunctive Adverbs			
accordingly	furthermore	instead	nevertheless
besides	however	meanwhile	otherwise
consequently	indeed	moreover	therefore

Commonly Used Transitional Expressions			
as a result	for example	for instance	that is
in addition	in other words	in conclusion	in fact

NOTE When a conjunctive adverb or a transitional expression joins clauses, it is preceded by a semicolon and followed by a comma. When it interrupts a clause, however, it is set off by commas.

EXAMPLES Dad got the snacks ready**; meanwhile,** Theo and I decorated the living room.

Dad got the snacks ready; Theo and I**, meanwhile,** decorated the living room.

23n. A semicolon (rather than a comma) may be needed to separate independent clauses joined by a coordinating conjunction when the clauses contain commas.

Use a semicolon in such a situation only to prevent confusion or misreading.

CONFUSING Our strongest defensive players are Carlos, Will, and Jared, and Kareem and Matt are excellent on offense.

CLEAR Our strongest defensive players are Carlos, Will, and Jared**;** and Kareem and Matt are excellent on offense.

As long as the sentence is not confusing or hard to read without a semicolon, a comma is enough.

EXAMPLE Otto, you are the sweetest, most lovable dog in the world, and I'm glad I found you.

NOTE Semicolons are also used between items in a series when the items contain commas.

EXAMPLE He was born on September 27, 1983; began school on September 4, 1988; and graduated from high school on May 17, 2001.

Exercise 11 Correcting Sentences by Adding Semicolons and Commas

Write the following sentences, adding semicolons and commas where they are needed.

EXAMPLE 1. The gym is on the ground floor the classrooms are above it.

1. The gym is on the ground floor; the classrooms are above it.

HELP Not all of the sentences in Exercise 11 need both semicolons and commas.

1. Scientists have explored almost all the lands on earth they are now exploring the floors of the oceans.
2. Some of the birds at the feeder were picky eaters; the blue jay for instance would eat only sunflower seeds.
3. St. Augustine, Florida, was the first European settlement in the United States the Spanish founded it in 1565.
4. Mike Powell set a world record for the long jump in 1991 his leap of 29 feet and 4½ inches beat Bob Beamon's 1968 record by 2 inches.
5. Some reptiles like a dry climate others prefer a wet climate.
6. We visited New Orleans Louisiana Natchez Mississippi and St. Louis Missouri.
7. In April 1912, a new, "unsinkable" ocean liner, the *Titanic*, struck an iceberg in the North Atlantic as a result roughly 1,500 persons lost their lives.
8. The members of the swim team who won first-place medals were Sam Foster, in the fifty-meter freestyle Philip Tucker, in the individual medley and Earl Sinclair, in the one-hundred-meter backstroke.

STYLE TIP

Semicolons do a better job if you do not use too many. Sometimes it is better to make two sentences out of a compound sentence or a heavily punctuated sentence rather than to use a semicolon.

ACCEPTABLE
Doubles tennis, as you know, is partly based on strategy; the two players must know each other's games, communicate well, and work together on their tactical approach.

BETTER
Doubles tennis, as you know, is partly based on strategy**.** The two players must know each other's games, communicate well, and work together on their tactical approach.

MECHANICS

9. Joanna, your team will include Fred Marty and Manny and Josie Sam and Phuong will be on my team.
10. The kind of tuba that wraps around the player's body is actually called a sousaphone it was named for John Philip Sousa, a famous band leader who came up with the idea for the shape.

Colons

23o. Use a colon before a list of items, especially after expressions like *as follows* or *the following.*

EXAMPLES Beyond talent lie all the usual words**:** discipline, love, luck, but, most of all, endurance.

James Baldwin, *The Writer's Chapbook*

Minimum equipment for camping is as follows**:** a bedroll, utensils for cooking and eating, warm clothing, sturdy shoes, a pocketknife, and a rope.

NOTE Do not use a colon between a verb and its object or between a preposition and its object.

INCORRECT Marcelo's hobbies include: fishing, hiking, and painting.

Last fall the Cohens traveled through: New York, Vermont, New Hampshire, and Maine.

CORRECT Marcelo's hobbies include fishing, hiking, and painting.

Last fall the Cohens traveled through New York, Vermont, New Hampshire, and Maine.

23p. Use a colon before a statement that explains or clarifies a preceding statement.

EXAMPLES Luis felt that he had accomplished something worthwhile**:** He had written and recorded his first song.

Mark Twain tried many jobs before becoming a successful writer**:** He was a printer's apprentice, a riverboat pilot, a soldier, and a silver miner.

23q. **Use a colon before a long, formal statement or quotation.**

EXAMPLE Patrick Henry concluded his revolutionary speech before the Virginia House of Burgesses with these ringing words**:** "Is life so dear, or peace so sweet as to be purchased at the price of chains and slavery? Forbid it, Almighty God! I know not what course others may take, but as for me, give me liberty or give me death!"

23r. **Use a colon in certain conventional situations.**

(1) Use a colon between the hour and the minute.

EXAMPLES 12**:**57 P.M. 4**:**08 A.M.

(2) Use a colon after the salutation of a business letter.

EXAMPLES Dear Ms. Gonzalez**:**

Dear Sir or Madam**:**

To Whom It May Concern**:**

(3) Use a colon between chapter and verse in Biblical references and between titles and subtitles.

EXAMPLES Matthew 6**:**9–13 "Easter**:** Wahiawa, 1959"

I Corinthians 13**:**1–2 *Akavak***:** *An Eskimo Journey*

Exercise 12 **Correcting Sentences by Adding Colons**

Write each of the following sentences, inserting a colon where it is needed.

EXAMPLE **1.** In Ruth 1 16, Ruth pledges her loyalty to Naomi, her mother-in-law.

1. In Ruth 1:16, Ruth pledges her loyalty to Naomi, her mother-in-law.

1. During the field trip, our teacher pointed out the following trees sugarberry, papaw, silver bell, and mountain laurel.
2. The first lunch period begins at 11 00 A.M.
3. This is my motto Laugh and the world laughs with you.
4. Using a recipe from *Miami Spice The New Florida Cuisine,* we made barbecue sauce.
5. The artist showed me how to make lavender Mix blue, white, and a little red.
6. The shortest verse in the Bible is John 11 35.

HELP

When a list of words, phrases, or subordinate clauses follows a colon, the first word of the list is lowercase. When an independent clause follows a colon, the first word of the clause begins with a capital letter.

EXAMPLES

All entries must include the following items**: a**n original photograph, a brief essay, and a self-addressed stamped envelope.

That reminds me of my favorite saying**: H**e who laughs last laughs best.

Reference Note

For more about **writing business letters,** see "Writing" in the Quick Reference Handbook.

7. Dear Senator Lupino
8. The train will leave at exactly 315.
9. When I look at the night sky I am reminded of lines from a poem called "Stars," by Sara Teasdale "And I know that I / Am honored to be / Witness / Of so much majesty."
10. The menu for the 100 P.M. lunch includes empanadas, egg rolls, curry, and hummus.

Review E Correcting a Paragraph by Adding Punctuation

Write the following paragraph, adding periods, question marks, exclamation points, commas, semicolons, and colons where they are needed.

EXAMPLE [1] Acadiana La isn't a town it's a region

1. *Acadiana, La., isn't a town; it's a region.*

[1] Known as Cajun country the region includes the twenty-two southernmost parishes of Louisiana [2] Did you know that the word *Cajun* is a shortened form of *Acadian* [3] Cajuns are descended from French colonists who settled along the Bay of Fundy in what is now eastern Canada they named their colony *Acadie* [4] After the British took over the area they deported nearly two thirds of the Acadians in 1755 many families were separated [5] Some Acadians took refuge in southern Louisiana's isolated swamps and bayous [6] They didn't remain isolated however They incorporated into their dialect elements of the following languages French English Spanish German and a variety of African and American Indian languages [7] In 1847 the American poet Henry Wadsworth Longfellow described the uprooting of the Acadians in *Evangeline* a long narrative poem that inspired Joseph Rusling Meeker to paint *The Land of Evangeline* which is shown to the left. [8] Today most people associate Cajun culture with hot spicy foods and lively fiddle and accordion music [9] Remembering their often tragic past Cajuns sum up their outlook on life in the following saying *Lâche pas la patate* which means "Don't let go of the potato." [10] What a great way to tell people not to lose their grip

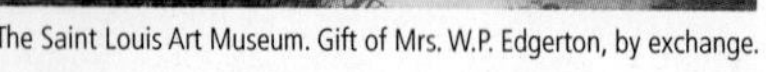
The Saint Louis Art Museum. Gift of Mrs. W.P. Edgerton, by exchange.

Chapter Review

A. Correcting Sentences by Adding Punctuation

Each of the following sentences contains at least one error in the use of periods, question marks, exclamation points, commas, semicolons, and colons. Write each sentence, correcting the punctuation errors.

1. Have you seen our principal Ms. O'Donnell today
2. We made a salad with the following vegetables from our garden lettuce cucumbers zucchini squash and cherry tomatoes
3. Running after the bus Dr Tassano tripped and fell in a puddle
4. My first pet which I got when I was six was a beagle
5. Come in Randy and sit down
6. The soft subtle colors of this beautiful Tabriz carpet are arranged in an intricate medallion pattern
7. Well I do know John 3 16 by heart
8. Does anyone know where the can opener is
9. The chickens clucked and the ducks squawked however the dogs didn't make a sound
10. Yes I recognize her She's in my math class
11. Wow That's the longest home run I've ever hit
12. After the rain stopped the blue jays hopped around the lawn
13. Wasn't President John F Kennedy assassinated in Dallas Tex on November 22 1963
14. Soy sauce which is made from soybeans flavors many traditional Chinese and Japanese foods
15. The first ones to arrive were Matt, Juan and Linda and Pat and Phil came later.
16. Preparing for takeoff the huge jetliner rolled toward the runway
17. In one of the barns we found an old butter churn
18. Did you see the highlights of the Cinco de Mayo Fiesta on the 6 00 news
19. Her address is 142 Oak Hollow Blvd Mendota CA 93640-2316
20. To get a better view of the fireworks Josh and I rode our bikes to Miller's Hill

MECHANICS

B. Correcting a Paragraph by Adding Periods, Question Marks, Exclamation Points, and Commas

Each sentence in the following paragraph contains at least one error in the use of periods, question marks, exclamation points, and commas. Write the paragraph, adding correct punctuation.

[21] Sixty miles south of Sicily is an ancient culturally diverse and quite fascinating island called Malta **[22]** After being a British colony for over 150 years Malta became an independent nation in 1964 **[23]** The Maltese are a Mediterranean people whose language Maltese is a West Arabic dialect interspersed with Italian words **[24]** Malta's history goes back to the Stone Age and the area has been colonized by Phoenician Greek Roman and Arab conquerors **[25]** Have you ever heard of the Knights of Malta **[26]** They successfully resisted a siege by the Ottoman Turks in the sixteenth century and Malta's capital Valletta is named after the Grand Master of the Knights at that time Jean de la Vallette **[27]** Valletta Malta's capital since 1571 is a compact city with narrow winding streets an ancient cathedral and a harbor on the Mediterranean Sea **[28]** With its sunny climate friendly people and multicultural heritage doesn't Malta sound like a great place for a vacation **[29]** Let's go **[30]** Well maybe not this year but dreams are free aren't they

C. Correctly Using Semicolons and Colons

Each of the following items contains errors in the use of semicolons or colons. Write each item, correcting the punctuation.

31. Emma felt shy however, she soon made new friends.

32. Additional supplies are as follows a ballpoint pen, some construction paper, scissors, and an eraser.

33. Dr. Termi has sent me letters from Dublin, Ireland Geneva, Switzerland Florence, Italy and Athens, Greece.

34. Our music class is very busy for example, Maria is giving a violin recital next week.

35. In the main hall we saw flags of five countries the United Kingdom, Canada, India, Jamaica, and South Africa.

MECHANICS

Writing Application

Using Correct Punctuation in a Business Letter

End Marks, Commas, Semicolons and Colons A local radio station is sponsoring a contest to select items to put in a time capsule. To enter the contest, write a business letter suggesting one item to include in the time capsule, which will be buried for one hundred years. In your letter, use punctuation marks correctly and follow the rules of business correspondence.

Prewriting List tangible items (ones you can touch) that show what life is like now in the United States. Next, choose the item you think would give people one hundred years from now the clearest picture of life today. Finally, make up a name, address, and call letters for the radio station.

Writing As you draft your letter, keep in mind that a business letter calls for a businesslike tone. Explain why the item you are suggesting should be included in the time capsule. Keep your letter brief, and stick to the point.

Revising To evaluate your letter, ask yourself the following questions: Is the letter easy to follow? Have I used standard English to present my ideas clearly and reasonably? Based on your answers to these questions, revise your letter to make it clearer and easier to follow.

Publishing Proofread your letter carefully, paying special attention to your use of end marks, commas, semicolons, and colons. Make sure that you have followed the proper form for a business letter. Type your letter on a computer, or handwrite a final copy and photocopy it. Compare it with those of your classmates. The class could vote on what ten items they would choose to put in a time capsule.

Reference Note

For more on **writing business letters,** see "Writing" in the Quick Reference Handbook.

VISION 2020
TIME CAPSULE
Sealed 9-25-1999
Open on 9-25-2019

CHAPTER

Punctuation

Underlining (Italics), Quotation Marks, Apostrophes, Hyphens, Parentheses, Brackets, Dashes

Diagnostic Preview

A. Proofreading Sentences for the Correct Use of Quotation Marks and Underlining (Italics)

Each of the following sentences requires underlining (italics), quotation marks, or both. Write each sentence correctly, inserting the appropriate punctuation.

EXAMPLE **1.** Ted, can you answer the first question? Ms. Simmons asked.

1. "Ted, can you answer the first question?" Ms. Simmons asked.

1. The best chapter in our vocabulary book is the last one, More Word Games.

2. "I answered all the questions, Todd said, but I think that some of my answers were wrong."

3. The Wizard of Oz was more exciting on the big movie screen than it was on our small television set.

4. Every Christmas Eve my uncle recites The Night Before Christmas for the children in the hospital.

5. There is a legend that the band on the Titanic played the hymn Nearer My God to Thee as the ship sank.

6. Play the Freddie Jackson CD again, Sam, Rebecca called.

7. Wendy wrote an article called Students, Where Are You? for our local newspaper, the Morning Beacon.
8. In the short story Thank You, M'am by Langston Hughes, a woman helps a troubled boy.
9. "Can I read Treasure Island for my report? Carmine asked.
10. Mr. Washington asked Connie, "Which flag also included the slogan Don't Tread on Me?"

B. Proofreading Sentences for the Correct Use of Apostrophes, Hyphens, Parentheses, Brackets, and Dashes

Each of the following sentences contains at least one error in the use of apostrophes, hyphens, parentheses, brackets, or dashes. Write each sentence correctly.

EXAMPLE 1. Ive been thinking about rivers names that come from American Indian words.

1. *I've been thinking about rivers' names that come from American Indian words.*

11. Boater's on the Missouri River may not know that *Missouri* means "people of the big canoes."
12. Have you ever heard the song about the Souths famous Shenandoah River?
13. The committee has voted to help keep the walkway clean a-long the Connecticut River.
14. I cant remember I wonder how many people have this same problem how many *i*s are in the word *Mississippi.*
15. Mount Vernon (the home of George Washington (1732–1799)) overlooks the Potomac River.
16. Alicia said, "Don't you remember their story about catching twenty two fish in the Arkansas River?"
17. Three fourths of the class couldnt pronounce the name *Monongahela* until we broke it into syllables Mo-non-ga-he-la.
18. Eliseo's oil painting of the Mohawk River was very good, but her's was better.
19. Ricardos guidebook the one he ordered last month states that the Suwannee is one of Floridas major rivers.
20. Shes lived in Massachusetts for thirty one years but has never before seen the Merrimack River.

Underlining (Italics)

COMPUTER TIP 

If you use a computer, you may be able to set words in italics. Most fonts can be set in italics.

Italics are printed letters that lean to the right, such as *the letters in these words.* In your handwritten or typewritten work, indicate italics by underlining. If your work were printed for publication, the underlined words would appear in italics. For example, if you were to write

Born Free is the story of a lioness that became a pet.

the printed version would look like this:

Born Free is the story of a lioness that became a pet.

Reference Note

For examples of **titles** that are not italicized but are enclosed in **quotation marks,** see page 667.

24a. Use underlining (italics) for titles and subtitles of books, plays, periodicals, works of art, films, television series, and long musical compositions and recordings.

Type of Title	Examples	
Books	*The Storyteller* *Lincoln: A Photobiography*	*Little Women* *The Adventures of Tom Sawyer*
Plays	*The Piano Lesson* *The Flying Tortilla Man*	*A Doll's House* *Visit to a Small Planet*
Periodicals	*The New York Times* *Scientific American* *Sky and Telescope*	*Hispanic* *Transitions Abroad* *The Nation*

TIPS & TRICKS

Generally, the title of an entire work (book, magazine, TV series) is italicized while the title of a part (chapter, article, episode) is enclosed in quotation marks.

NOTE Underline (or italicize) an article (*a, an,* or *the*) at the beginning of a title or subtitle only if it is the first word of the official title or subtitle.

EXAMPLES During vacation she read ***The** Woman Warrior,* by Maxine Hong Kingston. [The article *The* is part of the title.]

My parents subscribe to **the** *San Francisco Chronicle.* [The article *the* is not part of the official title.]

HELP

To find the official title of a newspaper or magazine, look at the masthead. In a newspaper, the masthead usually appears on the editorial page. In a magazine, the masthead can be found on one of the first few pages, usually following the table of contents.

MECHANICS

Type of Title	Examples	
Works of Art	*The Thinker*	*American Gothic*
Films	*The Wizard of Oz*	*Casablanca*
Television Series	*Dateline* *Boy Meets World*	*Wall Street Week* *Animaniacs*
Long Musical Compositions and Recordings	*Don Giovanni* *Fidelio*	*The Four Seasons* *Appalachian Spring*

24b. Use underlining (italics) for names of ships, trains, aircraft, and spacecraft.

Type of Title	Examples	
Ships	*Calypso*	*Titanic*
Trains	*Silver Meteor*	*Santa Fe Chief*
Aircraft	*Enola Gay*	*Air Force One*
Spacecraft	*Eagle*	*Columbia*

24c. Use underlining (italics) for words, letters, and numerals referred to as such.

EXAMPLES Jean sometimes confuses the words ***affect*** and ***effect.***

Don't forget to double the ***p*** when you add ***–ed.***

Does your number begin with a ***5*** or an ***8***?

Exercise 1 Using Underlining (Italics) in Sentences

Write and underline the words that should be italicized in each of the following sentences.

EXAMPLE **1.** Have you read The Call of the Wild?

1. The Call of the Wild

1. The magazine rack held current issues of National Wildlife, Time, Essence, Jewish Monthly, and Sports Illustrated.
2. Sometimes I forget to put the first o in the word thorough, and by mistake I write through.

Reference Note

For information on **capitalizing titles,** see page 619.

STYLE TIP

Writers sometimes use italics for emphasis, especially in written dialogue. The italic type shows how the sentence is supposed to be spoken. Read the following sentences aloud. Notice that by italicizing different words, the writer can change the meaning of the sentence.

EXAMPLES

"Are you *sure* the quarterback hurt his ankle?" asked Michelle. [Are you sure, not just guessing?]

"Are you sure the *quarterback* hurt his ankle?" asked Michelle. [Was it the quarterback, not some other player, who hurt his ankle?]

"Are you sure the quarterback hurt his *ankle*?" asked Michelle. [Did the quarterback hurt his ankle, not his knee?]

Italicizing (underlining) words for emphasis is a handy technique that should not be overused. It can quickly lose its impact.

3. The final number will be a medley of tunes from George Gershwin's opera Porgy and Bess.
4. Jerry Spinelli won the Newbery Medal for his book Maniac Magee, which is about an unusual athlete.
5. Picasso's painting Guernica is named for a Spanish town that was destroyed during the Spanish Civil War.
6. My father reads the Chicago Sun-Times because he likes Carl Rowan's column.
7. The first battle between ironclad ships took place between the Monitor and the Merrimack in 1862.
8. The Irish movie Into the West features the adventure of two brothers and their magical horse.
9. I had never traveled by train until we rode the Hill Country Flyer.
10. Melissa asked Christopher whether he and his family ever watch the show Nova.

Quotation Marks

24d. Use quotation marks to enclose a *direct quotation*—a person's exact words.

Be sure to place quotation marks both before and after a person's exact words.

EXAMPLES "Has anyone here swum in the Great Salt Lake?" asked my cousin.

Peggy Ann said, "I swam there last summer."

Do not use quotation marks for an ***indirect quotation***—a rewording of a direct quotation.

DIRECT QUOTATION	Kaya asked Christopher, "What is your interpretation of the poem?"
INDIRECT QUOTATION	Kaya asked Christopher what his interpretation of the poem is.
DIRECT QUOTATION	As Barbara Jordan said in her keynote address to the Democratic National Convention in 1976, "We are willing to suffer the discomfort of change in order to achieve a better future."
INDIRECT QUOTATION	Barbara Jordan said that people will put up with the discomfort of change to have a better future.

24e. A direct quotation generally begins with a capital letter.

EXAMPLES Brandon shouted, "**L**aura! Over here!"

Abraham Lincoln said, "**T**hose who deny freedom to others deserve it not for themselves."

24f. When the expression identifying the speaker interrupts a quoted sentence, the second part of the quotation begins with a lowercase letter.

EXAMPLES "Do you know," asked Angelo, "**w**hat the astronauts learned when they landed on the moon?"

"One thing they found," answered Gwen, "**w**as that the moon is covered by a layer of dust."

Notice in the examples above that each part of a divided quotation is enclosed in a set of quotation marks. In addition, the interrupting expression is set off by commas.

When the second part of a divided quotation is a complete sentence, it begins with a capital letter.

EXAMPLE "Any new means of travel is exciting," remarked Mrs. Perkins. "**S**pace travel is no exception."

Notice that in such cases a period, not a comma, follows the interrupting expression.

24g. A direct quotation is set off from the rest of the sentence by a comma, a question mark, or an exclamation point, but not by a period.

EXAMPLES Alyssa said**,** "Mrs. Batista showed us a short film about Narcissa Whitman."

"Was she one of the early settlers in the Northwest**?**" asked Delia.

"What an adventure**!**" exclaimed Iola.

24h. A period or a comma is placed inside the closing quotation marks.

EXAMPLES Ramón said, "Hank Aaron was a better player than Babe Ruth because he hit more home runs in his career**."**

"Hank Aaron never hit sixty homers in one year, though**,"** Paula responded.

24i. A question mark or an exclamation point is placed inside the closing quotation marks when the quotation itself is a question or an exclamation. Otherwise, it is placed outside.

EXAMPLES "Is the time difference between Los Angeles and Chicago two hours**?"** asked Ken. [The quotation is a question.]

Linda exclaimed, "I thought everyone knew that**!"** [The quotation is an exclamation.]

What did Jade Snow Wong mean in her story "A Time of Beginnings" when she wrote, "Like the waves of the sea, no two pieces of pottery art can be identical**"?** [The sentence, not the quotation, is a question.]

I'm so happy that Mom said, "You are allowed to stay out until 10:00 P.M. on Friday night**"!** [The sentence, not the quotation, is an exclamation.]

When both the sentence and a quotation at the end of that sentence are questions (or exclamations), only one question mark (or exclamation point) is used. It is placed inside the closing quotation marks.

EXAMPLE "What is the title of the Gwendolyn Brooks poem that begins "Oh mother, mother, where is happiness**?"**

Exercise 2 Correcting Sentences by Adding Capital Letters and Punctuation

Revise the following sentences by supplying capital letters and marks of punctuation as needed. If a sentence is already correct, write *C.*

EXAMPLE **1.** Of the early art of the Americas asked Julian which piece of art is your favorite?

1. "Of the early art of the Americas," asked Julian, "which piece of art is your favorite?"

1. Ms. Chung said, that of the Incas is probably my favorite, because it was beautiful and varied.
2. There are wonderful pictures in this book said Pedro. let's look at it.
3. The inlaid gold earrings are fantastic exclaimed Francine.

MECHANICS

4. The Incas' worship of the sun is expressed in many pieces of art said Tonya such as in this tapestry.
5. I found a picture of what the Inca capital of Cuzco looked like, Craig said. it is easy to see that it was a large, technologically advanced city.
6. Matina said that it was wonderful to be left so much art, but that it was a shame the Incas didn't have a written language.
7. They did leave *quipus* said Louella but no one completely understands their use; it's thought that the knotted strings assisted memory.
8. A bit like tying a string around your finger said Mahlon, but more complicated.
9. Cohila said lets make a *quipu* for the classroom.
10. We each need one for the algebra test laughed Marc.

Exercise 3 Correcting Sentences by Adding Capital Letters and Punctuation

Write the following sentences, supplying capital letters and marks of punctuation as needed.

EXAMPLE 1. Why she asked can't we leave now
1. *"Why," she asked, "can't we leave now?"*

1. Mom, will you take us to the soccer field asked Libby
2. Please hold my backpack for a minute, Dave Josh said I need to tie my shoelace
3. Cary asked What is pita bread
4. Alison answered It's a round, flat Middle Eastern bread
5. Run Run cried the boys a tornado is headed this way
6. Our cat caught a little rabbit and paid no attention when I yelled drop that
7. Have you ever eaten enchiladas made with homemade tortillas asked Martin
8. The computers are all ready to be used said Gary we'd better get to work
9. Oh no shouted Katrina not all of the chess pieces were put away with the board
10. If California is in the Pacific time zone, asked Ernesto in what time zone is Arizona

24j. When you write dialogue (conversation), begin a new paragraph each time the speaker changes.

EXAMPLE "Ay, no, señor!" Don Anselmo hastily blessed himself. "To bring a white horse into these mountains is not wise. *El Caballo Blanco* would not like it."

"*El Caballo Blanco* is dead. You yourself said this yesterday."

"Dead he may be in body, but the goatherds often see him on the trails in the moonlight, his hand on his gun, his hat on the back of his head, and his white horse between his knees."

"Have you ever seen him?"

Josefina Niggli, "The Quarry"

24k. When a quotation consists of several sentences, place quotation marks only at the beginning and at the end of the whole quotation.

EXAMPLES "Memorize all your lines for Monday. Be sure to have someone at home give you your cues. Enjoy your weekend!" said Ms. Goodwin.

Monica said, "We spent all day Saturday at the beach. In the morning, we went swimming in the surf. After lunch, we hiked over the dunes in search of seashells."

MECHANICS

Exercise 4 Correcting Dialogue by Adding Punctuation

Rewrite the following dialogue, adding commas, end marks, quotation marks, and paragraph indentions where necessary.

EXAMPLE **[1]** Which would you rather use, a pencil or a pen asked Jody

1. "Which would you rather use, a pencil or a pen?" asked Jody.

[1] Gordon, do you ever think about pencils Annie asked [2] I'm always wondering where I lost mine Gordon replied [3] Well said Annie let me tell you some of the things I learned about pencils [4] Okay Gordon said I love trivia [5] People have used some form of pencils for a long time Annie began [6] The ancient Greeks and Romans used lead pencils [7] However, pencils as

we know them weren't developed until the sixteenth century, when people started using graphite [8] What's graphite asked Gordon [9] Graphite is a soft form of carbon Annie explained that leaves a mark when it's drawn over most surfaces [10] Thanks for the information, Annie Gordon said Now, do you have a pencil I can borrow

24l. Use quotation marks to enclose titles and subtitles of short works such as short stories, poems, essays, articles, songs, episodes of television series, and chapters and other parts of books.

Reference Note

For examples of **titles that are italicized,** see page 660.

Type of Title	Examples
Short Stories	"A Worn Path" "The Rule of Names" "The Tell-Tale Heart" "A Rose for Emily"
Poems	"Mother to Son" "Birches" "Calling in the Cat" "Easter 1916"
Essays and Articles	"The Creative Process" "Free Speech and Free Air" "How to Make a Budget" "A Modest Proposal"
Songs	"Joy to the World" "Amazing Grace" "Duke of Earl" "Yesterday"
Episodes of Television Series	"Heart of a Champion" "The Trouble with Tribbles" "Journey's End"
Chapters and Other Parts of Books	"Learning About Reptiles" "English: Origins and Uses" "Creating a Federal Union"

Reference Note

Remember that the **titles of long musical works are italicized,** not enclosed in quotation marks. See the examples on page 661.

24m. Use single quotation marks to enclose a quotation within a quotation or a title of a short work within a quotation.

EXAMPLES "I said, 'The quiz will cover Unit 2 and your special reports,'" repeated Mr. Allyn.

"Which Shakespeare character speaks the line 'Good night, good night! Parting is such sweet sorrow'?" Carol asked.

Sharon said, "I just read 'Broken Chain.'"

Exercise 5 Correcting Sentences by Adding Quotation Marks

Write the following sentences, using quotation marks as needed.

EXAMPLE **1.** We sang Greensleeves for the assembly, said Hiu.

1. "We sang 'Greensleeves' for the assembly," said Hiu.

1. "Has anyone read the story To Build a Fire?" asked the teacher.
2. "I think Eileen said, Please go on without me," said Judy.
3. Do you know the poem To Make a Prairie?
4. Our chorus will sing When You Wish upon a Star today.
5. In the chapter Workers' Rights, the author discusses Cesar Chavez's efforts to help migrant workers.
6. "The first song I learned to accompany on guitar was Shenandoah," said Jack.
7. "When I was only seven I memorized Lewis Carroll's poem Jabberwocky," claimed Damita.
8. My favorite episode of *Nova* is the one titled The Doomsday Asteroid.
9. The magazine article How to Make the Most of Your Life contains very good advice.
10. "Danny, would you like to read Robert Frost's poem The Road Not Taken at graduation?" asked Dr. Washington.

Review A Correcting Sentences by Adding Punctuation and Capital Letters

Write the following sentences, using marks of punctuation and capital letters as needed. If a sentence is already correct, write *C.*

EXAMPLE 1. Did you read the article about the runner Jackie Joyner-Kersee in USA Weekend Lynn asked.

1. *"Did you read the article about the runner Jackie Joyner-Kersee in USA Weekend?" Lynn asked.*

1. Won't you stay pleaded Wynnie there will be music and refreshments later.
2. Hey, Jason, said Chen, you play the drums like an expert!
3. The girls asked whether we needed help finding our campsite.
4. Elise, do you know who said The only thing we have to fear is fear itself asked the teacher.
5. What a wonderful day for a picnic on the levee exclaimed Susan to Rafiq.
6. I've read Connie said that Thomas Jefferson loved Italian food and ordered pasta from Italy.
7. When President Lincoln heard of the South's defeat, he requested that the band play Dixie.
8. The latest issue of National Geographic has a long article on rain forests.
9. Langston Hughes's Dream Deferred is a subtle, thought-provoking poem.
10. What can have happened to Francine this time, Tina? Didn't she say, I'll be home before you leave? Justin asked.

Apostrophes

An ***apostrophe*** is used to form the possessive case of nouns and some pronouns, to indicate in a contraction where letters or numerals have been omitted, and to form some plurals.

Possessive Case

The ***possessive case*** of a noun or a pronoun shows ownership or possession.

Sandra's boat	an **hour's** time
Mother's job	**Julio's** sister
your book	**everyone's** choice

24n. To form the possessive case of a singular noun, add an apostrophe and an *s.*

EXAMPLES	a dog**'s** collar	one dollar**'s** worth
	a moment**'s** notice	Willis**'s** typewriter

HELP

A proper noun ending in *s* may take only an apostrophe to form the possessive case if the addition of *'s* would make the name awkward to pronounce.

EXAMPLES
Marjorie Kinnan Rawlings**'** novels
Hercules**'** feats
Mr. Fuentes**'** plans

MECHANICS

Exercise 6 Supplying Apostrophes for Possessive Nouns

Write each noun that should be in the possessive case in the following sentences. Then, add the apostrophe.

EXAMPLE 1. The dogs leash is made of nylon.
1. dog's

1. That trucks taillights are broken.
2. By the end of the demonstration, the judges were impressed with Veronicas project.
3. Last weeks travel story was about Mindanao, the second largest island of the Philippines.
4. Matthews dream is to have a palomino.
5. Robin, please pack your mothers books.
6. Several cats and dogs were adopted during the animal shelters open house.
7. When the Martins came to visit, we played my fathers favorite game, Yahtzee.
8. The science museums schedule of summer events did not list an astronomy class.
9. A roosters crowing could wake up the soundest sleeper.
10. Much of E. E. Cummings poetry appeals to both adults and children.

24o. To form the possessive case of a plural noun ending in *s*, add only the apostrophe.

EXAMPLES	actors**'** scripts	doctors**'** opinions
	customers**'** complaints	the Haines**'** invitations

To form the possessive case of a plural noun that does not end in *s*, add an apostrophe and an *s*.

EXAMPLES	women**'s** suits	geese**'s** noise
	sheep**'s** pasture	children**'s** books

NOTE In general, you should not use an apostrophe to form the plural of a noun.

INCORRECT The passenger's showed their tickets to the flight attendant.

CORRECT The **passengers** showed their tickets to the flight attendant. [plural]

Reference Note

For information on using an apostrophe and an *s* to form the **plurals of letters, numerals, symbols, and words used as words,** see page 675.

Exercise 7 Forming Plural Possessives

Correctly write each of the following plural possessives.

EXAMPLE **1.** artists paintings

1. artists' paintings

1. boys boots
2. women careers
3. friends comments
4. three days homework
5. girls parents
6. Joneses cabin
7. men shoes
8. children game
9. cities mayors
10. oxen yokes
11. sisters closet
12. schools playgrounds
13. teachers lounge
14. actors costumes
15. deer tracks
16. trees branches
17. birds nests
18. tadpoles ponds
19. Thomases house
20. classes schedules

24p. Do not use an apostrophe with possessive personal pronouns.

EXAMPLES These keys are **yours,** not **mine.**

Are these tapes **ours** or **theirs**?

His pantomime was good, but **hers** was better.

Reference Note

For more information about **possessive personal pronouns,** see page 545. For more about the **difference between *its* and *it's*,** see page 590.

NOTE The possessive case form of *it* is *its.* The expression *it's* is a contraction of the words *it is* or *it has.*

24q. To form the possessive case of some indefinite pronouns, add an apostrophe and an *s.*

EXAMPLES someone**'s** pencil

no one**'s** fault

anybody**'s** guess

HELP—For information on forming the plurals of nouns, see page 694.

Review B **Forming Singular Possessives and Plural Possessives**

Form the singular possessive and the plural possessive of each of the following nouns.

EXAMPLES **1.** citizen

1. citizen's; citizens'

2. city

2. city's; cities'

1. book	**6.** hero	**11.** hand	**16.** politician
2. puppy	**7.** elephant	**12.** roof	**17.** moose
3. donkey	**8.** tooth	**13.** hour	**18.** canoe
4. mouse	**9.** school	**14.** chalkboard	**19.** zoo
5. calf	**10.** family	**15.** foot	**20.** country

Contractions

24r. To form a contraction, use an apostrophe to show where letters or numerals have been omitted.

A ***contraction*** is a shortened form of a word, a numeral, or a group of words. The apostrophe in a contraction indicates where letters or numerals have been left out.

Common Contractions			
I am	I'm	they had	they'd
1993	'93	where is	where's
let us	let's	we are	we're
of the clock	o'clock	he is	he's
she would	she'd	you will	you'll

The word *not* can be shortened to *n't* and added to a verb, usually without changing the spelling of the verb.

EXAMPLES

is not	is**n't**	has not	has**n't**
are not	are**n't**	have not	have**n't**
does not	does**n't**	had not	had**n't**
do not	do**n't**	should not	should**n't**

MECHANICS

	was not . . . . wasn**'**t	would not . . . . . . wouldn**'**t
	were not . . . . . weren**'**t	could not . . . . couldn**'**t
EXCEPTIONS	will not . . . . **won'**t	cannot . . . . **can'**t

Do not confuse contractions with possessive pronouns.

Contractions	Possessive Pronouns
He said **it's** snowing. [*it is*]	**Its** front tire is flat.
It's been a long time. [*It has*]	
Who's next in line? [*Who is*]	**Whose** idea was it?
Who's swept? [*Who has*]	
You're writing an essay. [*You are*]	**Your** writing has improved.
They're not here. [*They are*]	**Their** dog is barking.
There's a trophy for first place. [*There is*]	This trophy is **theirs.**

Exercise 8 Forming Contractions

Form the contraction of each of the following pairs of words.

EXAMPLE **1.** he is

1. he's

1. will not
2. there is
3. who will
4. they are
5. who is
6. are not
7. it is
8. should not
9. let us
10. I have
11. you are
12. does not
13. he would
14. has not
15. we are
16. I am
17. had not
18. she is
19. you will
20. could not

Exercise 9 Correcting Contractions by Adding Apostrophes

The letter on the following page contains ten punctuation errors. Write each incorrect contraction, and add an apostrophe.

EXAMPLE **1.** When you visit Glacier National Park, youre in for a treat.

1. you're

STYLE  TIP

In formal writing, avoid using a contraction of a year. In informal writing, if the reader cannot determine the time period from the context of the sentence, it is best to write out the year.

EXAMPLE
The famous tenor toured Europe in '01. [Did the tenor tour in 1801, 1901 or 2001?]

REVISED
The famous tenor toured Europe in **1901.**

August 7, 2001

Dear Granddad,

Youll love the pictures Im sending you from here. Glacier National Park is awesome, and were having a wonderful time. Thank you for telling us about it. Weve been here two weeks now, but it doesnt seem like more than two days. We werent planning to spend all day yesterday canoeing on Swiftcurrent Lake, but its so beautiful we didnt want to go back to our hotel. Last night the rangers warned us to be careful on the trails because there are often bears. Just to be safe, we wont walk alone or after sundown, which is around seven o clock.

Love,

Cal

Cal

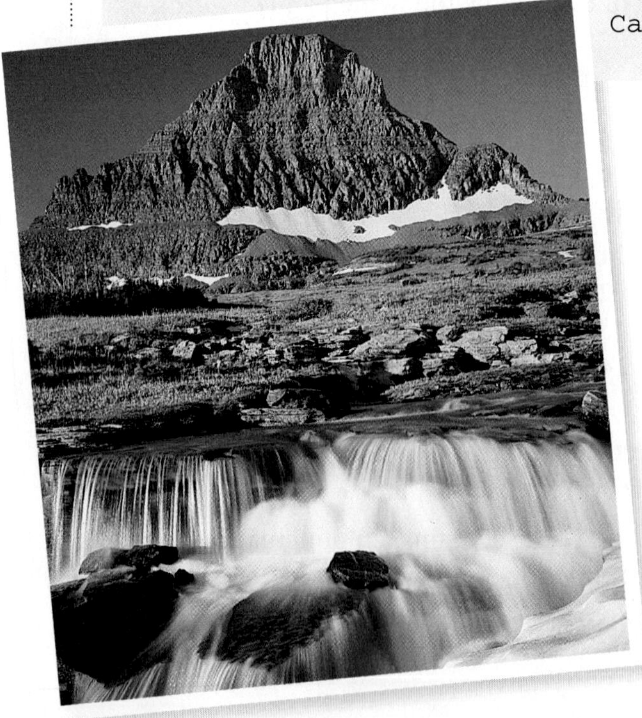

MECHANICS

Plurals

24s. Use an apostrophe and an *s* to form the plurals of letters, numerals, and symbols, and of words referred to as words.

EXAMPLES There are two *d*'s in the word *hidden.*

Your *2*'s look like backward *5*'s.

Jazz became quite popular in the 1920's.

Don't use too many *so*'s and *and*'s.

He wrote *$*'s before all the amounts.

STYLE TIP

In your reading, you may notice that an apostrophe is not always used in forming the kinds of plurals addressed by Rule 24s. Nowadays, many writers omit the apostrophe if the plural meaning is clear without it. However, to make sure that your writing is clear, you should always use an apostrophe.

Review C Correcting Sentences by Adding Apostrophes

Write the correct form of each item that requires an apostrophe in the following sentences.

EXAMPLE 1. Dont you know what youre doing?

1. Don't, you're

1. The girls didnt say when theyd be back.
2. Lets find out when the next game is.
3. My cousin Blanca usually gets As and Bs on her report card.
4. It isnt correct to use *&*s in your compositions.
5. Many of the scores on the math test were in the 80s and 90s.
6. They cant come to the bar mitzvah with us; they've been delayed.
7. Theyll meet us, if its all right to tell them where were going.
8. Whos signed up for the talent show?
9. Dont those *9*s look like *g*s to you?
10. Your capital *L*s and *I*s are hard to tell apart.

Hyphens

24t. Use a hyphen to divide a word at the end of a line.

EXAMPLES What percentage of U.S. households have sub-
scribed to cable television?

You can probably find the answer in the almanac in the library.

COMPUTER TIP

Some word-processing programs will automatically divide a word at the end of a line and insert a hyphen. Sometimes, such a division will break one of the rules of hyphenation.

Check a printout of your writing to see how the computer has hyphenated words at the ends of lines. If a hyphen is used incorrectly, revise the line by moving the word or by redividing the word and inserting a "hard" hyphen (one that the computer cannot move).

STYLE TIP

Hyphens are often used in compound names. In such cases, the hyphen is thought of as part of the spelling of the name.

EXAMPLES

Jean-Phillipe Rameau

Chiang Kai-shek

Henri Cartier-Bresson

Wilkes-Barre

If you are not sure whether a compound name is hyphenated, ask the person with that name or look in a reference source.

MECHANICS

When dividing a word at the end of a line, remember the following rules:

(1) Divide a word only between syllables.

INCORRECT Lisa wrote her science report on the tyra-
nnosaurs, the largest meat-eating dinosaurs.

CORRECT Lisa wrote her science report on the tyran-
nosaurs, the largest meat-eating dinosaurs.

NOTE If you are not sure how to divide a word into syllables correctly, look up the word in a dictionary.

(2) Do not divide a one-syllable word.

INCORRECT The fans stood and sang while the band played the school song.

CORRECT The fans stood and sang while the band played the school song.

(3) Divide an already hyphenated word at a hyphen.

INCORRECT Keisha and I went to the fair with our great-uncle James.

CORRECT Keisha and I went to the fair with our great-
uncle James.

(4) Do not divide a word so that one letter stands alone.

INCORRECT While moving to Chicago last week, Anthony i-
magined what the new house would be like.

CORRECT While moving to Chicago last week, Anthony imagined what the new house would be like.

24u. Use a hyphen with compound numbers from *twenty-one* to *ninety-nine* and with fractions used as modifiers.

EXAMPLES thirty-five students

forty-eighth state

one-third pint of milk

When a fraction is a noun, do not use a hyphen.

EXAMPLE **one third** of a pint

24v. Use a hyphen with the prefixes *all–, ex–, great–,* and *self–* and with the suffixes *–elect* and *–free* and with all prefixes before a proper noun or proper adjective.

EXAMPLES all-star president-elect

ex-principal sugar-free

great-aunt mid-September

self-confidence pro-American

24w. Hyphenate a compound adjective when it precedes the noun it modifies.

EXAMPLES a **well-worn** book [but *a book that is well worn*]

a **small-town** girl [but *a girl from a small town*]

Do not use a hyphen if one of the modifiers is an adverb that ends in *ly.*

EXAMPLES a **terribly bad** cold

a **nicely turned** phrase

NOTE Some compound adjectives are always hyphenated, whether they precede or follow the nouns they modify.

EXAMPLES a **brand-new** stereo

a stereo that is **brand-new**

Exercise 10 Hyphenating Numbers and Fractions

Write the following expressions, inserting hyphens as needed. If an expression is already correct, write *C.*

EXAMPLE **1.** thirty one days

1. thirty-one days

1. a two thirds majority
2. one half of the coconut
3. one hundred thirty five pages
4. Forty second Street
5. twenty two Amish quilts
6. one third cup of water
7. ninety nine years
8. fifty five dollars and twenty cents
9. three eighths of the pizza
10. the twenty first amendment

STYLE TIP

The prefix *half–* often requires a hyphen, as in *half-life, half-moon,* and *half-truth.* However, sometimes *half* is used without a hyphen, either as part of a single word (*halftone, halfway, halfback*) or as a separate word (*half shell, half pint, half note*). If you are not sure how to spell a word containing *half,* look up the word in a dictionary.

HELP

To find out whether a compound adjective is always hyphenated, look it up in a current dictionary.

Review D Adding Apostrophes, Hyphens, and Underlining (Italics)

Write the following sentences, inserting apostrophes, hyphens, and underlining as needed.

EXAMPLE 1. Isnt the preface to that edition of Frankenstein twenty four pages long?

1. Isn't the preface to that edition of Frankenstein twenty-four pages long?

1. Theres where they live.
2. Wholl go to next weeks showing of the film Small Change?
3. The Lockwood sisters golden retriever is named Storm.
4. One third of Hollys allowance goes into the bank.
5. The park on Fifty third Street has a well lit jogging trail.
6. Twenty six members of the student council (more than a three fourths majority) voted to change the school song.
7. Shelly said that shes always wanted to read Amy Tan's book The Joy Luck Club.
8. If two thirds of the class have scores below seventy five, well all have to retake the test.
9. Lets find out about Henry VIIIs flagship, the Mary Rose.
10. Ninety seven years ago my great grandparents left Scotland for the United States.

MECHANICS

TIP

Too many parenthetical expressions in a piece of writing can distract readers from the main idea. Keep your meaning clear by limiting the number of parenthetical expressions you use.

Parentheses

24x. Use parentheses to enclose material that is added to a sentence but is not considered of major importance.

EXAMPLES Mohandas K. Gandhi **(**1869–1948**)** led India's struggle for independence from British rule.

Mrs. Matsuo served us the sushi **(**soo' shē**)** that she had prepared.

Material enclosed in parentheses may range from a single word or number to a short sentence. A short sentence in parentheses may stand by itself or be contained within another sentence. Notice that a sentence within a sentence is not capitalized; such a sentence may be followed by a question mark or exclamation point, but not by a period.

EXAMPLES You should try the orange juice. **(It's freshly squeezed.)**

No, set that ladder **(watch out!)** over there.

My great-uncle Ed **(he's Grandma's brother)** is odd.

Brackets

24y. Use brackets to enclose an explanation or added information within quoted or parenthetical material.

EXAMPLES At the press conference, Detective Stamos stated, "We are following up on several leads regarding the **[**Mills Sporting Goods**]** robbery."

During the Revolutionary War, Mohawk leader Joseph Brant (his Indian name was Thayendanegea **[**1742–1807**]**) became a colonel in the British Army.

HELP

The brackets in the first example for 24y tell the reader that *Mills Sporting Goods* is not part of Detective Stamos's sentence but was added to the quotation for clarity.

Exercise 11 Writing Sentences with Parentheses and Brackets

For each of the following sentences, insert parentheses or brackets where they are needed. Be sure not to enclose any words or marks of punctuation that do not belong inside the parentheses or brackets.

EXAMPLE **1.** One popular pet is the house cat *Felis cattus.*

1. One popular pet is the house cat (Felis cattus).

1. The old fort it was used during the Civil War has been rebuilt and is open to the public.
2. The final speaker said, "If you don't allow them the umpires to do their jobs, we might as well not play the games."
3. The American writer Langston Hughes 1902–1967 is best known for his poetry.
4. Alligators use their feet and tails to dig water holes also called "gator holes" in marshy fields.
5. On the Sabbath my family eats braided bread called challah pronounced khä′lə.
6. Komodo dragons the largest of all monitor lizards can be found in Indonesia.
7. Antonin Dvořák 1841–1904 was a Czech composer who wrote beautiful symphonies.

MECHANICS

8. The town's historic district it dates from the nineteenth century is a popular meeting place.
9. Block print all addresses use blue or black ink.
10. The next president (he was Ulysses S. Grant 1822–1885) continued the Reconstruction program while trying to protect the rights of former slaves.

Dashes

Reference Note

For more information about **using commas with parenthetical expressions,** see page 643. For more about **using parentheses,** see page 678.

Many words and phrases are used *parenthetically;* that is, they break into the main thought of a sentence. Most parenthetical elements are set off by commas or parentheses.

EXAMPLES The tomato**, however,** is actually a fruit, not a vegetable.

The outcome **(which candidate would be elected governor?)** was in the hands of the voters.

Sometimes, parenthetical elements demand stronger emphasis. In such instances, a dash is used.

24z. Use a dash to indicate an abrupt break in thought or speech.

EXAMPLES Ms. Alonzo**—**she just left**—**will be one of the judges of the talent show.

"Right over here**—**oh, excuse me, Mr. Mills**—**you'll find the reference books," said the librarian.

Alisha began, "The burglar is**—**but I don't want to give away the ending."

Exercise 12 Writing Sentences with Dashes

For each of the following sentences, insert dashes where they are needed.

EXAMPLE 1. Paul Revere he imported hardware made beautiful jewelry and utensils.

1. Paul Revere—he imported hardware—made beautiful jewelry and utensils.

1. A beautiful grand piano it was once played by Chopin was on display in the museum.

MECHANICS

2. "I'd like the red no, give me the blue cycling shorts and white socks," said Josh.
3. Frederic Remington artist, historian, and lover of the frontier is famous for his paintings of the West.
4. On July 7, 1981, Sandra Day O'Connor she's the first female associate justice was nominated to the U.S. Supreme Court.
5. Cheryl wondered aloud, "Where in the world oh, my poor Muffy could that hamster be?"
6. Kohlrabi an odd-looking vegetable is part of the cabbage family.
7. You may cut some of the roses oh, here, use the garden shears to give to your mother.
8. We put up the banners don't tell me they've fallen down for the pep rally.
9. "The dog stop jumping on the people, Punkin doesn't bite," says our neighbor every time we visit her.
10. Most planets have Greek or Roman names Mercury, Venus, Mars, Jupiter, and Saturn were all Roman gods while the word *Earth* is Old English.

Review E Correcting Sentences by Adding Punctuation

Write the following sentences, supplying punctuation marks where needed. If a sentence is already correct, write *C.*

EXAMPLE 1. Stans going to the Washingtons Birthday cele bration in Laredo, Texas Teresa said.

1. *"Stan's going to the Washington's Birthday celebration in Laredo, Texas," Teresa said.*

1. Some say that Laredos festivities are the countrys biggest celebration of Washingtons birthday Juan said Isnt that surprising
2. No, not really said Frank The citys large Hispanic population chose to honor George Washington, whom they consider a freedom fighter
3. Teresa said The citizens there also have great respect for Washingtons abilities as a leader
4. Juan said that the annual event began back in the 1800's.
5. Did you know that theyve extended the birthday party to both sides of the Texas-Mexico border Teresa asked.

6. Thats right Juan said The citizens of Nuevo Laredo in Mexico really enjoy the celebration, too
7. Just look at the colorful costumes in the photograph exclaimed Teresa Can you tell what famous couple these people are portraying
8. Teresa continued Mrs. Serrano she's Juans aunt who lives in Houston has gone to the festivities in Laredo for the past twenty two years.
9. Today the Laredo Morning Times reported that a jalapeño-eating contest was part of this years celebration Anna re ported.
10. In honor of Washingtons birthday February 22, three fourths of our class read the book Washington by William Jay Jacobs, said Juan.

MECHANICS

Chapter Review

A. Proofreading Sentences for the Correct Use of Quotation Marks and Underlining (Italics)

Each of the following sentences contains at least one error in the use of quotation marks or underlining (italics). Write each sentence correctly.

1. Uncle Ned reads The Wall Street Journal every day.
2. Fill in all the information on the form, the secretary said.
3. How many times have you seen the movie version of Margaret Mitchell's novel Gone with the Wind?
4. Many of the students enjoyed the humor and irony in O. Henry's short story The Ransom of Red Chief.
5. My little sister asked, Why can't I have a hamster?
6. Please don't sing I've Been Working on the Railroad.
7. Last summer my older sister played in a band on a Caribbean cruise ship named Bright Coastal Star.
8. "Read James Baldwin's essay Autobiographical Notes, and answer both of the study questions," the teacher said.
9. Dudley Randall's poem Ancestors questions why people always seem to believe that their ancestors were aristocrats.
10. "That artist," Mr. Russell said, was influenced by the Cuban painter Amelia Pelaez del Casal.

B. Proofreading Sentences for the Correct Use of Apostrophes, Hyphens, Parentheses, and Dashes

Each of the following sentences contains at least one error in the use of apostrophes, hyphens, parentheses, or dashes. Write each sentence correctly.

11. Marsha is this years captain of the girls basketball team.
12. Susan B. Anthony 1820–1906 worked to give women the right to vote in the United States.
13. Id never heard of a Greek bagpipe before, but Mr. Protopapas played one at his great uncle's birthday party.

14. We couldn't have done the job without everyones help.
15. Hes strict about being on time.
16. On my older brothers next birthday, he will turn twenty one.
17. Wed have forgotten to turn off the computer if Maggie hadnt reminded us.
18. The recipe said to add two eggs and one quarter cup of milk.
19. My mothers office is on the twenty second floor.
20. Our dog he's a giant schnauzer is gentle and very well behaved.

C. Proofreading a Paragraph for the Correct Use of Punctuation

Write the following sentences, supplying punctuation marks and starting new paragraphs where needed. If a sentence is already correct, write *C.*

[21] "Im on my way to curling practice," announced Andy. **[22]** Really? said Lori. Whats curling, exactly? Ive heard of it, but I get it confused with hockey. **[23]** Actually, theres one main similarity, said Andy. Theyre both played indoors, on ice. **[24]** I don't know much about them, said Lori, but Im from South Texas, and we don't have too many ice sports down there! **[25]** Actually, said Andy, its in my blood. Im from Wisconsin, where curling is a well established tradition, and Ive played it since I was ten. **[26]** In fact, he continued, its been around since the 1800's, thanks to Scottish immigrants who brought the sport over with them. **[27]** Thats interesting, but how do you play it? asked Lori. **[28]** "It's not too complicated, as long as you don't let go of your stone," explained Andy. **[29]** Thats a round stone with a handle that you slide as far as possible across the rink toward the center of a circle, called the bottom. **[30]** Oh, I see! exclaimed Lori. It's a bit like shuffleboard, isnt it?

D. Writing Sentences with Brackets and Parentheses

The following sentences contain errors in the use of brackets and parentheses. Write the sentences, correcting the errors.

31. During the nineteenth century, novelist George Eliot pen name of Mary Ann Evans 1819–1880 wrote some of English literature's most important works.

MECHANICS

32. John Singer Sargent 1856–1925 was a prominent American painter of portraits and landscapes.

33. Fill in the entire application form type or print.

34. A common greeting among friends in France is "Salut!" pronounced sa-loo.

35. One of the nineteenth century's most eloquent defenders of civil rights was Frederick Douglass 1817–1895.

Writing Application

Using Quotation Marks in a Report

Using Correct Punctuation Your class is taking a survey of people's reading habits. Interview at least five people, and based on the information you gather, write a brief report about people and their reading habits. In your report, use underlining and quotation marks correctly.

Prewriting First, think of questions to ask. These questions could be about what, how often, when, and why people read. Next, select at least five people to interview. Record the name, age, and occupation of each person. As you conduct your interviews, write down or tape-record what people say. If you want to tape the interview, be sure to ask the interviewee for permission to do so. Jot down some notes to help you organize your information.

Writing In the first paragraph of your rough draft, include a statement that summarizes the main idea of your project and findings. Then, use people's answers to your survey questions to support your main idea.

Revising After you have finished your rough draft, take another look at your main idea. Add, cut, or rearrange details to present your findings clearly. State your conclusions in the last paragraph of your report.

Publishing Proofread your report for any errors in grammar, usage, and mechanics. Be sure that you have correctly used quotation marks and underlining for titles. You and your classmates may want to collect your reports in a binder or create multimedia presentations based on your findings.

Spelling

Improving Your Spelling

Diagnostic Preview

Proofreading for Misspelled Words and Words Often Confused

Identify and correct the errors in the following sentences.

EXAMPLE **1.** If you go too the store, pick up some of those lovly pears.

1. too—to, lovly—lovely

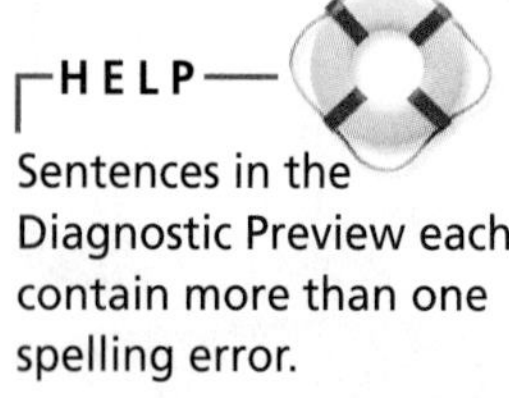

HELP—

Sentences in the Diagnostic Preview each contain more than one spelling error.

1. "Does a mature elephant wiegh more then a ton?" Andy asked Roseanne at the zoo.

2. "Your finally coming home!" my young sister happyly shouted over the phone.

3. They're plan to hold a fund-raiser met with the school board's approveal.

4. Our mother and father are very industryous people, and they are good parents, to.

5. Dr. Silvana adviced us to work harder weather we wanted to or not.

6. The editor in chiefs of the major newspapers met last Tuesday and agreed on a clear coarse of action to deal with the strike.

7. The Gobi, a large dessert in Asia, stretches across vast planes in China and Mongolia.

8. Our principle, Ms. Rios, who moved here last year, was formally the superintendent of schools in her hometown.

9. As long as the meaning of this paragraph is clear, it will be unecessary to change the paragraphs that preceed it.
10. The whether in the mountains can change several times dayly, so be prepared.

Good Spelling Habits

As your vocabulary grows, you may have difficulty spelling some new words. You can improve your spelling by using the following methods.

1. ***Pronounce words correctly.*** Pronouncing words carefully can often help you to spell them correctly.

EXAMPLES athlete: ath•lete [not *ath•e•lete*]

probably: prob•a•bly [not *pro•bly*]

library: li•brar•y [not *li•bar•y*]

2. ***Spell by syllables.*** When you have trouble spelling long words, divide them into syllables. A ***syllable*** is a word part that is pronounced as one uninterrupted sound.

EXAMPLES gymnasium: gym•na•si•um [four syllables]

representative: rep•re•sent•a•tive [five syllables]

Learning to spell the syllables of a word one at a time will help you master the spelling of the whole word.

3. ***Use a dictionary.*** When you are not sure about the spelling of a word, look it up in a dictionary. A dictionary will also tell you the correct pronunciations and syllable divisions of words.

4. ***Keep a spelling notebook.*** The best way to master words that give you difficulty is to list the words and review them frequently. Divide each page of a notebook into four columns.

COLUMN 1 Correctly write the words you frequently misspell.

COLUMN 2 Write the words again, dividing them into syllables and marking the accents. (If you are not sure how to do this, use a dictionary.)

STYLE TIP

In some names, marks that show how to say the word are as important as the letters are.

PEOPLE

Gréban	Jiménez
Luís	Döbereiner
Dvořák	Bjørn

PLACES

Alençon	Bâle
Cáceres	Espíritu Santo
El Faiyûm	João Pessoa

If you are not sure about the spelling of a name, ask the person with that name or look it up in a dictionary.

COLUMN 3	Write the words again, circling the parts that give you trouble.
COLUMN 4	Jot down any comments that may help you remember the correct spelling.

EXAMPLE

Correct Spelling	Syllables and Accents	Trouble Spot	Comments
escape	es•cape′	e(sc)ape	Pronounce correctly.
calendar	cal′•en•dar	calend(a)r	Think of days marked on the calendar.
casually	cas′•u•al•ly	casua(ll)y	Study rule 25e.

5. ***Proofread for careless spelling errors.*** Whenever you write, proofread your paper carefully for spelling errors and unclear letters. By slowly re-reading what you have written, you can correct careless errors such as uncrossed *t*'s, undotted *i*'s, and crossed *l*'s.

MECHANICS

TIPS & TRICKS

To help you spell words containing *ei* and *ie*, remember this rhyme:
I before *e* except after *c*
or when sounded like *a*,
as in *neighbor* and *weigh*.

If you use this rhyme, remember that "*i* before *e*" refers only to words in which these two letters are in the same syllable and stand for the sound of long e, as in the examples under Rule 25a.

Spelling Rules

ie and *ei*

25a. Write *ie* when the sound is long *e*, except after *c*.

EXAMPLES	ach**ie**ve	bel**ie**ve	ch**ie**f	f**ie**ld	p**ie**ce
	c**ei**ling	conc**ei**t	dec**ei**t	dec**ei**ve	rec**ei**ve
EXCEPTIONS	**ei**ther	l**ei**sure	n**ei**ther		
	prot**ei**n	s**ei**ze	sh**ei**k		

25b. Write *ei* when the sound is not long *e*, especially when the sound is long *a*.

EXAMPLES	for**ei**gn	forf**ei**t	h**ei**ght	sl**ei**gh	th**ei**r
	fr**ei**ght	n**ei**ghbor	r**ei**gn	v**ei**l	w**ei**gh
EXCEPTIONS	anc**ie**nt	consc**ie**nce	effic**ie**nt	sc**ie**nce	
	fr**ie**nd	misch**ie**f	pat**ie**nce	anx**ie**ty	

Exercise 1 Spelling Words with *ie* and *ei*

The following paragraph contains ten words with missing letters. Add the letters *ie* or *ei* to spell each numbered word correctly.

EXAMPLE Many people know **[1]** th____r signs in the Chinese zodiac.
1. their

My [**1**] n____ghbor, Mrs. Yee, told me about the Chinese zodiac signs. Not all Chinese people [**2**] bel____ve in the zodiac. My parents don't, and [**3**] n____ther do I, but I do think it is interesting. The Chinese zodiac is an [**4**] anc____nt set of twelve-year cycles named after different animals. According to Mrs. Yee, the [**5**] ch____f traits in your personality come from your animal sign. At first, I thought this notion was an odd [**6**] conc____t, but it is not hard to understand. For example, a tiger is supposed to [**7**] s____ze opportunities [**8**] f____rcely. That description perfectly fits my brother's [**9**] fr____nd Mike Chen, who was born in 1974. Mrs. Yee showed me a chart like the one on this page so that I could figure out the signs of all [**10**] ____ght members of my family.

–cede, –ceed, and *–sede*

25c. In English, the only word ending in *–sede* is *supersede*. The only words ending in *–ceed* are *exceed, proceed,* and *succeed.* Most other words with this sound end in *–cede.*

EXAMPLES con**cede** inter**cede** pre**cede** re**cede** se**cede**

Exercise 2 **Proofreading for Misspelled Words Ending in *–cede, –ceed,* and *–sede***

Each of the following sentences contains a misspelled word ending in *–cede, –ceed,* or *–sede.* Identify the errors, and spell the words correctly.

EXAMPLE **1.** The guitarist could not procede until the electricity came back on.

1. procede—proceed

1. Clarence Leo Fender succeded in changing the music business in the 1950s.
2. He improved the design of electric guitars, which quickly superceded acoustic guitars in popular music.
3. The great success of Fender's invention probably exceded his wildest dreams.
4. Music critics consede that a new era began with the invention of the electric guitar.
5. Concerts that preceeded Fender's invention were not nearly as loud as modern ones.

Adding Prefixes

Reference Note

Sometimes a prefix is used with a hyphen, as in *self-propelled.* For more about using **hyphens,** see page 675.

A ***prefix*** is a letter or group of letters added to the beginning of a word to create a different meaning.

EXAMPLES dis + honest = **dis**honest

un + selfish = **un**selfish

25d. When adding a prefix to a word, do not change the spelling of the word itself.

EXAMPLES mis + spell = mis**spell** over + rate = over**rate**

Exercise 3 **Spelling Words with Prefixes**

Spell each of the following words, adding the prefix given.

EXAMPLE **1.** un + wrap

1. unwrap

1. im + migrate
2. re + settle
3. un + certain
4. il + legal
5. semi + circle
6. in + sight
7. re + action
8. un + known
9. dis + belief
10. semi + finalist

Adding Suffixes

A ***suffix*** is a letter or group of letters added to the end of a word to create a different meaning.

EXAMPLES stay + ing = stay**ing**

comfort + able = comfort**able**

walk + ed = walk**ed**

25e. When adding the suffix *–ly* or *–ness* to a word, do not change the spelling of the word itself.

EXAMPLES slow + ly = **slow**ly dark + ness = **dark**ness

usual + ly = **usual**ly late + ness = **late**ness

shy + ly = **shy**ly shy + ness = **shy**ness

EXCEPTIONS For words that end in *y* and have more than one syllable, change the *y* to *i* before adding *–ly* or *–ness.*

happy + ly = happ**ily** lazy + ness = laz**iness**

25f. Drop the final silent e before adding a suffix beginning with a vowel.

EXAMPLES line + ing = **lin**ing

approve + al = **approv**al

EXCEPTIONS Keep the final silent e

- in a word ending in *ce* or *ge* before adding a suffix beginning with *a* or *o:*

  trace + able = tra**ceable**

  courage + ous = coura**geous**

- in *dye* before *–ing:* dy**eing**
- in *mile* before *–age:* mil**eage**

25g. Keep the final silent e before adding a suffix beginning with a consonant.

EXAMPLES hope + less = hop**e**less care + ful = car**e**ful

awe + some = aw**e**some love + ly = lov**e**ly

nine + ty = nin**e**ty amuse + ment = amus**e**ment

EXCEPTIONS nine + th = **nin**th argue + ment = **argu**ment

true + ly = **tru**ly whole + ly = **whol**ly

awe + ful = **aw**ful

Exercise 4 Spelling Words with Suffixes

Spell each of the following words, adding the suffix given.

EXAMPLE **1.** hope + ful

1. hopeful

1. natural + ly
2. adore + able
3. sure + ly
4. dry + ness
5. tease + ing
6. lucky + ly
7. tune + ful
8. notice + able
9. confine + ment
10. advantage + ous

25h. For words ending in *y* preceded by a consonant, change the *y* to *i* before any suffix that does not begin with *i.*

EXAMPLES cry + ed = cr**ied** duty + ful = dut**iful**

easy + ly = eas**ily** try + ing = tr**ying**

25i. For words ending in *y* preceded by a vowel, keep the *y* when adding a suffix.

EXAMPLES pray + ing = pra**ying** pay + ment = pa**yment**

obey + ed = obe**yed** boy + ish = bo**yish**

EXCEPTIONS day + ly = da**ily** lay + ed = la**id**

pay + ed = pa**id** say + ed = sa**id**

25j. Double the final consonant before adding a suffix beginning with a vowel if the word (1) has only one syllable or has the accent on the last syllable and (2) ends in a single consonant preceded by a single vowel.

EXAMPLES sit + ing = si**tt**ing refer + ed = refe**rr**ed

swim + er = swi**mm**er begin + er = begi**nn**er

drop + ed = dro**pp**ed forbid + en = forbi**dd**en

MECHANICS

Otherwise, the final consonant is usually not doubled before a suffix beginning with a vowel.

EXAMPLES sing + er = sin**g**er   final + ist = fina**l**ist

speak + ing = spea**k**ing   center + ed = cente**r**ed

NOTE In some cases, the final consonant may or may not be doubled.

EXAMPLES cancel + ed = cance**l**ed *or* cance**ll**ed

travel + er = trave**l**er *or* trave**ll**er

Most dictionaries list all the spellings above as correct.

HELP—
When you are not sure about the spelling of a word, it is best to look it up in a dictionary.

Exercise 5 Spelling Words with Suffixes

Spell each of the following words, adding the suffix given.

EXAMPLE **1.** study + ed
1. studied

1. tiny + est
2. trim + ing
3. dry + ing
4. pity + ful
5. display + ed
6. enjoy + ment
7. refer + al
8. jog + er
9. submit + ing
10. win + er

Review A Proofreading for Misspelled Words

Most of the following sentences contain a spelling error. Identify and correct each error. If a sentence is already correct, write *C.*

EXAMPLE **1.** The man shown on the next page is not Sam Houston or Jim Bowie, but he is a certifyed Texas hero.
1. certifyed—certified

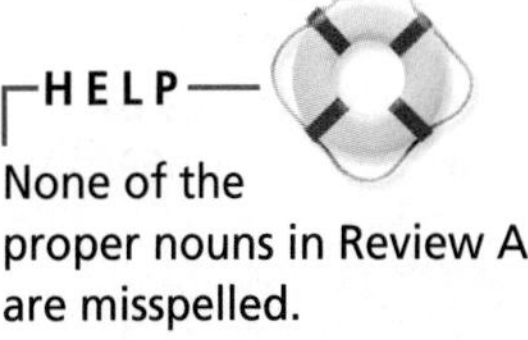

HELP—
None of the proper nouns in Review A are misspelled.

1. This industryous blacksmith is William Goyens.
2. In 1820, he moved from North Carolina to Texas, where he succeded in several businesses.
3. Goyens acheived his greatest fame as a negotiator with the Comanche and the Cherokee peoples.
4. He easily made freinds with the American Indians who traded in the small town of Nacogdoches.

William Goyens, tinted print (1820s). Courtesy of Hendrick-Long Publishing Co.

HELP
Make sure that you do not confuse the plural form of a noun with its possessive form. Generally, you should not use an apostrophe to form the plural of a word.

MECHANICS

Reference Note
For a discussion of **possessive forms of nouns,** see page 669.

5. Later, he assisted the Mexican government and then the Texas army in makking peace with their American Indian neighbors.
6. General Sam Houston asked Goyens to interceed on behalf of the settlers.
7. Because of Goyens's efforts, the Comanches and Cherokees agreed to remain on peacful terms with the settlers.
8. In addition to negotiating peace treaties, Goyens studyed law to protect his own and others' freedoms.
9. People started coming to him with their legal problems, and he unselfishly tried to help them.
10. William Goyens was truely an important force in shaping Texas history.

Forming the Plurals of Nouns

25k. To form the plurals of most nouns in English, add *s.*

SINGULAR	pest	isle	blue	opera	Taylor
PLURAL	pest**s**	isle**s**	blue**s**	opera**s**	Taylor**s**

25l. For nouns ending in *s, x, z, ch,* or *sh,* add *es.*

SINGULAR	gas	box	waltz	wrench	wish	Paz
PLURAL	gas**es**	box**es**	waltz**es**	wrench**es**	wish**es**	Paz**es**

NOTE Some one-syllable words ending in *z* double the final consonant when forming plurals.

EXAMPLES quiz fez
quiz**zes** fez**zes**

Exercise 6 Spelling the Plural Forms of Nouns

Spell the plural form of each of the following nouns.

EXAMPLE **1.** right
1. rights

1. dish
2. plumber
3. candle
4. watch
5. address
6. march
7. parade
8. republic
9. Gómez
10. tax

25m. **For nouns ending in *y* preceded by a vowel, add *s*.**

SINGULAR	valley	weekday	boy	journey	Murray
PLURAL	valley**s**	weekday**s**	boy**s**	journey**s**	Murray**s**

25n. **For nouns ending in *y* preceded by a consonant, change the *y* to *i* and add *es*.**

SINGULAR	puppy	library	lily	navy	story
PLURAL	pupp**ies**	librar**ies**	lil**ies**	nav**ies**	stor**ies**

EXCEPTIONS For proper nouns, add *s*.

Kennedy—Kennedy**s** Curry—Curry**s**

25o. **For some nouns ending in *f* or *fe*, add *s*. For others, change the *f* or *fe* to *v* and add *es*.**

SINGULAR	roof	sheriff	giraffe	knife	thief
PLURAL	roof**s**	sheriff**s**	giraffe**s**	kni**ves**	thie**ves**

HELP—When you are not sure about how to spell the plural of a noun ending in *f* or *fe*, look it up in a dictionary.

25p. **For nouns ending in *o* preceded by a vowel, add *s*.**

SINGULAR	radio	ratio	video	igloo	Romeo
PLURAL	radio**s**	ratio**s**	video**s**	igloo**s**	Romeo**s**

25q. **For nouns ending in *o* preceded by a consonant, add *es*.**

SINGULAR	tomato	potato	echo	hero
PLURAL	tomato**es**	potato**es**	echo**es**	hero**es**

EXCEPTIONS For musical terms and proper nouns, add *s*.

piano—piano**s** soprano—soprano**s**
solo—solo**s** Nakamoto—Nakamoto**s**

NOTE To form the plural of some nouns ending in *o* preceded by a consonant, you may add either *s* or *es*.

SINGULAR	domino	mosquito	banjo	flamingo
PLURAL	domino**s**	mosquito**s**	banjo**s**	flamingo**s**
	or	*or*	*or*	*or*
	domino**es**	mosquito**es**	banjo**es**	flamingo**es**

HELP—When you are in doubt about the way to form the plural of a noun ending in *o* preceded by a consonant, check the spelling in a dictionary.

25r. **Some nouns have irregular plural forms.**

SINGULAR	ox	goose	foot	tooth	child	mouse
PLURAL	ox**en**	g**ee**se	f**ee**t	t**ee**th	child**ren**	m**ice**

Reference Note

For more information on **compound nouns,** see page 346.

STYLE TIP

In your reading, you may notice that some writers do not use apostrophes to form the plurals of numerals, capital letters, symbols, and words used as words.

EXAMPLES

Their music is as popular today as it was in the **1970s.**

When dividing, remember to write ***Rs*** before the remainders in the quotients.

However, using an apostrophe is not wrong and may be necessary for clarity. Therefore, it is better to use the apostrophe.

HELP

Some words in Exercise 7 have more than one correct plural form. You need to give only one form for each word. You may want to use a dictionary to check your work.

MECHANICS

25s. For most compound nouns, form the plural of the last word in the compound.

SINGULAR	bookshelf	pull-up	blue jay	four-year-old
PLURAL	bookshel**ves**	pull-up**s**	blue jay**s**	four-year-old**s**

25t. For compound nouns in which one of the words is modified by the other word or words, form the plural of the word modified.

SINGULAR	sister-in-law	guest of honor	ninth-grader
PLURAL	sister**s**-in-law	guest**s** of honor	ninth-grader**s**

25u. For some nouns, the singular and the plural forms are the same.

SINGULAR AND PLURAL	aircraft	sheep
	deer	Sioux
	moose	Vietnamese

25v. For numerals, letters, symbols, and words used as words, add an apostrophe and *s*.

EXAMPLES The product of two ***4*'s** is twice the sum of four ***2*'s**.

Notice that the word *Mississippi* has four ***i*'s**, four ***s*'s**, and two ***p*'s**.

Write **$'s** before, not after, amounts of money.

This composition contains many ***us*'s** and ***them*'s**.

Exercise 7 Spelling the Plurals of Nouns

Spell the plural form of each of the following nouns.

EXAMPLE **1.** volcano

1. volcanoes or *volcanos*

1. monkey	**8.** child	**15.** drive-in
2. trophy	**9.** cargo	**16.** *t*
3. Massey	**10.** woman	**17.** salmon
4. diary	**11.** mother-in-law	**18.** spoonful
5. hoof	**12.** sit-up	**19.** @
6. proof	**13.** *8*	**20.** *him*
7. palomino	**14.** trout	

Spelling Numbers

25w. Spell out a number that begins a sentence.

EXAMPLE **Fifteen thousand** tickets to the Milton Nascimento concert went on sale.

25x. In a sentence, spell out numbers that can be written in one or two words. Use numerals for other numbers.

EXAMPLES Do you have **two** nickels for **one** dime?

Our school's concert band has **twenty-six** members.

The movie theater has **270** seats.

NOTE If you use several numbers, some short and some long, write them all the same way. Usually, it is better to write them all as numerals.

INCORRECT We sold eighty-six tickets to the fall dance and 121 tickets to the spring dance.

CORRECT We sold **86** tickets to the fall dance and **121** tickets to the spring dance.

25y. Spell out numbers used to indicate order.

EXAMPLE Our team placed **third** [not *3rd*] in the regional track meet this season.

Exercise 8 Spelling Numbers

Write each of the following sentences correctly. If a sentence is already correct, write *C*.

EXAMPLE **1.** 3 quarters were sitting on the table.

1. Three quarters were sitting on the table.

1. David was scheduled to be the 4th speaker at the banquet.
2. Kerry counted 349 pennies in her penny jar.
3. The new cafeteria had a capacity of over 300 people.
4. Shannon correctly answered 96 of the 125 items on the test.
5. 1286 tickets were sold for the weekend performances of the senior play.

Words Often Confused

Reference Note

If there is a word you cannot find in the following list, refer to the Glossary of Usage, Chapter 21, or look up the word in a dictionary.

People frequently confuse the words in each of the following groups. Some of these words are ***homonyms.*** The pronunciations of homonyms are the same, but their meanings and spellings are different. Others have the same or similar spellings but have different meanings.

accept	[verb] *to receive with consent; to give approval to* In 1964, Dr. Martin Luther King, Jr., *accepted* the Nobel Prize for peace.
except	[verb] *to leave out from a group;* [preposition] *other than; but* We were *excepted* from the requirement. Everyone *except* Ruben will be there.
advice	[noun] *a recommendation about a course of action* *Advice* may be easy to give but hard to follow.
advise	[verb] *to recommend a course of action; to give advice* I *advise* you to continue your music lessons.
affect	[verb] *to influence; to produce an effect upon* The eruption of Krakatau *affected* the sunsets all over the world.
effect	[noun] *the result of an action; consequence* The phases of the moon have an *effect* on the tides of the earth's oceans.
all ready	[adjective] *all prepared* The players are *all ready* for the big game in San Diego next week.
already	[adverb] *previously* Our class has *already* taken two field trips.
all right	[adjective] *satisfactory;* [adverb] *satisfactorily* Was my answer *all right*? Maria did *all right* in the track meet.

HELP

All right should be written as two words. The spelling *alright* is not standard English.

MECHANICS

Exercise 9 Using Words Often Confused

From the choices in parentheses, select the correct word or words for each of the following sentences.

EXAMPLE **1.** Anh and her family are (*all ready, already*) to celebrate Tet, the Vietnamese New Year.

1. *all ready*

1. Do you think my work is (*all right, alright*)?
2. The (*affect, effect*) of the victory was startling.
3. The scientists were (*all ready, already*) to watch the launching of the rocket.
4. Whose (*advice, advise*) are you going to take?
5. The coach (*advices, advises*) us to stick to the training rules.
6. Why did you (*accept, except*) Carla from the rule?
7. Her weeks of practice have finally (*affected, effected*) her game.
8. Juan has (*all ready, already*) learned how to water-ski.
9. The president offered most of the rebels a full pardon, which they (*accepted, excepted*), but the leaders were (*accepted, excepted*) from the offer.
10. Gabriel took my (*advice, advise*) and visited the home of Frederick Douglass in Washington, D.C.

altar	[noun] *a table for a religious ceremony* The *altar* was covered with lilies.
alter	[verb] *to change* The outcome of the election may *alter* the mayor's plan.
all together	[adjective] *in the same place;* [adverb] *at the same time* The family was *all together* then. Please sing *all together*, everybody.
altogether	[adverb] *entirely* Nishi seemed *altogether* thrilled to see us.
brake	[noun] *a device to stop a machine* Can you fix the *brake* on my bicycle?
break	[verb] *to fracture; to shatter* A high-pitched noise can *break* glass.

(continued)

COMPUTER TIP

Most word-processing programs have a spellchecker that can help you catch spelling mistakes. Remember, though, that a computer's spellchecker cannot point out homonyms that are used incorrectly. For example, if you use *affect* where you should use *effect*, the computer probably will not catch the mistake. Learn how to proofread your own writing, and never rely entirely on a spellchecker.

TIPS & TRICKS

To remember how to spell *capitol*, use this memory aid: There's a d**o**me on the capit**o**l.

(continued)

capital	[noun] *a city; the seat of a government* Olympia is the *capital* of Washington.
capitol	[noun] *building; statehouse* Where is the *capitol* in Albany?
choose	[verb; rhymes with *whose*] *to select* Did you *choose* speech or art as your elective?
chose	[verb; past tense of *choose*, rhymes with *grows*] *selected* Sara *chose* a red pen, not a blue one.

FRANK & ERNEST reprinted by permission of Newspaper Enterprise Association, Inc.

MECHANICS

Exercise 10 Using Words Often Confused

From the choices in parentheses, select the correct word or words for each of the following sentences.

EXAMPLE 1. Mr. Conway said he (*choose, chose*) teaching as a career because he wants to help young people.

1. *chose*

1. The building with the dome is the (*capital, capitol*).
2. By working (*all together, altogether*), we can succeed.
3. Alma (*choose, chose*) a difficult part in the school play.
4. Be careful not to (*brake, break*) those dishes.
5. That book is (*all together, altogether*) too complicated.
6. The candles on the (*altar, alter*) glowed beautifully.
7. Why did you (*choose, chose*) that one?
8. A car without a good emergency (*brake, break*) is a menace to pedestrians and other vehicles.
9. Will Carrie's accident (*altar, alter*) her plans?
10. Tallahassee is the (*capital, capitol*) of Florida.

clothes	[noun] *wearing apparel* One can learn much about a historical period by studying its styles of *clothes.*
cloths	[noun] *pieces of fabric* Some cleaning *cloths* are in the drawer.
coarse	[adjective] *rough; crude* The beach is covered with *coarse* brown sand.
course	[noun] *path of action; unit of study; route;* [also used in the expression *of course*] If you follow that *course,* you'll succeed. My mother is taking a *course* in accounting. The wind blew the ship slightly off its *course.* You know, of *course,* that I'm right.
complement	[noun] *something that completes or makes perfect;* [verb] *to complete or make perfect* The chef's kitchen features a full *complement* of appliances. The white tulips *complemented* the crystal vase.
compliment	[noun] *a remark that expresses approval, praise, or admiration;* [verb] *to praise someone* Mrs. Chung paid Miranda a *compliment* on her model of Notre Dame. The ambassador *complimented* Agent Makowski on her quick thinking.
consul	[noun] *a representative of a government in a foreign country* Who is the Guatemalan *consul* in Miami?
council	[noun] *a group of people who meet together* The mayor called a meeting of the city *council.*
counsel	[noun] *advice;* [verb] *to give advice* When choosing a career, seek *counsel* from your teachers. Ms. Jiménez *counseled* me to pursue a career in teaching.

(continued)

TIPS & TRICKS

You can remember the difference in spelling between *complement* and *compliment* by remembering that a compl**e**ment compl**e**tes a sentence.

MECHANICS

(continued)

councilor	[noun] *member of a council* The *councilors* discussed several issues.
counselor	[noun] *one who advises* Who is your guidance *counselor*?
desert	[noun, pronounced des′•ert] *a dry, sandy region* The Sahara is the largest *desert* in Africa.
desert	[verb, pronounced de•sert′] *to abandon; to leave* Most dogs will not *desert* a friend in trouble.
dessert	[noun, pronounced des•sert′] *the sweet, final course of a meal* Fruit salad is my favorite *dessert.*

Exercise 11 Using Words Often Confused

From the choices in parentheses, select the correct word for each of the following sentences.

EXAMPLE 1. Egypt, of (*course, coarse*), is an ancient country in northeastern Africa.

1. *course*

1. The student (*council, counsel*) voted to have "A Night on the Nile" as its dance theme.
2. In this photograph, many shoppers at an Egyptian market wear Western (*clothes, cloths*).

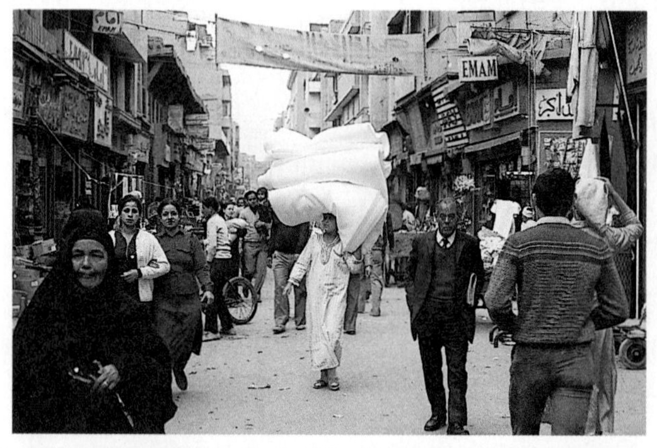

3. Others wear traditional garments, including (*clothes, cloths*) called *kaffiyehs* wrapped loosely around their heads.
4. In ancient Egypt, pharaohs did not always follow the advice of their friends and other wise (*councilors, counselors*).
5. The surfaces of some famous Egyptian monuments look (*coarse, course*) from years of exposure to wind and sand.

MECHANICS

6. In my geography (*coarse, course*), I learned that Nubians make up the largest minority group in Egypt's population.
7. The U.S. (*consul, council*) in Cairo welcomed the vice-president to Egypt.
8. Camels did not (*desert, dessert*) their owners when they crossed the Egyptian (*desert, dessert*).
9. Figs, grapes, and dates have been popular (*deserts, desserts*) in Egypt for a long time.
10. In Cairo, the confused tourists looked to their tour director for (*council, counsel*).

formally	[adverb] *with dignity; according to strict rules or procedures* The mayor delivered the speech *formally.*
formerly	[adverb] *previously; in the past* Adele Zubalsky was *formerly* the principal of the school.
hear	[verb] *to receive sounds through the ears* Dogs can *hear* sounds that people can't *hear.*
here	[adverb] *in this place* The treasure is buried *here.*
its	[possessive form of *it*] *belonging to it* Mount Fuji is noted for *its* beauty.
it's	[contraction of *it is* or *it has*] *It's* [It is] a good idea to relax. *It's* [It has] been a long time.
lead	[verb, rhymes with *feed*] *to go first; to be a leader* A small town in New Hampshire often *leads* the nation in filing its election returns.
led	[verb, past tense of *lead*] *went first* Mr. Tanaka *led* the scout troop back to camp.
lead	[noun, rhymes with *red*] *a heavy metal; graphite in a pencil* Many fishing nets are weighted with *lead* to hold them to the sea bottom. Is your mechanical pencil out of *lead*?

(continued)

MECHANICS

(continued)

loose	[adjective, rhymes with *moose*] ***not securely attached; not fitting tightly*** If the knot is too *loose,* the piñata will fall out of the tree.
lose	[verb, rhymes with *whose*] ***to suffer loss*** Vegetables *lose* some of their vitamins when they are cooked.

Exercise 12 Using Words Often Confused

From the choices in parentheses, select the correct word for each of the following sentences.

EXAMPLE **1.** Mary Beth did not (*loose, lose*) her Southern accent even after she moved to Boston.

1. lose

1. According to Ethan's map, (*its, it's*) a very long way from (*hear, here*) to the park.
2. The ancient Chinese, Greeks, and Romans used (*lead, led*) in their coins.
3. If you don't wait (*hear, here*), we may (*loose, lose*) you in the crowd.
4. "Before the club takes up any new business," said Mr. Burr, "the secretary (*formally, formerly*) reads the minutes of the previous meeting."
5. (*Its, It's*) too bad that the oak tree has lost (*its, it's*) leaves so early in the season.
6. Didn't you (*hear, here*) me, Charlotte? Come over (*hear, here*) right now!
7. The Chipmunks were ten runs behind, and it seemed certain that they were going to (*loose, lose*).
8. Venus Williams (*lead, led*) after the first set of the tennis match at the U.S. Open.
9. Our new mayor, Mr. Brown, was (*formally, formerly*) an actor but has been in politics for ten years now.
10. That (*loose, lose*) bolt could cause trouble if we have to fly during a storm.

passed	[verb, past tense of *pass*] *went by* The people in the car waved as they *passed* us.
past	[noun] *that which has gone by;* [preposition] *beyond;* [adjective] *ended* Some people long to live in the *past.* They walked *past* the dozing guard. He forgot his *past* concerns.
peace	[noun] *security and quiet order* We are striving for *peace* and prosperity.
piece	[noun] *a part of something* Some people can catch fish with a pole, a *piece* of string, and a bent pin.
plain	[adjective] *simple, common, unadorned;* [noun] *a flat area of land* The actors wore *plain* costumes. What is the difference between a prairie and a *plain*?
plane	[noun] *a tool; an airplane; a flat surface* The *plane* is useful in the carpenter's trade. Four single-engine *planes* are in the hangar. In geometry class, we learned how to measure the angles of *planes* such as squares and triangles.
principal	[noun] *the head of a school;* [adjective] *main or most important* The *principal* of the school is Mr. Arimoto. What are the *principal* exports of Brazil?
principle	[noun] *a rule of conduct; a main fact or law* Judge Rios is a woman of high *principle.* We discussed some of the basic *principles* of democracy.
quiet	[adjective] *still and peaceful; without noise* Let's find a *quiet* room so that we can study.
quite	[adverb] *wholly or entirely; to a great extent* Winters in New England can be *quite* severe.

Here's a way to remember the difference between *peace* and *piece*: You eat a p**ie**ce of p**ie.**

TIPS & TRICKS

Here is an easy way to remember the difference between *principal* and *principle:* The princi**pal** is your **pal.**

MECHANICS

Exercise 13 Using Words Often Confused

From the choices in parentheses, select the correct word for each of the following sentences.

EXAMPLE **1.** Summer (*passed, past*) by too quickly!
1. passed

1. In some Filipino villages, you can still find (*plain, plane*), practical houses built on bamboo stilts.
2. The summer was not (*quiet, quite*) over before the beginning of school brought a (*quiet, quite*) household once more.
3. This is a main (*principal, principle*) in mathematics.
4. On July 11, 1991, the moon (*passed, past*) between the earth and the sun, causing a total solar eclipse.
5. A (*plain, plane*) is a useful tool.
6. Save me a (*peace, piece*) of that blueberry pie.
7. The new (*principal, principle*) used to be a student here.
8. You can learn much from the (*passed, past*), Eduardo.
9. After the long war came a long period of (*peace, piece*).
10. Cattle were grazing on the (*plains, planes*).

shone	[verb, past tense of *shine*] *gleamed; glowed* The Navajo jeweler polished the silver-and-turquoise ring until it *shone.*
shown	[verb, past participle of *show*] *revealed* A model of the new school will be *shown* to the public next week.
stationary	[adjective] *in a fixed position* Most of the furnishings of a space station must be *stationary.*
stationery	[noun] *writing paper* I need a new box of *stationery.*
than	[conjunction used for comparisons] The Amazon River is longer *than* the Mississippi River.
then	[adverb] *at that time* If the baby is awake by four o'clock, we will leave *then.*

TIPS & TRICKS

Here is an easy way to remember the difference between *stationary* and *stationery*: You write a lett**er** on station**er**y.

MECHANICS

their	[possessive form of *they*] ***belonging to them*** *Their* team seems very skillful.
there	[adverb] ***at or in that place;*** [also used to begin a sentence] Go *there* in the fall when the leaves are turning. *There* were no objections.
they're	[contraction of *they are*] *They're* rehearsing for a summer production of *A Soldier's Story.*
threw	[verb, past tense of *throw*] ***tossed, pitched*** Our relief pitcher *threw* nine strikes in succession.
through	[preposition] ***in one side and out the other side, across*** The ship went *through* the series of locks in the Panama Canal.

Exercise 14 Using Words Often Confused

From the choices in parentheses, select the correct word for each of the following sentences.

EXAMPLE 1. (*There, Their*) are some truly amazing tunnels used for transportation throughout the world.

1. *There*

1. Take a good look at the workers in the photograph on the next page because (*there, they're*) part of history.
2. (*Their, They're*) labor helped link England with France by creating a tunnel under the English Channel.
3. A documentary about the tunnels through the Alps will be (*shone, shown*) at the library.
4. Huge exhaust fans had to be constructed to move the (*stationary, stationery*) air in the Holland Tunnel in New York.
5. To run railroad lines all across the United States, workers had to dig many tunnels (*threw, through*) mountains.
6. Used for blasting tunnels in mountainsides, explosives (*threw, through*) enormous boulders into the air.
7. The warm sun (*shone, shown*) brightly on the snowy top of Mont Blanc, but in the mountain's tunnel it was dark and chilly.

8. We rode the underground, or subway, into London, where I bought some (*stationary, stationery*).
9. Boston's subway is older (*than, then*) New York City's subway.
10. In Paris, we took the subway, called the *métro,* to the Eiffel Tower and (*than, then*) to the Louvre museum.

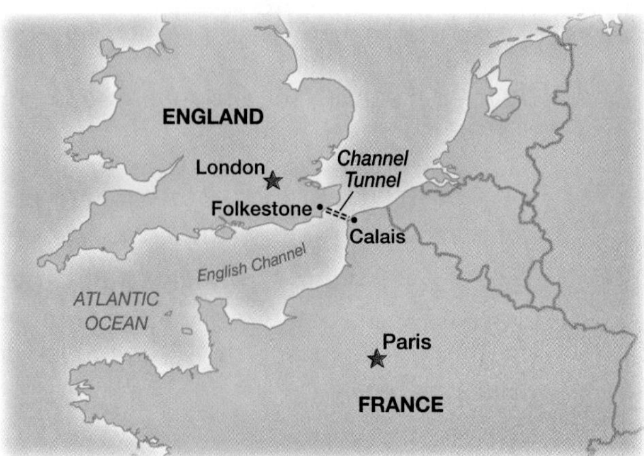

to	[preposition] *in the direction of; toward* [also part of the infinitive form of a verb] Marco Polo began his trip *to* China in 1271. Do you know how *to* make tortillas?
too	[adverb] *also; more than enough* We have lived in Iowa and in Alaska, *too.* It is *too* cold for rain today.
two	[noun] *cardinal number between one and three;* [adjective] *one more than one* I've got *two* of their CDs. She borrowed *two* dollars from me.
waist	[noun] *the middle part of the body* These pants are too big in the *waist.*
waste	[noun] *unused material;* [verb] *to squander* Most of the *waste* can be recycled. Don't *waste* your money on popcorn and soda.
weak	[adjective] *not strong; feeble* The patient is too *weak* to have visitors.
week	[noun] *seven days* Josh's bar mitzvah is planned for next *week.*

weather	[noun] *condition of the air or atmosphere* The *weather* is hot and humid.
whether	[conjunction] *if* Jessica wondered *whether* she should go.
who's	[contraction of *who is* or *who has*] *Who's* [Who is] representing the yearbook staff? *Who's* [Who has] read today's newspaper?
whose	[possessive form of *who*] *belonging to whom* *Whose* report are we hearing today?
your	[possessive form of *you*] *belonging to you* *Your* work in math is improving.
you're	[contraction of *you are*] *You're* right on time!

Exercise 15 Using Words Often Confused

From the choices in parentheses, select the correct word for each of the following sentences.

EXAMPLE 1. (*Your, You're*) class gets to visit Minnehaha Park in Minneapolis.

1. *Your*

1. Jason felt (*weak, week*) after skiing all day in the Sangre de Cristo Mountains of New Mexico.
2. (*Weather, Whether*) we'll go to the park or not depends on the (*weather, whether*).
3. (*Whose, Who's*) books are you carrying?
4. Find out (*whose, who's*) going to the annual football banquet if you can.
5. Learning (*to, too, two*) roll carved sticks for the Korean game of *yut* wasn't (*to, too, two*) difficult.
6. (*Your, You're*) off your course, captain.
7. We took (*to, too, two*) (*weaks, weeks*) for our trip to France and Switzerland last summer.
8. Twirl the hoop around your (*waste, waist*).
9. Would you enjoy a trip (*to, too, two*) Mars, Flo?
10. Aren't you using (*your, you're*) compass?

Review B Proofreading for Words Often Confused

Identify and correct each error in words often confused in the following sentences.

EXAMPLE 1. Anne Shirley, here portrayed by actress Megan Follows, found a pieceful life and a loving family on Prince Edward Island.

1. *pieceful—peaceful*

1. Does the scenery shone in the picture on this page appeal to you?
2. My family enjoyed the green hillsides and rugged seashore during our two-weak vacation there last summer.
3. Prince Edward Island is quite a beautiful spot, and its Canada's smallest province.
4. Everyone who lives there calls the island PEI, and now I do, to.
5. During our visit, the weather was quite pleasant, so I lead my parents all over PEI on foot.
6. We walked to several places of interest in Charlottetown, the capitol.
7. I got to chose our first stop, and I selected the farmhouse that's the setting for the novel *Anne of Green Gables.*
8. That novel's main character, Anne Shirley, is someone who's ideas I admire.
9. Walking around "The Garden Province," we passed many farms; the principle crop is potatoes.
10. Take my advise and visit Prince Edward Island if you get the chance.

Chapter Review

A. Proofreading for Misspelled and Misused Words

Most of the following sentences contain at least one error in spelling or in words often confused. Write the sentences, correcting each error. If a sentence is already correct, write *C*.

HELP
None of the proper nouns in the Chapter Review are misspelled.

1. 15,000 young salmon were released into the river last week by the fishing club.
2. Phil and his family drove one hundred thirty-five miles to visit his cousins.
3. "It is quiet foolish," said Mr. Vohra, "to hope for success but to do nothing."
4. The dog didn't get tired until the 5th time it had run around the house.
5. Finally, we succeded in getting the pig out of the backyard.
6. Last weak I felt ill, but now I'm fine.
7. How adoreable that puppy is!
8. We were relieved to discover that the storm had passed and that everyone was all right.
9. "Woodrow Wilson's most remarkable acheivement," said Mrs. Levine, "was to make a broken promise look like leadership by declaring war after promising piece."
10. Our neighbor, a city council member, agreed to interceed on our behalf.
11. How many waltzs did they dance back in old Vienna?
12. Fewer and fewer Inuit live in iglooes nowadays.
13. They told us the computer books were on one of the bookshelfs at the back.
14. Teddy has two brother-in-laws, and they're both nice.
15. The alter of a church is a table or stand used for religious services.
16. "Closing the deal now would be personally advantagous to you," the sales representative assured us.
17. After the mechanic put in a new alternator, the engine started very easyly.
18. Weren't oxes used in the old days to pull plows?

19. My little brother calls my sisters' boyfriends Romeoes.

20. "How many *n*s are there in *Tennessee*?" asked Kim.

B. Using Words Often Confused

From the choices in parentheses, choose the correct word or words for each of the following sentences.

21. A carelessly thrown baseball can (*brake, break*) a window.

22. New Delhi is the (*capitol, capital*) of India.

23. Turn up the sound so you can (*hear, here*) the program.

24. The car (*past, passed*) us at high speed.

25. We must not (*desert, dessert*) a friend in need.

26. All of the members of the United Nations Security (*Counsel, Council*) voted against intervention.

27. Our (*plain, plane*) finally took off after a two-hour delay.

28. I know that aardvarks eat ants, and I think they eat termites, (*to, two, too*).

29. (*Whose, Who's*) raincoat is on the coat rack?

30. At those prices, buying those new CDs would be a serious (*waist, waste*) of money.

C. Proofreading a Paragraph for Misspelled and Misused Words

Each sentence in the following paragraph contains at least one misspelled or misused word. Correctly write each incorrect word.

[31] My mother, who's birthplace is Alexandria, Virginia, has always wanted to go back there. **[32]** Last year, we finally traveled from our home in the Midwest too see where she was born. **[33]** Strolling around the Old Town section of Alexandria, a beautiful old city just outside Washington, D.C., we past many historic buildings. **[34]** Their were churches, homes, old taverns, and several shops on our tour. **[35]** At a building called Gadsby's Tavern, built in the 1770s, a man dressed in Colonial-era cloths greeted us. **[36]** He was a guide, and he lead us on a tour of the building, which is now a museum. **[37]** As one of the very few eighteenth-century taverns

MECHANICS

remaining in the United States, Gadsby's, he explained, is quiet a special place: George Washington, the Marquis de Lafayette, and Thomas Jefferson were some of the principle visitors. [**38**] When our guide told us that, it didn't take much for us to imagine those famous people climbing up the front steps to the lovly old tavern. [**39**] By the end of the day, Mother had shone us where she was born and had taken us to see the Potomac riverfront. [**40**] She said she would readyly move back to Alexandria, and we completely understood how she felt.

Writing Application

Using Words Correctly in an Essay

Correctly Using Words Often Confused Write a three-paragraph essay on the favorite hobbies of your family or your friends. Use at least five words from the Words Often Confused list in this chapter.

Prewriting First, make a list of family members or friends, and beside each name, write what you know about that person's favorite hobby or pastime. If you're not sure about someone's hobbies, ask him or her. Then, choose at least five words from the Words Often Confused list, and use them in your essay.

Writing As you jot down notes for your first draft, think about ways to organize your information. You could list the information by age of friend or family member, hobbies in common, variety of interests and pastimes, and so on.

Revising Ask a friend or classmate to read your essay. Is each person's hobby or pastime clearly described? Add, cut, or rearrange information to make your essay as clear and descriptive as possible.

Publishing Read through your essay to check for errors in grammar, usage, punctuation, and spelling. Have you used words often confused correctly? You and your classmates may want to share your essays with your class, either by reading them aloud or posting them on a class bulletin board or Web page.

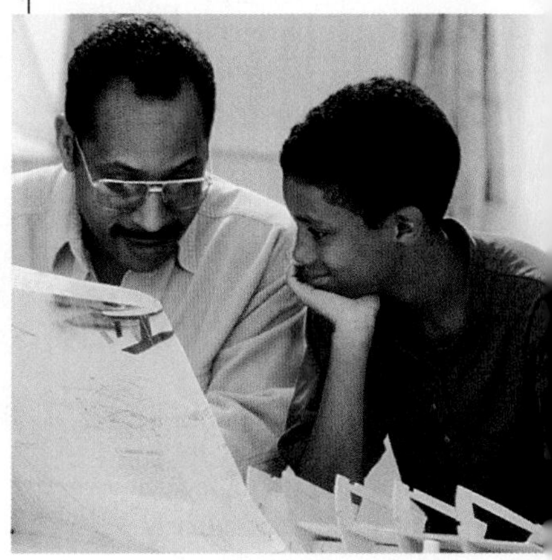

Spelling Words

emade
term
underground
handkerchief
large-scale
gingerbread
furthermore
heart attack
stagecoach
good-natured
headquarters
loudspeaker

- boarder
bard
stationary
principle
palette
stationery
burro
pallet
Capitol
burrow
foul
barred

- programming
refused
omitted
produced
acquired
abilities
submitted
justified
forbidding
petrified
nutrients
resources

- continue
profession
dramatic
despair
awe
professionally
continuous
strenuous
continuously
dramatically
desperately
strenuously

- conscious
excess
bizarre
finely
breadth
persecuted
conscience
prosecuted
futile
access
anecdote
feudal

- inspection
insisted
illustrated
advice
approved
agreeable
investigated
announcement
impressed
accomplished
affectionate
irresponsible

- suite
matinee
blouse
debris
surgeon
embarrassed
chauffeur
croquet
amateur
crochet
plateau
coup

- historic
ragged
magnetic
barefooted
democratic
passionate
rigid
contented
poetic
undersized
metallic
confederate

- symbolic
microphone
generation
cyclone
symptoms
genius
synonyms
generator
synthetic
genes
sympathetic
symphony

- physical
aroma
episode
marathon
chorus
pneumonia
rhythm
labyrinth
melancholy
philosophy
phenomenon
architecture

- chemical
scientists
sonar
instruments
atmosphere
experiments
hemisphere
environment
laser
probability
technological
molecules

- predicting
dictator
supported
verdict
dictionaries
reservation
preservation
conservation
observatory
indictment
emigrate
immigration

- combine
combination
patriots
patriotic
distribute
distribution
repeated
repetition
oblige
obligation
medicine
medicinal

- provisions
international
interview
telescopes
underlying
underneath
profitable
proceeds
intermediate
prosperity
interrupted
intercept

- abstract
transaction
absolute
extravagant
subdued
abolished
translation
submerged
transferred
transient
extraordinary
extraterrestrial

MECHANICS

- hesitate
demonstrate
investigate
delegate
concentrate
mandate
eliminate
advocate
simulate
participate
negotiate
phosphate

- multicolored
magnitude
equality
multitude
microscope
equation
multimedia
equator
microorganism
multicultural
magnificently
equivalent

- scattering
polluted
summoned
satellite
vaccination
intellectual
narrative
penniless
parallel
embassy
exaggerated
torrential

- tourism
loyalty
robbery
uncertainty
patriotism
cruelty
specialty
realism
novelty
optimism
mechanism
criticism

- occupation
obtained
offering
obviously
offensive
opportunity
obscure
occupant
obstacle
opposition
obsessions
occasionally

- perimeter
circumstances
permanently
circumference
perception
intrastate
introvert
perspective
periodic
peripheral
persuaded
circuit

- politics
sophisticated
metropolitan
optic
scholarship
philosopher
optical
optometrist
archaic
automatically
sophomore
archaeologist

- carnival
chipmunk
parakeet
monsoon
hickory
heroic
skeleton
spaghetti
walrus
yacht
macaroni
barbecue

- geographic
astronauts
geology
geometry
supervision
nautical
navigation
odometer
asterisk
altimeter
cosmonauts
seismometer

- spoonerism
malapropism
sequoia
boycott
mackintosh
frankfurter
pasteurize
Braille
Celsius
Fahrenheit
odyssey
zeppelin

- detained
sentimental
productive
deceived
attended
adjustments
justice
acceptable
acceptance
sensation
sensory
perceived

- yearling
diskette
luncheonette
particle
icicle
sapling
banquet
cabinet
bracelet
cassette
pamphlet
statuette

- duplicate
financial
complicated
vocal
conjunction
infinite
vocabulary
vocational
definitely
territorial
juncture
applicable

- igloo
karate
harpoon
kimono
kindergarten
caucus
toboggan
kayak
tundra
persimmon
hibachi
haiku

- historically
favorably
eventually
governmental
fortunately
economically
architectural
sensationally
naturalization
significantly
mysteriously
rhythmically

CHAPTER

Correcting Common Errors

Key Language Skills Review

This chapter reviews key skills and concepts that pose special problems for writers.

- **Sentence Fragments and Run-on Sentences**
- **Subject-Verb and Pronoun-Antecedent Agreement**
- **Verb Forms**
- **Pronoun Forms**
- **Comparison of Modifiers**
- **Misplaced and Dangling Modifiers**
- **Standard Usage**
- **Capitalization**
- **Punctuation—Commas, End Marks, Colons, Semicolons, Quotation Marks, and Apostrophes**
- **Spelling**

Most of the exercises in this chapter follow the same format as the exercises found throughout the grammar, usage, and mechanics sections of this book. You will notice, however, that two sets of review exercises are presented in standardized test formats. These exercises are designed to provide you with practice not only in solving usage and mechanics problems, but also in dealing with these kinds of problems on standardized tests.

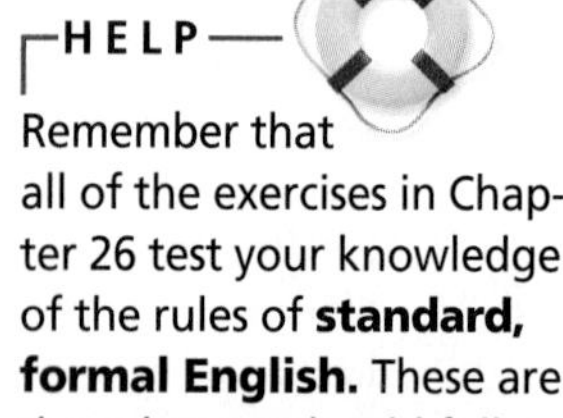

HELP

Remember that all of the exercises in Chapter 26 test your knowledge of the rules of **standard, formal English.** These are the rules you should follow in your school work.

Reference Note

For more about **standard** and **nonstandard English** and **formal** and **informal English,** see page 583.

Exercise 1 Identifying Word Groups as Sentence Fragments or Sentences

Identify each of the following word groups as either a *sentence fragment* or a *sentence.* If the word group is a fragment, correct it by adding or deleting words to make a complete sentence. You may need to change punctuation and capitalization, too.

EXAMPLE 1. Those basketballs over there.

1. Those basketballs over there are for tomorrow's game.

or

Please gather up those basketballs over there.

1. Fourteen years ago today.
2. In 1810, when Miguel Hidalgo started the independence movement in Mexico.
3. Drought and dust plagued Oklahoma and adjoining states in the 1930s.
4. If she decides to become a doctor.
5. Let us see what will happen next.
6. He thinks the 1997 movie about the *Titanic* is the best movie ever made.
7. Running in from the pouring rain.
8. When he wrote the letter to the editor.
9. To keep from using foam cups, my uncle Louis carries a reusable plastic cup.
10. Another example of being environmentally conscious.

HELP—Most of the word groups in Exercise 1 can be correctly revised in more than one way. You need to give only one revision for each word group.

Reference Note

For information on **sentence fragments,** see page 275.

Exercise 2 Correcting Sentence Fragments

Most of the groups of words on the following page are sentence fragments. If a word group is a fragment, correct it either by adding or deleting words to make a complete sentence or by attaching it to a complete sentence. You may need to change the punctuation and capitalization, too. If a word group is already a complete sentence, write *S.*

EXAMPLE 1. The movie about Cleopatra.

1. The movie about Cleopatra is playing downtown.

or

Have you seen the movie about Cleopatra?

HELP—Most of the word groups in Exercise 2 can be correctly revised in more than one way. You need to give only one revision for each word group.

Reference Note

For information on **sentence fragments,** see page 275.

1. Answered the telephone politely.
2. An armadillo's covering of bony plates like armor.
3. Because Alan prefers volleyball to any other team sport.
4. After the first winter snow.
5. Someone gave the museum those photographs of settlers in the Ozarks.
6. When she returns to the house this afternoon.
7. Delivering the package with postage due.
8. The recycling center accepting magazines and catalogs.
9. The kitten walked across the computer keyboard.
10. Moved here from Germany so that she could study at the institute.

HELP—Most of the sentences in Exercise 3 can be correctly revised in more than one way. You need to give only one revision for each sentence.

Reference Note

For information about **run-on sentences,** see page 277.

COMMON ERRORS

Exercise 3 Correcting Run-on Sentences

Correct each of the following run-on sentences by making two separate sentences or by combining the two parts of the run-on sentence to make one complete sentence. Be sure to use capitalization and punctuation correctly.

EXAMPLE 1. Sign language, or manual speech, is not new, in fact, it has a long history.

1. Sign language, or manual speech, is not new; in fact, it has a long history.

or

Sign language, or manual speech, is not new. In fact, it has a long history.

1. Some people may think that manual speech dates from this century the beginnings of manual speech go much further back.
2. An Italian physician played a very important role in the development of manual speech, I had never heard of him.
3. His name was Girolamo Cardano he lived during the sixteenth century.
4. Cardano proposed the theory that people unable to hear could learn to associate written symbols with objects or actions he thought that people who could not hear or speak could then use such symbols to communicate.
5. In the 1700s, Abbé Charles Michel de L'Epée opened the first free school for people with impaired hearing he devised a manual sign version of spoken French.

6. In 1778, Samuel Heinicke began a school in Germany for people unable to hear, it was the first such school to receive government recognition.
7. The first school in the United States for those unable to hear was founded in 1817 its founder was Thomas Hopkins Gallaudet, a minister from Philadelphia.
8. Laurent Clerc was the first deaf person to teach other deaf people in a school in the United States in 1816 he came to the United States to help Gallaudet found the Hartford School for the Deaf.
9. Gallaudet College is in Washington, D.C it is still the world's only liberal arts college specifically for people who are deaf or hard of hearing.
10. Today, American Sign Language is used by at least 500,000 people in the United States and Canada it is the fourth most common language in the United States.

Exercise 4 Correcting Sentence Fragments and Run-on Sentences

The following word groups contain sentence fragments, run-on sentences, and complete sentences. Identify each word group by writing *F* for a fragment, *R* for a run-on, or *S* for a complete sentence. If a word group is a fragment, correct it by adding or deleting words to make a complete sentence. Correct each run-on by making it into two separate sentences or by combining the two parts of the run-on to make one complete sentence. You may also need to change the punctuation and capitalization.

EXAMPLE 1. The old truck drove very slowly up the hill, a long line of cars followed it.

1. *R—The old truck drove very slowly up the hill. A long line of cars followed it.*

or

R—The old truck drove very slowly up the hill, and a long line of cars followed it.

1. One of the most famous photographs taken during World War II shows soldiers raising the U.S. flag at Iwo Jima.
2. I hope to travel to Asia someday, I want to climb the Himalayas.

HELP

Most of the sentences in Exercise 4 can be correctly revised in more than one way. You need to give only one revision for each sentence.

Reference Note

For information on **sentence fragments,** see page 275. For information on **run-on sentences,** see page 277.

3. To uproot the stumps of the trees we cut down in the front yard.
4. Some kinds of spiders, such as the bolas spider, that do not make webs.
5. We played a variety of music from different countries for the dancers.
6. Robin, my best friend since fourth grade.
7. Into the forest and across the valley they rode it took until sundown to reach the camp.
8. When a cicada comes out of the ground.
9. My mother's favorite movie is about the composer Mozart, I can't remember its title.
10. Sirius, which is the brightest star that can be seen from Earth at night.

HELP

Most of the word groups in Exercise 5 can be correctly revised in more than one way. You need to give only one revision for each word group.

Reference Note

For information on **sentence fragments,** see page 275. For information on **run-on sentences,** see page 277.

COMMON ERRORS

Exercise 5 Correcting Sentence Fragments and Run-on Sentences

The following paragraph contains sentence fragments, run-on sentences, and complete sentences. First, identify each numbered word group by writing *F* for a fragment, *R* for a run-on, or *S* for a complete sentence. Then, revise the paragraph to correct the fragments and run-ons.

EXAMPLE **[1]** The history of food a delicious subject.

1. *F—The history of food is a delicious subject.*

or

F—I just saw a documentary on the history of food, a delicious subject.

[**1**] There have been many milestones in the history of food production, the development of canned food is one of the most important. [**2**] Because canned goods fill our stores today. [**3**] Most people generally take these goods for granted. [**4**] The story of canned goods begins in the 1700s with Lazzaro Spallanzani his experiments in preserving food were some of the earliest to succeed. [**5**] Other early experimenters preserved vegetables, fruit, and meat in glass bottles. [**6**] Using processes in which the bottles of food were heated to very high temperatures. [**7**] Bottles later replaced with containers made of tin-plated iron. [**8**] Heat kills the bacteria that cause food to spoil. [**9**] As Louis Pasteur

discovered in the mid-1800s. [**10**] The development of this process, now called pasteurization, made eating canned food safer the eventual invention of the can opener made it easier!

Exercise 6 Identifying Verbs That Agree in Number with Their Subjects

For each of the following sentences, choose the form of the verb in parentheses that agrees with the subject.

EXAMPLE **1.** (*Do, Does*) you know much about clouds?
1. *Do*

1. Learning about clouds (*help, helps*) you predict the weather.
2. Some of the books that I used in my report about weather (*give, gives*) detailed information about clouds.
3. Water droplets and ice crystals (*form, forms*) clouds.
4. Many of us (*like, likes*) to look for faces and familiar shapes in clouds overhead.
5. One of the most common types of clouds (*is, are*) the cumulonimbus rain cloud.
6. People often (*call, calls*) these clouds thunderstorm clouds.
7. Clouds of this kind (*produce, produces*) tornadoes and hail at times.
8. My friends Jeffrey and Kate (*don't, doesn't*) remember the name of cloud formations that look like wisps of cotton.
9. Several of these cirrus clouds (*was, were*) in the sky yesterday.
10. Stratus clouds, which often produce drizzle, (*look, looks*) like smooth sheets.
11. The basic types of clouds (*include, includes*) cumulus, nimbus, stratus, and cirrus.
12. Many cloud names (*combine, combines*) these basic names.
13. A cumulonimbus cloud (*have, has*) combined characteristics of cumulus and nimbus.
14. Another type of cloud, which combines features of nimbus and stratus clouds, (*are, is*) called a nimbostratus.
15. Other combinations (*take, takes*) the names stratocumulus and cirrostratus.
16. This information (*sounds, sound*) complicated but is easy to learn and fun to use.

Reference Note

For information on **subject-verb agreement,** see page 476.

17. Think how impressed your friends will be when you say, "Those (*appear, appears*) to be nimbostratus clouds over there; we may get rain later."
18. Cloud names (*come, comes*) from Latin words such as *cumulus,* meaning "heap."
19. *Nimbus,* in Latin, (*mean, means*) "rainstorm"; nimbus clouds are dark and full of rain.
20. *Cirrus* and *stratus* (*derive, derives*) from Latin words meaning "to curl" and "to spread out."

Exercise 7 Proofreading Sentences for Correct Subject-Verb Agreement

Reference Note

For information on **subject-verb agreement,** see page 476.

Most of the following sentences contain errors in subject-verb agreement. If a verb does not agree with its subject, give the correct form of the verb. If a sentence is already correct, write *C.*

EXAMPLE 1. Spanish explorers and missionaries is important in New Mexico's history.

1. *are*

1. Spanish missions throughout New Mexico attracts many tourists nowadays.
2. Some of these missions has been in continuous use for centuries.
3. Two missions especially interests me.
4. I can't decide whether the Mission of San Agustin de Isleta or Santa Fe's Mission of San Miguel are my favorite.
5. Both of these beautiful missions date from the early seventeenth century.
6. Each of them have survived damage caused by fires and centuries of wear.
7. Antique objects and priceless art lends their beauty to these old missions.
8. One of the most noteworthy features of the Santa Fe mission is a bell.
9. The bell, which was brought to Santa Fe in the 1800s, were cast in 1356 in Spain.
10. Churches in Spain and Mexico was home to the bell before it was brought to New Mexico.

Exercise 8 Identifying Pronouns That Agree with Their Antecedents

For each of the following sentences, choose the pronoun or pair of pronouns in parentheses that agrees with its antecedent or antecedents.

EXAMPLE **1.** The horse and mule walked toward (*its, their*) owner.

1. their

1. Did your uncle or your father take (*his, their*) fishing license to the pier?
2. Does one of the coats have Kim's initials on (*their, its*) label?
3. Everyone has had (*his or her, their*) turn to play in the game.
4. Ms. Torres and Ms. Lawrence gladly accepted (*her, their*) Community Appreciation Certificates.
5. Anyone may recite (*his or her, their*) poem during the program tonight.
6. Did Alejandro or Tim put on (*his, their*) jacket?
7. Neither of my twin stepbrothers has had (*his, their*) first haircut.
8. Each of the twenty women cast (*their, her*) vote.
9. Neither Ramona nor Isabel recalled (*her, their*) dream from the night before.
10. The first grade and the second grade will be taking (*its, their*) field trip tomorrow.
11. Either Eileen or Alicia has forgotten (*their, her*) raincoat.
12. Did your brother and your cousin Brad intend to exchange (*his, their*) tickets?
13. The cat has eaten all of (*its, their*) food.
14. Carlton joined the band but then forgot to bring (*his, their*) guitar to practice.
15. Each of the women will need (*their, her*) copy of the newsletter.
16. Many U.S. presidents were reelected and therefore served (*his, their*) second terms.
17. The track team and the cross-country team have (*its, their*) competitions tomorrow.
18. Neither Chris nor Luke has had (*their, his*) bicycle repaired yet.
19. Has either Cristina or Rachael lost all of (*their, her*) baby teeth yet?
20. The cast and director hope (*his, their*) production succeeds.

Reference Note

For information on **pronoun-antecedent agreement,** see page 493.

COMMON ERRORS

Exercise 9 Proofreading Sentences for Correct Pronoun-Antecedent Agreement

Reference Note

For information on **pronoun-antecedent agreement,** see page 493.

Most of the following sentences contain errors in pronoun-antecedent agreement. Identify each incorrect pronoun, and supply the correct form or forms. If the sentence is already correct, write *C.*

EXAMPLE 1. Tintin, whose adventures spanned the globe, traveled with their dog, Snowy.

1. their—his

Snowy! It's up to you to save us now, Snowy ... You must carry this message and get help from the monastery . . .

HERGE/MOULINSART 1999

1. The Belgian cartoonist Georges Remi created the comic strip character Tintin in the 1920s and set their first adventures in the Soviet Union.
2. Everybody in class who had read Tintin stories had their favorite tales of the adventurous reporter.
3. Both of this character's closest companions, Captain Haddock and Professor Cuthbert Calculus, help his friend Tintin.
4. Each of these men has their own unusual characteristics.
5. Thomson and Thompson, detectives who look alike, add his own silliness to Tintin's travels.
6. Several of the students said that he or she had read the comic strip.
7. Which one of the seven girls remembered to bring their own copy of *Tintin in Tibet*?
8. Julia showed us her drawing of Tintin's dog, Snowy.
9. My grandparents still have some of his or her old Tintin books.
10. Did *Tintin's Travel Diaries* inspire James or Reginald to keep their own travel diary during the summer?

Exercise 10 Writing Correct Verb Forms

Reference Note

For information on **verb forms,** see page 506.

For each of the following sentences, fill in the blank with the correct past or past participle form of the verb given before the sentence.

EXAMPLE 1. *draw* Kevin has ____ a Japanese pagoda.

1. drawn

1. *hike* Most of the club members have ____ on the Appalachian Trail.
2. *know* I have ____ the Katsanos family for years.

3. *steal* Can you believe that Jean Valjean was put in prison because he had ____ a loaf of bread?
4. *try* The baby giraffe ____to stand immediately after its birth.
5. *spin* The car ____ around twice on the wet road.
6. *build* My dad and my sister have ____ a workbench.
7. *make* Who ____ this delicious Irish soda bread?
8. *swim* Our team has ____ in pools this size, but we prefer Olympic-size pools.
9. *suppose* Gary was ____ to rent a funny movie for us to watch tonight.
10. *shake* The wet puppy ____ itself and got water all over Phuong's dress.
11. *take* She ____ the opportunity to work in Nigeria.
12. *climb* They had ____ Mount McKinley before trying Mount Everest.
13. *join* To meet others with similar interests, many people have ____ clubs.
14. *think* They ____ Elena would like the new computer.
15. *write* Everything he ____ entertained his readers.
16. *play* The dogs have ____ with the toy so long that it is in shreds.
17. *show* The teacher has ____ the film to both classes.
18. *bring* We had ____ fry bread to go with the stew.
19. *stand* They have ____ by the window all morning, waiting for the rain to stop.
20. *go* The train to Seattle ____ by two hours ago.

Exercise 11 Proofreading for Correct Past and Past Participle Verb Forms

If a sentence contains an incorrect verb form, write the correct form. If a sentence is already correct, write *C*.

EXAMPLE 1. Have you ever saw a sundial?

1. *seen*

1. I have read Anne Frank's *The Diary of a Young Girl.*
2. The song that Ann and Brian sang use to be popular in the 1950s.
3. Caitlin begun swimming lessons around the age of six.
4. Ben perform that routine for the judges last year.

Reference Note

For information on **verb forms,** see page 506.

5. The lizard done its best to catch the fly, but the fly flew away unharmed.
6. Have you wrote a letter recently?
7. The performer telled jokes and stories while he danced.
8. Excited about her new idea, Marie gived up on her first plan.
9. Is it true that the winner actually run backward in the race?
10. Did Sara say that Bill "Bojangles" Robinson made up the word *copacetic,* which means "fine" or "excellent"?
11. The bells for class have rang already.
12. I buyed three CDs on sale yesterday.
13. During the storm, the billboards blowed down.
14. Hoping to get to home base, Sammi stealed third.
15. My second-grade teacher teached me how to tell time.
16. I'll never forget the times I have spent with my cousin.
17. The clothes that I haven't weared in a long time, I'll give to the thrift store.
18. Thank goodness they have leaved the lights on.
19. We have freezed the leftover tortillas to use next week.
20. The dog chased and bited its own tail.

Exercise 12 Proofreading for Correct Past and Past Participle Verb Forms

Reference Note

For information on **verb forms,** see page 506.

If a sentence contains an incorrect verb form, write the correct form. If a sentence is already correct, write *C.*

EXAMPLE 1. I have took several lessons in aikido.

1. taken

1. Aikido, a Japanese system of self-defense, has interest me for some time.
2. A month ago, I begun lessons at a local martial arts studio.
3. Every time I have went to class, I have been nervous, but I am finally becoming more confident.
4. Our instructor has teached us that the Japanese word *aikido* means "the way of blending energy."
5. He sayed that I can "accept" an attacker's energy and redirect the attack away from myself.
6. Today in class, I saw how redirecting an opponent's energy really works.
7. The aikido holds and movements I choosed played off my opponent's strength.

COMMON ERRORS

8. I maked these movements without using any unnecessary force.
9. My opponent lunged at me, but he losed his footing.
10. My instructor said that attackers are usually throwed off balance by such movements because a person under attack usually uses force to fight back.

Exercise 13 Identifying Correct Pronoun Forms

Choose the correct form of each pronoun in parentheses in the following sentences.

EXAMPLE 1. The new rules do not apply to any of (*us, we*) eighth-graders.

1. us

1. Please give (*her, she*) the sequins for the costume.
2. The new paramedics at the stadium are (*they, them*).
3. Sasha and (*him, he*) are good at trivia games.
4. Coach Mendoza adjusted the parallel bars for Paul and (*me, I*).
5. The usher showed (*us, we*) to our seats.
6. My sister and (*me, I*) will help Dad paint our house this summer.
7. A friend of ours sent (*us, we*) a new book of short stories by a popular Venezuelan author.
8. The retirement home where Brad's grandmother lives impressed (*him, he*).
9. Did you give the oranges and apples to (*they, them*) for the picnic?
10. The first ones to arrive there in the morning are always (*she and I, her and me*).

Reference Note

For information on **pronoun forms,** see page 536.

Exercise 14 Identifying Correct Pronoun Forms

Choose the correct form of the pronoun in parentheses in each of the following sentences.

EXAMPLE 1. Facts about first ladies interest (*me, I*).

1. me

1. Hillary Rodham Clinton wrote a book titled *It Takes a Village;* last week she autographed copies for (*us, we*).
2. James and (*I, me*) were surprised to learn that Lucy Hayes was the first president's wife to earn a college degree.

Reference Note

For information on **pronoun forms,** see page 536.

3. It was (*her, she*) who was nicknamed Lemonade Lucy.
4. The school librarian gave (*him, he*) an article about Grace Coolidge, who taught children with hearing impairments.
5. Jack showed Caroline, Heather, and (*me, I*) a picture of Mrs. Coolidge with Helen Keller.

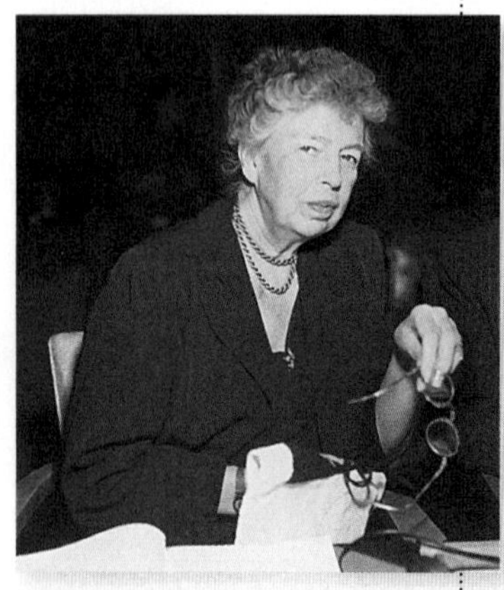

6. Tell (*them, they*) about Martha Washington's role as hostess of the new nation.
7. The artist who painted the portrait of the elegant Elizabeth Monroe could have been (*him, he*).
8. In a report on Edith Wilson, Nathaniel said that (*she, her*) sewed clothes to send to soldiers during World War I.
9. When she was a delegate to the United Nations, Eleanor Roosevelt, shown here, championed human rights and worked to secure (*it, them*) for all people.
10. With (*she, her*) as chairperson, the United Nations' Human Rights Commission drafted the Universal Declaration of Human Rights.

Exercise 15 Identifying Correct Pronoun Forms

Reference Note

For information on **pronoun forms,** see page 538.

Choose the correct form of the pronoun in parentheses in each of the following sentences.

EXAMPLE 1. Anika has a book that she asked David and (*I, me*) to read.
1. me

1. The book is *In a Sacred Manner I Live,* and David and (*I, me*) are eager to read it.
2. Several of (*we, us*) who are interested in American Indian writings are getting together to read the book aloud.
3. The writings are beautiful, and the wisdom contained in (*they, them*) should be shared.
4. For Anika and (*I, me*) the writings have special meaning because of our American Indian ancestry.
5. David says the stories are interesting for (*he, him*) because his great-grandmother was a Cherokee Indian.
6. The one who researched their family history was (*she, her*).
7. Asa, whose grandfather is Navajo, hopes (*he, him*) will speak to our group.
8. (*We, Us*) students all like the beautiful Navajo chant, "In Beauty May I Walk," which is in the book.

9. The editor of the book, Neil Philip, has published a collection of American Indian poems that (*he, him*) titled *Earth Always Endures.*
10. Our group discussions are such fun that (*we, us*) will get that book, too.

Exercise 16 Choosing Correct Regular and Irregular Modifiers

Choose the correct form of the modifier in parentheses in each of the following sentences.

EXAMPLE 1. *The Fantasticks* is Jorge's (*favorite, favoritest*) musical.

1. *favorite*

1. *The Fantasticks* has had the (*longer, longest*) run of any musical in New York City.
2. In fact, it is the (*oldest, older*) continuously running musical in the United States.
3. My aunt says that the performance she saw at New York's Sullivan Street Playhouse in 1996 was the (*better, best*) show of any she'd ever seen.
4. She told me that *The Fantasticks* was created by one of the (*most talented, talentedest*) teams of writers for the stage—Tom Jones and Harvey Schmidt.
5. Jones and Schmidt have also written other musicals, but *The Fantasticks,* which opened in New York City in 1960, is generally considered to be the (*popularest, most popular*) of their works.
6. Have you ever seen a musical with a character called something (*more strange, stranger*) than The Man Who Dies?
7. The play has both serious and funny songs; many people like the funny songs (*best, better*).
8. The Handyman, who appears only during the play's intermission, and The Mute, who has no lines to speak, are among the (*most odd, oddest*) roles in modern theater.
9. The students who put on our school's recent production of *The Fantasticks* performed (*good, well*).
10. If the play ever comes to your town, you might find it (*more, most*) enjoyable to see than a movie.

Reference Note

For information on **using modifiers correctly,** see page 554.

Exercise 17 Correcting Double Comparisons and Double Negatives

Reference Note

For information on **double comparisons,** see page 566. For information on **double negatives,** see page 567.

Identify the incorrect modifier in each of the following sentences. Then, rewrite the sentence to correct the error.

EXAMPLE **1.** Some of the most prettiest candles are made of beeswax.

1. Some of the prettiest candles are made of beeswax.

1. We wanted to rent a movie but couldn't find none that we all wanted to see.
2. Both Ted and I are learning Spanish, but I am more shyer about speaking it than he is.
3. Kim never wanted to go nowhere near the icy rapids.
4. People in cars are less safer when they do not wear seat belts.
5. We volunteered to help with the preschool art classes because there wasn't nobody else who had the time.
6. Of all the kinds of trees in our neighborhood, which do you think is the least commonest?
7. Moose are the most largest members of the deer family.
8. Don't never use the elevator to escape if the building you are in is on fire.
9. Carrie couldn't scarcely walk after she broke her toe.
10. Kudzu is a Japanese vine that grows more faster than many other plants.
11. We never get no interesting mail.
12. It was the most tiniest mouse that ever lived.
13. The storm couldn't have been more fiercer.
14. When Jake and Fido jog together, Jake can't hardly keep up.
15. Filing all the papers was the most best I could do.
16. You can't never be too careful about avoiding double negatives.
17. The Pacific Ocean is the most biggest ocean in the world.
18. None of us would never throw litter out of a car window.
19. Ostriches lay more bigger eggs than any other birds do.
20. The movie theater is less cleaner on Saturday afternoons.

Exercise 18 Revising Sentences to Correct Misplaced Modifiers

Reference Note

For information on **misplaced modifiers,** see page 569.

Each of the following sentences contains a misplaced modifier. Revise each sentence to correct the error.

EXAMPLE **1.** Bathing in the mud, the photographer snapped several photographs of the elephants.

1. The photographer snapped several photographs of the elephants bathing in the mud.

1. My dad said today we are going to the beach.
2. The children could see the bacteria using their microscope.
3. Richard saw the announcement for the book sale on the bulletin board.
4. Yesterday evening, I saw a raccoon going to check the mail.
5. I gave flowers to my friends that I had picked along the roadside.
6. Looming in the road ahead I saw a large moose.
7. I could see the constellations clearly sitting on the roof.
8. Leaning down to smell the flowers, the large grasshopper startled me.
9. Luís went to a baseball game using his season pass.
10. We watched a film about how volcanoes form in science class.

Exercise 19 Revising Sentences to Correct Misplaced and Dangling Modifiers

Each of the following sentences contains a misplaced or dangling modifier. Revise each sentence to correct the error.

Reference Note

For information on **misplaced and dangling modifiers,** see page 569.

EXAMPLE **1.** Growing in the root cellar, my aunt found a red mushroom.

1. My aunt found a red mushroom growing in the root cellar.

1. I read a book about how the Egyptian pyramids were built yesterday.
2. While making lunch for the visitors, the stove caught on fire.
3. The children played in the puddle with no boots on.
4. Don announced at the meeting he will be asking for volunteers.
5. Running to catch the bus, several books fell out of his backpack.
6. Wobbling, the crowd anxiously watched the tightrope walker.
7. My sister described the giraffe she had seen during our flight back to the United States.
8. Tired of the drought, the rain was greeted with loud cheers.

9. Sparkling in the sunlight, the mockingbird showed no interest in the sapphire ring.
10. While walking along the shoreline, a large, black fossilized shark's tooth caught my eye.

Exercise 20 Revising Sentences to Correct Misplaced and Dangling Modifiers

Reference Note

For information on **misplaced and dangling modifiers,** see page 569.

Each of the following sentences contains a misplaced or dangling modifier. Revise each sentence to correct the error.

EXAMPLE 1. Swimming in the pond, the cat watched the goldfish.

1. The cat watched the goldfish swimming in the pond.

1. Facing an election, the recent polls did not please the politician.
2. My uncle told me about armadillos on a car trip to Texas.
3. To expand the park, neighboring land has been donated.
4. Looking at the x-rays, my leg was bruised and not broken.
5. Wearing our swimsuits, the security guard let us into the pool area.
6. My mother showed me where she had gone to kindergarten when I was a little girl.
7. The mountain climbers looked at the glittering glacier with sunglasses on.
8. Checking the grocery list, the cart bumped a stack of cans.
9. Watching the sunset, a barking dog chased a cat through the yard.
10. We bought a bicycle from a local store that had ten speeds.

Exercise 21 Revising Sentences to Correct Misplaced and Dangling Modifiers

Reference Note

For information on **misplaced and dangling modifiers,** see page 569.

Each of the following sentences contains a misplaced or dangling modifier. Revise each sentence to correct the error.

EXAMPLE 1. Grabbing for the rope, the boat was swept away.

1. While we were grabbing for the rope, the boat was swept away.

1. Yelling "More! More!" the musicians returned to the stage in response to the cheering audience.
2. Wearing a hard hat, the falling icicle didn't hurt me.

3. Listening to the concert, her purse fell to the floor.
4. To enter the contest, many questions must be answered.
5. Lifted by the wind, capture was impossible.
6. After picking up the litter, the trash can was full.
7. Shining in the night sky, I tried to remember the names of some constellations.
8. The waves washed under the net while playing volleyball.
9. Using the can opener, the cat always knows it's time to be fed.
10. Driving carefully, the mountain road didn't seem as winding.

Exercise 22 Identifying Correct Usage

For each of the following sentences, choose the word or word group in parentheses that is correct according to the rules of formal, standard English.

EXAMPLE 1. About (*a, an*) hour before sunrise, the dam almost (*burst, busted*).

1. an, burst

1. (*Doesn't, Don't*) the long-term (*affects, effects*) of global warming concern you?
2. There (*use to, used to*) be (*fewer, less*) people jogging in my neighborhood.
3. (*Without, Unless*) we have permission, I don't think we ought to (*bring, take*) Dad's new CD player to the beach tomorrow.
4. Marshall (*would of, would have*) gone to the picnic in the park, but (*then, than*) he changed his mind.
5. We had a difficult time choosing (*between, among*) the two puppies playing together (*inside, inside of*) the large basket.
6. My clarinet playing has improved (*some, somewhat*), but I really (*had ought, ought*) to practice more.
7. Everyone (*accept, except*) John thinks the weather will be (*allright, all right*) for the powwow.
8. I (*try and, try to*) go to all of my aunt's softball games because her team plays so (*good, well*).
9. (*Who's, Whose*) going to sleep outside with so many of (*them, those*) mosquitoes around?
10. Randy talks (*like, as if*) he has to ride his bike a very long (*way, ways*) on his paper route.

Reference Note

For information on **common usage errors,** see page 580.

Reference Note

For information on **common usage errors,** see page 580.

Exercise 23 Correcting Errors in Usage

Each of the following sentences contains an error in the use of formal, standard English. Identify and correct each error.

EXAMPLE **1.** Patrick did so good at the spelling bee that he qualified for the national contest.

1. good—well

1. If the shrimp enchiladas taste badly, don't eat any more of them.

2. My stepsister said she would learn me how to play the piano.

3. Please bring these vegetables to your grandmother when you visit her this Friday.

4. I read where a waterspout is the name for a tornado that occurs over a lake or an ocean.

5. The cartoonist which works for our local newspaper has a wonderful sense of humor.

6. The *ruble* is an unit of currency used in both Russia and Tajikistan.

7. A friendly rivalry arose between all of the members of the soccer team.

8. Late last night, Jack saw a light shining somewheres across the river.

9. Mr. Catalano said that the smallest dinosaurs weren't scarcely larger than chickens.

10. I knew that we should of brought the umbrella with us when we left the house today.

11. Mr. Stevens would not except any final history papers turned in after Friday.

12. Alot of students wanted to work on the play.

13. Although he had less hits than Corey, Jorge scored more runs.

14. Maryanne wanted to know how come the bus was late.

15. Jan used smooth brush strokes on the painting, like the teacher had shown him.

16. Is a cheetah faster then a cougar?

17. Mrs. Koontz asked us to try and memorize our music for the concert by Monday.

18. The bus driver said we still had quite a ways to go before we arrived in St. Louis.

19. Whose going to the dance this weekend?

20. Don't forget to bring you're favorite book to class.

Exercise 24 Correcting Errors in Usage

Each of the following sentences contains an error in the use of formal, standard English. Identify and correct each error.

EXAMPLE 1. Our class has all ready read about the life of José Luis Muñoz Marín (1898–1980).

1. *all ready—already*

1. Where was Muñoz Marín born at?
2. I read in this here biography that he was born in San Juan, the capital of Puerto Rico.
3. For more then a quarter of a century, Muñoz Marín was Puerto Rico's chief political leader.
4. He worked to help the people of Puerto Rico build better lives for theirselves.
5. Like Muñoz Marín himself discovered, he had been born at a major turning point in the history of his country.
6. He must of been very popular, for he was elected governor four times.
7. When I read his biography, I learned how come he founded the Popular Democratic Party.
8. John F. Kennedy was the president which awarded Muñoz Marín the Presidential Medal of Freedom.
9. Its fascinating to think of Muñoz Marín's being both a poet and a politician.
10. Did you know that their is a U.S. postage stamp featuring Muñoz Marín?

Reference Note

For information on **common usage errors,** see page 580.

Grammar and Usage Test: Section 1

DIRECTIONS Read the paragraph below. For each numbered blank, select the word or word group that best completes the sentence. Indicate your response by shading in the appropriate oval on your answer sheet.

EXAMPLE The word *organic* __(1)__ "of or related to living things."

1. (A) it means
   (B) meant
   (C) is meaning
   (D) means

ANSWER 1. 

Scientists __(1)__ study the prehistoric world __(2)__ carbon dating to determine the age of organic materials such as wood and bone. All living things absorb carbon-14 from the environment into __(3)__ tissues. An organism that has died __(4)__ carbon-14 because __(5)__ no longer takes in air and food. Carbon-14 that was previously absorbed into the organism's tissues __(6)__ at a specific rate. Knowing the rate of breakdown, scientists measure the amount of carbon-14 in an organism's remains to determine how much time __(7)__ since the organism died. Scientists cannot use carbon dating to determine the age of organic material __(8)__ is __(9)__ about 120,000 years, because carbon-14 __(10)__ down and becomes untraceable after that length of time.

1. (A) which
   (B) who
   (C) whom
   (D) what

2. (A) they use
   (B) use
   (C) uses
   (D) used

3. (A) its
   (B) his or her
   (C) they're
   (D) their

4. (A) doesn't absorb no more
   (B) don't absorb more
   (C) doesn't absorb any more
   (D) don't absorb any more

5. (A) he
   (B) she
   (C) it
   (D) they

6. (A) it decays
   (B) decays
   (C) decay
   (D) were decaying

COMMON ERRORS

7. (A) passes
   (B) is passing
   (C) have passed
   (D) has passed

8. (A) that
   (B) what
   (C) who
   (D) whom

9. (A) more old then
   (B) older than
   (C) older then
   (D) more older than

10. (A) busts
    (B) busted
    (C) break
    (D) breaks

Grammar and Usage Test: Section 2

DIRECTIONS Either part or all of each of the following sentences is underlined. Using the rules of formal, standard English, choose the answer that correctly expresses the meaning of the underlined word or word group. If there is no error, choose A. Indicate your response by shading in the appropriate oval on your answer sheet.

EXAMPLE 1. The first Cuban-born woman to become a U.S. Army officer was Mercedes O. Cubria, whom served in the Women's Army Corps.

(A) whom
(B) who
(C) that
(D) which

ANSWER 1.    

1. In basketball, one kind of illegal dribbling is when a player stops dribbling and then begins dribbling again.
   (A) is when
   (B) is that
   (C) is because
   (D) occurs when

2. Karen's sandwich is more tastier than the one I brought.
   (A) more tastier than
   (B) more tastier then
   (C) tastier than
   (D) tastier then

COMMON ERRORS

3. Tonya said she had seen a hummingbird at her feeder in the mall today.
   (A) Tonya said she had seen a hummingbird at her feeder in the mall today.
   (B) In the mall today, Tonya said she had seen a hummingbird at her feeder.
   (C) Tonya said in the mall today she had seen a hummingbird at her feeder.
   (D) Tonya said in the mall today at her feeder she had seen a hummingbird.

4. Have the Glee Club and they set down to discuss the program?
   (A) Have the Glee Club and they set
   (B) Have the Glee Club and them sat
   (C) Have the Glee Club and they sat
   (D) Has the Glee Club and they sat

5. For many years, Matthew Henson accompanied Robert Peary on expeditions, together, in 1908, they set out for the North Pole.
   (A) expeditions, together, in 1908, they set
   (B) expeditions, together, in 1908, they setted
   (C) expeditions; together, in 1908, they setted
   (D) expeditions. Together, in 1908, they set

6. The reason you should wear a helmet is because it can prevent head injuries.
   (A) is because it
   (B) is that it
   (C) is that they
   (D) is when it

7. A dedicated and creative teacher, Anne Sullivan learned Helen Keller how to communicate effectively.
   (A) learned
   (B) taught
   (C) was learning
   (D) teached

8. Between Josh and him lay the exhausted puppy.
   (A) him lay
   (B) he lay
   (C) him laid
   (D) him has laid

9. The treasure that was buried in the abandoned mine.
   (A) The treasure that was buried in the abandoned mine.
   (B) The treasure found buried in the abandoned mine.
   (C) The treasure buried in the abandoned mine.
   (D) The treasure was buried in the abandoned mine.

10. Peering behind the bookcase, a secret passage was discovered by the detective.
   (A) Peering behind the bookcase, a secret passage was discovered by the detective.
   (B) Peering behind the bookcase, the detective discovered a secret passage.
   (C) The detective discovered a secret passage peering behind the bookcase.
   (D) While peering behind the bookcase, a secret passage was discovered by the detective.

COMMON ERRORS

Exercise 25 Correcting Errors in Capitalization

Reference Note

For information on **capitalization rules,** see page 602.

Each of the following word groups contains at least one error in capitalization. Correct the errors either by changing capital letters to lowercase letters or by changing lowercase letters to capital letters.

EXAMPLE **1.** central avenue in albuquerque, New mexico

1. Central Avenue in Albuquerque, New Mexico

1. venus and jupiter
2. my Aunt Jessica
3. wednesday morning
4. the Jewish holiday hanukkah
5. Thirty-Fifth street
6. the stone age
7. nobel peace prize
8. Minute maid® orange juice
9. spanish, earth science, and algebra I
10. secretary of state madeleine albright
11. the washington Monument
12. Portland, oregon
13. my Mother
14. the japanese fan
15. social studies and french
16. where fifty-first street crosses Collins avenue
17. Lake erie
18. president of the pta
19. the mexican flag
20. the thirteenth of october

Exercise 26 Correcting Errors in Capitalization

Reference Note

For information on **capitalization rules,** see page 602.

Each of the following sentences contains errors in capitalization. Correct the errors either by changing capital letters to lowercase letters or by changing lowercase letters to capital letters.

EXAMPLE **1.** many african americans lived and worked in the western United states after the civil war.

1. Many African Americans lived and worked in the western United States after the Civil War.

1. one of the most interesting people from that era is bill pickett, who was born on December 5, 1870.

COMMON ERRORS

2. His Father worked on ranches near austin, texas, and pickett grew up watching cowhands work.
3. Bill began performing rodeo tricks at County fairs, and in 1905 he joined the 101 wild west show in the region then called the oklahoma territory.
4. With this show, Pickett toured the united states, south america, canada, and great britain.
5. i wish i could have seen all the cowboys, cowgirls, horses, buffalo, and longhorn cattle that were part of the show!
6. My Uncle Larry told me that Pickett portrayed himself in a 1923 silent movie.
7. Pickett, who died in 1932, was later inducted into the national rodeo cowboy hall of fame.
8. in 1977, the university of oklahoma press published a biography, *bill pickett, bulldogger*, written by colonel bailey c. hanes.
9. a bronze statue of Bill Pickett was dedicated at the fort worth cowtown coliseum in 1987.
10. The Bill Pickett invitational rodeo, which tours all over the united states, draws rodeo talent from around the nation.

Exercise 27 Correcting Sentences by Adding Commas

Each of the following sentences lacks at least one comma. Write the word that comes before each missing comma, and add the comma.

Reference Note

For information on **using commas,** see page 633.

EXAMPLE 1. When the Spanish brought the first horses to North America the lives of many American Indians changed dramatically.

1. America,

1. Native peoples bred the Spanish horses and developed ponies that could survive on the stubby coarse grasses of the Great Plains.
2. These hardy ponies may not have been considered as beautiful as the Spanish horses but they were faster stronger and smarter.
3. Because horses were so highly valued they came to signify status and wealth.
4. These ponies which were useful in the daily activities of American Indians were also ridden into battle.
5. Before riding into a battle Crow warriors painted symbolic designs on themselves and on their ponies.

6. These designs might show that the rider possessed “medicine power” had been on successful horse raids or had lost someone special to him.
7. Just as designs did color had special meanings.
8. The color blue for example represented wounds; red which symbolized courage and bravery represented bloodshed.
9. Often painted on the pony’s flanks or under its eyes white clay stripes indicated the number of horses a warrior had captured.
10. Among the Plains Indians warriors who disgraced their enemies by tapping them at close range earned horizontal stripes called “coup” marks.

Exercise 28 Using Periods, Question Marks, Exclamation Points, and Commas Correctly

Reference Note

For information on **using end marks and commas,** see page 628.

The following sentences need periods, question marks, exclamation points, and commas. Write the word or numeral that comes before each missing punctuation mark, and add the proper punctuation.

EXAMPLE 1. Did you sign up for the class trip to Washington Baltimore and Roanoke

1. *Washington, Baltimore, Roanoke?*

1. What for instance would you suggest doing to improve wheelchair access to the theater
2. Well I was standing on the ladder but I still couldn’t reach the apples
3. Marta a friend of mine always recycles her aluminum cans and newspapers
4. When I draw with pastels charcoal or chalk I’m careful to wash my hands before touching anything else
5. Amy watch out for the wasp
6. Is the Spanish Club meeting scheduled for today or tomorrow Lee
7. Adela wrote one letter on May 19 2001 and another on October 5 2001
8. Mr N Q Galvez Ms Alma Lee and Dr Paul M Metz spoke at the nutrition seminar last week
9. What a great idea that is Edward
10. My friends and I like to hike in the mountains water-ski on the lake and jog along the park trails

Exercise 29 Using Semicolons and Colons Correctly

The following sentences lack necessary colons and semicolons. Write the word or numeral that comes before and after each missing punctuation mark, and add the proper punctuation.

EXAMPLE 1. Friday is the day for the band concert all of my family is attending.

1. concert; all

1. I put bread in the oven at 4 15 it should be done soon.
2. We have been keeping the highway clean for three years naturally, no one in the club litters.
3. My brother's favorite movie is *Homeward Bound The Incredible Journey.*
4. We gathered driftwood, shells, and rocks and we bought sand, glass, and paint for the sculpture.
5. My stepsister Sarah, who is deaf, uses the following electronic devices a doorbell that makes the lights flicker, a telephone that converts speech to written words, and a television with closed captioning.
6. The counselor used Proverbs 15 1 as the basis for her talk.
7. To paint the clubhouse we needed the following brushes, paint, masking tape, and water.
8. We are going to Dallas for the rally however, first we need to raise the money.
9. The swimmers will compete in three divisions backstroke, breaststroke, sidestroke.
10. Her business letter began as follows, "To Whom It May Concern I am a student at Lincoln Middle School."

Reference Note

For information on using **semicolons,** see page 649. For information on using **colons,** see page 652.

Exercise 30 Correcting Sentences by Adding Quotation Marks, Other Marks of Punctuation, and Capital Letters

Revise the following sentences by supplying capital letters and marks of punctuation as needed.

EXAMPLE 1. Diane asked where is Denali National Park?

1. Diane asked, "Where is Denali National Park?"

1. Gloria Estefan is my favorite singer said Stephen but I haven't heard her newest song yet.
2. Aunt Caroline exclaimed what a beautiful origami swan that is!

Reference Note

For information on **using quotation marks,** see page 662. For information on **using other punctuation marks,** see page 663. For information on **using capital letters,** see page 663.

3. To block some of the traffic noise Russell commented the city should plant some trees along this street.
4. The first episode of that new television series is called Once upon a Twice-Baked Potato.
5. Did you see that Francis asked. That player bumped the soccer ball into the goal with his heel
6. Beverly asked why doesn't Janet want to be president of the club?
7. I'll go with you Dee said that sack of birdseed will be too heavy for you to carry back by yourself.
8. I just finished reading the chapter titled Noah Swims Alone, and I really enjoyed it Shawn said.
9. Did Stephanie actually yell I'm out of here before she left the room asked Joel.
10. Jonathan said You've Got a Friend in Me is one of the songs in the movie *Toy Story*.

Exercise 31 Proofreading a Dialogue for Correct Punctuation

Reference Note

For information on **punctuating dialogue,** see page 666.

Correct any errors in the use of quotation marks and other marks of punctuation in the following dialogue. Also, correct any capitalization errors, and begin a new paragraph each time the speaker changes.

EXAMPLES **[1]** Guess what! Henry exclaimed This Saturday I'm going with my youth group to work on a Habitat for Humanity project **[2]** What is Habitat for Humanity Lynn asked

1. "Guess what!" Henry exclaimed. "This Saturday I'm going with my youth group to work on a Habitat for Humanity project."

2. "What is Habitat for Humanity?" Lynn asked.

[**1**] It's an organization that renovates and builds houses for people who are poor and do not own homes Henry replied. [**2**] Oh, now I remember Lynn said. Many volunteers help with the work, right [**3**] Yes that's true Henry answered and the people who will live in the houses also help with the renovating or building of these houses

[**4**] Are they required to help paint, hammer, and do whatever else needs to be done? Lynn asked. [**5**] Yes, and over an extended period of time, they also pay back the building costs Henry explained

[6] Lynn asked Isn't it expensive to build a house [7] Well Henry responded it does take a lot of money, but volunteer labor, donated construction materials, and skillful management keep the cost of building affordable.

[8] How long has Habitat for Humanity existed, and who started it Lynn asked [9] Our youth group leader told us that Millard and Linda Fuller started Habitat for Humanity in Georgia in 1976 Henry replied.

[10] Hey, I think I'll go with you to work on the building project Lynn said.

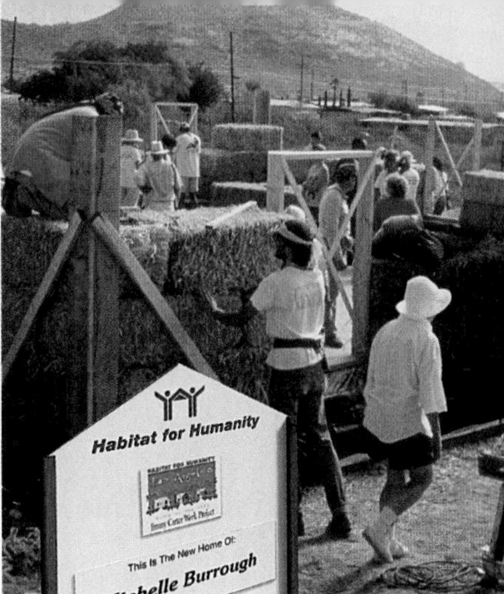
Habitat for Humanity
This Is The New Home Of:
Michelle Burrough

Exercise 32 Correcting Sentences by Adding Apostrophes

Write the correct form of each word that requires an apostrophe in the following sentences. If a sentence is already correct, write *C*.

EXAMPLE 1. Didnt the womens team win the tournament last year, too?

1. *Didn't, women's*

Reference Note

For information on **using apostrophes,** see page 669.

1. Theyre looking for Rodneys bucket of seashells that he gathered at the beach.
2. Its anybodys guess who will win!
3. Im glad you enjoyed staying at the Caldwells cabin last weekend.
4. If you help me wash my car this afternoon, I will help you wash yours tomorrow.
5. Isnt ten dollars worth going to be enough?
6. I havent a clue about that.
7. Charles Dickens "A Christmas Carol" is a story that youll really enjoy.
8. The mens clothing shop is closed today.
9. Lets go swimming next Wednesday.
10. Tonyas Mexican casserole is always a hit at the churchs annual cook-off.

Exercise 33 Correcting Spelling Errors

If a word in the list on the following page is spelled incorrectly, write the correct spelling. If a word is already correctly spelled, write *C*.

EXAMPLE 1. superceed

1. *supersede*

Reference Note

For information on **spelling rules,** see page 688.

1. fryed
2. receed
3. brief
4. wifes
5. tempoes
6. Lopezs
7. freewayes
8. casualy
9. disfigureing
10. mother-in-laws
11. dimmer
12. sliegh
13. receipt
14. mishapen
15. manageing
16. measurment
17. denys
18. ratioes
19. sheeps
20. tablescloth
21. thiefs
22. freight
23. intersede
24. imature
25. courageous
26. monkies
27. aircrafts
28. deer
29. commander in chiefs
30. switchs

Exercise 34 Using Words Often Confused

Reference Note

For information on **words often confused,** see page 698.

Choose the correct word or words from the choices in parentheses in each of the following sentences.

EXAMPLE 1. My brother's (*advise, advice*) is usually good.
1. advice

1. When will you hear (*whether, weather*) your poem has been (*accepted, excepted*) for publication?
2. We have (*all ready, already*) planned the field trip.
3. Do you think we will need to (*alter, altar*) our plans?
4. If you could (*choose, chose*) any place in the world to visit, where would you go?
5. Did the town (*counsel, council, consul*) meet today?
6. I'd rather experience the (*piece, peace*) and quiet of the beach (*then, than*) the noise and crowds of the city.
7. (*Its, It's*) good manners to hold the door open for anyone (*whose, who's*) hands are full.
8. The floats (*shown, shone*) brightly in the sunlight as the parade (*passed, past*) our house.
9. If the (*whether, weather*) is bad, will that (*effect, affect*) our party, or are we having the party indoors?
10. Before turning in plastic bags for recycling, we reuse them (*to, too, two*) or three times.
11. (*You're, Your*) collection of glass animals is fascinating.
12. The (*course, coarse*) texture of this cloth bothers me.
13. Some people prefer to live in the (*dessert, desert*).
14. Ms. Chen will be (*formally, formerly*) installed as president.
15. Mr. Martinez (*led, lead*) us through the museum.

16. Logan has been (*excepted, accepted*) by the architecture program at Rice University.
17. Jamie (*through, threw*) the stick for Chauncey to fetch.
18. Isaiah prefers (*plane, plain*) cloth for his shirts.
19. No matter how much she practiced, Kate couldn't get the music (*quiet, quite*) right.
20. The wind and lightning have (*past, passed*), but it is still raining.

Exercise 35 Proofreading for Errors in Spelling and Words Often Confused

HELP

No proper nouns in Exercise 35 are misspelled.

Reference Note

For information on **spelling rules,** see page 688. For information on **common usage errors,** see page 580.

For each of the following sentences, correct any error in spelling or words often confused.

EXAMPLE 1. Have you noticeed the advertisments for the exhibit of rare manuscripts?

1. *noticed, advertisements*

1. The manuscript known as the *Book of Kells* was produced in Ireland around the 8th century.
2. At that time, printing presss had not yet been invented, and manuscripts had too be written by hand.
3. Christian scribes, who created books of great beauty for monasterys and churchs, copied and illustrated the Gospels in the *Book of Kells.*
4. The beauty of it's illustrations distinguishes the *Book of Kells* from other copys of the Gospels.
5. The book's drawings, made with great care and artistry, display vibrant and harmonyous colors.
6. The rich, interlaceing patterns of decoration, which are sometimes wraped around still other patterns, often contain figures of animals and people.
7. These ornate drawings do not yeild there secrets to casual readers.
8. Many of the anceint illustrations express they're meanings threw symbols.
9. Those symbols include butterflys, oxes, eagles, mouses, lions, and fish.
10. Unfortunatly, many pages of the manuscript are missing, perhaps lost or destroied by Viking warriors during raids.

COMMON ERRORS

Mechanics Test: Section 1

DIRECTIONS Each numbered item below contains an underlined group of words. Choose the answer that shows the correct capitalization, punctuation, and spelling of the underlined part. If there is no error, choose answer D (Correct as is). Indicate your response by shading in the appropriate oval on your answer sheet.

EXAMPLE Thank you very **[1]** much Mr. and Mrs. Fernandez for a great visit.

(A) much Mr. and Mrs. Fernandez,
(B) much, Mr. and Mrs. Fernandez,
(C) much Mr. and Mrs. Fernandez;
(D) Correct as is

ANSWER **1.**  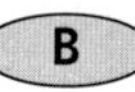  

1201 Palm Circle
[**1**] Jacksonville Fla. 32201

[**2**] April 11 2001

[**3**] Dear Mr. and Mrs. Fernandez,

I am so glad that you and Pedro invited me to stay at your home this [**4**] past weekend, I had a great time. The [**5**] whether I think was perfect for the activities you planned. The [**6**] picnic lunches volleyball games, and boat rides were so much fun! I especially enjoyed going fishing in your boat [**7**] the ugly duckling.

Next weekend my parents are going to have a barbecue party to celebrate [**8**] my aunt Jessicas birthday. If you would like to join us this coming [**9**] Saturday at 5:30 P.M. please give us a call sometime this week.

[**10**] Sincerely yours,

Todd Grinstead

Todd Grinstead

1. (A) Jacksonville, FL 32201
   (B) Jacksonville Fla 32201
   (C) Jacksonville FL 32201
   (D) Correct as is

2. (A) April, 11 2001
   (B) April Eleventh 2001
   (C) April 11, 2001
   (D) Correct as is

3. (A) Dear Mr. and Mrs. Fernandez:
   (B) Dear Mr and Mrs Fernandez:
   (C) Dear Mr. and Mrs Fernandez,
   (D) Correct as is

4. (A) passed weekend; I had
   (B) past weekend; I had
   (C) passed weekend, I had
   (D) Correct as is

5. (A) weather, I think, was
   (B) weather, I think was
   (C) whether, I think was
   (D) Correct as is

6. (A) picnic lunchs,
   (B) picnic lunchs
   (C) picnic lunches,
   (D) Correct as is

7. (A) *the Ugly Duckling.*
   (B) *The Ugly Duckling.*
   (C) "The Ugly Duckling."
   (D) Correct as is

8. (A) my Aunt Jessica's
   (B) my Aunt Jessicas'
   (C) my aunt Jessica's
   (D) Correct as is

9. (A) Saturday, at 5:30 P.M.
   (B) Saturday at 5:30 P.M.,
   (C) Saturday, at 530 P.M.,
   (D) Correct as is

10. (A) Sincerely yours',
    (B) Sincerly yours,
    (C) Sincerely yours:
    (D) Correct as is

Mechanics Test: Section 2

DIRECTIONS Each of the sentences on the following page contains an underlined word or group of words. Choose the answer that shows the correct capitalization, punctuation, and spelling of the underlined part. If there is no error, choose answer D (Correct as is). Indicate your response by shading in the appropriate oval on your answer sheet.

EXAMPLE 1. King Louis Philippe of France created the foreign legion in 1831.

(A) Foreign Legion
(B) Foriegn Legion
(C) foriegn legion
(D) Correct as is

ANSWER 1.    

COMMON ERRORS

1. My music teacher, Mrs. O'Henry will sing two solos at our school's talent show.

(A) Mrs. O'Henry, will sing two soloes
(B) Mrs. O'Henry will sing two solos
(C) Mrs. O'Henry, will sing two solos
(D) Correct as is

2. "Do we have enough pickets to build the fence," asked Michelle.

(A) fence"
(B) fence?"
(C) fence"?
(D) Correct as is

3. Last Friday my sister-in-laws nephew stopped by.

(A) my sister-in-law's
(B) my sister's-in-law
(C) my sister-in-law
(D) Correct as is

4. The short story Over the Fence is about three oxen and a frog.

(A) 'Over the Fence' is about three oxes
(B) 'Over The Fence' is about three oxen
(C) "Over the Fence" is about three oxen
(D) Correct as is

5. Turn left on Ninety-eighth Street.

(A) Ninty-eighth Street
(B) Ninety-Eighth Street
(C) Ninety-eighth street
(D) Correct as is

6. Roberto Clemente twice lead the Pittsburgh Pirates to victory in the World Series.

(A) lead The Pittsburgh Pirates
(B) led the Pittsburgh Pirates
(C) led the Pittsburgh pirates
(D) Correct as is

7. "How many of you," asked Mr. Reynolds "have seen a painting by the young Chinese artist Wang Yani?"

(A) Mr. Reynolds, "have
(B) Mr. Reynolds," have
(C) Mr. Reynolds, "Have
(D) Correct as is

8. Those who studied for the test of course, did better than those who did not.

(A) Those, who studied for the test,
(B) Those, who studied for the test
(C) Those who studied for the test,
(D) Correct as is

9. "Did you say that "it's time to go?" asked Raul.

(A) say, that 'it's time to go'?"
(B) say that it's time to go?"
(C) say that 'Its time to go'?"
(D) Correct as is

10. My younger sister excels in the following classes Art II, social studies, and English.

(A) classes: Art II, social studies,
(B) classes, Art II, Social Studies,
(C) classes art II, social studies,
(D) Correct as is

COMMON ERRORS

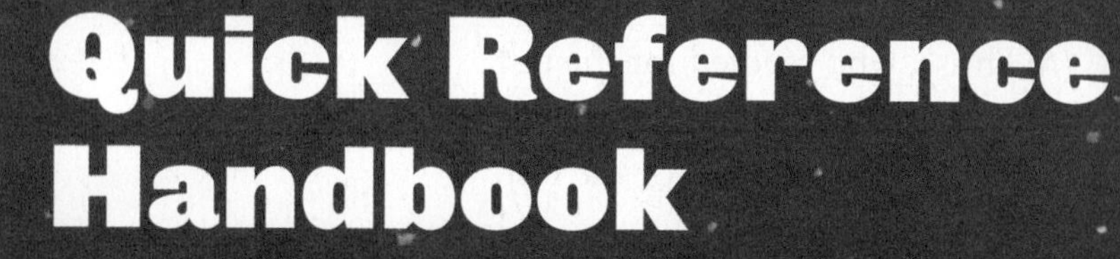
Quick Reference
Handbook

The Dictionary

Types and Contents

Types of Dictionaries Different types of dictionaries contain different kinds of information. However, all dictionaries contain certain general features.

Types of Dictionaries

An **abridged** dictionary is one that is shortened or condensed. It contains most of the words you are likely to use or encounter in your reading or writing.

EXAMPLE

Merriam-Webster's Collegiate Dictionary, Tenth Edition

A **specialized** dictionary defines words or terms that are used in a particular profession, field, or area of interest.

EXAMPLE

Stedman's Medical Dictionary

An **unabridged** dictionary contains nearly all the words in use in a language.

EXAMPLE

Webster's Third International Unabridged Dictionary

Dictionary Entry A dictionary entry defines a word and provides other information about it. The parts of the dictionary entry on the next page are labeled and explained below.

1. **Entry word** The entry word shows the correct spelling of a word and how it is divided into syllables. The entry word may also tell whether the word is capitalized and provide alternate spellings.
2. **Pronunciation** The pronunciation of a word is shown by the use of accent marks and either phonetic symbols or diacritical marks. Each ***phonetic symbol*** represents a different sound. ***Diacritical marks*** are special symbols placed above the letters to show how they sound. A pronunciation key located in the front of a dictionary explains diacritical marks and phonetic symbols.
3. **Part-of-speech labels** The part-of-speech labels (usually in abbreviated form) indicate how the entry word should be used in a sentence. Some words may be used as more than one part of speech. In this case, a part-of-

Sample Dictionary Entry

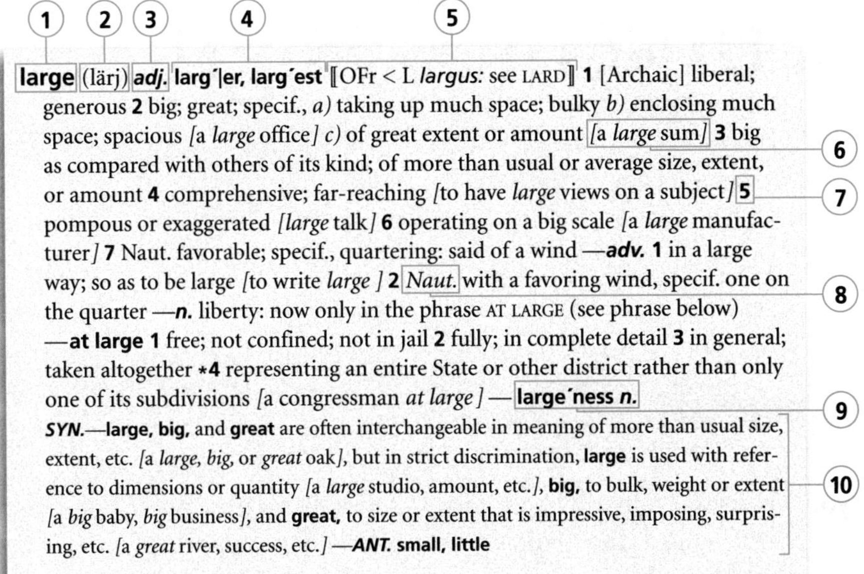

large (lärj) ***adj.*** **larg´|er, larg´est** ⟦OFr < L *largus:* see LARD⟧ **1** [Archaic] liberal; generous **2** big; great; specif., *a)* taking up much space; bulky *b)* enclosing much space; spacious *[a large* office*]* *c)* of great extent or amount *[a large* sum*]* **3** big as compared with others of its kind; of more than usual or average size, extent, or amount **4** comprehensive; far-reaching *[*to have *large* views on a subject*]* **5** pompous or exaggerated *[large* talk*]* **6** operating on a big scale *[*a *large* manufacturer*]* **7** Naut. favorable; specif., quartering: said of a wind —***adv.*** **1** in a large way; so as to be large *[*to write *large]* **2** *Naut.* with a favoring wind, specif. one on the quarter —***n.*** liberty: now only in the phrase AT LARGE (see phrase below) —**at large 1** free; not confined; not in jail **2** fully; in complete detail **3** in general; taken altogether ⋆**4** representing an entire State or other district rather than only one of its subdivisions *[*a congressman *at large]* — **large´ness *n.***

SYN.—**large, big,** and **great** are often interchangeable in meaning of more than usual size, extent, etc. *[*a *large, big,* or *great* oak*]*, but in strict discrimination, **large** is used with reference to dimensions or quantity *[*a *large* studio, amount, etc.*]*, **big,** to bulk, weight or extent *[*a *big* baby, *big* business*]*, and **great,** to size or extent that is impressive, imposing, surprising, etc. *[*a *great* river, success, etc.*]* —***ANT.*** **small, little**

speech label is provided before each numbered or lettered series of definitions. In the sample entry, *large* can be used as an adjective, an adverb, or a noun, depending on the meaning.

4. **Other forms** For some words the dictionary shows spellings of plural forms of nouns, tenses of verbs, or the comparative forms of adjectives and adverbs.
5. **Etymology** The ***etymology*** is the origin and history of a word. It tells how the word or its parts entered the English language.
6. **Examples** A dictionary may demonstrate how the defined word is used in phrases or sentences.
7. **Definitions** If a word has more than one meaning, each definition is numbered or lettered.
8. **Special usage labels** These labels identify the contexts in which some words have additional, specialized meanings, such as *Naut.* (nautical).
9. **Related word forms** These are various forms of the entry word, usually created by adding suffixes or prefixes.
10. **Synonyms and antonyms** Sometimes synonyms or antonyms of a word are listed at the end of its entry. ***Synonyms*** are words that have similar meanings. ***Antonyms*** are words that have opposite meanings.

Document Design

Manuscript Style

Whether you write your paper by hand or use a word-processing program, your teacher has a certain way he or she wants you to set up your paper. Use the guidelines below to prepare a typed or handwritten paper that is neat and easy to read.

Guidelines for Manuscript Style

1. Use only one side of each sheet of paper.

2. Type your paper using a word processor, or write it neatly in blue or black ink.

3. For handwritten papers, ask your teacher if he or she wants you to skip lines. For typed papers, many teachers prefer that you double-space your assignment.

4. Leave one-inch margins at the top, bottom, and sides of your paper.

5. The first line of every paragraph should be indented five spaces. You can set the **tab** button on a word processor to indent five spaces automatically.

6. Number all pages in the top right-hand corner. Do not number the first page.

7. Make sure your pages look neat and clean. For handwritten papers, you may want to use correction fluid to correct your mistakes. If you have several mistakes on one page, however, write out the page again. For typed papers, you can make corrections and print out a clean copy.

8. Use the heading your teacher prefers for your name, your class, the date, and the title of your paper. Your teacher may prefer that a title page include this information. If so, place the information your teacher requests on a separate sheet of paper. Place the information in the center of the sheet, with only one piece of information on each line (such as the title of your paper). Be sure to center-align the text, too (see page 757).

Desktop Publishing

To attract a reader, you must create a document that is easy to read and pleasing to the eye. You can create attractive reports, newsletters, and other documents by using desktop publishing. ***Desktop publishing*** is a way of using a personal computer to design documents that combine neatly arranged text and eye-catching graphics. Even if you do not have access to a computer, you can use many of the ideas discussed on the following pages to create a well-designed handwritten document.

To create a professional-looking document, you will need to make many important decisions about text and graphics. The following section explains how you can create attractive page layouts and use type effectively. For information about how graphics can make your ideas clear to readers, see page 761.

Page Layout

Page layout is the design of a page in a document. It involves the text and graphics on each page, as well as the balance of white and dark space. Consider these elements when you create a page layout for your document.

Alignment The arrangement of lines of text on a page is called ***alignment.*** Properly aligning your text can help you produce a neat, easy-to-read document. Examples of the different types of alignment follow.

- **Center-aligned** Text that is ***center-aligned*** is centered on an invisible line down the middle of the page or column. You might find titles and other short pieces of information centered.

EXAMPLE

These lines are center-aligned.
They are centered on an
imaginary line down the middle
of the column.

- **Left-aligned** When a section of text is ***left-aligned,*** each line begins at the left margin of the page or column. Most text in English is left-aligned, since English words are read from left to right.

EXAMPLE

These lines of text are left-
aligned. Notice that each line
begins at the left margin of
the column.

- **Right-aligned** Text that is ***right-aligned*** lines up against the right margin of the page or column. Right alignment can make text difficult to read, so it is only used with small amounts of text. For instance, quotes that are pulled from a piece of writing may be right-aligned so they stand out from the rest of the text.

EXAMPLE

These lines of text are
right-aligned. All of the text
is lined up against the right
margin of the column.

- **Justified** When several lines of text are ***justified,*** the lines form a straight edge along the left and right margins. Spaces must be added to the lines to ensure that each edge lines up. (Since the last line in justified text may have only a few words, the last line may be shorter than the other lines.) Justified text often appears in

QUICK REFERENCE HANDBOOK

books, newspapers, and magazines. Justifying text makes a document easy to read and neat.

EXAMPLE

This text is justified. Each line of text forms a straight edge along the right and left margins of the column.

- **Ragged** Text that is ***ragged*** lines up only on one side of the page. Use ragged text for your reports.

EXAMPLE

These lines are left-aligned and ragged. Each line forms a neat edge on the left but not on the right.

Bullet A ***bullet*** (•) is a large dot or other symbol that is most commonly used to separate items in a list. You can use bullets to attract a reader's eye to important information. The following bulleted list gives some guidelines for using bullets.

- Be sure your bulleted list contains at least two items.
- Make sure each item in your list is parallel. For example, if the first item is a noun phrase, each item that follows should be a noun phrase. Each item in this bulleted list begins with an imperative sentence, which is a sentence that gives a command.
- Line up text within a bulleted item beneath the first word, not beneath the bullet. For example, all of the text after the first line of this bulleted item lines up beneath the word *Line.*

Contrast The term ***contrast*** describes the balance of light and dark areas on a page. The dark areas of a page have text, pictures, and other graphics. The light areas have very little text and few or no graphics. A page with high contrast—in other words, one with a balance of light and dark areas—is easier to read than a page with low contrast.

Emphasis ***Emphasis*** is a way of stressing what is important on a page. You can emphasize important information by using color, text size, graphics, or boxes around the text. Pick only the most important items to emphasize. If too many items are emphasized on a single page, the technique loses its effect.

Gutter A ***gutter*** is the inner margin of space from the printed area of a page to the book's binding.

Headers and Footers ***Headers*** and ***footers*** are lines of text that give information about a document. Headers are at the top of the page, and footers are at the bottom. Headers and footers often contain information such as the following.

- name of writer
- name of publication
- date of publication
- chapter or section title
- page numbers

Headings and Subheadings Titles within the sections of a document are called ***headings*** and ***subheadings.*** They may also be called ***heads*** and ***subheads.*** The purpose of headings and subheadings is to make the organization of a document clear to the reader.

- ***Headings*** are titles used to describe a major section of text. A heading appears at the beginning of a section of text and often appears in large, bold, or capital letters. (See also **Type** on this page.)

- ***Subheadings*** are more specific headings within a major section. A writer uses subheadings to break a major section into smaller sections so readers can find the information they need. To call attention to subheadings, a writer sometimes sets subheadings in a different size, design, or style of type than that of the main text.

EXAMPLE

The Great Outdoors	heading
Vacationers find outdoor trips fun, economical	subheading
Say the word "vacation" and what once came to mind were pictures of hotels, historical landmarks, and tourist traps. Now, however, more people are vacationing outdoors.	text

Indentation When you ***indent*** text, you move the text a few spaces to the right of the left margin. Indentation at the beginning of a paragraph is commonly five spaces or half an inch.

Margins The ***margin*** of a page is the blank space at the top, bottom, and sides that surrounds the text or graphics. Word-processing programs commonly set side margins at 1.25 inches and top and bottom margins at 1 inch. You can change your margins to fit more or less text on the page. However, you should always check with your teacher before changing the margins on your paper. (See also **White Space** on this page.)

Pull-quote See page 142.

Rules Vertical and horizontal lines in a document are knows as ***rules.*** Rules can separate columns or set off text from other elements, such as a headline or graphic.

Title and Subtitle A document's ***title*** is its name. ***Subtitles*** are secondary, more descriptive titles. Sometimes, subtitles follow the title and a colon. However, if the subtitle is on its own line, no colon is necessary. In a book, the title and subtitle appear on a separate page at the beginning.

EXAMPLE

Changes of Life

Some Insects Metamorphose into Other Forms

White Space On a page, an area where there is no text or graphics is called ***white space.*** Using white space properly cannot only make a page look neater, but it can also make a page easier to read. White space is most commonly limited to the margins; the gutter; and the spaces between words, lines, and columns. (See also **Contrast** on page 758.)

Type

Type refers to the letters, numbers, and other characters in printed text. Using a computer program to create your document allows you to experiment with different designs and sizes of type to find the perfect presentation. As you design your document, think about these elements of type.

Font The term ***font*** is used to describe a set of characters (such as numbers, letters, and punctuation marks) of a particular design and size. For example, 12-point Palatino is a font. The font size is 12 points (see below); the font design is called Palatino. Font is also called *typeface.*

Font Size The size of type in a document is called the ***font size,*** or ***point size.*** The font size is measured in points. A point is $\frac{1}{72}$ of an inch. The main text of a school assignment is usually printed in 10- or 12-point type. Captions are usually printed in slightly smaller point sizes, one to three points smaller than the main text. Headlines and titles may be printed in a range of point sizes, from 14 points in a standard document to 72 points in a poster.

Title	24 point
Text	12 point
Caption	9 point

Font Style The ***font style*** is the way type is printed. You can use a font style to create emphasis. You can also use font styles to conform to mechanics rules, which tell when to use capitals, italic type, and so on. Examples of common font styles follow.

- **Boldface** A ***boldface*** word is written in thick, heavy type. Boldface can be used to emphasize information.

  EXAMPLE

  This sentence is written in boldface type.

- **Capital letters** A ***capital*** (or ***uppercase***) ***letter*** is most often used to conform to rules of mechanics. For example, capitals usually signal proper names, the beginnings of sentences, titles, and so on. Titles and headings sometimes appear in all capital letters. To call attention to information, a writer will sometimes put a word or a sentence in text in all capital letters. However, this strategy should be used sparingly.

- **Condensed** When type is ***condensed,*** the letters in a word have less space between them. In justified text, writers sometimes use condensed type to save space.

  EXAMPLE

  This sentence is written in condensed type.

- **Expanded** When type is ***expanded,*** the letters in a word have more space between them. Expanded type can be used to draw attention to information. Writers use expanded type to fill up space, especially when text is justified.

  EXAMPLE

  This sentence is written in expanded type.

- **Italics** A word written in ***italic*** type has a slanted style. Italic type, like boldface, can be used to create emphasis. It is also used in conventional situations, such as when referring to titles in text. (See also page 660.)

  EXAMPLE

  This sentence is written in italic type.

- **Lowercase letters** A ***lowercase*** letter is neither a capital nor a small capital. Lowercase letters are the most frequently used letters.

- **Shadow** A word written in ***shadow*** style makes the word appear to cast shadows. Shadow style is more appropriate for titles and headings than it is for regular text.

  EXAMPLE

  This sentence is written in shadow type.

- **Small capitals** Use ***small capitals*** when writing abbreviations referring to time. For example, when typing the time *5:00 P.M.* and the year *A.D. 1776,* you should use small capitals.

Leading Another word for *line spacing,* or the distance between lines of text, is called ***leading*** (rhymes with *heading*). Most formal documents you create for your teacher are double-spaced. Double-spacing your document makes it easier for your teacher to read your assignment and make comments and corrections. Books, magazines, and newspapers that are written for a general audience are usually single-spaced.

Legibility A document that is ***legible*** is one that contains text and graphics that are clear and easily recognizable. A document with high legibility uses a simple, easy-to-read font size and design, such as twelve-point Palatino, for the main text. A highly legible document also contains well-designed graphics.

Typeface See **Font** on page 759.

Graphics

Graphics, such as charts, graphs, tables, diagrams, and illustrations, are a great way to communicate. Graphics can

- show information
- explain a process or show how to do something
- show how something looks, works, or is organized
- show developments over a period of time

The most effective graphic is one that supports and communicates the same information as the text on the page where the graphic appears.

Arrangement and Design

Arranging your graphics and text in an organized, pleasing way can be difficult. Use the tips below to help you arrange and design graphics that are effective and informative.

Accuracy Make sure that your graphics contain ***accurate,*** or true, information. Use information from reliable sources only.

Color Using ***color*** in your graphics makes the graphics more interesting to your readers. You can use colors to do the following.

- Attract your reader's attention.
- Stress important information.
- Group items on a page.
- Organize information on a page or throughout a document.

Think about these hints as you use color in your document.

- *Plan out a color scheme for your document.* A color scheme is a collection of two or more colors that work well together.
- *Use complementary colors.* Colors opposite each other on the color wheel (see below) are complementary. Colors that are too close to each other appear to blend together, while colors opposite each other tend to stand out.
- *Do not overuse warm colors.* Reds, oranges, yellows, and other warm tones can be overpowering. Use warm colors sparingly for emphasis.
- *Use cool colors.* Blue, green, and other cool colors make readers feel calm. Cool colors work well as backgrounds.

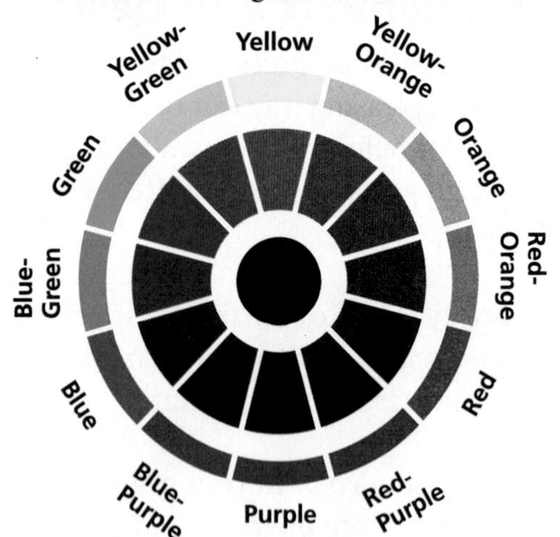

A ***color wheel*** demonstrates how different colors in the spectrum relate to each other. The ***primary colors*** are red, blue, and yellow. All other colors are formed by combining primary colors or by mixing them with black or white. When you create a color scheme, combine complementary reds, blues, and yellows.

Focus The subject of a graphic is called its ***focus.*** Use the following questions to help you make sure your graphic has a clear focus.

- *Is the subject of the graphic clear?* Make sure your graphic contains a clear title that describes the subject.
- *Does the graphic contain distracting information?* Details that do not make your idea clearer can be distracting. Crop or trim out the distracting details to refocus the graphic.
- *Is the entire subject shown, or are parts hidden?* Make sure your graphic shows the important parts of the subject.
- *Does the graphic need labels?* Using labels can make your graphic easier to understand. However, make sure not to use too many labels. Too many labels can confuse the reader.

The focus of your graphic should support the text next to which the graphic appears.

Labels, Captions, and Titles Add ***labels, captions,*** and ***titles*** to graphics to make them easier to understand. ***Labels*** identify the important parts of a graphic. Labels are connected to the graphic with thin lines called *rules.* ***Captions*** are sentences that explain a graphic, especially if the graphic is a photograph or illustration. Captions appear beside, above, or below the graphic and are commonly set one to three points smaller than the text surrounding the graphic. Even if your graphic contains no labels or captions, it should have a clear ***title.***

Types of Graphics

Use the following information to choose the best graphics for your document. Once you decide on the type of graphics you want for your document, you can create the graphics by computer or by hand.

Chart A ***chart*** demonstrates the relationship between pieces of information. Two common types of charts are flowcharts and pie charts.

- ***Flowcharts*** show a sequence of events. Each box in a flowchart contains text. The boxes appear in order from right to left or from top to bottom. Many flowcharts include arrows to show the direction in which to read.

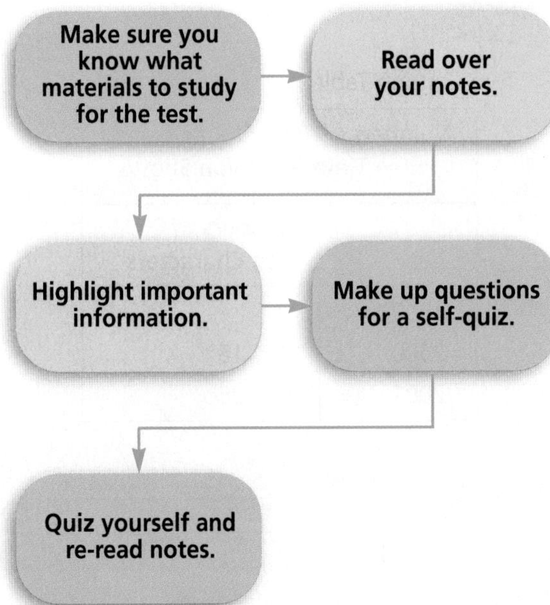

- ***Pie charts*** demonstrate how the parts of a whole relate to each other. Pie charts are often used to show comparisons. The largest wedge starts at the top, and the other wedges are arranged clockwise in decreasing order of size. (See also **Charts** on page 785.)

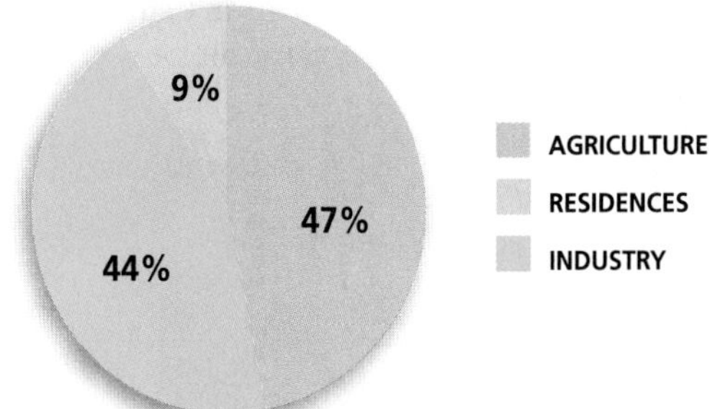

Diagram A ***diagram*** uses pictures and symbols, such as circles and arrows, to compare abstract ideas, show a process, or provide instruction. As with all of the graphics in this section, a diagram can be drawn by hand or by computer. (See also ***Diagrams*** on page 785.)

Graph A ***graph*** shows how something changes over a period of time. The horizontal axis of a *line graph* or *bar graph* usually shows periods or points in time. The vertical axis shows amounts.

EXAMPLES

Line Graph

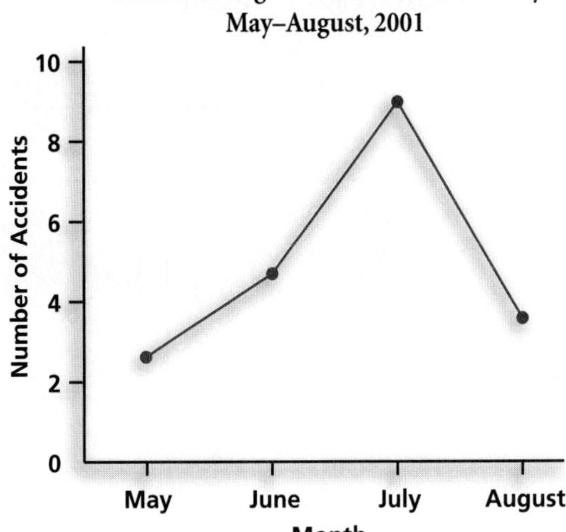

Bar Graph

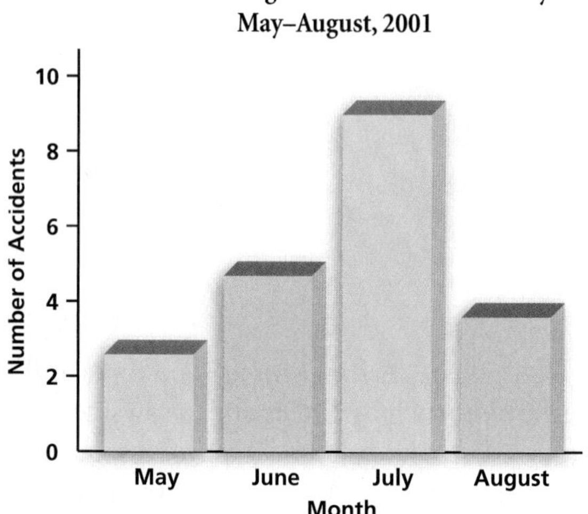

Illustration An ***illustration*** is a drawing or photograph that shows readers an unfamiliar or hard-to-picture event or object; what something or someone looks like; how to do something; or how something works. (See also **Diagram** on page 763.)

Storyboard A ***storyboard*** illustrates a series of actions. Storyboards are frequently used to plan a video segment, movie, or TV commercial. As seen below, storyboards contain boxes, each representing one scene in the story. A small sketch in the box depicts the main action of the scene, and text may appear inside the box or as a caption.

Table ***Tables*** show information without analysis or interpretation. It is up to readers to read the information and then draw their own conclusions. For example, after studying the following tables, a reader could conclude that the number of teen characters in prime time television programs rose for three years and that the greatest number of teen characters on any single channel was ten. A reader might also predict that the number of teen characters on television will continue to increase in the future.

EXAMPLES

Two-Column Table

Numbers of Teen Characters on Prime Time Television Shows	
Year	Numbers of Teen Characters
1999	7
2000	18
2001	26

Nothing to do?

There's a place with a door that's open for you.

Have you been to the library lately?

Three-Column Table

Ages of Characters on Prime Time Television Shows by Local Channel		
Channel	**Ages 0–12**	**Ages 13–19**
24	1	9
38	5	10
18	10	7

When making a table, make sure to organize information logically and label information clearly so that your readers will understand your point.

Time Line A ***time line*** demonstrates events that happened over a period of time. Like a graph, a time line has an axis which can be horizontal or vertical. The points along the axis of a time line show points in time. The events that happen during a specific year or period of years are described above, below, or to the side of the date. Time lines may also include small pictures or illustrations.

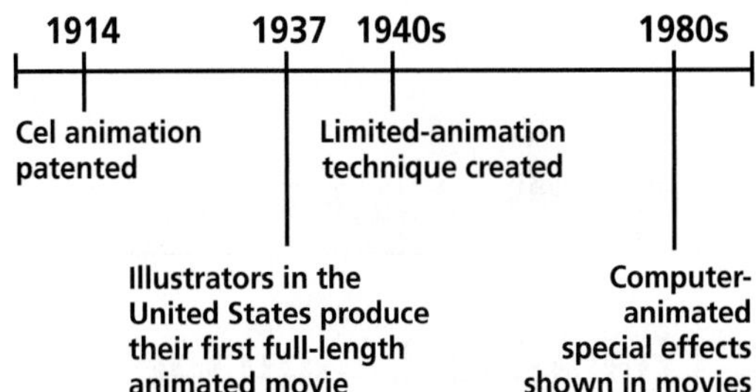

QUICK REFERENCE HANDBOOK

The History of English

Origins and Uses

A Changing Language

English and dozens of other languages have the same ancestor, a language that was spoken over six thousand years ago in Europe. For example, the English word *mother* is similar to the French word *mère,* the German word *Mutter,* and the Spanish word *madre.*

English has been a written language for about 1,300 years. Its history can be divided into three major stages: *Old English, Middle English,* and *Modern English.* You would recognize some of Middle English, but Old English has changed so much that you would probably have a hard time translating it.

Changes in Meaning Over time, words take on new meanings as people use the words in different ways. For example, the word *silly* meant "happy or blessed" in Old English. In Middle English, the word *silly* meant "harmless" and then evolved into meaning "foolish."

Changes in Pronunciation Modern words are also pronounced differently from Old and Middle English words. These pronunciation changes explain why some words are not spelled as they sound. For example, the word *knight* used to be pronounced with a beginning *k* sound. We have kept the spelling, but changed the pronunciation. Vowel sounds have also changed. In the thirteenth century, *meek* would have sounded like *make, boot* like *boat,* and *mouse* like *moose.*

Changes in Spelling Spelling is one of the most obvious changes in English. Some changes are subtle, but others are dramatic. You would probably recognize the Old English word *catt* as the present-day *cat.* However, the Old English word *hwit,* from which we get the modern word *white,* has undergone a more dramatic change in spelling.

Word Origins English has a large vocabulary of over 600,000 words, but it can take credit for only about 15 percent of those words. The other 85 percent have been invented from proper names or borrowed.

- **Borrowed words** English is a language that loves to borrow words from other languages and cultures. For example, our word *sky* comes from the Norse word *sky.* We also borrowed the word *paper* from the Latin word *papyrus.* From the French, we took *faceon* and changed it into *fashion.* Here are some other examples of borrowed words.

EXAMPLES

African: gumbo, okra, safari

Dutch: boss, sleigh, waffle

Native American: chipmunk, moose, totem

Spanish: avocado, patio, tamale

- **Words from names** Proper names are another source of new words in English. Many objects are named after the people who invented or inspired them or after the places from which they come. The *graham cracker* is named for Sylvester Graham, the minister who invented the graham cracker. *Sardines* come from Sardinia, an island in the Mediterranean Sea. *Teddy bears* were named after the twenty-sixth U. S. president, Theodore ("Teddy") Roosevelt.

Dialects of American English

Different groups of people speak different forms, or varieties, of American English called ***dialects.*** Dialects differ from one another in pronunciation, grammar, and vocabulary. Everyone uses a dialect, and no dialect is better or worse than another.

Ethnic dialects Your cultural heritage can make a difference in how you speak. The English used by a particular cultural group is called an ***ethnic dialect.*** Like a regional dialect, an ethnic dialect is a shared language that many (but not all) members of a group have in common. The most widely spoken American ethnic dialects are the English of many African Americans and the Spanish-influenced English of many people from Mexico, Central America, Cuba, and Puerto Rico. Many words from these dialects have become part of the general American vocabulary. For example, *jazz* and *jukebox* come from African American dialect, and *bronco* and *mesa* come from Hispanic English.

Regional dialects People from a particular region of the country tend to talk alike. In other words, they use the same ***regional dialect.*** The chart below shows three of the major regional dialects in the United States. The fourth, *Western,* is still developing. The chart shows some examples of the differences among the dialects. Not everyone in a region uses that region's dialect. Also, people in one region may use words and expressions that are considered part of another region's dialect.

	Northern	Midland	Southern
Vocabulary	pail	bucket	bucket
Grammar	ten pound	ten pounds	ten pound
Pronunciation	*greasy* with an *s* sound	*greasy* with a *z* sound	*greasy* with a *z* sound

QUICK REFERENCE HANDBOOK

Standard American English

Many Americans use more than one variety of English. They speak a regional or ethnic dialect at home and use ***standard American English*** at school or work. Standard American English is the most widely used and accepted variety of American English. It is the variety you usually hear on radio and television and read in books and magazines. It is the form people are expected to use in school and business situations. This textbook will help you understand the rules for using standard American English. Expressions that are labeled *nonstandard* in **Part 3: Grammar, Usage, and Mechanics** are not considered *standard* usage. *Nonstandard* does not mean wrong language. It means language that is inappropriate in situations where standard English is expected.

Two Types of English

Since American English has many different forms, you need to choose your words carefully to suit your purpose, audience, and situation. Different situations can affect the way you speak or write. Because of the situation, you must choose the correct type of English—either formal or informal—to match your purpose and audience.

Formal English ***Formal English*** is the language you would use for important occasions such as public speeches, graduation ceremonies, and serious reports. Formal English often includes long sentences and precise words. It usually does not include contractions such as *don't* or *isn't.*

Informal English ***Informal English*** is used in everyday speaking and writing. You probably use informal English when you talk with family members or friends and when you write personal letters or journal entries. Informal English uses short sentences that are easy to understand. It also includes contractions and conversational expressions. You should be familiar with two uses of informal English: *colloquialisms* and *slang.*

- **Colloquialisms** ***Colloquialisms*** are the colorful, widely-used expressions in conversational language. They are not appropriate in more formal situations. Many colloquialisms have meanings that are different from the basic meanings of the words.

EXAMPLES

That movie **gave me the creeps.**

Bernice is a **real sport.**

- **Slang** ***Slang*** is often the special vocabulary of specific groups, such as musicians, teenagers, or military recruits. Slang consists of made-up words or old words used in new ways. Because of slang's limited use, it usually has a short life. The examples below are all considered slang, but they might seem out-of-date to you now.

EXAMPLES

crib: the place a person lives

hang out: spend time at a place

get into: enjoy, be interested in

The Library/ Media Center

Using Print and Electronic Sources

Maybe you think of the library, or media center, as a place for getting information for completing school assignments. The library, however, is also a place for getting information for your personal use. At the library, you can read the latest magazines, check out the next book in your favorite fiction series, or research the value of a baseball card collection. Understanding how to use print and electronic sources will help you find information quickly and efficiently.

Call Number Libraries give a number and letter code—a ***call number***—to each book. The *call number* tells you how the book has been classified and where to find it in the library. Most school libraries use the **Dewey Decimal Classification system** to classify and arrange books according to their subjects. The system assigns numbers to books according to ten categories. For example, history books are assigned numbers in the 900s. Biographies usually do not have Dewey Decimal system numbers and are placed in a separate sections. Biographies are alphabetized according to the subjects' last names. If there are several books about the same person, the biographies are then arranged according to the last names of the authors. Fiction books are also kept in a separate section and are arranged alphabetically by the authors' last names. Some libraries arrange books using the Library of Congress Classification system.

Card Catalog The traditional ***card catalog*** is a cabinet of small drawers containing three types of cards: title cards, author cards, and subject cards. The cards are arranged alphabetically, and each type of card is in a separate section of the cabinet. The card catalog allows you to search for a book by title, by author, or by subject. Only nonfiction books have subject cards, however; fiction books are generally listed by title and author only. A *"See"* or *"See also"* card tells you where to find additional information on a subject. The parts of a card are labeled and explained on the next page.

Information in the Card Catalog

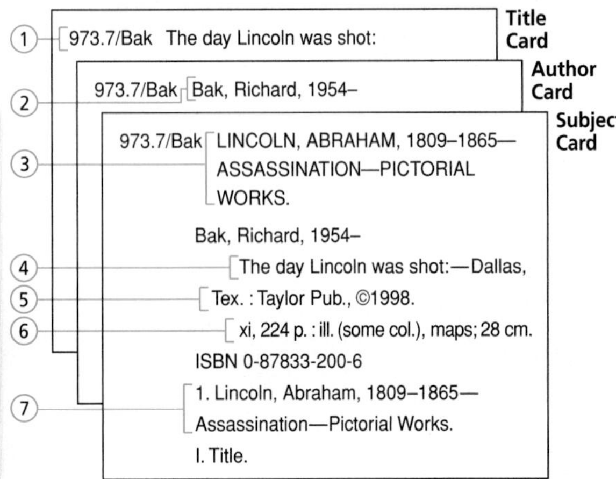

1. **Call Number**
   The number assigned to a book by the Dewey Decimal or Library of Congress Classification system
2. **Author**
   Author's full name, last name first
3. **Subject**
   General subject of a book; subject card may show specific headings
4. **Title**
   Full title and subtitle of a book
5. **Publisher**
   Publisher's name and place and date of publication
6. **Physical Description**
   Description of the book, such as its size and number of pages, and whether it is illustrated
7. **Cross-references**
   Refers to other headings or related topics under which a book is listed

Many libraries now use electronic or online card catalogs instead of the traditional card catalog. (See also **Online Card Catalog** on page 772.)

CD-ROMs *CD-ROM* (Compact Disc-Read Only Memory) is a CD that holds large amounts of visual and audio information that can be retrieved by computer. Since one CD-ROM can hold about 250,000 pages of printed text, many encyclopedias, dictionaries, and indexes come on CD-ROMs. Another advantage of CD-ROMs is that they allow you to conduct searches. They may also provide interactive graphics and audio. (For some specific CD-ROM titles, see the **Reference Works** chart on page 773.)

Indexes An index lists topics, sources, or authors alphabetically and tells where to find information on them. An index may apply to a single book, a series of books, or a whole body of different publications. For example, when looking for recent magazine articles, you might use the *Readers' Guide to Periodical Literature.* This index lists articles, poems, and stories from more than two hundred magazines and journals (periodicals). Articles are listed alphabetically by author and by subject in boldface, capitalized headings. A key at the front of the *Readers' Guide* explains the meanings of the abbreviations used in the entries. The printed and online versions of the *Readers' Guide* give the same information. Both versions sometimes provide ***abstracts,*** or summaries, of the articles.

On the following page are examples of *Readers' Guide* entries. The first example is from the print version and shows several entries for subjects beginning with *C.* The second example shows how one of these entries would appear in the online version.

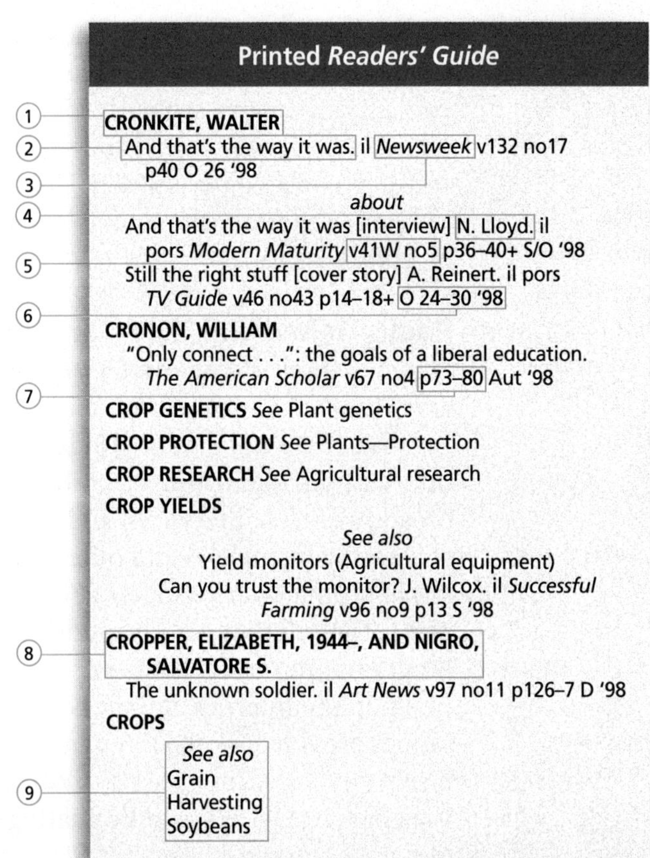

1 **Subject entry**
2 **Title of article**
3 **Name of magazine**
4 **Author of article**
5 **Volume number of magazine**
6 **Date of magazine**
7 **Page reference**
8 **Author entry**
9 **Subject cross-reference**

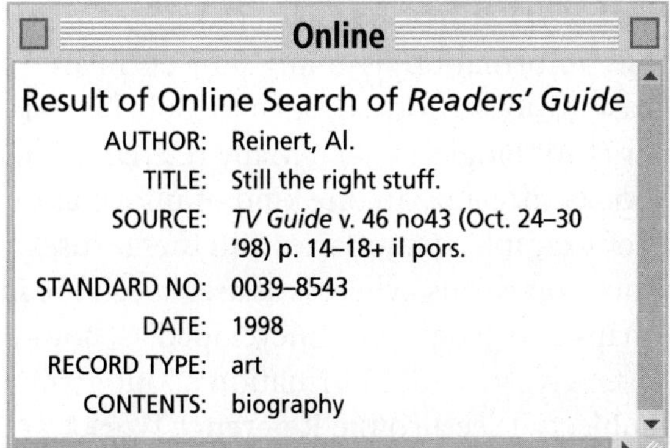

Internet The ***Internet*** is an international network of computers. Through the use of modems, the network allows users to display, view, send, and retrieve information from computers anywhere in the world. Developed in the 1960s by researchers who wanted to share data, the Internet is now used by millions of people and contains information on almost any topic. There are many ways to view material on the Internet, including FTP (File Transfer Protocol), Gopher, Telnet, and *World Wide Web browsers.* The most popular place to begin research is the World Wide Web. (See also **Browser** and **World Wide Web** on page 774.)

Microforms ***Microforms*** are photographically reduced articles from various publications. The two most common kinds of microforms are *microfilm* (a roll or reel of film) and *microfiche* (a sheet of film). A special projector enlarges the images to a readable size. Microforms are especially useful when you are researching historical subjects. You can see articles from the actual newspapers and magazines published at the time of an event.

Online Card Catalog An ***online card catalog*** is a catalog of a library's holdings, stored on a computer. To find the book you want, type in the title, author, or subject of the book. The computer will display the results of the search, as shown below.

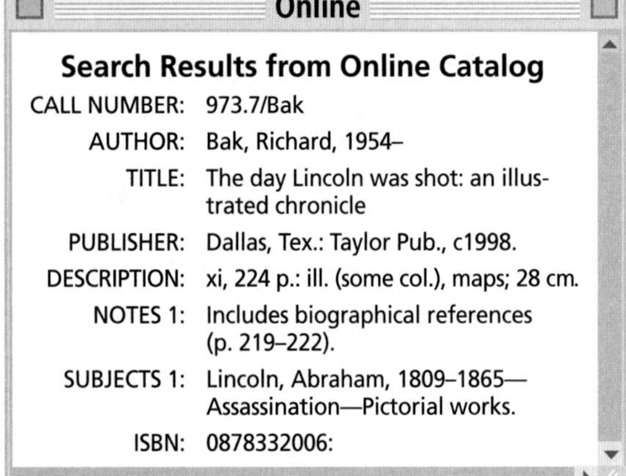

Online

Search Results from Online Catalog

CALL NUMBER:	973.7/Bak
AUTHOR:	Bak, Richard, 1954–
TITLE:	The day Lincoln was shot: an illustrated chronicle
PUBLISHER:	Dallas, Tex.: Taylor Pub., c1998.
DESCRIPTION:	xi, 224 p.: ill. (some col.), maps; 28 cm.
NOTES 1:	Includes biographical references (p. 219–222).
SUBJECTS 1:	Lincoln, Abraham, 1809–1865—Assassination—Pictorial works.
ISBN:	0878332006:

Online Databases An ***online database*** is a collection of information that can be accessed only by a computer. Most databases are created for specific groups of people or organizations, such as universities, libraries, or businesses. Some databases require a subscription, which means that users must pay to use the database. Other databases may be accessed free of charge through the World Wide Web.

Online Sources An ***online source*** is a source of information that is retrieved by computer. When you use a modem to connect to the Internet, you are online.

Periodicals Publications that are published at regular intervals are called ***periodicals.*** Libraries carry scholarly journals, popular magazines, newspapers, and consumer-related periodicals. These periodicals are used for both research and pleasure by library visitors.

Radio, Television, Film, and Video You may think of ***radio, television, film,*** and ***video*** as sources of entertainment. However, they can also be good sources of information. Radio and television often broadcast news, interviews, and documentaries. Documentaries and other educational programs are also found on film or video. Listings that describe radio and TV programs appear in newspapers and sometimes on the Internet. Be sure to check the ratings provided for the films and videos before viewing them. (See also **Critical Viewing** on page 824, and **Evaluating Media Messages** on page 825.)

Reference Books Reference books contain information on many subjects in an easy-to-locate format, such as alphabetical or chronological order. Many reference books specialize in one kind of information. For example, dictionaries and thesauruses focus on words, whereas atlases specialize in maps and geography. Encyclopedias, however, give general information about many subjects. (See also the **Reference Works** chart on page 773.)

Reference Sources The chart on the next page describes common reference sources and gives specific examples of each type of source.

Reference Works		
Type	**Description**	**Example**
Encyclopedias	▪ multiple volumes ▪ articles arranged alphabetically by subject ▪ contain general information ▪ may have index or annuals	*Collier's Encyclopedia* *Compton's Encyclopedia* *The World Book Multimedia Encyclopedia™*
General Biographical References	▪ information about the lives and accomplishments of outstanding people	*Current Biography Yearbook* *Dictionary of American Biography* *Biography Index* (database) *Webster's New Biographical Dictionary*
Special Biographical References	▪ information about people noted for accomplishments in various fields or for membership in specific groups	*American Men & Women of Science* *Contemporary Authors® on CD-ROM* *Mexican American Biographies*
Atlases	• maps and geographical information	*Atlas of World Cultures* *National Geographic Atlas of the World*
Almanacs	▪ up-to-date information about current events, facts, statistics, and dates	*The Information Please Almanac, Atlas and Yearbook* *The World Almanac and Book of Facts*
Books of Quotations	▪ famous quotations indexed or grouped by subject	*Bartlett's Familiar Quotations* *The Oxford Dictionary of Quotations*
Books of Synonyms	▪ list of more vivid or more exact words to express ideas	*Roget's International Thesaurus* *Webster's New Dictionary of Synonyms*
Literary References	▪ information about various works of literature	*Granger's Index to Poetry* *Short Story Index* *Subject Index to Poetry* *Gale Literary Index CD-ROM*

Vertical File A *vertical file* is a special file containing up-to-date materials such as newspaper clippings or informative pamphlets from the government and other sources.

World Wide Web (*WWW* or *the Web*) Think of the ***World Wide Web*** as a galaxy of linked documents within the Internet universe. The linked documents are ***Web sites*** or ***Web pages*** and contain text, graphics, video, and sometimes sound. The linked documents are joined by connections known as *hyperlinks.* The following terms will help you understand the workings of the World Wide Web.

- **Browser** The software that allows computers to enter and navigate the Web is known as a ***browser.*** The browser helps viewers find, read, save, download, and explore Web sites; it also helps viewers use the links between sites. Jumping from site to site with the aid of a browser is known as ***browsing*** or ***surfing.*** (See also **Web Site** on the next page.)

- **Hyperlink** Clicking on a ***hyperlink*** connects the user to a new Web site or area on the Internet. Hyperlinks, also known as *links,* are words, headings, or symbols that are underlined or are set in a different color than the core text.

- **Search Engine** When you want to search for specific information on the Web, a ***search engine*** provides a list of sites that contain the keywords you enter. (See also **World Wide Web, Searching,** on page 775.)

- **URL** (***U***niform ***R***esource ***L***ocator) The ***URL*** is like a street address for a document on the Web. Instead of numbers and street names, URLs use a specific format, which may include abbreviations, numbers, words, and punctuation. The parts of the address are explained below.

1 2 3

http://go.hrw.com/ndNSAPI.nd/gohrw_rls1/pHome

1. The language used by the Internet service
2. The ***hostname.*** The hostname is made up of a series of "domains." Each domain gives your computer more and more specific information when you send it out to look for a Web site. In the example above, *com* tells your computer that the Web site you want is a part of a commercial network. In the same example, *hrw* is the name of the company whose computer contains the Web site, and *go* is the specific machine within *hrw* that contains the Web site.

   Here are abbreviations and descriptions of the most common networks:

Common Networks on the World Wide Web	
com	commercial or individual
edu	educational
gov	governmental
net	administrative
org	usually nonprofit organization

3. The specific request for the file or piece of information that you want. Not all addresses will have this part.

Web Site (or Web Page)

A ***Web site*** is a location on the Web that contains linked pages. The ***home page*** is the first page on a Web site; it usually gives an overview of the major areas in the site. Usually, the home page also includes hyperlinks that connect to other sites. The sample home page to the right is a typical example of what you would see if you had located a Web site with a browser.

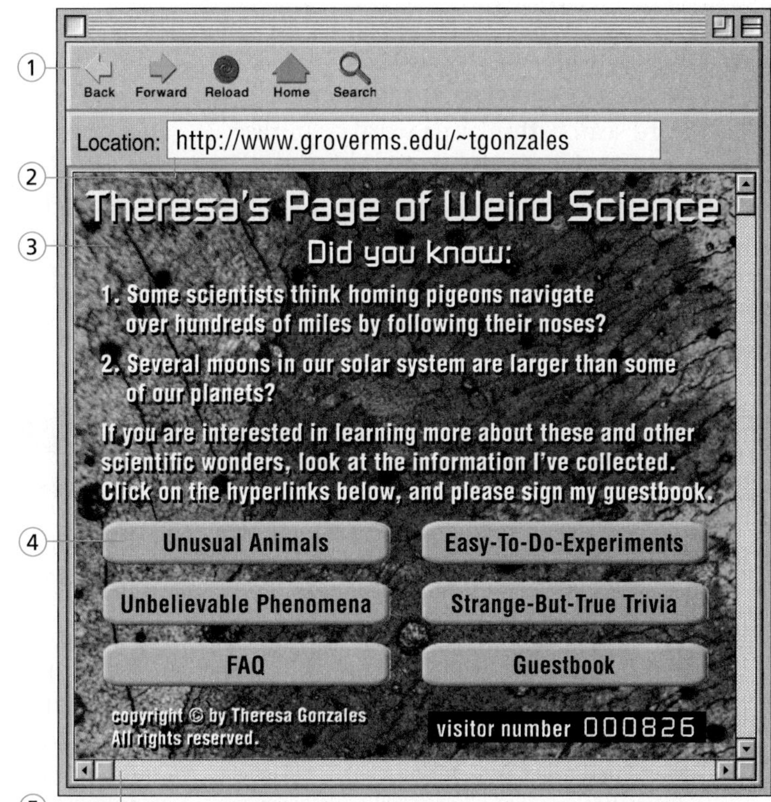

1. **Toolbar buttons** Click toolbar buttons to perform different functions, such as search, print, move forward or back to different pages, and see or hide images.
2. **Location window** This box shows the address, or the URL, of the site at which you are looking.
3. **Content area** This area shows the main text, images, hyperlinks, and other parts of a Web page.
4. **Hyperlink** Click these buttons to connect to other Web sites and information available within this site.
5. **Scroll bar** Clicking along the horizontal or vertical scroll bar (or on the arrows at either end) allows you to move left to right or up and down in the image area.

World Wide Web, Searching Finding the right information quickly on the Web means knowing how to search. To find information, you can use *directories* and *search engines.*

Directories If you want to use a table of contents to the Web, you might consult a directory. A ***directory*** breaks down the World Wide Web into broad categories, such as *Travel* and *Sports.* Subcategories are listed under the general categories, and these subcategories are broken down into even more specific sub-subcategories. You search a directory by narrowing down a general topic to a specific one.

Search Engines A ***search engine*** allows you to search the Web for sites that contain a specific word or phrase. Looking for sites that contain specific words or phrases is known as a ***keyword search.*** To conduct a keyword search, think of a word or phrase that is related to the subject you want to find. Then, type the keyword or phrase in the search space and hit the return key or the search or find button. A list of sites will appear, with the most relevant matches at the top.

If the number of matches for a search is too great, you may need to narrow your search. To narrow the search to a manageable number of matches or to increase the matches, learn to *refine* your search. The strategies below can help you; keep in mind, however, that different search engines may use slightly different commands. Consult the Help section of your search engine for specific commands.

Refining a Keyword Search

Strategy	Example
▪ **Make your keywords specific instead of general.** A general keyword can produce many irrelevant matches.	If you are interested in group dances, type *Macarena* instead of *dance*.
▪ **Use quotation marks.** Putting quotation marks around your keyword or phrase tells the search engine to find sites with exact matches of your words.	Enter "Revolutionary War" to find sites about the fight for United States independence rather than sites about revolutionary cleaning products or the Korean War.
▪ **Use *AND.*** When you put the word *AND* between your keywords, the search engine will find only Web sites that contain all words connected by *AND*.	For sites that mention both Wolfgang Amadeus Mozart and Antonio Vivaldi, enter *Wolfgang Amadeus Mozart AND Antonio Vivaldi.*
▪ **Use *NOT* between keywords** to make sure that the search engine does not pull up sites that deal with topics that are similar but unrelated.	Enter *Apollo NOT Greek god* to find Web sites about the Apollo Theater, not the Greek god Apollo.
▪ **Use *OR.*** To broaden your search, use *OR* to let the search engine know that you would accept sites that contain any of your keywords.	If you want sites that discuss either vegetarian or low-fat diets, enter *vegetarian OR low-fat diets.*

To choose the most useful sites from a list of search results, make predictions. Use sites with names that fit your topic, and avoid sites you think are selling products. If a site seems promising, go to its home page and make more predictions. Look for professional-looking graphics, clear organization, and relevant categories. If you see amateurish text or graphics or no sign of your specific topic, move on to another site on your list.

World Wide Web, Web Site Evaluation Information from the World Wide Web may sound accurate or official. The Web, however, is not monitored for accuracy in the way most newspapers, books, or television programs are. Therefore, you must be critical of the information you find there. The chart below lists questions you can use to ***evaluate*** a Web site's value as a source of information.

Evaluating Web Sites
Who created or sponsored the Web site? Knowing a Web site's creator or sponsor will tell you much about the accuracy of the site's information. The Web site's home page should identify its sponsor. Use only Web sites that are affiliated with reputable organizations, such as government agencies, universities, and museums. The Web sites for these organizations will usually belong in the *edu, gov,* or *org* networks. National news organizations also provide reliable information on the Web.
When was the page first posted and is it frequently updated? Information that is current and frequently updated lets you know that the Web site's sponsor pays attention to recent changes. The dates of its first posting and updates usually appear at the bottom of the home page, along with the creator's e-mail address.
To what other Web pages is the site linked? Sometimes you can judge a Web site by its links. Sites with accurate information will be linked or affiliated with reputable sites.
Does the Web site present information objectively? An objective site will present ideas from both sides of an issue. If a site contains strong language or opinions, consider using a different site.
Is the Web site well designed? A well-designed Web site with legible type, clear graphics, and working links shows that the sponsor has put time and effort into the site. The written content of the site should also be well organized and use proper spelling, punctuation, and grammar.

Reading and Vocabulary

Reading

Skills and Strategies

You can use the following skills and strategies to become a more effective reader.

Author's Point of View, Determining The author's attitude about a subject is called the ***point of view.*** An author's point of view, or ***bias,*** is often shaped by his or her beliefs. As a reader, determining an author's point of view can help you get more meaning from the text. (See also page 246.)

EXAMPLE Students should be required to take physical education each year. PE gives students daily physical exercise and teaches them how to play a variety of sports. PE will help students develop the lifelong habit of physical fitness, which is an important part of a healthy lifestyle. This knowledge is just as important as history or math.

Author's point of view: Students should be required to take physical education each year.

Author's Purpose, Determining An author has a reason to write about the subject. An author's reason is called the ***purpose.*** To inform, to influence, to express oneself, and to entertain are the major purposes for writing. (See also page 22.)

EXAMPLE An important part of making your schedule is choosing an elective. Students have four choices: band, art, Latin, and choir. To make a good choice, consider your interests, abilities, and future plans. Electives are also a good way to explore new interests, so you might want to branch out in a new direction. Choosing the right elective can make your schedule and your year great.

Author's purpose: To inform students about choosing electives

Cause-and-Effect Relationships, Analyzing When you read, you may find yourself asking, "Why?" and "What happened?" You are examining causes and effects with these questions. A ***cause*** makes something happen. An ***effect*** is what happens as a result of that cause. (See also page 90.)

EXAMPLE Brace yourself for the changes that come with braces! First, your mouth feels different with all those wires, bands, and appliances. Since your mouth feels so different, you may find that you have to learn new ways to talk and eat.

Analysis: Braces are the *cause* that makes the following *effects* happen: your mouth feels different; you find new ways to talk and eat.

Clue Words, Using To connect ideas smoothly, a writer uses certain ***clue words.*** A writer usually chooses clue words based on the text structure he or she is using. Use these clue words to help you identify a writer's organizational pattern. (See also **Text Structures** on page 783.)

Clue Words

Cause-effect Pattern

as a result	so that
because	therefore
consequently	this led to
if . . . then	thus
since	

Chronological Order Pattern

after	not long after
as	now
before	second
finally	then
first	when

Comparison-contrast Pattern

also	not only . . . but also
although	on the other hand
as well as	similarly
but	unless
either . . . or	yet
however	

Listing Pattern

also	most important
for example	to begin with
in fact	

Problem-solution Pattern

as a result	this led to
nevertheless	thus
therefore	

Drawing Conclusions When you read, you encounter two sets of information: the information in the text and the information you already know. When you add information you already know to information in a text to make a judgment about the text, you are ***drawing conclusions.*** As you read, gather information and connect it to your experiences to understand the text better. (See also page 54.)

EXAMPLE Carrie stood on the street corner in the early morning light. She glanced again at her history notes, trying to put the wait to good use. She was tempted to open her lunch box and eat her sandwich. Two other students sat on their backpacks, watching the cars whiz past the corner.

Conclusion: Carrie and the students are waiting for the school bus.

Fact and Opinion, Distinguishing A ***fact*** is information that can be proved true. An ***opinion*** expresses a personal belief or attitude, so it cannot be proved true or false. Writers often use facts to support their opinions. A reader who can tell fact from opinion will not be easily misled. (See also page 162.)

EXAMPLE

Fact: A tunnel under the English Channel, nicknamed the Chunnel, connects England and France.

Opinion: Driving in a tunnel is dangerous.

Generalizations, Forming A reader forms a ***generalization*** by combining information in a text with personal experience, current events, or cultural backgrounds to make a judgment about the world in general. (See also page 122.)

EXAMPLE Three new soccer leagues have sprung up in the city of Fairview in the last decade. Each year the number of teams grows. Boys and girls ages four to fourteen try to hone their skills in weekly practices and games. Parents who never played the game themselves are becoming knowledgeable and enthusiastic fans of the sport.

Generalization: Soccer is becoming a popular sport for many American families.

Implied Main Idea, Identifying Sometimes the main idea of a passage is not directly stated; instead it is ***implied*** or suggested. In this case, you, the reader, have to analyze the details and decide what overall meaning these details express. (See also page 21 and **Stated Main Idea** on page 782.)

EXAMPLE Masoud Karkehabadi graduated from high school in California at age seven. He was so interested in Parkinson's disease that he started doing research to find a cure when he was just eleven. At the ripe old age of thirteen, Masoud graduated from college and planned to start medical school at fourteen.

Implied main idea: Masoud Karkehabadi was very intelligent.

Making Inferences An ***inference*** is an educated guess based on information in the text and on your prior knowledge and experience. As you read, you make decisions about ideas and details that writers do not directly reveal. *Generalizations, conclusions,* and *predictions* are three types of inferences.

EXAMPLE The traffic on the interstate slowed to a crawl and then stopped. After fifteen long minutes, Miriam turned off the ignition and got out. She could barely see a tow truck and the flashing blue light of a patrol car ahead of the long line of cars. "Great," she said as she leaned against the car door.

Inference: A car accident is preventing traffic from moving, and Miriam will be delayed.

Paraphrasing ***Paraphrasing*** is the act of restating someone else's ideas in your own words. Using paraphrasing when you read may help you to understand the author's meaning better. Unlike a summary, which includes only the main points, a paraphrase is a complete retelling of an author's ideas. (See also **summarizing** on page 783.) For this reason, a paraphrase is usually about the same length as the original. Be sure to avoid *plagiarism* with both paraphrasing and summarizing. Plagiarism occurs when you use an author's exact words without quotation marks, then publish those words as your own. (See the chart on page 812 for paraphrasing guidelines.)

EXAMPLE Helping Hearts is not just any business. This is a candle-making business with a big heart and a big purpose: helping Romanian orphans. Valorie Darling and Arielle Ring of Spokane, Washington, started the business when they were both eleven years old. The two girls started selling handmade beeswax candles that they first made as Christmas presents. During its first year, Helping Hearts donated about $8,000 to Romanian charities.

Paraphrasing: Two eleven-year-olds are using their candle-making business to help Romanian orphanages. Valorie Darling and Arielle Ring of Spokane, Washington, were making beeswax candles for holiday gifts when they decided to start selling their home-made candles. They named their business Helping Hearts, and in the first year they donated about $8,000 to charities in Romania.

Persuasive Techniques, Analyzing
Writers who use ***persuasive techniques*** try to convince readers to think or act in a certain way. Some persuasive techniques rely on faulty reasoning or emotional appeals. As you read persuasive writing, look for sound, logical reasoning and facts to help you decide whether you agree or disagree with the writer's opinion. (See also page 207.)

EXAMPLE Valleyview Middle School needs more dress choice days for its students. The school now allows only two dress choice days. However, in a student survey, 98 percent of students said they would like to have at least four dress choice days per year. Students could become depressed if forced to wear the same school uniform day after day. Better schoolwork and attendance would occur with more dress choice days.

Analysis: The second and third sentences state facts that support the opinion in the first sentence. The second-to-last sentence contains an emotional appeal. (It appeals to the reader's heart.) The last sentence contains faulty reasoning. (No evidence supports this conclusion.)

Predicting ***Predicting*** is the act of deciding what you think will happen next in a text. You can make accurate predictions by examining the text and relying on your own knowledge and experience. As you read on, you can confirm or adjust your predictions.

EXAMPLE Alex glanced at his watch after he made the final corrections to his report. He had just ten minutes to print out the report before he had to leave for school. He hit the print command and sat back to watch. Suddenly, the printer beeped and then stopped. The ink cartridge was empty, and Alex knew he didn't have another one.

Prediction: Alex will not be able to print out his report. He will either be late to school or will have to hand in his report late.

Problem-Solution Relationships, Analyzing A ***problem*** is an unanswered question. A ***solution*** is an attempt to answer that question. When an author writes about a problem, he or she may propose, or suggest, one or more solutions. To analyze the problem in a problem-solution paper, ask yourself what the problem is, who has the problem, and why it is a problem. Then, look for the solution(s) the author suggests. Finally, analyze the solution(s) by deciding if the solution(s) could work.

EXAMPLE For years, DeLee Springs has provided people of all ages with a safe place to swim and socialize. However, because the city's new budget does not provide the funds to pay a full-time lifeguard, DeLee Springs is in danger of closing to the public. To prevent this from happening, I suggest that our class start a fund-raising campaign. As students, we might not have the money to pay a lifeguard, but businesspeople in our community do. If a businessperson does not want to donate directly, we could simply ask him or her to put out a donation jar.

Analysis: The problem is that DeLee Springs could close. The problem affects the members of the community, because many people in the community enjoy the springs. The solution the author suggests is for students to start a fund-raising campaign. Since DeLee Springs only needs one lifeguard, and businesspeople in the community would probably want to help, this solution seems like it could work.

Reading Log, Using a When you write down ideas, questions, and reactions to your reading, you are creating a ***reading log.*** A reading log, which can be a notebook or journal, can help you understand what you read. Because readers have different experiences, interests, beliefs, and opinions, no two reading logs will be alike.

Reading Rate, Adjusting The speed at which you read is called your ***reading rate.*** How quickly or how slowly you read depends upon your purpose for reading. Adjusting your reading rate to suit your purpose, as shown in the chart below, helps you to be a more efficient reader.

SQ3R *SQ3R* is a popular reading and study strategy. SQ3R stands for five steps in the reading process:

S ***Survey*** the entire text. Look briefly at each page—the headings, titles, illustrations, charts, and the material in boldface and italics.

Q ***Question*** yourself as you do your survey. What should you know after completing your reading? Make a list of questions to be answered.

R ***Read*** the entire selection. Think of answers to your questions as you read.

R ***Recite*** in your own words answers to each question.

R ***Review*** the material by re-reading quickly, looking over the questions, and recalling the answers.

Stated Main Idea and Supporting Details, Identifying The most important point or focus of a passage is the ***main idea.*** A topic sentence often reveals

Reading Rates According to Purpose

Reading Rate	Purpose	Example
Scanning	Reading for specific details or key words	Looking for the name of the main river in central Africa in a geography textbook
Skimming	Reading for main points	Reviewing charts, headings, and graphs in your science textbook the night before a test
Reading for mastery	Reading to understand and remember	Taking notes on a chapter in your history textbook to study for a test
Reading at a comfortable speed	Reading for enjoyment	Reading a newspaper article about interesting people or events

a paragraph's main idea. The main idea of an essay is usually included in the essay's introduction or conclusion. ***Supporting details*** support or explain the main idea.

NOTE A stated main idea is also called an explicit main idea. (See also **Implied Main Idea** on page 780.)

EXAMPLE

Henry O. Flipper finally recovered his good name 118 years after being accused of a crime he did not commit. In February 1999, President Clinton pardoned Flipper in a ceremony attended by Flipper's family. The first African American to graduate from the U.S. Military Academy at West Point, Flipper was born a slave in 1856. Flipper was wrongly dismissed from the army for "conduct unbecoming an officer."

Main idea: It took 118 years for Henry Flipper to be cleared of a crime he did not commit.

Supporting details: Flipper was born a slave in 1856. He was wrongly dismissed from the army. President Clinton pardoned him in 1999.

Summarizing A ***summary*** gives a brief restatement of only the most important points of a selection. In contrast, a *paraphrase* restates almost all of the ideas in a passage. (See also **Paraphrasing** on page 780). Summarizing helps a reader understand a passage's key points. (See the chart on page 812 for summarizing guidelines.)

EXAMPLE A creative librarian in Kenya has figured out a way to get books to isolated desert villages. Wycliffe Oluoch employed three camels to carry library books to village students. The camels, accompanied by four people, now make up the Mobile Camel Library. Carrying about 400 pounds of books, the camels travel to villages two times a month. Students are thrilled when they spy the Mobile Camel Library headed their way.

Summary: Wycliffe Oluoch created the Camel Library to deliver library books to students in isolated villages in Kenya.

Text Structures, Analyzing The pattern a writer uses to organize ideas or events is called a *text structure.* The five major patterns of organization are cause-effect, chronological order, comparison-contrast, listing, and problem-solution. Recognizing these structures will help you to understand a text and its ideas better. Use the following guidelines when analyzing text structures.

1. Search the text for the main idea. Look for clue words that signal a specific pattern of organization (see the **Clue Words** chart on page 779).
2. Study the text for other important ideas. Think about how the ideas connect, and look for an obvious pattern.
3. Remember that a writer might use one organizational pattern throughout an entire text or might combine patterns.
4. Use a **graphic organizer** to map the relationships among the ideas. Your graphic organizer may look like one of the following text structures.
   - ***Cause-effect pattern*** explains why something happens (causes) or shows the results of something (effects). (See also page 778.) The example on the next page shows how a week at camp (cause) led to new friends, increased confidence, and new skills (effects).

Causal Chain

Attended Camp Minnehaha
↓
Lived in cabin with people from different places
↓
Tried new activities like rock climbing
↓
made new friends | increased confidence | learned new skills

- ***Chronological order pattern*** shows events or ideas happening in sequence. (See also page 55). The following example shows the sequence for sending e-mail.

Sequence Chain

Log on to Internet provider → Type in recipient's address in "To" header → Write message in e-mail → Click the "Send" button

- ***Comparison-contrast pattern*** points out similarities and/or differences. A Venn diagram is one graphic organizer you can use to see similarities and differences between two topics. Similarities appear where the two circles overlap, and differences appear where the circles do not overlap. The following example compares right whales and white sharks.

Venn Diagram

Differences: Right Whales	Similarities	Differences: White Sharks
▪ use lungs to breathe ▪ sideways tail fin ▪ type of mammal ▪ use baleen to strain food	▪ backbone ▪ live in water ▪ animals	▪ use gills to breathe ▪ vertical tail fin ▪ type of fish ▪ use teeth to grab food

- ***Listing pattern*** presents material according to certain criteria such as size, location, importance, or relatedness. The following example lists details about the items in a closet according to their location.

List

1. floor: shoes, dirty clothes, backpack, crumpled papers
2. clothes rod: shirts, pants, coats, ties
3. shelves: suitcases, sleeping bag, boxes, blankets

- ***Problem-solution pattern*** identifies at least one problem, offers one or more solutions to the problem(s), and explains the outcomes and the final results. The following example illustrates how one school dealt with the problem of raising money for a school trip.

Problem: Money Needed for Trip	
Solution	**Result**
bake sale	Not many people participated. We raised very little money.
car wash	Several students and parents volunteered. This solution helped raise most of the money for the trip.

Transitional Words and Phrases, Using Words or phrases that connect ideas and make writing smooth are called ***transitions.*** Transitions may be words or phrases. As a reader, your ability to recognize transitions will help you to understand how all the ideas in a selection fit together. (See page 309 for chart of transitional words and phrases.)

Visuals and Graphics, Interpreting ***Visuals*** and ***graphics*** convey complex information in a simple, visual format by using pictures or symbols. Most often, they provide a clear comparison of different but related points of information. As a reader, your task is to interpret the information presented in a visual or graphic and draw your own conclusions.

- **Elements of an effective visual:**

1. The **body** presents information in the form of a graph, chart, time line, diagram, or table; the body is specific to the type of information or data that is presented.
2. **Labels** identify and give meaning to the information shown in the graphic.
3. A **legend,** or **key,** identifies special symbols, color coding, scales, or other features readers need to recognize in order to read the graphic; the legend appears as a small box placed near the body.
4. The **source** identifies where the information contained in the graphic was found; knowing the source helps readers evaluate the accuracy of the graphic.
5. A **title** identifies the subject or main idea of the graphic.

- **Examples of common visuals, such as charts, diagrams, graphs, tables, and time lines:**

1. **Charts** show how parts of a whole are related. The emphasis in a **pie chart** is always on the proportions of the sections, not on the specific amounts of each section nor on the value of the whole pie.

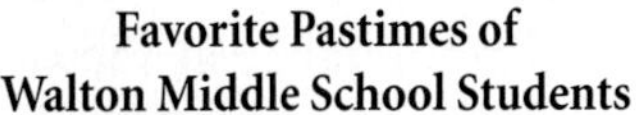

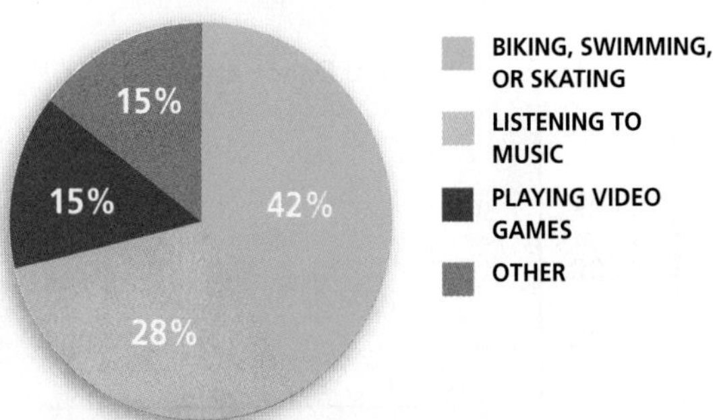

2. **Diagrams** use symbols (such as circles or arrows) or pictures to compare ideas, show a process, or provide instruction. Keep in mind that diagrams should not be used to present numerical data. The shapes and forms used in diagrams are generally not

accurate ways to represent amounts. The diagram below uses a picture to show the paths electrons take around the nucleus of an atom.

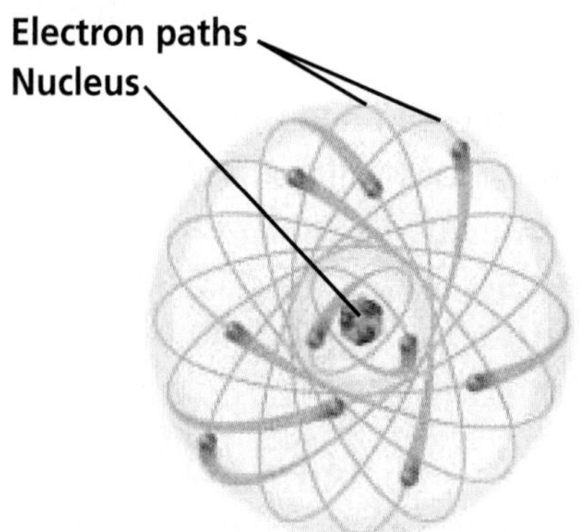

3. **Graphs** show changes or trends over time. The horizontal axis in a **line graph** or **bar graph** indicates points in time, and the vertical axis shows quantities. The vertical axis on a line or bar graph should begin at zero. The bar graph below shows changes in the number of students who attended the annual school dance at Victory Middle School. (See also page 763.)

School Dance Attendance

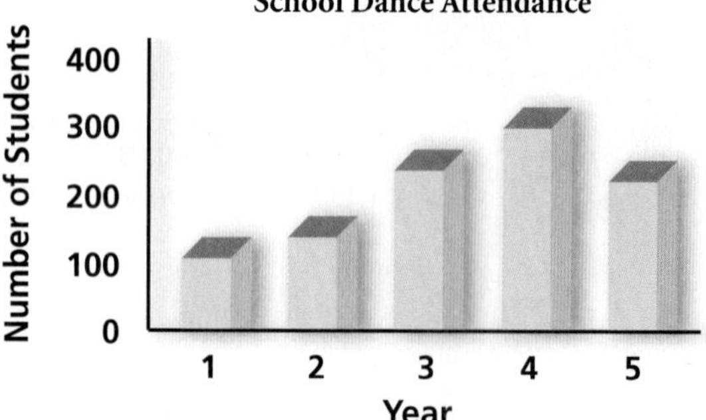

4. **Tables** provide information in its simplest form. They do not show trends and patterns in data. Readers must draw their own conclusions about any relationships in the data. The following table illustrates one student's daily homework schedule.

Daily Homework

Class	Assignment	Status
English	complete page 54	finished
Science	read pages 8–12	haven't started
Math	worksheet	finished

5. **Time lines** identify events that take place over the course of time. Events are identified or described on one side of the time line, and the time divisions or periods are indicated on the other side.

Major Events in Early Space Travel

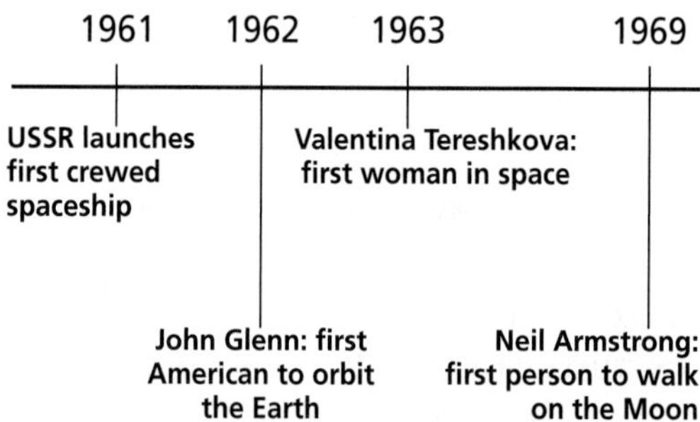

Tips for interpreting visuals.

1. **Always read the title, labels, and legend** of any visual or graphic before analyzing the data it presents.
2. **Draw your own conclusions,** and compare them to those of the writer.
3. **Think about the information that is *not* included** in the graphic. Is important information left out because it does not match the author's conclusions?

Vocabulary

Context Clues Sometimes the ***context*** of an unfamiliar word will give you clues to its meaning. The context is the group of words or sentences surrounding the word. Here are some common types of context clues.

How to Use Context Clues
Type of Clue
Definitions and Restatements: Look for words that define the term or restate it in other words. *The **appalling** condition of the starving dog filled Ana with dismay and shock.*
Examples: Look for examples used in context that reveal the word's meaning. *Potters, weavers, and other **artisans** donated their products to the crafts fair.*
Synonyms: Look for clues that indicate an unfamiliar word is similar in meaning to a familiar word or phrase. *His guilt and regret showed that his **remorse** was real.*
Antonyms or Contrasts: Look for clues that indicate an unfamiliar word is opposite in meaning to a familiar word. *The shiny, new sports car seemed out of place in front of the **dilapidated** house.*
Cause and Effect: Look for clues that indicate an unfamiliar word is related to the cause or is the result of an action, feeling, or idea. *After skipping breakfast and lunch, Yolanda was **famished.***

Word Bank A list of words that you gather from your reading, listening, and viewing is known as a ***word bank.*** Creating a word bank can help you increase your vocabulary. Check your dictionary for the meaning of each new word.

Word Meanings Words have layers of meanings that can change depending on how the words are used. Use the following definitions and examples to help you make sure that your words say what you want them to say.

- **Clichés and tired words** ***Clichés*** and ***tired words*** are phrases or words that have lost their freshness and force because of overuse.

  EXAMPLES *Pretty as a picture, home sweet home, hot as fire,* and *burned to a crisp* are clichés. *Nice, good, pretty, wonderful, terrific,* and *great* are tired words.

- **Denotation and connotation** The dictionary definition of a word is its ***denotation***—its actual meaning. A word's ***connotation*** is an additional meaning, feeling, or association suggested by the word. Because connotations often stir people's feelings, they can have powerful effects on the listener or reader.

  EXAMPLES The words *inexpensive* and *cheap* have similar denotative meanings, but they suggest different ideas. *Inexpensive* suggests an item that is affordable because of its low price. *Cheap,* on the other hand, has a negative connotation that suggests an item that is poorly made and of little value.

- **Euphemisms** A ***euphemism*** is a way of sugarcoating a word or phrase that might be considered too direct or blunt.

Some euphemisms are used as a courtesy to avoid offending people. Euphemisms are also used to mislead people—to hide unpleasant truths or misrepresent the facts.

EXAMPLES

Euphemism	More Direct Term
powder room	bathroom
pre-owned	used
passed away	died
negative outcome	failure

- **Figurative language** ***Figurative language*** creates mental pictures for the reader by going beyond the literal meaning of words. The following chart shows the most common types of figurative language.

Type of Figurative Language	Example
A **metaphor** says that something *is* something else.	*The in-line skates were the rockets that propelled him.*
Personification gives human characteristics to nonhuman things.	*The tree heard the thunder and shook in fear.*
A **simile** compares two basically unlike things, using the words *like* or *as.*	*The city lights shimmered like stars in a far-off galaxy.*

- **Idioms** ***Idioms*** are phrases that mean something different from the literal meanings of the words. Idioms often do not follow the usual rules of grammar, and they make no sense if translated word-for-word into another language.

EXAMPLES

Mr. Ware will not *put up with* any excuses.

The dog *made off with* all my freshly baked cookies.

She *fell for* Maria's explanation.

- **Jargon** ***Jargon*** is a special language used by a group of people who share the same profession, occupation, hobby, or field of study. Jargon is effective only if the reader or listener is familiar with its special meaning. Note in the following example how the single word *run* can mean different things to different groups.

EXAMPLE **Run**

Baseball players—a point scored

Farmers—an outdoor enclosure for animals, such as chickens

Musicians—a rapid sequence of notes

Journalists—the printing of the newspaper

- **Loaded words** ***Loaded words*** deliberately provoke strong feeling, either positive or negative. A writer or speaker who wants to prejudice you for or against something may use loaded words.

EXAMPLES

A *gourmet* meal and *luxurious* surroundings made quite an impression on the staff.

An *overpriced* meal and *wasteful* surroundings made quite an impression on the staff.

- **Multiple meanings** Since a word can have more than one meaning, you need to consider all of its definitions. Keep in mind the context in which you read or heard the word, because the context will determine the meaning you choose. Then, try each definition in that context until you find the one that fits.

  EXAMPLE She invested all of her **capital** in the stock market. (As shown by the following definitions, the third definition for *capital* as a noun best fits the meaning in context.)

  capital (kap'ət'l) *adj.* **1.** first and most important **2.** excellent; first-rate **3.** punishable by or involving death. —*n.* **1.** capital letter. **2.** the official seat of government of a city or town. **3.** money or property owned or used for business purposes by a person or corporation.

Word Origins See **The History of English** on page 766.

Word Parts Most English words are made up of smaller units called word parts. (Words that cannot be divided into parts are called **base words.** *Plate, grind,* and *large* are examples of base words.) The three types of word parts are ***roots, prefixes,*** and ***suffixes.*** Knowing the meanings of these word parts can help you determine the meanings of many unfamiliar words.

- **Roots** The ***root*** is the foundation on which a word is built. It carries the word's core meaning, and it is the part to which prefixes and suffixes are added. Many words in English have Greek and Latin roots, as the following chart shows.

Commonly Used Roots

Roots	Meanings	Examples
Greek		
-chron-	time	chronology, chronic
-graph-	write, writing	biography, graphic
-log(ue)-, -logy-	study, word	logical, astrology
-micr-	small	microfilm, microscopic
-phono-	sound	symphony, phonetic
Latin		
-aud-	hear	audience, audible
-bene-	well, good	beneficial, benefit
-gen-	birth, kind, origin	genetic, general
-magni-	large	magnificent, magnify
-mal-	bad	malfunction, malice
-ped-	foot	pedicure, pedal
-pend-, -pens-	hang, weigh	pendulum, expense
-vid-, -vis-	see	video, vision

- **Prefixes** A ***prefix*** is a word part that is added before a root. The word that is created from a prefix and a root combines the meanings of both its parts.

Commonly Used Prefixes		
Prefixes	**Meanings**	**Examples**
Greek		
anti-	against, opposing	antiwar, anticlimax
dia-	through, across, between	diameter, diagonal
syn-, sym-, syl-, sys-	together, with	synthesis, symmetric, syllable, system
Latin and French		
bi-	two	bisect, bimonthly
co-	with, together	coexist, codependent
de-	away from, off, down	debone, debug
in-, im-	in, into, within	introduce, imprison
inter-	between, among	interpersonal, intersect
non-	not	nonprofit, nonfat
post-	after, following	postnasal, postgraduate
pre-	before	prepayment, preview
re-	back, backward, again	reverse, return, recur
sub-	under, beneath	submarine, substandard
trans-	across	transplant, translate
Old English		
mis-	badly, not, wrongly	mistake, mislead
over-	above, excessive	overhead, overstate
un-	not, reverse of	uneven, unlock

Suffixes A ***suffix*** is a word part that is added after a root. Often, adding or changing a suffix will change both a word's meaning and its part of speech, as in *please/pleasure.*

Commonly Used Suffixes		
Suffixes	**Meanings**	**Examples**
Greek, Latin, and French		
Nouns		
-ance, -ancy	act, quality	admittance, constancy
-ity	state, condition	reality, sincerity
-ment	result, act of, state of being	judgment, fulfillment
-tion	action, condition	rotation, election
Adjectives		
-able	able, likely	readable, lovable
-ible	able, likely	flexible, digestible
-ous	character-ized by	dangerous, malicious

Commonly Used Suffixes		
Suffixes	**Meanings**	**Examples**
Verbs		
-ate	to become, to cause to be	captivate, activate
-fy	to make, to cause to be	liquefy, simplify
-ize	to make, to cause to be	socialize, motorize
Old English		
Nouns		
-dom	state, condition	stardom, freedom
-hood	state, condition	manhood, sisterhood
-ness	quality, state	brightness, kindness
Adjectives		
-en	made of	earthen, golden
-ish	like, tending to be	bookish, childish
Verbs		
-en	to cause to be	shorten, soften

Words to Learn Use the three words in the list below to increase vocabulary this year. Make it a habi unfamiliar words from this list regularly.

abuse
acceptance
access
accessible
accessory
accommodations
activate
adapt
adept
adequate
adjacent
advantageous
advent
aeronautics
agenda
aggressive
alliance
anonymous
anthology
antibiotics
anxiety
appalling
apt
aristocrat
aroma
arrogant
articulate
artisan
aspiration
assumption
attain
automation

badger
baffle
bankrupt
barbarism
basis
baste
bewilder
blockade
boisterous
boycott
braggart
burly

calamity
calculation
capital
casual
catastrophe
category
censorship
charitable
circulate
circumnavigate
clarify
climax
colossal
commute
complement
condemn
confederation
confide
confiscate
congest
consecutive
considerate
contagious
contemporary
controversy
convert

creative
customary

decade
deceased
deceive
dedicate
deduction
defy
delegate
demolish
denial
deport
depose
derive
descend
detach
dictate
diction
dilapidated
dilute
diminish
dingy
diplomat
disagreeable
discord
dismantle
dispatch
dispense
dissect
distraction
durable

eccentric
ecology
elegant
eligible
embarrass
emigrate
eminent
emphasize
endorse
enhance
epidemic
erosion

essay
evacuate
exaggeration
exertion
extensive

falter
famine
famished
feasible
feline
ferocious
fictitious
folklore
foresight
foreword
fragile
fragment
fraudulent
frequency

gallery
generate
glorify
gnarled
gracious
grieve

hamper
harmonious
haughty
haven
hilarious
hospitable
humidity
humiliate
hydraulic
hypothesis

illuminate
immense
immigrate
impel
imperative
imply
impose

improvise
impulsive
incite
inclination
incomparable
inconsiderate
indelible
inevitable
inflexible
ingenious
inherit
insoluble
integrity
intelligible
intensity
intentional
intercept
intervene
intolerance
intrigue
invariable
irk
isolation

jeopardize
jubilation

knoll

liable
liberate
literal

malfunction
malnutrition
manageable
maroon
memento
menace
menagerie
miscellaneous
misdeed
modify
monopoly
morale
motivate

multicolored
multitude
mutual
myriad
mystical

nationality
naturalization
negligent
neutral
notify
nourish
novelty

obituary
obscure
occupant
occurrence
omission
optimism
ordeal

pacify
parasitic
persistent
petition
petty
pewter
phenomenon
photogenic
picturesque
pious
planetarium
pleasantry
populate
posterity
potential
prearrange
predicament
premier
premiere
presume
primitive
privilege
probable
probation

propaganda
proposal
prosecute
provision
pulverize
pun

quaint
quench

rebate
recuperate
refuge
regime
remorse
remote
resolute
respiration
restore
restrain
revelation
rigid
riotous
romantic
ruthless

sable
salutation
sanctuary
sarcasm
satire
saturate
secluded
sedate
sincerity
spacious
strategy
successor
summit
superficial
sustain
synthetic

tangible
tariff
tarnish
technology
temperament
testify
therapy
thrifty
thrive
titanic
transit
tumult

unique
upbraid
urban
urgent

valid
valor
verify
vitality

warranty

Speaking and Listening

Speaking

Use the strategies in this section to become a more effective speaker in formal speeches and oral interpretations as well as in informal speaking situations.

Formal Speaking

Formal speeches are given at specific times and places and for specific reasons. The purpose for giving a formal speech may be to inform, to persuade, or to entertain.

Content of a Formal Speech A formal speech is given at an arranged time and place, which allows you time to prepare what you will say. The steps in preparing your speech are very similar to the steps in the writing process. The following steps can help you write an effective speech.

1. **Select a topic.** Sometimes you will speak on an assigned topic, but other times you may be able to choose the topic for your speech. Use one of the methods in the next column to find a topic that will interest both you and your audience.
   - Consider turning one of your written compositions into a speech.
   - Brainstorm a list of topics.
   - Ask teachers, friends, and classmates for ideas about topics.
   - Look over past journal entries.
   - Flip through magazines, newspapers, and books for ideas.
2. **Identify purpose and occasion.** The ***purpose*** of your speech is what you want the speech to accomplish. The purpose of your speech will influence your presentation. For example, you may need to adapt your word choice to suit your purpose. The chart on the next page describes some of the most common purposes for formal speeches. The ***occasion*** of your speech is determined by when and where it takes place. The event at which you are speaking also influences your speech. Use the questions on the next page to help you understand how the occasion of your speech will affect it.

Purposes for Speaking	
Purpose	**Examples of Speech Titles**
To inform give facts or explain how to do something	▪ What Makes an Airplane Fly ▪ How to Make Your Home a Safer Place ▪ How to Make Paper Airplanes
To persuade attempt to change listeners' opinions or get them to take action	▪ Why Getting Suntans May be a Bad Idea ▪ Why Students Should Learn CPR ▪ Recycle Now!
To entertain relate an amusing or interesting story or incident	▪ My First Experience Riding a Bicycle ▪ My Mom, the Superhero ▪ Mud Puddles and Mud Pies

- ***Is the occasion formal or informal?*** When you speak for a formal occasion, such as eighth-grade graduation, you need to speak carefully. Pronounce words correctly and use **standard formal English.** If the occasion is less formal, for example, a banquet for your track team, you can probably worry less about formal language and word choice.
- ***When will you give your speech?*** The date and time of day affect your speech. If you give your speech on a certain holiday or observance, you can connect your ideas to that date. The time of day can also affect your speech. If you are speaking when people may be tired, such as the early morning or after a meal, include lots of surprising, attention-getting information.
- ***Where will your speech be given?*** Where you speak also affects your preparation. Will you have a microphone and a podium on which to place your notes, or will you have to speak without the benefit of a microphone?
- ***What other conditions might affect your speech?*** What are the time limits for your speech? Have you been given a specific topic, or can you choose your own? Can you use notes? Find out about these and any other restrictions for your speech.

3. **Analyze the audience.** When you plan your speech, you also need to consider your audience's needs and interests. You will need to use a vocabulary and manner of speaking that they will understand and avoid using slang, jargon, or technical terms. If you are adapting a piece you have written, consider how your listening audience will be different from the audience you had in mind when you wrote the piece. The questions in the chart on the next page will help you analyze your audience.

Thinking About Your Audience

Questions about audience	Answer	Your speech will need
What does the audience already know about this subject?	very little	to provide background details to inform your listeners about your topic
	a little	to include at least some background detail
	a lot	to focus on lesser-known facts
How interested will the audience be in this subject?	very interested	to maintain your listeners' interest with surprising information throughout the speech
	only a little interested	to stick to parts of the topic in which your listeners are most interested
	uninterested	to convince your listeners that this topic is important

4. **Gather information.** You will need to find information about your topic that will interest your audience and fit the purpose and occasion for your speech. Depending on your topic, the information in your speech may come from your own memories, from previous writing assignments you have done, or from more formal research. (See also **Library/ Media Center** beginning on page 769 and **Arranging Ideas** on page 841.)

5. **Organize your speech notes.** In order to speak directly to your listeners, rather than reading a report aloud to them, you will need to make note cards. Look over the information you have gathered, and prepare an outline of the main points you want to make in your speech. Then, make a note card for each main point, using the pointers in the chart in the next column.

How to Create Speech Note Cards

1. Write each major point on a separate note card, then add notes to remind you of evidence, elaborations, and examples you want to use to support that point.

2. Make a special note card for anything that you plan to read word for word, such as a quotation or a series of dates or statistics that would be hard to memorize.

3. Include a special note card to indicate when to show a chart, diagram, model, or other visual materials.

4. Number your completed cards to keep them in order.

6. **Use media.** Media such as ***audiovisuals*** and ***electronic media*** are resources that can enhance your speech such as:
   - electronic media (graphic images, audio files, and text presentations)

- audio recordings (cassettes or compact discs)
- pre-recorded videotapes or videodiscs
- short films
- slides or filmstrips
- visuals such as charts, graphs, illustrations, and diagrams

Use the following questions to help you decide whether to use audiovisuals or electronic media in your presentation.

Evaluating the Use of Media in Speeches

1. *Will media help you make a point more clearly?* Some ideas are best explained with a visual, so using a chart or poster can help communicate your ideas easily.

2. *Will the media help the audience remember a point?* Media can help emphasize points you especially want your audience to remember.

3. *Will the media distract the audience while you are speaking?* Don't overuse media in your speech. The audience might pay more attention to the media than to your speech.

When you use media, make sure the materials are easy for your audience to see and hear. Always have your materials ready to use. For example, have audio clips cued up and ready to play. Make sure posters, charts, and other visuals are large enough for your audience to read. (See also **Graphics** on page 761.)

Delivery of a Formal Speech Use the following pointers to deliver a speech effectively.

1. **Rehearse.** Rehearsing your speech gives you confidence and helps you spot mistakes. Use these strategies to make your practice productive.
   - Practice your speech in front of an audience of friends and family members. Practicing with an audience will prepare you for the actual speech situation.
   - Present your speech just as you hope to deliver it. Use hand gestures and eye contact. Be natural.
   - Evaluate your performance. Ask yourself and your practice audience for honest feedback. Use this feedback to make changes. You might revise your speech's organizational structure, or you may simply need to rearrange a few sentences to clarify your meaning. Then, practice some more. (See also **Listening to Evaluate** on page 807.)
   - Plan additional rehearsals. Give yourself enough time for several rehearsals before you give your speech. Practice does make perfect!
2. **Deliver the speech to your audience.** When you speak effectively, you use your voice and your gestures to help convey your meaning to your listeners. Here are some pointers to use when you are speaking.
   - Be prepared. Organize your material carefully. Make sure your note cards and other special information and visuals are ready before you speak.
   - Remember your purpose. Focus on what you want to tell your audience

and how you want them to react instead of worrying about your performance.

- Explain ideas clearly and directly, using the active voice. For example, say "The space shuttle carries a crew of astronauts," not "A crew of astronauts is carried by the space shuttle."
- Use nonverbal signals, sometimes called **body language,** which are an important part of communicating effectively. The following chart lists some nonverbal elements you can use in your speech.

Nonverbal Signals
Eye contact *Examples or Meanings* Look directly into the eyes of your audience members *Functions* ▪ Helps to convey honesty or sincerity ▪ Can communicate intensity
Facial Expression *Examples or Meanings* Wink, make eye contact, raise an eyebrow, smile, frown, or sneer *Functions* ▪ Reveals your feelings ▪ Can emphasize certain words
Gestures *Examples or Meanings* Give the thumbs up (approval, encouragement), shrug (uncertainty), nod the head (agreement), shake the head (disagreement) *Functions* ▪ Can sometimes replace words ▪ Emphasizes words or phrases ▪ Adds meaning to the speech
Posture *Examples or Meanings* Stand tall and straight *Functions* ▪ Gives an attitude of confidence and poise

- Use verbal elements. The expressive qualities of your voice can enhance communication with your audience. Practice the tips below.

Verbal Elements	Definition
Diction	*Enunciate,* or pronounce words clearly, when you speak to help your listeners understand you.
Emphasis (or stress)	Your voice naturally stresses some words and phrases when you speak. Emphasize words that are important in your message.
Mood (or tone)	Your speech must make your listeners feel certain emotions. Mood usually applies to oral interpretations of literature, but it may also apply to a formal speech.
Pause	Pauses are the small silences in your speech. They can emphasize a point you are making or help listeners catch up.
Pitch	Your voice naturally changes pitch—or modulates—when you speak. Saying some words higher

Verbal Elements	Definition
	and others lower gives listeners cues about your meaning. For example, you might raise your pitch to connect two related ideas, or show juncture.
Rate	Your rate, or tempo, of speaking is normally faster than the speed you will need to use when giving a formal speech. Talking more slowly during a speech helps listeners hear and understand more easily.
Volume	Although you may normally speak quietly, you need to speak fairly loudly when you give a speech. Be loud enough to be heard by all of your listeners. Consider speaking more loudly or softly to emphasize certain points.

In order to make your speech effective, consider the **audience** and the **setting** (time and place) and adapt one or all of the elements above to suit them.

Other Formal Speaking Situations

Here are some specific formal speaking situations and tips for giving each type of speech.

- **Announcements** Use an announcement to present a brief message to many people at once. Write down what you will say, get your listeners' attention, and read the message loudly, clearly, and slowly.
- **Introductions** To prepare to introduce someone to an audience, learn biographical details about the person. When introducing, clearly pronounce the person's name and title. Then, give important and interesting information about the person. Be respectful, and welcome the person you introduce.
- **Workplace speaking** In the world of work, you will encounter a variety of speaking situations, including talking with customers, sharing information at meetings, and giving co-workers instructions. In all of these situations, you should speak clearly and politely and get to the point quickly.

Informal Speaking

Informal speaking occurs in casual situations in which you have personal contact with your audience. In formal speaking situations, the speaker is more distant from the audience. Informal speaking tends to be informative or social.

Group Discussion Group discussions occur when a group of people meet together for a particular purpose. In group discussions, members share their own ideas, information, experiences, and insights, and build on ideas presented by other members of the group. The elements of a group discussion are listed below.

1. **Setting a Purpose** In many of your classes and in future work situations, you will work with others in groups to accomplish a specific purpose. This purpose may be one of the following items.

- to discuss and share ideas
- to cooperate in group learning
- to solve a problem
- to arrive at a group decision or to make a group recommendation

Once your group decides on a purpose, find out how much time will be allowed and figure out what you will need to accomplish within the time limit.

2. **Understanding Roles and Responsibilities** Everyone involved in a group discussion has a specific role. As the chart below shows, each role has special responsibilities. For example, your group may choose a recorder, with the responsibility of taking notes during the discussion. All group members should take the role of active participants—listening as well as contributing to the discussion—and should express agreement or disagreement with others in an appropriate way.

   Usually, a group creates an ***agenda***, or outline of the order of topics, to follow in a discussion. The agenda may be created by the chairperson or by the entire group.

Impromptu Speaking Sometimes you need to speak to a group of people without having time to plan what you will say. This is called an ***impromptu speech***. Remember the following points.

1. Consider your purpose. Are you trying to inform your audience? Do you want to persuade them?
2. Consider your topic. What are the main ideas you need to say? What do you want your audience to remember after you have finished speaking? Do you have time to add details that support or explain your main ideas?
3. Consider your audience. Does what you are saying suit the time, the place, and audience you are addressing?

When you are called on to give an impromptu speech, stay calm and focus on what you need to accomplish.

Speaking Socially Although speaking socially requires less preparation and less careful diction than some other types of speaking, you can improve your social-speaking skills. The guidelines on the next page will

Responsibilities of Group Members

Chairperson	▪ Announce the topic and set the agenda. ▪ Follow the agenda. ▪ Encourage each member to participate. ▪ Help group members stay on track and avoid disagreements.
Recorder	▪ Take notes about important information. ▪ Prepare a final report.
Participant	▪ Take an active part in the discussion. ▪ Ask questions and pay attention to what others have to say. ▪ Cooperate and share information.

help you speak more effectively when giving directions, making introductions, and speaking on the telephone.

Giving Directions or Instructions

1. Divide the instructions or directions into clear, understandable steps.

2. Tell your listener the steps in order.

3. Check to be sure that your listener understands all of the instructions or directions.

Making Social Introductions

1. Be confident. Introduce yourself to other people.

2. When introducing others, identify them by name.

3. When you are introducing others, you should speak first to

- an older person before a younger person
- the person you know best

Speaking on the Telephone

1. Call people at times that are convenient for them.

2. Identify yourself, and state your reason for calling.

3. Be polite. Keep your call to a reasonable length.

Oral Interpretation

When you perform an ***oral interpretation,*** you read a piece of literature expressively to your listeners. You use facial expressions, vocal techniques, and body language to interpret and express the basic meaning of the literary work. Follow these steps to prepare and present an oral interpretation.

1. **Selecting Material** When choosing materials for an oral interpretation, you usually know the purpose, audience, occasion, and length of time for your presentation. You might choose to interpret a short poem or four to six stanzas of a longer poem. The poem you choose should tell a story (such as an epic poem) or have a speaker (using the word *I* or featuring a conversation between two characters). You might use a short story, or a part of a story, that has a beginning, a middle, and an end and that has one or more characters who talk during the story. You could use part of a play, such as a scene between two characters or a dramatic monologue. Other options include giving your own interpretation of part of a famous speech or sharing a personal narrative you have written about an event or experience in your life.

2. **Adapting Material** You may be able to find just the right piece of literature that is already the perfect length. Often, though, you will need to shorten a work. This shortened version is called a ***cutting.***

How to Make a Cutting

1. Follow the story in time order.

2. Cut dialogue tags, such as *she whispered sadly*. Instead, use these clues to tell you how to act out the characters' words.

3. Cut parts that don't contribute to the portion of the story you are telling.

3. **Presenting an Oral Interpretation** After you have chosen a piece to present, you

will need to take the following steps.

- **Prepare a *reading script.*** A reading script is usually typed (double-spaced). It can then be marked to help you with your interpretative reading. For example, you can underline words you want to emphasize.
- **Write an introduction.** You may need to introduce your interpretation. You might tell your listeners something about the author of your selection, tell about important events that have already taken place in the story, or describe the setting. You will also need to tell listeners if your scene is told from the **point of view** of a certain character. If so, you should provide some background information about that character by describing his or her personality or appearance or by contrasting the character with another character.
- **Rehearse your presentation.** Practice interpreting the scene in several different ways, and choose the most effective way to interpret the passage. Use your voice to show your meaning. Vary your body movements and your voice to show that you are portraying different characters and to show important character traits.

QUICK REFERENCE HANDBOOK

Listening

Hearing is not the same as listening. Listening is an active process that involves understanding what you hear. When you hear new information, listening for understanding can be challenging. This section can help you listen more effectively.

Basics of the Listening Process

Just as you use different skills before, while, and after you read, the listening process involves skills for preparing to listen, listening, and responding to what you have heard.

Before Listening Before you begin to listen, take steps to prepare yourself to get the most out of your listening experience.

1. **Know why you are listening.** Keeping your purpose in mind as you listen helps you to become a more effective listener. You hear things differently depending on why you are listening. For example, if you listen to your friends talking, you may only pay enough attention to follow the topic. However, if you listen to directions to a new friend's house, you will probably need to pay closer attention in order to find your way. Common purposes for listening are
   - for enjoyment or entertainment
   - to gain information or solve a problem
   - to understand information or an explanation
   - to evaluate or form an opinion
2. **Limit distractions.** Listening requires concentration. Sometimes, you may get

distracted by your environment or by your own emotions. Use the steps below to help you focus on the message.

Eliminating Barriers to Effective Listening

- *Be positive, and focus on the speaker.* Begin with a positive attitude, and make sure you relax. Tell yourself that you are going to focus on the speaker for the next few minutes. Mentally put aside distracting thoughts, plans, or worries as you listen.
- *Think about the message.* As you listen, concentrate on what the speaker is saying. Try not to focus on mannerisms, clothing, or annoyances that may distract you.
- *Adjust to your physical environment.* Classrooms and other listening settings can sometimes be too hot or too cold. Bringing along a sweater can help you be more comfortable. As you choose a place to sit, make sure you can see and hear the speaker and are away from distractions.

Listening Listening effectively involves not only paying attention to the information presented, but also giving feedback to the speaker. Nonverbal elements, such as your facial expressions and body language, can tell the speaker when you are listening and when you are not. Follow these guidelines to respond politely and effectively to a speaker.

- *Respect the speaker.* Show respect for the speaker's cultural, racial, and religious background.
- *Do not interrupt.* Pay attention, and save your questions or comments until the speaker has finished.
- *Do not judge too soon.* Wait to hear the speaker's whole message before you make judgments.
- *Ask appropriate questions.* Use a voice loud enough for all to hear. To help the speaker understand your question, **summarize** or **paraphrase** the part of the speech that you are questioning. (See also **summarizing** and **paraphrasing** on page 812.)
- *Take notes of the speaker's main points.* Taking notes helps you remember important information and organize your ideas. Focus on capturing the speaker's main points as well as your own thoughts in your notes. Some listeners like to organize a speaker's ideas in outline form; others prefer to use graphic organizers. Later, use your notes to reflect, ask questions, or make comments. (See also **Notes on reading or lectures** on page 811.)

Responding to a Speaker After listening to a speech, you have an opportunity to respond. Your feedback can help the speaker know how the speech went. Choose one or more of these ways to respond to a speaker.

- *Ask questions to clarify details.* If something in the speech was not clear, ask about it. Your question gives the speaker a chance to explain, which can help you and others understand confusing information.
- *Give positive feedback.* Encourage the speaker with a compliment about one or two specific things that he or she did

well. Even if you do not agree with the speaker, you may be able to praise his or her humor or use of media.

- *Offer constructive criticism.* Constructive, or helpful, information can help speakers improve their presentations. In a polite way, mention something you did not understand or something you wish the speaker had included.
- *Remember the power of nonverbal feedback.* Body language is sometimes louder than words. Staying in your seat until after the speech is over shows interest and respect. Listening attentively to questions and answers communicates appreciation. Remember that a smile can say more than words.
- *Find out what other audience members thought of the speech.* Discussing the speech may help you rethink your response to it or your understanding of it. It may also help you learn something you missed.

Listening with a Purpose

Depending on your purpose for listening, different strategies may help you listen more effectively. The following section provides tips for listening to appreciate or to be entertained, listening to gain information, and listening to evaluate a speech.

Listening to Appreciate You usually listen to appreciate when you listen to literature, including works of fiction, poetry, and drama, and when you listen to oral tradition, such as family stories.

- **Listening to Literature** Listening to literature is similar to reading it. Reading literature means getting ready to read, reading, and thinking about what you have read. You can use similar steps when you listen to literature, as the following chart shows.

Listening to Literature
Before you listen ▪ Prepare to understand background information about the piece of literature. What is the selection about? What is the title? Who is the author? What kind of literature is it? ▪ Make predictions about what you will hear. Use your questions to help you predict what you will hear. Don't worry about whether your predictions are correct.
As you listen ▪ Visualize mental images of what you hear as the literature is read. ▪ Jot down notes, questions, or ideas you have as you listen. ▪ Relate what you hear to similar experiences or feelings you have had.

QUICK REFERENCE HANDBOOK

Listening to Literature

After you listen

- Confirm or adjust your predictions. How did your predictions change as you listened?
- Respond personally to the selection. What did you like about the selection? Did you learn anything? What did you feel while listening?
- Identify and analyze the literary elements that appeared in the literature. Did the selection use imagery, allusion, suspense, or rhythm? What was the theme, or message, of the selection? How did the literary elements add to the selection's meaning?
- Look over the questions you had before you listened. Were they answered? If not, how can you find the answers?
- Summarize the selection. What happened in the selection? What did you learn through this listening experience?

Listening to Oral Tradition ***Oral tradition*** is a way that people pass down their culture and history, usually through storytelling. Oral traditions always involve both speakers and listeners. Listening to fairy tales or folk tales, for example, makes you a participant in the oral tradition. Use the following tips to be an active listener of these important stories.

Strategies for Listening to Oral Tradition

1. Identify common elements in the stories. Many folk tales and fairy tales have similar characters, settings, themes or messages, or plots. As you listen, think about other stories with similar elements. How are the two stories alike? How are they different?

2. Compare versions of the same story. Different storytellers tell the same story differently. By emphasizing certain parts or changing wording, a storyteller makes the story he or she tells unique. Compare the story you hear now with the story as you have read or heard it before. What is different between the two stories?

3. Look for similarities and differences between the story and the storyteller's region or cultural background. Many cultures tell folk tales about superheroes. Each version, however, is unique to the storyteller's culture. For example, "Oni and the Great Bird" tells about Oni, a West African superhero who saves people from a giant eagle. Superman is a similar superhero from the United States; many elements of this story link it to the United States. Listen for ways that the story you are hearing matches or is different from the storyteller's culture or region.

4. Identify slang or sayings from specific regions and cultures. As you listen to the story, identify words or phrases used in specific regions or by people of specific cultures. What do these phrases add to the story?

Listening to Comprehend To get the information you need from a spoken message, use the following steps.

How to Listen for Information

Find major ideas.

What are the most important points? Listen for clue words, such as *major, main, most important,* or similar words.

Identify support.

What dates, names, or facts does the speaker use to support main ideas? Listen for the words *for example* or *for instance.*

Distinguish between facts and opinions.

A ***fact*** is a statement that can be proved true. (Earth is the third planet.) An ***opinion*** is a belief or a judgment about something. It cannot be proved true. (Soccer is more fun than basketball.)

Note comparisons and contrasts.

Are some details compared or contrasted with others? Compare the speaker's ideas and information with what you have heard elsewhere.

Understand cause and effect.

Does the speaker say or hint that some events cause others to occur? that some events are the result of others?

Predict outcomes and draw conclusions.

What reasonable inferences can you make from the evidence in the speech?

LQ2R The LQ2R study method helps you listen for information.

L *Listen* carefully to information as it is being presented.

Q *Question* yourself as you listen. Make a list, mentally or in your notes, of questions as they occur to you.

R *Recite* mentally the answers to your questions as you discover them, or jot down notes as you listen.

R *Re-listen* as the speaker concludes the presentation. Major points may be summed up or listed again.

***5W-How?* Questions** When you listen for information, you need to listen for details that answer the basic *5W-How?* questions: *Who? What? When? Where? Why?* and *How?* For example, when you take a telephone message, you will need to get important details from the caller, such as

- the caller's name
- whom the call is for
- the caller's message
- the caller's telephone number

Listening to Instructions Usually, instructions or directions involve a series of steps. When you listen to instructions, ask questions to be sure you understand all the steps you will need to follow.

Strategies for Listening to Instructions

1. *Listen for the order of steps.* Identify words that tell you when each step ends and the next one begins, such as *first, second, next, then,* and *last.*

2. *Identify the number of steps in the process.* If the instructions are long and complicated, take notes.

3. *Visualize each step.* Imagine yourself actually performing the action. Try to

Strategies for Listening to Instructions

get a mental image of what you should be doing at each step.

4. *Review the steps.* When the speaker is finished, be sure you understand the instructions.

Listening to Evaluate Evaluating a speech means judging its content, delivery, and impact on the audience. You should base your evaluation on how well the speech meets certain criteria. The chart below lists questions you can use to evaluate a speech. Because every speech is unique, though, it is always a good idea to generate your own criteria for evaluating a speech's content, delivery, and impact. Add your own questions to those listed below, and use them to evaluate your own presentations as well as those given by other people.

Points to Interpret and Evaluate

Interpret the speaker's message

- Can you pinpoint the main idea of the speech?
- Can you explain why the message of the speech is important?

Interpret the speaker's point of view

- Is the speaker's perspective or attitude toward the subject clear?

Evaluate the clarity of the speech

- Is the speech organized logically?
- Can you identify each of the main points of the speech?

Analyze the speaker's trustworthiness

- Did the speaker use outside sources of information to verify information?
- Are the sources respectable or credible?

Evaluate the speaker's delivery

- Can you hear the speaker?
- Does the speaker speak clearly?
- Does the speaker use gestures and facial expressions well?
- Does the speaker use visual materials?

Interpret the speaker's nonverbal messages

- Does the speaker use nonverbal elements to emphasize points?
- Do nonverbal gestures match the speaker's words?

Interpret the speaker's purpose

- Why is the speaker giving the speech?
- Is the speech given primarily to inform, persuade, or entertain?

Identify the persuasive techniques

- Does the speaker try to convince you by using reasons and evidence, by appealing to your emotions, or both?
- Does the speaker use propaganda? For example, does the speaker try to make you feel that because everyone is doing something, you should, too? Does the speaker try to make you feel that he or she understands you?

Summarize the speaker's ideas

- Does the speech have a strong beginning and ending?

Special Listening Situations

Group Discussions See **Group Discussion** on page 799.

Interviews An ***interview*** usually takes place between two people, an interviewer and the person being interviewed (called the *interviewee*). The purpose of an interview is to gather information. Follow these suggestions to conduct an effective interview.

Strategies for Interviewing

Before the Interview

- Decide what information you most want to know.
- Make a list of questions.
- Make an appointment, and be on time.

During the Interview

- Be polite, and be patient. Give the interviewee time to answer each question.
- When you ask a question, listen to the answer. If you're not sure you understand, ask another question to clear up your confusion.
- If you are planning to quote the person directly, ask for permission first.
- Respect the interviewee's opinion. You may ask the other person to explain an opinion, but be polite even if you disagree.
- Conclude by thanking the interviewee.

After the Interview

- Review your notes, and write a summary while you still remember the interview clearly.

Media Messages *Media* refers to a wide range of communication forms, including television, radio, newspapers, magazines, and the Internet. Because the media reach vast numbers of people, they are often called mass communication. The different forms of media are used to inform, to persuade, or to entertain. Sometimes, it is difficult to tell whether a program is designed for entertainment, information, or persuasion. Listeners must carefully analyze the messages they hear in media.

- **Analyzing Media Messages** Many messages in the media are designed to be persuasive. However, that purpose may be disguised by making the message seem entertaining or informative. To understand the true purpose of a message, ask yourself the questions below.

Guidelines for Analyzing Media Messages

1. *What purpose does the message seem to have?* Listen to the message. How is it presented? Is it being presented by an authority? Does the message sound true to you?

2. *Is the information in the message accurate and up-to-date?* Where does the information come from? If no sources are given, you should not trust the information.

3. *What kind of language does the message use?* Does the language try to persuade you to do something, with phrases such as "you should . . ."? Does it evaluate things with words such as *better* or *best*?

4. *What are the underlying values or assumptions of the message?* Does the

Guidelines for Analyzing Media Messages

message present a balanced picture, or does it support one side of an issue? Think about what the message does *not* say. For example, a program on alternative medical practices that tells only about the successes would present an unbalanced message.

5. *What is your opinion of the message?* Draw on your experience, knowledge, and instincts to decide what you think about the message. If you think the message may not be completely accurate, you may want to find out more information on your own. Especially when viewing or listening to advertising, be careful to distinguish among fact, opinion, and fiction.

Identifying Lack of Objectivity in the Media The terms defined in the following chart will help you evaluate media messages. They describe some ways in which a message can be less than objective or truthful.

Evaluating Media Messages

Bias	A *bias* is a preference or inclination. A biased program may present only one side of an issue or downplay information in favor of the other side. A biased listener may not pay attention to information that doesn't support his or her opinion.
Misleading Information	*Misleading Information* bends facts or statistics to support an idea. A speaker may use misleading information to support a point, especially if the point is already popular with the audience.
Prejudice	*Prejudice* is pre-judgment or belief based on preconceived notions, rather than facts or reason. Prejudiced speakers or listeners will ignore facts that go against their beliefs.
Propaganda	*Propaganda* is a form of persuasion that deliberately discourages people from thinking for themselves. Propaganda uses incorrect information and emotional appeal to support a one-sided message. Propaganda does not allow people to disagree. (See also page 828.)

Studying and Test Taking

Studying

Skills and Strategies

The purpose of learning good study skills is to help you absorb information a little bit at a time and avoid long study sessions the night before an assignment is due. Practicing good study habits will help you earn better grades, finish homework on time, and do well on tests. Studying will also make you more likely to remember what you have learned—even long after the assignment is over. (See also **"Test Taking"** on page 814.)

Making a Study Plan To make effective use of your study time, plan a study schedule. Try some of the following suggestions.

1. **Know your assignments.** Write down your assignments for each class, and be sure to write down their due dates. If you have a question about the instructions for an assignment, ask your teacher before you leave class.
2. **Make a plan.** Tackle large assignments one piece at a time. Break them into smaller steps, and set a deadline to help you finish each step.
3. **Concentrate when you study.** Find a time and place where you can work every day without distractions. Focus only on your assignments.

Organizing and Remembering Information Different study skills allow you to organize information in ways that make it easy to remember. The strategies listed below can help you as you study.

- **Classifying** ***Classifying*** is a way to organize items by arranging them into categories. The name of the category, or group, describes the relationship between the items. If you break your notes into categories, you will have an easier time learning the material. For example, if you were studying Harriet Tubman, you might divide your notes into the following categories: childhood, education, work during Civil War, and later life.

- **Graphic organizers** ***Graphic organizers*** make information easier to remember by putting it into a visual framework, such as a map, chart, or diagram. (See also page 842.)

- **Memorization** Sometimes you need to ***memorize*** information for a test or quiz. It is easiest to memorize material if you practice in frequent, short, focused sessions. Use the following tips to develop your memorization skills.

How to Memorize

Memorize only the most important information. Minor details are not as important as main ideas. Identify those main ideas and memorize them.

Rehearse the material in several different ways. Read your notes out loud. Then, read them silently. Copy a section of your notes, and then write that section from memory. Experiment with different techniques until you find the ones that work best for you.

Play memory games. Find clever ways to make ideas memorable. Write a song or jingle to help you remember facts and details, or form a word from the first letters of important terms.

- **Notes on reading or lectures** Textbooks and lectures are usually well organized. If you take careful ***notes*** from these sources, your notes will already be organized when you need to study for a test or write a paper. Use the following suggestions to take good notes.

How to Take Study Notes

1. Recognize and record main ideas as headings in your notes. In a lecture, listen for key words and phrases used by the speaker, such as *first, therefore,* and *most important*. These words usually introduce main ideas. In a textbook, pay attention to chapter headings, subheadings, lists, charts, time lines, and illustrations.

2. Summarize what you hear or read. Write down the information in your own words, using abbreviations to save time.

3. Note important examples that are likely to make you remember the main ideas.

4. Review your notes soon after you take them. Be sure your information is complete and accurate before you begin to study.

Look at the following example. A student took these study notes after reading a passage about Garrett Morgan. The notes include the main points of the passage. They are grouped with headings that identify the key ideas.

Biography
Famous African American inventor
Born 1877 in Kentucky
Grew up on farm; finished only 6th grade
Moved to Ohio
Started sewing-machine repair shop, then garment shop
Achievements
Made money with his work

(continued)

(continued)

Possibly first black man in Cleveland to own a car
Invented modern traffic signal
Invented the Safety Hood, patented in 1914
Saved men trapped in tunnel; given gold medal
WWI—Safety Hood became gas mask; saved lives

Outline An ***outline*** can help you organize important ideas and information. When you make an outline, you group ideas together in an organized pattern to show their relationship to one another. (See also **Outlines** on page 842.)

Paraphrasing When you ***paraphrase,*** you restate someone else's ideas in your own words. Paraphrasing can help you understand and remember difficult material. (See also **Paraphrasing** on page 780.)

How to Paraphrase

1. **Read the selection carefully.**
2. **Be sure you understand the main idea** of the selection. Look up unfamiliar words in a dictionary.
3. **Determine the tone** of the selection. (What is the attitude of the writer toward the subject of the selection?)
4. **Identify the speaker in fictional material.** (Is the writer or a character within the selection speaking?)
5. **Write your paraphrase in your own words.** Shorten long sentences or stanzas and use your own, familiar vocabulary, but follow the same order of ideas used in the selection.
6. **Check** to be sure that your paraphrase expresses the same ideas as the original text.

SQ3R ***Survey, Question, Read, Recite,*** and ***Review,*** or ***SQ3R,*** is a strategy designed to help you study reading materials carefully. (See also **SQ3R** on page 782.)

Summarizing A ***summary*** is like a paraphrase because it, too, requires restating someone else's ideas in your own words. However, a **summary** condenses the original material, presenting only the most important points. (See also **Summarizing** on page 783.)

How to Summarize

1. **Skim the selection.**
2. **Re-read the passage closely** and look for the main ideas and supporting details.
3. **Write your summary** in your own words. Include only the writer's main ideas and most important supporting points.
4. After you write your draft, **evaluate and revise your summary,** checking to see that you have covered the most important points. Make sure that the information is clearly expressed and that the ideas follow each other logically.

Here is a summary a student wrote of the reading selection on pages 87–89.

Millions of Americans, including 17 percent of middle and high school students, suffer from some degree of hearing loss. Listening to loud music increases the chances that young people will lose some of their hearing. Loud music impairs hearing by damaging the cilia, the hairlike structures in the inner ear that detect vibrations and carry them to the auditory nerve. Once the cilia are damaged, they never completely recover. Hearing experts are not sure exactly what noise levels cause hearing damage, but they agree that constant exposure to noise over 85 decibels is dangerous. One teenager, Kate LaVail, who suffers from impaired hearing, is doing her part to help others avoid hearing loss by passing out earplugs at concerts.

■ **Writing to learn** ***Writing*** is a tool that can help you learn material. It can help you organize your ideas, analyze problems, record your observations, and plan your work. The following chart shows some of the different ways writing can help you learn.

Types of Writing for Different Purposes

Type of Writing	Purpose	Example
Freewriting	To help you **focus** your thoughts	Write for five minutes to brainstorm ideas for an essay.
Autobiographies	To help you **examine** important events in your life	Write about a personal event that showed you the importance of honesty.
Diaries	To help you **recall** your feelings and impressions	Write about your reaction to an idea a classmate raised during class or to a character in a book.
Journals and Learning Logs	To help you to **record** your observations, ideas, descriptions, and questions	Jot down questions about a topic during prewriting to help generate features for an essay.
	To help you **define** or **analyze** information or **discover** the solution to a problem	Write about a problem at school or in your community. Explore the situation and possible solutions.

Test Taking

Studying for Tests

Two of the most common types of tests you take in school are essay tests and objective tests. The information that follows can help you prepare for them.

Essay tests *Essay tests* measure how well you understand the material you have learned in class. Most essay tests require you to write an answer that is usually a paragraph or more in length.

How to Study for Essay Tests

1. **Read the required chapters** in your textbook carefully.
2. **Identify the main points and important details** from your reading, and arrange them in an outline.
3. **Brainstorm questions** that might appear on the test, and prepare answers to them.
4. **Evaluate and revise your practice answers.** Use your notes and textbook to make sure your answers are correct, and use the Writing Workshops in this book to help in writing your answers.

Objective tests *Objective tests* measure your ability to remember specific information, such as names, dates, terms, and definitions. Most questions on an objective test have only one correct answer. Multiple-choice, short-answer, and true/false questions often appear on objective tests.

How to Study for Objective Tests

1. **Scan your textbook and class notes** to highlight important terms and facts. Then, find the study questions in your textbook and answer them.
2. **Study the information in more than one form.** For instance, if you are responsible for identifying the countries in Central and South America on a map, you can make an unlabeled map and practice labeling the areas on the map you made.
3. **Practice and repeat factual information.** Note which items you have difficulty with, and review them.
4. If possible, **review your notes** one more time shortly before the test.

Types of Test Questions

The following tips and strategies can help you answer different types of questions found on tests.

Analogy questions *Analogy questions* measure your ability to analyze word relationships. Analogy questions ask you to recognize the relationship between a pair of words and to identify a second pair of words with the same relationship. Some analogy questions are multiple-choice, as in the example below.

EXAMPLE

Directions: Select the appropriate pair of words to complete the analogy.

1. SHEEP : LAMB :: ____________
   A. sparrow : finch
   B. cub : bear
   C. horse : foal
   D. feather : tail

Occasionally, an analogy question may appear as a fill-in-the-blank question.

EXAMPLE

Directions: Complete the following analogy.

2. PARAGRAPH : ESSAY :: petal : flower .

How to Answer Analogy Questions

1. Analyze the first pair of words. Identify the relationship between the first set of items. In Example 1, the relationship between a *sheep* and a *lamb* is that of a grown animal to a young animal.

2. Express the analogy in sentence or question form. The first example could be expressed as, "A *sheep* is a grown *lamb,* just as a ______ is a grown ______." Fill the blanks with the possible answers to see which makes sense. For instance, if you fill in the sentence with answer B, you find that the order of the terms is reversed. A *bear* is older than a *cub,* not the other way around.

3. Find the best available choice to complete the analogy. For a multiple-choice analogy, choose the pair of words that shares the same relationship as the pair given in the question. For a fill-in-the-blank analogy, select a word or words that have the same relationship existing between the first pair of words.

The following chart shows you some of the most common types of analogy relationships. Many other types of analogies are possible because there are many ways that two things can be related.

Analogy Examples

A word to its synonym
DIFFICULT : HARD :: easy : simple

A word to its antonym
YOUNG : OLD :: smooth : rough

A thing to its cause
EROSION : WIND :: flood : rain

A thing to its effect
SOAP : CLEAN :: mud : dirty

A part of something to the whole of something
FINGER : HAND :: toe : foot

A whole thing to a part of that thing
CAR : TIRE :: house : window

A thing to a characteristic of that thing
BENCH : HARD :: cushion : soft

A thing to its use
SHOVEL : DIGGING :: scissors : cutting

An action to the person who performs the action
ARGUE : LAWYER :: teach : instructor

A location to a related location
LONDON : ENGLAND :: Mexico City : Mexico

Essay questions *Essay questions* cannot be answered in one or two words or even one or two sentences. Usually they require you to write a paragraph or more. Your essay should include a main idea statement, supporting details, and a conclusion. Following are steps you can take to answer essay questions. (For sample essay questions, see the chart **Key Verbs That Appear in Essay Questions** below.)

1. **Scan the directions on the test.** If you can choose from several questions, pick the one you think you can answer best. Then, decide how much time you will spend preparing and writing your answer. If you need to answer more than one question, set aside time for each one.
2. **Read the questions carefully.** Some questions have more than one part. Be sure to answer the whole question.
3. **Pay attention to the key verbs in the questions.** The verbs in an essay question

Key Verbs That Appear in Essay Questions		
Key Verb	**Task**	**Sample Question**
analyze	Take something apart and see how each part works.	Analyze the effects of global warming.
compare	Point out likenesses.	Compare lions and house cats.
contrast	Point out differences.	Contrast the topographic features of Earth and Moon.
define	Give specific details that make something unique.	Define the word *epicenter* as it is used in science class.
demonstrate (also *show*)	Provide examples to support a point.	Demonstrate how tropical rain forests benefit medical research.
describe	Give a picture in words.	Describe the narrator in the short story "The Moustache."
discuss	Examine in detail.	Discuss Pueblo culture.
explain	Give reasons.	Explain why John F. Kennedy was such a popular president.
identify	Point out characteristics.	Identify the types of clouds.
interpret	Give the meaning or significance of something.	Interpret the impact of the development of the telephone.
list (also *outline*)	Give all steps in order or all details about a subject.	List the events that caused the Mexican Revolution.
persuade	Form an opinion on an issue and support it.	Persuade the city council that a public park should be created.
summarize	Give a brief overview of the main points.	Summarize Odysseus' encounter with the Cyclops.

let you know what task you need to perform. Become familiar with the key verbs that commonly appear on essay tests.

4. **Use prewriting strategies to brainstorm your answer.** After considering the key verbs in the question, jot down notes or create an outline of what you are going to say and how you are going to say it.
5. **Evaluate and revise your answer after you write.** On a test, you probably will not have time to write more than one draft of your answer. Try to leave yourself a few minutes to proofread your answer. Correct any spelling, punctuation, or grammatical errors, and make sure you have answered every part of the question.

Qualities of a Good Essay Answer
The essay is well organized.
The main ideas and supporting points are clearly presented.
The sentences are complete and clear.
There are no distracting errors in spelling, punctuation, or grammar.

Matching questions *Matching questions* ask you to match the items in one list with items in another list.

EXAMPLE

Directions: Match the World War II leaders in the right-hand column to their countries in the left-hand column.

C	**1.** United States	**A.** Stalin
D	**2.** Great Britain	**B.** Hitler
A	**3.** Soviet Union	**C.** Roosevelt
B	**4.** Germany	**D.** Churchill
E	**5.** Italy	**E.** Mussolini

How to Answer Matching Questions

1. Read the directions carefully. Some tests contain items that will not be used at all. Other test directions tell you that you can use an item more than once.

2. Scan the columns to identify related items. Match the items that you know first. Then, spend more time considering the items about which you are less sure.

3. Complete the matching process. Make an educated guess on any remaining items.

Multiple-choice questions *Multiple-choice questions* ask you to select a correct answer from among a number of choices.

EXAMPLE

1. Which of the following was not discovered or developed during the seventeenth century A.D.?
   A. telescope
   B. microscope
   C. Laws of Planetary Motion
   (D.) gunpowder

How to Answer Multiple-Choice Questions

1. Read the question or statement carefully. Make sure you understand the question or statement completely before considering your choices. Always look for qualifiers, such as *not* or *always,* because these words limit the answer.

2. Read all the possible answers before making a choice. Quickly eliminate the choices that you know

(continued)

QUICK REFERENCE HANDBOOK

(continued)

How to Answer Multiple-Choice Questions

are incorrect. Eliminating choices improves your chances of choosing correctly from among the remaining choices. Consider the remaining choices carefully and choose the one that makes the most sense even if you are not absolutely sure of the correct response.

On-demand reading questions An on-demand question is one for which you cannot study in advance. ***On-demand reading questions*** ask you about a reading passage. Some of the answers to the questions may be found in the passage. Others will come from conclusions you draw based on your own experiences or understanding of the passage.

EXAMPLE

Directions: Read the passage below, and answer the question that follows.

Many breads are made with yeast, a small one-celled organism that creates carbon dioxide when it is mixed with sugar. The carbon dioxide bubbles cause the dough to rise, or grow tall, and become less dense than it was before. Other breads rise because their dough contains baking powder.

1. Which of the following is the best title for this passage?
   A. "How to Make Bread"
   B. "Baking with Yeast"
   C. "Helpful Organisms"
   (D.) "What Makes Bread Rise"

How to Answer On-Demand Reading Questions

1. Read the passage carefully. As you read, identify the main idea and important details.

2. Read the questions that follow the reading passage. Most of the time, the questions that follow a passage in an on-demand reading test are multiple-choice questions. (See also **Multiple-choice Questions** on page 817.)

3. Compare the language in the question to language in the reading passage. You can match words from the questions to words in the passage to help find an answer.

4. If the language of the question is not in the reading passage, you must draw your own conclusions. The reading passage in the example to the left does not give the title directly. However, you can conclude that the passage is telling you methods for making dough rise. Therefore, the best title would be choice *D.*

On-demand writing questions ***On-demand writing questions*** are essay questions. They are found on many state writing tests. Usually these questions are broad and related to your experience. They ask you to write a persuasive, informative, narrative, or descriptive essay. You cannot study for the content of an on-demand writing question, but you can prepare by writing a practice essay and asking for feedback from your teacher or classmates.

EXAMPLE

Some cities are establishing laws to prevent teenagers from being on city streets after a certain hour. Write an essay in which you persuade the mayor that this law is or is not a good idea.

How to Answer On-Demand Writing Questions

1. Read the question carefully, and determine what it is asking. Analyze the verbs carefully to find out whether your answer should be persuasive, informative, or descriptive. (See also **Key Verbs That Appear in Essay Questions** on page 816.)

2. Plan your answer. Use a prewriting technique to help you plan before you begin writing. (See **Prewriting Techniques** on page 839.)

3. Evaluate and revise your answer after you write. Make sure that your answer has a clear topic sentence. Also make sure it has supporting details, transitions between ideas, and a conclusion.

Reasoning or logic questions

Reasoning or ***logic questions*** measure your reasoning abilities more than your knowledge of a specific subject. Reasoning or logic questions often appear on standardized tests. They may ask you to identify the relationship between several items, to identify a pattern in a sequence of numbers, or to predict the next item in a series of images or numbers.

EXAMPLE

What comes next?

1 2 3 4 ______

In this sequence, a different square is missing each time from a box of four squares. Therefore, the last drawing in the series should show a square missing in the only position from which a square had not yet been removed.

How to Answer Reasoning or Logic Questions

1. Be sure you understand the instructions. Reasoning or logic questions are usually multiple-choice, but some require you to write a response or to draw a picture.

2. Analyze the relationship implied in the question. Examine the question to gather information about the relationship shared by the items.

3. Draw reasonable conclusions. Evaluate the relationship of the items to decide your answer.

Sentence-completion questions

Sentence-completion questions test your knowledge of vocabulary words. These questions ask you to choose an answer that correctly completes the meaning of a sentence.

EXAMPLE

1. As we reached the mountaintop, we felt elated, but our joy was hindered slightly by ______________ after the steep climb.

   A. resting

   (B.) breathlessness

   C. happiness

   D. exercise

How to Answer Sentence-Completion Questions

1. Read the sentence carefully. Make sure you understand the words in the sentence. Some sentences may contain clues to the meaning of the word or words that go in the blanks. In the example on the previous page "after the steep climb" is a clue that the correct answer is *breathlessness*. The words "our joy was hindered" tell you that the answer has negative connotations. The only answer that makes sense in the sentence and has negative connotations is *breathlessness.* (For more on **connotations,** see page 787.)

2. Rule out incorrect answer choices. If you can immediately rule out any answer choices, mark through them.

3. Fill in the blank with the remaining choices, and choose the best answer. If you are not sure which choice is correct, use each one in the blank of the sentence and choose the answer that makes the most sense.

Short-answer questions ***Short-answer questions*** ask you to write brief, precise answers to show what you have learned. Some short-answer questions (such as fill-in-the-blank questions) are shorter than others, requiring a reply of only one or two words. Others require you to write one or two sentences.

EXAMPLE How does the temperature on Mars compare to the temperature on Earth?

Answer: Mars is much colder than Earth, with temperatures as low as –220°F at its north and south poles.

How to Answer Short-Answer Questions

1. Read the question carefully. Some questions have more than one part. Be sure to answer the entire question.

2. Plan your answer. Briefly decide what ideas and details you need to include in the answer.

3. Be as specific as possible. Write a full, exact answer.

4. Budget your time. Answer the questions you know first. Save time for more difficult questions.

True/false questions ***True/false questions*** ask you to determine whether a given statement is true or false.

EXAMPLE

1. (T) F The Earth is always rotating.

How to Answer True-False Questions

1. Read the statement carefully. Remember that the whole statement is false if any part of it is false.

2. Look for word clues. Words such as *always* and *never* are qualifiers and limit a statement. A statement is true only if it is entirely and always true.

Viewing and Representing

Understanding Media Terms

People who work in or write about the media often use ***jargon,*** a special language that helps them communicate quickly. This section may contain terms that are familiar to you but that are used in an unfamiliar or technical way. Understanding the terms in this section will help you evaluate the media messages you see and hear. It will also help you create your own media messages.

The section is divided into three parts: Electronic Media Terms, General Media Terms, and Print Media Terms. Terms that apply to both print media and electronic media are defined under Print Media Terms only. If you are looking for terms relating to the Internet or the World Wide Web, you will find them in the "Library/Media Center" section beginning on page 769. Terms relating to the use of type and graphics in page layout can be found in "Document Design" beginning on page 756.

Electronic Media Terms

Advertising See **Advertising** on page 828.

Animation ***Animation*** is the art of making photographs of drawings appear to move. Animators use film or video images recorded at a rate of twenty-four frames per second, making small changes from image to image to create the illusion of movement. Many types of media messages, such as cartoons, movies, and advertisements use animation.

Broadcasting ***Broadcasting*** is transmitting radio or television content over a wide area through the airwaves. ***Commercial broadcasting*** is done for profit. Broadcasters sell advertisers air time in which to persuade the audience to buy their products or services. ***Public broadcasting*** is non-profit broadcasting. In the United States, the Public Broadcasting Service (PBS), which has more than three hundred member stations, is funded mostly by corporations and individual viewers and listeners. Some funds are also provided by the federal government.

Byline See **Byline** on page 829.

Cable Television *Cable television* uses powerful antennas to receive television signals that are then delivered to homes and businesses through cables. Users pay to receive cable television.

Camera Angle The *camera angle* is the angle at which a camera is pointed at a subject. A high angle makes the subject look small, while a low angle makes the subject look tall and seem powerful. A tilted angle makes the subject appear off balance.

Camera Shot A *camera shot* is a single, continuous image recorded by a movie camera or video camera. These are three of the most common shots used in film or video production:

- **Close-up shot** A close-up shot is made from very close to the subject—for example, a flower.
- **Medium shot** A medium shot is made from a midrange distance—for example, a person from the waist up.
- **Long shot** A long shot is made from far away—for example, a park from a helicopter.

Commercial Broadcasting See **Broadcasting** on page 821.

Copy See **Copy** on page 829.

Credits The *credits* are a list of the names of people who worked on a presentation. The list usually appears at the end of a television program, film, or video.

Demographics See **Demographics** on page 829.

Digital Editing See **Digital Editing** on page 829.

Documentary A *documentary* is a film or television program that interprets actual events. A documentary usually includes elements like interviews and footage of actual events taking place. Some documentaries may include reenactments of events using actors, as well as voice-over narration. A documentary's primary purpose may be to inform, to persuade, to entertain, or to make money. Some documentaries have more than one purpose. For example, a documentary about endangered animals and cultures in the rain forest may have the dual purposes of informing and persuading.

Editor See **Editor** on page 829.

Feature News See **Feature News** on page 829.

Film *Film* is a material on which sounds and images may be recorded. Filmed sounds and images are crisp and clear, last a long time, and can be presented on a large screen. Images on film can also appear more sophisticated than images recorded on videotape, but film is more expensive to buy and develop than videotape is. (See also **Videotape** on page 823.)

Hard News See **Hard News** on page 829.

Internet The *Internet* is a global network of computers that makes it possible for computer users all over the world to communicate. Its use requires a computer and a modem, a device that connects the computer with a telephone or cable line.

Internet service providers charge monthly fees for access to the Internet. (See also **"The Library/Media Center"** beginning on page 769.)

Lead See **Lead** on page 830.

Marketing See **Marketing** on page 830.

Medium See **Medium** on page 830.

Message See **Message** on page 827.

News See **News** on page 830.

Newsmagazine See **Newsmagazine** on page 830.

Photography See **Photography** on page 830.

Producer A ***producer*** is the person who oversees the production of a television or radio program or a movie. The producer is responsible for developing the overall message, finding appropriate materials, organizing a crew or staff, finding and budgeting funding, and keeping the production on schedule. (See also **Production** on page 831.)

Production See **Production** on page 831.

Public Broadcasting See **Broadcasting** on page 821.

Reporter See **Reporter** on page 831.

Script A ***script*** is the text that is to be spoken during a film, a play, or a television or radio program. It may include voice-over narration as well as dialogue. Scripts for films and television programs also include information about the images to be shown. The script for a news broadcast is called *copy.*

Soft News See **Soft News** on page 831.

Sound In film and video, sound is all of the recorded material that you hear, including dialogue, music, sound effects, and so on. In addition to the obvious purpose of conveying "talk," producers and filmmakers use sound to achieve various goals. One role of sound is to create an illusion. For example, when you see two actors talking outside of a building, the background noise may convince you that the actors are standing near a busy street, even if no traffic is visible. Another role of sound is to create mood. For example, the music that a video producer selects to accompany visual images can tell the audience whether to feel cheerful, frightened, anxious, and so on.

Source See **Source** on page 831.

Storyboard A ***storyboard*** is a series of drawings displayed on a large board showing the sequence of the shots and scenes in a script. A storyboard may also include audio and visual cues.

Target Audience See **Target Audience** on page 831.

Text See **Text** on page 831.

Videotape A ***videotape*** is a magnetic tape on which images and sounds may be recorded. Videotape is a relatively inexpensive medium. The equipment needed to record with videotape is also more accessible and easier to use than film equipment. However, the images recorded on videotape have less *resolution,* or clarity, than filmed images, and videotape does not last as long as film. (See also **Film** on page 822.)

General Media Terms

Audience An ***audience*** is the group of people to whom a media message is presented. Advertisers try to reach audiences they think they can persuade to buy their products or services. (See also **Advertising** on page 828; **Demographics** on page 829; **Target Audience** on page 831.)

Authority ***Authority*** refers to how knowledgeable and well qualified the source of a message seems. A message that appears to come from an expert source will seem authoritative to you. For example, a message about the effects of pollution on marine life would have more authority coming from a marine biologist than from a visitor at the beach.

Bias A ***bias*** is a preference for one side of an issue, either for it or against it. People who are biased may ignore information that does not support their views. (See also **Point of View** on page 828.)

Context ***Context*** is everything that surrounds a media message. For example, the context of a television commercial may include the other commercials shown during a program and the program itself. Viewers' interpretations of a message may be influenced by the context in which the message appears.

Credibility ***Credibility*** is the quality of being believable. Audience members determine a speaker's credibility. (See also **Message** on page 827. See also page 807.)

Critical Viewing ***Critical viewing*** means analyzing, interpreting, and evaluating visual messages in the mass media. Such messages may take a range of forms, from films and television programs to still photographs and editorial cartoons. Keep these five key concepts in mind as you view messages.

Concept 1: All messages are somebody's creation.

Every visual message is the product of many choices by the message maker. In creating a visual message, an artist, photographer, or filmmaker must decide which elements (words, images, sounds) to include, which ones to leave out, and how to arrange and sequence the elements selected. Understanding how visual messages are constructed will help you analyze the message and appreciate the skill that went into creating it.

Concept 2: Messages are a reflection of reality.

Every visual message is a version of reality, not reality itself. In a sales brochure, for example, everything from the photographs to the type size is carefully packaged. Realizing that all visual messages are versions of reality helps you evaluate how authentic (true to life) a particular message seems.

Concept 3: Each individual interprets messages differently.

Viewers' prior knowledge and experience determine the way they interpret visual messages. Because people's prior knowledge and experience differ, viewers interpret the same message differently. Connecting a message to your own knowledge and experience will help you shape and express your interpretation of it.

Concept 4: Messages usually have more than one purpose.

The person who creates a visual message has a purpose. Usually, that purpose is to inform, to persuade, to entertain, or to express thoughts and feelings. Most visual messages in the mass media also have another underlying purpose: to make money for the people who created the messages and for the owners and operators of the media. Recognizing the underlying moneymaking purpose of visual messages in the mass media will help you understand how messages are intended to affect you.

Concept 5: The medium shapes the message.

Each visual medium has its own strengths and weaknesses. For example, a still photograph captures only a single moment, but it can be studied at length. Film offers moving images as well as sound, but the scenes are fleeting, not permanent. The creators of visual messages try to take advantage of a particular medium's strengths and to play down its weaknesses. Understanding how the medium shapes the message will help you understand why the message maker used certain elements and why the message affects you the way it does.

Evaluating Media Messages The following questions are based on the five key concepts of critical viewing explained previously. They will help you analyze, interpret, and evaluate visual messages in the mass media.

- Through what medium is the message delivered?
- Who created the message?
- What seems to be the main purpose of the message? If there is also an underlying purpose, what is it?
- What elements (words, images, or sounds) does the message include?
- How are those elements arranged and sequenced?
- How skillfully are the elements presented?
- What may have been left out of the message?
- How is the version of reality presented in the message similar to and different from what I know from my own knowledge and experience?
- How authentic (true to life) does the message seem? Why?
- What does the message bring to mind?
- How does it make me feel about the world? about myself? about other people?
- How does the medium help shape the message?

Feedback ***Feedback*** is an audience's response to a message. The response may be either immediate or delayed. Applause is an example of immediate feedback; filling out an evaluation form is an example of delayed feedback.

Formula A ***formula*** is a long-established approach or model. In film and television, it refers to a typical way of presenting material or combining characters. Local news programs, for example, often follow the formula of pairing a male anchor with a female anchor.

Genre A *genre* is a type or category of media product. Media products in the same genre share certain characteristics or conventions. Examples of genres common on television include

- children's programming
- documentary
- drama
- game show
- infomercial
- music video
- news broadcast
- sitcom (situation comedy)
- soap opera
- talk show

Illustration An *illustration* is a picture created to decorate or explain something. Drawings, paintings, photographs, and computer-generated artwork can all be illustrations. Illustrations are made up of some or all of the following elements.

- **Color** Color can create a certain mood or highlight an important part of an illustration.
- **Form** The three-dimensional effect of an illustration is its form. An illustration is more realistic if it appears to have depth and weight. Illustrators often use shadows and bright spots to create the illusion of three dimensions on paper.
- **Line** Everything you see around you has some sort of line. Some lines are obvious, like the vertical line made when walls meet. Other lines are more subtle—for example, the lines made by the shingles on a roof. Illustrators also use line to show depth and to show viewers where the horizon line in the drawing is.
- **Shape** Shape is an object's two-dimensional outline. Lines can come together to make a shape. All of the shapes in an illustration are connected to each other in some way.

Images An *image* is a visual representation of something. It may be a painting, a photograph, a sculpture, or a moving picture, among other things.

- A ***still image,*** such as a photograph, allows viewers to notice detail and spend time considering the image. Still images may also be easier than moving images for message makers to manipulate, such as by cropping or using a computer program.
- A ***moving image*** is a series of still images projected quickly onto a television or film screen. A moving image may show an actual event (called *documentary footage*), or it may show an event arranged by the filmmaker or video producer (a *dramatization*). Documentary footage includes scenes shown on the evening news. Dramatizations include fictional movies. Both kinds of moving images are the filmmaker or video producer's version of an event, not reality.

To analyze how message makers create effects using images, consider the points in the chart on the next page.

Media Law The First Amendment of the U. S. Constitution prohibits Congress

Creating Effects with Images	
Technique	**Definition/Effects**
Color	Color can emphasize certain parts of an image or tell viewers how they should feel about the image. When a spot of color suddenly appears in a black-and-white movie, the director wants viewers to pay special attention to that part of the image. Different colors are associated with different moods. An image may use color to affect the viewer—for example, photographing an image through a blue filter may make a viewer feel calm.
Juxtaposition	Juxtaposition involves putting two or more images next to each other to create more meaning than the individual images would have. For example, a drama may juxtapose a scene in the present time with a flashback to earlier events that provides clues about what is happening in the present.
Slow or fast motion	When an image moves faster or slower than its normal speed, it draws attention and creates an effect. Making an image move faster than normal can create a comic effect, while slowing an image down can create a tense, dramatic effect.

from passing laws that would limit the freedom of the press. Therefore, except during wartime, the United States government seldom uses *censorship.* ***Censorship*** refers to any attempt by a government or other group to control people's access to literature or the mass media.

However, laws do exist that regulate, or control, the media. The Federal Communications Commission (FCC) enforces laws regulating electronic media. In addition, a person whose reputation has been damaged by the publication of a false statement may sue the publisher. Finally, the author or publisher of a media message may seek copyright protection in order to guard against the ***plagiarism,*** or theft, of that message.

The growing use of the Internet has raised many new questions about the regulation of the media. These questions will be the subject of debate for years to come.

Media Literacy ***Media literacy*** is the ability to access, analyze, evaluate, and communicate messages in a wide variety of forms. (See also **Critical Viewing** on page 824.)

Message A ***message*** is a communication sent to an audience. The **content** of a message is the information it presents. (See also **Credibility** on page 824; **Realism** on page 828; **Source** on page 831.)

Multimedia Presentation A ***multimedia presentation*** is any presentation that involves two or more forms of media. For example, when you give an oral presentation including visuals (such as slides, transparencies, or posters), you are giving a multimedia presentation—one medium is your voice and the other is the visuals you use to support your presentation. A multimedia presentation that involves the use of presentation software or Web sites is sometimes called a ***technology presentation.***

Newsworthiness ***Newsworthiness*** is the quality that makes a news event seem worth reporting. An event is considered newsworthy if it meets certain criteria. Among those criteria are:

- **timeliness** Timely events or issues are ones that are happening now or that people are interested in now.
- **impact** Events or issues with impact are ones that directly affect people's lives.
- **human interest** Human interest stories are about basic needs or are stories that affect the audience's emotions.
- **celebrity angle** Stories with a celebrity angle are stories about famous people.

An event that meets one or more of these criteria is more likely to be covered by the news media.

Persuasion See **Propaganda** on this page.

Point of View In the news media, ***point of view*** is the way a message maker approaches a topic. Point of view is shaped by a person's background and values. A person's point of view affects how he or she sees an issue or topic. A news reporter writing about a new school might focus on the up-to-date features it will provide. Another reporter might focus on how traffic in the area is expected to increase.

In photography, point of view refers to the photographer's approach to his or her subject. Choices that affect the photographer's point of view include selecting the subject and the camera angle. (See also **Bias** on page 824 and **Propaganda** below.)

Propaganda Originally, ***propaganda*** meant the use of lies and misleading information to affect public opinion. For this reason, the word *propaganda* has a negative connotation. *Propaganda* still often refers to efforts to persuade that involve bending, distorting, or hiding the truth. However, some propaganda techniques, such as the emotional appeal, are widely considered acceptable for use in commercials, public service announcements, and political campaigns. (See also **Persuasive Techniques** on page 254, **Advertising** below, **Bias** on page 824, and **Point of View** on this page.)

Realism ***Realism*** is representing people and things just as they appear to be, without making them seem more pleasant or acceptable than they are.

Stereotypes ***Stereotypes*** are beliefs about all the members of a particular group. Such beliefs do not take into account how different any two people are. For example, one stereotype about teenagers is that they are all sleepyheads. Of course, this is not true of many teenagers. Stereotypes are usually based on too little evidence or on false or misleading information.

Print Media Terms

Advertising ***Advertising*** is the use of text, images, or both to persuade an audience to buy, use, or accept a product, service, image, or idea. Advertisers buy time or space in the media to promote their products and services. (See also **Marketing** on page 830.)

Byline A ***byline*** is a credit line that states the name of the writer or reporter of a television or radio presentation or of a newspaper or magazine article.

Copy ***Copy*** is the text presented in a media message. (See also **Script** on page 823.)

Demographics ***Demographics*** are the characteristics of a particular audience. They may include gender, cultural heritage, age, education, and income. Advertisers use demographics to target audiences likely to buy their products and services. For example, a particular brand of jeans may be targeted at teenage females. (See also **Audience** on page 824, and **Target Audience** on page 831.)

Digital Editing ***Digital editing*** is the use of computer technology to alter a digitized (or computer) image before it is presented to an audience. For example, a fashion photographer may scan photographs into a computer program to digitally edit images of models to make their skin clearer. A photograph of a person may be taken in a studio and then edited to make it appear that he or she is on a beach or in some other setting.

Editor An ***editor*** is a journalist who may supervise reporters. Editors choose which news stories to present, check the accuracy of facts, and correct errors. (See also **Newsworthiness** on page 828.)

Editorial Cartoon An ***editorial cartoon*** is a cartoon, usually found in the editorial section of a newspaper, that reflects the cartoonist's opinion of a current event. Editorial cartoonists use exaggeration and caricature to make their points. (See also page 269.)

Feature News ***Feature news*** (also called *soft news*) refers to news stories whose primary purpose is to entertain. Feature stories, which may or may not be timely, may be about ordinary people or celebrities or about events, animals, places, or products. An example of a feature news story is one that highlights a high school student winning a scholarship for dog training. (See also **Hard News** below and **Soft News** on page 831.)

Font A ***font*** is a style of lettering that is used for printing text. (See also **Font** on page 759.)

Hard News ***Hard news*** refers to fact-based stories about current events. Such stories answer the basic *5W-How?* questions about important subjects such as natural disasters and scientific discoveries. An example of a hard news story is one that provides updates on a military crisis. (See also **Feature News** above and **Soft News** on page 831.)

Headline A ***headline*** is the title of a newspaper article. Usually, headlines are set in large, boldface type. A headline has two purposes: to attract the reader's attention and to inform the reader about the content of the article.

EXAMPLE

State Chess Champions Return Today

(See also **"Document Design."**)

Lead A ***lead*** is the first sentence or opening paragraph of a news story. A hard news story's lead may contain the major facts of the story, answering the *5W-How?* questions. It usually tries to hook the audience's attention with a surprising or unusual fact or image.

EXAMPLE Students at Briar Woods Junior High are healthier than anyone expected. During the past month, the students in eighth-grade health and science classes have conducted surveys and tests to gauge the health of the student body. The eighth-graders have examined the student body's eating and exercise habits, physical endurance, and emotional well-being. Today the project reports were due, and it seems that as a student body, Briar Woods passes.

Marketing ***Marketing*** is the process of moving goods or services from a producer to consumers. It includes

- identifying what consumers want or need
- designing, packaging, and pricing the product
- arranging how and where the product will be sold
- promoting the product to a target audience through advertising or other means

(See also **Advertising** on page 828, **Demographics** on page 829, and **Target Audience** on page 831.)

Medium A ***medium*** is the means through which a message is communicated. *Medium* is the singular form of the noun *media.* In general, modern media can be grouped into two categories: print media, such as newspapers and magazines, and electronic media, such as radio and television, audio and video recordings, film, and the Internet. The mass media are the media that reach a large audience.

Message See **Message** on page 827.

News ***News*** is the presentation of current information considered likely to interest or affect a news medium's audience. Local news media focus on news of regional interest. National news media, with their greater resources, cover national and world issues and events.

Newsmagazine In the print media a ***newsmagazine*** is a publication, usually issued weekly, that focuses on recent events and issues. In television the term is used for a program, aired one or more times a week, on which the news is analyzed and interpreted.

Photography ***Photography*** is the process of recording an image on film with a camera. Photographs, like all media messages, are selective and incomplete. A photographer makes a number of choices about how to communicate through film.

For example, before a photographer shoots pictures, he or she selects color or black-and-white film, camera angles, and lighting. After a photograph is developed, a photographer or film editor may enhance a selected idea or image by cropping it, digitally editing it, or adding a caption to it. (See also **Digital Editing** on page 829.)

Political Cartoon See **Editorial Cartoon** on page 829.

Production ***Production*** is the process of creating a publication, a film, a video, or a radio or television program. The process is carried out in three stages.

- ***Preproduction*** involves obtaining and polishing copy or scripts, raising and budgeting funds, hiring staff and crew, and planning schedules.
- During **production,** the work is filmed, recorded, or printed.
- The finishing touches are added during ***post-production.*** Films and tapes are edited, soundtracks are recorded, and sound and special effects are added. Books and newspapers are bound or gathered. Post-production also includes marketing and distribution.

(See also **Marketing** on page 830.)

Reporter A ***reporter*** is a journalist who gathers information and, working with editors, creates electronic or print reports.

Soft News ***Soft news*** is general-interest material, such as sports and travel stories, presented in a news format. The purpose of soft news is to entertain. (See also **Feature News** and **Hard News** on page 829.)

Source A ***source*** is a person or a publication from which a journalist receives information or ideas. Much of the information journalists report comes from sources. Journalists rely on individuals and publications they believe are credible and have authority. (See also **Authority** and **Credibility** on page 824 and **Message** on page 827.)

Target Audience A ***target audience*** is a portion of the population for which a product or message is designed. Children are the target audience for toy commercials. Teens are the target audience for ads for certain brands of clothing. (See also **Demographics** on page 829.)

Text ***Text*** refers to the words, printed or spoken, used to create a message. (See also **Message** on page 827.)

Writing

Skills, Structures, and Techniques

You can use the following ideas and information to become a more effective writer:

Applications See **Forms** on page 834.

Composition A ***composition*** is made up of paragraphs and has three main parts: the ***introduction,*** the ***body,*** and the ***conclusion.*** Think of the parts of a composition as a team. These parts each have a specific job as team members of the composition. Together they communicate the writer's main idea.

- **Introduction** Your composition's ***introduction*** has two jobs: It must catch the reader's attention and present the main idea, or thesis, of the composition.
  1. **Catch the reader's attention.** Your introduction should make a good first impression so your readers will want to read on. Here are three techniques writers use to grab their reader's attention.

How to Catch Your Reader's Attention

Ask a question.

Do you like to exercise and have fun? Do you like having people cheer for you? If so, why not participate in sports this summer?

Tell an anecdote.

I played my first junior league game last summer. I remember how nervous I became when it was my turn to bat. Standing at the plate, I felt my knees trembling as I waited for the ball. The pitch came in fast and low, but somehow I managed to hit it. Although I only got to first base, this was one of the most exciting moments I've ever experienced.

State an intriguing or startling fact.

Experts say that approximately forty million school-age boys and girls play organized sports.

2. **Present the main idea statement, or thesis.** A ***main idea statement*** sums up in one or two sentences the main idea of your composition. Every detail in each paragraph ties into this main idea. Including your main idea statement in the introduction keeps both you and your readers on track. Here are some strategies for helping you write a main idea statement.

How to Write a Main Idea Statement

Ask yourself what your topic is.
topic: playing sports

Look at your prewriting notes. What do the facts and details suggest might be your main idea about your topic?
Playing sports gives boys and girls more than just an opportunity to have fun.

Be specific. Sharpen your focus and present a clear main idea statement.
Playing sports gives boys and girls a chance to have fun, but it also provides them with the opportunity to learn responsibility and good sportsmanship.

■ **Body** The ***body's*** job is to state the composition's main points. Each point in the body should support the main idea statement. To help the reader understand the ideas in your composition, the body must have *coherence* and *unity.*

1. ***Coherence*** makes your composition smooth and easy to understand. To arrange your ideas so readers can easily see how the ideas are related, use ***transitional expressions.*** (See also page 303.)
2. ***Unity*** occurs when all of the details of your composition support the main idea statement. Make sure you have unity by removing any details that do not support the main idea statement. (See also page 301.)

■ **Conclusion** The ***conclusion*** should let your readers know that your composition has come to an end.

How to Write a Conclusion

Refer to your introduction.
If you enjoy having fun while getting exercise, consider joining a local sports league this summer.

Restate the main idea in different words.
Fun, fairness, and a sense of responsibility are three of the many benefits of playing sports.

Close with a final idea.
Before I started playing sports, my idea of a good summer was staying indoors playing video games. Video games are fun, but they are no match for an afternoon game of baseball.

E-mail When you use the computer to send and receive mail, you are using electronic mail, or ***e-mail.*** E-mail is most often used to write personal or informal letters or to send business letters. Informal language and format are often appropriate when you write to a friend or relative.

However, when you write to someone you do not know well for business or research purposes, you should follow the guidelines listed below. Online etiquette, or "Netiquette," is just as important in cyberspace as good manners and proper form are in the real world.

E-Mail Guidelines
Keep your message short. Limiting yourself to one full screen or less of text shows consideration for your reader's time.
Pay attention to how the e-mail looks. Using bulleted lists and indentation makes e-mail easy to read, especially if you are raising more than one question or point.
Use standard English. Make sure you follow the rules for proper grammar, spelling, and punctuation.
Use a formal opening and closing when writing to someone you do not know. For example, "Dear Ms. Phelan" and "Sincerely, Jose Martinez" would be appropriate.
Be polite in your messages—even when you are tempted to be rude. Be aware that a person who receives a message from you may choose to forward it to other people.
Do not shout in your messages. CAPITALS CONVEY SHOUTING. People might misinterpret your tone if you use capitals. To show emphasis, place asterisks (*) on either side of the important word. For example, "What *time* is the concert?"
Never use *emoticons* in formal e-mails. ***Emoticons*** are combinations of symbols that, when you tilt your head to the left, resemble faces. They are a kind of shorthand to communicate feelings or reactions. For example, the emoticon :-) suggests laughter or "Just teasing." Use them in informal e-mails only.
Make sure you enter the correct address to avoid sending your e-mail to the wrong person.
Announce the topic of your message by filling in the subject line before you send a message. This helps your readers to know which e-mails should be opened first.
Ask permission of the original sender before forwarding e-mail. Private e-mails are usually intended for your eyes only.

Forms A ***form*** is a document that requests personal information. Throughout your life, you will be asked to fill out many different forms. For example, an ***application*** is a form you will fill out to ask or apply for something. You might fill out an application to request membership in a school organization, to apply for a library card, or to join a sports league. On the next page is an example of an application for a savings account.

FIRST NATIONAL BANK
Savings Account Application

Today's Date January 3, 2000

Do you have accounts with First National Bank? YES ____ NO X

Amount of deposit for new account $225.00

Account Information

Legal Name John Michael Watson Home Phone # 555-0131

Address 1522 Seahorse Lane Laurel Hill, Florida 32567

Driver's License # N/A Date of Birth 05-22-88 S.S.N 423-55-2215

Employer self Phone # 555-0131 Position lawn mower

Employer's Address same as home address Length of Employment 2 years

Mother's Maiden Name Jackson

If you follow a few standard guidelines, you should be able to fill out most forms accurately and completely.

Guidelines for Filling Out Forms

Look over the entire form before you begin.

Notice any special instructions, such as "Please print clearly," or "Use a pencil."

Read each item carefully.

Supply all the information requested. If the information requested does not apply to you, use a dash or the symbol *N/A,* which means "not applicable."

Proofread your form to check for errors and to make sure you did not leave any items blank.

Letters Writing a ***letter*** is an important way of communicating your ideas to others. To write an effective letter, keep in mind that the type of letter you write depends on your specific purpose and audience.

Types of Letters

A **business letter** is written to request a product or service, or to voice appreciation or a complaint.

The **audience** for a business letter is a business or organization.

An **informal** or **personal** letter is written to express thanks or regret, or to provide information about an event.

The **audience** for an informal or personal letter may include friends, relatives, or social acquaintances.

Letters, Business A ***business letter*** is a formal letter that takes care of a business-related matter. How a business letter looks and sounds is very important.

- **Appearance of a business letter** The appearance of a business letter should follow these guidelines.
  1. Use unlined 8½" x 11" paper.
  2. Type your letter if possible (single-spaced, leaving an extra line between

paragraphs). Otherwise, neatly write the letter by hand, using black or blue ink. Check for typing errors and misspellings.

3. Center your letter on the paper with equal margins on the sides and at the top and bottom.
4. Use only one side of the paper. If your letter will not fit on one page, leave a one-inch margin at the bottom of the first page, and carry over at least two lines onto the second page.

Envelopes All letters—personal or business—need to be sent in a properly addressed envelope. Use the following steps to complete an envelope.

1. Put your address in the top left-hand corner. Include your name, street address, city, state, and ZIP Code.
2. Write the correct name and address of the person to whom you are writing in the center of the envelope. Be sure to include the ZIP Code and to use the correct two-letter abbreviation for the state, such as IA for Iowa.
3. Place the correct postage in the upper right-hand corner of the envelope.

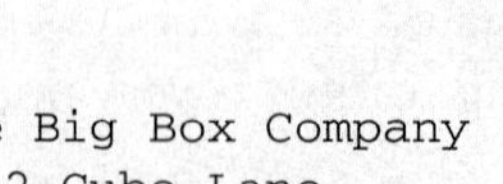

Terry Slade
1254 Country Road
Princeton, TX 75407
The Big Box Company
1522 Cube Lane
New York, NY 10023

Parts of a business letter The following explains each of the six parts of a business letter.

1. The **heading** usually has three lines: your street address; your city, state, and ZIP Code; and the date the letter was written.
2. The **inside address** gives the name and address of the person or company to whom you are writing. If you are directing your letter to someone by name, use a courtesy title (such as *Mr.*, *Ms.*, or *Mrs.*) or a professional title (such as *Dr.* or *Professor*) in front of the person's name. After the person's name, include the person's business title (such as *Vice President* or *Manager*).
3. The **salutation** is your greeting. If you are writing to a specific person, begin with *Dear,* followed by a courtesy title or a professional title and the person's name.
4. The **body,** which is the main part of your letter, contains your message. If your letter contains more than one paragraph, leave a blank line between paragraphs.
5. The **closing** of your letter should include a standard word or phrase such as *Sincerely, Yours truly,* or *Respectfully yours.*
6. Your **signature** should be in ink below the closing. Type or print your name neatly just below your signature.

Forms for business letters The six parts of a business letter are usually arranged on the page in one of two forms, or styles. In the ***block form,*** every part of the letter begins at the left margin, and paragraphs are not indented. In the ***modified block form,*** the heading, the closing, and your signature are placed to the right of the center of the page. However, the other parts of the letter begin at the left margin, and paragraphs are indented.

Block Style

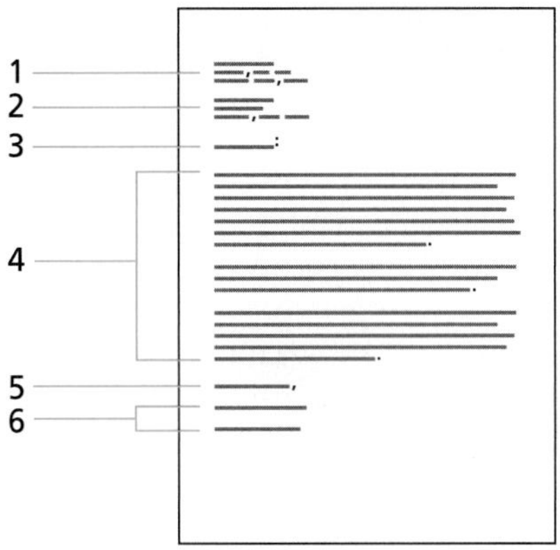

Modified Block Style

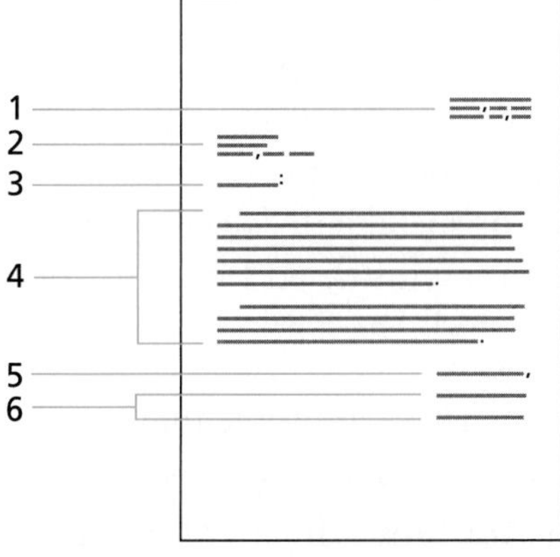

■ **Types of business letters** There are three types of business letters.

1. **The appreciation or commendation letter** You write an ***appreciation*** or ***commendation letter*** to express appreciation, gratitude, or praise for a person, group, or organization. When you write an appreciation or commendation letter, be sure to state exactly why you are pleased. Here is a sample appreciation letter.

5021 Treeside Road
Danbury, CT 06814

Water Control Board
2101 Webster Street, Suite 500
Poughkeepsie, NY 12603

Dear Sir or Madam:

I am writing this letter to thank all of you at the Water Control Board for your help with our team project. The information we gained firsthand on our tour of the facilities was very helpful to our research efforts.

We realize how busy you are with your work, so the time and patience you gave to our group is greatly appreciated.

Sincerely,

Sarah Lands

2. **The complaint or adjustment letter** If an error has been made or you have a specific complaint, you may write a ***complaint*** or ***adjustment letter***. When you are writing a complaint or adjustment letter, remember these points.

Tips for Writing a Complaint or Adjustment Letter
Send your complaint as soon as possible.
Explain why you are unhappy, how you were affected, and what solution you believe will correct the problem.
Keep the tone of your letter calm and courteous.

The following is the body of a complaint or adjustment letter.

> On April 30, I ordered a pair of green, heavy-duty swim fins. In your spring catalog, these fins are item number 820. This morning, however, I received a big, yellow, inflatable sea serpent, which I am returning to you. Please exchange the sea serpent for the swim fins.
>
> Thank you for your help.

3. **The request or order letter** A ***request letter***—also known as a **letter of inquiry**—asks for sample materials or information about a product or service. An ***order letter*** asks for something specific, such as an item of merchandise from a catalog with a missing order form. Remember the following tips when writing a request or order letter.

Tips for Writing a Request or Order Letter
Clearly state your request.
If you are requesting information, enclose a self-addressed, stamped envelope.
Make your request well in advance of the time you need it.
When ordering merchandise, include size, color, brand name, and cost.

At the top of the next column is the body of a request letter to the Department of State Parks in Wyoming.

> My family is planning a two-week vacation in Wyoming in July. We'd like to visit Yellowstone National Park, Jackson Lake, and Grand Teton National Park. Please send me any information--free brochures, pamphlets, or maps--that might help us on the trip. We would be interested in any information about attractions, such as museums or caverns, that lie on our route.
>
> We'll be driving down from Bozeman in a large camper, so we would also appreciate a list of campsites and fees.

Letters, Informal or Personal Sometimes an informal or personal letter is the most appropriate way to communicate a personal message. Unlike a business letter, a personal or social letter need not include a heading or an inside address, but you should include the date.

- **Types** There are three main types of informal or personal letters.
  1. **Invitations** In an informal invitation, include specific information about the occasion, the time and place, and any other special details your guest might need to know.
  2. **Letters of Regret** A letter of regret is written to inform someone that you will not be able to accept an invitation. You should make a special effort to respond in writing to invitations that include the letters *R.S.V.P.* (in French, an abbreviation for "please reply"). Be sure to send a letter of regret in a timely manner so that the

host will know how many people will attend the occasion.

3. **Thank-you letters** These are letters that tell someone that you appreciate his or her taking time, trouble, or expense to do something for you. Always mail a thank-you letter promptly, and try to say something personal. You might mention that you are aware of the person's effort, or you might tell why the gift is special to you.

Memo A ***memo,*** or memorandum, is a written message used when conducting business within an organization. For example, a person might send a memo to co-workers to remind them about a meeting or to inform them of a new policy. Memos should state the subject, give important details, and tell what actions need to be taken. An organization often has a set format for memos.

```
Greengrow, Inc.
MEMO

Date:     July 13, 2001
To:       Landscaping Staff
From:     Gina Williams, Schedule
          Coordinator
Subject:  Schedules During August

Please let me know by the end of
this week about any vacation
plans you may have in August. I
expect to be short-staffed dur-
ing this month, and I would like
to let our customers know in
advance about any changes to
their usual lawn-cutting service
schedule.

Thank you for your cooperation.
```

Prewriting Techniques Using one or more of the following ***prewriting techniques*** will help you find and explore ideas about which you would like to write. You might practice these techniques in a writer's notebook or journal so you can keep track of your ideas.

Many of these strategies involve the use of ***graphic organizers.*** A graphic organizer is a visual that helps you organize ideas and information. Graphic organizers are helpful in prewriting steps, gathering information, and organizing details, especially details from multiple sources.

1. **Generating ideas** You can generate ideas for writing by using the following strategies.
   - **Asking the *5W-How?* questions** Reporters often get information for news stories by asking the ***5W-How? questions:*** *Who? What? Where? When? Why?* and *How?* You can use these same questions to explore a topic. The example below shows you how this process might work for a report on a local environmental club. The notes in parentheses tell where the student would go to look for answers.

     EXAMPLE

     TOPIC: How Gorillas Might Be Saved from Extinction

     WHO? Who is working on the effort to save gorillas from extinction? (Check the library for names and addresses of groups.)

     WHAT? What is needed to save the gorillas? (Read books and articles; interview a zoo director.)

     WHAT? What is done with money given to save gorillas? (Contact groups working to save gorillas.)

QUICK REFERENCE HANDBOOK

WHERE? Where do gorillas live? (Check in an encyclopedia.)

WHY? Why are gorillas in danger? (Read books and articles; interview a zoo director.)

HOW? How can we save gorillas? (Check in a book, or call the education department at a zoo.)

- **Brainstorming** When you ***brainstorm,*** you write what comes to mind in response to a word or idea without stopping to judge what is said. You can brainstorm alone, but group or partner brainstorming is more fun because hearing other people's ideas helps you think of even more ideas. When you brainstorm, follow these steps:

Guidelines for Brainstorming
Write down a subject at the top of a piece of paper. (In a group, use the chalkboard.)
List every idea about the subject that comes to mind. (In a group, have one person list the ideas.)
Keep going until you run out of ideas.

Teen Culture

clothes—how different groups dress
bad movies
relationships with parents
favorite TV shows
hairstyles
slang
friends
favorite magazines
favorite music and movies
hangouts—skating rink
concerts and stars
peer pressure

- **Clustering** ***Clustering*** (sometimes called *webbing*) is a form of brainstorming in which you list ideas in circles and connect them with lines that show how the ideas fit together. To make a cluster diagram, follow these guidelines:

Guidelines for Clustering
Write your subject on your paper and circle it.
Around the subject, write whatever ideas about it occur to you. Circle these ideas.
Draw lines connecting the ideas with the subject.
When your ideas make you think of related ideas, connect them with lines.

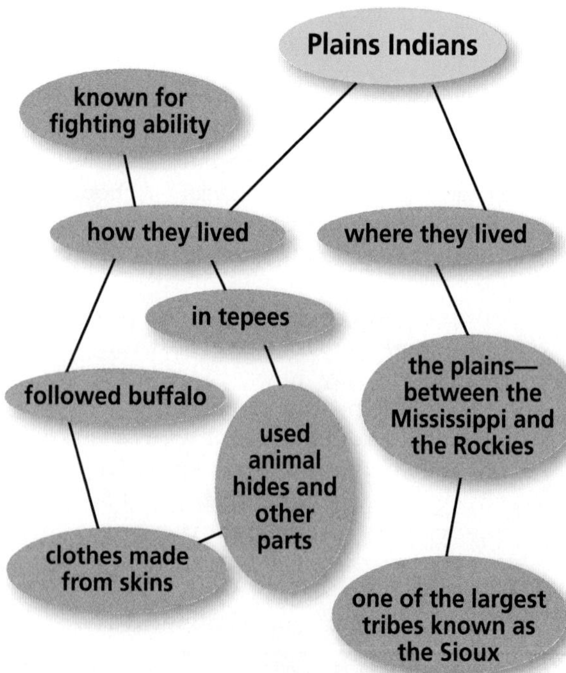

QUICK REFERENCE HANDBOOK

- **Freewriting** ***Freewriting*** is the act of writing whatever pops into your head. When you are freewriting, you do not judge ideas or worry about wording or punctuation. Freewriting can loosen you up for later writing or can give you ideas for topics.

Guidelines for Freewriting

Guidelines for Freewriting
Set a time limit of three to five minutes, and keep writing until the time is up.
Start with a subject that is important to you.
If you get stuck, just write anything. The important thing is to keep your pen moving.

Pioneers. Worked hard outside. Kids worked hard, too. Remember pictures of Abe Lincoln splitting logs as a child. Simple life. Families close. Good. Close to nature, but hard life. People died young—too hard. No doctors. Kids died, too. Pioneers. Going across plains. Oxen and horses. Wild animals. Built own houses. Wish I was a pioneer. Snakes. Wolves. Glad I wasn't a pioneer.

- **Imagining** Can you imagine that you are someone else or somewhere else? Imagining gives you creative ideas for your writing. Jump-start your imagination with ***"What if?" questions.*** "What if?" questions can be silly or serious. Here are examples.

  What if I became a grown-up overnight?
  What if something in my life—such as TV—did not exist?
  What if people could fly like birds?
  What if everyone looked exactly alike?

- **Writer's journal** A ***writer's journal*** can help you record your experiences, feelings, and ideas. When you need a subject to write about, you can turn to your journal for ideas.

Guidelines for Keeping a Journal
Write daily, keeping your journal handy.
Let your imagination run free. Write down dreams, songs, poems, and story ideas. Include drawings.
Forget about grammar and punctuation. Only your thoughts matter.

2. **Gathering ideas** Use the following strategies to gather ideas for writing.
   - **Listening with a focus** By listening with a focus, you can get information from speeches, radio and TV programs, interviews, audiotapes, or videotapes. Make a list of questions about your topic. Then, as you listen, jot down answers to your questions and write down main ideas and important details.
   - **Reading with a focus** Read sources such as books, magazines, newspapers, and brochures to gather information. Before you read a source, look for your topic in the table of contents and index. Then, skim the pages until you find information you can use. After finding information, slow down and take notes.

3. **Arranging ideas** After you have gathered ideas for your writing, you can use one or more of the following strategies to organize your ideas.

- **Charts** A **chart** helps you arrange information into categories. To create a chart for a particular subject, think about how you can divide the subject into parts or categories. Then, list details about each part or category. In the following chart—which is set up in table format—the writer's topic is musical instruments. The writer divided the topic into three categories and listed details about each one.

Musical Instruments

Name	Type of Instrument	How It Makes Sound
harp	stringed	by plucking the strings
clarinet	woodwind	by blowing into or through a tube
kettle-drum	percussion	by striking the drumhead

- **Conceptual mapping** ***Conceptual mapping*** resembles clustering in form but is used to organize ideas. A conceptual map is also helpful for determining whether you have enough support for each main idea. Notice how the conceptual map at the bottom of the page groups main ideas and supporting ideas.
- **Outlines** An ***outline*** shows how the main points and details of your composition fit together. Completing an outline will not only help you organize your writing into paragraphs, but it will also help you decide whether you have enough information for your composition. An outline can be written in sentence or topic form. A ***topic outline*** states ideas in single words or brief phrases. A ***sentence outline*** states ideas in complete sentences. In addition, an outline can be either ***formal*** or ***informal.***

Use a ***formal outline*** for major assignments, such as important compositions or research reports. A formal outline, which uses Roman numerals, should be an accurate reflection of the order and main content of your completed composition. At the top of the next page is a formal topic outline for a composition on what makes a good movie.

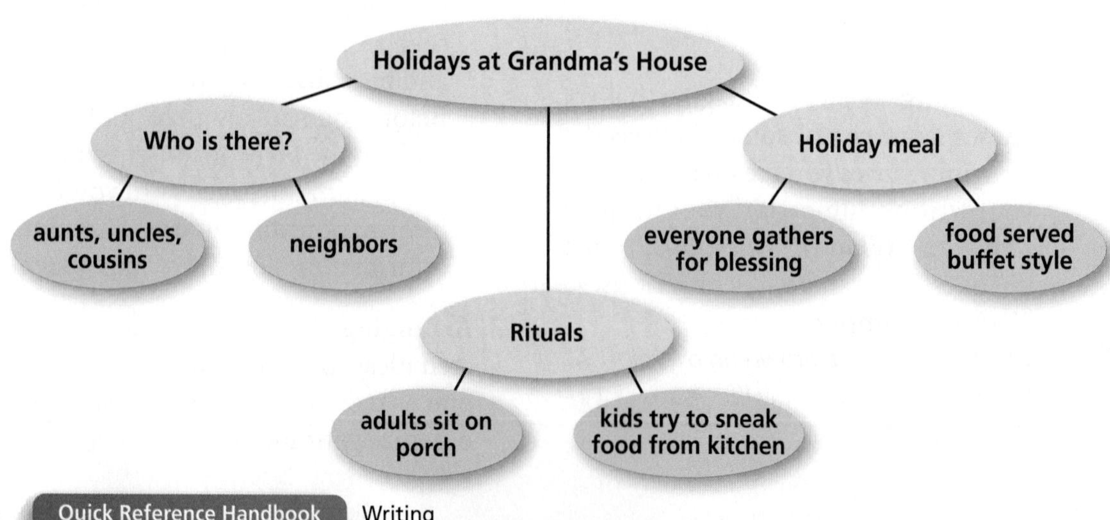

```
Title: Good Movies
  I. Plot
     A. Strong beginning
     B. Interesting plot
        developments
 II. Characters
     A. Real and interesting
     B. Sympathetic in some way
III. Special features
     A. Special effects
     B. Interesting or unusual
        settings
     C. Music
```

You can use an ***informal outline*** to make an early plan of your composition. Use an informal outline to *group* and *order* your ideas in a logical way. *Grouping* helps you arrange your details and eliminate ones that do not fit. *Ordering* helps you think about the best way to organize your ideas. The writer of the example below grouped details about what makes a good movie. Then, she arranged the groups according to their ***order of importance.*** (For other methods of ordering, see page 303.)

NOTE An informal outline can be used as the basis for a formal outline.

STRONG PLOT
interesting beginning, high interest level

STRONG CHARACTERS
real and interesting people, sympathetic to viewers

SPECIAL FEATURES
special effects, unusual settings, different time periods, music

- **Sequence chain** When you want to see how one event leads to another, you can create a **sequence chain.** For example, the events in a story or the steps in a process would be easy to see in a sequence chain. (See page 784 for an example of a sequence chain.)
- **Time line** A ***time line*** organizes information chronologically on a horizontal or a vertical line. The first or earliest events go on the left end of the time line. The most recent or latest events go on the right end of the time line. The following time line lists some of the major events of Paul Robeson's acting and singing career.

Appeared in *Showboat*	Starred in Shakespeare's *Othello*	Appeared in *King Solomon's Mines*
1928	1930	1937

- **Venn diagram** A Venn diagram uses overlapping circles to show how two subjects are alike and different. The area where the two circles overlap shows how the subjects are alike; the remaining areas show how the subjects are different.

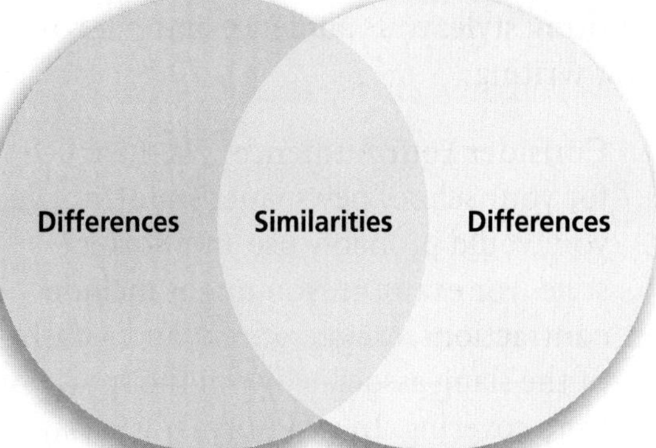

(See also page 784.)

QUICK REFERENCE HANDBOOK

SYMBOLS FOR REVISING AND PROOFREADING		
SYMBOL	**EXAMPLE**	**MEANING OF SYMBOL**
≡	at Scott lake	Capitalize a lowercase letter.
/	a gift for my Uncle	Lowercase a capital letter.
∧	cost ∧ cents (fifty)	Insert a missing word, letter, or punctuation mark.
∧——	by ∧their house (our)	Replace something.
℘	What day is is it?	Leave out a word, letter, or punctuation mark.
∽	recieved	Change the order of letters.
¶	¶ The last step is	Begin a new paragraph.
⊙	Please be patient⊙	Add a period.
∧ (comma)	Yes∧that's right.	Add a comma.

Revising and Proofreading Symbols When you are revising and proofreading your work, indicate any changes you need to make by using the symbols shown above.

Style You make choices every day about how to fix your hair, how to dress, and how to speak. These choices contribute to your personal style. Many factors affect your personal style—your family and friends, for example. When you write, you make choices about what words to use and how to arrange those words in sentences. These choices contribute to your writing style. Two important factors affect your writing style: your audience and purpose for writing.

- **Consider Your Audience** In an article for your school newspaper's sports page, you would probably use an informal style. For example, you might include contractions, exaggerations, and a dash of the slang associated with the sport you were covering. In an informative essay about the same sport written for your teacher, you would use a formal style. You would eliminate contractions and slang and avoid exaggeration, using precise words instead.

- **Consider Your Purpose** You also adjust your style according to your purpose for writing. The purpose of the sports-page article mentioned above is to entertain as well as inform. By exaggerating occasionally and using a bit of colorful slang from the sports world, you present the facts in an entertaining way. If you were writing an article for your school newspaper's front page, however, your primary purpose would be to inform—and inform quickly. You would need to get right to the point, using precise language and the fewest words possible. In this situation, exaggeration and slang would undercut your purpose.

Transitions To show readers how ideas are connected, writers use ***transitional expressions*** in their writing. (See page 309 for a chart of transitional expressions.)

Voice The way a piece of writing "sounds" is its ***voice.*** As you develop your writing skills, your voice will be something that you and your audience can recognize in everything you write. However, even a professional writer with a strong writing voice makes adjustments to that voice to fit the audience and purpose of a composition.

- **Consider Your Audience** If you were writing an essay to persuade an audience of teachers to eliminate weekend homework, you would probably want to aim for a reasonable-sounding, matter-of-fact voice. For example, you might not argue that homework interferes with your leisure time, because that might come across as whiny. Instead, you might offer reasons that would appeal to teachers. For example, you might suggest they spend their weekends relaxing instead of working. In a letter to the student council, however, you might use the very arguments that you would avoid for an audience of teachers. Thinking about how your ideas "sound" to your audience is a good way to think about voice.

- **Consider Your Purpose** When you write to express your feelings, as in a journal entry, you do not need to worry about how you sound. Just let "the real you" come out. When writing to inform or persuade, however, you usually want to aim for a voice that sounds fair and reasonable. You can achieve that by supporting your main idea or opinion, and by elaborating on your support as thoroughly as you possibly can. Make the reader think: "You've done your homework!"

mmar at a Glance

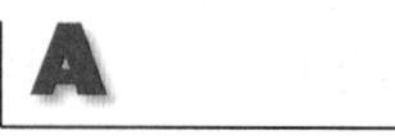

A

HELP

Grammar at a Glance is an alphabetical list of special terms and expressions with examples and references to further information. When you encounter a grammar or usage problem in the revising or proofreading stage of your writing, look for help in this section first. You may find all you need to know right here. If you need more information, **Grammar at a Glance** will show you where in the book to turn for a more complete explanation. If you do not find what you are looking for in **Grammar at a Glance,** turn to the index.

abbreviation An abbreviation is a shortened form of a word or a phrase.

■ **capitalization of**

TITLES USED WITH NAMES	**M**rs.	**G**ov.	**J**r.	**M.D.**	
KINDS OF ORGANIZATIONS	**C**o.	**I**nc.	**A**ssn.	**C**orp.	
PARTS OF ADDRESSES	**B**lvd.	**S**t.	**A**ve.	**P.O. B**ox	
NAMES OF STATES	[without ZIP Codes]			**A**riz. **C**onn.	**M**d. **N. M**ex.
	[with ZIP Codes]			**AZ** **CT**	**MD** **NM**
TIMES	**A.M.**	**P.M.**	**B.C.**	**A.D.**	

■ **punctuation of** (See page 631.)

WITH PERIODS	(See preceding examples.)				
WITHOUT PERIODS	MVP	PBS	USAF	NASA	
	kg	mi	qt	C	cm
	[Exception: inch = in.]				

action verb An action verb expresses physical or mental activity. (See page 373.)

EXAMPLE She **hoped** Myron **would leave** on time.

active voice Active voice is the voice a verb is in when it expresses an action done by its subject. (See page 520. See also **voice.**)

EXAMPLE Peggy **climbed** the old oak tree.

adjective An adjective modifies a noun or a pronoun. (See page 358.)

EXAMPLE Arthur likes **action-packed crime** thrillers.

adjective clause An adjective clause is a subordinate clause that modifies a noun or a pronoun. (See page 444.)

EXAMPLE The actor **who starred in that TV film** is Robert Duvall.

adjective phrase A prepositional phrase that modifies a noun or a pronoun is called an adjective phrase. (See page 417.)

EXAMPLE The clothes **from Italy** are the best **in the store.**

adverb An adverb modifies a verb, an adjective, or another adverb. (See page 381.)

EXAMPLE **Usually,** the linguini is **very** good here.

adverb clause An adverb clause is a subordinate clause that modifies a verb, an adjective, or an adverb. (See page 447.)

EXAMPLE They stayed **until darkness fell.**

adverb phrase A prepositional phrase that modifies a verb, an adjective, or an adverb is called an adverb phrase. (See page 419.)

EXAMPLE **In the afternoon,** we will go **to the park.**

agreement Agreement is the correspondence, or match, between grammatical forms. Grammatical forms agree when they have the same number and gender.

- **of pronouns and antecedents** (See page 493.)

SINGULAR **Ernesto** is saving **his** money to buy a new pair of in-line skates.

PLURAL Having tuned **their** instruments, the mariachi band **members** were ready to rehearse.

SINGULAR **Everyone** in the science class is hard at work on **his or her** ecology project.

PLURAL **All** of the science students are hard at work on **their** ecology projects.

QUICK REFERENCE HANDBOOK

SINGULAR	**Neither Julie nor Erin** was pleased with **her** performance in the piano recital.
PLURAL	**Julie and Erin** were not pleased with **their** performances in the piano recital.

of subjects and verbs (See page 476.)

SINGULAR	The space shuttle **commander is** optimistic that the rescue mission will be successful.
SINGULAR	The space shuttle **commander,** as well as her crew members, **is** optimistic that the rescue mission will be successful.
PLURAL	The space shuttle crew **members are** optimistic that the rescue mission will be successful.
PLURAL	The space shuttle crew **members,** as well as their commander, **are** optimistic that the rescue mission will be successful.
SINGULAR	Does Charlene know that **each** of these library books **is** overdue?
PLURAL	Does Charlene know that **all** of these library books **are** overdue?
SINGULAR	**Either Ben or Cameron is** in charge of ticket sales.
PLURAL	**Both Ben and Cameron are** in charge of ticket sales.
SINGULAR	Here **is** a **recipe** for making the famous Korean dish kimchi.
PLURAL	Here **are** the **ingredients** you will need for making the famous Korean dish kimchi.
SINGULAR	***Little Heroes* is** a heartwarming movie.
PLURAL	The young **heroes** in the movie **are** an eleven-year-old girl named Charley and her dog, Fuzz.
SINGULAR	**Gymnastics is** not yet a part of our school's athletics program.
PLURAL	The **Summer Olympics are** not **held** in the same year as the Winter Olympics.
SINGULAR	A common **problem** at picnics **is** ants.
PLURAL	**Ants are** a common problem at picnics.

antecedent An antecedent is the word or words that a pronoun stands for. (See page 351.)

EXAMPLE **Tamara** told **Ben** and **Tracy** **she** was thinking of **them.** [*Tamara* is the antecedent of *she*. *Ben* and *Tracy* are the antecedents of *them.*]

apostrophe

- **to form contractions** (See page 672. See also **contractions.**)

  EXAMPLES can't they'll o'clock '99

- **to form plurals of letters, numerals, symbols, and words used as words** (See page 675.)

  EXAMPLES dotting *i*'s and crossing *t*'s writing *R*'s and *B*'s

  in the 1900's learning the ABC's

  using *and*'s instead of *&*'s or +'s

- **to show possession** (See page 669.)

  EXAMPLES the student's schedule

  the students' schedules

  children's toys

  someone's backpack

  Tommy and Eric's pet-sitting service

  Katrina's and Simon's paper routes

  one year's [or twelve months'] salary

appositive An appositive is a noun or a pronoun placed beside another noun or pronoun to identify or describe it. (See page 432.)

EXAMPLE The great soccer player **Pelé** is also a composer and businessman.

appositive phrase An appositive phrase consists of an appositive and its modifiers. (See page 432.)

EXAMPLE Mrs. Grabovski, **our upstairs neighbor,** has become a good friend to our family.

article The articles, *a, an,* and *the,* are the most frequently used adjectives. (See page 359.)

EXAMPLE **A** favorite cartoon character around **the** world, and **an** ageless hero, is **the** Belgian reporter Tintin.

B

bad, badly (See page 585.)

NONSTANDARD This sour milk smells badly.

STANDARD This sour milk smells **bad.**

base form The base form, or infinitive, is one of the four principal parts of a verb. (See page 506.)

EXAMPLE We saw him **leave** the building.

brackets (See page 679.)

EXAMPLES According to an African proverb, "It is not only giants **[**extraordinary people**]** that do great things **[**heroic deeds**]**."

The United States Congress comprises the House of Representatives (435 members **[**each up for reelection every two years**]**) and the Senate (100 members **[**each up for reelection every six years**]**).

C

capitalization

- **of abbreviations** (See page 607. See also **end marks.**)
- **of first words** (See page 604.)

EXAMPLES **M**any students are in favor of attending school year-round.

Mr. Inouye told us, "**T**he Hawaiian alphabet consists of five vowels and seven consonants."

Dear Ms. Evans:

Sincerely yours,

- **of proper nouns and proper adjectives** (See page 606 and 616.)

EXAMPLES Have you ever visited **Canada**? [proper noun]

I can sing the **Canadian** national anthem. [proper adjective]

Proper Noun	**Common Noun**
Alfred the **G**reat	leader
South **A**merica	continent
Saudi **A**rabia	country
San **M**iguel **C**ounty	county
Saskatchewan **P**rovince	province
Galápagos **I**slands	islands
Gulf of **T**onkin	body of water
Mount **P**inatubo	mountain
Chaco **C**ulture **N**ational **H**istorical **P**ark	park
Sherwood **F**orest	forest
Mammoth **C**ave	cave
Zion **C**anyon	canyon
the **S**outheast	region
Forty-second **S**treet	street
Democratic **P**arty (or **p**arty)	political party
Battle of **S**an **J**uan **H**ill	historical event
Super **B**owl	special event
Presidents' **D**ay	holiday
January, **T**hursday	calendar items
Quapaw **S**ioux	people
Taoism	religion
Buddhist	religious follower
God (*but* the **g**od **A**pollo)	deity
Hanukkah	holy day
Koran	sacred writing
Statue of **L**iberty	monument
Texas **C**ommerce **T**ower	building
Spingarn **M**edal	award
Neptune	planet
Beta **C**rucis	star
Ursa **M**inor	constellation
***S**candinavian **S**tar*	ship
***E**nterprise*	spacecraft

QUICK REFERENCE HANDBOOK

■ **of titles** (See page 619.)

EXAMPLES **S**enator Ben Nighthorse Campbell [preceding a name]

Ben Nighthorse Campbell, a **s**enator from Colorado [following a name]

Thank you, **S**enator. [direct address]

Uncle Omar [*but* my uncle Omar]

***T**he **W**orld's **G**ame: **A** **H**istory of **S**occer* [book]

***M**ythic **W**arriors: **G**uardian of the **L**egend* [TV series]

***D**og **B**arking at the **M**oon* [work of art]

***T**he **T**hree-**C**ornered **H**at* [musical composition]

"**M**y **O**ld **K**entucky **H**ome" [song]

"**T**he **L**egend of **S**leepy **H**ollow" [short story]

"**E**legy for the **G**iant **T**ortoises" [poem]

***T**een **P**eople* [magazine]

the ***S**t. **L**ouis **P**ost-**D**ispatch* [newspaper]

***D**ennis the **M**enace* [comic strip]

case of pronouns Case is the form a pronoun takes to show how it is used in a sentence. (See page 536.)

NOMINATIVE For social studies, **she** and **I** built a model of the White House.

The chairperson of the dance committee is **he.**

Either basketball player, Carmen or **she,** is an excellent point guard.

We eighth-graders are learning how beneficial the rain forests are.

Is I. M. Pei the architect **who** designed the Mile High Center in Denver, Colorado?

Do you know **who** the new exchange student is?

We have known Ramon longer than **she.** [subject of an elliptical clause meaning *longer than she has known Ramon*]

OBJECTIVE My parents took **me** to Memphis, Tennessee, to visit the museum honoring the legacy of Dr. Martin Luther King, Jr., and his civil rights efforts.

Ms. Wu read **us** the Cambodian folk tale "Judge Rabbit and the Tree Spirit."

The final footrace was between Lupe and **him.**

The reward money was divided equally among the three rescuers, Leo, Chen, and **her.**

In the locker room, Coach Alvarez showed **us** players the videotape of last night's game.

One leader about **whom** I would like to know more is Kofi Annan, who was elected secretary-general of the United Nations in 1997.

We have known Ramon longer than **her.** [direct object of an elliptical clause meaning *longer than we have known her*]

POSSESSIVE **Your** camera takes better pictures than **mine** does.

clause A clause is a group of words that contains a subject and a verb and is used as part of a sentence. (See page 439.)

EXAMPLES While Molly sang a song [subordinate clause]

Brendan played the pipes [independent clause]

colon (See page 652.)

- **before lists**

EXAMPLES The Nobel prizes are awarded each year to those who have made the greatest contributions in the following fields**:** chemistry, physics, medicine or physiology, economics, literature, and world peace.

Only four women have been featured on United States currency**:** Martha Washington, the first first lady; Matoaka, better known as Pocahontas; Susan B. Anthony, a pioneer in the women's rights movement; and Sacajawea, the American Indian guide of Lewis and Clark.

- **before statements that explain or clarify**

EXAMPLE This is one of the most popular computers**:** It is inexpensive, easy to use, and comes in designer colors.

- **before a long, formal statement or quotation**

EXAMPLE Mark Twain's philosophy was simple and straight-forward**:** "Let us so live that when we come to die even the undertaker will be sorry."

- **in conventional situations**

EXAMPLES 10**:**15 P.M.

Exodus 20**:**3–17

*Heart of Lions***:** *The History of American Bicycle Racing*

Dear Ms. Zahn**:**

comma (See page 633.)

- **in a series**

EXAMPLES In 1999, the lira**,** the franc**,** the deutsche mark**,** and eight other currencies were all replaced by a currency called the euro.

A good night's sleep in the cool**,** crisp**,** clean mountain air had invigorated the weary rock climbers.

- **in compound sentences**

EXAMPLES The highest point in the United States is Mount McKinley in Alaska**,** and the lowest is Death Valley in California.

I have read *The Education of Little Tree***,** but I have not seen the film version of the book.

- **with nonessential phrases and clauses**

EXAMPLES Eileen Collins**,** a lieutenant colonel in the United States Air Force**,** was the first woman to command a space shuttle mission.

Halley's comet**,** named for the scientist Edmund Halley**,** orbits the sun about every seventy-six years.

The name *Minnesota* comes from the Dakota Sioux word *mnisota***,** which means "cloudy or milky water."

- **with introductory elements**

EXAMPLES On her way to her karate lesson**,** Courtney stopped by the library to return a book for her grandfather.

After he had graduated from college**,** my brother Giovanni joined the Peace Corps.

- **with interrupters**

EXAMPLES The most impressive exhibit at the art gallery, in my opinion, is the one called "Ancient Art of Olmec Mexico."

"May 5, of course, is the day on which the Cinco de Mayo Fiesta will be held," the mayor reminded her staff.

- **in conventional situations**

EXAMPLES On Saturday, August 19, 2000, Mr. Diaz and his daughter began their hot-air balloon trip from Savannah, Georgia, to Cheyenne, Wyoming.

Please ship this package to 701 Loyola Ave., Portsmouth, New Hampshire, on 12 January 2001.

comma splice A comma splice is a run-on sentence in which only a comma separates two complete sentences. (See **fused sentence, run-on sentence.**)

COMMA SPLICE This baseball card is valued at two hundred dollars, to some collectors it may be worth more than that.

REVISED This baseball card is valued at two hundred dollars, **and** to some collectors it may be worth more than that.

REVISED This baseball card is valued at two hundred dollars; **t**o some collectors it may be worth more than that.

REVISED This baseball card is valued at two hundred dollars. **T**o some collectors it may be worth more than that.

comparison of modifiers (See page 559.)

- **comparison of adjectives and adverbs**

Positive	Comparative	Superlative
short	shorter	shortest
lucky	luckier	luckiest
valuable	**more (less)** valuable	**most (least)** valuable
swiftly	**more (less)** swiftly	**most (least)** swiftly
bad/badly	**worse**	**worst**

- **comparing two**

EXAMPLES Of Venus and Mars, which planet is **farther** from Earth?

My sister keyboards **faster** and **more accurately** than I.

Don't you think that Kaya and Russell perform this routine **more gracefully** than **any other** couple in the dance company?

- **comparing more than two**

EXAMPLES Weighing approximately ninety tons, the seismosaurus was the **largest** dinosaur.

Of the four golfers, Chen plays **most skillfully.**

complement A complement is a word or word group that completes the meaning of a verb. (See page 399. See also **direct object, indirect object, subject complement, predicate nominative,** and **predicate adjective**)

EXAMPLES The teacher asked **everyone** in the room three **questions.**

It's an old **car,** but it is **fast.**

complex sentence A complex sentence has one independent clause and at least one subordinate clause. (See page 465.)

EXAMPLES Aboriginal art, which is the artwork of the Australian Aborigines, includes cave paintings, rock engravings, and tree carvings.

If we are going to make gazpacho for dinner tonight, I want you to promise that you'll help in the kitchen.

compound-complex sentence A compound-complex sentence has two or more independent clauses and at least one subordinate clause. (See page 467.)

EXAMPLE My pen pal e-mails me a poem every week; sometimes it is one that he has composed, but most of the time it is one that a famous poet, such as Langston Hughes or Robert Frost, has written.

Our aunt Junko came to visit us last week, and with her she brought a new computer game, which she had helped to design.

compound sentence A compound sentence has two or more independent clauses but no subordinate clauses. (See page 462.)

EXAMPLES The first person to reach the North Pole was the American explorer Robert Peary, and the first to reach the South Pole was Roald Amundsen, an explorer from Norway.

The Big Dipper consists of seven stars; it is part of the constellation Ursa Major.

conjunction A conjunction joins words or groups of words. (See pages 389 and 448.)

EXAMPLES Lucy Devereux **and** Millie Ramos are best friends, **but** they live on opposite sides of town.

Either the dog **or** the cat knocked over this plant.

When she heard the news, Ling volunteered to help.

contraction A contraction is a shortened form of a word, a numeral, or a group of words. Apostrophes in contractions indicate where letters or numerals have been omitted. (See page 672. See also **apostrophe.**)

EXAMPLES

you've [you have]	where's [where is]
who's [who is *or* who has]	they're [they are]
wouldn't [would not]	it's [it is *or* it has]
can't [cannot]	won't [will not]
'39–'45 war [1939–1945 war]	o'clock [of the clock]

dangling modifier A dangling modifier is a modifying word, phrase, or clause that does not clearly and sensibly modify a word or a word group in a sentence. (See page 569.)

DANGLING Searching the Internet for information about American Indian customs, an article about the Shawnee leader Tenskwatawa, Chief Tecumseh's brother, captured my interest. [Is the article searching the Internet?]

REVISED **Searching the Internet for information about American Indian customs, I** found an interesting article about the Shawnee leader Tenskwatawa, Chief Tecumseh's brother.

REVISED **While I was searching the Internet for information about American Indian customs,** an article about the Shawnee leader Tenskwatawa, Chief Tecumseh's brother, captured my interest.

dash (See page 680.)

EXAMPLE My friend Rico**—**his real name is Federico**—**wants to be a marine biologist.

declarative sentence A declarative sentence makes a statement and is followed by a period. (See page 339.)

EXAMPLE Whales and dolphins are marine mammals**.**

direct object A direct object is a word or word group that receives the action of the verb or shows the result of the action. A direct object answers the question *Whom?* or *What?* after a transitive verb. (See page 401.)

EXAMPLE Did you read the **newspaper** today?

double comparison A double comparison is the nonstandard use of two comparative forms (usually *more* and *–er*) or two superlative forms (usually *most* and *–est*) to express comparison. In standard usage, the single comparative form is correct. (See page 566.)

NONSTANDARD Devon would have had a more better time on the camping trip if he had not forgotten his allergy medication.

STANDARD Devon would have had a **better** time on the camping trip if he had not forgotten his allergy medication.

double negative A double negative is the nonstandard use of two negative words to express a single negative idea. (See page 567.)

NONSTANDARD This morning, my throat was so sore that I couldn't hardly swallow.

STANDARD This morning, my throat was so sore that I **could hardly** swallow.

NONSTANDARD The tickets to the local science center to see the documentary *Africa's Elephant Kingdom* won't cost the students nothing.

STANDARD The tickets to the local science center to see the documentary *Africa's Elephant Kingdom* **won't cost** the students **anything.**

STANDARD The tickets to the local science center to see the documentary *Africa's Elephant Kingdom* **will cost** the students **nothing.**

double subject A double subject occurs when an unnecessary pronoun is used after the subject of a sentence. (See page 589.)

NONSTANDARD Dr. Yaeger, who lives next door to me, she is one of the veterinarians at the animal clinic.

STANDARD **Dr. Yaeger,** who lives next door to me, **is** one of the veterinarians at the animal clinic.

end marks (See page 629.)

- **with sentences**

EXAMPLES Jambalaya, a spicy Creole dish, is made of rice, vegetables, and various kinds of meat**.** [declarative sentence]

Have you ever eaten jambalaya**?** [interrogative sentence]

Wow**!** [interjection] What a hot, spicy dish this is**!** [exclamatory sentence]

Pass the jambalaya, please**.** [imperative sentence]

Sit down**!** [strong imperative sentence]

- **with abbreviations** (See page 631. See also **abbreviations.**)

EXAMPLES One of the guest speakers was Jesse Jackson, Jr**.**

Wasn't one of the guest speakers Jesse Jackson, Jr.**?**

essential clause/essential phrase An essential, or restrictive, clause or phrase is necessary to the meaning of a sentence and is not set off by commas. (See page 639.)

EXAMPLES Participants **who have not received an I.D. card** must come to the front desk. [essential clause]

Students **entered in the relay race** should meet with Coach Peterson. [essential phrase]

exclamation point (See **end marks.**)

exclamatory sentence An exclamatory sentence expresses strong feeling and is followed by an exclamation point. (See page 339.)

EXAMPLE I've never been so surprised**!**

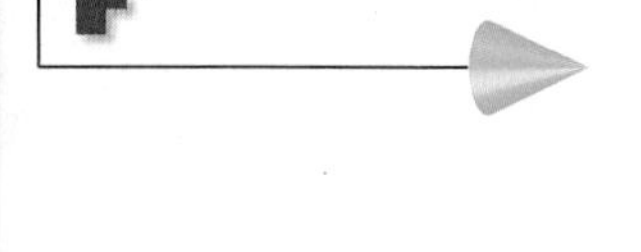

fragment (See **sentence fragment.**)

fused sentence A fused sentence is a run-on sentence in which no punctuation separates complete sentences. (See **comma splice, run-on sentence.**)

FUSED The Underground Railroad was not an actual railroad it was a network of people who helped fugitive slaves secure their freedom.

REVISED The Underground Railroad was not an actual railroad**. I**t was a network of people who helped fugitive slaves secure their freedom.

REVISED The Underground Railroad was not an actual railroad**;** it was a network of people who helped fugitive slaves secure their freedom.

G

gerund A gerund is a verb form ending in *–ing* that is used as a noun. (See page 425.)

EXAMPLE **Singing** is her main interest.

gerund phrase A gerund phrase consists of a gerund and its modifiers and complements. (See page 426.)

EXAMPLE They improved the insulation of the apartment by **adding solar screens to the windows.**

good, well (See page 558.)

EXAMPLE The gymnast's performance on the uneven parallel bars was especially **good.** [*not* well]

hyphen (See page 675.)

- **for division of words**

EXAMPLE The labor leader Cesar Chavez worked hard to organ**-**ize the migrant farm workers in the United States.

- **in compound numbers**

EXAMPLE Wasn't the price of a postage stamp twenty**-**three cents?

- **with prefixes and suffixes**

EXAMPLES The construction of the new high school should be completed by mid**-**June.

The speech will be given by the club's president**-**elect, Catherine French.

H

I

imperative sentence An imperative sentence gives a command or makes a request and is followed by either a period or an exclamation point. (See page 339.)

EXAMPLES All those in favor, say "Aye**.**"

Sit down**!**

independent clause An independent clause (also called a *main clause*) expresses a complete thought and can stand by itself as a sentence. (See page 440.)

EXAMPLE Because she wanted to celebrate spring, **Josie bought a bouquet of daffodils and placed them in a vase on the hallway table.**

indirect object An indirect object is a word or word group that often comes between a transitive verb and its direct object and tells to whom or to what or for whom or for what the action of the verb is done. (See page 403.)

EXAMPLE Roman told **Natalya** and **Stefan** a fascinating tale of old Warsaw. [The direct object is *tale.*]

infinitive An infinitive is a verb form, usually preceded by *to,* that is used as a noun, an adjective, or an adverb. (See page 428.)

EXAMPLE These apples are the kind **to bake.**

infinitive phrase An infinitive phrase consists of an infinitive and its modifiers and complements. (See page 429.)

EXAMPLE Dr. Matissot is the one **to ask about matters of French grammar.**

interjection An interjection expresses emotion and has no grammatical relation to the rest of the sentence. (See page 391.)

EXAMPLE **Wow!** That's some fish!

interrogative sentence An interrogative sentence asks a question and is followed by a question mark. (See page 339.)

EXAMPLE Is *Petrushka* a ballet by Igor Stravinsky**?**

intransitive verb An intransitive verb is a verb that does not take an object. (See page 379.)

EXAMPLE The crowd **cheered** for a full five minutes.

irregular verb An irregular verb is a verb that forms its past and past participle in some way other than by adding *d* or *ed* to the base form. (See page 508. See also **regular verb.**)

Base Form	Present Participle	Past	Past Participle
be	[is] being	was, were	[have] been
bring	[is] bringing	brought	[have] brought
build	[is] building	built	[have] built
burst	[is] bursting	burst	[have] burst
choose	[is] choosing	chose	[have] chosen
cost	[is] costing	cost	[have] cost
drive	[is] driving	drove	[have] driven
grow	[is] growing	grew	[have] grown
speak	[is] speaking	spoke	[have] spoken
swim	[is] swimming	swam	[have] swum

italics (See **underlining.**)

its, it's (See page 590.)

EXAMPLES One of **its** [Hawaii's] nicknames is the Aloha State.

It's [It is] located in the North Pacific.

It's [It has] been a U.S. state since 1959.

lie, lay (See page 523.)

EXAMPLES For nearly one hundred years, the wrecked ship **lay** on the ocean floor.

Before we set out the food, we **laid** a clean tablecloth on the picnic table.

linking verb A linking verb connects the subject with a word that identifies or describes the subject. (See page 374.)

EXAMPLE Before long, the sea **became** rough and choppy.

misplaced modifier A misplaced modifier is a word, phrase, or clause that seems to modify the wrong word or words in a sentence. (See page 569.)

MISPLACED The explorers discovered a sack of old Spanish gold coins winding their way through a maze of stalagmites and stalactites. [Are the coins winding their way through a maze?]

REVISED **Winding their way through a maze of stalagmites and stalactites,** the explorers discovered a sack of old Spanish gold coins.

REVISED The explorers, **winding their way through a maze of stalagmites and stalactites,** discovered a sack of old Spanish gold coins.

modifier A modifier is a word or group of words that makes the meaning of another word more specific. (See page 556.)

EXAMPLE **Suddenly,** a **tiny** rabbit appeared **on the lawn.**

The book **that I just finished reading** is about Tiger Woods.

N

nonessential clause/nonessential phrase A nonessential, or nonrestrictive, clause or phrase adds information not necessary to the main idea in the sentence and is set off by commas. (See page 639.)

EXAMPLES That man, **who lives across the street from us,** has some strong opinions. [nonessential clause]

The scouts, **exhausted by the hike,** dozed by the campfire. [nonessential phrase]

noun A noun names a person, place, thing, or idea. (See page 345.)

EXAMPLE On **Friday,** the lead **car** in the **expedition** blew a **gasket,** and the **team** wasted no **time** in contacting **Colonel MacPherson** at **headquarters** over the **radio.**

noun clause A noun clause is a subordinate clause used as a noun. (See page 450.)

EXAMPLE **How she won the race** is an amazing story.

number Number is the form a word takes to indicate whether the word is singular or plural. (See page 475.)

SINGULAR	foot	I	essay	solo
PLURAL	feet	we	essays	solos

object of a preposition An object of a preposition is the noun or pronoun that ends a prepositional phrase. (See page 416.)

EXAMPLE The timid deer ran from **us.** [*From us* is a prepositional phrase.]

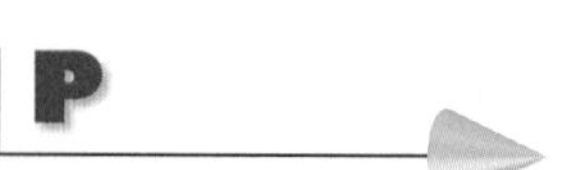

parentheses (See page 678.)

EXAMPLES The Heimlich maneuver **(**see the diagram below**)** is an emergency technique that can be used to help a person who is choking.

The Heimlich maneuver is an emergency technique that can be used to help a person who is choking. **(S**ee the diagram below**.)**

participial phrase A participial phrase consists of a participle and any complements and modifiers it has. (See page 422.)

EXAMPLE They were surprised to find their goat Daisy **grazing in the neighbors' yard.**

participle A participle is a verb form that can be used as an adjective. (See page 421.)

EXAMPLE Colin calmed the **snarling** dog.

passive voice The passive voice is the voice a verb is in when it expresses an action done to its subject. (See page 520. See also **voice.**)

EXAMPLE We **were told** to meet him here.

period (See **end marks.**)

phrase A phrase is a group of related words that does not contain both a verb and its subject and that is used as a single part of speech. (See page 415.)

EXAMPLES The court chamberlain **had been thinking** recently **about his position.** [*Had been thinking* is a verb phrase. *About his position* is a prepositional phrase.]

Running swiftly, the gazelle escaped **from the cheetah.** [*Running swiftly* is a participial phrase. *From the cheetah* is a prepositional phrase.]

To know me is **to love me.** [*To know me* and *to love me* are infinitive phrases.]

Painting the bedroom is our next project. [*Painting the bedroom* is a gerund phrase.]

predicate The predicate is the part of a sentence that says something about the subject. (See page 329.)

EXAMPLE They **spent all their leisure time painting the apartment.**

predicate adjective A predicate adjective is an adjective that completes the meaning of a linking verb and that modifies the subject of the verb. (See page 407.)

EXAMPLE Of all the cities the Podestas visited in the United States, Santa Fe seemed **friendliest** and most **hospitable.**

predicate nominative A predicate nominative is a noun or pronoun that completes the meaning of a linking verb and identifies or explains the subject of the verb. (See page 405.)

EXAMPLE The highest jumper in that heat was **Oscar.**

prefix A prefix is a word part that is added before a base word or root. (See page 690.)

EXAMPLES un + important = **un**important

il + legal = **il**legal

re + construct = **re**construct

pre + recorded = **pre**recorded

self + conscious = **self-**conscious

ex + governor = **ex-**governor

mid + Atlantic = **mid-**Atlantic

pre + Revolution = **pre-**Revolution

preposition A preposition shows the relationship of a noun or a pronoun to some other word in a sentence. (See page 386.)

EXAMPLE **From** July 6 **until** July 14 each year, the running **of** the bulls takes place **in** Pamplona, the capital **of** Navarre province **in** northeastern Spain.

prepositional phrase A prepositional phrase includes a preposition, a noun or pronoun called the object of the preposition, and any modifiers of that object. (See page 416. See also **object of a preposition.**)

EXAMPLE Riding **on a fast horse,** the pony express carrier never lingered.

pronoun A pronoun is used in place of one or more nouns or pronouns. (See page 351.)

EXAMPLES Zita told Patrick **her** frank opinion of **his** plan.

Someone helped **himself** or **herself** to my yogurt.

That is a good idea, Jeremy.

question mark (See **end marks.**)

quotation marks (See page 662.)

- **for direct quotations**

EXAMPLE "Take nothing but pictures," our nature guide reminded us, "and leave nothing but footprints."

- **with other marks of punctuation** (See also preceding example.)

EXAMPLES "What is the capital of Uruguay?" asked Albert.

Doesn't the word *fortuitous* mean "occurring by chance"?

The teacher asked, "What are the names of the speaker's children in Li Po's poem 'Letter to His Two Small Children'?"

- **for titles**

EXAMPLES "Raymond's Run" [short story]

"Quiet Night Thoughts" [short poem]

"When You Wish upon a Star" [song]

regular verb A regular verb is a verb that forms its past and past participle by adding *d* or *ed* to the base form. (See page 507. See also **irregular verb.**)

Base Form	Present Participle	Past	Past Participle
ask	[is] asking	asked	[have] asked
believe	[is] believing	believed	[have] believed
drown	[is] drowning	drowned	[have] drowned
risk	[is] risking	risked	[have] risked
suppose	[is] supposing	supposed	[have] supposed
use	[is] using	used	[have] used

QUICK REFERENCE HANDBOOK

rise, raise (See page 525.)

EXAMPLES For nine days in a row, the temperature **rose** higher than 100°F.

Adjusting the thermostat, Mother **raised** the temperature in the room to 78°F.

run-on sentence A run-on sentence is two or more complete sentences run together as one. (See page 277. See also **comma splice** and **fused sentence.**)

RUN-ON Ms. Micklewhite, Tom's supervisor, told Tom he was at the top of the list for a promotion however, she said that the promotion might mean Tom would have to relocate to Chicago.

REVISED Ms. Micklewhite, Tom's supervisor, told Tom he was at the top of the list for a promotion**. H**owever, she said that the promotion might mean Tom would have to relocate to Chicago.

REVISED Ms. Micklewhite, Tom's supervisor, told Tom he was at the top of the list for a promotion**;** however**,** she said that the promotion might mean Tom would have to relocate to Chicago.

semicolon (See page 649.)

- **in compound sentences with no conjunction**

  EXAMPLE In 1993, Vicki Van Meter became the youngest girl to pilot an airplane across the United States**;** she was eleven years old.

- **in compound sentences with conjunctive adverbs or transitional expressions**

  EXAMPLE The Hubble Space Telescope, which entered Earth's orbit in 1990, has proved to be a valuable resource for astronomers**;** for example, in 1996, the telescope provided them views of the surface of the planet Pluto.

- **between items in a series when the items contain commas**

  EXAMPLE Joshua made a chart that classifies the different species of dinosaurs as carnivorous, or meat eating**;** herbivorous, or plant eating**;** or omnivorous, or meat eating and plant eating.

sentence A sentence is a group of words that contains a subject and a verb and expresses a complete thought. (See page 324.)

EXAMPLE Many children are curious about animals of all species. (S: children; V: are)

sentence fragment A sentence fragment is a group of words that is punctuated as if it were a complete sentence but that does not contain both a subject and a verb or that does not express a complete thought. (See pages 275 and 324.)

FRAGMENT Sweeping across the Sahara, a hot, violent wind called a simoom.

SENTENCE Sweeping across the Sahara, a hot, violent wind called a simoom causes the formation of huge sand dunes.

FRAGMENTS The reason for building the Great Wall of China. To protect the country from invaders.

SENTENCE The reason for building the Great Wall of China was to protect the country from invaders.

simple sentence A simple sentence has one independent clause and no subordinate clauses. (See page 460.)

EXAMPLES The French expression *joie de vivre* means "joy of living."

Emilia and Jeffrey are running for class president.

sit, set (See page 521.)

EXAMPLES The students **sat** quietly, listening to an audiotape of the Japanese folk tale "Green Willow."

Did you see who **set** this package on my desk?

stringy sentence A stringy sentence is a sentence that has too many independent clauses. Usually, the clauses are strung together with coordinating conjunctions like *and* or *but.* (See page 288.)

STRINGY In Roman mythology, Arachne was a peasant girl, and she was a skillful weaver, too, and she claimed that her skill was superior to that of the goddess Minerva.

REVISED In Roman mythology, Arachne, a peasant girl who was a skillful weaver, claimed that her skill was superior to that of the goddess Minerva.

QUICK REFERENCE HANDBOOK

subject The subject tells whom or what a sentence is about. (See page 327.)

EXAMPLE ***The Jungle*** by Upton Sinclair is a strong criticism of the meat-packing industry in the early years of the twentieth century.

subject complement A subject complement is a word or word group that completes the meaning of a linking verb and identifies or modifies the subject. (See page 405.)

EXAMPLES Before he emigrated, my great-grandfather was a **farmer.**

He was always very **resourceful.**

subordinate clause A subordinate clause (also called a *dependent clause*) contains a subject and verb but does not express a complete thought and cannot stand alone as a sentence. (See page 441. See also **adjective clause, adverb clause, noun clause.**)

EXAMPLES The student **who studies hardest** will get the highest score. [adjective clause]

That they came back to win in the final two minutes didn't surprise the team. [noun clause]

While you write your names, I will hand out the papers. [adverb clause]

suffix A suffix is a word part that is added after a base word or root. (See page 691.)

EXAMPLES

safe + ly = safe**ly**	lucky + ly = lucki**ly**
open + ness = open**ness**	portray + ing = portray**ing**
move + able = mov**able**	peace + able = peace**able**
begin + er = beginn**er**	dream + er = dream**er**

tense of verbs The tense of verbs indicates the time of the action or state of being expressed by the verb. (See page 516.)

Present Tense	
I take	we take
you take	you take
he, she, it takes	they take
Past Tense	
I took	we took
you took	you took
he, she, it took	they took
Future Tense	
I will (shall) take	we will (shall) take
you will (shall) take	you will (shall) take
he, she, it will (shall) take	they will (shall) take
Present Perfect Tense	
I have taken	we have taken
you have taken	you have taken
he, she, it has taken	they have taken
Past Perfect Tense	
I had taken	we had taken
you had taken	you had taken
he, she, it had taken	they had taken
Future Perfect Tense	
I will (shall) have taken	we will (shall) have taken
you will (shall) have taken	you will (shall) have taken
he, she, it will (shall) have taken	they will (shall) have taken

transitive verb A transitive verb is an action verb that takes an object. (See page 379.)

EXAMPLE Jill **passed** the exam.

QUICK REFERENCE HANDBOOK

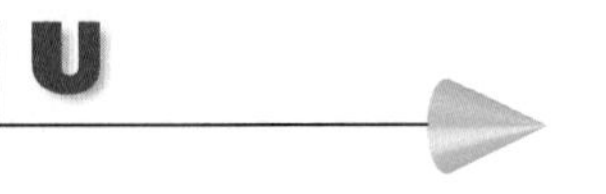

U

underlining (italics) (See page 660.)

- **for titles**

EXAMPLES *The Deep End of the Ocean* [book]

USA Today [periodical]

The Potato Eaters [work of art]

Rhapsody in Blue [long musical composition]

- **for words, letters, and symbols used as such and for foreign words**

EXAMPLES Notice that the *f* sounds in the word *photography* are spelled *ph.*

The friendly, gracious server at the French restaurant wished us *bon appétit.*

V

verb A verb expresses an action or a state of being. (See page 371.)

EXAMPLES Tamara **walks** to school every day.

Tamara **is** in school today.

verbal A verbal is a form of a verb used as a noun, an adjective, or an adverb. (See page 421. See also **participle, gerund,** and **infinitive.**)

EXAMPLES **Smiling,** Mr. Patel invited us in.

I liked his **yodeling.**

It's not easy **to yodel** well.

verbal phrase A verbal phrase consists of a verbal and any modifiers and complements it has. (See page 421. See also **participial phrase, gerund phrase,** and **infinitive phrase.**)

EXAMPLES **Experienced in foreign-car repair,** Darryl was soon hired by a big local dealership and began **to specialize in transmissions.**

He liked **working there.**

verb phrase A verb phrase consists of a main verb and at least one helping verb. (See page 372.)

EXAMPLE **"Should** I **speak** to her?" wondered Mrs. Callaghan.

voice Voice is the form a transitive verb takes to indicate whether the subject of the verb performs or receives the action. (See page 520.)

ACTIVE VOICE Vincent van Gogh **painted** *The Night Café* in 1888.

PASSIVE VOICE *The Night Café* **was painted** by Vincent van Gogh in 1888.

well (See ***good, well.***)

who, whom (See page 545.)

EXAMPLES Everyone **who** has applied for the job is well qualified.

Everyone **whom** I have interviewed for the job is well qualified.

wordiness Wordiness is the use of more words than necessary or the use of fancy words where simple ones will do. (See page 290.)

WORDY Theo Marshall, who is the athlete who regularly plays the position of quarterback for their football team, will not play in the game that is scheduled for tonight due to the fact that he sprained his ankle during the practice that was held yesterday.

REVISED Theo Marshall, their regular quarterback, will not play in tonight's game because he sprained his ankle during yesterday's practice.

Diagramming Appendix

Diagramming Sentences

A ***sentence diagram*** is a picture of how the parts of a sentence fit together. It shows how the words in the sentence are related.

Subjects and Verbs

Reference Note

For information on **subjects and verbs,** see Chapter 10.

To diagram a sentence, first find the simple subject and the verb (simple predicate), and write them on a horizontal line. Then, separate them with a vertical line.

EXAMPLES The reporter dashed to the fire.

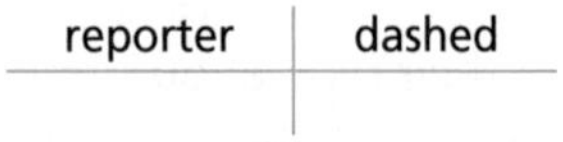

reporter | dashed

Have you been studying?

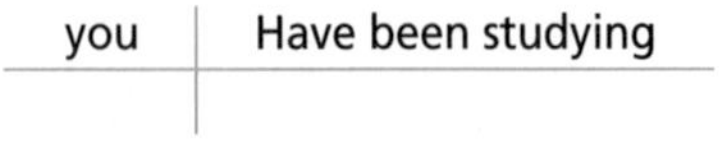

you | Have been studying

Notice that a diagram shows the capitalization but not the punctuation of a sentence.

Understood Subjects

To diagram an imperative sentence, place the understood subject *you* in parentheses on the horizontal line.

EXAMPLE Listen to the beautiful music.

Reference Note

For information on **understood subjects,** see page 339.

Exercise 1 Diagramming Simple Subjects and Verbs

Diagram only the simple subjects and the verbs in the following sentences.

EXAMPLE **1.** Midas is a character in Greek mythology.

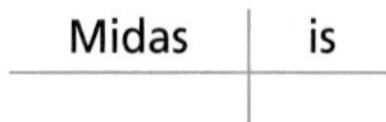

1. Midas ruled the kingdom of Phrygia.
2. One of the gods gave Midas the power to turn anything into gold.
3. Soon this gift became a curse.
4. Do you know why?
5. Read the story of King Midas in a mythology book.

Compound Subjects

EXAMPLES **Vines** and **weeds** grew over the old well.

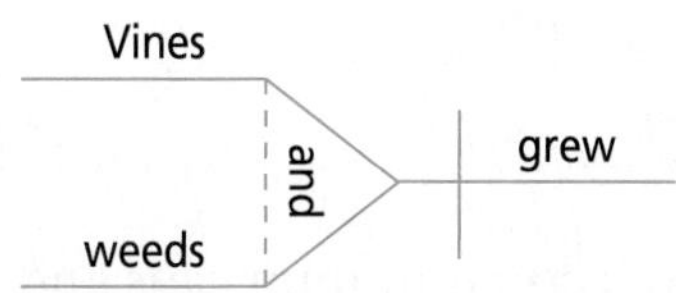

Either **Daphne** or **Teresa** plans to report on Thailand.

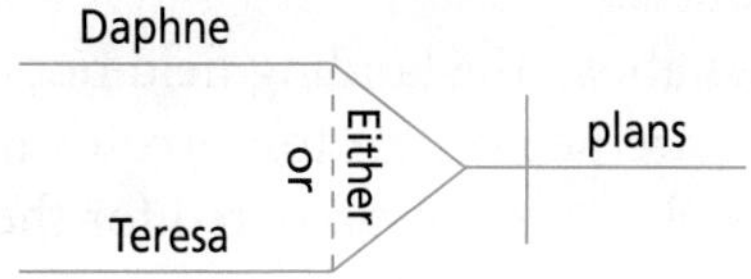

Reference Note

For information on **compound subjects,** see page 335.

Compound Verbs

Reference Note

For information on **compound verbs,** see page 336.

EXAMPLE We **ran** to the corner and barely **caught** the bus.

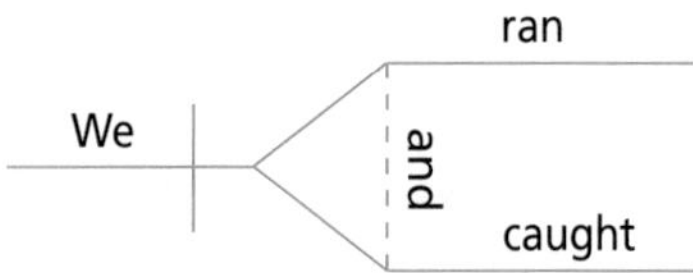

Compound Subjects and Compound Verbs

EXAMPLE **Ken** and **LaDonna dived** into the water and **swam** across the pool.

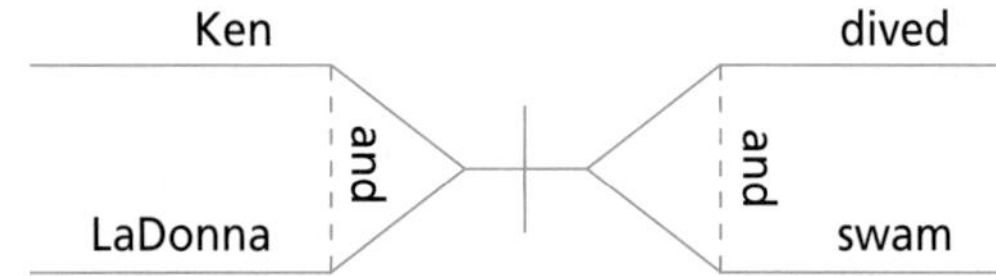

Exercise 2 Diagramming Compound Subjects and Verbs

Diagram the compound subjects and the verbs in the following sentences.

EXAMPLE **1.** Nikki and Chris chopped the cilantro and added it to the salsa.

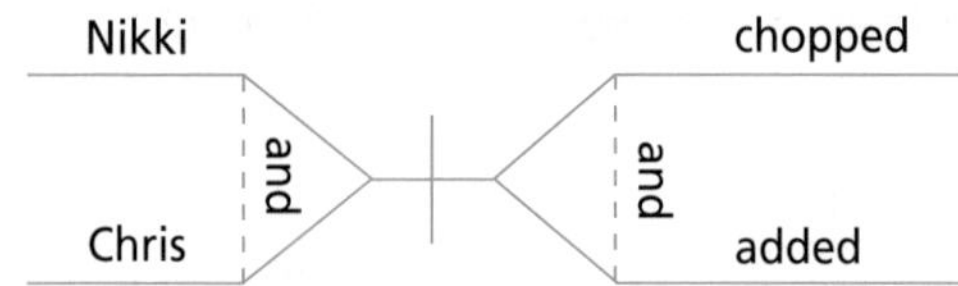

1. Mr. Carrington collects aluminum cans and returns them for recycling.
2. The students and the faculty combined their efforts and defeated the proposal.
3. The plane circled above the landing field but did not descend.
4. Pencil and paper are needed for tomorrow's math assignment.
5. Angela Bassett and her costar prepared for the scene.

Adjectives and Adverbs

Both adjectives and adverbs are written on slanted lines below the words they modify.

Adjectives

EXAMPLE **bright** star **a special** person **her favorite** class

star
bright

person
a special

class
her favorite

Two or more adjectives joined by a connecting word are diagrammed this way:

EXAMPLE a **lovely** and **quiet** place

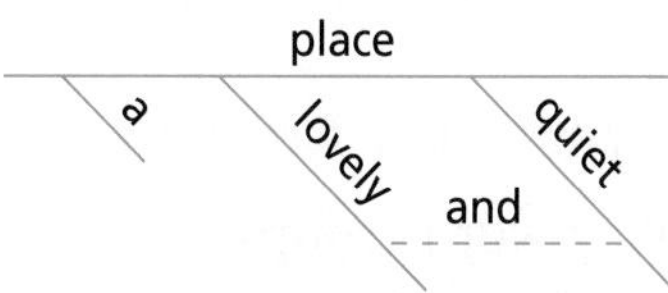

Exercise 3 **Diagramming Adjectives**

Diagram the following word groups.

EXAMPLE **1.** that old clock

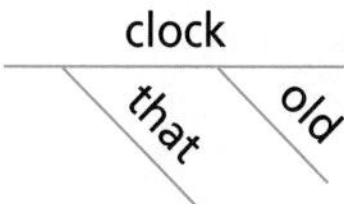

1. mighty warrior
2. long, exciting movie
3. my final offer
4. short and funny story
5. the slow but persistent turtle

Reference Note

For information on **adjectives** and **adverbs,** see page 358 and page 381.

HELP

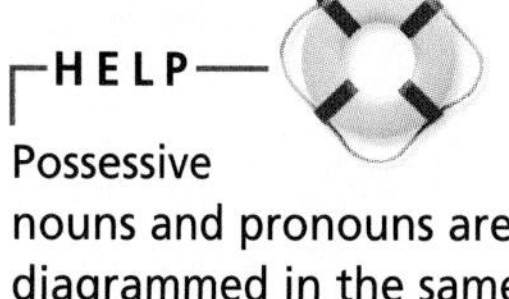

Possessive nouns and pronouns are diagrammed in the same way adjectives are.

Adverbs

Reference Note

For information on **adverbs,** see page 381.

EXAMPLES studies **hard** does **not** exercise **daily**

studies
hard

does exercise
not
daily

When an adverb modifies an adjective or another adverb, it is placed on a line connected to the word it modifies.

EXAMPLES **extremely** strong wind tried **rather** hard

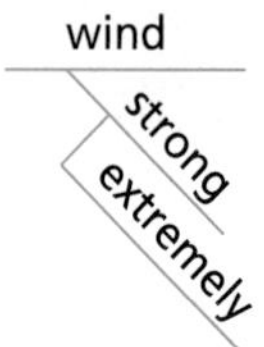

Exercise 4 Diagramming Adverbs

Diagram the following word groups.

EXAMPLE **1.** very seldom breaks

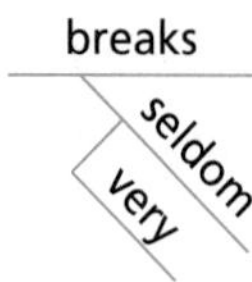

1. answered quickly
2. listened quite intently
3. dangerously sharp curve
4. may possibly happen
5. never plans very carefully

Review A Diagramming Sentences That Contain Adjectives and Adverbs

Diagram the following sentences.

EXAMPLE **1.** The blue car quickly swerved left.

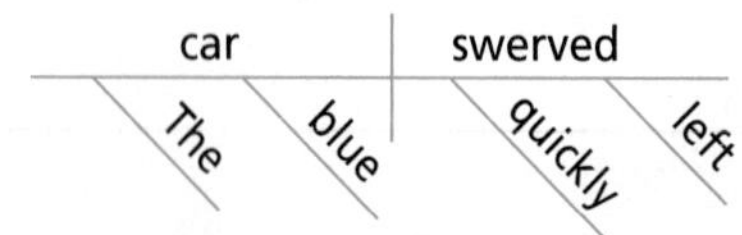

1. Our turn finally came.
2. We are definitely leaving tomorrow.
3. The anxious motorist drove too fast.
4. The shutters rattled quite noisily.
5. The new car had not been damaged badly.

Objects

Direct Objects

A direct object is diagrammed on the horizontal line with the subject and verb. A vertical line separates the direct object from the verb. Notice that this vertical line does not cross the horizontal line.

EXAMPLE The rain cleaned the **street.**

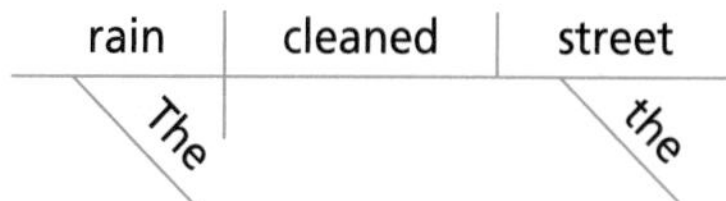

Reference Note

For information on **objects,** see page 401.

Reference Note

For information on **direct objects,** see page 401.

Compound Direct Objects

EXAMPLE We sold **lemonade** and **oranges.**

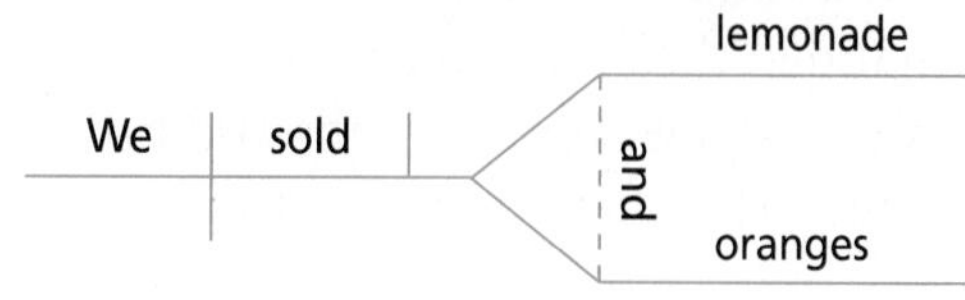

Reference Note

For information on **compound direct objects,** see page 402.

Indirect Objects

To diagram an indirect object, write it on a short horizontal line below the verb. Connect the indirect object to the verb by a slanted line.

EXAMPLE The artist showed **me** his painting.

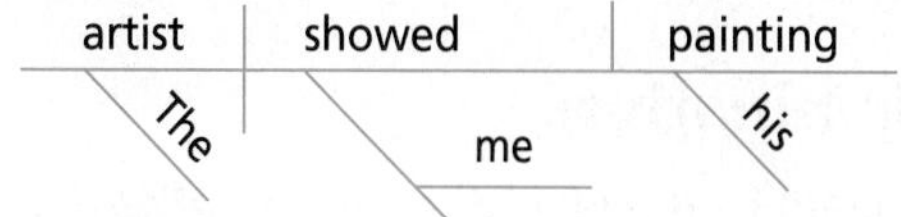

Reference Note

For information on **indirect objects,** see page 403.

Compound Indirect Objects

> **Reference Note**
> For information on **compound indirect objects,** see page 403.

EXAMPLE The company gave **Jean** and **Corey** summer jobs.

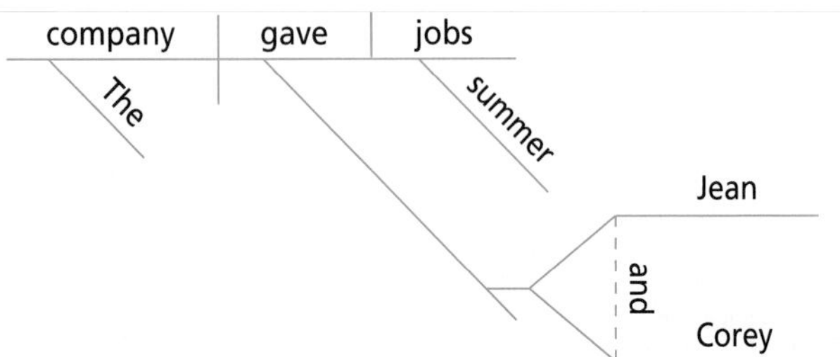

Exercise 5 Diagramming Sentences That Contain Direct Objects and Indirect Objects

> **HELP**
> Some sentences in Exercise 5 do not contain an indirect object.

Diagram the following sentences.

EXAMPLE **1.** They gave her a present.

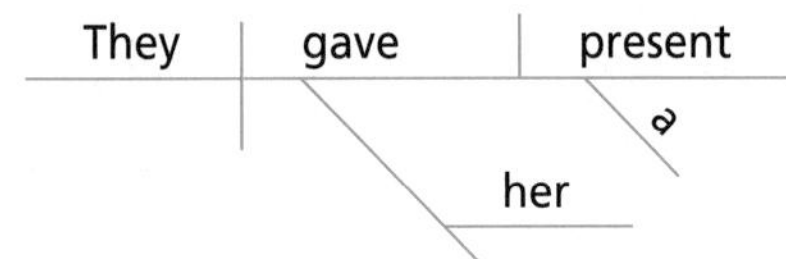

1. The judges awarded the prizes.
2. Cara's sister taught her the rules.
3. The cashier handed the children balloons.
4. Plácido Domingo signed photographs and programs.
5. Snow gives motorists and pedestrians trouble.

Subject Complements

> **Reference Note**
> For information on **subject complements,** see page 405.

A subject complement is placed on the horizontal line with the simple subject and the verb. The subject complement comes after the verb and is separated from it by a line slanting toward the subject. This slanted line shows that the complement refers to the subject.

Predicate Nominatives

> **Reference Note**
> For information on **predicate nominatives,** see page 405.

EXAMPLE William Least Heat-Moon is an **author.**

William Least Heat-Moon | is \ author
an

Compound Predicate Nominatives

EXAMPLE The contestants are **Joan** and **Dean.**

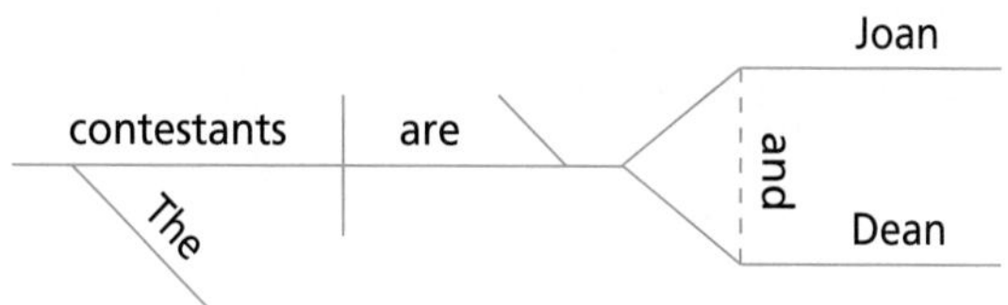

Reference Note

For information on **compound predicate nominatives,** see page 406.

Predicate Adjectives

EXAMPLE The river looked **deep.**

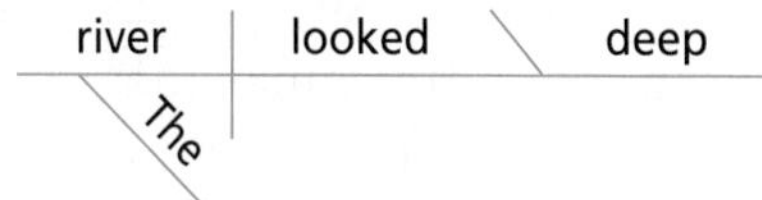

Reference Note

For information on **predicate adjectives,** see page 407.

Compound Predicate Adjectives

EXAMPLE This Chinese soup tastes **hot** and **spicy.**

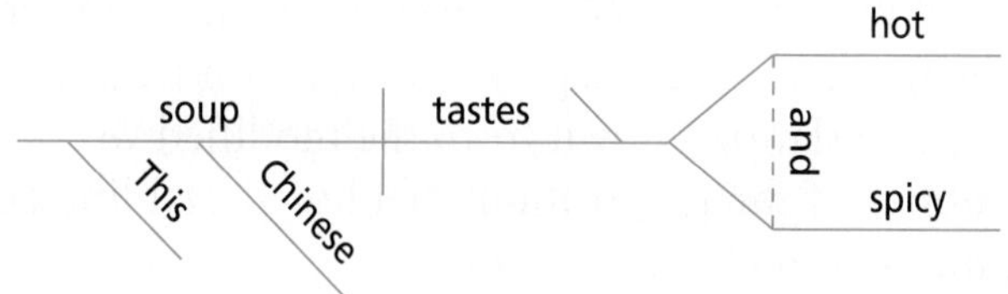

Reference Note

For information on **compound predicate adjectives,** see page 407.

Exercise 6 Diagramming Sentences That Contain Subject Complements

Diagram the following sentences.

EXAMPLE 1. Some dogs are good companions.

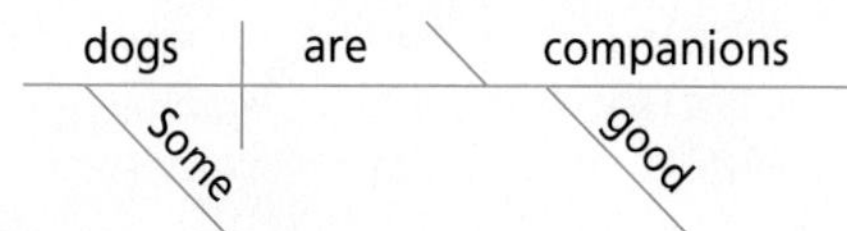

1. My shoes looked dusty.
2. Sir Francis Drake was a brave explorer.
3. The air grew cold and damp.
4. The chimpanzees seemed tired but happy.
5. My favorite months are September and May.

Review B Diagramming Sentences That Contain Complements

Diagram the following sentences.

EXAMPLE 1. That cockatiel is friendly.

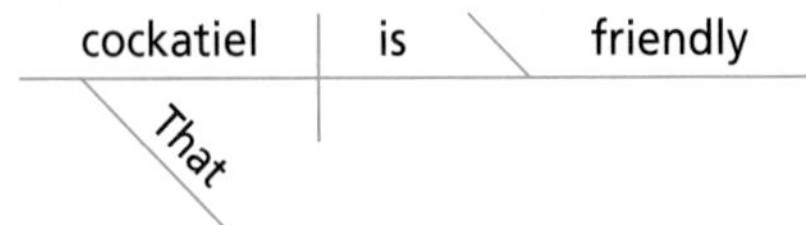

1. Her mother was an airplane mechanic.
2. Don and Maria rehearsed their parts.
3. The legend's origin remains mysterious and strange.
4. My favorite Mexican foods are empanadas and enchiladas.
5. The girls made themselves bracelets and necklaces.

Phrases

Reference Note

For information on **phrases,** see Chapter 14. For information on **prepositional phrases,** see page 416.

Prepositional Phrases

Prepositional phrases are diagrammed below the word or word group they modify. Write the preposition that introduces the phrase on a line slanting down from the modified word. Then, write the object of the preposition on a horizontal line extending from the slanting line.

Reference Note

For information on **adjective phrases,** see page 417.

Adjective Phrases

EXAMPLES paintings **by famous artists**

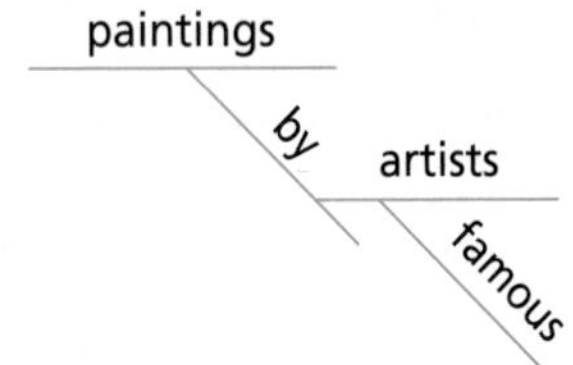

cloth **from Costa Rica and Guatemala**

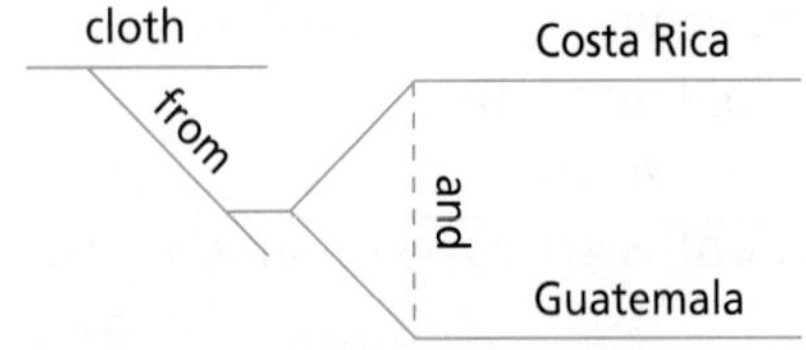

Adverb Phrases

EXAMPLES walked **along the road**

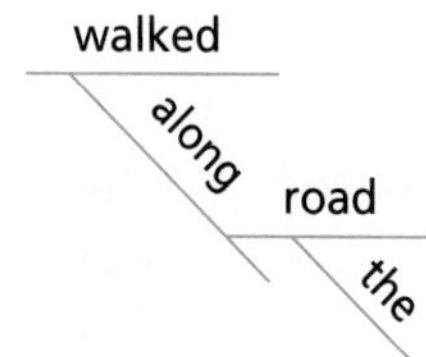

went **with Hollis and Dave**

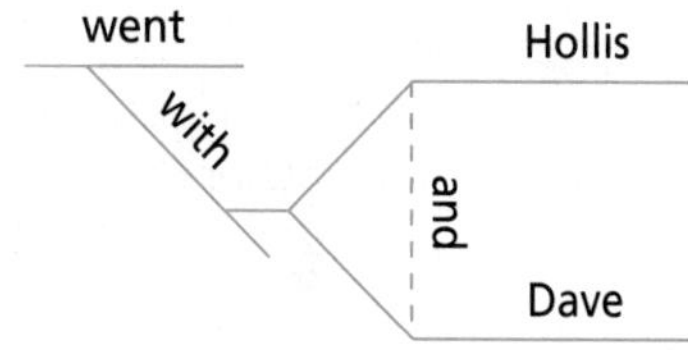

When a prepositional phrase modifies the object of another prepositional phrase, the diagram looks like this:

EXAMPLE camped on the side **of a mountain**

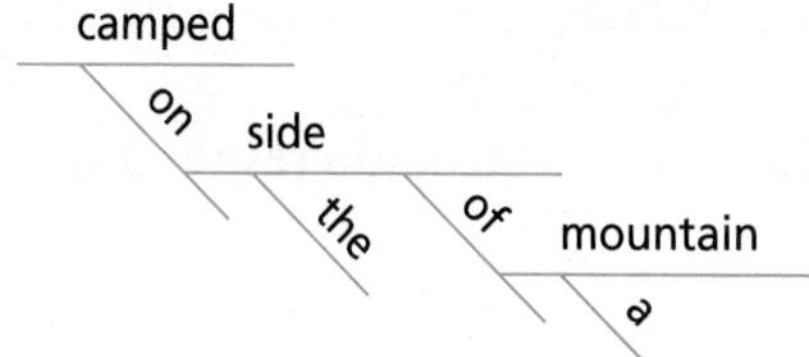

Reference Note

For information on **adverb phrases,** see page 419.

Exercise 7 Diagramming Prepositional Phrases

Diagram the following word groups.

EXAMPLE 1. drove through the Maine woods

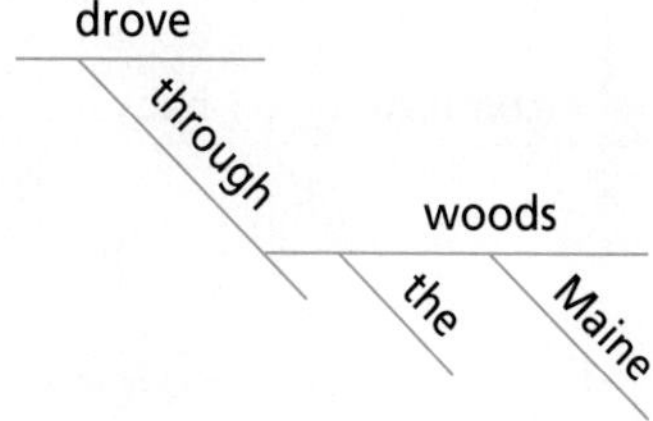

1. invited to the celebrations
2. a glimpse of the famous ruler

3. one of the people in the room
4. drove to a village near Paris
5. wrote about the Vietnamese and their history

Review C **Diagramming Sentences That Contain Prepositional Phrases**

Diagram the following sentences.

EXAMPLE **1.** The steep slopes of the mountains are covered with forests.

1. The number of whales decreases annually.
2. Hundreds of animal species are being protected by concerned citizens.
3. Citrus fruits are grown in California and Florida.
4. Many historic events have been decided by sudden changes in the weather.
5. The defeat of the Spanish Armada resulted from a violent ocean storm.

Reference Note

For information on **verbals** and **verbal phrases,** see page 421.

Verbals and Verbal Phrases

Participles and Participial Phrases

Participles are diagrammed in the same way as other adjectives.

EXAMPLE José comforted the **crying** baby.

Participial phrases are diagrammed as follows:

EXAMPLE **Shaking the manager's hand,** Teresa accepted her new job.

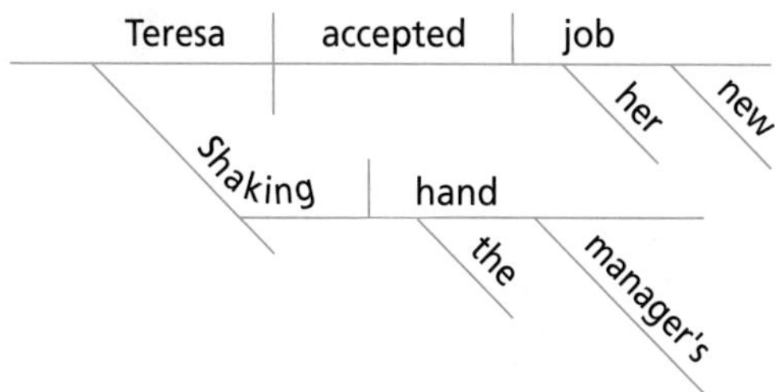

Notice that the participle has a direct object (*the manager's hand*), which is diagrammed in the same way that the direct object of a main verb is.

Reference Note

For information on **participles** and **participial phrases,** see page 421.

Gerunds and Gerund Phrases

EXAMPLES I enjoy **swimming.** [gerund used as direct object]

Being slightly ill is no excuse for **missing two days of piano practice.** [Gerund phrases used as subject and as object of preposition. The first gerund has a subject complement (*ill*); the second gerund has a direct object (*days*).]

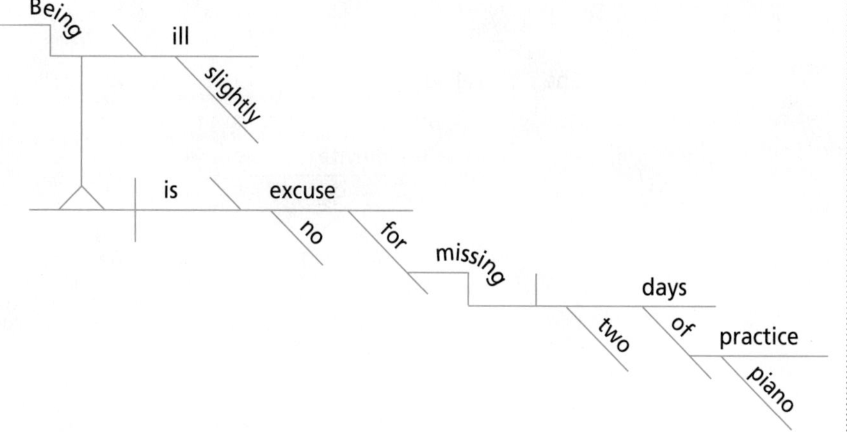

Reference Note

For information on **gerunds** and **gerund phrases,** see page 425.

Reference Note

For information on **infinitives** and **infinitive phrases,** see page 428.

Infinitives and Infinitive Phrases

EXAMPLES **To write** is her ambition. [infinitive used as subject]

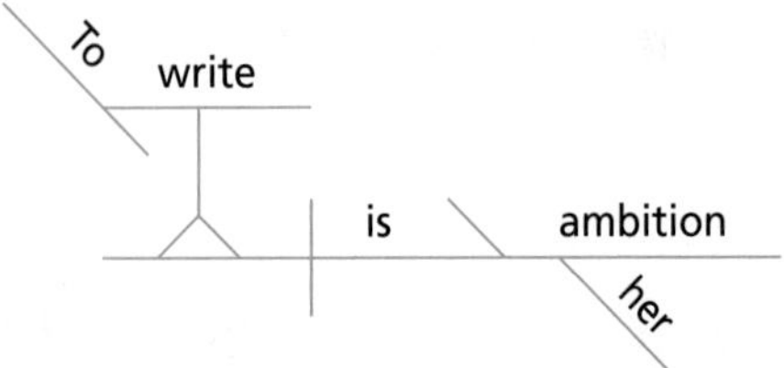

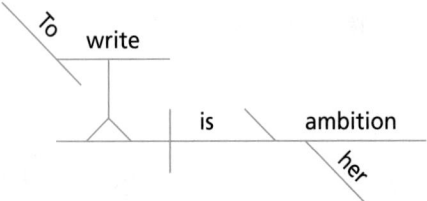

He was the first one **to solve that tricky problem.** [infinitive phrase used as adjective]

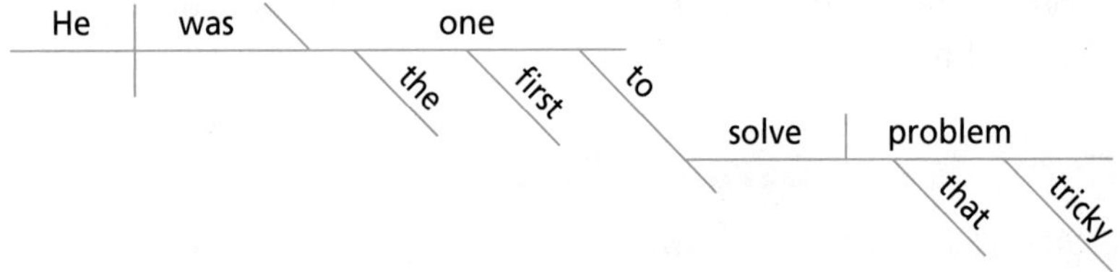

Marge was hoping **to go with us.** [infinitive phrase used as direct object]

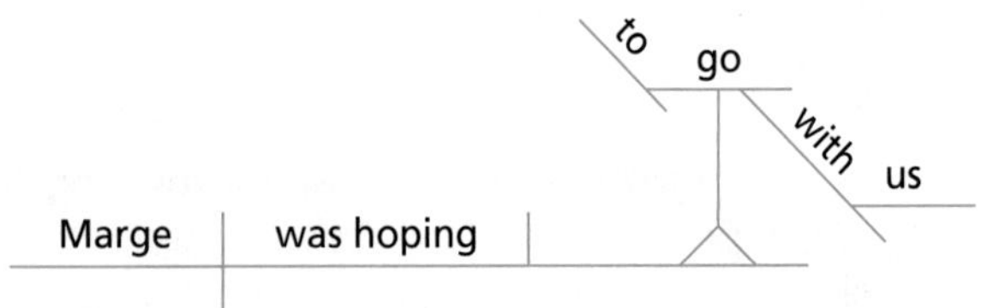

She called **to invite us over.** [infinitive phrase used as adverb]

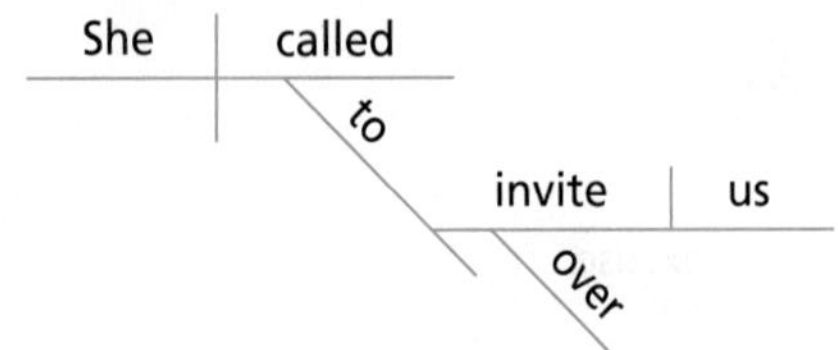

Exercise 8 Diagramming Sentences That Contain Verbal Phrases

Diagram the following sentences.

EXAMPLE **1.** I heard them **laughing.**

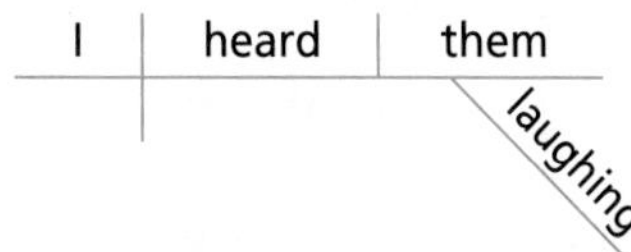

1. Taking that shortcut will cut several minutes off the trip.
2. I want to watch television tonight.
3. That is my cat licking its paws.
4. Checking the time, Wynetta rushed to the gym.
5. Did they say what to do about this?

Appositives and Appositive Phrases

To diagram an appositive or an appositive phrase, write the appositive in parentheses after the word it identifies.

Reference Note

For information on **appositives** and **appositive phrases,** see page 432.

EXAMPLES Our cousin **Iola** is a chemical engineer.

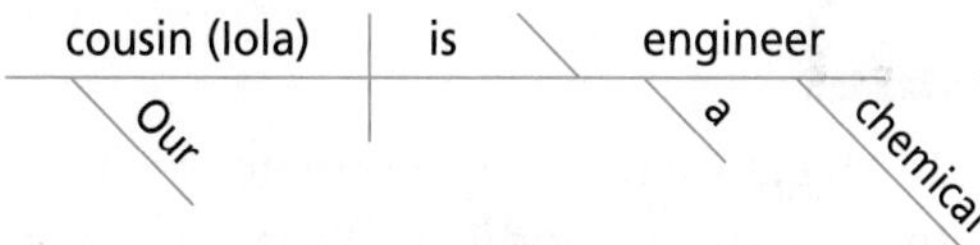

Jerry Seinfeld, **the popular comedian,** is also the author of a best-selling book.

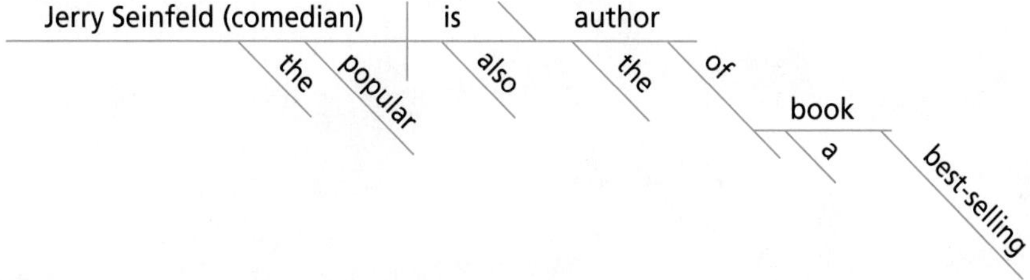

Subordinate Clauses

Reference Note

For information on **adjective clauses,** see page 444.

HELP

The relative pronouns are *who, whom, whose, which,* and *that.*

Reference Note

For information on **relative pronouns,** see page 444.

Adjective Clauses

Diagram an adjective clause by connecting it with a broken line to the word it modifies. Draw the broken line between the relative pronoun and the word to which it relates.

EXAMPLE The grade **that I got yesterday** pleased my parents.

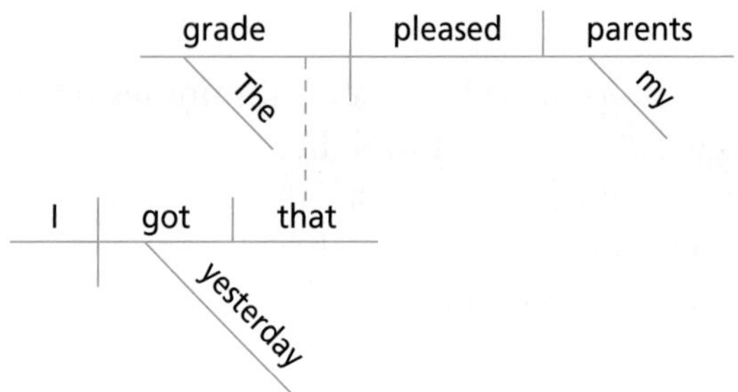

NOTE A relative pronoun relates an adjective clause to the word the clause modifies. The relative pronouns are *that*, *which*, *who*, *whom*, and *whose*.

Reference Note

For information on **adverb clauses,** see page 447.

Adverb Clauses

Diagram an adverb clause by using a broken line to connect the adverb clause to the word it modifies. Place the subordinating conjunction that introduces the adverb clause on the broken line.

EXAMPLE **When I got home from school,** I ate an apple.

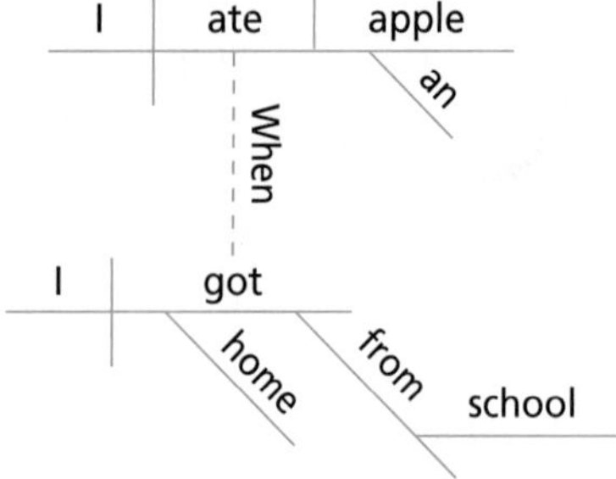

NOTE An adverb clause is introduced by a subordinating conjunction. Some common subordinating conjunctions include *because*, *before*, *since*, *though*, and *whether*.

Noun Clauses

Diagram a noun clause by connecting it to the independent clause with a solid line.

EXAMPLE Olivia knew **what she wanted.** [The noun clause is the direct object of the independent clause. The word *what* is the direct object in the noun clause.]

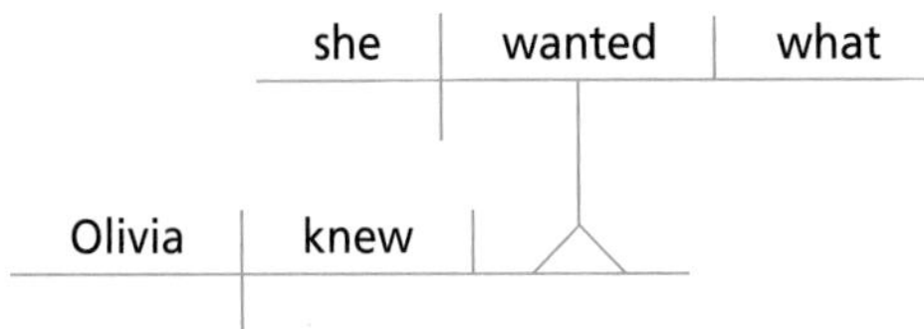

When the introductory word of the noun clause does not have a specific function in the noun clause, the sentence is diagrammed in this way:

EXAMPLE The problem is **that they lost the map.** [The noun clause is the predicate nominative of the independent clause. The word *that* has no function in the noun clause.]

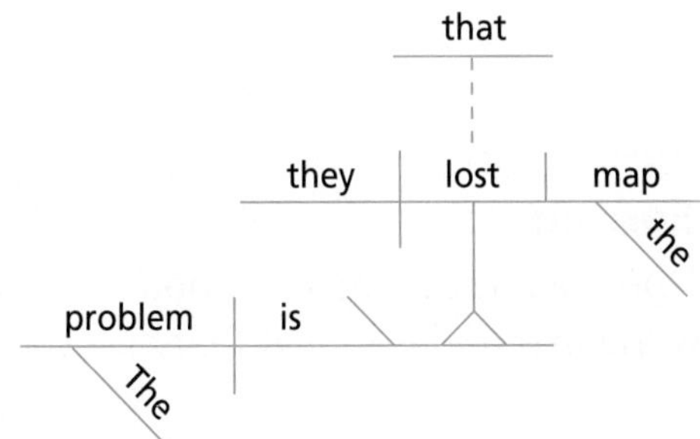

Reference Note

For information on **noun clauses,** see page 451.

Exercise 9 **Diagramming Sentences That Contain Subordinate Clauses**

Diagram the sentences on the following page.

EXAMPLE **1.** The box that contained the treasure was wooden.

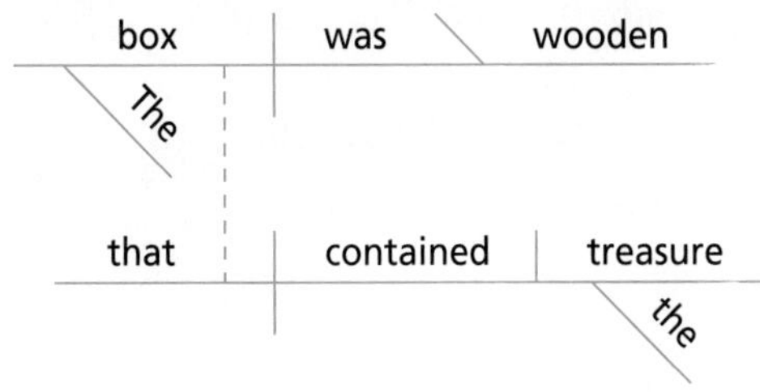

1. The test that we took on Friday was hard.
2. If I had not studied on Thursday night, I could not have answered half of the questions.
3. Our teacher announced what would be on the test.
4. Several friends of mine were not paying attention when the teacher gave the assignment.

Sentences Classified According to Structure

Simple Sentences

Reference Note

For information on **simple sentences,** see page 460.

EXAMPLE Tracy is building a birdhouse in industrial arts class. [one independent clause]

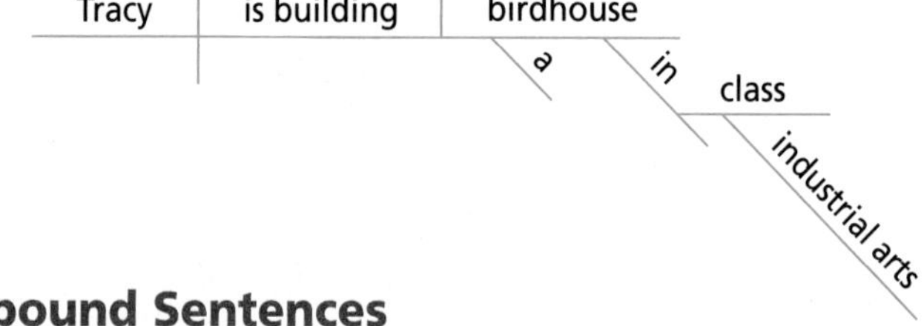

Compound Sentences

Reference Note

For information on **compound sentences,** see page 462.

The second independent clause in a compound sentence is diagrammed below the first and is joined to it by a coordinating conjunction.

EXAMPLE Darnell threw a good pass, but Clay did not catch it. [two independent clauses]

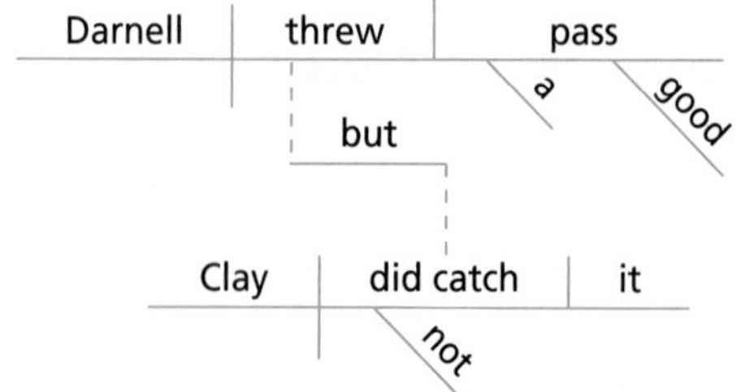

Exercise 10 Diagramming Compound Sentences

Diagram the following compound sentences.

EXAMPLE 1. A strange dog chased us, but the owner came to our rescue.

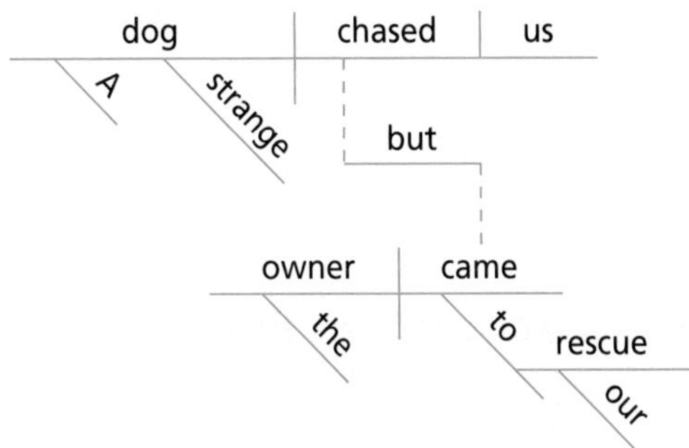

Reference Note
For information about **coordinating conjunctions,** see page 389.

1. I want a motorboat, but Jan prefers a sailboat.
2. The bus stopped at the restaurant, and all of the passengers went inside.
3. Our club is very small, but it is growing.
4. Shall we meet you at the station, or will you take a taxi?
5. In Arizona the temperature is often high, but the humidity always remains low.

Complex Sentences

EXAMPLE Before they left the museum, Lester and Jessica visited the exhibit of masks from Nigeria and the Ivory Coast. [one subordinate clause and one independent clause]

Reference Note
For information on **complex sentences,** see page 465.

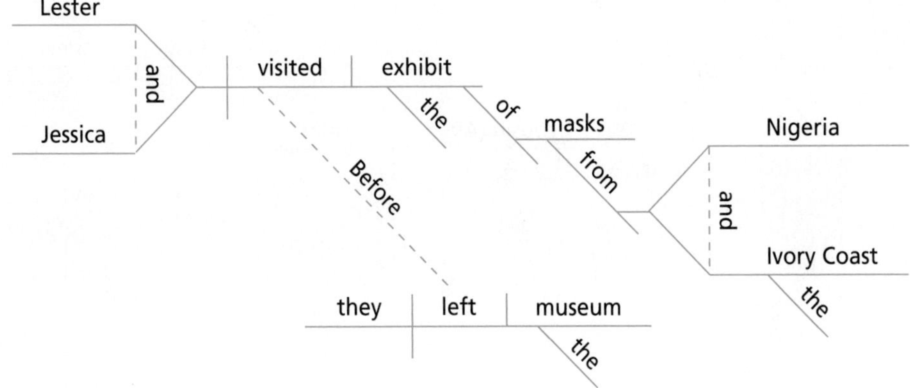

Exercise 11 Diagramming Complex Sentences

Diagram the following complex sentences.

EXAMPLE 1. As night fell, the storm grew worse.

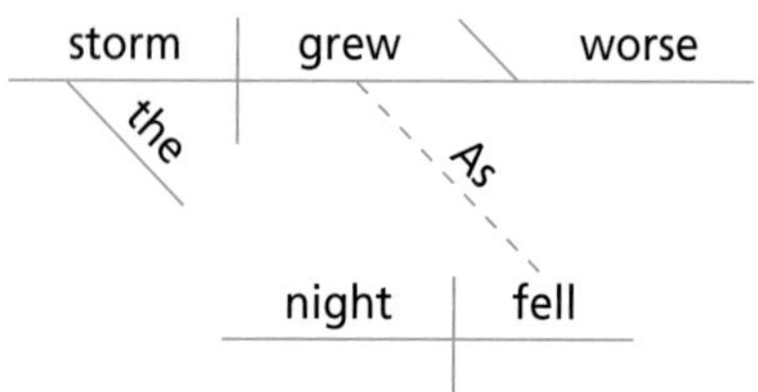

1. One book that has won a Pulitzer Prize is *Pilgrim at Tinker Creek.*
2. Go whenever you like.
3. The satellite will be launched if the weather remains good.
4. The knight in black armor fought whoever would challenge him.
5. Alexander the Great, who conquered most of the known world, died at the age of thirty-three.

Compound-Complex Sentences

Reference Note

For information on **compound-complex sentences,** see page 467.

EXAMPLE Hamako, whose father is a musician, studies piano, but her cousin Akio prefers to play tennis. [two independent clauses and one subordinate clause]

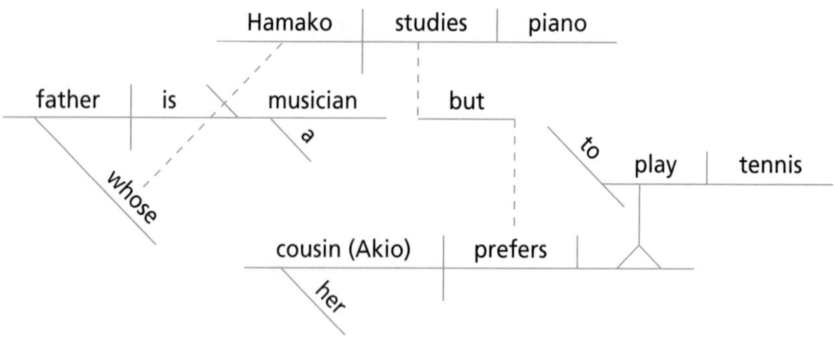

Review D Diagramming Sentences

Diagram the following sentences.

EXAMPLE 1. The room that Carrie painted had been white, but she changed the color.

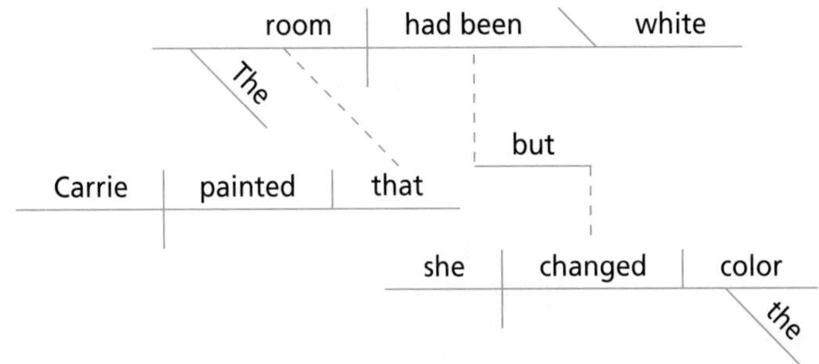

1. Diego Rivera and Frida Kahlo were two important Mexican artists of the twentieth century.
2. Mom wanted to fly to Utah, but Dad and I wanted to drive there.
3. Our new neighbors, the Chens, come from Taiwan, which is an island off the coast of China.
4. For my report, I wrote about Katherine Anne Porter and Eudora Welty, two Southern authors.
5. When I returned to the store, the purple shirt had been sold, so I bought the blue one.

INDEX

C

E

H

I

M

P

Q

S

T

U

V

ACKNOWLEDGMENTS

For permission to reprint copyrighted material, grateful acknowledgment is made to the following sources:

The Advertising Council and United Negro College Fund: Slogan "A mind is a terrible thing to waste®" from the **Ad Council** Web site, at http://www.adcouncil.org.

Gwendolyn Brooks: From "the sonnet-ballad" from *Blacks* by Gwendolyn Brooks. Copyright © 1987, 1991 by Gwendolyn Brooks. Published by The David Company. Reissued by Third World Press, 1991.

Curtis Brown, Ltd.: From "Strange and Terrible Monsters of the Deep" by William Wise from *Boys' Life*, February 1978. Copyright © 1978 by The Boy Scouts of America.

California Milk Producers Advisory Board: Slogan "Milk. It does a body good.®" Trademark registered 1985 by California Milk Producers Advisory Board dba California Milk Advisory Board.

Carus Publishing Company, 30 Grove Street, Suite C, Peterborough, NH 03458: From "Word Stories: Brazil" from "Fun With Words" from *Calliope: 1494: Portugal and Spain Divide the World*, vol. 8, no. 8, April 1998. Copyright © 1998 by Cobblestone Publishing. From "Daniel 'Chappie' James, Jr.: Never Give Up" by Alexis O'Neill from *Cobblestone: Tuskegee Airmen*, February 1997. Copyright © 1997 by Cobblestone Publishing.

Joan Daves Agency as agent for the proprietor: From *Apples* by Frank Browning. Copyright © 1998 by Frank Browning.

Franklin Associates for the USEPA: Graph "Solid Waste Generated Per Person" from *Junior Scholastic*, vol. 100, no. 16, April 13, 1998. Copyright © 1998 by Franklin Associates, Ltd.

HarperCollins Publishers, Inc.: "An Elephant Is Hard to Hide" from *Something Big Has Been Here* by Jack Prelutsky. Copyright © 1990 by Jack Prelutsky.

Henry Holt and Company, LLC: From *It's Hard to Read a Map with a Beagle on Your Lap* by Marilyn Singer. Copyright © 1993 by Marilyn Singer.

Alfred A. Knopf, Inc. a division of Random House, Inc.: From "Along the Colorado" from *The Secret Worlds of Colin Fletcher* by Colin Fletcher. Copyright © 1989 by Colin Fletcher. From "Dreams" from *Collected Poems* by Langston Hughes. Copyright © 1994 by the Estate of Langston Hughes.

Ray Lincoln Literary Agency, Elkins Park House, 107–B, Elkins Park, PA 19027: From "The Big Bang" from *Mount St. Helens: A Sleeping Volcano Awakens* by Marian T. Place. Copyright © 1981 by Marian T. Place.

Ben Mikaelsen: From "Bear in the Family" by Ben Mikaelsen from *Voices from the Middle*, vol. 5, no. 2, April 1998. Copyright © 1998 by Ben Mikaelsen.

National Crime Prevention Council: Slogan "Take A Bite Out Of Crime®." Registered by the National Crime Prevention Council.

The New York Times Company: From "That Day in Dallas" by Russell Freedman from *The New York Times Book Review*, November 16, 1997. Copyright © 1997 by The New York Times Company.

NOVA Online, WGBH Educational Foundation: From "Special Effects: Titanic and Beyond" by Kelly Tyler from *NOVA* Web site at www.pbs.org/nova. Copyright © 1998 by NOVA Online. NOVA Online is produced for PBS by the WGBH Science Unit. Major funding for NOVA is provided by the Park Foundation, The Northwestern Mutual Life Foundation, and Iomega Corporation.

Perseus Books Publishers, a member of Perseus Books, L.L.C.: From *When I Was Puerto Rican* by Esmeralda Santiago. Copyright © 1993 by Esmeralda Santiago.

Purple Room Publishing: From "Don't Bring Camels in the Classroom" from *My Foot Fell Asleep* by Kenn Nesbitt. Copyright © 1998 by Kenn Nesbitt.

Random House Children's Books, a division of Random House, Inc.: From "The Dog and His Shadow" from *Aesop's Fables*, retold by Anne Terry White. Copyright © 1964 by Anne Terry White.

Marian Reiner: "Growing Up" from *The Little Hill* by Harry Behn. Copyright 1949 by Harry Behn; copyright renewed © 1977 by Alice L. Behn.

Rourke Publications, Inc.: From *Responsible Pet Care: Dogs* by Pam Jameson. Copyright © 1989 by Rourke Publications, Inc.

Scholastic Inc.: From "I Can't Hear You! Listen Up: Save Your Hearing by Acting Now" by Bob Hugel from *Scholastic Choices,* vol. 13, no. 6, March 1998. Copyright © 1998 by Scholastic Inc.

Charol Shakeshaft: From "Should Public School Students Wear Uniforms?" by Carol Shakeshaft from *Newsday,* p. A 45, March 10, 1996. Copyright © 1996 by Charol Shakeshaft.

Time Inc.: From "Under Attack" by Michael D. Lemonick from *Time,* vol. 150, no. 6, August 11, 1997. Copyright © 1997 by Time Inc.

United Nations Publication Board: Graph "Major Sources of Ocean Pollution" from *The State of the Marine Environment,* United Nations Environment Program, 1990. Copyright © 1990 by the United Nations.

U. S. Army and Army Reserve: Slogan "Be All You Can Be®" for the United States Army.

The University of North Carolina Press: From *Mexican Village* by Josefina Niggli. Copyright © 1945 by the University of North Carolina Press; copyright renewed © 1972 by Josefina Niggli.

Wiley Publishing, Inc.: Entry for "large" from *Webster's New World™ College Dictionary,* Fourth Edition. Copyright © 2000, 1999 by Wiley Publishing, Inc.

H. W. Wilson Company: From "Cronkite, Walter" to "Crops" from *The Reader's Guide to Periodical Literature,* February 1999. Copyright © 1999 by H. W. Wilson Company.

SOURCES CITED:

From *The Diary of a Young Girl: The Definitive Edition* by Anne Frank, edited by Otto H. Frank and Mirjam Pressler, translated by Susan Massotty. Published by Doubleday, New York, 1991.

From *The Diary of Anne Frank: The Critical Edition,* edited by David Barnouw and Gerrold van der Stroom, translated by Arnold J. Pomerans and B.M. Mooyaart-Doubleday. Published by Doubleday, New York, NY, 1989.

From *Nisei Daughter* by Monica Sone. Published by Little, Brown and Company, Boston, 1953.

Screen shot from FirstSearch® database, at http://firstsearch.org. FirstSearch and World Cat are registered trademarks of OCLC Online Computer Library Center, Incorporated and for World Cats. Published by OCLC Online Computer Library Center, Inc., Dublin, OH, 1999.

PHOTO CREDITS

Abbreviations used: (tl)top left, (tc)top center, (tr)top right, (l)left, (cl)center left, (c)center, (cr)center right, (r)right, (bl)bottom left, (bc)bottom center, (br)bottom right.

COVER: Scott Van Osdol/HRW Photo.

TABLE OF CONTENTS: Page viii (br), Scott Van Osdol/HRW Photo; ix, John Langford/HRW Photo; x, SuperStock; xii, Painting by John Jude Palencar ©1999; xiv, Randal Alhadeff/HRW Photo; xv, Jack de Coningh/Animals Animals; xvi, Image Copyright ©2001 PhotoDisc, Inc.; xvii, xviii, SuperStock; xix, Image Copyright ©2001 PhotoDisc, Inc.; xx, Stephen Simpson/Getty Images/FPG; xxi, Alan Schein/Corbis Stock Market; xxii, Image Copyright ©2001 PhotoDisc, Inc.; xxiv, Paul Nehrenz/Getty Images/The Image Bank; xxv, U.S. Postal Service.

PART OPENERS: Page xxii, 1, 260, 261, 298, 299, 678, 679, Kazu Nitta/The Stock Illustration Source, Inc.

TAKING TESTS: Page 2, Rob Cage/Getty Images/Taxi; 4, Stephen Frink/CORBIS; 7, J.B. Diederich/Contact Press Images/PictureQuest.

CHAPTER 1: Page 16, Scott Van Osdol/HRW Photo; 28, Digital Image Copyright ©2004 PhotoDisc.

CHAPTER 2: Page 48, John Langford/HRW Photo; 52, Museo Gregoriano Egizio/Art Resource, NY; 60, Spencer Jones/Getty Images/Taxi.

CHAPTER 3: Page 82, Telegraph Colour Library/Getty Images/FPG; 99, Creatas; 114 (cr), Nick Vedros/Vedros & Associates/Getty Images/Stone; 133, Anne Frank Center USA.

CHAPTER 4: Page 136, © AFF/Anne Frank Stichting, Amsterdam, 1992. Viking Press.

CHAPTER 5: Page 156, Painting by John Jude Palencar ©1999; 159 (cl), NOVA Online; 159 (br), Everett Collection; 161, NRG Public Relations; 165, Digital Image Copyright ©2004 Eyewire.

CHAPTER 6: Page 206, Jonathan Nourok/PhotoEdit; 234, Nello Giambi/Getty Images/Stone.

CHAPTER 7: Page 238, Randal Alhadeff/HRW (boy), Image Copyright ©2001 PhotoDisc, Inc. (Golden Gate Bridge), Corbis Images (Rockies), Image Copyright ©2001 PhotoDisc, Inc. (cactus), Corbis Images (beach), Images Copyright ©2001 PhotoDisc, Inc. (St. of Liberty, fireworks), Texas Department of Transportation (Alamo); 241, The Conservancy of Southwest Florida, Inc.; 244, ©1998 George & Judy Manna/Photo Researchers, Inc.; 245 (tc), (tr), Steve Smith/Getty Images/FPG; 245 (c), (cr), Robert E. Daemmrich/Getty Images/Stone; 253, David Pollack/CORBIS; 258, Peter Van Steen/HRW Photo; 261, Mary Kate Denny/PhotoEdit; 262, Victoria Smith/HRW Photo; 270 (cl), AP/Wide World Photos.

CHAPTER 8: Page 274, Chromo Sohm/Sohm/Stock Boston; 277, Helen Brush/Everett Collection; 279, SuperStock; 281, Express Newspapers/Hulton Archive/Getty Images; 283, SuperStock; 284, Image Copyright ©2001 PhotoDisc, Inc.; 287, Owen Franken/Stock Boston; 289, Hulton Archive/Getty Images; 291, Image Copyright ©2001 PhotoDisc, Inc.; 293, SuperStock.

CHAPTER 9: Page 296, Ralph A. Reinhold/Animals Animals; 298, Collier/Condit/Stock Boston; 301, Bridgeman Art Library; 302, HRW Photo Library/Seaver Center; 304, John Cancalosi/Stock Boston; 307, Courtesy of the U.S. Air Force Museum; 308 (bl), SuperStock; 308 (tl), Jack de Coningh/Animals Animals; 311, Scala/Art Resource, NY; 312, Lynda Richardson/CORBIS; 315, The Granger Collection, New York; 316, SuperStock; 325, The Granger Collection, New York.

CHAPTER 10: Page 329, Image Copyright ©2001 PhotoDisc, Inc.; 332, Red-figure amphora, showing the slaying of Medusa by Perseus/British Museum, London/Bridgeman Art Library; 335, Image Copyright ©2001 PhotoDisc, Inc.; 337, AP/Wide World Photos; 343, Geoff Langan/Getty Images/Taxi.

CHAPTER 11: Page 346, William S. Soule/National Anthropological Archives/National Museum of Natural History/Smithsonian Institute; 350, Alan Schein/Corbis Stock Market; 356, Derek Redfearn/Getty Images/The Image Bank; 358, Courtesy Concord Jazz; 363 (cr), Ken Dequaine/The Picture Cube; 363 (bc), George Cassidy/The Picture Cube; 369, RNT Productions/CORBIS.

CHAPTER 12: Page 376, Phototone/Letraset; 378, Image Copyright ©2001 PhotoDisc, Inc.; 382 (cl), Image Copyright ©2001 PhotoDisc, Inc.; 382 (b), Image Copyright ©2001 PhotoDisc, Inc.; 385, Corbis Stock Market; 385 (tr), Frank Schreider/Photo Researchers, Inc.; 388, Corbis Images; 391, Stephen Simpson/Getty Images/FPG; 394, Bonnie Timmons/Getty Images/The Image Bank; 400, The Granger Collection, New York.

CHAPTER 13: Page 404, Professional Rodeo Cowboy Assoc.; 406 (tl) (cl) (bl), Barry L. Runk/Grant Heilman Photography; 406 (br), SuperStock; 409, Earl Kogler/HRW Photo; 413, Howard Grey/Getty Images/Stone.

CHAPTER 14: Page 417, Courtesy of Hubert Ausbie; 420, Autry Museum of Western Heritage, Los Angeles; 425 (tr), SuperStock; 425, (cl) (c), Bob Daemmrich Photography; 431, Cahokia Mounds State Historical Site; 437, Stephen Frink/CORBIS.

CHAPTER 15: Page 453, (br) (cr), The Museum of Appalachia, Norris, Tennessee; 457, Barbara Peacock/Getty Images/Taxi.

CHAPTER 16: Page 461, Musee de'l Armee, Paris/Art Resource, NY; 463, Stock Editions/HRW Photo; 464, Everett Collection; 469, Michelle Bridwell/Frontera Fotos; 473, David Young-Wolff/PhotoEdit.

CHAPTER 17: Page 478, Diana Lyn/Shooting Star International; 482, A. Scibilia/Art Resource, NY; 486, Eric Beggs/HRW Photo; 490, Rob Atkins/Getty Images/The Image Bank; 500, Rayli McLinde/Shooting Star International; 503, Bettmann/CORBIS.

CHAPTER 18: Page 515, Stock Editions/HRW Library Photo; 519, ©1997 Radlund & Associates for Artville; 524, 526, Image Copyright ©2001 PhotoDisc, Inc.; 528 (bl), Steve Allen/Peter Arnold, Inc.; 528 (bc), Jerry Jacka Photography; 530, Image Copyright ©2001 PhotoDisc, Inc.; 533, Jeff Greenberg/PhotoEdit.

CHAPTER 19: Page 537 (cr) (bc) (br), Michael Ochs Archives/Venice, CA; 540 (bl) (cl), Fielder Kownslar/IBM Corporation; 549, Everett Collection; 553, Gregory Pace/CORBIS Sygma.

CHAPTER 20: Page 564, Bob Daemmrich/Stock Boston; 565, Image Copyright ©2001 PhotoDisc, Inc.; 568, SuperStock; 576, Copyright ©1998-2001 EyeWire, Inc. All rights reserved; 579, Victoria Smith/HRW.

CHAPTER 21: Page 585, SuperStock; 591, Corbis Images; 595, Chris Falkenstein; 597, Al Tielemans/Duomo Photography; 601, Joseph Sohm: Chromo Sohm Inc./CORBIS.

CHAPTER 22: Page 609, Corbis Images; 612, Wolfgang Kaehler Photography; 615, Paul Nehrenz/Getty Images/The Image Bank; 618, Courtesy of McGraw-Hill; 627, Jeff Greenberg/PhotoEdit.

CHAPTER 23: Page 633, Mike Powers; 638, Kjell B. Sandved/Photo Researchers, Inc.; 641, Everett Collection; 645, U.S. Postal Service; 649, Image Copyright ©2001 PhotoDisc, Inc.; 657, Reed Saxon/AP/Wide World Photos.

CHAPTER 24: Page 665, Werner Forman Archive/Museum für Völkerkunde, Berlin/Art Resource, NY; 666, Image Copyright ©2001 PhotoDisc, Inc.; 674, Larry Ulrich/Getty Images/Stone; 682, Michael Sullivan/TexaStock; 685 (tr), G & M David de Lossy/Getty Images/The Image Bank; 685 (r), Andreas Pollok/Getty Images/Stone; 685 (br), Digital Image Copyright ©2004 PhotoDisc.

CHAPTER 25: Page 694 (tl), Courtesy of Hendrick-Long Publishing Co.; 702, SuperStock; 708, Reuters/Pascal Rossignol/Hulton Archive/Getty Images; 710 (cl), SuperStock; 710 (bl), Richard Sullivan/Shooting Star International; 713, Jose Luis Pelaez, Inc./CORBIS.

CHAPTER 26: Page 717, 718, Image Copyright ©2001 PhotoDisc, Inc.; 726, Courtesy of Franklin Delano Roosevelt Library Historical Pictures Service; 741 (tr), Image Copyright ©2001 PhotoDisc, Inc.; 741 (br), Theodor Gentilz; 745, Copyright 1996 David Eisenberg/Development Center for Appropriate Technology; 747, Trinity College Dublin Library.

ILLUSTRATION CREDITS

TABLE OF CONTENTS: Page ix (cl), Will Nelson; xi (cl), Steve Dininno; xiii (cl), Sandra Shap.

CHAPTER 2: Page 48 (c), Will Nelson; 48 (all), HRW; 77 (all), Leslie Kell; 78 (b), Network Graphics; 79 (t), Leslie Kell.

CHAPTER 3: Page 89 (tl), Network Graphics; 114 (all), Leslie Kell.

CHAPTER 4: Page 116 (all), Steven Dininno.

CHAPTER 5: Page 177 (all), 178 (b), Leslie Kell.

CHAPTER 6: Page 202 (all), Sandra Shap; 210 (c), 219 (t), HRW.

CHAPTER 7: Page 238 (all), 245 (all), 260 (br), 269 (cr), HRW.

CHAPTER 15: Page 443 (c), Ortelius Design; 449 (b), Judy Love.

CHAPTER 17: Page 490 (bc), Uhl Studios, Inc.

CHAPTER 18: Page 514 (b), Ortelius Design.

CHAPTER 20: Page 562 (c), Leslie Kell; 575 (b), Judy Love.

CHAPTER 21: Page 592 (bc), Uhl Studios, Inc.; 598 (bl), Ortelius Design.

CHAPTER 25: Page 688 (t), Leslie Kell; 689 (c), Richard Murdock; 708 (c), Ortelius Design.

QRH: Page 764 (b), HRW; 775 (tr), Leslie Kell; 786 (tl), Stephen Durke/Washington-Artists' Represents; 51 (all), 52 (all), 53 (all), 159 (all), 160 (all), 161 (all), Leslie Kell.